WHITAKER'S SCOTTISH A

A & C BLACK

LONDON

WHITAKER'S SCOTTISH ALMANACK

A & C BLACK

LONDON

A & C Black (Publishers) Ltd
37 Soho Square, London W1D 3QZ
ISBN 0-7136-6758-3
Whitaker's Almanack published annually since 1868
© 4th edition A & C Black (Publishers) Ltd

Designed by: Fiona Pike
Jacket photographs: © Corbis
Typeset by: Parliamentary Press, The Stationery Office,
  London
Printed and bound in the EU by: William Clowes Ltd.
  Beccles, Suffolk

A CIP catalogue record for this book is available from the British Library.

EDITORIAL STAFF
Editor-in-Chief: Lauren Simpson
Editors: Jill Laidlaw; Vanessa White; Inna Ward

Contributors: Alan Boyd (the Government of Scotland); Duncan Murray (Legal Notes); Karen Turner (the Scottish Economy).

Other titles in the Whitaker's Almanack range:
Whitaker's Almanack
Whitaker's Concise Almanack
Whitaker's Almanack Pocket Reference
Whitaker's Olympic Almanack

PREFACE TO THE 4TH EDITION

Welcome to the fourth edition of *Whitaker's Scottish Almanack,* the first to be published by A&C Black Publishers Ltd., whose prestigious stable of reference works includes *Who's Who* and *The Writers' and Artists' Yearbook.*

In 1999, for the first time in nearly 300 years, the world witnessed self-government in Scotland, the culmination of over 20 years hard work and determination by people striving to restore Scotland as a nation with its own constitutional identity. The first edition of *Whitaker's Scottish Almanack* was published to coincide with the first elections of the Scottish Parliament, to celebrate a historic chapter in Scottish life and to provide readers with a work of reference that reflects our ever-changing world. Four years on, with the second parliamentary elections under the nation's belt, the fourth edition of *Whitaker's Scottish Almanack* continues to provide an invaluable account of recent political events. With a budget of over £20 billion and an ambitious legislative programme for 2003–4, the Scottish Parliament continues to evolve, highlighting more than ever the need for accurate and timely reference material.

Yet *Whitaker's Scottish Almanack* is not merely a guide to the government of Scotland. It also presents wide-ranging information on the people, places and institutions of Scotland be they legal, environmental, cultural, religious or connected with business, media and public services.

So whether you live, work or study in Scotland, are planning a visit or are just interested in finding out about who's who and what's what in Scotland, *Whitaker's Scottish Almanack* is a comprehensive reference tool packed with an abundance of reliable facts and figures.

NEW FOR THIS EDITION

- May 2003 election results
- Bills passed by the Scottish Parliament 1999–2003
- The legislative programme for 2003–4
- Scottish food and drink
- History of the Scottish banking system
- Crime and legal statistics
- More biographies of key Scottish figures from sport and the arts
- Directory listings of magazines, newspapers and independent production companies

As ever, *Whitaker's Scottish Almanack* was compiled with the assistance of several Scots, all experts in their field, who offer a real insight into Scotland's infrastructure, people and places. I would like to thank the contributors, editors and the many hundreds of individuals and organisations throughout Scotland without whose help we would not be able to produce such a unique publication.

Lauren Simpson
Editor-in-Chief
A&C Black Publishers Ltd
37 Soho Square
London
W1D 3QZ

Tel: 020 7287 5385
Fax: 020 7734 6856
Email: whitakers@acblack.com
Web: www.acblack.com

CONTENTS

RELIGIOUS SCOTLAND

SCOTLAND AND THE WORLD

SOCIETIES AND INSTITUTIONS

GOVERNED SCOTLAND

GOVERNED SCOTLAND

The first session of Scottish Parliament was officially opened by the Queen on 1 July 1999, from which date devolution became effective, the Scottish Parliament and Scottish Administration assuming their full powers under the Scotland Act 1998.

The second general election for membership of the Scottish Parliament was held on 1 May 2003. The 129 Members of the Scottish Parliament (MSPs) were elected to office for a fixed term of four years.

PRE-DEVOLUTION GOVERNMENT

Scotland's parliament and administration developed in medieval times and were firmly established by 1603, when James VI of Scotland acceded to the English throne following the death of Elizabeth I of England. Despite the union of the crowns, the independence of the two countries' parliamentary systems was unaffected until 1707, when the Act of Union unified the two parliaments and transferred the government of Scotland to Westminster.

From the late 19th century the office of Secretary of State for Scotland (formerly the Secretary for Scotland) increased in importance, and became a Cabinet post in 1926. Over that period the Scottish Office also grew in size and importance. It provided the government departments in Scotland for education, health, local government, housing, economic development, agriculture and fisheries, home affairs, and law and order. Although required to operate within overall levels of funding set down by Westminster, the Scottish Office under the Secretary of State for Scotland and the Scottish Office ministers enjoyed a freedom of operation and flexibility of budget far greater than the departments of state in Whitehall. The 'Scottish Block' comprised a total allocation of money to Scotland with the Secretary of State being able to set his own spending priorities within the overall budget.

MOVEMENT TOWARDS DEVOLUTION

However, the concept of Scottish home rule did not die with the Union. Following the general election in October 1974, which saw the Scottish National Party return 11 MPs to Westminster, the Scottish home rule movement gained fresh momentum. Legislation was put in place to establish a Scottish assembly (the Scotland Act 1978) but the required

qualified majority did not materialise at the referendum held in March 1979. During the 1980s, support for a measure of home rule continued and a Scottish Constitutional Convention was established in 1989. The Convention, which included representatives from many political parties and other bodies representative of Scottish public life, produced a blueprint for a Scottish Parliament. The Labour government returned at the general election in May 1997 promised constitutional reform as one of its legislative priorities and an early referendum on the establishment of a Scottish Parliament.

The government published a White Paper, *Scotland's Parliament*, in July 1997. This document set out in detail the Government's proposals to devolve to a Scottish Parliament the power to legislate in respect of all matters not specifically reserved to Westminster. It further proposed limited tax-raising powers, a single-chamber Parliament with powerful committees, and also considered the Scottish Parliament's relationship with Westminster and the European Union. It proposed a measure of proportional representation for the first time in a British legislative body.

In a referendum held in Scotland on 11 September 1997, almost 75 per cent of those voting agreed 'that there should be a Scottish Parliament'. On the question that 'the Scottish Parliament should have tax-varying powers', almost two-thirds voted for the proposition. The Scotland Bill was introduced to the House of Commons on 17 December 1997. The Bill completed its Commons stages on 20 May 1998 after 32 days of debate and was subjected to 17 days of line-by-line scrutiny in the House of Lords before receiving royal assent on 19 November 1998. The Government itself tabled 670 amendments to the Bill.

In November 1997 the Government announced the establishment of an all-party Consultative Steering Group to take forward consideration of how the Scottish Parliament might operate in practice and to develop proposals for rules of procedure and standing orders; the Group reported to the Secretary of State in January 1999. The report enshrined four main principles: sharing the power; accountability; accessibility and participation; and equal opportunities. It proposed a modern, accessible and participative Parliament which would operate in a different manner from Westminster.

POST-DEVOLUTION GOVERNMENT

The Scottish Parliament is a subordinate legislature and can only legislate in respect of matters devolved to it. Westminster is sovereign and could, in theory, repeal the Scotland Act and do away with the Scottish Parliament, although all political parties are working to ensure that the Parliament works effectively. The role of the monarch is unchanged and Acts of the Scottish Parliament require royal assent before becoming law.

DEVOLVED POWERS

The Scottish Parliament is empowered to pass primary legislation (known as Acts of the Scottish Parliament) and Scottish Ministers can also make secondary legislation in respect of devolved matters. The principal devolved matters are: health, education, local government, social work and housing, planning, economic development, tourism, some aspects of transport, most aspects of criminal and civil law, the criminal justice and prosecution system, police and fire services, environment, natural and built heritage, agriculture and fisheries, food standards, forestry, sport, and the arts. The Scottish Parliament is also responsible for implementing European Community legislation in respect of matters devolved to it (see below). It is an absolute requirement that all laws of the Scottish Parliament, whether in the form of primary or secondary legislation, and all actions of the Scottish Executive must comply with the European Convention on Human Rights, which has been given effect by the Human Rights Act, as well as being consistent with EU law.

RESERVED POWERS

Despite the extent of devolved powers, a substantial range of matters are reserved to Westminster, including the constitution, foreign affairs, defence, the civil service, financial and economic matters, transport regulation, social security, employment and equal opportunities. The Secretary of State and the law officers may challenge in the courts the right of the Scottish Parliament to legislate in respect of any of these areas. Such challenges will ultimately be dealt with by the Judicial Committee of the Privy Council, which has assumed a new role as Scotland's principal constitutional court and is the final arbiter in disputes between Westminster and Edinburgh regarding legislative competence.

THE SCOTTISH EXECUTIVE

The Scottish Executive is the government in Scotland in respect of all devolved matters. The Scottish Executive comprises the First Minister, the law officers (the Lord Advocate and the Solicitor-General for Scotland) and other ministers appointed by the First Minister. The members of the Scottish Executive are referred to collectively as the Scottish Ministers. The Scottish Ministers assumed their full powers on 1 July 1999, the day on which were transferred to them powers and duties and other functions relating to devolved matters which were previously exercised by Ministers of the Crown. The transfer of powers was achieved by a series of Statutory Instruments.

The Scottish law officers, the Lord Advocate and the Solicitor-General for Scotland are entitled to participate, but not vote, in the proceedings of the Parliament even if they are not MSPs. As at June 2003 no MSP had yet been appointed as law officer. In addition to being the senior law officer in Scotland, the Lord Advocate continues to be the independent head of the systems of criminal prosecution and investigation of deaths in Scotland and this independence is entrenched in the Scotland Act 1998.

The Secretary of State for Scotland continues to be a member of the UK Government and is not a member of the Scottish Executive. The Scotland Act recognises that the UK Government will continue to need advice on Scots law, whether relating to reserved or devolved matters. To that end, a new law officer post in the UK Government, the Advocate-General for Scotland, was created in 1999. The first holder of this post is Dr Lynda Clark, QC, MP, who at the date of her appointment was the first ever female law officer.

The Scottish Ministers are supported by staff who were initially drawn from the staff of the Former Scottish Office and its agencies. On 1 July 1999 the departments of the Scottish Office transferred to the Scottish Executive. This name reflects the fact that the departments of the Scottish Office now work to the First Minister and his ministerial team. The structure of the Scottish Executive now reflects Scottish ministerial portfolios (for details, see Scottish Executive section).

All officials of the Executive hold office under the Crown on terms and conditions of service determined in accordance with the provisions of the Civil Service Management Code and remain members of the Home Civil Service. Established arrangements for interchange with other government departments also remain in place.

THE LEGISLATURE

The Scottish Parliament is a single-chamber legislature with 129 members. Of these, 73 represent constituencies and are elected on a first-past-the-post system. These constituencies are the same as for elections to Westminster with the exception of Orkney and Shetland, which comprise separate constituencies in the Scottish Parliament. In addition, 56 regional members (seven members for each of the eight former Scottish constituencies in the European Parliament) are elected on a proportional basis; this is intended to ensure that the overall composition of the Scottish Parliament reflects closely the total number of votes cast for each of the political parties. Each elector casts two votes, one for a constituency member and one for the party of his or her choice.

The Scottish Parliament has a fixed term of four years; governments cannot hold snap general elections. Elections will normally be held on the first Thursday in May, although there is a limited measure of flexibility should this date prove unsuitable. Extraordinary general elections can be held in exceptional circumstances, such as failure of the Parliament to nominate a First Minister within 28 days or if the Parliament itself resolves that it should be dissolved with the support of at least two-thirds of the members.

The Parliament is responsible for agreeing its own methods of operation and has adopted its own standing orders which are kept under regular review.

THE LEGISLATIVE PROCESS

There are three stages to the legislative process: pre-parliamentary procedure, parliamentary procedure, and procedure leading up to royal assent.

Under the pre-parliamentary procedure, before a Bill may be introduced to the Parliament, a member of the Scottish Executive must make a written statement to the effect that the Bill is within the legislative competence of the Scottish Parliament. Furthermore, the Presiding Officer must also certify that the provisions of the Bill would be within the legislative competence of the Parliament.

All Bills on introduction must be accompanied by a Financial Memorandum setting out the best estimates of the administrative, compliance and other costs to which the provisions of the Bill give rise, best estimates of time-scales over which such costs are expected to arise, and an indication of the margins of uncertainty in such estimates.

Furthermore, government Bills must be accompanied by explanatory notes summarising the provisions of the Bill, and a Policy Memorandum which sets out the policy objectives of the Bill, what alternative ways of meeting these objectives were considered, a summary of any consultation undertaken on the objectives of the Bill, and an assessment of the effects of the Bill on equal opportunities, human rights, island communities, local government, sustainable development and any

other matter which the Scottish Ministers consider relevant.

The parliamentary procedure has three stages: a general debate on the principle of the Bill with an opportunity to vote (analogous to the second reading debate in the House of Commons); detailed consideration of the Bill with the opportunity to move amendments (analogous to the Committee stage); and a final stage at which the Bill can be passed or rejected (analogous to the third reading).

After a Bill completes its parliamentary procedure, the Presiding Officer submits it for royal assent. There is an in-built delay of four weeks before royal assent is granted to allow one of the law officers or the Secretary of State to challenge the competency of the Parliament to pass the Act.

COMMITTEES

As the Scottish Parliament is a single chamber, there is no body such as the House of Lords to undertake detailed scrutiny of legislation. Instead, the Scottish Parliament has powerful all-purpose committees to undertake substantial pre-legislative scrutiny. These committees combine the role of Westminster standing and select committees and have power to:

- consider and report on policy and administration of the Scottish Administration
- conduct enquiries
- scrutinise primary, secondary and proposed EU legislation
- initiate legislation
- scrutinise financial proposals of the Scottish Executive (including taxation, estimates, appropriation and audit)
- scrutinise procedures relating to the Parliament and its members

Ministers are required to inform committees of the Government's legislative intentions in their areas of interest, and to discuss which relevant bodies should be involved in the pre-legislative consultation process. In practice, the Committees have operated with considerable success and have taken evidence from interested bodies and individuals on a wide range of matters. Scottish Ministers have also been required to account to the Committees for matters within their portfolios. Most Committee business is undertaken in public.

MANAGEMENT OF PARLIAMENT

The management of the business of the Parliament is undertaken by the Parliamentary Bureau. This meets in private and its main functions are to:

- prepare the programme of business of the Parliament

- timetable the daily order of business for the plenary session
- timetable the progress of legislation in committees
- propose the remit, membership, duration and budget of parliamentary committees

On certain days the Parliamentary Bureau gives priority to:

- business of the committees
- business chosen by political parties which are not represented in the Scottish Executive
- private members' business.

The management of the business of Parliament as a corporate entity is the responsibility of the Scottish Parliamentary Corporate Body. This has legal powers to hold property, make contracts and handle money and also to bring or defend legal proceedings by or against the Scottish Parliament. It also employs staff engaged in the running of the Parliament who are not civil servants.

BUDGET AND RUNNING COSTS

The budget approved by the Parliament for 2003–4 is £23 billion. This is due to rise to almost £26 billion in 2005–6. The UK Government has agreed to the continuing application of the Barnett Formula to allow for uprating of the Parliament's budget in line with increases for corresponding matters for the rest of the UK. In addition, the Parliament has limited power to vary the basic rate of income tax by a maximum of 3 pence although this power has not yet been used. The only other financial powers held by the Scottish Parliament relate to the manner in which local authorities raise revenue, presently by way of council tax and business rates.

The Scottish Parliament will be permanently housed in a custom-built building under construction at Holyrood, Edinburgh. The project has been beset by problems and completion is not now expected until 2004. The cost has risen from an original estimate of £40 million to a figure in excess of £370 million. The final cost may well be even greater. Until the new Parliament building is completed, the Scottish Parliament is occupying the Church of Scotland General Assembly buildings at The Mound, Edinburgh.

The total running costs of the Parliament for financial year 2003–4 as set out in the Budget (Scotland) Act 2003 including salaries and allowances for MSPs, staff costs, accommodation costs and payments in respect of the Scottish Parliamentary Commissioner for Administration, are estimated at around £108 million.

SALARIES AND ALLOWANCES

The salaries of MSPs are a matter for the Scottish Parliament. Enhanced salaries are payable to the Scottish Ministers and there is a system of allowances to cover MSPs' expenses in carrying out constituency and parliamentary work.

THE JUDICIARY

The role of the judiciary is specifically acknowledged in the Scotland Act and there are detailed proposals for the appointment and removal of judges. Judges are likely to be increasingly involved in matters of political significance, including legal challenges to legislation passed by the Scottish Parliament and issues arising out of the European Convention on Human Rights.

Due to their increasing involvement in matters of political sensitivity, the procedures for removing judges have been made more rigorous. Judges can only be removed from office by the Queen on the recommendation of the First Minister following a resolution of the Parliament. Parliament may only pass such a motion following a written report by an independent tribunal concluding that the person in question is unfit for office by reason of inability, neglect of duty or misbehaviour.

RELATIONSHIP WITH THE UK GOVERNMENT

The devolution settlement has resulted in changes to the UK constitutional framework. The role of the Secretary of State for Scotland is diminished to the extent that he or she will only represent Scotland's interests with regard to reserved matters; there is no guarantee that the Secretary of State will continue to have a place in the Cabinet.

A system of concordats has been put in place to ensure that the business of government in Scotland and at the UK level is conducted smoothly. The concordats are non-statutory bilateral agreements between the Scottish Executive and the UK Government which cover a range of administrative procedures relating to devolution. They are intended to ensure that good working relationships and communications continue between the Scottish administration and UK government departments.

They set out the principles on which working relationships will be based rather than prescribe the details of what those relationships should be. Concordats are intended to ensure that consultation takes place in relation to proposals for legislative and executive action, including advance notification.

There are likely to be further changes in future, for example, the number of Scottish MPs at

Westminster is expected to be reduced following the next review of electoral areas carried out by the Boundary Commission for Scotland. As the legislation stands, this would also have the consequence of reducing the number of MSPs. However, it is possible that the Scotland Act will be amended to maintain the number of MSPs at 129. If the number is reduced on a par with the number of MPs elected to Westminster, estimates suggest that the number of MSPs could drop to around 110. However, exact numbers will only be known after the Boundary Commission completes its work. This possible reduction in numbers is already causing concern in view of the extent of the workload of Committees of the Scottish Parliament in particular and the UK Government has indicated that it will keep this matter under review.

RELATIONSHIP WITH THE EU

Relations with the EU remain a reserved matter. While the Scottish Parliament has responsibility for scrutinising European legislation affecting Scotland and the Scottish Executive has the responsibility for applying that legislation in Scotland, it is the UK Government that represents Scottish interests in the Council of Ministers; this includes areas such as farming and fishing, where Scottish Office ministers may previously have led UK delegations. The Government has indicated that Scottish Ministers might be able to participate, on behalf of the UK, in EU meetings. It has indicated that it sees UK and Scottish Ministers agreeing a common line prior to negotiating with other EU member states.

One of the concerns expressed about the proposed relationship between the Scottish Executive and the EU institutions is accountability. Scottish Ministers are not members of the UK Parliament and are therefore not accountable to Westminster. As Scotland is not a member state of the EU, the responsibility for ensuring compliance with EU legislation rests with the UK Government. There is potential for conflict between the Scottish Parliament and Westminster with regard to the implementation of European legislation. In that event the proposed concordats between the Scottish Parliament and Westminster will be tested.

Any financial penalties imposed by the EU for non-observance of an EU measure, even in respect of devolved matters, will be met by the UK. Where the fault is due to the failure of the Scottish Executive to implement EU legislation in respect of devolved matters, the financial consequences will be met out of the Scottish Block.

THE LEGISLATIVE PROGRAMME OF THE SCOTTISH PARLIAMENT

In its first session (1999–2003) a total of 62 bills were passed by the Parliament. Prior to the commencement of the Scottish Parliament, Westminster generally passed two or three Scottish bills each year. Of the 62 bills passed, 50 were Executive Bills (including four Budget Bills), eight were Member's Bills, three were Committee Bills and one was a Private Bill.

BILLS PASSED IN THE FIRST SESSION 1999–2003
Abolition of Feudal Tenure etc. (Scotland)
Abolition of Poindings and Warrant Sales
Adults with Incapacity (Scotland)
Agricultural Holdings (Scotland)
Bail, Judicial Appointments etc. (Scotland)
Budget (Scotland)
Budget (Scotland) (No. 3)
Budget (Scotland) (No. 2)
Budget (Scotland) (No. 4)
Building (Scotland)
Census Amendment (Scotland)
Commissioner for Children and Young People (Scotland)
Community Care and Health (Scotland)
Convention Rights (Compliance) (Scotland)
Council of the Law Society of Scotland
Criminal Justice (Scotland)
Criminal Procedure (Scotland)
Debt Arrangement and Attachment (Scotland)
Dog Fouling (Scotland)
Education (Disability Strategies and Pupils' Records) (Scotland)
Education (Graduate Endowment and Student Support) (Scotland) (No. 2)
Education and Training (Scotland)
Erskine Bridge Tolls
Ethical Standards in Public Life etc. (Scotland)
Freedom of Information (Scotland)
Fur Farming (Prohibition) (Scotland)
Homelessness (Scotland)
Housing (Scotland)
International Criminal Court (Scotland)
Land Reform (Scotland)
Leasehold Casualties (Scotland)
Local Government in Scotland
Marriage (Scotland)
Mental Health (Care and Treatment)
Mental Health (Public Safety and Appeals) (Scotland)
Mortgage Rights (Scotland)
National Galleries of Scotland
National Parks (Scotland)
Police and Fire Services (Finance) (Scotland)
Protection from Abuse (Scotland)

Protection of Children (Scotland)
Protection of Wild Mammals (Scotland)
Public Appointments and Public Bodies (Scotland)
Public Finance and Accountability (Scotland)
Regulation of Care (Scotland)
Regulation of Investigatory Powers
Salmon and Freshwater Fisheries (Consolidation) (Scotland)
Salmon Conservation (Scotland)
School Education (Amendment) (Scotland)
Scottish Local Authorities (Tendering) (Scotland)
Scottish Local Government (Elections)
Scottish Parliamentary Standards Commissioner
Scottish Public Services Ombudsmen
Scottish Qualifications Authority
Sea Fisheries (Shellfish) Amendment (Scotland)
Sexual Offices (Procedure and Evidence) (Scotland)
Standards in Scotland's Schools
Title Conditions (Scotland)
Transport (Scotland)
University of St Andrews (Postgraduate Medical Degrees)
Water Environment and Water Services (Scotland)
Water Industry (Scotland)

Further details and summaries of all bills can be found in a paper entitled "*Summaries of Bills Passed by the Scottish Parliament in the First Session*" (SP Paper 846) available on the Scottish Parliament website at www.scottish.parliament.uk.

THE GENERAL ELECTION MAY 2003

The second general election for the Scottish Parliament was held on 1 May 2003. Once again, no party was elected with an overall majority. Several days after the election a coalition deal was finalised between Labour and the Liberal Democrats which cleared the way for Jack McConnell (Labour) to be re-elected as First Minister with Jim Wallace (Liberal Democrat) as Deputy First Minister and Minister for Enterprise and Lifelong Learning. The number of Ministers has been trimmed down; the Cabinet now consists of 11 Ministers, with 19 Ministers in total (including the First Minister) – 5 of them Liberal Democrats.

THE PARTNERSHIP AGREEMENT

The negotiations between the coalition partners resulted in a broad ranging agreement with concessions on each side. Most controversially the Partnership Agreement contains plans for proportional representation for local government. The agreement includes:

ENTERPRISE AND LIFELONG LEARNING
- Grow renewable energy industries
- Extend "Enterprise in Education" to every school
- Create a strategy for the construction industry
- Introduce a national tourism registration scheme
- Legislate on personal bankruptcy and diligence to modernise the law
- Establish Business Improvement Districts and Urban Regeneration Companies

EDUCATION
- 200 more schools to be renewed by 2006
- 53,000 more teachers by 2007
- Class sizes of 20 pupils in S1–S2 Maths and English
- End system of national testing for 5–14 year olds
- Reform of the school curriculum

CHILDREN AND YOUNG PEOPLE
- Increased access to sport and leisure facilities
- Review of the Children's Hearings system

JUSTICE
- Introduce a Fire Services Bill
- Introduce civil orders requiring parents to act in the best interests of their children
- Establish a Scottish Human Rights Commission

TRANSPORT
- Deliver rail links to Glasgow and Edinburgh airports
- Complete central Scotland motorway network and the Aberdeen West Peripheral Road
- Extend concessionary fares on public transport for older people and people with disabilities
- Support construction of the Borders Rail line
- Review tolls on the Skye Bridge
- Agree a new ScotRail franchise

RURAL
- Implement land management contracts
- Implement the Organic Action Plan
- Implement reformed Common Fisheries Policy
- Reduce the number of bodies regulating the aquaculture industry
- Set up an urgent review of the management of all fisheries within the 12-mile coastal zone

HEALTH
- Treatment for coronary heart disease patients within 18 weeks of diagnosis, from 2004
- Legislation to abolish NHS Trusts and establish Community Health Partnerships
- Double the resources for tackling alcohol abuse
- Free eye and dental checks for all before 2007

SOCIAL JUSTICE

- 18,000 new homes for rent and low cost ownership by 2006
- Action against racism and sectarianism

SPORT, CULTURE AND THE ARTS

- Introduce a Gaelic Language Bill
- Develop six multi-sport facilities across Scotland

THE LEGISLATIVE PROGRAMME FOR 2003–4

On 28 May 2003, First Minister Jack McConnell announced the Scottish Executive's Legislative programme for the year ahead. The proposals include:

JUSTICE AND HOME AFFAIRS

- Vulnerable Witnesses Bill particularly aiming to protect children under 16, victims of rape and their families
- Court Reform Bill to improve efficiency in the High Court
- Anti-Social Behaviour Bill to introduce anti-social behaviour orders and tagging for under 16s – as well as imposing Parenting Orders and banning the sale of spray paint to young people

HEALTH AND COMMUNITY CARE

- NHS Reform Bill to abolish the NHS Trusts in Scotland and to establish Community Health Partnerships
- Primary Medical Services Bill depending on GP agreement to implement new contracts for providers of general medical services

EDUCATION

- Education (Additional Support for Learning) Bill to reform provision for children with special educational needs
- Education (School Meals) Bill to safeguard the current entitlement of children to free school meals
- a third education bill on Ministerial Power of Direction will give Ministers powers to intervene, based on Inspectorate reports

LOCAL GOVERNMENT

- Local Government Bill to increase democratic participation and to introduce STV for the next local government elections in Scotland

ENVIRONMENT

- Nature Conservation Bill to place a duty on local authorities to conserve biodiversity, reform the SSSI System and build on wildlife crime measures
- Strategic Environmental Assessment Bill to ensure that new strategies, programmes and plans are properly considered in the public sector
- Water Services Bill following upon consultation regarding a new regulatory framework for public water and sewerage services

OTHER MATTERS

- Consultation on proposals for the establishment of a new Strategic Transport Authority
- Gaelic Language (Scotland) Bill to secure the status of Gaelic in Scots Law
- Fire Services Bill to give Fire Brigades and Authorities statutory responsibility for fire prevention and to increase local control over services
- Budget Bill to give statutory authority to spend monies from the Scottish Consolidated Fund. This Bill is required annually

Up to date information on the progress of all Bills can be found on the Scottish Parliament website at www.scottish.parliament.uk

THE SCOTTISH EXECUTIVE

The Scottish Executive is the government of Scotland in respect of all devolved matters. The Scottish Executive consists of the First Minister, the law officers (the Lord Advocate and the Solicitor-General for Scotland), and the other Scottish Ministers appointed by the First Minister. The First Minister is also able to appoint junior ministers to assist the Scottish Ministers.

SCOTLAND OFFICE

On 12 June 2003 the Prime Minister announced a number of changes to the UK government, including the integration of the Scotland Office into the Department for Constitutional Affairs. The Rt. Hon. Alistair Darling was appointed Secretary of State for Scotland and Secretary of State for Transport. He is responsible for Scottish Affairs, advised by the Scotland Office.

THE SCOTTISH MINISTERS

First Minister: The Rt. Hon. Jack McConnell, MSP *(Lab.)*

Deputy First Minister and Minister for Enterprise and Lifelong Learning: Jim Wallace, QC, MP, MSP *(LD)*
Areas of responsibility: alongside the First Minister, responsible for the development, implementation and presentation of Scottish Executive policies; as Enterprise Minister, responsible for economy, business and industry, including Scottish Enterprise, European Structural Funds, trade and inward investment, energy (including renewable energy), further and higher education, lifelong learning, training and science.

Minister for Justice: Cathy Jamieson, MSP *(Lab.)*
Areas of responsibility: criminal justice, youth justice, victim support, criminal justice social work, police, prisons, sentencing policy, courts, law reform.

Minister for Education and Young People: Peter Peacock, MSP *(Lab.)*
Areas of responsibility: school education, nurseries, childcare, Gaelic, children's services, social work, the Scottish Qualifications Authority, HM Inspectorate of Education.

Minister for Health and Community Care: Malcolm Chisholm, MP, MSP *(Lab.)*
Areas of responsibility: NHS, community care, health service reform, health improvement, health promotion, public health, allied healthcare services, acute, primary and mental health services, performance, quality and improvement framework and food safety.

Minister for Environment and Rural Development: Ross Finnie, MSP *(LD)*
Areas of responsibility: environment and natural heritage, land reform, water, sustainable development, agriculture, fisheries, rural development including aquaculture and forestry.

Minister for Finance and Public Services: Andy Kerr, MSP *(Lab.)*
Areas of responsibility: the Scottish budget, public service delivery, modernising government including civil service reform, local government, cities and community planning.

Minister for Communities: Margaret Curran, MSP *(Lab.)*
Areas of responsibility: anti-social behaviour, poverty, housing and area regeneration, land use, building standards, equality issues, voluntary sector, religious and faith organisations, charity law.

Minister for Parliamentary Business: Patricia Ferguson, MSP *(Lab.)*
Areas of responsibility: Parliamentary affairs and the management of Executive business in the Parliament

Minister for Tourism, Culture and Sport: Frank McAveety, MSP *(Lab.)*
Areas of responsibility: tourism, culture and the arts, sport, major events strategy, built heritage, architecture, Historic Scotland, lottery funding.

Minister for Transport: Nicol Stephen, MSP *(LD)*
Areas of responsibility: transport policy and delivery, public transport, rail services, air and ferry services

Lord Advocate: Colin Boyd, QC *(Lab.)*

JUNIOR MINISTERS

Deputy Minister for Enterprise and Lifelong Learning: Lewis Macdonald, MSP *(Lab.)*
Deputy Minister for Justice: Hugh Henry, MSP *(Lab.)*
Deputy Minister for Education and Young People: Euan Robson, MSP *(LD)*
Deputy Minister for Health and Community Care: Tom McCabe, MSP *(Lab.)*
Deputy Minister for Environment and Rural Development: Allan Wilson, MSP *(Lab.)*
Deputy Minister for Finance and Public Services: Tavish Scott, MSP *(LD)*
Deputy Minister for Communities: Mary Mulligan, MSP *(Lab.)*
Deputy Minister for Parliamentary Business: Tavish Scott, MSP *(LD)*
Solicitor-General: Elish Angiolini, QC

DEPARTMENTS OF THE SCOTTISH EXECUTIVE

St Andrew's House, Regent Road, Edinburgh EH1 3DG
Tel: 0131-556 8400; Enquiry line: 08457-741741
Fax: 0131-244 8240 Email: ceu@scotland.gov.uk and
scottish.ministers@scotland.gov.uk
Web: www.scotland.gov.uk
Permanent Secretary: J. Elvidge

The Scottish Executive Ministers are supported by staff largely drawn from the staff of the Scottish Office, as constituted before devolution, and its agencies. On 1 July 1999 the departments of the Scottish Office transferred to the Scottish Executive and now work to the First Minister and his ministerial team. All officials of the Executive hold office under the Crown on terms and conditions of service determined in accordance with the provisions of the Civil Service Management Code and remain members of the Home Civil Service.

On 1 July 1999 the Scottish Office changed its name to the Scottish Executive and its departments were renamed; some reassignment of responsibilities also took place. Current departmental responsibilities are:

SCOTTISH EXECUTIVE DEVELOPMENT DEPARTMENT – anti-social behaviour, housing and area regeneration, building better cities, area regeneration (Communities Scotland), homelessness, inquiry reporters, planning and building standards, building control, analytical services, social justice, social inclusion, voluntary issues, equality

SCOTTISH EXECUTIVE EDUCATION DEPARTMENT – schools, teachers, pupil support and inclusion, additional support needs, new educational developments, qualifications, assessment and curriculum, schools inspectorate, social work services inspectorate, policy co-ordination, children and young people, families, early education and childcare, young people and looked after children, information, analysis and communications, tourism, sport, the arts and culture, architectural policy, review of Historic Scotland

SCOTTISH EXECUTIVE ENTERPRISE, TRANSPORT AND LIFELONG LEARNING DEPARTMENT – enterprise and industrial affairs, business growth and innovation, Scotland enterprise and industrial affairs enterprise and industry division, energy, telecommunications, digital inclusion and corporate services, European Structural Funds, Scottish Development International, analytical services, enterprise networks, lifelong learning, transitions to work, skills for life and work, higher education and science, further and adult

education, Funding for Learners, the student awards agency for Scotland, transport, trunk roads network management, trunk roads design and construction

SCOTTISH EXECUTIVE HEALTH DEPARTMENT – directorate of service policy and planning, health planning and quality, primary care, community care, mental health, health improvement, order people, performance management and finance, analytical services, performance management, property and capital planning, computing and IT strategy, human resources, partnership and employment practice, workforce and policy, learning, development and careers, nursing, chief scientist office, professional staff, public health, substance misuse, centre for change and innovation, national waiting times unit, research and policy development initiative

SCOTTISH EXECUTIVE JUSTICE DEPARTMENT – police and community safety, criminal justice, community justice, criminal justice, criminal procedure, parole and life sentence review, single agency project, civil and international, HM chief inspector of prisons, HM chief inspector of fire services, HM chief inspector of constabulary, Scottish prison service

SCOTTISH EXECUTIVE ENVIRONMENT AND RURAL AFFAIRS DEPARTMENT – agricultural and biological research, food and agriculture, land use and rural policy, agricultural policy, farm business restructuring, CAP management, information systems, animal health and welfare, economics & statistics, veterinary, Scottish agricultural science agency, fisheries and rural development, scottish fisheries protection agency, environment

SCOTTISH EXECUTIVE FINANCE AND CENTRAL SERVICES DEPARTMENT – cabinet secretariat, office of the chief economic adviser, office of the chief researcher, local government, finance and performance, external relations, media and communications, Scottish Executive EU office, finance, change to deliver, expenditure, audit and accountancy services, Scottish public pensions agency, corporate development, changing to deliver, 21st century government

SCOTTISH EXECUTIVE CORPORATE SERVICES – central support functions, including human resources, equal opportunities, the Modernising Government agenda

SCOTTISH EXECUTIVE LEGAL AND PARLIAMENTARY SERVICES DEPARTMENT – The Crown Office and Procurator Fiscal Service is headed by the Lord Advocate, who is assisted by the Solicitor General for Scotland. They are the Scottish Law Officers and members of the Scottish Executive. The department provides Scotland's independent public prosecution and deaths investigation service. The Chief Executive is responsible to the Lord Advocate for the management of the department.

SCOTTISH EXECUTIVE CORPORATE SERVICES
Saughton House, Broomhouse Drive, Edinburgh EH11 3XD Tel: 0131-556 8400

Principal Establishment Officer and Head of Corporate Services: Agnes Robson
Head of Personnel: Sally Cruthers

DIRECTORATE OF CORPORATE SERVICES
Saughton House, Broomhouse Drive, Edinburgh EH11 3XD. Tel: 0131-556 8400

Principal Establishment Officers:
Head of Corporate Services: Agnes Robson
Director of HR: Sally Cruthers
Head of Accommodation: Paul Rhodes
Director of Information Technology: Paul Gray
Chief Quantity Surveyor: Alastair Wyllie
Director of Procurement and Commercial Services: Nick Bowd

DIRECTORATE OF CORPORATE DEVELOPMENT
Director: Clive Martlew

SCOTTISH EXECUTIVE FINANCE AND CENTRAL SERVICES
St Andrew's House, Regent Road, Edinburgh EH1 3DG
Tel: 0131-244 5598 Fax: 0131-248 5536
Acting Head of Department and Chief Economic Advisor: Dr Andrew Goudie
Principal Finance Officer: P. Collings
Assistant Directors of Finance: Mrs J. Young; S. Rosie; D. N. G Reid; A. Stobart
Head of Audit and Accountancy Services Division: Mrs A. Wright
Constitution and Parliamentary Secretariat: Michael Lugton
Head of Cabinet Secretariat Division: Liz Lewis
Legal Secretary to the Lord Advocate: Patrick Layden

EXTERNAL RELATIONS DIVISION
Head of Division: George Calder

LOCAL GOVERNMENT GROUP
Head: C. Smith

MEDIA AND COMMUNICATIONS GROUP
Head of Marketing and New Media: R. Williams
Head of News: A. Baird

SCOTTISH EXECUTIVE DEVELOPMENT DEPARTMENT
Victoria Quay, Edinburgh EH6 6QQ
Tel: 0131-244 0763 Fax: 0131-244 0785
Email: ps/dd@scotland.gov.uk
Web: www.scotland.gov.uk
Head of Department: Mrs Nicola S. Munro
Group Heads: Mike Neilson; Jim Mackinnon; Neil Jackson; James McCulloch; Mark Batho;
Division Heads: Geoff Huggins; Lindsay Manson; Phil Cornish; Alan Denham; Tom Williamson; Ian Duncan; Maureen McGinn; Neil Jackson; Kay Barton; Yvonne Strachan; Neville MacKay; F. Duffy; R. Grant; C. Macintosh

INQUIRY REPORTERS
2 Greenside Lane, Edinburgh EH1 3AG
Tel: 0131-244 5649
Chief Reporter: J. M. McCulloch

SCOTTISH EXECUTIVE EDUCATION DEPARTMENT
Victoria Quay, Edinburgh EH6 6QQ
Tel: 08457-741741 Fax: 0131-244 8240
Head of Department: M. Ewart
Head of Group: Philip Rycroft; Colin MacLean; John Mason
Heads of Division: C. Reeves; J. Fraser; E. Emberson; D. Henderson; M. Gibson; F. Osowska; S. Smith; V. Cox; R. Gwyon, P. Scrimgeour, R. Irvine; J. Brown
Chief Inspector of Social Work Services for Scotland: A. Skinner
Assistant Chief Inspectors: K. Vincent; G. Ottley; M. Miller; J. Knox
Senior Chief Inspector of Schools: G. Donaldson

SCOTTISH EXECUTIVE ENTERPRISE, TRANSPORT AND LIFELONG LEARNING DEPARTMENT
Meridian Court, 5 Cadogan Street, Glasgow G2 6AT
Tel: 0141-248 4778 Fax: 0141-242 5665
Head of Department: E. W. Frizzell

BUSINESS INTERESTS AND IMPROVING REGULATION
Meridian Court, 5 Cadogan Street, Glasgow G2 6AT
Tel: 0141-248 2855

LIFELONG LEARNING GROUP

Europa Building, 450 Argyle Street, Glasgow G2 8LG
Tel: 0131-556 8400
Head of Group: M. Batho
Division Heads: K. Doran; L. M. A. Hunter;
  G. Troup; J. Rigg; H. Jones

ENTERPRISE AND INDUSTRIAL AFFAIRS

Meridian Court, 5 Cadogan Street, Glasgow G2 6AT
Tel: 0131-556 8400
Head of Group: Graeme Dickson
Division Heads: R. Naysmith; I. J. C. Howie;
  W. Malone; D. A. Stewart; D. McLafferty

ENTERPRISE NETWORKS

Meridian Court, 5 Cadogan Street, Glasgow G2 6AT
Tel: 0131 556 8400
Head of Division: J. Morgan

SCOTTISH DEVELOPMENT INTERNATIONAL

150 Broomielaw, Atlantic Quay, Glasgow G2 8LU
Tel: 0141-248 2700
Head of Group: M. Togner
Division Heads: D. Taylor; B. Shaw; D. McFadyen;
J. Amour

TRANSPORT GROUP

Victoria Quay, Edinburgh EH6 6QQ Tel: 0131-556 8400
Head of Group: J. Martin
Division Heads: J. Pryce; J. Ross; K. Hogg; D. Hart;
  J. Barton; J. Howison

SCOTTISH EXECUTIVE HEALTH DEPARTMENT

St Andrew's House, Regent Road, Edinburgh EH1 3DG
Tel: 0131-244 2440 Fax: 0131-244 2162

NATIONAL HEALTH SERVICE IN SCOTLAND MANAGEMENT EXECUTIVE

Chief Executive: T. Jones
Director Performance Management and Finance:
  J. Aldridge
Director of Human Resources: M. Butler
Director of Nursing: Miss A. Jarvie
Director of Service Policy and Planning: I. W. Gordon
Director of Waiting Times Unit: J. Connaghan
Heads of Community Care: T. Teale; J. A. Rennie
Director of Health Improvement: Mrs P. Whittle
Chief Medical Officer: Dr Armstrong
Computing and IT Strategy, NHS: C. B. Knox
Head of Property and Capital Planning: D. Hastie
Chief Pharmacist: W. Scott
Chief Scientist: Prof. R. Jung
Chief Dental Officer: F. Watkins

SCOTTISH EXECUTIVE JUSTICE DEPARTMENT

St Andrew's House, Regent Road, Edinburgh EH1 3DG
Tel: 0131-244 2122 Fax: 0131-244 2121
Head of Department: J. D. Gallagher
Group Heads: C. Baxter; Mrs M. H. Brannan;
  Mrs V. Macniven
Division Heads: P. Beaton; R. Scott; Mrs R.
  Menlowe; Mrs E. Carmichael; D. Henderson;
  Mrs W. Dickson; C. Imrie; A. Quinn;
  J. Rowell; I. Snedden

SCOTTISH EXECUTIVE ENVIRONMENT AND RURAL AFFAIRS DEPARTMENT

Pentland House, 47 Robb's Loan, Edinburgh EH14 1TY
Tel: 0131-556 8400 Fax: 0131-244 6116
Head of Department: J. S. Graham
Group heads: D. F. Middleton (*Food and Agriculture*);
  Dr P. Brady (*Fisheries*); M. Foulis (*Environment*);
  A. J. Rushworth (*Agricultural and Biological
  Research*);
A. J. Robertson (*Chief Agricultural Officer*)
Division/unit heads: Dr J. R. Wildgoose; I. R.
  Anderson; A. Sim; L. Roxborough; B. Pearson;
  A. G. Dickson; Ms J. Dalgleish; D. Rogers;
  P. Wright; E. Mitchell; A. J. Cameron; Dr A. Scott
  (*Environment Group*)
Division heads: J. Hutchison; D. J. Greig (*Fisheries and
  Rural Development*); B. Aiken; R. McLachlan;
  I. Bainbridge; T. Hooton; D. Carmichael;
  J. Hooker; N. Harvey; L. Saunderson
Assistant Chief Agricultural Officers: W. A. Aitken;
  J. Henderson; A. Robb
Senior Rural Economist: A. Moxey

SCOTTISH EXECUTIVE LEGAL AND PARLIAMENTARY SERVICES DEPARTMENT

25 Chambers Street, Edinburgh EH1 1LA
Tel: 0131-226 2626 Fax: 0131-226 6564
*Head of Department and Chief Executive of the Crown
  Office:* R. Gordon.

THE SCOTTISH PARLIAMENT

The Scottish Parliament, Edinburgh EH99 1SP
Tel: 0131-348 5000 (switchboard);
0845-278 1999 (general enquiries);
0131-348 5415 (textphone)
Web: www.scottish.parliament.uk

Useful Email addresses:

Public Information
sp.info@scottish.parliament.uk

Media Enquiries
sp.media@scottish.parliament.uk

Schools and Colleges
education.service@scottish.parliament.uk

Gaelic Service
Gaidhlig@scottish.parliament.uk

Business in the Debating Chamber
chamber.office@scottish.parliament.uk

Business in Committees
committee.office@scottish.parliament.uk

Recruitment and Placement Enquiries
personnel.office@scottish.parliament.uk

Petitions
petitions@scottish.parliament.uk

Office of the Presiding Officer
presiding.officer@scottish.parliament.uk

Enquiries regarding the Website
webmaster@scottish.parliament.uk

Note: at the time of going to press, no formal date had been announced for the opening of the new Scottish Parliament building at Holyrood. However, according to the Scottish Parliament Press Office, MSPs and Parliament staff will begin moving from the Parliament's temporary home on the Mound early in 2004.

FACTS AND FIGURES
Elections: 6 May 1999, turnout was 59 per cent of the electorate; 1 May 2003, turnout was 49.4 per cent of the electorate

Official opening: 1 July 1999 at Edinburgh Assembly Hall

Devolved responsibilities: education, health, law, environment, economic development, local government, housing, police, fire services, planning, financial assistance to industry, tourism, some transport, heritage and the arts, sport, agriculture, forestry, fisheries, food standards
Powers: can introduce primary legislation; can raise or lower income tax by up to three pence in the pound
Number of members: 129

STATE OF THE PARTIES
as at 21 May 2003

	Constituency MSPs	Regional MSPs	Total
Labour	46	4	50
SNP	9	18	27
Conservative	3	15	18
Liberal Democrats	13	4	17
Green	0	7	7
Scottish Socialist	0	6	6
Scottish Senior Citizens Unity Party	0	1	1
Independent†	2	1	3
Total	73	56	129

† Independents are: Dennis Canavan, Margo MacDonald and Dr Jean Turner

SALARIES
from 1 April 2003

	Office holders salary	Total salary
First Minister	£71,433	£120,748
Scottish Ministers	£37,056	£86,371
Presiding Officer	£37,056	£86,371
Junior Scottish Minister	£23,210	£72,525
Deputy Presiding Officers	£23,210	£72,525
Lord Advocate	£48,418	£97,728
Solicitor-General	£35,006	£84,321
MSPs	n/a	£49,315

OFFICERS
The Presiding Officer: The Rt. Hon. George Reid, MSP
Deputy Presiding Officers: Patricia Godman, MSP (*Lab.*); Murray Tosh (*C.*)

THE PARLIAMENTARY BUREAU
The Parliamentary Bureau consists of the Presiding Officer and representatives of each political party, or any group in the Parliament which has five or more members. The representatives are nominated by the leader of each party. One of the main functions of the Parliamentary Bureau is to propose the establishment, remit, membership and duration of any committee or sub-committee.

Members (as at July 2003)
The Presiding Officer
Mark Ballard (*Green*)
Patricia Ferguson (*Lab.*)
Bill Aitken (*C.*)
Bruce Crawford (*Green*)
Carolyn Leckie (*SSP*)
Tavish Scott (*LD*)

SCOTTISH PARLIAMENTARY CORPORATE BODY (SPCB)

The SPCB is responsible for ensuring that the Scottish Parliament is provided with the property, staff and services it requires.
Members (as at July 2003)
The Presiding Officer
Robert Brown, MSP (*LD*)
Duncan McNeill, MSP (*Lab.*)
John Scott, MSP (*C.*)
Andrew Welsh, MSP (*SNP*)

THE COMMITTEES

The committees of the Scottish Parliament and their membership as at May 2003:

AUDIT
Rhona Brankin (*Lab.*)
Susan Deacon (*Lab.*)
Robin Harper (*Green*)
Margaret Jamieson (*Lab.*)
George Lyon (*LD*)
Kenny MacAskill (*SNP*)
*Brian Monteith (*C.*)

COMMUNITIES
Cathie Craigie (*Lab.*)
Donald Gorrie (*LD*)
Patrick Harvie (*Green*)
*Johann Lamont (*Lab.*)
Maureen Macmillan (*Lab.*)
Campbell Martin (*SNP*)
Mary Scanlon (*C.*)
Elaine Smith (*Lab.*)
Stewart Stevenson (*SNP*)

EDUCATION
Wendy Alexander (*Lab.*)
Rhona Brankin (*Lab.*)
*Robert Brown (*LD*)
Rosemary Byrne (*SSP*)
Lord James Douglas-Hamilton (*C.*)
Fiona Hyslop (*SNP*)
Adam Ingram (*SNP*)
Kenneth Macintosh (*Lab.*)
Dr Elaine Murray (*Lab.*)

ENTERPRISE AND CULTURE
Brian Adam (*SNP*)
Richard Baker (*Lab.*)
Chris Ballance (*Green*)
Susan Deacon (*Lab.*)
Murdo Fraser (*C.*)
Christine May (*Lab.*)
*Alasdair Morgan (*SNP*)
Jamie Stone (*LD*)
Mike Watson (*Lab.*)

ENVIRONMENT AND RURAL DEVELOPMENT
*Sarah Boyack (*Lab.*)
Roseanna Cunningham (*SNP*)
Rob Gibson (*SNP*)
Karen Gillon (*Lab.*)
Alex Johnstone (*C.*)
Maureen Macmillan (*Lab.*)
Alasdair Morrison (*Lab.*)
Nora Radcliffe (*LD*)
Eleanor Scott (*Green*)

EQUAL OPPORTUNITIES
Shiona Baird (*Green*)
Frances Curran (*SSP*)
Marlyn Glen (*Lab.*)
Marilyn Livingstone (*Lab.*)
Campbell Martin (*SNP*)
Nanette Milne (*C.*)
*Cathy Peattie (*Lab.*)
Elaine Smith (*Lab.*)

EUROPEAN AND EXTERNAL RELATIONS
Dennis Canavan (*Ind.*)
Margaret Ewing (*SNP*)
Phil Gallie (*C.*)
Jon Home Robertson (*Lab.*)
Gordon Jackson (*Lab.*)
*Richard Lochhead (*SNP*)
Alasdair Morrison (*Lab.*)
Irene Oldfather (*Lab.*)
Keith Raffan (*LD*)

FINANCE
Wendy Alexander (*Lab.*)
Ted Brocklebank (*C.*)
Fergus Ewing (*SNP*)
Kate Maclean (*Lab.*)
*Des McNulty (*Lab.*)
Jim Mather (*SNP*)
Dr Elaine Murray (*Lab.*)
Jeremy Purvis (*LD*)
John Swinburne (*SSCUP*)

HEALTH
David Davidson (*C.*)
Helen Eadie (*Lab.*)
*Christine Grahame (*SNP*)
Janis Hughes (*Lab.*)
Kate Maclean (*Lab.*)
Duncan McNeil (*Lab.*)
Shona Robison (*SNP*)
Mike Rumbles (*LD*)
Dr Jean Turner (*Ind.*)

JUSTICE I
Bill Butler (*Lab.*)
Marlyn Glen (*Lab.*)
*Pauline McNeill (*Lab.*)
Michael Matheson (*SNP*)
Margaret Mitchell (*C.*)
Stewart Maxwell (*SNP*)
Margaret Smith (*LD*)

JUSTICE II
Jackie Baillie (*Lab.*)
Scott Barrie (*Lab.*)
Colin Fox (*SSP*)
*Annabel Goldie (*C.*)
Mike Pringle (*LD*)
Nicola Sturgeon (*SNP*)
Karen Whitefield (*Lab.*)

LOCAL GOVERNMENT AND TRANSPORT
Dr Sylvia Jackson (*Lab.*)
Rosie Kane (*SSP*)
Michael McMahon (*Lab.*)
Bruce McFee (*SNP*)
Paul Martin (*Lab.*)
*Bristow Muldoon (*Lab.*)
David Mundell (*C.*)
Iain Smith (*LD*)
Andrew Welsh (*SNP*)

PROCEDURES
Richard Baker (*Lab.*)
Mark Ballard (*Green*)
Cathie Craigie (*Lab.*)
Bruce Crawford (*SNP*)
Karen Gillon (*Lab.*)
Jamie McGrigor (*C.*)
*Iain Smith (*LD*)

PUBLIC PETITIONS
Jackie Baillie (*Lab.*)
Helen Eadie (*Lab.*)
Linda Fabiani (*SNP*)
Carolyn Leckie (*SSP*)
*Michael McMahon (*Lab.*)
John Farquhar Munro (*LD*)
John Scott (*C.*)
Mike Watson (*Lab.*)
Sandra White (*SNP*)

STANDARDS
Bill Butler (*Lab.*)
Alex Fergusson (*C.*)
Donald Gorrie (*LD*)
Kenneth Macintosh (*Lab.*)
*Tricia Marwick (*SNP*)
Alex Neil (*SNP*)
Karen Whitefield (*Lab.*)

SUBORDINATE LEGISLATION
Gordon Jackson (*Lab.*)
*Dr Sylvia Jackson (*Lab.*)
Stewart Maxwell (*SNP*)
Christine May (*Lab.*)
Mike Pringle (*LD*)
Murray Tosh (*C.*)

*Convener

SCOTTISH PARLIAMENT ELECTIONS

1 May 2003

CONSTITUENCIES

ABERDEEN CENTRAL
(Scotland North East Region)
E. 49,477 T. 20,964 (42.37%)

Lewis Macdonald, (*Lab.*)	6,835	(32.60%)
Richard Lochhead, (*SNP*)	5,593	(26.68%)
Eleanor Anderson, (*LD*)	4,744	(22.63%)
Alan Butler, (*C.*)	2,616	(12.48%)
Andy Cumbers, (*SSP*)	1,176	(5.61%)

*Lab. Maj.*1,242 (5.92%)
2.13% swing Lab. to SNP

ABERDEEN NORTH
(Scotland North East Region)
E. 52,898 T. 25,027 (47.31%)

Brian Adam, (*SNP*)	8,381	(33.49%)
Elaine Thomson, (*Lab.*)	7,924	(31.66%)
John Reynolds, (*LD*)	5,767	(23.04%)
Jim Gifford, (*C.*)	2,311	(9.23%)
Katrine Trolle, (*SSP*)	644	(2.57%)

SNP Maj. 457 (1.83%)
1.63% swing Lab. to SNP

ABERDEEN SOUTH
(Scotland North East Region)
E. 58,204 T. 30,124 (51.76%)

Nicol Stephen, (*LD*)	13,821	(45.88%)
Richard Baker, (*Lab.*)	5,805	(19.27%)
Ian Duncan, (*C.*)	5,230	(17.36%)
Maureen Watt, (*SNP*)	4,315	(14.32%)
Keith Farnsworth, (*SSP*)	953	(3.16%)

LD Maj. 8,016 (26.61%)
10.77% swing Lab. to LD

ABERDEENSHIRE WEST AND KINCARDINE
(Scotland North East Region)
E. 62,542 T. 31,636 (50.58%)

Mike Rumbles, (*LD*)	14,553	(46.00%)
David Davidson, (*C.*)	9,154	(28.94%)
Ian Angus, (*SNP*)	4,489	(14.19%)
Kevin Hutchens, (*Lab.*)	2,727	(8.62%)
Alan Manley, (*SSP*)	713	(2.25%)

LD Maj. 5,399 (17.07%)
5.33% swing C. to LD

AIRDRIE AND SHOTTS
(Scotland Central Region)
E. 56,680 T. 25,086 (44.26%)

Karen Whitefield, (*Lab.*)	14,209	(56.64%)
Gil Paterson, (*SNP*)	5,232	(20.86%)
Alan Melville, (*C.*)	2,203	(8.78%)
Fraser Coats, (*SSP*)	2,096	(8.36%)
Kevin Lang, (*LD*)	1,346	(5.37%)

Lab. Maj. 8,977 (35.78%)
4.37% swing SNP to Lab.

ANGUS
(Scotland North East Region)
E. 60,608 T. 29,789 (49.15%)

Andrew Welsh, (*SNP*)	13,251	(44.48%)
Alex Johnstone, (*C.*)	6,564	(22.03%)
John Denning, (*Lab.*)	4,871	(16.35%)
Dick Speirs, (*LD*)	3,802	(12.76%)
Bruce Wallace, (*SSP*)	1,301	(4.37%)

SNP Maj. 6,687 (22.45%)
1.66% swing SNP to C.

ARGYLL AND BUTE
(Highlands and Islands Region)
E. 48,330 T. 27,948 (57.83%)

George Lyon, (*LD*)	9,817	(35.13%)
David Petrie, (*C.*)	5,621	(20.11%)
Jim Mather, (*SNP*)	5,485	(19.63%)
Hugh Raven, (*Lab.*)	5,107	(18.27%)
Des Divers, (*SSP*)	1,667	(5.96%)
David Walker, (*SPA*)	251	(0.90%)

LD Maj. 4,196 (15.01%)
1.68% swing LD to C.

AYR
(Scotland South Region)
E. 55,523 T. 31,591 (56.90%)

John Scott, (*C.*)	12,865	(40.72%)
Rita Miller, (*Lab.*)	10,975	(34.74%)
James Dornan, (*SNP*)	4,334	(13.72%)
Stuart Ritchie, (*LD*)	1,769	(5.60%)
James Stewart, (*SSP*)	1,648	(5.22%)

C. Maj. 1,890 (5.98%)
3.02% swing Lab. to C.

BANFF AND BUCHAN
(Scotland North East Region)
E. 55,358 T. 26,149 (47.24%)

Stewart Stevenson, (*SNP*)	13,827	(52.88%)
Stewart Whyte, (*C.*)	5,463	(20.89%)
Ian Brotchie, (*Lab.*)	2,885	(11.03%)
Debra Storr, (*LD*)	2,227	(8.52%)
Alan Buchan, (*SPA*)	907	(3.47%)
Alice Rowan, (*SSP*)	840	(3.21%)

SNP Maj. 8,364 (31.99%)
1.80% swing SNP to C.

CAITHNESS, SUTHERLAND AND EASTER ROSS
(Highlands and Islands Region)
E. 40,462 T. 21,127 (52.21%)

Jamie Stone, (*LD*)	7,742	(36.65%)
Deirdre Steven, (*Lab.*)	5,650	(26.74%)
Rob Gibson, (*SNP*)	3,692	(17.48%)
Alan McLeod, (*C.*)	2,262	(10.71%)
Gordon Campbell, (*Ind.*)	953	(4.51%)
Frank Ward, (*SSP*)	828	(3.92%)

LD Maj. 2,092 (9.90%)
3.48% swing LD to Lab.

CARRICK, CUMNOCK AND DOON VALLEY
(Scotland South Region)
E. 65,102 T. 34,366 (52.79%)

Cathy Jamieson, (*Lab. Co-op*)	16,484	(47.97%)
Phil Gallie, (*C.*)	9,030	(26.28%)
Adam Ingram, (*SNP*)	5,822	(16.94%)
Murray Steele, (*SSP*)	1,715	(4.99%)
Caron Howden, (*LD*)	1,315	(3.83%)

Lab. Co-op Maj. 7,454 (21.69%)
3.20% swing Lab. Co-op to C.

CLYDEBANK AND MILNGAVIE
(Scotland West Region)
E. 51,327 T. 26,514 (51.66%)

Des McNulty, (*Lab.*)	10,585	(39.92%)
Jim Yuill, (*SNP*)	6,051	(22.82%)
Rod Ackland, (*LD*)	3,224	(12.16%)
Mary Leishman, (*C.*)	2,885	(10.88%)
Dawn Brennan, (*SSP*)	1,902	(7.17%)
Danny McCafferty, (*Ind.*)	1,867	(7.04%)

Lab. Maj. 4,534 (17.10%)
1.49% swing SNP to Lab.

CLYDESDALE
(Scotland South Region)
E. 63,675 T. 32,442 (50.95%)

Karen Gillon, (*Lab.*)	14,800	(45.62%)
John Brady, (*SNP*)	8,129	(25.06%)
Alastair Campbell, (*C.*)	5,174	(15.95%)
Fraser Grieve, (*LD*)	2,338	(7.21%)
Owen Meharry, (*SSP*)	1,422	(4.38%)
David Morrison, (*SPA*)	579	(1.78%)

Lab. Maj. 6,671 (20.56%)
5.30% swing SNP to Lab.

COATBRIDGE AND CHRYSTON
(Scotland Central Region)
E. 51,521 T. 23,862 (46.32%)

Elaine Smith, (*Lab.*)	13,422	(56.25%)
James Gribben, (*SNP*)	4,851	(20.33%)
Donald Reece, (*C.*)	2,041	(8.55%)
Gordon Martin, (*SSP*)	1,911	(8.01%)

Doreen Nisbet, (*LD*)	1,637	(6.86%)

Lab. Maj. 8,571 (35.92%)
0.73% swing SNP to Lab.

CUMBERNAULD AND KILSYTH
(Scotland Central Region)
E. 48,667 T. 24,404 (50.14%)

Cathie Craigie, (*Lab.*)	10,146	(41.58%)
Andrew Wilson, (*SNP*)	9,626	(39.44%)
Kenny McEwan, (*SSP*)	1,823	(7.47%)
Hugh O'Donnell, (*LD*)	1,264	(5.18%)
Margaret McCulloch, (*C.*)	978	(4.01%)
Christopher Donohue, (*Ind.*)	567	(2.32%)

Lab. Maj. 520 (2.13%)
5.89% swing Lab. to SNP

CUNNINGHAME NORTH
(Scotland West Region)
E. 55,319 T. 28,631 (51.76%)

Allan Wilson, (*Lab.*)	11,142	(38.92%)
Campbell Martin, (*SNP*)	7,755	(27.09%)
Peter Ramsay, (*C.*)	5,542	(19.36%)
John Boyd, (*LD*)	2,333	(8.15%)
Sean Scott, (*SSP*)	1,859	(6.49%)

Lab. Maj. 3,387 (11.83%)
1.25% swing Lab. to SNP

CUNNINGHAME SOUTH
(Scotland South Region)
E. 49,877 T. 22,772 (45.66%)

Irene Oldfather, (*Lab.*)	11,165	(49.03%)
Michael Russell, (*SNP*)	5,089	(22.35%)
Rosemary Byrne, (*SSP*)	2,677	(11.76%)
Andrew Brocklehurst, (*C.*)	2,336	(10.26%)
Iain Dale (*LD*)	1,505	(6.61%)

Lab. Maj. 6,076 (26.68%)
1.78% swing SNP to Lab.

DUMBARTON
(Scotland West Region)
E. 55,575 T. 28,823 (51.86%)

Jackie Baillie, (*Lab.*)	12,154	(42.17%)
Iain Docherty, (*SNP*)	5,542	(19.23%)
Eric Thompson, (*LD*)	4,455	(15.46%)
Murray Tosh, (*C.*)	4,178	(14.50%)
Les Robertson, (*SSP*)	2,494	(8.65%)

Lab. Maj. 6,612 (22.94%)
4.61% swing SNP to Lab.

DUMFRIES
(Scotland South Region)
E. 61,517 T. 32,110 (52.20%)

Elaine Murray, (*Lab.*)	12,834	(39.97%)
David Mundell, (*C.*)	11,738	(36.56%)
Andrew Wood, (*SNP*)	3,931	(12.24%)
Clare Hamblen, (*LD*)	2,394	(7.46%)

John Dennis, (*SSP*) 1,213 (3.78%)
Lab. Maj. 1,096 (3.41%)
3.05% swing Lab. to C.

DUNDEE EAST
(Scotland North East Region)
E. 53,876 *T.* 26,348 (48.90%)

Shona Robison, (*SNP*)	10,428	(39.58%)
John McAllion, (*Lab.*)	10,338	(39.24%)
Edward Prince, (*C.*)	3,133	(11.89%)
Clive Sneddon, (*LD*)	1,584	(6.01%)
James Gourlay, (*Ind.*)	865	(3.28%)

SNP Maj. 90 (0.34%)
4.68% swing Lab. to SNP

DUNDEE WEST
(Scotland North East Region)
E. 51,387 *T.* 25,003 (48.66%)

Kate McLean, (*Lab.*)	8,234	(32.93%)
Irene McGugan, (*SNP*)	7,168	(28.67%)
Ian Borthwick, (*Ind.*)	4,715	(18.86%)
Shona Ferrier, (*LD*)	1,878	(7.51%)
Jim McFarland, (*SSP*)	1,501	(6.00%)
Victoria Roberts, (*C.*)	1,376	(5.50%)
Morag MacLachlan, (*SPA*)	131	(0.52%)

Lab. Maj. 1,066 (4.26%)
1.92% swing SNP to Lab.

DUNFERMLINE EAST
(Scotland Mid and Fife Region)
E. 51,220 *T.* 23,154 (45.20%)

Helen Eadie, (*Lab. Co-op*)	11,552	(49.89%)
Janet Law, (*SNP*)	4,262	(18.41%)
Stuart Randall, (*C.*)	2,485	(10.73%)
Brian Stewart, (*Local Hospital*)	1,890	(8.16%)
Linda Graham, (*SSP*)	1,537	(6.64%)
Rodger Spillane, (*LD*)	1,428	(6.17%)

Lab. Co-op Maj. 7,290 (31.48%)
1.08% swing SNP to Lab. Co-op

DUNFERMLINE WEST
(Scotland Mid and Fife Region)
E. 53,915 *T.* 25,240 (46.81%)

Scott Barrie, (*Lab.*)	8,664	(34.33%)
David Wishart, (*Local Hospital*)	4,584	(18.16%)
Brian Goodall, (*SNP*)	4,392	(17.40%)
Jim Tolson, (*LD*)	3,636	(14.41%)
Jim Mackie, (*C.*)	1,868	(7.40%)
Andy Jackson, (*SSP*)	923	(3.66%)
Alastair Harper, (*Ind.*)	714	(2.83%)
Damien Quigg, (*Ind. Q*)	459	(1.82%)

Lab. Maj. 4,080 (16.16%)

EAST KILBRIDE
(Scotland Central Region)
E. 65,472 *T.* 34,087 (52.06%)

Andy Kerr, (*Lab.*)	13,825	(40.56%)
Linda Fabiani, (*SNP*)	8,544	(25.07%)
Grace Campbell, (*C.*)	3,785	(11.10%)
Carolyn Leckie, (*SSP*)	2,736	(8.03%)
Colin McCartney, (*Ind.*)	2,597	(7.62%)
Alex Mackie, (*LD*)	2,181	(6.40%)
John Houston, (*Ind. Houston*)	419	(1.23%)

Lab. Maj. 5,281 (15.49%)
0.08% swing Lab. to SNP

EAST LOTHIAN
(Scotland South Region)
E. 59,227 *T.* 31,204 (52.69%)

John Home Robertson, (*Lab.*)	13,683	(43.85%)
Judy Hayman, (*LD*)	5,508	(17.65%)
Stewart Thomson, (*C.*)	5,459	(17.49%)
Tom Roberts, (*SNP*)	5,174	(16.58%)
Hugh Kerr, (*SSP*)	1,380	(4.42%)

Lab. Maj. 8,175 (26.20%)
6.95% swing Lab. to LD

EASTWOOD
(Scotland West Region)
E. 67,051 *T.* 38,889 (58.00%)

Ken Macintosh, (*Lab.*)	13,946	(35.86%)
Jackson Carlaw, (*C.*)	10,244	(26.34%)
Allan Steele, (*LD*)	5,056	(13.00%)
Stewart Maxwell, (*SNP*)	4,736	(12.18%)
Margaret Hinds, (*Local Health*)	3,163	(8.13%)
Steve Oram, (*SSP*)	1,504	(3.87%)
Martyn Greene, (*SPA*)	240	(0.62%)

Lab. Maj. 3,702 (9.52%)
2.42% swing C. to Lab.

EDINBURGH CENTRAL
(Lothians Region)
E. 60,824 *T.* 28,014 (46.06%)

Sarah Boyack, (*Lab.*)	9,066	(32.36%)
Andy Myles, (*LD*)	6,400	(22.85%)
Kevin Pringle, (*SNP*)	4,965	(17.72%)
Peter Finnie, (*C.*)	4,802	(17.14%)
Catriona Grant, (*SSP*)	2,552	(9.11%)
James O'Neill, (*SPA*)	229	(0.82%)

Lab. Maj. 2,666 (9.52%)
5.98% swing Lab. to LD

EDINBURGH EAST AND MUSSELBURGH
(Lothians Region)
E. 57,704 *T.* 29,044 (50.33%)

Susan Deacon, (*Lab.*)	12,655	(43.57%)
Kenny MacAskill, (*SNP*)	6,497	(22.37%)
John Smart, (*C.*)	3,863	(13.30%)
Gary Peacock, (*LD*)	3,582	(12.33%)

Derek Durkin, (*SSP*) 2,447 (8.43%)
Lab. Maj. 6,158 (21.20%)
1.53% swing SNP to Lab.

EDINBURGH NORTH AND LEITH
(Lothians Region)
E. 60,501 *T.* 28,734 (47.49%)

Malcolm Chisholm, (*Lab.*)	10,979	(38.21%)
Anne Dana, (*SNP*)	5,565	(19.37%)
Ian Mowat, (*C.*)	4,821	(16.78%)
Sebastian Tombs, (*LD*)	4,785	(16.65%)
Bill Scott, (*SSP*)	2,584	(8.99%)

Lab. Maj. 5,414 (18.84%)
1.13% swing Lab. to SNP

EDINBURGH PENTLANDS
(Lothians Region)
E. 58,534 *T.* 33,382 (57.03%)

David McLetchie, (*C.*)	12,420	(37.21%)
Iain Gray, (*Lab.*)	10,309	(30.88%)
Ian McKee, (*SNP*)	5,620	(16.84%)
Simon Clark, (*LD*)	3,943	(11.81%)
Frank O'Donnell, (*SSP*)	1,090	(3.27%)

C. Maj. 2,111 (6.32%)
6.80% swing Lab. to C.

EDINBURGH SOUTH
(Lothians Region)
E. 60,366 *T.* 31,196 (51.68%)

Mike Pringle, (*LD*)	10,005	(32.07%)
Angus Mackay, (*Lab.*)	9,847	(31.56%)
Gordon Buchan, (*C.*)	5,180	(16.60%)
Alex Orr, (*SNP*)	4,396	(14.09%)
Shirley Gibb, (*SSP*)	1,768	(5.67%)

LD Maj. 158 (0.51%)
7.61% swing Lab. to LD

EDINBURGH WEST
(Lothians Region)
E. 60,136 *T.* 33,301 (55.38%)

Margaret Smith, (*LD*)	14,434	(43.34%)
James Douglas-Hamilton, (*C.*)	8,520	(25.58%)
Carol Fox, (*Lab.*)	5,046	(15.15%)
Alyn Smith, (*SNP*)	4,133	(12.41%)
Pat Smith, (*SSP*)	993	(2.98%)
Bruce Skivington, (*SPA*)	175	(0.53%)

LD Maj. 5,914 (17.76%)
3.37% swing C. to LD

FALKIRK EAST
(Scotland Central Region)
E. 56,175 *T.* 27,559 (49.06%)

Cathy Peattie, (*Lab.*)	14,235	(51.65%)
Keith Brown, (*SNP*)	7,576	(27.49%)
Thomas Calvert, (*C.*)	2,720	(9.87%)
Karen Utting, (*LD*)	1,651	(5.99%)

Mhairi McAlpine, (*SSP*) 1,377 (5.00%)
Lab. Maj. 6,659 (24.16%)
6.20% swing SNP to Lab.

FALKIRK WEST
(Scotland Central Region)
E. 52,122 *T.* 26,400 (50.65%)

Dennis Canavan, (*Falkirk W*)	14,703	(55.69%)
Michael Matheson, (*SNP*)	4,703	(17.81%)
Lee Whitehill, (*Lab.*)	4,589	(17.38%)
Iain Mitchell, (*C.*)	1,657	(6.28%)
Jacqueline Kelly, (*LD*)	748	(2.83%)

Falkirk W Maj. 10,000 (37.88%)
0.34% swing SNP to Falkirk W

FIFE CENTRAL
(Scotland Mid and Fife Region)
E. 57,633 *T.* 25,597 (44.41%)

Christine May, (*Lab. Co-op*)	10,591	(41.38%)
Tricia Marwick, (*SNP*)	7,829	(30.59%)
Andrew Rodger, (*Ind.*)	2,258	(8.82%)
James North, (*C.*)	1,803	(7.04%)
Elizabeth Riches, (*LD*)	1,725	(6.74%)
Morag Balfour, (*SSP*)	1,391	(5.43%)

Lab. Co-op Maj. 2,762 (10.79%)
7.81% swing Lab. Co-op to SNP

FIFE NORTH EAST
(Scotland Mid and Fife Region)
E. 58,695 *T.* 29,282 (49.89%)

Iain Smith, (*LD*)	13,479	(46.03%)
Ted Brocklebank, (*C.*)	8,424	(28.77%)
Capre Ross-Williams, (*SNP*)	3,660	(12.50%)
Gregor Poynton, (*Lab.*)	2,353	(8.04%)
Carlo Morelli, (*SSP*)	1,366	(4.66%)

LD Maj. 5,055 (17.26%)
1.59% swing C. to LD

GALLOWAY AND UPPER NITHSDALE
(Scotland South Region)
E. 51,651 *T.* 29,635 (57.38%)

Alex Fergusson, (*C.*)	11,332	(38.24%)
Alasdair Morgan, (*SNP*)	11,233	(37.90%)
Norma Hart, (*Lab.*)	4,299	(14.51%)
Neil Wallace, (*LD*)	1,847	(6.23%)
Joy Cherkaoui, (*SSP*)	709	(2.39%)
Graham Brockhouse, (*SPA*)	215	(0.73%)

C. Maj. 99 (0.33%)
4.70% swing SNP to C.

GLASGOW ANNIESLAND
(Glasgow Region)
E. 50,795 *T.* 22,165 (43.64%)

Bill Butler, (*Lab. Co-op*)	10,141	(45.75%)
Bill Kidd, (*SNP*)	3,888	(17.54%)
Bill Aitken, (*C.*)	3,186	(14.37%)

Charlie McCarthy, (*SSP*)   2,620   (11.82%)
Iain Brown, (*LD*)   2,330   (10.51%)
Lab. Co-op Maj. 6,253 (28.21%)
5.19% swing Lab. Co-op to SNP

GLASGOW BAILLIESTON
(Glasgow Region)
E. 46,346 *T.* 18,270 (39.42%)

Margaret Curran, (*Lab.*)   9,657   (52.86%)
Lachlan McNeill, (*SNP*)   3,479   (19.04%)
Jim McVicar, (*SSP*)   2,461   (13.47%)
Janette McAlpine, (*C.*)   1,472   (8.06%)
David Jackson, (*LD*)   1,201   (6.57%)
Lab. Maj. 6,178 (33.81%)
10.43% swing SNP to Lab.

GLASGOW CATHCART
(Glasgow Region)
E. 49,017 *T.* 22,307 (45.51%)

Mike Watson, (*Lab.*)   8,742   (39.19%)
David Ritchie, (*SNP*)   3,630   (16.27%)
Richard Cook, (*C.*)   2,888   (12.95%)
Malcolm Wilson, (*SSP*)   2,819   (12.64%)
Pat Lally, (*Local Health*)   2,419   (10.84%)
Tom Henery, (*LD*)   1,741   (7.80%)
Robert Wilson, (*Parent Ex*)   68   (0.30%)
Lab Maj. 5,112 (22.92%)
1.50% swing SNP to Lab.

GLASGOW GOVAN
(Glasgow Region)
E. 48,635 *T.* 21,136 (43.46%)

Gordon Jackson, (*Lab.*)   7,834   (37.06%)
Nicola Sturgeon, (*SNP*)   6,599   (31.22%)
Jimmy Scott, (*SSP*)   2,369   (11.21%)
Faisal Butt, (*C.*)   1,878   (8.89%)
Paul Graham, (*LD*)   1,807   (8.55%)
Razaq Dean. (*Ind.*)   226   (1.07%)
John Foster, (*CPPDS*)   215   (1.02%)
Asif Nasir, (*SPA*)   208   (0.98%)
Lab. Maj. 1,235 (5.84%)
0.41% swing Lab. to SNP

GLASGOW KELVIN
(Glasgow Region)
E. 56,038 *T.* 22,080 (39.40%)

Pauline McNeill, (*Lab.*)   7,880   (35.69%)
Sandra White, (*SNP*)   4,591   (20.79%)
Douglas Herbison, (*LD*)   3,334   (15.10%)
Andy Harvey, (*SSP*)   3,159   (14.31%)
Gawain Towler, (*C.*)   1,816   (8.22%)
Alistair McConnachie, (*Ind. Green*) 1,300   (5.89%)
Lab. Maj. 3,289 (14.90%)
0.32% swing Lab. to SNP

GLASGOW MARYHILL
(Glasgow Region)
E. 49,119 *T.* 18,243 (37.14%)

Patricia Ferguson, (*Lab.*)   8,997   (49.32%)
Bill Wilson, (*SNP*)   3,629   (19.89%)
Donnie Nicolson, (*SSP*)   2,945   (16.14%)
Arthur Sanderson, (*LD*)   1,785   (9.78%)
Robert Erskine, (*C.*)   887   (4.86%)
Lab. Maj. 5,368 (29.42%)
5.31% swing SNP to Lab.

GLASGOW POLLOK
(Glasgow Region)
E. 47,134 *T.* 21,538 (45.70%)

Johann Lamont, (*Lab. Co-op*)   9,357   (43.44%)
Tommy Sheridan, (*SSP*)   6,016   (27.93%)
Kenneth Gibson, (*SNP*)   4,118   (19.12%)
Ashraf Anjum, (*C.*)   1,012   (4.70%)
Isabel Nelson, (*LD*)   962   (4.47%)
Robert Ray, (*Parent Ex*)   73   (0.34%)
Lab. Co-op Maj. 3,341 (15.51%)
3.35% swing Lab. Co-op to SSP

GLASGOW RUTHERGLEN
(Glasgow Region)
E. 49,512 *T.* 23,554 (47.57%)

Janis Hughes, (*Lab.*)   10,794   (45.83%)
Robert Brown, (*LD*)   4,491   (19.07%)
Anne McLaughlin, (*SNP*)   3,511   (14.91%)
Gavin Brown, (*C.*)   2,499   (10.61%)
Bill Bonnar, (*SSP*)   2,259   (9.59%)
Lab. Maj. 6,303 (26.76%)
0.21% swing LD to Lab.

GLASGOW SHETTLESTON
(Glasgow Region)
E. 46,730 *T.* 16,547 (35.41%)

Francis McAveety, (*Lab. Co-op*)   9,365   (56.60%)
Jim Byrne, (*SNP*)   3,018   (18.24%)
Rosie Kane, (*SSP*)   2,403   (14.52%)
Dorothy Luckhurst, (*C.*)   982   (5.93%)
Lewis Hutton, (*LD*)   779   (4.71%)
Lab. Co-op Maj. 6,347 (38.36%)
5.87% swing SNP to Lab. Co-op

GLASGOW SPRINGBURN
(Glasgow Region)
E. 49,551 *T.* 18,573 (37.48%)

Paul Martin, (*Lab.*)   10,963   (59.03%)
Frank Rankin, (*SNP*)   2,956   (15.92%)
Margaret Bean, (*SSP*)   2,653   (14.28%)
Alan Rodger, (*C.*)   1,233   (6.64%)
Charles Dundas, (*LD*)   768   (4.14%)
Lab. Maj. 8,007 (43.11%)
5.36% swing SNP to Lab.

GORDON
(Scotland North East Region)
E. 60,686 T. 28,798 (47.45%)

Nora Radcliffe, (*LD*)	10,963	(38.07%)
Nanette Milne, (*C.*)	6,892	(23.93%)
Alasdair Allan, (*SNP*)	6,501	(22.57%)
Ellis Thorpe, (*Lab.*)	2,973	(10.32%)
John Sangster, (*SSP*)	780	(2.71%)
Steven Mathers, (*Ind.*)	689	(2.39%)

LD Maj. 4,071 (14.14%)
1.48% swing LD to C.

GREENOCK AND INVERCLYDE
(Scotland West Region)
E. 46,045 T. 23,781 (51.65%)

Duncan McNeil, (*Lab.*)	9,674	(40.68%)
Ross Finnie, (*LD*)	6,665	(28.03%)
Tom Chalmers, (*SNP*)	3,532	(14.85%)
Tricia McCafferty, (*SSP*)	2,338	(9.83%)
Charles Dunlop, (*C.*)	1,572	(6.61%)

Lab. Maj. 3,009 (12.65%)
1.20% swing Lab. to LD

HAMILTON NORTH AND BELLSHILL
(Scotland Central Region)
E. 51,965 T. 24,195 (46.56%)

Michael McMahon, (*Lab.*)	12,812	(52.95%)
Alex Neil, (*SNP*)	4,907	(20.28%)
Charles Ferguson, (*C.*)	2,625	(10.85%)
Shareen Blackhall, (*SSP*)	1,932	(7.99%)
Siobhan Mathers, (*LD*)	1,477	(6.10%)
Gordon McIntosh, (*SPA*)	442	(1.83%)

Lab. Maj. 7,905 (32.67%)
7.36% swing SNP to Lab.

HAMILTON SOUTH
(Scotland Central Region)
E. 45,749 T. 20,518 (44.85%)

Tom McCabe, (*Lab.*)	9,546	(46.53%)
John Wilson, (*SNP*)	4,722	(23.01%)
Margaret Mitchell, (*C.*)	2,601	(12.68%)
Willie O'Neil, (*SSP*)	1,893	(9.23%)
John Oswald, (*LD)*	1,756	(8.56%)

Lab. Maj. 4,824 (23.51%)
2.09% swing Lab. to SNP

INVERNESS EAST, NAIRN AND LOCHABER
(Highlands and Islands Region)
E. 66,694 T. 34,795 (52.17%)

Fergus Ewing, (*SNP*)	10,764	(30.94%)
Rhoda Grant, (*Lab.*)	9,718	(27.93%)
Mary Scanlon, (*C.*)	6,205	(17.83%)
Patsy Kenton, (*LD*)	5,622	(16.16%)
Steve Arnott, (*SSP*)	1,661	(4.77%)
Thomas Lamont, (*Ind.*)	825	(2.37%)

SNP Maj. 1,046 (3.01%)
0.98% swing Lab. to SNP

KILMARNOCK AND LOUDOUN
(Scotland Central Region)
E. 61,055 T. 31,520 (51.63%)

Margaret Jamieson, (*Lab.*)	12,633	(40.08%)
Danny Coffey, (*SNP*)	11,423	(36.24%)
Robin Traquair, (*C.*)	3,295	(10.45%)
Ian Gibson, (*LD*)	1,571	(4.98%)
Colin Rutherford, (*SSP*)	1,421	(4.51%)
May Anderson, (*Ind.*)	404	(1.28%)
Matthew Donnelly, (*Ind.*)	402	(1.28%)
Lyndsay McIntosh, (*SPA*)	371	(1.18%)

Lab. Maj. 1,210 (3.84%)
1.59% swing Lab. to SNP

KIRKCALDY
(Scotland Mid and Fife Region)
E. 49,653 T. 21,939 (44.18%)

Marilyn Livingstone, (*Lab. Co-op*)	10,235	(46.65%)
Colin Welsh, (*SNP*)	5,411	(24.66%)
Alex Cole-Hamilton, (*LD*)	2,417	(11.02%)
Mike Scott-Hayward, (*C.*)	2,332	(10.63%)
Rudi Vogels, (*SSP*)	1,544	(7.04%)

Lab. Co-op Maj. 4,824 (21.99%)
3.10% swing SNP to Lab. Co-op

LINLITHGOW
(Lothians Region)
E. 54,113 T. 27,645 (51.09%)

Mary Mulligan, (*Lab.*)	11,548	(41.77%)
Fiona Hyslop, (*SNP*)	9,578	(34.65%)
Gordon Lindhurst, (*C.*)	3,059	(11.07%)
Martin Oliver, (*LD*)	2,093	(7.57%)
Steve Nimmo, (*SSP*)	1,367	(4.94%)

Lab. Maj. 1,970 (7.13%)
0.77% swing Lab. to SNP

LIVINGSTON
(Lothians Region)
E. 65,421 T. 30,557 (46.71%)

Bristow Muldoon, (*Lab.*)	13,327	(43.61%)
Peter Johnston, (*SNP*)	9,657	(31.60%)
Lindsay Paterson, (*C.*)	2,848	(9.32%)
Paul McGreal, (*LD*)	2,714	(8.88%)
Robert Richard, (*SSP*)	1,640	(5.37%)
Stephen Milburn, (*SPA*)	371	(1.21%)

Lab. Maj. 3,670 (12.01%)
0.67% swing SNP to Lab.

MIDLOTHIAN
(Lothians Region)
E. 48,319 T. 23,556 (48.75%)

Rhona Brankin, (*Lab. Co-op*)	11,139	(47.29%)
Graham Sutherland, (*SNP*)	5,597	(23.76%)
Jacqui Bell, (*LD*)	2,700	(11.46%)
Rosemary MacArthur, (*C.*)	2,557	(10.85%)
Bob Goupillot, (*SSP*)	1,563	(6.64%)

Lab. Co-op Maj. 5,542 (23.53%)
2.48% swing SNP to Lab. Co-op

MORAY
(Highlands and Islands Region)
E. 58,242 T. 26,981 (46.33%)

Margaret Ewing, (*SNP*)	11,384	(42.19%)
Tim Wood, (*C.*)	6,072	(22.50%)
Peter Peacock, (*Lab.*)	5,157	(19.11%)
Linda Gorn, (*LD*)	3,283	(12.17%)
Norma Anderson, (*SSP*)	1,085	(4.02%)

SNP Maj. 5,312 (19.69%)
3.24% swing C. to SNP

MOTHERWELL AND WISHAW
(Scotland Central Region)
E. 51,785 T. 25,388 (49.03%)

Jack McConnell, (*Lab.*)	13,739	(54.12%)
Lloyd Quinan, (*SNP*)	4,480	(17.65%)
Mark Nolan, (*C.*)	2,542	(10.01%)
John Milligan, (*SSP*)	1,961	(7.72%)
John Swinburne, (*SSCUP*)	1,597	(6.29%)
Keith Legg, (*LD*)	1,069	(4.21%)

Lab. Maj. 9,259 (36.47%)
9.92% swing SNP to Lab.

OCHIL
(Scotland Mid and Fife Region)
E. 55,596 T. 30,416 (54.71%)

George Reid, (*SNP*)	11,659	(38.33%)
Richard Simpson, (*Lab.*)	11,363	(37.36%)
Malcolm Parkin, (*C.*)	2,946	(9.69%)
Catherine Whittingham, (*LD*)	2,536	(8.34%)
Felicity Garvie, (*SSP*)	1,102	(3.62%)
Flash Gordon Approaching, (*Loony*)	432	(1.42%)
William Whyte, (*ND*)	378	(1.24%)

SNP Maj. 296 (0.97%)
2.25% swing Lab. to SNP

ORKNEY
(Highlands and Islands Region)
E. 15,487 T. 8,004 (51.68%)

Jim Wallace, (*LD*)	3,659	(45.71%)
Christopher Zawadski (*C.*)	1,904	(23.79%)
John Mowat (*SNP*)	1,056	(13.19%)
John Aberdein (*SSP*)	914	(11.42%)
Richard Meade (*Lab.*)	471	(5.88%)

LD Maj. 1,755 (21.93%)
14.93% swing LD to C.

PAISLEY NORTH
(Scotland West Region)
E. 44,999 T. 22,206 (49.35%)

Wendy Alexander, (*Lab.*)	10,631	(47.87%)
George Adam, (*SNP*)	6,321	(28.47%)
Allison Cook, (*C.*)	1,871	(8.43%)
Brian O'Malley, (*LD*)	1,705	(7.68%)
Sean Hurl, (*SSP*)	1,678	(7.56%)

Lab. Maj. 4,310 (19.41%)
1.39% swing SNP to Lab.

PAISLEY SOUTH
(Scotland West Region)
E. 49,818 T. 24,984 (50.15%)

Hugh Henry, (*Lab.*)	10,190	(40.79%)
Bill Martin, (*SNP*)	7,737	(30.97%)
Eileen McCartin, (*LD*)	3,517	(14.08%)
Mark Jones, (*C.*)	1,775	(7.10%)
Frances Curran, (*SSP*)	1,765	(7.06%)

Lab. Maj. 2,453 (9.82%)
2.42% swing Lab. to SNP

PERTH
(Scotland and Mid Fife Region)
E. 61,957 T. 31,614 (51.03%)

Roseanna Cunningham, (*SNP*)	10,717	(33.90%)
Alexander Stewart, (*C.*)	9,990	(31.60%)
Robert Ball, (*Lab.*)	5,629	(17.81%)
Gordon Campbell, (*LD*)	3,530	(11.17%)
Philip Stott, (*SSP*)	982	(3.11%)
Thomas Burns, (*Ind.*)	509	(1.61%)
Ken Buchanan, (*SPA*)	257	(0.81%)

SNP Maj. 727 (2.30%)
1.56% swing SNP to C.

RENFREWSHIRE WEST
(Scotland West Region)
E. 50,963 T. 28,302 (55.53%)

Patricia Godman, (*Lab.*)	9,671	(34.17%)
Bruce McFee, (*SNP*)	7,179	(25.37%)
Annabel Goldie, (*C.*)	6,867	(24.26%)
Alison King, (*LD*)	2,902	(10.25%)
Gerry MaCartney, (*SSP*)	1,683	(5.95%)

Lab. Maj. 2,492 (8.81%)
0.15% swing SNP to Lab.

ROSS, SKYE AND INVERNESS WEST
(Highlands and Islands Region)
E. 55,777 T. 28,971 (51.94%)

John Farquhar Munro, (*LD*)	12,495	(43.13%)
David Thompson, (*SNP*)	5,647	(19.49%)
Maureen MacMillan, (*Lab.*)	5,464	(18.86%)
Jamie McGrigor, (*C.*)	3,772	(13.02%)
Anne McLeod, (*SSP*)	1,593	(5.50%)

LD Maj. 6,848 (23.64%)
6.66% swing SNP to LD

ROXBURGH AND BERWICKSHIRE
(Scotland South Region)
E. 45,625 T. 22,511 (49.34%)

Euan Robson, (*LD*)	9,280	(41.22%)
Sandy Scott, (*C.*)	6,790	(30.16%)
Roderick Campbell, (*SNP*)	2,816	(12.51%)
Sam Held, (*Lab.*)	2,802	(12.45%)
Graeme McIver, (*SSP*)	823	(3.66%)

LD Maj. 2,490 (11.06%)
0.90% swing LD to C.

SHETLAND
(Highlands and Islands Region)
E. 16,677 *T.* 8,645 (51.84%)

Tavish Scott, (*LD*)	3,989	(46.14%)
Willie Ross, (*SNP*)	1,729	(20.00%)
John Firth, (*C.*)	1,281	(14.82%)
Peter Hamilton, (*Lab.*)	880	(10.18%)
Peter Andrews, (*SSP*)	766	(8.86%)

LD Maj. 2,260 (26.14%)
7.00% swing LD to SNP

STIRLING
(Scotland and Mid Fife Region)
E. 52,087 *T.* 29,647 (56.92%)

Sylvia Jackson, (*Lab.*)	10,661	(35.96%)
Brian Monteith, (*C.*)	7,781	(26.25%)
Bruce Crawford, (*SNP*)	5,645	(19.04%)
Kenyon Wright, (*LD*)	3,432	(11.58%)
Margaret Stewart, (*SSP*)	1,486	(5.01%)
Keith Harding, (*SPA*)	642	(2.17%)

Lab. Maj. 2,880 (9.71%)
1.25% swing Lab. to C.

STRATHKELVIN AND BEARSDEN
(Scotland West Region)
E. 61,905 *T.* 35,736 (57.73%)

Jean Turner, (*Ind.*)	10,988	(30.75%)
Brian Fitzpatrick, (*Lab.*)	10,950	(30.64%)
Jo Swinson, (*LD*)	4,950	(13.85%)
Fiona McLeod, (*SNP*)	4,846	(13.56%)
Rory O'Brien, (*C.*)	4,002	(11.20%)

Ind Maj. 38 (0.11%)

TAYSIDE NORTH
(Scotland Mid and Fife Region)
E. 62,697 *T.* 33,343 (53.18%)

John Swinney, (*SNP*)	14,969	(44.89%)
Murdo Fraser, (*C.*)	10,466	(31.39%)
Gordon MacRae, (*Lab.*)	3,527	(10.58%)
Bob Forrest, (*LD*)	3,206	(9.62%)
Rosie Adams, (*SSP*)	941	(2.82%)
George Ashe, (*SPA*)	234	(0.70%)

SNP Maj. 4,503 (13.51%)
1.24% swing C. to SNP

TWEEDDALE, ETTRICK AND LAUDERDALE
(Scotland South Region)
E. 50,912 *T.* 26,700 (52.44%)

Jeremy Purvis, (*LD*)	7,197	(26.96%)
Christine Grahame, (*SNP*)	6,659	(24.94%)
Catherine Maxwell Stuart, (*Lab.*)	5,757	(21.56%)
Derek Brownlee, (*C.*)	5,686	(21.30%)
Norman Lockhart, (*SSP*)	1,055	(3.95%)
Alex Black, (*SPA*)	346	(1.30%)

LD Maj. 538 (2.01%)
5.63% swing LD to SNP

WESTERN ISLES
(Highlands and Islands Region)
E. 21,205 *T.* 12,387 (58.42%)

Alasdair Morrison, (*Lab.*)	5,825	(47.03%)
Alasdair Nicholson, (*SNP*)	5,105	(41.21%)
Frank Warren, (*C.*)	612	(4.94%)
Conor Snowden, (*LD*)	498	(4.02%)
Joanne Telfer, (*SSP*)	347	(2.80%)

Lab. Maj. 720 (5.81%)
4.59% swing Lab. to SNP

REGIONS

GLASGOW
E. 492,877 *T.* 39.42%

Lab.	77,040	(39.65%)
SNP	34,894	(17.96%)
SSP	31,116	(16.02%)
C.	15,299	(7.87%)
LD	14,839	(7.64%)
Green	14,570	(7.50%)
SSCUP	4,750	(2.44%)
Soc. Lab.	3,091	(1.59%)
ProLife	2,477	(1.27%)
SUP	2,349	(1.21%)
BNP	2,344	(1.21%)
SPA	612	(0.32%)
UK Ind.	552	(0.28%)
CPPDS	345	(0.18%)

Lab. Maj. 42,146 (21.69%)
1.64% swing SNP to Lab.

ADDITIONAL MEMBERS
Bill Aitken, (*C.*)
Robert Brown, (*LD*)
Sandra White, (*SNP*)
Nicola Sturgeon, (*SNP*)
Patrick Harvie, (*Green*)
Tommy Sheridan, (*SSP*)
Rosie Kane, (*SSP*)

HIGHLANDS AND ISLANDS
E. 322,874 *T.* 52.22%

SNP	39,497	(23.43%)
Lab.	37,605	(22.30%)
LD	31,655	(18.78%)
C.	26,989	(16.01%)
Green	13,935	(8.27%)
SSP	9,000	(5.34%)
UK Ind.	1,947	(1.15%)
SASSDR	1,822	(1.08%)
CPFRI	1,768	(1.05%)
Soc. Lab.	1,617	(0.96%)
PRSP	1,438	(0.85%)
SPA	793	(0.47%)

Ind.	353	(0.21%)
Rural	177	(0.10%)

SNP Maj. 1,892 (1.12%)
0.57% swing SNP to Lab.

ADDITIONAL MEMBERS
Jamie McGrigor, (*C.*)
Mary Scanlon, (*C.*)
Peter Peacock, (*Lab.*)
Maureen MacMillan, (*Lab.*)
Jim Mather, (*SNP*)
Rob Gibson, (*SNP*)
Eleanor Scott, (*Green*)

LOTHIANS
E. 525,918 *T.* 50.52%

Lab.	65,102	(24.50%)
SNP	43,142	(16.24%)
C.	40,173	(15.12%)
Green	31,908	(12.01%)
LD	29,237	(11.01%)
Ind.	27,144	(10.22%)
SSP	14,448	(5.44%)
PP	5,609	(2.11%)
Lib.	2,573	(0.97%)
Soc. Lab.	2,181	(0.82%)
UK Ind.	1,057	(0.40%)
Witchery	964	(0.36%)
SPA	879	(0.33%)
ProLife	608	(0.23%)
Ind. C.	383	(0.14%)
Ind. A	184	(0.07%)
Ind. Gatensbury	78	(0.03%)

Lab. Maj. 21,960 (8.27%)
1.89% swing SNP to Lab.

ADDITIONAL MEMBERS
Lord James Douglas-Hamilton, (*C.*)
Kenny MacAskill, (*SNP*)
Fiona Hyslop, (*SNP*)
Robin Harper, (*Green*)
Mark Ballard, (*Green*)
Margo MacDonald, (*Ind.*)
Colin Fox, (*SSP*)

SCOTLAND CENTRAL
E. 541,191 *T.* 48.61%

Lab.	106,318	(40.41%)
SNP	59,274	(22.53%)
C.	24,121	(9.17%)
SSP	19,016	(7.23%)
SSCUP	17,146	(6.52%)
LD	15,494	(5.89%)
Green	12,248	(4.66%)
Soc. Lab.	3,855	(1.47%)
SUP	2,147	(0.82%)

Ind.	1,265	(0.48%)
SPA	1,192	(0.45%)
UK Ind.	1,009	(0.38%)

Lab. Maj. 47,044 (17.88%)
3.19% swing SNP to Lab.

ADDITIONAL MEMBERS
Margaret Mitchell, (*C.*)
Donald Gorrie, (*LD*)
Alex Neil, (*SNP*)
Michael Matheson, (*SNP*)
Linda Fabiani, (*SNP*)
John Swinborne, (*SSCUP*)
Carolyn Leckie, (*SSP*)

SCOTLAND MID AND FIFE
E. 503,453 *T.* 49.68%

Lab.	63,239	(25.29%)
SNP	57,631	(23.04%)
C.	43,941	(17.57%)
LD	30,112	(12.04%)
Green	17,147	(6.86%)
SSP	11,401	(4.56%)
PP	8,380	(3.35%)
FHC	5,064	(2.02%)
SLH	4,662	(1.86%)
UK Ind.	2,355	(0.94%)
Soc. Lab.	2,273	(0.91%)
SPA	1,191	(0.48%)
Christian	1,064	(0.43%)
Ind. Gray	996	(0.40%)
Ind.	637	(0.25%)

Lab. Maj. 5,608 (2.24%)
1.22% swing Lab. to SNP

ADDITIONAL MEMBERS
Murdo Fraser, (*C.*)
Brian Monteith, (*C.*)
Ted Brocklebank, (*C.*)
Keith Raffan, (*LD*)
Bruce Crawford, (*SNP*)
Tricia Marwick, (*SNP*)
Mark Ruskell, (*Green*)

SCOTLAND NORTH EAST
E. 505,036 *T.* 48.25%

SNP	66,463	(27.28%)
Lab.	49,189	(20.19%)
LD	45,831	(18.81%)
C.	42,318	(17.37%)
Green	12,724	(5.22%)
SSP	10,226	(4.20%)
PP	5,584	(2.29%)
Fishing	5,566	(2.28%)
Soc. Lab.	2,431	(1.00%)
UK Ind.	1,498	(0.61%)
SPA	941	(0.39%)
Ind.	902	(0.37%)

SNP Maj. 17,274 (7.09%)
0.10% swing Lab. to SNP

ADDITIONAL MEMBERS
David Davidson, (C.)
Alex Johnstone, (C.)
Nanette Milne, (C.)
Marlyn Glen, (Lab.)
Richard Baker, (Lab.)
Richard Lochhead, (SNP)
Shiona Baird, (Green)

SCOTLAND SOUTH
E. 503,109 *T.* 52.33%

Lab.	78,955	(29.99%)
C.	63,827	(24.24%)
SNP	48,371	(18.37%)
LD	27,026	(10.26%)
Green	15,062	(5.72%)
SSP	14,228	(5.40%)
PP	9,082	(3.45%)
Soc. Lab.	3,054	(1.16%)
UK Ind.	1,889	(0.72%)
SPA	1,436	(0.55%)
Rural	355	(0.13%)

Lab. Maj. 15,128 (5.75%)
1.83% swing Lab. to C.

ADDITIONAL MEMBERS
Phil Gallie, (C.)
David Mundell, (C.)
Christine Grahame, (SNP)
Alasdair Morgan, (SNP)
Adam Ingram, (SNP)
Chris Ballance, (Green)
Rosemary Byrne, (SSP)

SCOTLAND WEST
E. 483,002 *T.* 61.53%

Lab.	83,931	(28.24%)
LD	71,580	(24.09%)
SNP	50,387	(16.96%)
C.	40,261	(13.55%)
SSP	18,591	(6.26%)
Green	14,544	(4.89%)
SSCUP	7,100	(2.39%)
ProLife	3,674	(1.24%)
Soc. Lab.	3,155	(1.06%)
UK Ind.	1,662	(0.56%)
SUP	1,617	(0.54%)
SPA	674	(0.23%)

Lab. Maj. 12,351 (4.16%)
11.70% swing Lab. to LD

ADDITIONAL MEMBERS
Annabel Goldie, (C.)
Murray Tosh, (C.)
Ross Finnie, (LD)
Campbell Martin, (SNP)
Bruce McFee, (SNP)
Stewart Maxwell, (SNP)
Frances Curran, (SSP)

MEMBERS OF THE SCOTTISH PARLIAMENT AS AT MAY 2003

*Adam, Brian, *SNP, Glasgow, Aberdeen North*, Maj. 457

*Aitken, Bill, *C., Glasgow region*

*Alexander, Wendy, *Lab., Paisley North*, Maj. 4,310

*Baillie, Jackie, *Lab., Dumbarton*, Maj. 6,612

Baird, Shiona, *Green, Scotland North East region*

Baker, Richard, *Lab., Scotland North East region*

Ballance, Chris, *Green, Scotland South region*

Ballard, Mark, *Green, Lothians region*

*Barrie, Scott, *Lab., Dunfermline West*, Maj. 4,080

*Boyack, Sarah, *Lab., Edinburgh Central*, Maj. 2,666

*Brankin, Rhona, *Lab. Co-op, Midlothian*, Maj. 5,542

Brocklebank, Ted, *C., Scotland Mid region*

*Brown, Robert E, *LD, Glasgow region*

*Butler, Bill, *Lab. Co-op, Glasgow Anniesland*, Maj. 6,253

Byrne, Rosemary, *SSP, Scotland South region*

*Canavan, Dennis, *Ind., Falkirk West*, Maj. 10,000

*Chisholm, Malcolm, *Lab., Edinburgh North and Leith*, Maj. 5,414

*Craigie, Cathie, *Lab., Cumbernauld and Kilsyth*, Maj. 520

*Crawford, Bruce, *SNP, Scotland Mid region*

*Cunningham, Roseanna, *SNP, Perth*, Maj. 727

Curran, Frances, *SSP, Scotland West region*

•Curran, Margaret, *Lab., Glasgow Baillieston*, Maj. 6,178

*Davidson, David, *C., Scotland North East region*

*Deacon, Susan, *Lab., Edinburgh East and Musselburgh*, Maj. 6,158

*Douglas-Hamilton, James, *C., Lothians region*

*Eadie, Helen, *Lab. Co-op, Dunfermline East*, Maj. 7,290

*Ewing, Fergus, *SNP, Inverness East, Nairn and Lochaber*, Maj. 1,046

*Ewing, Margaret, *SNP, Moray*, Maj. 5,312

*Fabiani, Linda, *SNP, Scotland Central region*

*Ferguson, Patricia, *Lab., Glasgow Maryhill*, Maj. 5,368

*Fergusson, Alex, C., *Galloway and Upper Nithsdale*, Maj. 99

*Finnie, Ross, *LD, Scotland West region*

Fox, Colin, *SSP, Lothians region*

*Fraser, Murdo, *C., Scotland Mid region*

*Gallie, Phil, *C., Scotland South region*

Gibson, Rob, *SNP, Highland region*

*Gillon, Karen, *Lab., Clydesdale*, Maj. 6,671

Glen, Marlyn, *Lab., Scotland North East region*

*Godman, Patricia, *Lab., Renfrewshire West*, Maj. 2,492

*Goldie, Annabel, *C., Scotland West region*

*Gorrie, Donald, *LD, Scotland Central region*

*Grahame, Christine, *SNP, Scotland South region*

*Harper, Robin, *Green, Lothians region*

Harvie, Patrick, *Green, Glasgow region*

*Henry, Hugh, *Lab., Paisley South*, Maj. 2,453

*Home Robertson, John, *Lab., East Lothian*, Maj. 8,175

*Hughes, Janis, *Lab., Glasgow Rutherglen*, Maj. 6,303

*Hyslop, Fiona, *SNP, Lothians region*

*Ingram, Adam, *SNP, Scotland South region*

*Jackson, Gordon, *Lab., Glasgow Govan*, Maj. 1,235

*Jackson, Sylvia, *Lab., Stirling*, Maj. 2,880

*Jamieson, Cathy, *Lab. Co-op, Carrick, Cumnock and Doon Valley*, Maj. 7,454

*Jamieson, Margaret, *Lab. Co-op, Kilmarnock and Loudoun*, Maj. 1,210

*Johnstone, Alex, *C., Scotland North East region*

Kane, Rosie, *SSP, Glasgow region*

*Kerr, Andy, *Lab., East Kilbride*, Maj. 5,281

*Lamont, Johann, *Lab. Co-op, Glasgow Pollok*, Maj. 3,341

Leckie, Carolyn, *SSP, Scotland Central region*

*Livingstone, Marilyn, *Lab. Co-op, Kirkcaldy*, Maj. 4,824

*Lochhead, Richard, *SNP, Scotland North East region*

*Lyon, George, *LD, Argyll and Bute*, Maj. 4,196

*MacAskill, Kenny, *SNP, Lothians region*

*MacDonald, Lewis, *Lab., Aberdeen Central*, Maj. 1,242

*MacDonald, Margo, *Ind., Lothians region*

*Macintosh, Kenneth, *Lab., Eastwood*, Maj. 3,702

*Maclean, Kate, *Lab., Dundee West*, Maj. 1,066

*MacMillan, Maureen, *Lab., Highland region*

Martin, Campbell, *SNP, Scotland West region*

*Martin, Paul, *Lab., Glasgow Springburn*, Maj. 8,007

*Marwick, Tricia, *SNP, Scotland Mid region*

Mather, Jim, *SNP, Highland region*

*Matheson, Michael, *SNP, Scotland Central region*

Maxwell, Stewart, *SNP, Scotland West region*

May, Christine, *Lab. Co-op, Fife Central*, Maj. 2,762

*McAveety, Frank, *Lab. Co-op, Glasgow Shettleston*, Maj. 6,347

*McCabe, Tom, *Lab., Hamilton South*, Maj. 4,824

*McConnell, Jack, *Lab., Motherwell and Wishaw*, Maj. 9,259

McFee, Bruce, *SNP, Scotland West region*

*McGrigor, Jamie, *C., Highland region*

*McLetchie, David, *C., Edinburgh Pentlands*, Maj. 2,111

*McMahon, Michael, *Lab., Hamilton North and Bellshill*, Maj. 7,905

*McNeil, Duncan, *Lab., Greenock and Inverclyde*, Maj. 3,009

*McNeill, Pauline, *Lab., Glasgow Kelvin*, Maj. 3,289

*McNulty, Des, *Lab., Clydebank and Milngavie*, Maj. 4,534

Milne, Nanette, *C., Scotland North East region*

Mitchell, Margaret, *C., Scotland Central region*

*****Monteith,** Brian, *C., Scotland Mid region*

*****Morgan,** Alasdair, *SNP, Scotland South region*

*****Morrison,** Alasdair, *Lab., Western Isles,* Maj. 720

*****Muldoon,** Bristow, *Lab., Livingston,* Maj. 3,670

*****Mulligan,** Mary, *Lab., Linlithgow,* Maj. 1,970

*****Mundell,** David, *C., Scotland South region*

Munro, John F., *LD, Ross, Skye and Inverness West,* Maj. 6,848

*****Murray,** Elaine, *Lab., Dumfries,* Maj. 1,096

*****Neil,** Alex, *SNP, Scotland Central region*

*****Oldfather,** Irene, *Lab., Cunninghame South,* Maj. 6,076

*****Peacock,** Peter, *Lab., Highland region*

*****Peattie,** Cathy, *Lab., Falkirk East,* Maj. 6,659

Pringle, Mike, *LD, Edinburgh South,* Maj. 158

Purvis, Jeremy, *LD, Tweeddale, Ettrick and Lauderdale,* Maj. 538

*****Radcliffe,** Nora, *LD, Gordon,* Maj. 4,071

*****Raffan,** Keith, *LD, Scotland Mid region*

*****Reid,** George, *SNP, Ochil,* Maj. 296

*****Robison,** Shona, *SNP, Dundee East,* Maj. 90

*****Robson,** Euan, *LD, Roxburgh and Berwickshire,* Maj. 2,490

*****Rumbles,** Mike, *LD, Aberdeenshire West Kincardine,* Maj. 5,399

Ruskell, Mark, *Green, Scotland Mid region*

*****Scanlon,** Mary, *C., Highland region*

Scott, Eleanor, *Green, Highland*

*****Scott,** John, *C., Ayr,* Maj. 1,890

*****Scott,** Tavish, *LD, Shetland,* Maj. 2,260

*****Sheridan,** Tommy, *SSP, Glasgow region*

*****Smith,** Elaine, *Lab., Coatbridge and Chryston,* Maj. 8,571

*****Smith,** Iain, *LD, Fife North East,* Maj. 5,055

*****Smith,** Margaret, *LD, Edinburgh West,* Maj. 5,914

*****Stephen,** Nicol, *LD, Aberdeen South,* Maj. 8,016

*****Stevenson,** Stewart, *SNP, Banff and Buchan,* Maj. 8,364

*****Stone,** Jamie, *LD, Caithness, Sutherland and Easter Ross,* Maj. 2,092

*****Sturgeon,** Nicola, *SNP, Glasgow region*

Swinburne, John, *SSCUP, Scotland Central region*

*****Swinney,** John, *SNP, Tayside North,* Maj. 4,503

*****Tosh,** Murray, *C., Scotland West region*

Turner, Dr Jean, *Ind., Strathkelvin and Bearsden,* Maj. 38

*****Wallace,** Jim, *LD, Orkney,* Maj. 1,755

*****Watson,** Mike (Lord Watson of Invergowrie), *Lab., Glasgow Cathcart,* Maj. 5,112

*****Welsh,** Andrew, *SNP, Angus,* Maj. 6,687

*****White,** Sandra, *SNP, Glasgow region*

*****Whitefield,** Karen, *Lab., Airdrie and Shotts,* Maj. 8,977

*****Wilson,** Allan, *Lab., Cunninghame North,* Maj. 3,387

*Sitting MP

SCOTTISH PARLIAMENT CONSTITUENCIES AND REGIONS

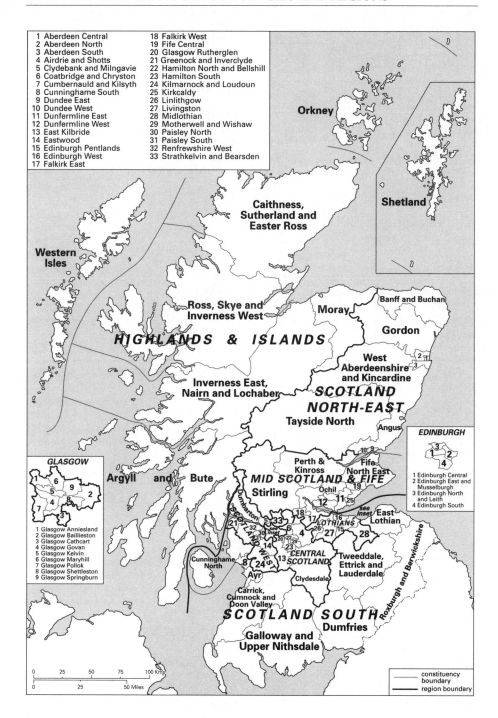

1 Aberdeen Central
2 Aberdeen North
3 Aberdeen South
4 Airdrie and Shotts
5 Clydebank and Milngavie
6 Coatbridge and Chryston
7 Cumbernauld and Kilsyth
8 Cunninghame South
9 Dundee East
10 Dundee West
11 Dunfermline East
12 Dunfermline West
13 East Kilbride
14 Eastwood
15 Edinburgh Pentlands
16 Edinburgh West
17 Falkirk East

18 Falkirk West
19 Fife Central
20 Glasgow Rutherglen
21 Greenock and Inverclyde
22 Hamilton North and Bellshill
23 Hamilton South
24 Kilmarnock and Loudoun
25 Kirkcaldy
26 Linlithgow
27 Livingston
28 Midlothian
29 Motherwell and Wishaw
30 Paisley North
31 Paisley South
32 Renfrewshire West
33 Strathkelvin and Bearsden

GLASGOW

1 Glasgow Anniesland
2 Glasgow Baillieston
3 Glasgow Cathcart
4 Glasgow Govan
5 Glasgow Kelvin
6 Glasgow Maryhill
7 Glasgow Pollok
8 Glasgow Shettleston
9 Glasgow Springburn

EDINBURGH

1 Edinburgh Central
2 Edinburgh East and
  Musselburgh
3 Edinburgh North
  and Leith
4 Edinburgh South

constituency
boundary
region boundary

SCOTTISH PARLIAMENT ELECTIONS

on 6 May 1999

CONSTITUENCIES

ABERDEEN CENTRAL
(Scotland North East region)
E. 52,715 *T.* 50.26%

L. Macdonald, *Lab.*	10,305
R. Lochhead, *SNP*	7,609
Ms E. Anderson, *LD*	4,403
T. Mason, *C.*	3,655
A. Cumbers, *SSP*	523

Lab. majority 2,696

ABERDEEN NORTH
(Scotland North East region)
E. 54,553 *T.* 51.00%

Ms E. Thomson, *Lab.*	10,340
B. Adam, *SNP*	9,942
J. Donaldson, *LD*	4,767
I. Haughie, *C.*	2,772

Lab. majority 398

ABERDEEN SOUTH
(Scotland North East region)
E. 60,579 *T.* 57.26%

N. Stephen, *LD*	11,300
M. Elrick, *Lab.*	9,540
Ms N. Milne, *C.*	6,993
Ms I. McGugan, *SNP*	6,651
S. Sutherland, *SWP*	206

LD majority 1,760

ABERDEENSHIRE WEST AND KINCARDINE
(Scotland North East region)
E. 60,702 *T.* 58.87%

M. Rumbles, *LD*	12,838
B. Wallace, *C.*	10,549
Ms M. Watt, *SNP*	7,699
G. Guthrie, *Lab.*	4,650

LD majority 2,289

AIRDRIE AND SHOTTS
(Scotland Central region)
E. 58,481 *T.* 56.79%

Ms K. Whitefield, *Lab.*	18,338
G. Paterson, *SNP*	9,353
P. Ross-Taylor *C.*	3,177
D. Miller, *LD*	2,345

Lab. majority 8,985

ANGUS
(Scotland North East region)
E. 59,891 *T.* 57.66%

A. Welsh, *SNP*	16,055
R. Harris, *C.*	7,154
I. McFatridge, *Lab.*	6,914
R. Speirs, *LD*	4,413

SNP majority 8,901

ARGYLL AND BUTE
(Highlands and Islands region)
E. 49,609 *T.* 64.86%

G. Lyon, *LD*	11,226
D. Hamilton, *SNP*	9,169
H. Raven, *Lab.*	6,470
D. Petrie, *C.*	5,312

LD majority 2,057

AYR
(Scotland South region)
E. 56,338 *T.* 66.48%

I. Welsh, *Lab.*	14,263
P. Gallie, *C.*	14,238
R. Mullin, *SNP*	7,291
Ms E. Morris, *LD*	1,662

Lab. majority 25

BANFF AND BUCHAN
(Scotland North East region)
E. 57,639 *T.* 55.06%

A. Salmond, *SNP*	16,695
D. Davidson, *C.*	5,403
M. Mackie, *LD*	5,315
Ms M. Harris, *Lab.*	4,321

SNP majority 11,292

CAITHNESS, SUTHERLAND AND EASTER ROSS
(Highlands and Islands region)
E. 41,581 *T.* 62.60%

J. Stone, *LD*	10,691
J. Hendry, *Lab.*	6,300
Ms J. Urquhart, *SNP*	6,035
R. Jenkins, *C.*	2,167
J. Campbell, *Ind.*	554
E. Stewart, *Ind.*	282

LD majority 4,391

CARRICK, CUMNOCK AND DOON VALLEY
(Scotland South region)
E. 65,580 *T.* 62.66%

Ms C. Jamieson, *Lab. Co-op.*	19,667
A. Ingram, *SNP*	10,864
J. Scott, *C.*	8,123
D. Hannay, *LD*	2,441

Lab. Co-op. majority 8,803

CLYDEBANK AND MILNGAVIE
(Scotland West region)
E. 52,461 T. 63.55%

D. McNulty, *Lab.*	15,105
J. Yuill, *SNP*	10,395
R. Ackland, *LD*	4,149
Ms D. Luckhurst, *C.*	3,688
Lab. majority 4,710	

CLYDESDALE
(Scotland South region)
E. 64,262 T. 60.61%

Ms K. Turnbull, *Lab.*	16,755
Ms A. Winning, *SNP*	12,875
C. Cormack, *C.*	5,814
Ms S. Grieve, *LD*	3,503
Lab. majority 3,880	

COATBRIDGE AND CHRYSTON
(Scotland Central region)
E. 52,178 T. 57.87%

Ms E. Smith, *Lab.*	17,923
P. Kearney, *SNP*	7,519
G. Lind, *C.*	2,867
Ms J. Hook, *LD*	1,889
Lab. majority 10,404	

CUMBERNAULD AND KILSYTH
(Scotland Central region)
E. 49,395 T. 61.97%

Ms C. Craigie, *Lab.*	15,182
A. Wilson, *SNP*	10,923
H. O'Donnell, *LD*	2,029
R. Slack, *C.*	1,362
K. McEwan, *SSP*	1,116
Lab. majority 4,259	

CUNNINGHAME NORTH
(Scotland West region)
E. 55,867 T. 59.95%

A. Wilson, *Lab.*	14,369
Ms K. Ullrich, *SNP*	9,573
M. Johnston, *C.*	6,649
C. Irving, *LD*	2,900
Lab. majority 4,796	

CUNNINGHAME SOUTH
(Scotland South region)
E. 50,443 T. 56.06%

Ms I. Oldfather, *Lab.*	14,936
M. Russell, *SNP*	8,395
M. Tosh, *C.*	3,229
S. Ritchie, *LD*	1,717
Lab. majority 6,541	

DUMBARTON
(Scotland West region)
E. 56,090 T. 61.86%

Ms J. Baillie, *Lab.*	15,181
L. Quinan, *SNP*	10,423
D. Reece, *C.*	5,060
P. Coleshill, *LD*	4,035
Lab. majority	4,758

DUMFRIES
(Scotland South region)
E. 63,162 T. 60.93%

Ms E. Murray, *Lab.*	14,101
D. Mundell, *C.*	10,447
S. Norris, *SNP*	7,625
N. Wallace, *LD*	6,309
Lab. majority 3,654	

DUNDEE EAST
(Scotland North East region)
E. 57,222 T. 55.33%

J. McAllion, *Lab.*	13,703
Ms S. Robison, *SNP*	10,849
I. Mitchell, *C.*	4,428
R. Lawrie, *LD*	2,153
H. Duke, *SSP*	530
Lab. majority 2,854	

DUNDEE WEST
(Scotland North East region)
E. 55,725 T. 52.19%

Ms K. MacLean, *Lab.*	10,925
C. Cashley, *SNP*	10,804
G. Buchan, *C.*	3,345
Ms E. Dick, *LD*	2,998
J. McFarlane, *SSP*	1,010
Lab. majority 121	

DUNFERMLINE EAST
(Scotland Mid and Fife region)
E. 52,087 T. 56.94%

Ms H. Eadie, *Lab. Co-op.*	16,576
D. McCarthy, *SNP*	7,877
Ms C. Ruxton, *C.*	2,931
F. Lawson, *LD*	2,275
Lab. Co-op. majority 8,699	

DUNFERMLINE WEST
(Scotland Mid and Fife region)
E. 53,112 T. 57.75%

S. Barrie, *Lab.*	13,560
D. Chapman, *SNP*	8,539
Ms E. Harris, *LD*	5,591
J. Mackie, *C.*	2,981
Lab. majority 5,021	

EAST KILBRIDE
(Scotland Central region)
E. 66,111 *T.* 62.49%

A. Kerr, *Lab.*	19,987
Ms L. Fabiani, *SNP*	13,488
C. Stevenson, *C.*	4,465
E. Hawthorn, *LD*	3,373

Lab. majority 6,499

EAST LOTHIAN
(Scotland South region)
E. 58,579 *T.* 64.16%

J. Home Robertson, *Lab.*	19,220
C. Miller, *SNP*	8,274
Ms C. Richard, *C.*	5,941
Ms J. Hayman, *LD*	4,147

Lab. majority 10,946

EASTWOOD
(Scotland West region)
E. 67,248 *T.* 67.51%

K. Macintosh, *Lab.*	16,970
J. Young, *C.*	14,845
Ms R. Findlay, *SNP*	8,760
Ms A. McCurley, *LD*	4,472
M. Tayan, *Ind.*	349

Lab. majority 2,125

EDINBURGH CENTRAL
(Lothians region)
E. 65,945 *T.* 56.73%

Ms S. Boyack, *Lab.*	14,224
I. McKee, *SNP*	9,598
A. Myles, *LD*	6,187
Ms J. Low, *C.*	6,018
K. Williamson, *SSP*	830
B. Allingham, *Ind. Dem.*	364
W. Wallace, *Braveheart*	191

Lab. majority 4,626

EDINBURGH EAST AND MUSSELBURGH
(Lothians region)
E. 60,167 *T.* 61.48%

Ms S. Deacon, *Lab.*	17,086
K. MacAskill, *SNP*	10,372
J. Balfour, *C.*	4,600
Ms M. Thomas, *LD*	4,100
D. White, *SSP*	697
M. Heavey, *Ind. You*	134

Lab. majority 6,714

EDINBURGH NORTH AND LEITH
(Lothians region)
E. 62,976 *T.* 58.19%

M. Chisholm, *Lab.*	17,203
Ms A. Dana, *SNP*	9,467
J. Sempill, *C.*	5,030
S. Tombs, *LD*	4,039
R. Brown, *SSP*	907

Lab. majority 7,736

EDINBURGH PENTLANDS
(Lothians region)
E. 60,029 *T.* 65.97%

I. Gray, *Lab.*	14,343
D. McLetchie, *C.*	11,458
S. Gibb, *SNP*	8,770
I. Gibson, *LD*	5,029

Lab. majority 2,885

EDINBURGH SOUTH
(Lothians region)
E. 64,100 *T.* 62.61%

A. MacKay, *Lab.*	14,869
Ms M. MacDonald, *SNP*	9,445
M. Pringle, *LD*	8,961
I. Whyte, *C.*	6,378
W. Black, *SWP*	482

Lab. majority 5,424

EDINBURGH WEST
(Lothians region)
E. 61,747 *T.* 67.34%

Ms M. Smith, *LD*	15,161
Lord J. Douglas-Hamilton, *C.*	10,578
Ms C. Fox, *Lab.*	8,860
G. Sutherland, *SNP*	6,984

LD majority 4,583

FALKIRK EAST
(Scotland Central region)
E. 57,345 *T.* 61.40%

Ms C. Peattie, *Lab.*	15,721
K. Brown, *SNP*	11,582
A. Orr, *C.*	3,399
G. McDonald, *LD*	2,509
R. Stead, *Soc. Lab.*	1,643
V. MacGrain, *SFPP*	358

Lab. majority 4,139

FALKIRK WEST
(Scotland Central region)
E. 53,404 T. 63.04%

D. Canavan, *Falkirk W.*	18,511
R. Martin, *Lab.*	6,319
M. Matheson, *SNP*	5,986
G. Miller, *C.*	1,897
A. Smith, *LD*	954

Falkirk W. majority 12,192

FIFE CENTRAL
(Scotland Mid and Fife region)
E. 58,850 T. 55.82%

H. McLeish, *Lab.*	18,828
Ms P. Marwick, *SNP*	10,153
Ms J. A. Liston, *LD*	1,953
K. Harding, *C.*	1,918

Lab. majority 8,675

FIFE NORTH EAST
(Scotland Mid and Fife region)
E. 60,886 T. 59.03%

I. Smith, *LD*	13,590
E. Brocklebank, *C.*	8,526
C. Welsh, *SNP*	6,373
C. Milne, *Lab.*	5,175
D. Macgregor, *Ind.*	1,540
R. Beveridge, *Ind.*	737

LD majority 5,064

GALLOWAY AND UPPER NITHSDALE
(Scotland South region)
E. 53,057 T. 66.56%

A. Morgan, *SNP*	13,873
A. Fergusson, *C.*	10,672
J. Stevens, *Lab.*	7,209
Ms J. Mitchell, *LD*	3,562

SNP majority 3,201

GLASGOW ANNIESLAND
(Glasgow region)
E. 54,378 T. 52.37%

D. Dewar, *Lab.*	16,749
K. Stewart, *SNP*	5,756
W. Aitken, *C.*	3,032
I. Brown, *LD*	1,804
Ms A. Lynch, *SSP*	1,000
E. Boyd, *Soc. Lab.*	139

Lab. majority 10,993

GLASGOW BAILLIESTON
(Glasgow region)
E. 49,068 T. 48.32%

Ms M. Curran, *Lab.*	11,289
Ms D. Elder, *SNP*	8,217
J. McVicar, *SSP*	1,864
Ms K. Pickering, *C.*	1,526
Ms J. Fryer, *LD*	813

Lab. majority 3,072

GLASGOW CATHCART
(Glasgow region)
E. 51,338 T. 52.55%

M. Watson, *Lab.*	12,966
Ms M. Whitehead, *SNP*	7,592
Ms M. Leishman, *C.*	3,311
C. Dick, *LD*	2,187
R. Slorach, *SWP*	920

Lab. majority 5,374

GLASGOW GOVAN
(Glasgow region)
E. 53,257 T. 49.52%

G. Jackson, *Lab.*	11,421
Ms N. Sturgeon, *SNP*	9,665
Ms T. Ahmed-Sheikh, *C.*	2,343
M. Aslam Khan, *LD*	1,479
C. McCarthy, *SSP*	1,275
J. Foster, *Comm. Brit.*	190

Lab. majority 1,756

GLASGOW KELVIN
(Glasgow region)
E. 61,207 T. 46.34%

Ms P. McNeill, *Lab.*	12,711
Ms S. White, *SNP*	8,303
Ms M. Craig, *LD*	3,720
A. Rasul, *C.*	2,253
Ms H. Ritchie, *SSP*	1,375

Lab. majority 4,408

GLASGOW MARYHILL
(Glasgow region)
E. 56,469 T. 40.75%

Ms P. Ferguson, *Lab.*	11,455
W. Wilson, *SNP*	7,129
Ms C. Hamblen, *LD*	1,793
G. Scott, *SSP*	1,439
M. Fry, *C.*	1,194

Lab. majority 4,326

GLASGOW POLLOK
(Glasgow region)
E. 47,970 T. 54.37%

J. Lamont, *Lab. Co-op.*	11,405
K. Gibson, *SNP*	6,763
T. Sheridan, *SSP*	5,611
R. O'Brien, *C.*	1,370
J. King, *LD*	931
Lab. Co-op. majority 4,642	

GLASGOW RUTHERGLEN
(Glasgow region)
E. 51,012 T. 56.89%

Ms J. Hughes, *Lab.*	13,442
T. Chalmers, *SNP*	6,155
R. Brown, *LD*	5,798
I. Stewart, *C.*	2,315
W. Bonnar, *SSP*	832
J. Nisbet, *Soc. Lab.*	481
Lab. majority 7,287	

GLASGOW SHETTLESTON
(Glasgow region)
E. 50,592 T. 40.58%

F. McAveety, *Lab. Co-op.*	11,078
J. Byrne, *SNP*	5,611
Ms R. Kane, *SSP*	1,640
C. Bain, *C.*	1,260
L. Clarke, *LD*	943
Lab. Co-op. majority 5,467	

GLASGOW SPRINGBURN
(Glasgow region)
E. 55,670 T. 43.77%

P. Martin, *Lab.*	14,268
J. Brady, *SNP*	6,375
M. Roxburgh, *C.*	1,293
M. Dunnigan, *LD*	1,288
J. Friel, *SSP*	1,141
Lab. majority 7,893	

GORDON
(Scotland North East region)
E. 59,497 T. 56.51%

Ms N. Radcliffe, *LD*	12,353
A. Stronach, *SNP*	8,158
A. Johnstone, *C.*	6,602
Ms G. Carlin-Kulwicki, *Lab.*	3,950
H. Watt, *Ind.*	2,559
LD majority 4,195	

GREENOCK AND INVERCLYDE
(Scotland West region)
E. 48,584 T. 58.95%

D. McNeil, *Lab.*	11,817
R. Finnie, *LD*	7,504
I. Hamilton, *SNP*	6,762
R. Wilkinson, *C.*	1,699
D. Landels, *SSP*	857
Lab. majority 4,313	

HAMILTON NORTH AND BELLSHILL
(Scotland Central region)
E. 53,992 T. 57.82%

M. McMahon, *Lab.*	15,227
Ms K. McAlorum, *SNP*	9,621
S. Thomson, *C.*	3,199
Ms J. Struthers, *LD*	2,105
Ms K. McGavigan, *Soc. Lab.*	1,064
Lab. majority 5,606	

HAMILTON SOUTH
(Scotland Central region)
E. 46,765 T. 55.43%

T. McCabe, *Lab.*	14,098
A. Ardrey, *SNP*	6,922
Ms M. Mitchell, *C.*	2,918
J. Oswald, *LD*	1,982
Lab. majority 7,176	

INVERNESS EAST, NAIRN AND LOCHABER
(Highlands and Islands region)
E. 66,285 T. 63.10%

F. Ewing, *SNP*	13,825
Ms J. Aitken, *Lab.*	13,384
D. Fraser, *LD*	8,508
Ms M. Scanlon, *C.*	6,107
SNP majority 441	

KILMARNOCK AND LOUDOUN
(Scotland Central region)
E. 61,454 T. 64.03%

Ms M. Jamieson, *Lab.*	17,345
A. Neil, *SNP*	14,585
L. McIntosh, *C.*	4,589
J. Stewart, *LD*	2,830
Lab. majority 2,760	

KIRKCALDY
(Scotland Mid and Fife region)
E. 51,640 T. 54.88%

Ms M. Livingstone, *Lab. Co-op.*	13,645
S. Hosie, *SNP*	9,170
M. Scott-Hayward, *C.*	2,907
J. Mainland, *LD*	2,620
Lab. Co-op. majority 4,475	

LINLITHGOW
(Lothians region)
E. 54,262 *T.* 62.26%

Ms M. Mulligan, *Lab.*	15,247
S. Stevenson, *SNP*	12,319
G. Lindhurst, *C.*	3,158
J. Barrett, *LD*	2,643
Ms I. Ovenstone, *Ind.*	415
Lab. majority 2,928	

LIVINGSTON
(Lothians region)
E. 62,060 *T.* 58.93%

B. Muldoon, *Lab.*	17,313
G. McCarra, *SNP*	13,409
D. Younger, *C.*	3,014
M. Oliver, *LD*	2,834
Lab. majority 3,904	

MIDLOTHIAN
(Lothians region)
E. 48,374 *T.* 61.51%

Ms R. Brankin, *Lab. Co-op.*	14,467
A. Robertson, *SNP*	8,942
J. Elder, *LD*	3,184
G. Turnbull, *C.*	2,544
D. Pryde, *Ind.*	618
Lab. Co-op. majority 5,525	

MORAY
(Highlands and Islands region)
E. 58,388 *T.* 57.50%

Mrs M. Ewing, *SNP*	13,027
A. Farquharson, *Lab.*	8,898
A. Findlay, *C.*	8,595
Ms P. Kenton, *LD*	3,056
SNP majority 4,129	

MOTHERWELL AND WISHAW
(Scotland Central region)
E. 52,613 *T.* 57.71%

J. McConnell, *Lab.*	13,955
J. McGuigan, *SNP*	8,879
W. Gibson, *C.*	3,694
J. Milligan, *Soc. Lab.*	1,941
R. Spillane, *LD*	1,895
Lab. majority 5,076	

OCHIL
(Scotland Mid and Fife region)
E. 57,083 *T.* 64.58%

R. Simpson, *Lab.*	15,385
G. Reid, *SNP*	14,082
N. Johnston, *C.*	4,151
Earl of Mar and Kellie, *LD*	3,249
Lab. majority 1,303	

ORKNEY
(Highlands and Islands region)
E. 15,658 *T.* 56.95%

J. Wallace, *LD*	6,010
C. Zawadzki, *C.*	1,391
J. Mowat, *SNP*	917
A. Macleod, *Lab.*	600
LD majority 4,619	

PAISLEY NORTH
(Scotland West region)
E. 49,020 *T.* 56.61%

Ms W. Alexander, *Lab.*	13,492
I. Mackay, *SNP*	8,876
P. Ramsay, *C.*	2,242
Ms T. Mayberry, *LD*	2,133
Ms F. Macdonald, *SSP*	1,007
Lab. majority 4,616	

PAISLEY SOUTH
(Scotland West region)
E. 53,637 *T.* 57.15%

H. Henry, *Lab.*	13,899
W. Martin, *SNP*	9,404
S. Callison, *LD*	2,974
Ms S. Laidlaw, *C.*	2,433
P. Mack, *Ind.*	1,273
Ms J. Forrest, *SWP*	673
Lab. majority 4,495	

PERTH
(Scotland Mid and Fife region)
E. 61,034 *T.* 61.27%

Ms R. Cunningham, *SNP*	13,570
I. Stevenson, *C.*	11,543
Ms J. Richards, *Lab.*	8,725
C. Brodie, *LD*	3,558
SNP majority 2,027	

RENFREWSHIRE WEST
(Scotland West region)
E. 52,452 *T.* 64.89%

Ms P. Godman, *Lab.*	12,708
C. Campbell, *SNP*	9,815
Ms A. Goldie, *C.*	7,243
N. Ascherson, *LD*	2,659
A. McGraw, *Ind.*	1,136
P. Clark, *SWP*	476
Lab. majority 2,893	

ROSS, SKYE AND INVERNESS WEST
(Highlands and Islands region)
E. 55,845 T. 63.42%

J. Farquhar-Munro, *LD*	11,652
D. Munro, *Lab.*	10,113
J. Mather, *SNP*	7,997
J. Scott, *C.*	3,351
D. Briggs, *Ind.*	2,302
LD majority 1,539	

ROXBURGH AND BERWICKSHIRE
(Scotland South region)
E. 47,639 T. 58.52%

E. Robson, *LD*	11,320
A. Hutton, *C.*	7,735
S. Crawford, *SNP*	4,719
Ms S. McLeod, *Lab.*	4,102
LD majority 3,585	

SHETLAND
(Highlands and Islands region)
E. 16,978 T. 58.77%

T. Scott, *LD*	5,435
J. Wills, *Lab.*	2,241
W. Ross, *SNP*	1,430
G. Robinson, *C.*	872
LD majority 3,194	

STIRLING
(Scotland Mid and Fife region)
E. 52,904 T. 67.68%

Ms S. Jackson, *Lab.*	13,533
Ms A. Ewing, *SNP*	9,552
B. Monteith, *C.*	9,158
I. Macfarlane, *LD*	3,407
S. Kilgour, *Ind.*	155
Lab. majority 3,981	

STRATHKELVIN AND BEARSDEN
(Scotland West region)
E. 63,111 T. 67.17%

S. Galbraith, *Lab.*	21,505
Ms F. McLeod, *SNP*	9,384
C. Ferguson, *C.*	6,934
Ms A. Howarth, *LD*	4,144
Ms M. Richards, *Anti-Drug*	423
Lab. majority 12,121	

TAYSIDE NORTH
(Scotland Mid and Fife region)
E. 61,795 T. 61.58%

J. Swinney, *SNP*	16,786
M. Fraser, *C.*	12,594
Ms M. Dingwall, *Lab.*	5,727
P. Regent, *LD*	2,948
SNP majority 4,192	

TWEEDDALE, ETTRICK AND LAUDERDALE
(Scotland South region)
E. 51,577 T. 65.37%

I. Jenkins, *LD*	12,078
Ms C. Creech, *SNP*	7,600
G. McGregor, *Lab.*	7,546
J. Campbell, *C.*	6,491
LD majority 4,478	

WESTERN ISLES
(Highlands and Islands region)
E. 22,412 T. 62.26%

A. Morrison, *Lab.*	7,248
A. Nicholson, *SNP*	5,155
J. MacGrigor, *C.*	1,095
J. Horne, *LD*	456
Lab. majority 2,093	

REGIONS

GLASGOW
E. 531,956 T. 48.19%

Lab.	112,588	(43.92%)
SNP	65,360	(25.50%)
C.	20,239	(7.90%)
SSP	18,581	(7.25%)
LD	18,473	(7.21%)
Green	10,159	(3.96%)
Soc. Lab.	4,391	(1.71%)
ProLife	2,357	(0.92%)
SUP	2,283	(0.89%)
Comm. Brit.	521	(0.20%)
Humanist	447	(0.17%)
NLP	419	(0.16%)
SPGB	309	(0.12%)
Choice	221	(0.09%)
Lab. majority 47,228		

(May 1997, *Lab. maj.* 166,061)

ADDITIONAL MEMBERS
W. Aitken, *C.*
R. Brown, *LD*
Ms D. Elder, *SNP*
Ms S. White, *SNP*
Ms N. Sturgeon, *SNP*
K. Gibson, *SNP*
T. Sheridan, *SSP*

HIGHLANDS AND ISLANDS
E. 326,553 T. 61.76%

SNP	55,933	(27.73%)
Lab.	51,371	(25.47%)
LD	43,226	(21.43%)
C.	30,122	(14.94%)
Green	7,560	(3.75%)
Ind. Noble	3,522	(1.75%)
Soc. Lab.	2,808	(1.39%)
Highlands	2,607	(1.29%)
SSP	1,770	(0.88%)
Mission	1,151	(0.57%)
Int. Ind.	712	(0.35%)
NLP	536	(0.27%)
Ind. R.	354	(0.18%)

SNP majority 4,562
(May 1997, LD maj. 1,388)

ADDITIONAL MEMBERS
J. MacGrigor, C.
Mrs M. Scanlon, C.
Ms M. MacMillan, Lab.
P. Peacock, Lab.
Ms R. Grant, Lab.
Mrs W. Ewing, SNP
D. Hamilton, SNP

LOTHIANS
E. 539,656 T. 61.25%

Lab.	99,908	(30.23%)
SNP	85,085	(25.74%)
C.	52,067	(15.75%)
LD	47,565	(14.39%)
Green	22,848	(6.91%)
Soc. Lab.	10,895	(3.30%)
SSP	5,237	(1.58%)
Lib.	2,056	(0.62%)
Witchery	1,184	(0.36%)
ProLife	898	(0.27%)
Rights	806	(0.24%)
NLP	564	(0.17%)
Braveheart	557	(0.17%)
SPGB	388	(0.12%)
Ind. Voice	256	(0.08%)
Ind. Ind.	145	(0.04%)
Anti-Corr.	54	(0.02%)

Lab. majority 14,823
(May 1997, Lab. maj. 101,991)

ADDITIONAL MEMBERS
Rt. Hon. Lord James Douglas Hamilton, C.
D. McLetchie, C.
Rt. Hon. Sir David Steel, LD
K. MacAskill, SNP
Ms M. MacDonald, SNP
Ms F. Hyslop, SNP
R. Harper, Green

SCOTLAND CENTRAL
E. 551,733 T. 59.90%

Lab.	129,822	(39.28%)
SNP	91,802	(27.78%)
C.	30,243	(9.15%)
Falkirk W.	27,700	(8.38%)
LD	20,505	(6.20%)
Soc. Lab.	10,956	(3.32%)
Green	5,926	(1.79%)
SSP	5,739	(1.74%)
SUP	2,886	(0.87%)
ProLife	2,567	(0.78%)
SFPP	1,373	(0.42%)
NLP	719	(0.22%)
Ind. Prog.	248	(0.08%)

Lab. majority 38,020
(May 1997, Lab. maj. 143,376)

ADDITIONAL MEMBERS
Mrs L. McIntosh, C.
D. Gorrie, LD
A. Neil, SNP
M. Matheson, SNP
Ms L. Fabiani, SNP
A. Wilson, SNP
G. Paterson, SNP

SCOTLAND MID AND FIFE
E. 509,387 T. 60.01%

Lab.	101,964	(33.36%)
SNP	87,659	(28.68%)
C.	56,719	(18.56%)
LD	38,896	(12.73%)
Green	11,821	(3.87%)
Soc. Lab.	4,266	(1.40%)
SSP	3,044	(1.00%)
ProLife	735	(0.24%)
NLP	558	(0.18%)

Lab. majority 14,305
(May 1997, Lab. maj. 54,087)

ADDITIONAL MEMBERS
N. Johnston, *C.*
B. Monteith, *C.*
K. Harding, *C.*
K. Raffan, *LD*
B. Crawford, *SNP*
G. Reid, *SNP*
Ms P. Marwick, *SNP*

SCOTLAND NORTH EAST
E. 518,521 *T.* 55.05%

SNP	92,329	(32.35%)
Lab.	72,666	(25.46%)
C.	52,149	(18.27%)
LD	49,843	(17.46%)
Green	8,067	(2.83%)
Soc. Lab.	3,557	(1.25%)
SSP	3,016	(1.06%)
Ind. Watt.	2,303	(0.81%)
Ind. SB	770	(0.27%)
NLP	746	(0.26%)

SNP majority 19,663
(May 1997, *Lab. maj.* 17,518)

ADDITIONAL MEMBERS
D. Davidson, *C.*
A. Johnstone, *C.*
B. Wallace, *C.*
R. Lochhead, *SNP*
Ms S. Robison, *SNP*
B. Adam, *SNP*
Ms I. McGugan, *SNP*

SCOTLAND SOUTH
E. 510,634 *T.* 62.35%

Lab.	98,836	(31.04%)
SNP	80,059	(25.15%)
C.	68,904	(21.64%)
LD	38,157	(11.99%)
Soc. Lab.	13,887	(4.36%)
Green	9,468	(2.97%)
Lib.	3,478	(1.09%)
SSP	3,304	(1.04%)
UK Ind.	1,502	(0.47%)
NLP	775	(0.24%)

Lab. majority 18,777
(May 1997, *Lab. maj.* 79,585)

ADDITIONAL MEMBERS
P. Gallie, *C.*
D. Mundell, *C.*
M. Tosh, *C.*
A. Fergusson, *C.*
M. Russell, *SNP*
A. Ingram, *SNP*
Ms C. Creech, *SNP*

SCOTLAND WEST
E. 498,466 *T.* 62.27%

Lab.	119,663	(38.55%)
SNP	80,417	(25.91%)
C.	48,666	(15.68%)
LD	34,095	(10.98%)
Green	8,175	(2.63%)
SSP	5,944	(1.91%)
Soc. Lab.	4,472	(1.44%)
ProLife	3,227	(1.04%)
Individual	2,761	(0.89%)
SUP	1,840	(0.59%)
NLP	589	(0.19%)
Ind. Water	565	(0.18%)

Lab. majority 39,246
(May 1997, *Lab. maj.* 115,995)

ADDITIONAL MEMBERS
A. Goldie, *C.*
J. Young, *C.*
R. Finnie, *LD*
L. Quinan, *SNP*
Ms F. McLeod, *SNP*
Ms K. Ullrich, *SNP*
C. Campbell, *SNP*

BY ELECTIONS

AYR *(16 March 2000)*
T. 57.0%

J. Scott, *C.*	12,580
SNP	9,236
Lab.	7,054
SNP	1,345
LD	800
Green	460
Ind.	186
UK Ind.	113
ProLife	111
Ind	15

Majority, 3,344

GLASGOW ANNIESLAND *(November 23 2000)*
T. 20,221

Bill Butler, *Lab.*	9,838
Tom Chalmers, *SNP*	4,462
Kate Pickering, *C.*	2,148
R. Kane, *Scottish Socialist Party*	1,429
Judith Fryer, *LD*	1,384
Alasdair Whitelaw, *Green*	662
Murdo Ritchie, *Lab.*	298

Majority, 5,376

BANFF AND BUCHAN *(7 June 2001)*
T. 30,838

Stewart Stevenson, *SNP*	15,386
Ted Brocklebank *C.*	6,819
Megan Harris, *Lab.*	4,597
Canon Kenyon Wright, *LD*	3,231
Peter Anderson, *SSP*	682

Majority, 8,567

STRATHKELVIN AND BEARSDEN
(7 June 2001)
T. 41,734

Brian Fitzpatrick, *Lab.*	15,401
Jean M. Turner, *Ind.*	7,275
John Morrison, *LD*	7,147
Janet E. Law, *SNP*	6,457
Charles Ferguson, *C.*	5,037

Majority, 8,126

SCOTTISH CONSTITUENCIES IN THE UK PARLIAMENT

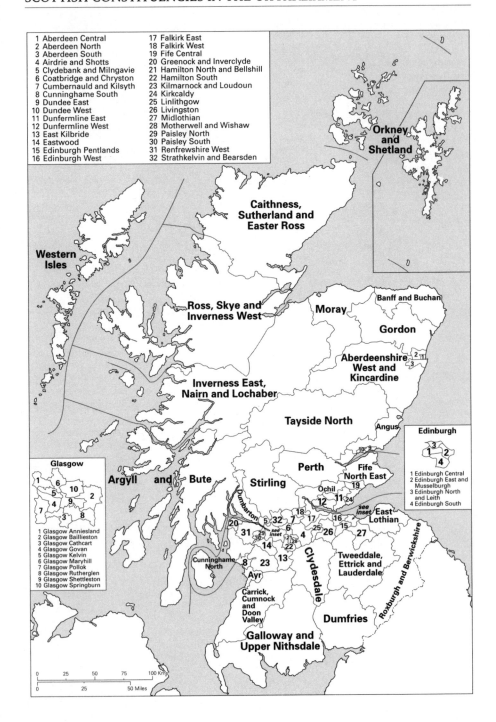

1 Aberdeen Central
2 Aberdeen North
3 Aberdeen South
4 Airdrie and Shotts
5 Clydebank and Milngavie
6 Coatbridge and Chryston
7 Cumbernauld and Kilsyth
8 Cunninghame South
9 Dundee East
10 Dundee West
11 Dunfermline East
12 Dunfermline West
13 East Kilbride
14 Eastwood
15 Edinburgh Pentlands
16 Edinburgh West

17 Falkirk East
18 Falkirk West
19 Fife Central
20 Greenock and Inverclyde
21 Hamilton North and Bellshill
22 Hamilton South
23 Kilmarnock and Loudoun
24 Kirkcaldy
25 Linlithgow
26 Livingston
27 Midlothian
28 Motherwell and Wishaw
29 Paisley North
30 Paisley South
31 Renfrewshire West
32 Strathkelvin and Bearsden

Orkney and Shetland

Caithness, Sutherland and Easter Ross

Western Isles

Ross, Skye and Inverness West

Moray

Banff and Buchan

Gordon

Aberdeenshire West and Kincardine

Inverness East, Nairn and Lochaber

Tayside North

Angus

Edinburgh

1 Edinburgh Central
2 Edinburgh East and Musselburgh
3 Edinburgh North and Leith
4 Edinburgh South

Perth

Fife North East

Glasgow

1 Glasgow Anniesland
2 Glasgow Baillieston
3 Glasgow Cathcart
4 Glasgow Govan
5 Glasgow Kelvin
6 Glasgow Maryhill
7 Glasgow Pollok
8 Glasgow Rutherglen
9 Glasgow Shettleston
10 Glasgow Springburn

Argyll and Bute

Stirling

Ochil

East Lothian

Cunninghame North

Ayr

Clydesdale

Tweeddale, Ettrick and Lauderdale

Roxburgh and Berwickshire

Carrick, Cumnock and Doon Valley

Dumfries

Galloway and Upper Nithsdale

0   25   50   75   100 Km
0   25   50 Miles

UK PARLIAMENT ELECTIONS

as at 7 June 2001

SCOTTISH CONSTITUENCIES

*Sitting MP

ABERDEEN CENTRAL
E. 50,098   T. 26,429 (52.75%)   Lab. hold
*Frank Doran, *(Lab.)*   12,025
Wayne Gault, *(SNP)*   5,379
Ms Eleanor Anderson, *(LD)*   4,547
Stewart Whyte, *(C.)*   3,761
Andy Cumbers, *(SSP)*   717
Lab. maj 6,646, (25.15%)
4.24% swing Lab. to SNP
1997: Lab. maj 10,801 (30.32%)

ABERDEEN NORTH
E. 52,746   T. 30,357 (57.55%)   Lab. hold
*Malcolm Savidge, *(Lab.)*   13,157
Dr Alasdair Allan, *(SNP)*   8,708
Jim Donaldson, *(LD)*   4,991
Richard Cowling, *(C.)*   3,047
Ms Shona Forman, *(SSP)*   454
Lab. maj 4,449 (14.66%)
5.70% swing Lab. to SNP
1997: Lab. maj 10,010 (26.06%)

ABERDEEN SOUTH
E. 58,907   T. 36,890 (62.62%)   Lab. hold
*Ms Anne Begg, *(Lab.)*   14,696
Ian Yuill, *(LD)*   10,308
Moray Macdonald, *(C.)*   7,098
Ian Angus, *(SNP)*   4,293
David Watt, *(SSP)*   495
Lab. maj 4,388 (11.89%)
2.13% swing LD to Lab.
1997: Lab. maj 3,365 (7.64%)

ABERDEENSHIRE WEST & KINCARDINE
E. 61,180   T. 37,914 (61.97%)   LD hold
*Sir Robert Smith, *(LD)*   16,507
Tom Kerr, *(C.)*   11,686
Kevin Hutchens, *(Lab.)*   4,669
John Green, *(SNP)*   4,634
Alan Manley, *(SSP)*   418
LD maj 4,821 (12.72%)
3.28% swing C. to LD
1997: LD maj 2,662 (6.16%)

AIRDRIE & SHOTTS
E. 58,349   T. 31,736 (54.39%)   Lab. hold
*Ms Helen Liddell, *(Lab.)*   18,478
Ms Alison Lindsay, *(SNP)*   6,138
John Love, *(LD)*   2,376
Gordon McIntosh, *(C.)*   1,960
Ms Mary Dempsey, *(Scot U)*   1,439
Kenny McGuigan, *(SSP)*   1,171
Chris Herriot, *(Soc. Lab.)*   174
Lab. maj 12,340 (38.88%)
0.73% swing SNP to Lab.
1997: Lab. maj 15,412 (37.42%)

ANGUS
E. 59,004   T. 35,013 (59.34%)   SNP hold
Michael Weir, *(SNP)*   12,347
Marcus Booth, *(C.)*   8,736
Ian McFatridge, *(Lab.)*   8,183
Peter Nield, *(LD)*   5,015
Bruce Wallace, *(SSP)*   732
SNP maj 3,611 (10.31%)
6.67% swing SNP to C.
1997: SNP maj 10,189 (23.66%)

ARGYLL & BUTE
E. 49,175   T. 30,957 (62.95%)   LD hold
Alan Reid, *(LD)*   9,245
Hugh Raven, *(Lab.)*   7,592
David Petrie, *(C.)*   6,436
Ms Agnes Samuel, *(SNP)*   6,433
Des Divers, *(SSP)*   1,251
LD maj 1,653 (5.34%)
9.60% swing LD to Lab.
1997: LD maj 6,081 (17.03%)

AYR
E. 55,630   T. 38,560 (69.32%)   Lab. hold
*Ms Sandra Osborne, *(Lab.)*   16,801
Phil Gallie, *(C.)*   14,256
Jim Mather, *(SNP)*   4,621
Stuart Ritchie, *(LD)*   2,089
James Stewart, *(SSP)*   692
Joseph Smith, *(UK Ind.)*   101
Lab. maj 2,545 (6.60%)
4.01% swing Lab. to C.
1997: Lab. maj 6,543 (14.62%)

BANFF & BUCHAN

E. 56,496   T. 30,806 (54.53%)   SNP hold
*Alex Salmond, *(SNP)*   16,710
Alexander Wallace, *(C.)*   6,207
Edward Harris, *(Lab.)*   4,363
Douglas Herbison, *(LD)*   2,769
Ms Alice Rowan, *(SSP)*   447
Eric Davidson, *(UK Ind.)*   310
SNP maj 10,503 (34.09%)
1.06% swing C. to SNP
1997: SNP maj 12,845 (31.97%)

CAITHNESS, SUTHERLAND & EASTER ROSS

E. 41,225   T. 24,867 (60.32%)   LD hold
Viscount John Thurso, *(LD)*   9,041
Michael Meighan, *(Lab.)*   6,297
John Macadam, *(SNP)*   5,273
Robert Rowantree, *(C.)*   3,513
Ms Karn Mabon, *(SSP)*   544
Gordon Campbell, *(Ind.)*   199
LD maj 2,744 (11.03%)
1.64% swing Lab. to LD
1997: LD maj 2,259 (7.75%)

CARRICK, CUMNOCK & DOON VALLEY

E. 64,919   T. 40,107 (61.78%)
                                               Lab Co-op hold
*George Foulkes, *(Lab Co-op)*   22,174
Gordon Miller, *(C.)*   7,318
Tom Wilson, *(SNP)*   6,258
Ms Amy Rogers, *(LD)*   2,932
Ms Amanda McFarlane, *(SSP)*   1,058
James McDaid, *(Soc. Lab.)*   367
Lab Co-op maj 14,856 (37.04%)
2.90% swing Lab. Co-op to C.
1997: Lab. maj 21,062 (42.84%)

CLYDEBANK & MILNGAVIE

E. 52,534   T. 32,491 (61.85%)   Lab. hold
*Tony Worthington, *(Lab.)*   17,249
Jim Yuill, *(SNP)*   6,525
Rod Ackland, *(LD)*   3,909
Dr Catherine Pickering, *(C.)*   3,514
Ms Dawn Brennan, *(SSP)*   1,294
Lab. maj 10,724 (33.01%)
0.54% swing Lab. to SNP
1997: Lab. maj 13,320 (34.08%)

CLYDESDALE

E. 64,423   T. 38,222 (59.33%)   Lab. hold
*Jimmy Hood, *(Lab.)*   17,822
Jim Wright, *(SNP)*   10,028
Kevin Newton, *(C.)*   5,034
Ms Moira Craig, *(LD)*   4,111
Paul Cockshott, *(SSP)*   974
Donald MacKay, *(UK Ind.)*   253
Lab. maj 7,794 (20.39%)
5.01% swing Lab. to SNP
1997: Lab. maj 13,809 (30.41%)

COATBRIDGE & CHRYSTON

E. 52,178   T. 30,311 (58.09%)   Lab. hold
*Tom Clarke, *(Lab.)*   19,807
Peter Kearney, *(SNP)*   4,493
Alistair Tough, *(LD)*   2,293
Patrick Ross-Taylor, *(C.)*   2,171
Ms Lynne Sheridan, *(SSP)*   1,547
Lab. maj 15,314 (50.52%)
0.39% swing Lab. to SNP
1997: Lab. maj 19,295 (51.30%)

CUMBERNAULD & KILSYTH

E. 49,739   T. 29,699 (59.71%)   Lab. hold
*Ms Rosemary McKenna, *(Lab.)*   16,144
David McGlashan, *(SNP)*   8,624
John O'Donnell, *(LD)*   1,934
Ms Alison Ross, *(C.)*   1,460
Kenny McEwan, *(SSP)*   1,287
Thomas Taylor, *(Scot Ref)*   250
Lab. maj 7,520 (25.32%)
2.78% swing Lab. to SNP
1997: Lab. maj 11,128 (30.89%)

CUNNINGHAME NORTH

E. 54,993   T. 33,816 (61.49%)   Lab. hold
*Brian Wilson, *(Lab.)*   15,571
Campbell Martin, *(SNP)*   7,173
Richard Wilkinson, *(C.)*   6,666
Ross Chmiel, *(LD)*   3,060
Sean Scott, *(SSP)*   964
Ms Louise McDaid, *(Soc. Lab.)*   382
Lab. maj 8,398 (24.83%)
3.51% swing Lab. to SNP
1997: Lab. maj 11,039 (26.84%)

CUNNINGHAME SOUTH

E. 49,982   T. 28,009 (56.04%)   Lab. hold

*Brian Donohoe, *(Lab.)*	16,424
Bill Kidd, *(SNP)*	5,194
Mrs Pam Paterson, *(C.)*	2,682
John Boyd, *(LD)*	2,094
Ms Rosemary Byrne, *(SSP)*	1,233
Bobby Cochrane, *(Soc. Lab.)*	382

Lab. maj 11,230 (40.09%)
0.93% swing Lab. to SNP
1997: Lab. maj 14,869 (41.95%)

DUMBARTON

E. 56,267   T. 33,994 (60.42%)

Lab. Co-op hold

*John McFall, *(Lab. Co-op)*	16,151
Iain Robertson, *(SNP)*	6,576
Eric Thompson, *(LD)*	5,265
Peter Ramsay, *(C.)*	4,648
Les Robertson, *(SSP)*	1,354

Lab Co-op maj 9,575 (28.17%)
0.89% swing SNP to Lab. Co-op
1997: Lab. maj 10,883 (26.38%)

DUMFRIES

E. 62,931   T. 42,586 (67.67%)   Lab. hold

*Russell Brown, *(Lab.)*	20,830
John Charteris, *(C.)*	11,996
John Ross Scott, *(LD)*	4,955
Gerry Fisher, *(SNP)*	4,103
John Dennis, *(SSP)*	702

Lab. maj 8,834 (20.74%)
0.64% swing C. to Lab.
1997: Lab. maj 9,643 (19.47%)

DUNDEE EAST

E. 56,535   T. 32,358 (57.24%)   Lab. hold

Iain Luke, *(Lab.)*	14,635
Stewart Hosie, *(SNP)*	10,160
Alan Donnelly, *(C.)*	3,900
Raymond Lawrie, *(LD)*	2,784
Harvey Duke, *(SSP)*	879

Lab. maj 4,475 (13.83%)
5.38% swing Lab. to SNP
1997: Lab. maj 9,961 (24.58%)

DUNDEE WEST

E. 53,760   T. 29,242 (54.39%)   Lab. hold

*Ernie Ross, *(Lab.)*	14,787
Gordon Archer, *(SNP)*	7,987
Ian Hail, *(C.)*	2,656
Ms Elizabeth Dick, *(LD)*	2,620
Jim McFarlane, *(SSP)*	1,192

Lab. maj 6,800 (23.25%)
3.65% swing Lab. to SNP
1997: Lab. maj 11,859 (30.56%)

DUNFERMLINE EAST

E. 52,811   T. 30,086 (56.97%)   Lab. hold

*Gordon Brown, *(Lab.)*	19,487
John Mellon, *(SNP)*	4,424
Stuart Randall, *(C.)*	2,838
John Mainland, *(LD)*	2,281
Andy Jackson, *(SSP)*	770
Tom Dunsmore, *(UK Ind.)*	286

Lab. maj 15,063 (50.07%)
0.60% swing Lab. to SNP
1997: Lab. maj 18,751 (51.26%)

DUNFERMLINE WEST

E. 54,293   T. 30,975 (57.05%)   Lab. hold

*Ms Rachel Squire, *(Lab.)*	16,370
Brian Goodall, *(SNP)*	5,390
Russell McPhate, *(LD)*	4,832
James Mackie, *(C.)*	3,166
Ms Kate Stewart, *(SSP)*	746
Alastair Harper, *(UK Ind.)*	471

Lab. maj 10,980 (35.45%)
0.77% swing SNP to Lab.
1997: Lab. maj 12,354 (33.91%)

EAST KILBRIDE

E. 66,572   T. 41,690 (62.62%)   Lab. hold

*Adam Ingram, *(Lab.)*	22,205
Archie Buchanan, *(SNP)*	9,450
Ewan Hawthorn, *(LD)*	4,278
Mrs Margaret McCulloch, *(C.)*	4,238
David Stevenson, *(SSP)*	1,519

Lab. maj 12,755 (30.59%)
2.52% swing Lab. to SNP
1997: Lab. maj 17,384 (35.63%)

EAST LOTHIAN

E. 58,987   T. 36,871 (62.51%)   Lab. hold

Mrs Anne Picking, *(Lab.)*	17,407
Hamish Mair, *(C.)*	6,577
Ms Judy Hayman, *(LD)*	6,506
Ms Hilary Brown, *(SNP)*	5,381
Derrick White, *(SSP)*	624
Jake Herriot, *(Soc. Lab.)*	376

Lab. maj 10,830 (29.37%)
1.68% swing Lab. to C.
1997: Lab. maj 14,221 (32.74%)

EASTWOOD

E. 68,378	T. 48,368 (70.74%)	Lab. hold
*Jim Murphy, (Lab.)		23,036
Raymond Robertson, (C.)		13,895
Allan Steele, (LD)		6,239
Stewart Maxwell, (SNP)		4,137
Peter Murray, (SSP)		814
Dr Manar Tayan, (Ind.)		247

Lab. maj 9,141 (18.90%)
6.35% swing C. to Lab.
1997: Lab. maj 3,236 (6.19%)

EDINBURGH CENTRAL

E. 66,089	T. 34,390 (52.04%)	Lab. hold
*Alistair Darling, (Lab.)		14,495
Andrew Myles, (LD)		6,353
Alastair Orr, (C.)		5,643
Dr Ian McKee, (SNP)		4,832
Graeme Farmer, (Green)		1,809
Kevin Williamson, (SSP)		1,258

Lab. maj 8,142 (23.68%)
5.15% swing Lab. to LD
1997: Lab. maj 11,070 (25.90%)

EDINBURGH EAST & MUSSELBURGH

E. 59,241	T. 34,454 (58.16%)	Lab. hold
*Dr Gavin Strang, (Lab.)		18,124
Rob Munn, (SNP)		5,956
Gary Peacock, (LD)		4,981
Peter Finnie, (C.)		3,906
Derek Durkin, (SSP)		1,487

Lab. maj 12,168 (35.32%)
0.41% swing SNP to Lab.
1997: Lab. maj 14,530 (34.50%)

EDINBURGH NORTH & LEITH

E. 62,475	T. 33,234 (53.20%)	Lab. hold
Mark Lazarowicz, (Lab.)		15,271
Sebastian Tombs, (LD)		6,454
Ms Kaukab Stewart, (SNP)		5,290
Iain Mitchell, (C.)		4,626
Ms Catriona Grant, (SSP)		1,334
Don Jacobsen, (Soc. Lab.)		259

Lab. maj 8,817 (26.53%)
3.67% swing Lab. to LD
1997: Lab. maj 10,978 (26.81%)

EDINBURGH PENTLANDS

E. 59,841	T. 38,932 (65.06%)	Lab. hold
*Dr Lynda Clark, (Lab.)		15,797
Sir Malcolm Rifkind, (C.)		14,055
David Walker, (LD)		4,210
Stewart Gibb, (SNP)		4,210
James Mearns, (SSP)		555
William McMurdo, (UK Ind.)		105

Lab. maj 1,742 (4.47%)
3.08% swing Lab. to C.
1997: Lab. maj 4,862 (10.63%)

EDINBURGH SOUTH

E. 64,012	T. 37,166 (58.06%)	Lab. hold
*Nigel Griffiths, (Lab.)		15,671
Ms Marilyne MacLaren, (LD)		10,172
Geoffrey Buchan, (C.)		6,172
Ms Heather Williams, (SNP)		3,683
Colin Fox, (SSP)		933
Ms Linda Hendry, (LCA)		535

Lab. maj 5,499 (14.80%)
7.19% swing Lab. to LD
1997: Lab. maj 11,452 (25.54%)

EDINBURGH WEST

E. 61,895	T. 39,478 (63.78%)	LD hold
John Barrett, (LD)		16,719
Ms Elspeth Alexandra, (Lab.)		9,130
Iain Whyte, (C.)		8,894
Alyn Smith, (SNP)		4,047
Bill Scott, (SSP)		688

LD maj 7,589 (19.22%)
2.59% swing LD to Lab.
1997: LD maj 7,253 (15.22%)

FALKIRK EAST

E. 57,633	T. 33,702 (58.48%)	Lab. hold
*Michael Connarty, (Lab.)		18,536
Ms Isabel Hutton, (SNP)		7,824
Bill Stevenson, (C.)		3,252
Ms Karen Utting, (LD)		2,992
Tony Weir, (SSP)		725
Raymond Stead, (Soc. Lab.)		373

Lab. maj 10,712 (31.78%)
0.20% swing Lab. to SNP
1997: Lab. maj 13,385 (32.18%)

FALKIRK WEST

E. 53,583	T. 30,891 (57.65%)	Lab. hold
*Eric Joyce, (Lab.)		16,022
David Kerr, (SNP)		7,490
Simon Murray, (C.)		2,321
Hugh O'Donnell, (LD)		2,203
William Buchanan, (Ind. B)		1,464
Ms Mhairi McAlpine, (SSP)		707
Hugh Lynch, (Ind.)		490
Ronnie Forbes, (Soc. Lab.)		194

Lab. maj 8,532 (27.62%)
4.15% swing Lab. to SNP
2000 Dec by-election: Lab. maj 705 (3.61%)
1997: Lab. maj 13,783 (35.92%)

FIFE CENTRAL

E. 59,597	T. 32,512 (54.55%)	Lab. hold
John MacDougall, (Lab.)		18,310
David Alexander, (SNP)		8,235
Ms Elizabeth Riches, (LD)		2,775
Jeremy Balfour, (C.)		2,351
Ms Morag Balfour, (SSP)		841

Lab. maj 10,075 (30.99%)
1.33% swing Lab. to SNP
1997: Lab. maj 13,713 (33.64%)

FIFE NORTH EAST

E. 61,900	T. 34,692 (56.05%)	LD hold
*Menzies Campbell, (LD)		17,926
Mike Scott-Hayward, (C.)		8,190
Ms Claire Brennan, (Lab.)		3,950
Ms Kris Murray-Browne, (SNP)		3,596
Keith White, (SSP)		610
Mrs Leslie Von Goetz, (LCA)		420

LD maj 9,736 (28.06%)
1.66% swing C. to LD
1997: LD maj 10,356 (24.75%)

GALLOWAY & UPPER NITHSDALE

E. 52,756	T. 35,914 (68.08%)	C. gain
Peter Duncan, (C.)		12,222
Malcolm Fleming, (SNP)		12,148
Thomas Sloan, (Lab.)		7,258
Neil Wallace, (LD)		3,698
Andy Harvey, (SSP)		588

C. maj 74 (0.21%)
6.80% swing SNP to C.
1997: SNP maj 5,624 (13.39%)

GLASGOW ANNIESLAND

E. 53,290	T. 26,722 (50.14%)	Lab. hold
*John Robertson, (Lab.)		15,102
Grant Thoms, (SNP)		4,048
Christopher McGinty, (LD)		3,244
Stewart Connell, (C.)		2,651
Charlie McCarthy, (SSP)		1,486
Ms Katherine McGavigan, (Soc. Lab.)		191

Lab. maj 11,054 (41.37%)
1.68% swing Lab. to SNP
2000 Nov by-election: Lab. maj 6,337 (31.35%)
1997: Lab. maj 15,154 (44.73%)

GLASGOW BAILLIESTON

E. 49,268	T. 23,261 (47.21%)	Lab. hold
*Jimmy Wray, (Lab.)		14,200
Lachlan McNeill, (SNP)		4,361
David Comrie, (C.)		1,580
Jim McVicar, (SSP)		1,569
Charles Dundas, (LD)		1,551

Lab. maj 9,839 (42.30%)
2.15% swing Lab. to SNP
1997: Lab. maj 14,840 (46.59%)

GLASGOW CATHCART

E. 52,094	T. 27,386 (52.57%)	Lab. hold
Tom Harris, (Lab.)		14,902
Mrs Josephine Docherty, (SNP)		4,086
Richard Cook, (C.)		3,662
Tom Henery, (LD)		3,006
Ronnie Stevenson, (SSP)		1,730

Lab. maj 10,816 (39.49%)
1.80% swing SNP to Lab.
1997: Lab. maj 12,245 (35.90%)

GLASGOW GOVAN

E. 54,068	T. 25,284 (46.76%)	Lab. hold
*Mohammad Sarwar, (Lab.)		12,464
Ms Karen Neary, (SNP)		6,064
Bob Stewart, (LD)		2,815
Mark Menzies, (C.)		2,167
Willie McGartland, (SSP)		1,531
John Foster, (Comm)		174
Badar Mirza, (Ind.)		69

Lab. maj 6,400 (25.31%)
8.14% swing SNP to Lab.
1997: Lab. maj 2,914 (9.04%)

GLASGOW KELVIN

E. 61,534   T. 26,802 (43.56%)   Lab. hold
*George Galloway, (Lab.)   12,014
Ms Tamsin Mayberry, (LD)   4,754
Frank Rankin, (SNP)   4,513
Miss Davina Rankin, (C.)   2,388
Ms Heather Ritchie, (SSP)   1,847
Tim Shand, (Green)   1,286
Lab. maj 7,260 (27.09%)
4.85% swing Lab. to LD
1997: Lab. maj 9,665 (29.60%)

GLASGOW MARYHILL

E. 55,431   T. 22,231 (40.11%)   Lab. hold
Ms Ann McKechin, (Lab.)   13,420
Alex Dingwall, (SNP)   3,532
Stuart Callison, (LD)   2,372
Gordon Scott, (SSP)   1,745
Gawain Towler, (C.)   1,162
Lab. maj 9,888 (44.48%)
1.76% swing Lab. to SNP
1997: Lab. maj 14,264 (47.99%)

GLASGOW POLLOK

E. 49,201   T. 25,277 (51.37%)
                                   Lab. Co-op hold
*Ian Davidson, (Lab. Co-op)   15,497
David Ritchie, (SNP)   4,229
Keith Baldassara, (SSP)   2,522
Ms Isabel Nelson, (LD)   1,612
Rory O'Brien, (C.)   1,417
Lab. Co-op maj 11,268 (44.58%)
1.27% swing SNP to Lab. Co-op
1997: Lab. maj 13,791 (42.04%)

GLASGOW RUTHERGLEN

E. 51,855   T. 29,213 (56.34%)
                                   Lab. Co-op hold
*Tommy McAvoy, (Lab. Co-op)   16,760
Ms Anne McLaughlin, (SNP)   4,135
David Jackson, (LD)   3,689
Malcolm Macaskill, (C.)   3,301
Bill Bonnar, (SSP)   1,328
Lab Co-op maj 12,625 (43.22%)
0.48% swing SNP to Lab. Co-op
1997: Lab. maj 15,007 (42.25%)

GLASGOW SHETTLESTON

E. 51,557   T. 20,465 (39.69%)   Lab. hold
*David Marshall, (Lab.)   13,235
Jim Byrne, (SNP)   3,417
Ms Rosie Kane, (SSP)   1,396
Lewis Hutton, (LD)   1,105
Campbell Murdoch, (C.)   1,082
Murdo Ritchie, (Soc. Lab.)   230
Lab. maj 9,818 (47.97%)
5.60% swing Lab. to SNP
1997: Lab. maj 15,868 (59.18%)

GLASGOW SPRINGBURN

E. 55,192   T. 24,104 (43.67%) Speaker hold
*Michael Martin, (Speaker)   16,053
Sandy Bain, (SNP)   4,675
Ms Carolyn Leckie, (SSP)   1,879
Daniel Houston, (Scot U)   1,289
Richard Silvester, (Ind.)   208
Speaker maj 11,378 (47.20%)
1997: Lab. maj 17,326 (54.87%)

GORDON

E. 59,996   T. 35,001 (58.34%)   LD hold
*Malcolm Bruce, (LD)   15,928
Mrs Nanette Milne, (C.)   8,049
Mrs Rhona Kemp, (SNP)   5,760
Ellis Thorpe, (Lab.)   4,730
John Sangster, (SSP)   534
LD maj 7,879 (22.51%)
2.97% swing C. to LD
1997: LD maj 6,997 (16.57%)

GREENOCK & INVERCLYDE

E. 47,884   T. 28,419 (59.35%)   Lab. hold
David Cairns, (Lab.)   14,929
Chic Brodie, (LD)   5,039
Andrew Murie, (SNP)   4,248
Alistair Haw, (C.)   3,000
Davey Landels, (SSP)   1,203
Lab. maj 9,890 (34.80%)
3.77% swing Lab. to LD
1997: Lab. maj 13,040 (37.59%)

HAMILTON NORTH & BELLSHILL

E. 53,539   T. 30,404 (56.79%)   Lab. hold
*Dr John Reid, (Lab.)   18,786
Chris Stephens, (SNP)   5,225
Bill Frain Bell, (C.)   2,649
Keith Legg, (LD)   2,360
Ms Shareen Blackall, (SSP)   1,189
Steve Mayes, (Soc. Lab.)   195
Lab. maj 13,561 (44.60%)
0.16% swing Lab. to SNP
1997: Lab. maj 17,067 (44.92%)

HAMILTON SOUTH

E. 46,665   T. 26,750 (57.32%)   Lab. hold

*Bill Tynan, *(Lab.)*	15,965
John Wilson, *(SNP)*	5,190
John Oswald, *(LD)*	2,381
Neil Richardson, *(C.)*	1,876
Ms Gena Mitchell, *(SSP)*	1,187
Ms Janice Murdoch, *(UK Ind.)*	151

Lab. maj 10,775 (40.28%)
3.85% swing Lab. to SNP
1999 Sep by-election: Lab. maj 556 (2.86%)
1997: Lab. maj 15,878 (47.98%)

INVERNESS EAST, NAIRN & LOCHABER

E. 67,139   T. 42,461 (63.24%)   Lab. hold

*David Stewart, *(Lab.)*	15,605
Angus MacNeil, *(SNP)*	10,889
Ms Patsy Kenton, *(LD)*	9,420
Richard Jenkins, *(C.)*	5,653
Steve Arnott, *(SSP)*	894

Lab. maj 4,716 (11.11%)
3.10% swing SNP to Lab.
1997: Lab. maj 2,339 (4.90%)

KILMARNOCK & LOUDOUN

E. 61,049   T. 37,665 (61.70%)   Lab. hold

*Des Browne, *(Lab.)*	19,926
John Brady, *(SNP)*	9,592
Donald Reece, *(C.)*	3,943
John Stewart, *(LD)*	3,177
Jason Muir, *(SSP)*	1,027

Lab. maj 10,334 (27.44%)
6.07% swing SNP to Lab.
1997: Lab. maj 7,256 (15.30%)

KIRKCALDY

E. 51,559   T. 28,157 (54.61%)

                                        Lab. Co-op hold

*Dr Lewis Moonie, *(Lab. Co-op)*	15,227
Ms Shirley-Anne Somerville, *(SNP)*	6,264
Scott Campbell, *(C.)*	3,013
Andrew Weston, *(LD)*	2,849
Dougie Kinnear, *(SSP)*	804

Lab Co-op maj 8,963 (31.83%)
0.60% swing SNP to Lab. Co-op
1997: Lab. maj 10,710 (30.63%)

LINLITHGOW

E. 54,599   T. 31,655 (57.98%)   Lab. hold

*Tam Dalyell, *(Lab.)*	17,207
Jim Sibbald, *(SNP)*	8,078
Gordon Lindhurst, *(C.)*	2,836
Martin Oliver, *(LD)*	2,628
Eddie Cornoch, *(SSP)*	695
Ms Helen Cronin, *(R & R Loony)*	211

Lab. maj 9,129 (28.84%)
0.75% swing SNP to Lab.
1997: Lab. maj 10,838 (27.33%)

LIVINGSTON

E. 64,850   T. 36,033 (55.56%)   Lab. hold

*Robin Cook, *(Lab.)*	19,108
Graham Sutherland, *(SNP)*	8,492
Gordon Mackenzie, *(LD)*	3,969
Ian Mowat, *(C.)*	2,995
Ms Wendy Milne, *(SSP)*	1,110
Robert Kingdon, *(UK Ind.)*	359

Lab. maj 10,616 (29.46%)
1.02% swing SNP to Lab.
1997: Lab. maj 11,747 (27.43%)

MIDLOTHIAN

E. 48,625   T. 28,724 (59.07%)   Lab. hold

David Hamilton, *(Lab.)*	15,145
Ian Goldie, *(SNP)*	6,131
Ms Jacqueline Bell, *(LD)*	3,686
Robin Traquair, *(C.)*	2,748
Bob Goupillot, *(SSP)*	837
Terence Holden, *(ProLife)*	177

Lab. maj 9,014 (31.38%)
1.69% swing SNP to Lab.
1997: Lab. maj 9,870 (28.00%)

MORAY

E. 58,008   T. 33,223 (57.27%)   SNP hold

Angus Robertson, *(SNP)*	10,076
Mrs Catriona Munro, *(Lab.)*	8,332
Frank Spencer-Nairn, *(C.)*	7,677
Ms Linda Gorn, *(LD)*	5,224
Ms Norma Anderson, *(SSP)*	821
Bill Jappy, *(Ind.)*	802
Nigel Kenyon, *(UK Ind.)*	291

SNP maj 1,744 (5.25%)
8.25% swing SNP to Lab.
1997: SNP maj 5,566 (14.00%)

MOTHERWELL & WISHAW

E. 52,418	T. 29,673 (56.61%)	Lab. hold
*Frank Roy, *(Lab.)*		16,681
Jim McGuigan, *(SNP)*		5,725
Mark Nolan, *(C.)*		3,155
Iain Brown, *(LD)*		2,791
Stephen Smellie, *(SSP)*		1,260
Ms Claire Watt, *(Soc Lab)*		61

Lab. maj 10,956 (36.92%)
1.00% swing SNP to Lab.
1997: Lab. maj 12,791 (34.93%)

OCHIL

E. 57,554	T. 35,303 (61.34%)	Lab. hold
*Martin O'Neill, *(Lab.)*		16,004
Keith Brown, *(SNP)*		10,655
Alasdair Campbell, *(C.)*		4,235
Paul Edie, *(LD)*		3,253
Ms Pauline Thompson, *(SSP)*		751
Flash Gordon Approaching, *(Loony)*		405

Lab. maj 5,349 (15.15%)
2.26% swing SNP to Lab.
1997: Lab. maj 4,652 (10.63%)

ORKNEY & SHETLAND

E. 31,909	T. 16,733 (52.44%)	LD hold
Alistair Carmichael, *(LD)*		6,919
Robert Mochrie, *(Lab.)*		3,444
John Firth, *(C.)*		3,121
John Mowat, *(SNP)*		2,473
Peter Andrews, *(SSP)*		776

LD maj 3,475 (20.77%)
6.48% swing LD to Lab.
1997: LD maj 6,968 (33.72%)

PAISLEY NORTH

E. 47,994	T. 27,153 (56.58%)	Lab. hold
*Ms Irene Adams, *(Lab.)*		15,058
George Adam, *(SNP)*		5,737
Ms Jane Hook, *(LD)*		2,709
Craig Stevenson, *(C.)*		2,404
Jim Halfpenny, *(SSP)*		982
Robert Graham, *(ProLife)*		263

Lab. maj 9,321 (34.33%)
1.61% swing Lab. to SNP
1997: Lab. maj 12,814 (37.54%)

PAISLEY SOUTH

E. 53,351	T. 30,536 (57.24%)	Lab. hold
*Douglas Alexander, *(Lab.)*		17,830
Brian Lawson, *(SNP)*		5,920
Brian O'Malley, *(LD)*		3,178
Andrew Cossar, *(C.)*		2,301
Ms Frances Curran, *(SSP)*		835
Ms Patricia Graham, *(ProLife)*		346
Terence O'Donnell, *(Ind.)*		126

Lab. maj 11,910 (39.00%)
2.44% swing SNP to Lab.
1997 Nov by-election: Lab. maj 2,731 (11.65%)
1997: Lab. maj 12,750 (34.13%)

PERTH

E. 61,497	T. 37,816 (61.49%)	SNP hold
Ms Annabelle Ewing, *(SNP)*		11,237
Miss Elizabeth Smith, *(C.)*		11,189
Ms Marion Dingwall, *(Lab.)*		9,638
Ms Vicki Harris, *(LD)*		4,853
Frank Byrne, *(SSP)*		899

SNP maj 48 (0.13%)
3.46% swing SNP to C.
1997: SNP maj 3,141 (7.05%)

RENFREWSHIRE WEST

E. 52,889	T. 33,497 (63.33%)	Lab gain
James Sheridan, *(Lab.)*		15,720
Ms Carol Puthucheary, *(SNP)*		7,145
David Sharpe, *(C.)*		5,522
Ms Clare Hamblen, *(LD)*		4,185
Ms Arlene Nunnery, *(SSP)*		925

Lab. maj 8,575 (25.60%)
2.77% swing SNP to Lab.
1997: Lab. maj 7,979 (20.05%)

ROSS, SKYE & INVERNESS WEST

E. 56,522	T. 34,812 (61.59%)	LD hold
*Charles Kennedy, *(LD)*		18,832
Donald Crichton, *(Lab.)*		5,880
Ms Jean Urquhart, *(SNP)*		4,901
Angus Laing, *(C.)*		3,096
Dr Eleanor Scott, *(Green)*		699
Stuart Topp, *(SSP)*		683
Philip Anderson, *(UK Ind.)*		456
James Crawford, *(Country)*		265

LD maj 12,952 (37.21%)
13.57% swing Lab. to LD
1997: LD maj 4,019 (10.06%)

ROXBURGH & BERWICKSHIRE

E. 47,059	T. 28,797 (61.19%)	LD hold
*Archy Kirkwood, *(LD)*		14,044
George Turnbull, *(C.)*		6,533
Ms Catherine Maxwell-Stuart, *(Lab.)*		4,498
Roderick Campbell, *(SNP)*		2,806
Ms Amanda Millar, *(SSP)*		463
Peter Neilson, *(UK Ind.)*		453

LD maj 7,511 (26.08%)
1.73% swing C. to LD
1997: LD maj 7,906 (22.63%)

STIRLING

E. 53,097	T. 35,930 (67.67%)	Lab. hold
*Ms Anne McGuire, *(Lab.)*		15,175
Geoff Mawdsley, *(C.)*		8,901
Ms Fiona Macaulay, *(SNP)*		5,877
Clive Freeman, *(LD)*		4,208
Dr Clarke Mullen, *(SSP)*		1,012
Mark Ruskell, *(Green)*		757

Lab. maj 6,274 (17.46%)
1.27% swing C. to Lab.
1997: Lab. maj 6,411 (14.93%)

STRATHKELVIN & BEARSDEN

E. 62,729	T. 41,486 (66.14%)	Lab. hold
John Lyons, *(Lab.)*		19,250
Gordon Macdonald, *(LD)*		7,533
Calum Smith, *(SNP)*		6,675
Murray Roxburgh, *(C.)*		6,635
Willie Telfer, *(SSP)*		1,393

Lab. maj 11,717 (28.24%)
7.44% swing Lab. to LD
1997: Lab. maj 16,292 (32.77%)

TAYSIDE NORTH

E. 61,645	T. 38,517 (62.48%)	SNP hold
Peter Wishart, *(SNP)*		15,441
Murdo Fraser, *(C.)*		12,158
Thomas Docherty, *(Lab.)*		5,715
Ms Julia Robertson, *(LD)*		4,363
Ms Rosie Adams, *(SSP)*		620
Ms Tina MacDonald, *(Ind.)*		220

SNP maj 3,283 (8.52%)
0.30% swing SNP to C.
1997: SNP maj 4,160 (9.13%)

TWEEDDALE, ETTRICK & LAUDERDALE

E. 51,966	T. 33,217 (63.92%)	LD hold
*Michael Moore, *(LD)*		14,035
Keith Geddes, *(Lab.)*		8,878
Andrew Brocklehurst, *(C.)*		5,118
Richard Thomson, *(SNP)*		4,108
Norman Lockhart, *(SSP)*		695
John Hein, *(Lib.)*		383

LD maj 5,157 (15.53%)
5.86% swing Lab. to LD
1997: LD maj 1,489 (3.81%)

WESTERN ISLES

E. 21,807	T. 13,159 (60.34%)	Lab. hold
*Calum MacDonald, *(Lab.)*		5,924
Alasdair Nicholson, *(SNP)*		4,850
Douglas Taylor, *(C.)*		1,250
John Horne, *(LD)*		849
Ms Joanne Telfer, *(SSP)*		286

Lab. maj 1,074 (8.16%)
7.02% swing Lab. to SNP
1997: Lab. maj 3,576 (22.20%)

MEMBERS FOR SCOTTISH SEATS

*Member of last Parliament

*Adams, Irene K., (b. 1948), Lab., Paisley North, maj. 9,321

*Alexander, Douglas, (b. 1967), Lab., Paisley South, maj. 11,910

Barrett, John, (b. 1954), LD, Edinburgh West, maj. 7,589

*Begg, Anne, (b. 1955), Lab., Aberdeen South, maj. 4,388

*Brown, Rt. Hon. Gordon, (b. 1951), Lab., Dunfermline East, maj. 15,063

*Brown, Russell, (b. 1951), Lab., Dumfries, maj. 8,834

*Browne, Des, (b. 1952), Lab., Kilmarnock and Loudoun, maj. 10,334

*Bruce, Malcolm G., (b. 1944), LD, Gordon, maj. 7,879

Cairns, David, (b. 1966), Lab., Greenock and Inverclyde, maj. 9,890

*Campbell, Rt. Hon. Menzies, CBE, QC, (b. 1941), LD, Fife North East, maj. 9,736

Carmichael, Alistair, (b. 1965), LD, Orkney and Shetland, maj. 3,475

*Clark, Lynda, QC, (b. 1949), Lab., Edinburgh Pentlands, maj. 1,742

*Clarke, Rt. Hon. Thomas, CBE, (b. 1941), Lab., Coatbridge and Chryston, maj. 15,314

*Connarty, Michael, (b. 1947), Lab., Falkirk East, maj. 10,712

*Cook, Rt. Hon. Robin, (b. 1946), Lab., Livingston, maj. 10,616

*Dalyell, Tam, (b. 1932), Lab., Linlithgow, maj. 9,129

*Darling, Rt. Hon. Alistair, (b. 1953), Lab., Edinburgh Central, maj. 8,142

*Davidson, Ian G., (b. 1950), Lab. Co-op., Glasgow Pollok, maj. 11,268

*Donohoe, Brian, (b. 1948), Lab., Cunninghame South, maj. 11,230

*Doran, Frank, (b. 1949), Lab., Aberdeen Central, maj. 6,646

Duncan, Peter, (b. 1965), C., Galloway and Upper Nithsdale, maj. 74

Ewing, Annabelle, (b. 1960), SNP, Perth, maj. 48

*Foulkes, George, (b. 1942), Lab. Co-op., Carrick, Cumnock and Doon Valley, maj. 14,856

*Galloway, George, (b. 1954), Lab., Glasgow Kelvin, maj. 7,260

*Griffiths, Nigel, (b. 1955), Lab., Edinburgh South, maj. 5,499

Hamilton, David, (b. 1950), Lab., Midlothian, maj. 9,014

Harris, Tom, (b. 1964), Lab., Glasgow Cathcart, maj. 10,816

*Hood, James, (b. 1948), Lab., Clydesdale, maj. 7,794

*Ingram, Rt. Hon. Adam, (b. 1947), Lab., East Kilbride, maj. 12,755

Joyce, Eric, (b. 1960), Lab., Falkirk West, maj. 8,532

*Kennedy, Rt. Hon. Charles P., (b. 1959), LD, Ross, Skye and Inverness West, maj. 12,952

*Kirkwood, Archibald J., (b. 1946), LD, Roxburgh and Berwickshire, maj. 7,511

Lazarowicz, Mark, (b. 1953), Lab., Edinburgh North and Leith, maj. 8,817

*Liddell, Rt. Hon. Helen, (b. 1950), Lab., Airdrie and Shotts, maj. 12,340

Luke, Iain, (b. 1951), Lab., Dundee East, maj. 4,475

Lyons, John, (b. 1950), Lab., Strathkelvin and Bearsden, maj. 11,717

*MacDonald, Calum A., (b. 1956), Lab., Western Isles, maj. 1,074

MacDougall, John, (b. 1947), Lab., Fife Central, maj. 10,075

*Marshall, David, (b. 1941), Lab., Glasgow Shettleston, maj. 9,818

*Martin, Rt. Hon. Michael J., (b. 1945), Speaker, Glasgow Springburn, maj. 11,378

*McAvoy, Thomas M., (b. 1943), Lab. Co-op., Glasgow Rutherglen, maj. 12,625

*McFall, John, (b. 1944), Lab. Co-op., Dumbarton, maj. 9,575

*McGuire, Anne, (b. 1949), Lab., Stirling, maj. 6,274

McKechin, Ann, (b. 1961), Lab., Glasgow Maryhill, maj. 9,888

*McKenna, Rosemary, CBE, (b. 1941), Lab., Cumbernauld and Kilsyth, maj. 7,520

*Moonie, Dr Lewis, (b. 1947), Lab. Co-op., Kirkcaldy, maj. 8,963

*Moore, Michael, (b. 1965), LD, Tweeddale, Ettrick and Lauderdale, maj. 5,157

*Murphy, Jim, (b. 1967), Lab., Eastwood, maj. 9,141

*O'Neill, Martin, (b. 1945), Lab., Ochil, maj. 5,349

*Osborne, Sandra, (b. 1956), Lab., Ayr, maj. 2,545

Picking, Anne, (b. 1958), Lab., East Lothian, maj. 10,830

Reid, Alan, (b. 1954), LD, Argyll and Bute, maj. 1,653

*Reid, Rt. Hon. Dr John, (b. 1947), Lab., Hamilton North and Bellshill, maj. 13,561

Robertson, Angus, (b. 1969), SNP, Moray, maj. 1,744

Robertson, John, (b. 1952), Lab., Glasgow Anniesland, maj. 11,054

*Ross, Ernest, (b. 1942), Lab., Dundee West, maj. 6,800

*Roy, Frank, (b. 1958), *Lab., Motherwell and Wishaw,*
maj. 10,956

*Salmond, Alex, (b. 1954), *SNP, Banff and Buchan,*
maj. 10,503

*Sarwar, Mohammed, (b. 1952), *Lab., Glasgow
Govan,* maj. 6,400

*Savidge, Malcolm, (b. 1946), *Lab., Aberdeen North,*
maj. 4,449

Sheridan, Jim, (b. 1952), *Lab., Renfrewshire West,*
maj. 8,575

*Smith, Sir Robert, Bt. (b. 1958), *LD, Aberdeenshire
West and Kincardine,* maj. 4,821

*Squire, Rachel, (b. 1954), *Lab., Dunfermline West,*
maj. 10,980

*Stewart, David, (b. 1956), *Lab., Inverness East,
Nairn and Lochaber,* maj. 4,716

*Strang, Rt. Hon. Dr Gavin, (b. 1943), *Lab.,
Edinburgh East and Musselburgh,* maj. 12,168

Thurso, John, (b. 1953), *LD, Caithness, Sutherland
and Easter Ross,* maj. 2,744

Tynan, Bill, (b. 1940), *Lab., Hamilton South,*
maj. 10,775

Weir, Michael, (b. 1957), *SNP, Angus, maj.* 3,611

*Wilson, Brian, (b. 1948), *Lab., Cunninghame North,*
maj. 8,398

Wishart, Peter, (b. 1962), *SNP, Tayside North,*
maj. 3,283

*Worthington, Anthony, (b. 1941), *Lab., Clydebank
and Milngavie,* maj. 10,724

*Wray, James, (b. 1938), *Lab., Glasgow Baillieston,*
maj. 9,839

ABBREVIATIONS OF PARTY NAMES

Anti-Corr.	Anti-Corruption, Mobile Home Scandal, Roads
Anti-Drug	Independent Anti-Drug Party
AS	Anti-sleaze
C.	Conservative
Ch. U.	Christian Nationalist
CPPDS	Communist Party Peace Democracy Socialism
BNP	British National Party
Comm. Brit.	Communist Party of Britain
D. Nat.	Democratic Nationalist
Falkirk W.	MP for Falkirk West
Green	Green Party
Highlands	Highlands and Islands Alliance
Ind.	Independent
Ind. Dem.	Independent Democrat
Ind. Ind.	Independent Independent
Ind. Prog.	Independent Progressive
Ind. Voice	Independent Voice for Scottish Parliament
Ind. Water	Independent Labour Keep Scottish Water Public
Individual	Independent Individual
Ind. You	Independent of London: Independent for You
Lab.	Labour
Lab. Co-op.	Labour Co-operative
LD	Liberal Democrat
Lib.	Liberal
Local Health	Local Health Concern
Loony	Official Monster Raving Loony Party
Mission	Scottish People's Mission
NLP	Natural Law Party
Parent Ex	Parent Excluded
ProLife	ProLife Alliance
Ref.	Referendum Party
SCU	Scottish Conservative Unofficial
SFPP	Scottish Families and Pensioners Party
SLI	Scottish Labour Independent
SLU	Scottish Labour Unofficial
SNP	Scottish National Party
Soc. Lab.	Socialist Labour Party
SPA	Scottish People's Alliance
SPGB	Socialist Party of Great Britain
SSA	Scottish Socialist Alliance
SSOCUP	Scottish Senior Citizens' Unity Party
SSP	Scottish Socialist Party
SUP	Scottish Unionist Party
SWP	Socialist Workers Party
UK Ind.	UK Independence Party
Witchery	Witchery Tour Party
WRP	Workers' Revolutionary Party

E. Electorate
T. Turnout

OTHER GOVERNMENT DEPARTMENTS, PUBLIC BODIES AND EXECUTIVE AGENCIES

This section details executive agencies of the Scottish Executive, regulatory bodies, tribunals and other statutory independent organisations and non-governmental public bodies. UK Civil Service departments and public bodies are included where their remit continues to extend to Scotland.

ACCOUNTS COMMISSION

110 George Street, Edinburgh EH2 4LH
Tel: 0131-477 1234 Fax: 0131-477 4567
Web: www.accounts-commission.gov.uk

The Accounts Commission is responsible for securing the audit of 32 councils and 34 joint boards. The Commission also promotes value for money and assists audited bodies to achieve efficient and effective use of their resources. In addition the Commission is responsible for ensuring the annual publication of performance information about councils.
Chairman: Alastair MacNish

ADJUDICATOR'S OFFICE

Haymarket House, 28 Haymarket, London SW1Y 4SP
Tel: 020-7930 2292 Fax: 020-7930 2298
Email: adjudicators@gtnet.gov.uk
Web: www.adjudicatorsoffice.gov.uk

The Adjudicator's Office investigates complaints about the way the Inland Revenue (including the Valuation Office Agency) and Customs and Excise have handled an individual's affairs.
The Adjudicator: Dame Barbara Mills, DBE, QC

ADVISORY COMMITTEE ON SITES OF SPECIAL SCIENTIFIC INTEREST

c/o Scottish Natural Heritage, 12 Hope Terrace,
Edinburgh EH9 2AS
Tel: 0131-447 4784 Fax: 0131-446 2277

The Committee advises Scottish Natural Heritage in cases where there are sustained scientific objections to the notification of Sites of Special Scientific Interest.
Chairman: Prof. W. Ritchie
Secretary: D. Howell

ADVISORY, CONCILIATION AND ARBITRATION SERVICE

Regional Office, 151 West George Street,
Glasgow G2 7JJ Tel: 08457-474747 or
0141-248 1400 Fax: 0141-221 4697
Web: www.acas.org.uk

The Advisory, Conciliation and Arbitration Service (ACAS) promotes the improvement of industrial relations in general, provides facilities for conciliation, mediation and arbitration as means of avoiding and resolving industrial disputes, and provides advisory and information services on industrial relations matters to employers, employees and their representatives.
Director, Scotland: Frank Blair

THE APPEALS SERVICE

Glasgow Office: Wellington House,
134–136 Wellington Street, Glasgow G2 2XL
Tel: 0141-354 8400 Fax: 0141-354 8463
Web: www.appeals-service.gov.uk

The Service is responsible for the functioning of tribunals hearing appeals concerning child support assessments, social security benefits and vaccine damage payments. Judicial authority for the service rests with the President, while administrative responsibility is exercised by the Appeals Service Agency, which is an executive agency of the Department for Work and Pensions.
President: His Hon. Judge Michael Harris
Chief Executive, Appeals Service Agency: N. Ward
Regional Chairman for Scotland: K. Kirkwood
Operation Director for Scotland: B. Craig

AUDIT SCOTLAND

110 George Street, Edinburgh EH2 4LH
Tel: 0131-477 1234 Fax: 0131-477 4567

Audit Scotland was set up on 1 April 2000. It provides audit and other services to the Accounts Commission and the Auditor General. Its principal work is the external audit of the Scottish Executive, local authorities, NHS bodies and further education colleges to ensure the proper, efficient and effective use of public funds. Audit Scotland carries out financial and regularity audits to ensure that public sector bodies adhere to the highest standards of financial management and governance and performance audits to ensure that these bodies achieve the best possible value for money. All of Audit Scotland's work concerning the 32 local authorities, fire and police boards is carried out for the Accounts Commission while its other work is undertaken for the Auditor General.
Auditor General: Robert W. Black
Controller of Audit: Ronnie Hinds
Secretary: William F. Magee

THE BANK OF ENGLAND

Threadneedle Street, London EC2R 8AH
Tel: 020-7601 4444 Fax: 020-7601 5460
Email: enquiries@bankofengland.co.uk
Web: www.bankofengland.co.uk

The Bank of England is the banker of the UK Government and manages the note issue. Since 1997 its Monetary Policy Committee has had responsibility for setting short-term interest rates to meet the Government's inflation target. As the central reserve bank of the country, the Bank keeps the accounts of British banks, who maintain with it a proportion of their cash resources, and of most overseas central banks.
Governor: M. A. King
Chief Cashier: Merlyn Lowther

SCOTLAND AGENCY
19 St Vincent Place, Glasgow G1 2DT
Tel: 0141-221 7972
Scotland Agent: Tony Strachan
Deputy Agent: Catriona Brown

BOUNDARY COMMISSION FOR SCOTLAND

3 Drumsheugh Gardens, Edinburgh EH3 7QJ
Tel: 0131-538 7200 Fax: 0131-538 7240
Email: secretariat@bcomm-scotland.gov.uk
Web: www.bcomm-scotland.gov.uk

The Commission is required by law to keep the parliamentary constituencies in Scotland under review. The latest review was completed in 1995 and its proposals took effect at the 1997 general election. The next review is due to be completed by 2006.
Chairman (ex officio): The Speaker of the House of Commons
Deputy Chairman: The Hon. Lady Cosgrove
Secretary: R. Smith

BRITISH BROADCASTING CORPORATION

Broadcasting House, Portland Place, London W1A 1AA
Tel: 020-7580 4468 Fax: 020-7637 1630

The BBC is the UK's public broadcasting organisation. It is financed by revenue from receiving licences for the home services and by grant-in-aid from Parliament for the World Service (radio). For services, *see* Media section.

BBC SCOTLAND
BBC Broadcasting House, Queen Margaret Drive, Glasgow G12 8DG. Tel: 0141-339 8844
National Governor for Scotland: Sir Robert Smith
Controller, BBC Scotland: John McCormick

BRITISH WATERWAYS

Willow Grange, Church Road, Watford, Herts WD17 4QA. Tel: 01923-201120 Fax: 01923-201400
Email: enquiries.hq@britishwaterways.co.uk
Web: www.britishwaterways.co.uk

British Waterways conserves and manages over 2,000 miles/3,250 km of canals and rivers in Great Britain. Its responsibilities include maintaining the waterways and structures on and around them; looking after wildlife and the waterway environment; and ensuring that canals and rivers are safe and enjoyable places to visit.
Chairman (part-time): G. Greener
Chief Executive: D. Fletcher

SCOTTISH OFFICE
Canal House, Applecross Street, Glasgow G4 9SP
Tel: 0141-332 6936 Fax: 0141-331 1688

BUILDING STANDARDS ADVISORY COMMITTEE

Scottish Executive Building Standards Division,
2-H Victoria Quay, Edinburgh EH6 6QQ
Tel: 0131-244 7440 Fax: 0131-244 0404

The Committee advises the Scottish Ministers on questions relating to their functions under Part II of the Building (Scotland) Act 1959.
Chairman: Dr S. Thorburn, OBE, FREng
Secretary: A. Murchison

CENTRAL ADVISORY COMMITTEE ON JUSTICES OF THE PEACE (SCOTLAND)

1st Floor, West Rear, St Andrews House, Regent Road, Edinburgh EH1 3DG
Tel: 0131-244 2691 Fax: 0131-244 2623

The Committee advises and makes recommendations as to problems arising in relation to the appointment and distribution of justices of the peace and the work of JPs in general and of the district court in particular.
Chairman: The Rt. Hon. Lord Gill

CERTIFICATION OFFICE FOR TRADE UNIONS AND EMPLOYERS' ASSOCIATIONS

180 Borough High Street, London SE1 1LW
Tel: 020-7210 3734/5 Fax: 020-7210 3612
Web: www.certoffice.org

The Certification Office is an independent statutory authority responsible for receiving and scrutinising annual returns from trade unions and employers' associations; for investigating allegations of financial irregularities in the affairs of a trade union or employers' association; for dealing with complaints concerning trade union elections; for ensuring observance of statutory requirements governing political funds and trade union mergers; and for certifying the independence of trade unions.
Chairman: D. Cockburn

SCOTTISH OFFICE

58 Frederick Street, Edinburgh EH2 1LN
Tel: 0131-226 3224 Fax: 0131-200 1300
Assistant Certification Officer for Scotland:
J. L. J. Craig

CHILD SUPPORT AGENCY

National Helpline: PO Box 55 Brierley Hill,
West Midlands DY5 1YL. Tel: 08457-133133
Fax: 08457-138924
Falkirk Child Support Agency Centre: Parklands,
Callendar Business Park, Falkirk FK1 1XT
Tel: 08457-136000 Fax: 08457-136134
The Agency is an agency of the Department of Work and Pensions. It is responsible for implementing the 1991 and 1995 Child Support Acts and for the assessment and collection (or arrangement of direct payment) of child support maintenance. From June 1999 the Chief Executive took over the responsibilities of the Chief Child Support Officer when that office was abolished.
Area Director: Gerry Rooney

CMPS (CENTRE FOR MANAGEMENT AND POLICY STUDIES)

1 St Colme Street, Edinburgh EH3 6AA
Tel: 0131-220 8267 Fax: 0131-220 8367
Web: www.cmps.gov.uk

The College provides training in management and professional skills for the public and private sectors.

COMMISSION FOR RACIAL EQUALITY SCOTLAND

The Tun, 12 Jackson's Entry, Edinburgh EH8 8PJ
Tel: 0131-524 2000 Fax: 0131-542 2001
Email: scotland@cre.gov.uk Web: www.cre.gov.uk

The Commission was established in 1977, under the Race Relations Act 1976, to work towards the elimination of discrimination and promote equality of opportunity and good relations between different racial groups. It is funded by the Home Office.
Head of CRE, Scotland: Dharmendra Kanani

COMMISSIONER FOR LOCAL ADMINISTRATION IN SCOTLAND

23 Walker Street, Edinburgh EH3 7HX
Tel: 0131-225 5300 Fax: 0131-225 9495

The Local Commissioner for Scotland is the local government ombudsman for Scotland, responsible for investigating complaints from members of the public against local authorities and certain other authorities. The Commissioner is appointed by the Crown on the recommendation of the First Minister.
Local Commissioner: Ian F. Smith

COMMON SERVICES AGENCY FOR NHS SCOTLAND (CSA)

Trinity Park House, South Trinity Road, Edinburgh
EH5 3SE. Tel: 0131-552 6255 Fax: 0131-552 8651

The CSA is part of NHS Scotland, supporting patient care by providing and co-ordinating national and regional services.
Chairman: Graeme Millar
Chief Executive: Stuart Bain

COMMUNITIES SCOTLAND

Thistle House, 91 Haymarket Terrace, Edinburgh
EH12 5HE. Tel: 0131-313 0044 Fax: 0131-313 2680
Web: www.communitiesscotland.gov.uk

Communities Scotland is a Scottish Executive agency, reporting directly to Ministers. Its overall aim is to improve the quality of life for people in Scotland by working with others to create sustainable, healthy and attractive communities. It does this by generating neighbourhoods, empowering communities and improving the effectiveness of investment.
Chief Executive: Bob Millar

COMMUNITY FUND

2nd Floor, Highlander House, 58 Waterloo Street,
Glasgow G2 7BB
Tel: 0141-223 8600; 0870-2402391
Fax: 0131-221 7120
Email: enquiries.scotland@community-fund.org.uk
Web: www.community-fund.org.uk

Community Fund gives Lottery money to charities and voluntary groups to help those in the greatest need. There are 17 board members appointed by the Culture Secretary, who are responsible for strategic direction and grant-making.

COMPANIES HOUSE (SCOTLAND)

37 Castle Terrace, Edinburgh EH1 2EB
Tel: 0870-333 3636 Fax: 0131-535 5820
Web: www.companieshouse.gov.uk

Companies House is an executive agency of the Department of Trade and Industry. It incorporates companies, registers company documents and provides company information.
Registrar for Scotland: J. Henderson

EDINBURGH SEARCH ROOM

Tel: 0870-333 3636 Fax: 0131-535 5820

COMPETITION COMMISSION

New Court, 48 Carey Street, London WC2A 2JT
Tel: 020-7271 0100

The role of the Competition Commission is to investigate and report on mergers and markets which are referred to it by the Office of Fair Trading or the regulators of utilities.
Chairman: Sir Derek Morris
Secretary and Chief Executive: R. Foster

COPYRIGHT TRIBUNAL

Harmsworth House, 13–15 Bouverie Street,
London EC4Y 8DP Tel: 020-7596 6510
Minicom: 0845-922 2250 Fax: 020-7596 6526

The Copyright Tribunal resolves disputes over copyright licences, principally where there is collective licensing.

The chairman and two deputy chairmen are appointed by the Lord Chancellor. Up to eight ordinary members are appointed by the Secretary of State for Trade and Industry.
Chairman: Christopher Tootal
Secretary: Jill Durdin

COURT OF THE LORD LYON

HM New Register House, Edinburgh EH1 3YT
Tel: 0131-556 7255 Fax: 0131-557 2148

The Court of the Lord Lyon is the Scottish Court of Chivalry (including the genealogical jurisdiction of the Ri-Sennachie of Scotland's Celtic Kings). The Lord Lyon King of Arms has jurisdiction, subject to appeal to the Court of Session and the House of Lords, in questions of heraldry and the right to bear arms. The Court also administers the Scottish Public Register of All Arms and Bearings and the Public Register of All Genealogies. Pedigrees are established by decrees of Lyon Court and by letters patent. As Royal Commissioner in Armory, the Lord Lyon grants patents of arms (which constitute the grantee and heirs noble in the Noblesse of Scotland) to 'virtuous and well-deserving' Scots and to petitioners (personal or corporate) in the Queen's overseas realms of Scottish connection, and issues birthbrieves.
Lord Lyon King of Arms: Robin O. Blair, LVO, WS

HERALDS

Albany: J. A. Spens, MVO, RD, WS
Rothesay: Sir Crispin Agnew of Lochnaw, Bt., QC
Ross: C. J. Burnett, FSA Scot.

HERALD EXTRAORDINARY

Orkney: Sir Malcolm Innes of Edingight, KCVO, WS

PURSUIVANTS

Unicorn: Alastair Campbell of Airds, FSA Scot.
Carrick: Mrs C. G. W. Roads, MVO, FSA Scot.
Bute: W. David. H. Sellar, FSA Scot.

PURSUIVANTS EXTRAORDINARY

Orkney: Sir Malcolm Innes of Edingight, KCVO, WS
Linlithgow: J. C. G George, FSA Scot.
Lyon Clerk and Keeper of Records:
  Mrs C. G. W. Roads, MVO, FSA Scot.
Procurator-Fiscal: G. A. Way of Plean, SSC
Herald Painter: Mrs J. Phillips
Macer: H. Love

CRIMINAL INJURIES COMPENSATION AUTHORITY

Tay House, 300 Bath Street, Glasgow G2 4LN
Tel: 0141-331 2726 Fax: 0141-331 2287
Web: www.cica.gov.uk

All applications for compensation for personal injury arising from crimes of violence in Scotland are dealt with by the Authority.
Chief Executive of the Criminal Injuries Compensation Authority: H. Webber

CROFTERS COMMISSION
4–6 Castle Wynd, Inverness IV2 3EQ
Tel: 01463-663450 Fax: 01463-711820
Email: info@crofterscommission.org.uk
Web: www.crofterscommission.org.uk

The Crofters Commission is a non-departmental public body established in 1955. It advises the Scottish Ministers on all matters relating to crofting, and works with other organisations and with communities to develop and promote thriving crofting communities. It also aims to simplify legislation. It administers the Crofting Counties Agricultural Grants Scheme, Croft Entrant Scheme, and livestock improvement schemes.
Chairman: David Green
Chief Executive: Shane Rankin

THE CROWN ESTATE
6 Bell's Brae, Edinburgh EH4 3BT
Tel: 0131-260 6070 Fax: 0131-260 6090

The Crown Estate manages property held 'in the right of the Crown'. In Scotland this includes commercial property, agricultural land, half of the foreshore and almost all the seabed to the twelve-mile territorial limit. The Crown Estate Commissioners manage the Estate under the provisions of the Crown Estate Act of 1961. The entire net surplus is paid to the Treasury.
Edinburgh Office Manager: Ian Pritchard

CUSTOMS AND EXCISE
Scotland, 44 York Place, Edinburgh EH1 3JW
Tel: 0131-469 7300 Fax: 0131-469 7340
Web: www.hmce.gov.uk

HM Customs and Excise is responsible for collecting and administering customs and excise duties and VAT, and advises the Chancellor of the Exchequer on any matters connected with them. The Department is also responsible for preventing and detecting the evasion of revenue laws and for enforcing a range of prohibitions and restrictions on the importation of certain classes of goods. In addition, the Department undertakes certain agency work on behalf of other departments, including the compilation of UK overseas trade statistics from customs import and export documents.
Head of Business Services for Scotland: Ian Mackay

DEER COMMISSION FOR SCOTLAND
Knowsley, 82 Fairfield Road, Inverness IV3 5LH
Tel: 01463-231751 Fax: 01463-712931
Email: enquiries@deercom.com
Web: www.dcs.gov.uk

The Deer Commission for Scotland has the general functions of furthering the conservation, control and sustainable management of deer in Scotland. It has the statutory duty, with powers, to prevent damage to agriculture, forestry and habitat by deer. It is funded by the Scottish Executive.
Chairman (part-time): A. Raven
Members: G. Campbell; D. Irwin-Houston;
  R. Cooke; J. Duncan-Millar; Prof. J. Milne;
  Sir Michael Strang Steel; J. Mackintosh;
  Dr P. Ratcliffe; Prof. S. Walker
Director: N. Reiter
Technical Director: Dr D. Balharry

DRIVER AND VEHICLE LICENSING AGENCY
Longview Road, Morriston, Swansea SA6 7JL
Tel: 0870-240 0009 (drivers); 0870-240 0010 (vehicles)

The Agency is an executive agency of the Department of Transport, Local Governmment and the Regions (DTLR). It is responsible for the issuing of driving licences, the registration and licensing of vehicles in Great Britain, and the collection and enforcement of vehicle excise duty in the UK. The Agency also offers for sale attractive registration marks through the sale of Marks scheme.
Chief Executive: Clive Bennett

EDINBURGH VEHICLE REGISTRATION OFFICE
Saughton House, Broomhouse Drive, Edinburgh EH11 3XE Tel: 0131-455 7919 Fax: 0131-443 2478
Scottish Area Manager: D. Drury

DRIVING STANDARDS AGENCY
Stanley House, Talbot Street, Nottingham NG1 5GU
Tel: 0115-901 2500 Fax: 0115-901 2510
Web: www.dsa.gov.uk

The Agency is responsible for carrying out theory and practical driving tests for car drivers, motorcyclists, bus and lorry drivers and for maintaining the registers of Approved Driving Instructors and Large Goods Vehicle Instructors, as well as supervising Compulsory Basic Training (CBT) for learner motorcyclists. There are five area offices, which manage over 430 practical test centres across Britain.

EMPLOYMENT APPEAL TRIBUNAL
Divisional Office, 52 Melville Street, Edinburgh
EH3 7HF Tel: 0131-225 3963

The Employment Appeal Tribunal hears appeals on a question of law arising from any decision of an employment tribunal. A tribunal consists of a high court judge and two lay members, one from each side of industry.
Scottish Chairman: The Hon. Lord Johnston
Deputy Registrar: J. H. Sadler

EMPLOYMENT TRIBUNALS
Central Office (Scotland), Eagle Building, 215 Bothwell Street, Glasgow G2 7TS Tel: 0141-204 0730
Fax: 0141-204 0732 Email: glasgowet@ets.gov.uk
Web: www.employmenttribunals.gov.uk

Employment tribunals deal with matters of employment law, redundancy, dismissal, contract disputes, sexual, racial and disability discrimination, and related areas of dispute which may arise in the workplace. A central registration unit records all applications and maintains a public register.
   Chairmen are appointed by the Lord President of the Court of Session and lay members by the Secretary of State for Trade and Industry.
President: C. Milne

EQUAL OPPORTUNITIES COMMISSION
St Stephens House, 279 Bath Street, Glasgow, G2 4JL
Tel: 0845-601 5901 Fax: 0141-248 5834
Email: scotland@eoc.org.uk Web: www.eoc.org.uk

The Commission works towards the elimination of discrimination on the grounds of sex or marital status and to promote equality of opportunity between men and women generally. It is responsible to the Department for Work and Pensions.

EXTRA PARLIAMENTARY PANEL
The Scotland Office, Dover House, Whitehall, London SW1A 2AU Tel: 020-7270 6758 Fax: 020-7270 6812
Email: scottishsecretary@scotland.gsi.gov.uk
Web: www.scottishsecretary.gov.uk

The Panel hears evidence for and against draft provisional orders in private legislation procedure at an inquiry, and makes recommendations as to whether an order should proceed, be amended or be refused.

FISHERIES COMMITTEE (ELECTRICITY)
Pentland House, 47 Robb's Loan, Edinburgh EH14 1TY
Tel: 0131-244 5245 Fax: 0131-244 6313

The Committee advises and assists the Scottish Ministers and any person engaging in, or proposing to engage in, the generation of hydro-electric power on any question relating to the effect of hydro-electric works on fisheries or stocks of fish.
Chairman: James Cockburn

FISHERIES RESEARCH SERVICES
Marine Laboratory, PO Box 101, Victoria Road, Aberdeen AB11 9DB
Tel: 01224-876544 Fax: 01224-295511

The Agency provides scientific information and advice on marine and freshwater fisheries, aquaculture and the protection of the aquatic environment and its wildlife.
Chief Executive and Director: Dr Robin Cook
Deputy Chief Executive and Deputy Director: Dr Ron Stagg

FRESHWATER FISHERIES LABORATORY
Faskally, Pitlochry, Perthshire PH16 5LB
Tel: 01796-472060 Fax: 01796-473523

Senior Principal Scientific Officers: Malcolm Beveridge, Ph.D; Colin Moffat, Ph.D, FRSC; Nick Bailey; Bill Turrell, Ph.D, FRMS
Inspector of Salmon and Freshwater Fisheries for Scotland: David Dunkley

FORESTRY COMMISSION SCOTLAND
Silvan House, 231 Corstorphine Road, Edinburgh EH12 7AT Tel: 0131-334 0303 Fax: 0131-314 6152
Email: fcscotland@forestry.gsi.gov.uk
Web: www.forestry.gov.uk/scotland

The Forestry Commission is the Government Department responsible for forestry policy in Great Britain. It reports directly to forestry Ministries to whom it is responsible for advice on forestry policy and for the implementation of that policy. It manages nearly 1 million hectares of public forests throughout Great Britain. The Secretary of State for the Environment, Food and Rural Affairs has responsibility for forestry in England, Scottish Ministers have responsibility for forestry in Scotland, and the National Assembly for Wales has responsibility for forestry in Wales. For matters affecting forestry in Britain as a whole, all three have equal responsibility but the Secretary of State for the Environment, Food and Rural Affairs takes the lead.

The Commission's principal objectives are to protect Britain's forests and woodlands; expand Britain's forest area; enhance the economic value of the forest resources; conserve and improve the biodiversity, landscape and cultural heritage of forests and woodlands; develop opportunities for woodland recreation; and increase public understanding of and community participation in forestry.

Chairman of National Committee for Scotland:
  Andrew Raven

FOREST RESEARCH

Alice Holt Lodge, Wrecclesham, Farnham, Surrey GU10 4LU Tel: 01420-22255 Fax: 01420-23653
Email: ahl@forestry.gsi.gov.uk
Web: www.forestry.gov.uk/research

Forest Research provides research, development and advice to the forestry industry in support of the development and implementation of forestry policy.
Chief Executive: Prof. Jim Lynch

NORTHERN RESEARCH STATION

Roslin, Midlothian EH25 9SY
Tel: 0131-445 2176 Fax: 0131-445 5124
Email: nrs@forestry.gsi.gov.uk

GENERAL REGISTER OFFICE FOR SCOTLAND

New Register House, Edinburgh EH1 3YT
Tel: 0131-334 0380 Fax: 0131-314 4400
Email: records@gro-scotland.gov.uk
Web: www.gro-scotland.gov.uk

The General Register Office for Scotland is part of the devolved Scottish Administration. It is the office of the Registrar General for Scotland, who has responsibility for civil registration and the taking of censuses in Scotland and has in his custody the statutory registers of births, deaths, still births, adoptions, marriages and divorces; the old parish registers (recording births, deaths and marriages, etc., before civil registration began in 1855); and records of censuses of the population in Scotland (*see* also Legal Notes).
Registrar General: J. N. Randall
Deputy Registrar General: P. M. Parr
Census Manager: D. A. Orr
Heads of Branch: D. B. L. Brownlee; F. D. Garvie;
  G. Compton; G. W. L. Jackson; F. G. Thomas

GENERAL TEACHING COUNCIL FOR SCOTLAND

Clerwood House, 96 Clermiston Road, Edinburgh EH12 6UT Tel: 0131-314 6000 Fax: 0131-314 6001
Email: gtcs@gtcs.org.uk Web: www.gtcs.org.uk

The General Teaching Council for Scotland was set up under the Teaching Council (Scotland) Act 1965. It was the first such body for teachers in the UK and one of the first teaching councils in the world. One of the fundamental principles underlying the work of the Council is that of professional self-government. The principal aims of the Council are: to contribute to improving the quality of education and learning; to maintain and enhance professional standards in schools and colleges in collaboration with partners that include teachers, parents and the Scottish Executive; to be recognised as a voice and advocate for the teaching profession; and to contribute to the development of a world class educational system in Scotland.

HANNAH RESEARCH INSTITUTE

Hannah Research Park, Ayr KA6 5HL
Tel: 01292-674000 Fax: 01292-674003

The institute aims to generate and integrate new knowledge to improve lifelong health and prevent lifestyle-related diseases in Scotland
Chairman of the Institute Council:
  Prof. Sir Graeme Davies
Director: Prof. Malcolm Peaker

HEALTH EDUCATION BOARD FOR SCOTLAND

Woodburn House, Canaan Lane, Edinburgh EH10 4SG
Tel: 0131-536 5500 Fax: 0131-536 5501

Undertakes health initiatives on a national level, concentrating on areas such as coronary heart disease, cancer, stroke, smoking, diet, physical activity, sexual health and HIV/AIDS, drug and alcohol misuse, dental health, accidents, mental health and health inequalities.
Chair: Lesley Hinds
Acting Chief Executive: Graham Robertson

HEALTH AND SAFETY EXECUTIVE

Scotland Office, Belford House, 59 Belford Road, Edinburgh EH4 3UE
Tel: 0131-247 2000 Fax: 0131-247 2121
Web: www.hse.gov.uk

The Health and Safety Executive enforces health and safety law in the majority of industrial premises. The Executive advises the Health and Safety Commission in its major task of laying down safety standards through regulations and practical guidance for many industrial processes. The Executive is also the licensing authority for nuclear installations and the reporting officer on the severity of nuclear incidents in Great Britain.

Aberdeen Office: Lord Cullen House, Fraser Place, Aberdeen AB25 3UB
Tel: 01224-252500 Fax: 01224-252525

Glasgow Office: 375 West George Street, Glasgow G2 4LW Tel: 0141-275 3000 Fax: 0141-275 3100

Inverness Office: Longman House, 28 Longman Road, Longman Industrial Estate, Inverness IV1 1SF
Tel: 01463-718101 Fax: 01463-713459

Hazardous Installations Directorate: 6th Floor, St Anne's House, University Road, Bootle, Merseyside L20 3RA
Tel: 0151-951 4000 Fax: 0151-951 4236

HERITAGE LOTTERY FUND (SCOTLAND)
28 Thistle Street, Edinburgh EH2 1EN
Tel: 0131-225 9450 Fax: 0131-225 9454
Web: www.hlf.org.uk

The Heritage Lottery Fund is the designated distributor of the heritage share of proceeds from the National Lottery. The Scottish office receives and assesses all applications for projects based in Scotland. A Committee for Scotland makes decisions on grant requests up to £2 million; the main board of trustees in London is responsible for decisions on larger applications, with input from the Committee for Scotland. The Fund is keen to attract good quality applications from new audiences that have not previously been involved with their heritage.
Chairman, Committee for Scotland:
  Sir Angus Grossart, CBE
Manager, Scotland: Colin McLean

HM CHIEF INSPECTOR OF PRISONS FOR SCOTLAND
Saughton House, Broomhouse Drive, Edinburgh EH11 3XD Tel: 0131-244 8481 Fax: 0131-244 8446
HM Chief Inspector of Prisons: C. Fairweather, OBE

HM INSPECTORATE OF CONSTABULARY
1st Floor West, St. Andrew's House, Regent Road, Edinburgh EH1 3DG Tel: 0131-244 5614
HM Chief Inspector of Constabulary:
  Sir Roy Cameron, QPM, MPhil

HM INSPECTORATE OF EDUCATION IN SCOTLAND
T1 Spur, Saughton House, Broomhouse Drive, Edinburgh EH11 3XD Tel: 0131-244 7120
HM Senior Chief Inspector: G. H. C. Donaldson

HM INSPECTORATE OF FIRE SERVICES
St Andrew's House, Regent Road, Edinburgh EH1 3DG.
Tel: 0131-244 2342
HM Chief Inspector of Fire Services: D. Davis, QFSM

HIGHLANDS AND ISLANDS ENTERPRISE
Cowan House, Inverness Retail and Business Park, Inverness IV2 7GF
Tel: 01463-234171 Fax: 01463-244469
Email: hie.general@hient.co.uk
Web: www.hie.co.uk

Highlands and Islands Enterprise (HIE) was set up under the Enterprise and New Towns (Scotland) Act 1991. Its role is to design, direct and deliver enterprise development, training, careers guidance, environmental and social projects and services. HIE is made up of a strategic core body and ten local enterprise companies to which many of its individual functions are delegated.
Chief Executive: S. Cumming

HILL FARMING ADVISORY COMMITTEE FOR SCOTLAND
c/o Room 248, Pentland House, Robb's Loan, Edinburgh EH14 1TY
Tel: 0131-244 5248 Fax: 0131-244 3110
Web: www.scotland.gov.uk

The Committee advises the Minister for Environment and Rural Affairs on matters relating to hill farmers.
Chairman: Mr D. Crawley
Secretary: Miss A. McLure

HISTORIC ENVIRONMENT ADVISORY COUNCIL FOR SCOTLAND

Longmore House, Salisbury Place, Edinburgh EH9 1SH
Tel: 0131-668 8810 Fax: 0131-668 8788
Web: www.historic-scotland.gov.uk

The Historic Environment Advisory Council for Scotland provides advice to Scottish Ministers on issues affecting the historic environment and how the functions of the Scottish Ministers exercisable in relation to the historic environment may be exercised effectively. In this context, historic environment means any or all structures and places in Scotland of historical, archaeological or architectural interest or importance.
Chair: Elizabeth Burns, OBE
Secretary: Dr Malcolm Bangor-Jones

HISTORIC SCOTLAND

Longmore House, Salisbury Place, Edinburgh EH9 1SH
Tel: 0131-668 8600 Fax: 0131-668 8669
Web: www.historic-scotland.gov.uk

Historic Scotland is an executive agency of the Education Department. The agency's role is to protect Scotland's historic monuments, buildings and lands, and to promote public understanding and enjoyment of them.
Chief Executive: G. N. Munro
Directors: S. Adams; I. Maxwell; O. Kelly; B. O'Neil; L. Petrie
Chief Inspector of Ancient Monuments: Dr D. J. Breeze
Chief Inspector, Historic Buildings: R. Emerson, FSA, FSA Scot.

HORSERACE BETTING LEVY APPEAL TRIBUNAL FOR SCOTLAND

Fyfe Ireland W.S., Orchard Brae House, 30 Queensferry Road, Edinburgh EH4 2HG
Tel: 0131-343 2500 Fax: 0131-343 3166

The tribunal considers appeals by bookmakers in Scotland against the assessments made by the Horserace Betting Levy Board.
Secretary: Fiona Cumming

IMMIGRATION AND NATIONALITY DIRECTORATE

Glasgow Office: Public Enquiry Office, Festival Court, 200 Brand Street, Govan, Glasgow G51 1AR

The Immigration and Nationality Directorate is part of the Home Office and has the remit of effectively regulating entry into and settlement in the UK, in the interests of sustainable growth and social inclusion. It is also the responsibility of the Immigration and Nationality Directorate to deter and detect people who break immigration rules or whose presence in the UK would not be to the public good. In serious cases, Immigration Officers have legal powers to detain people and remove them from the country. The Immigration and Asylum Act 1999 provides for the appointment of judicial officers by the Lord Chancellor's Department to hear and determine appeals brought under the Act. The Immigration Appellate Authorities process these appeals.

INDEPENDENT REVIEW SERVICE FOR THE SOCIAL FUND

4th Floor, Centre City Podium, 5 Hill Street, Birmingham B5 4UB
Tel: 0121-606 2100 Fax: 0121-606 2180
Email: sfc@irs-review.org.uk
Web: www.irs-review.org.uk

The Independent Review Service for the Social Fund carries out independent reviews for dissatisfied customers of the discretionary social fund. It came into existence in 1988 and is a scheme of one-off payments of grants and loans intended to meet the needs of the poorest in society.
Social Fund Commissioner: Sir Richard Tilt

INFORMATION COMMISSIONER'S OFFICE

Wycliffe House, Water Lane, Wilmslow, Cheshire SK9 5AF Tel: 01625-545745 Fax: 01625-524510

The Data Protection Act 1998 sets rules for processing personal information and applies to some paper records as well as those held on computers. It is the Commissioner's duty to compile and maintain the register of data controllers and provide facilities for members of the public to examine the register; promote observance of the data protection principles; and disseminate information to the public about the Act and her function under the Act. The Commissioner also has the power to produce codes of practice. The Commissioner reports annually to parliament on the performance of his functions under the Act and has obligations to assess the breaches of the Act. The information commissioner is also responsible for freedom of information.
Commissioner: Richard Thomas

INFORMATION TRIBUNAL

Information Tribunal Secretariat, 1.51 Selbourne House, 54–60 Victoria Street, London SW1E 6QW
Tel: 020-7210 0614

The Information Tribunal (previously the Data Protection Tribunal, and renamed by the Freedom of Information Act 2000) determines appeals against decisions of the Information Commissioner under the Data Protection Act 1998 and the Freedom of Information Act 2000. All members are appointed by the Lord Chancellor's Department. The chair and deputy chairmen must be legally qualified. The lay members are appointed according to experience representing the interests of data users or data subjects. A Tribunal consists of a legally qualified chairman sitting with equal numbers of lay members representing the interests of data users and data subjects.
Chairman: D. G. M. Marks
Secretary: C. Mercer

INLAND REVENUE (SCOTLAND)

Clarendon House, 114–116 George Street, Edinburgh EH2 4LH Tel: 0131-473 4000

The Board of Inland Revenue administers and collects direct taxes and advises the Chancellor of the Exchequer on policy questions involving them. The Department's Valuation Office is an executive agency responsible for valuing property for tax purposes.
Director: D. R. Hinstridge

EDINBURGH STAMP OFFICE

Grayfield House, Spur X, 5 Bankhead Avenue, Edinburgh EH11 4AE
Tel: 0131-442 3161 Fax: 0131-442 3038
Operations Manager: Liz Webb

SOLICITOR'S OFFICE

Clarendon House, 114-116 George Street, Edinburgh EH2 4LH
Tel: 0131-473 4053 Fax: 0131-473 4143
Solicitor: D. S. Wishart

VALUATION OFFICE AGENCY

50 Frederick Street, Edinburgh EH2 1NG
Tel: 0131-465 0701 Fax: 0131-465 0799
Email: scotlandse.vo@voa.gov.uk
Chief Valuer: Scotland: A. Ainslie

Inland Revenue RPCS Capital Taxes, IR Charities and IR Trusts are based at:
Meldrum House, 15 Drumsheugh Gardens, Edinburgh EH3

JOBCENTRE PLUS

Argyll House, 3 Lady Lawson Street, Edinburgh EH3 9SD Tel: 0131-221 4000 Fax: 0131-221 4004
Web: www.jobcentreplus.gov.uk

Jobcentre Plus is an executive agency of the Department for Work and Pensions. Its aims are to help people without jobs to find work and employers to fill their vacancies.
Acting Director for Scotland: Douglas Kerr

JUDICIAL COMMITTEE OF THE PRIVY COUNCIL

Downing Street, London SW1A 2AJ
Tel: 020-7276 0485 Fax: 020-7276 0460
Email: judicial.committee@pco.x.gsi.gov.uk
Web: www.privycouncil.gov.uk

Following devolution, the Judicial Committee of the Privy Council is the final arbiter in disputes raising issues as to the legal competence of things done or proposed by the Scottish Parliament or Executive. The members of the Judicial Committee include the Lord Chancellor, the Lords of Appeal in Ordinary, other Privy Counsellors who hold or have held high judicial office in the United Kingdom and (except in devolution cases) certain judges from the Commonwealth.
Registrar of the Privy Council: J. A. C. Watherston
Chief Clerk: F. G. Hart

JUSTICES OF THE PEACE ADVISORY COMMITTEES

c/o Spur IWR, St Andrew's House, Regent Road, Edinburgh EH1 3DG
Tel: 0131-244 2693 Fax: 0131-244 2623

The committees, of which there are 32, keep under review the strength of the Commissions of the Peace in Scotland and advise on the appointment of new justices of the peace. Each committee has its own chairman and secretary. The Scottish Executive provides central advice to the committees.

LANDS TRIBUNAL FOR SCOTLAND

1 Grosvenor Crescent, Edinburgh EH12 5ER
Tel: 0131-225 7996 Fax: 0131-226 4812
Email: mailbox@lands-tribunal-scotland.org.uk
Web: www.lands-tribunal-scotland.org.uk

The Lands Tribunal for Scotland determines a broad range of questions relating to the valuation of land, including rating appeals, the discharge or variation of title conditions, questions of disputed compensation following compulsory purchase and disputes relating to tenants' rights to buy. It also

deals with appeals against the Keeper of the Land Register of Scotland. The president is appointed by the Lord President of the Court of Session.
President: The Hon. Lord McGhie
Members: A. R. MacLeary, FRICS; J. N. Wright, QC (part time)
Clerk: N. M. Tainsh

LEARNING AND TEACHING SCOTLAND

Glasgow: 74 Victoria Crescent Road, Glasgow G12 9JN. Tel: 0131-337 5000 Fax: 0131-337 5050
Dundee: Gardyne Road, Dundee DD5 1NY
Tel: 01382-443600 Fax: 01382-443645
General Enquiries: 08700-100297
Email: enquiries@ltscotland.org.uk
Web: www.ltscotland.com

Learning and Teaching Scotland is sponsored by the Scottish Executive Education Department and provides advice, support, resources and staff development to enhance the quality of educational experiences with a view to improving attainment and achievement and promoting lifelong learning. Learning and Teaching Scotland is required to advise the Scottish Executive on any aspect of the learning experiences of children up to the age of 18, and on any related issue. Learning and Teaching Scotland also provides guidance and support on the curriculum for schools, local education authorities and others.

LORD ADVOCATE'S OFFICE

Crown Office, 25 Chambers Street, Edinburgh EH1 1LA Tel: 0131-226 2626 Fax: 0131-226 6910

Lord Advocate: The Rt. Hon. Colin Boyd, QC
  Private Secretary: Kirsten Davidson
Solicitor-General for Scotland: Elish Angiolini, QC
  Private Secretary: Robbie Kent
Legal Secretary to the Law Officers: P. J. Layden, QC, TD

MARITIME AND COASTGUARD AGENCY

Spring Place, 105 Commercial Road, Southampton SO15 1EG Tel: 0870-600 6505
Email: infoline@mcga.gov.uk

The Agency is an executive agency of the Department of Transport, formed in 1998 by the merger of the Coastguard Agency and the Marine Safety Agency. Its role is to develop, promote and enforce high standards of marine safety; to minimise loss of life amongst seafarers and coastal users and to respond to maritime emergencies 24 hours a day.
Chief Executive: M. Storey

HM COASTGUARD SCOTLAND

Aberdeen, 4th Floor Marine House, Blaikies Quay, Aberdeen AB11 5PB Tel: 01224-592334

Forth, Fifeness, Crail, Fife KY10 3XN
Tel: 01333-450666

Shetland, The Knab, Knab Road, Lerwick, Shetland ZE1 0AX Tel: 01595-692976

Stornaway, Clan Macquarrie House, Battery Point, Stornaway, Isle of Lewis Tel: 01851-729988

MENTAL WELFARE COMMISSION FOR SCOTLAND

K Floor, Argyle House, 3 Lady Lawson Street, Edinburgh EH3 9SH
Tel: 0131-222 6111 Fax: 0131-222 6112
Email: enquiries@mwcscot.org.uk
Web: www.mwcscot.org.uk

The Commission protects the mentally disordered by the investigation of irregularities and by visiting patients in hospitals and in the community, and reports as appropriate to the relevant authorities. There are 22 commissioners.
Chairman: Ian J. Miller, OBE
Vice-Chairman: Mrs. M. Ross
Commissioners (part-time): Norma Bennie;
  Prof. D. J. G. Bain; Faith Cotter; Lynne Edwards;
  Bill Gent, OBE; Dr Pramod Jauhar; Dr Shainool
  Jiwa; Tom Keenan; Revd. Canon Joe Morrow;
  Malcolm D. Murray; Corrinna Penrose; Dr Linda
  Pollock; Archie Robb; Margaret Ross;
  Sheriff Gordon Shiach; Dr Margaret Whoriskey
Director: Dr James A. T. Dyer

MOREDUN RESEARCH INSTITUTE

Pentlands Science Park, Bush Lane, Penicuik, Midlothian EH26 0PZ
Tel: 0131-445 5111 Fax: 0131-445 6111

Conducts research into the control of animal diseases that impair welfare or threaten public health.
Chair: Prof. Sir J. Armour
Director: Prof. Quintin McKellar

NATIONAL ARCHIVES OF SCOTLAND

HM General Register House, Edinburgh EH1 3YY
Tel: 0131-535 1403 Fax: 0131-535 1360
Email: enquiries@nas.gov.uk

Formerly known as the Scottish Record Office, the history of the National Archives of Scotland can be traced back to the 13th century. It keeps the administrative records of pre-Union Scotland, the registers of central and local courts of law, the public registers of property rights and legal documents, and many collections of local and church records and private archives. Certain groups of records, mainly the modern records of government departments in Scotland, the Scottish railway records, the plans collection, and private archives of an industrial or commercial nature, are preserved in the branch repository at the West Register House in Charlotte Square. The National Register of Archives for Scotland is based in the West Register House.
Keeper of the Records of Scotland: G. P. MacKenzie
Deputy Keepers: D. Brownlee; Dr P. D. Anderson

NATIONAL GALLERIES OF SCOTLAND

73 Belford Road, Edinburgh EH4 3DS
Tel: 0131-624 6200 Fax: 0131-343 3250
Email: pressinfo@nationalgalleries.org
Web: www.nationalgalleries.org

The National Galleries of Scotland comprise the National Gallery of Scotland, the Scottish National Portrait Gallery, the Scottish National Gallery of Modern Art, the Dean Gallery and the Royal Scottish Academy Building. There are also outstations at Paxton House, Berwickshire and Duff House, Banffshire.
Chairman: Brian Ivory, CBE
Trustees: Valerie Atkinson; Anne Bonnar;
   Gavin Gemmell; Ian McKenzie Smith;
   Richard Thomson; Marc Ellington;
   Ruth Wishart; Liz Cameron
Director: T. Clifford
Keeper of Conservation: M. Gallagher
Head of Press and Information: Patricia Convery
Head of Education: Ms M. Finn
Registrar: Miss A. Buddle
Secretary: Ms E. Anderson
Buildings: R. Galbraith
Director, National Gallery of Scotland: M. Clarke
Director, Scottish National Portrait Gallery:
   J. Holloway
Curator of Photography: Miss S. F. Stevenson
*Director, Scottish National Gallery of Modern Art and
   Dean Gallery:* R. Calvocoressi

NATIONAL HEALTH SERVICE TRIBUNAL (SCOTLAND)

49 Craiglockhart Road North, Edinburgh EH14 1BT
Tel: 0131-443 2575 Fax: 0131-443 2575

The tribunal considers representations that the continued inclusion of a doctor, dentist, optometrist or pharmacist on a health board's list would be prejudicial to the efficiency of the service concerned. The tribunal sits when required and is composed of a chairman, one lay member, and one practitioner member drawn from a representative professional panel. The chairman is appointed by the Lord President of the Court of Session, and the lay member and the members of the professional panel are appointed by the First Minister.
Chairman: M. G. Thomson, QC
Lay member: J. D. M. Robertson, CBE
Clerk: W. Bryden, SSC

NATIONAL LIBRARY OF SCOTLAND

George IV Bridge, Edinburgh EH1 1EW
Tel: 0131-226 4531 Fax: 0131-622 4803
Email: enquiries@nls.uk Web: www.nls.uk

The Library, which was founded as the Advocates' Library in 1682, became the National Library of Scotland in 1925. It is funded through the Scottish Executive. It contains about seven million printed and new media items, 1.6 million maps, 25,000 periodicals and annual titles and 120,000 volumes of manuscripts. It has an unrivalled Scottish collection.

The Reading Room is for reference and research which cannot conveniently be pursued elsewhere. Admission is by ticket.
Chairman of the Trustees:
   Prof. Michael Anderson, OBE, FBA, FRSA
Librarian and Secretary to the Trustees:
   Martyn Wade, MLIB, MCLIP
Secretary of the Library: M. C. Graham
Director of General Collections: C. Newton
Director of Special Collections:
   M. C. T. Simpson, Ph.D.
Director of Public Services: A. M. Marchbank, Ph.D.

NATIONAL MUSEUMS OF SCOTLAND

Chambers Street, Edinburgh EH1 1JF
Tel: 0131-225 7534 Fax: 0131-220 4819
Email: feedback@nms.ac.uk Web: www.nms.ac.uk

The National Museums of Scotland comprise the Royal Museum of Scotland, the National War Museum of Scotland, the Museum of Scottish Country Life, Shambellie House Museum of

Costume and the Museum of Scotland. Total funding from the Scottish Executive for 2002–3 was £17.3 million.

BOARD OF TRUSTEES
Chairman: Lord Wilson of Tillyhorn, KT, GCMB, Ph.D, FRSE.
Members: J. A. G. Fiddes; OBE, DUniv, FRICS, DipTP; Grenville S. Johnston, OBE; Prof. Michael Lynch, Ph.D, FRSE, FSA Scot; Christina Macaulay; Anne MacLean; Neena Mahal, DCG; Prof. Aubrey Manning, OBE, Dphil, FRSE, FIBiol; Sir Neil McIntosh, CBE; Prof. James Murray, CEng, FIMechE, FIEE; Ian Ritchie, CBE, FREng, FRSE, FBCS; A. J. C. Smith FFA, FCIA

OFFICERS
Director: Dr Gordon Rintoul, Ph.D
Director of Public Programmes: Mary Bryden, FRSA
Director of Facilities Management and Projects: Stephen Elson, FSA Scot
Director of Marketing and Development: Colin McCallum, MICFM
Director of Collections: Jane Carmichael
Director of Finance and Resources: Andrew Patience
Head of Corporate Policy and Performance: Sheila McClure
Managing Director, NMSE: Peter Williamson, HD, MHCIMA

NHS EDUCATION FOR SCOTLAND
22 Queen Street, Edinburgh EH2 1NT
Tel: 0131-226 7371 Fax: 0131-225 9970
2nd Floor, Hanover Buildings, 66 Rose Street, Edinburgh EH2 2NN
Tel: 0131-225 4365 Fax: 0131-225 5891
3rd Floor, 2 Central Quay, 89 Hydepark Street, Glasgow G3 8BN
Tel: 0141-223 1400 Fax: 0141-223 1403
Web: www.nes.scot.nhs.uk

NHS Education for Scotland came into being on 1 April 2002 and covers the areas of hospital training, dentistry, general practice, clinical pathology, nursing, midwifery and health visiting and pharmacy. It aims to contribute to the highest quality of health care in the NHS in Scotland by promoting best practice in the education and lifelong learning of all its staff.
Chair: Ann Markham, OBE
Chief Executive: Dr Graham Buckley

NHS QUALITY IMPROVEMENT SCOTLAND
Edinburgh Office, Elliott House, 8-10 Hillside Crescent, Edinburgh, EH7 5EA
Tel: 0131- 623 4300 Fax: 0131-623 4299
Email: comments@nhshealthquality.org

A special health board established in 2003 to improve the quality of healthcare in Scotland. It is responsible for setting standards, monitoring performance and providing NHS Scotland with advice, guidance and support on effective clinical practice and service improvements.
Chairman: Lord Naren Patel
Chief Executive: Dr David Steel

NORTHERN LIGHTHOUSE BOARD
84 George Street, Edinburgh EH2 3DA
Tel: 0131-473 3100 Fax: 0131-220 2093
Email: enquiries@nlb.org.uk Web: www.nlb.org.uk

The Northern Lighthouse Board is the general lighthouse authority for Scotland and the Isle of Man. The present board owes its origin to an Act of Parliament passed in 1786. At present the Commissioners operate under the Merchant Shipping Act 1894 and are 19 in number.

The Commissioners control 83 major automatic lighthouses, 118 minor lights and many lighted and unlighted buoys. They have a fleet of two motor vessels.

COMMISSIONERS
The Lord Advocate
The Solicitor-General for Scotland
The Lord Provosts of Edinburgh, Glasgow and Aberdeen
The Provost of Inverness
The Convener of Argyll and Bute Council
The Sheriffs-Principal of North Strathclyde, Tayside, Central and Fife, Grampian, Highlands and Islands, South Strathclyde, Dumfries and Galloway, Lothians and Borders, and Glasgow and Strathkelvin
Capt. D. M. Cowell
Adm. Sir Michael Livesay, KCB
P. Mackay, CB
Capt. Kenneth MacLeod
Dr A. Cubie, CBE

Chief Executive: Capt. J. B. Taylor, RN
Director of Finance: D. Gorman
Director of Engineering: M. Waddell
Director of Operations and Navigational Requirements: G. Platten

OFFICE OF THE ACCOUNTANT IN BANKRUPTCY

George House, 126 George Street, Edinburgh EH2 4HH Tel: 0131-473 4600 Helpline 0845-7626171 Fax: 0131-473 4737 Email: info@aib.co.uk Web: www.aib.gov.uk

The office is responsible for administering the process of personal bankruptcy (sequestration) and recording corporate insolvencies in Scotland. *Accountant in Bankruptcy:* Gillian Thompson

OFFICE OF COMMUNICATIONS

Riverside House, 2A Southwark Bridge Road, London SE1 9HA Tel: 020-7981 3000 Fax: 020-7981 3333 Email: wwwenq@ofcom.org.uk Web: www.ofcom.org.uk

Ofcom is the regulator for the communications industry and was established by the Office of Communications Act 2002. Ofcom replaces the following regulators: the Independent Television Commission, the Broadcasting Standards Commission, the Office of Telecommunications (Oftel), the Radio Authority and the Radiocommunications Agency. Until Ofcom's regulatory powers are fully operational, any queries about current regulatory issues should be addressed to the relevant regulator, details below. *Chair:* Lord Currie *Chief Executive:* Stephen Carter

Broadcasting Standards Commission: 7 The Sanctuary, London SW1P 3JS. Tel: 020-7808 1000 Web: www.bsc.org.uk

Oftel: 50 Ludgate Hill, London EC4M 7JJ Web: www.oftel.gov.uk

Radio Authority: Holbrook House, 14 Great Queen Street, London WC2B 5DG. Tel: 020-7430 2724 Web: www.radioauthority.org.uk

Radiocommunications Agency: Wyndham House, 189 Marsh Wall, London E14 9SX. Tel: 020-7211 0211 Web: www.radio.gov.uk

Independent Television Commission: 33 Foley Street, London W1W 7TL. Web: www.itc.gov.uk

OFFICE OF GAS AND ELECTRICITY MARKETS (SCOTLAND)

Regent Court, 70 West Regent Street, Glasgow G2 2QZ Tel: 0141-331 2678 Fax: 0141-331 2777

The Office of Gas and Electricity Markets (Ofgem) is the independent regulatory body for the gas and electricity supply industries following the merger of the Office of Gas Supply and the Office of Electricity Regulation in 1999. Its functions are to promote competition and to protect customers' interests in relation to prices, security of supply and quality of services. *Chairman and Chief Executive:* C. McCarthy *Director for Scotland:* D. Halldearn

OFFICE OF THE SOCIAL SECURITY AND CHILD SUPPORT COMMISSIONERS

23 Melville Street, Edinburgh EH3 7YP Tel: 0131-225 2201 Fax: 0131-220 6782 Web: www.osscsc.gov.uk

The Social Security Commissioners are the final statutory authority to decide appeals relating to entitlement to social security, including housing and council tax and benefits. The Child Support Commissioners are the final statutory authority to decide appeals relating to child support. Appeals may be made in relation to both matters only on a point of law. *Chief Social Security Commissioner and Chief Child Support Commissioner (London):* His Hon. Judge M. Harris *Senior Commissioner for Scotland:* M. W. Walker, QC

PARLIAMENTARY AND HEALTH SERVICE OMBUDSMAN

Millbank Tower, Millbank, London SW1P 4QP Tel: 0845-015 4022; 020-7217 4163 (Parliamentary Ombudsman); 020-7217 4051 (Health Service Ombudsman) Email: opca.enquiries@ombudsman.gsi.gov.uk (parliamentary); ohsh.enquiries@ombudsman.gsi.gov.uk (health service)

The Parliamentary Ombudsman and the Health Service Ombudsman undertake independent investigations into complaints about government departments, a range of other public bodies and the National Health Service. The Parliamentary Ombudsman investigates complaints that injustice has been caused by the maladministration on the part of the government departments or other public bodies. The Health Service Ombudsman investigates complaints that a hardship or injustice has been caused by the NHS's failure to provide a service, by a failure in service, or by maladministration.

Parliamentary and Health Service Ombudsman:
  Ann Abraham

PAROLE BOARD FOR SCOTLAND

Saughton House, Broomhouse Drive, Edinburgh
EH11 3XD Tel: 0131-244 8373 Fax: 0131-244 6974
Web: www.scottishparoleboard.gov.uk

The Board is an independent body which directs and advises Scottish Ministers on the release of prisoners on licence, and related matters.
Chairman: D. J. J. McManus
Vice-Chairman: Mrs M. Casserly
Secretary: H. P. Boyle

PATENT OFFICE

Cardiff Road, Newport NP10 8QQ
Tel: 08459-500505 (enquiries); 01633-811010 (search and advisory service) Fax: 01633-814444
Email: enquiries@patent.gov.uk
Web: www.patent.gov.uk

The Patent Office is an executive agency of the Department of Trade and Industry. The duties of the Patent Office are to administer the Patent Acts, the Registered Designs Act and the Trade Marks Act, and to deal with questions relating to the Copyright, Designs and Patents Act 1988. It aims to stimulate the innovation and competitiveness of industry. The Search and Advisory Service carries out commercial searches through patent information.

PENSIONS APPEAL TRIBUNALS FOR SCOTLAND

20 Walker Street, Edinburgh EH3 7HS
Tel: 0131-220 1404 Fax: 0131-226 2596
Email: info@patscotland.org.uk

The Pensions Appeal Tribunals are responsible for hearing appeals from ex-servicemen or women and widows who have had their claims for a war pension rejected by the Secretary of State for Social Security. The Entitlement Appeal Tribunals hear appeals in cases where the Secretary of State has refused to grant a war pension. The Assessment Appeal Tribunals hear appeals against the Secretary of State's assessment of the degree of disablement caused by an accepted condition. The tribunal members are appointed by the President of the Court of Session
President: C. N. McEachran, QC
Secretary: W. Barclay

REGISTERS OF SCOTLAND

Meadowbank House, 153 London Road, Edinburgh
EH8 7AU Tel: 08456-070161 Fax: 0131-479 3688
Email: customer.services@ros.gov.uk
Web: www.ros.gov.uk

Registers of Scotland is the executive agency responsible for compiling and maintaining records relating to property and further legal documents in Scotland. Information from these public registers can be obtained through personal visits, by post, fax or via email.

The agency holds 15 registers; two property registers (General Register of Sasines and Land Register of Scotland), which form the chief security in Scotland of the rights of land and other heritable (or real) property; and the remaining 13 grouped under the collective name of the Chancery and Judicial Registers (Register of Deeds in the Books of Council and Session; Register of Protests; Register of Judgments; Register of Service of Heirs; Register of the Great Seal; Register of the Quarter Seal; Register of the Prince's Seal; Register of Crown Grants; Register of Sheriffs' Commissions; Register of the Cachet Seal; Register of Inhibitions and Adjudications; Register of Entails; Register of Hornings).
Keeper of the Registers: A. W. Ramage
Deputy Keeper: A. G. Rennie
Managing Director: F. Manson

RENT ASSESSMENT PANEL FOR SCOTLAND

140 West Campbell Street, Glasgow G2 4TZ
Tel: 0141-572 1170 Fax: 0141-572 1171

Provides members for the Rent Assessment Committees.
President: John M. Barton

ROWETT RESEARCH INSTITUTE

Greenburn Road, Bucksburn, Aberdeen AB21 9SB

The institute carries out research into nutrition in animals and humans to identify how this can improve sustainable agriculture, food quality and human health.
Chair: Dr James Stewart
Director: Prof. Peter Morgan

ROYAL BOTANIC GARDEN EDINBURGH

20A Inverleith Row, Edinburgh EH3 5LR
Tel: 0131-552 7171 Fax: 0131-248 2901
Email: press@rbge.org.uk
Web: www.rbge.org.uk

The Royal Botanic Garden Edinburgh (RBGE) originated as the Physic Garden, established in 1670 beside the Palace of Holyroodhouse. The Garden moved to its present 28-hectare site at Inverleith, Edinburgh, in 1821. There are also three other Gardens: Benmore Botanic Garden near Dunoon, Argyll; Logan Botanic Garden, near Stranraer, Wigtownshire; and Dawyck Botanic Garden, near Stobo, Peeblesshire. Since 1986, RBGE has been administered by a board of trustees established under the National Heritage (Scotland) Act 1985. It receives an annual grant from the Scottish Executive Environment and Rural Affairs Department.

RBGE is an international centre for scientific research on plant diversity and for horticulture education and conservation. It has an extensive library and a herbarium with over two million dried plant specimens.

Chairman of the Board of Trustees: Dr P. Nicholson
Regius Keeper: Prof. Stephen Blackmore

ROYAL COMMISSION ON THE ANCIENT AND HISTORICAL MONUMENTS OF SCOTLAND

John Sinclair House, 16 Bernard Terrace, Edinburgh
EH8 9NX Tel: 0131-662 1456 Fax: 0131-662 1477
Email: nmrs@rcahms.gov.uk
Web: www.rcahms.gov.uk

The Royal Commission was established in 1908 and is appointed to provide for the survey and recording of ancient and historical monuments connected with the culture, civilisation and conditions of life of people in Scotland from the earliest times. It is funded by the Scottish Executive.

The Commission compiles and maintains the National Monuments Record of Scotland as the national record of the archaeological and historical environment.

Chairman: Mrs K. Dalyell, FRSAS
Commissioners: Dr B. E. Crawford, FSA;
Miss A. C. Riches, OBE, FSA; J. W. T. Simpson;
Dr A. M. Mackay; Dr J. Murray;
Dr A. Macdonald; Prof. C. D. Morris, FSA, FRSE;
Dr S. Nenadic; G. Masterton, CEng

ROYAL FINE ART COMMISSION FOR SCOTLAND

Bakehouse Close, 146 Canongate, Edinburgh EH8 8DD
Tel: 0131-556 6699 Fax: 0131-556 6633
Email: plan@royfinartforsco.gov.uk
Web: www.futurescotland.org

The Commission was established in 1927 and advises ministers and local authorities on the visual impact and quality of design of construction projects. It is an independent body and gives its opinions impartially.

Chairman: The Rt. Hon. the Lord Cameron of Lochbroom, FRSE
Secretary: C. Prosser

ROYAL MAIL GROUP ADVISORY BOARD FOR SCOTLAND

10 Brunswick Road, Edinburgh EH7 5XX
Tel: 0131-500 8099 Fax: 0131-550 8109
Email: scottish.affairs@royalmail.com
Web: www.royalmailgroup.com

The Royal Mail Group Advisory Board for Scotland was set up to represent its three brands: Royal Mail, Post Office and Parcelforce Worldwide. The board is made up of executive members including the Director of Scottish Affairs and two non-executive members from the world of business. Its Scottish Affairs team deals directly with the Scottish Parliament, the Scottish Executive and the Scotland Office as well as former groups throughout the country to address and focus on Scottish issues.

Chairman: Lesley Sawers

SCOTLAND OFFICE

Dover House, Whitehall, London, SW1A 2AU
Tel: 020-7270 6754 Fax: 020-7270 6812
Email: scottish.secretary@scotland.gov.uk
Edinburgh Office: 1 Melville Crescent, Edinburgh EH3 7HW. Tel: 0131-244 9010
Glasgow Office: 1st Floor Meridian Court,
5 Cadogan Street, Glasgow G2 6AT
Tel: 0141-242 5958

The Scotland Office supports the Secretary of State for Scotland, who represents Scottish interests in the Cabinet on matters reserved to the UK Parliament and the Advocate General (a UK Law Officer and adviser to the UK Government on Scottish Law).

Secretary of State for Scotland:
The Rt. Hon. Alistair Darling, MP

SCOTTISH ADVISORY COMMITTEE ON DISTINCTION AWARDS

Secretariat: c/o Scottish Health Service Centre, Crewe Road South, Edinburgh EH4 2LF
Tel: 0131-623 2539 Fax: 0131-623 2518
Email: committee@shsc.csa.scot.nhs.uk

The Scottish Advisory Committee on Distinction Awards was set up in 1998 and acts on behalf of Scottish Ministers in deciding which individual medical and dental practitioners in the NHS in Scotland should receive distinction awards for their outstanding professional work.
Secretary: Margaret Brown

SCOTTISH ADVISORY COMMITTEE ON THE MEDICAL WORKFORCE

Health Department, St Andrews House, Edinburgh EH1 3DG Tel: 0131-244 2430 Fax: 0131-244 2837

The Committee advises on all matters relating to medical workforce planning in Scotland, other than matters concerning terms and conditions of service.
Chairman: Dr Robert Cairncross
Secretary: Michelle Williamson

SCOTTISH AGRICULTURAL SCIENCE AGENCY (SASA)

82 Craigs Road, East Craigs, Edinburgh EH12 8NJ
Tel: 0131-244 8890 Fax: 0131-244 8988
Email: info@sasa.gsi.gov.uk

SASA provides government with scientific information and advice on agricultural and horticultural crops, and the environment. It performs statutory and regulatory functions in relation to seed certification, plant health, bee health, plant variety registration, crop improvement, genetically modified organisms and the protection of crops, food and the environment.
Director: Dr R. Hay
Head of Administration: Mrs S. M. Quinn

SCOTTISH AGRICULTURAL WAGES BOARD

Pentland House, 47 Robb's Loan, Edinburgh EH14 1TY
Tel: 0131-244 6397 Fax: 0131-244 6551

The Board fixes minimum wage rates, holiday entitlements and other conditions for agricultural workers in Scotland.
Chairman: Christine Davis, CBE
Secretary: Ronnie Grady

SCOTTISH ARTS COUNCIL

12 Manor Place, Edinburgh EH3 7DD
Tel: 0131-226 6051 Fax: 0131-225 9833
Email: help.desk@scottisharts.org.uk
Web: www.scottisharts.org.uk

The Scottish Arts Council is the lead body for the funding, development and advocacy of the arts in Scotland. It offers a unique national perspective on the provision and management of the arts which seeks to balance the needs of all arts sectors and all communities in Scotland. Its expertise and experience in developing sound policy and good practice includes the ability to make links between the intrinsic value of the arts and their instrumental value in delivering social and economic benefits at a national level. It also offers a focus on research, information provision and international working. The Scottish Arts Council has a total budget of £60m for 2003–4; £38m from the Scottish Executive and £22m from the National Lottery Fund through the Department for Culture, Media and Sport.
Chairman: James Boyle
Members (as at July 2003): Joanna Baker; Elizabeth Cameron; Dale Idiens; Louise Mitchell; John Scott Moncrieff; John Mulgrew; Bill Speirs
Director: Graham Berry

SCOTTISH CHARITIES OFFICE

25 Chambers Street, Edinburgh EH1 1LA
Tel: 0131-226 2626 Fax: 0131-226 6912

The Scottish Charities Office is responsible for the supervision and regulation of charities in Scotland with the aim of enhancing the integrity and effectiveness of charities.
Director: B. M. Logan

SCOTTISH CHILDREN'S REPORTER ADMINISTRATION

Ochil House, Springkerse Business Park, Stirling FK7 7XE Tel: 01786-459533 Fax: 01786-459533

The Scottish Children's Reporter Administration supports the Principal Reporter in his statutory functions in relation to children who may be in need of compulsory measures of care and provides suitable accommodation and facilities for children's hearings.
Chairman: Douglas Bulloch
Principal Reporter: Allan Miller

SCOTTISH COMMITTEE OF THE COUNCIL ON TRIBUNALS

44 Palmerston Place, Edinburgh EH12 5BJ
Tel: 0131-220 1236 Fax: 0131-225 4271
Email: sccot@gtnet.gov.uk
Web: www.council-on-tribunals.gov.uk

The Council on Tribunals is an independent body that advises on and keeps under review the constitution and working of administrative tribunals, and considers and reports on administrative procedures relating to statutory inquiries. Some 70 tribunals are currently under the Council's supervision. It is consulted by and advises government departments on a wide range of subjects relating to adjudicative procedures. The Scottish Committee of the Council generally considers Scottish tribunals and matters relating only to Scotland.
Chairman: R. J. Elliot, DKS
Members: The Parliamentary Commissioner for Administration (ex officio); Mrs B. Bruce; D. Graham; Mrs M. Wood; Mrs E. Cameron; S. Mannion; Mrs A. Watson
Secretary: Mrs E. M. MacRae

SCOTTISH CONVEYANCING AND EXECUTRY SERVICES BOARD

1 St John's Place, Leith, Edinburgh EH6 7EL
Tel: 0131-555 6525 Fax: 0131-553 5011
Web: www.scesb.co.uk

The Scottish Conveyancing and Executry Services Board exists to encourage the creation of a new breed of conveyancing and executry practitioners who can offer the public a highly qualified, specialist service. It aims to make the public and the legal world fully aware of the value that SCESB-registered practitioners have to offer.
Chairman: Alistair C. Clark
Secretary: Eric Simmons

SCOTTISH COURT SERVICE

Hayweight House, 23 Lauriston Street, Edinburgh EH3 9DQ Tel: 0131-229 9200 Fax: 0131-221 6895
Email: enquiries@scotscourts.gov.uk

The Scottish Court Service is an executive agency within the Justice Department and is responsible for the provision and maintenance of Court Houses, supporting the judiciary in the Supreme and Sheriff Courts and for supplying trained staff, administrative and organisational services.
Chief Executive: J. Ewing

SCOTTISH CRIMINAL CASES REVIEW COMMISSION

5th Floor, Portland House, 17 Renfield Street, Glasgow G2 5AH Tel: 0141-270 7030 Fax: 0141-270 7023
Email: info@sccrc.org.uk

The Commission is a non-departmental public body which was established on 1 April 1999. It considers alleged miscarriages of justice in Scotland and refers cases meeting the relevant criteria to the High Court for determination. Members are appointed by Her Majesty The Queen on the recommendation of the Scottish Ministers; staff are appointed by the Commission.
Chairperson: The Very Revd Graham Forbes
Members: Prof. P. Duff; Sir G. Gordon, CBE, QC; W. Taylor, QC; D. Belfall; J. Mackay; R. Anderson, QC
Chief Executive: C. A. Kelly

SCOTTISH CROP RESEARCH INSTITUTE (SCRI)

Invergowrie, Dundee DD2 5DA
Tel: 01382-562731 Fax: 01382-562426

SCRI is an international centre for research on agricultural, horticultural and industrial crops.
Chair: James E. Godfrey
Director: Prof. John R. Hillman

SCOTTISH DEVELOPMENT INTERNATIONAL

Atlantic Quay, 150 Broomielaw, Glasgow G2 8LU
Tel: 0141-228 2828
Director: D. Macdonald

SCOTTISH ENTERPRISE

Atlantic Quay, 150 Broomielaw, Glasgow G2 8LU.
Tel 0141-248 2700 Fax 0141-221 3217
Email: scotent.co.uk Web: www.scotent.co.uk

Scottish Enterprise was established in 1991 and its purpose is to create jobs and prosperity for the people of Scotland. It is funded largely by the Scottish Executive and is responsible to the Scottish Minister for Enterprise and Lifelong Learning. Working in partnership with the private and public sectors, Scottish Enterprise aims to further the development of Scotland's economy, to enhance the skills of the Scottish workforce and to promote Scotland's international competitiveness. Through Locate in Scotland, Scottish Enterprise is concerned with attracting firms to Scotland, and through Scottish Trade International it helps Scottish companies to compete in world export markets. Scottish Enterprise has a network of 13 local

enterprise companies that deliver economic development services at local level.
Chairman: Sir Ian Robinson
Chief Executive: Robert Crawford

SCOTTISH ENVIRONMENT PROTECTION AGENCY

Erskine Court, The Castle Business Park, Stirling
FK9 4TR Tel: 01786-457700 Fax: 01786-446885
Email: publicaffairs@sepa.org.uk
Web: www.sepa.org.uk

The Scottish Environment Protection Agency is Scotland's environmental regulator, responsible for preventing and controlling pollution to land, air and water. Its main aim is to provide an efficient and integrated environmental protection system for Scotland which will improve the environment and contribute to the Government's goal of sustainable development. It has 21 offices throughout Scotland. It receives funding from the Scottish Executive.
Chairman: K. Collins
Chief Executive: Campbell Gemmell
Director of Finance and Corporate Support: J. Ford
Acting Director of Strategic Planning: C. MacDonald
Director of Operations: W. Halcrow
Director of Public Affairs and Corporate
  Communications: J. Beveridge

SCOTTISH FIRE SERVICES COLLEGE

Main Street, Gullane, East Lothian EH31 2HG
Tel: 01620-842236 Fax: 01620-843045
Director: R. Virtue
Head of College: J. Robson

SCOTTISH FISHERIES PROTECTION AGENCY

Pentland House, 47 Robb's Loan, Edinburgh EH14 1TY
Tel: 0131-556 8400 Fax: 0131-244 6086

An executive agency of the Rural Affairs Department, it enforces fisheries law and regulations in Scottish waters and ports.
Chief Executive: Capt. P. Du Vivier, RN
Director of Corporate Strategy and Resources:
  J. B. Roddin
Director of Operations: C. Ralph
Marine Superintendent: Capt. W. A. Brown
Director Coastal Fisheries Inspectorate: A. Stewart

SCOTTISH FURTHER EDUCATION FUNDING COUNCIL

Donaldson House, 97 Haymarket Terrace,
Edinburgh EH12 5HD
Tel: 0131-313 6500 Web: www.sfefc.ac.uk

The Scottish Further Education Funding Council came into being on 1 July 1999 and its remit includes: responsibility for funding Scotland's further education colleges; monitoring the financial health of the sector; advising the First Minister on funding matters and supporting his duty to secure adequate and efficient provision of further education in Scotland.
Chair: Esther Roberton
Chief Executive: Roger McClure

SCOTTISH FURTHER EDUCATION UNIT

Argyll Court, Castle Business Park, Stirling FK9 4TY
Tel: 01786-892000 Fax: 01786-892001
Email: sfeu@sfeu.ac.uk Web: www.sfeu.ac.uk

The Scottish Further Education Unit helps Scotland's further education colleges tackle their most challenging operational and developmental issues. In doing so, it seeks to raise standards of practice in the further education sector in Scotland.
Chair: Chris Hunter
Chief Executive: Alison Reid

SCOTTISH HIGHER EDUCATION FUNDING COUNCIL

Donaldson House, 97 Haymarket Terrace, Edinburgh
EH12 5HD Tel: 0131-313 6500
Web: www.shefc.ac.uk

The Scottish Higher Education Funding Council seeks to respond constructively to Scottish Executive policy for Scottish higher education, promote and support developments that benefit the Scottish higher education system and understand and respond to the needs of higher education.
Chair: Dr Chris Masters
Chief Executive: Roger McClure

SCOTTISH HOSPITAL ENDOWMENTS RESEARCH TRUST

Princes Exchange, 1 Earl Grey Street, Edinburgh,
EH3 9EE Tel: 0131-659 8800 Fax: 0131-228 8118
Web: www.shert.com or www.shert.org.uk

The Trust holds endowments, donations and bequests and makes grants from these funds to improve health standards by funding research into the cause, diagnosis, treatment and prevention of all

forms of illness and genetic disorders and into the advancement of medical technology. It also engages in fundraising activities.
Chairman: Prof. S. Moira Brown
Secretary: Turcan Connell

SCOTTISH HOSPITAL TRUST

Princes Exchange, 1 Earl Grey Street, Edinburgh EH3 9EE Tel: 0131-228 8111 Fax: 0131-228 8118

The Trust distributes endowments from property to Health Boards, NHS Trusts and the State Hospital Carstairs.
Chairman: D. C. Richie
Secretary: Turcan Connell

SCOTTISH INDUSTRIAL DEVELOPMENT ADVISORY BOARD

Meridian Court, 5 Cadogan Street, Glasgow G2 6AT
Tel: 0141-242 5674 Fax: 0141-242 5691
Web: www.rsascotland.gov.uk

The Board advises the Scottish Ministers on the exercise of their powers under Section 7 of the Industrial Development Act 1982.
Chairman: Vikram Lall
Secretary: Peter Ford

SCOTTISH LAND COURT

1 Grosvenor Crescent, Edinburgh EH12 5ER
Tel: 0131-225 3595 Fax: 0131-226 4812

The Scottish Land Court deals with a wide variety of cases relating to agriculture, including crofts and small holdings.
Chairman: The Hon. Lord McGhie, QC
Principal Clerk: K. Graham

SCOTTISH LAW COMMISSION

140 Causewayside, Edinburgh EH9 1PR
Tel: 0131-668 2131 Fax: 0131-662 4900
Email: info@scotlawcom.gov.uk
Web: www.scotlawcom.gov.uk

The Commission keeps the law in Scotland under review and makes proposals for its development and reform. It is responsible to the Scottish Ministers through the Scottish Executive Justice Department.
Chairman (part-time): The Hon. Lord Eassie
Commissioners (full-time): Prof. G. Maher;
  Prof. K. G. C. Reid; Prof. J. Thomson
Secretary: Miss J. McLeod

SCOTTISH LEGAL AID BOARD

44 Drumsheugh Gardens, Edinburgh EH3 7SW
Tel: 0131-226 7061 Fax: 0131-220 4878
Email: general@slab.org.uk
Web: www.slab.org.uk

The Scottish Legal Aid Board was set up under the Legal Aid (Scotland) Act 1986 to manage legal aid in Scotland. The Board is a non-departmental public body whose members are appointed by the First Minister.
Chairman: Mrs J. Couper
Chief Executive: L. Montgomery

SCOTTISH LEGAL SERVICES OMBUDSMAN

17 Waterloo Place, Edinburgh EH1 3DL
Tel: 0131-556 9123 Fax: 0131-556 9292
Email: ombudsman@slso.org.uk
Web: www.scot-legal-ombud.org.uk

The Office of the Scottish Legal Services Ombudsman investigates complaints against practitioners.
Scottish Legal Services Ombudsman:
  Mrs L. Costelloe Baker

SCOTTISH MEDICAL PRACTICES COMMITTEE

Scottish Health Service Centre, Crewe Road South, Edinburgh EH4 2LF Tel: 0131-623 2532

The Committee ensures that there is an adequate number of GPs providing general medical services in Scotland.
Chairman: Dr G. McIntosh, MBE
Secretary: Christopher Graham

SCOTTISH NATURAL HERITAGE

12 Hope Terrace, Edinburgh EH9 2AS
Tel: 0131-447 4784 Fax: 0131-446 2277
Email: enquiries@snh.gov.uk Web: www.snh.org.uk

Scottish Natural Heritage was established in 1992 under the Natural Heritage (Scotland) Act 1991. It provides advice on nature conservation to all those whose activities affect wildlife, landforms and features of geological interest in Scotland, and seeks to develop and improve facilities for the enjoyment and understanding of the Scottish countryside. It is funded by the Scottish Executive.
Chairman: Dr J. Markland, CBE
Chief Executive: Dr I. Jardine
Directors of Strategy and Operations: J. Thomson
  (West); A. Bachell (East); Dr. J. Watson (North)
Directors of Corporate Services: Mr I. Edgeler;
  Prof C. A. Galbraith (Scientific Advisory Services)

SCOTTISH OCEANIC AREA CONTROL CENTRE

Atlantic House, Sherwood Road, Prestwick KA9 2NR
Tel: 01292-479800 Fax: 01292-692733

National Air Traffic Services (NATS) provides safety by ensuring aircraft flying in UK airspace, and over the eastern part of the North Atlantic, are safely separated. Safety is NATS' first and foremost priority but it also aims to provide the service in an efficient and expeditious way.

The two centres situated in Atlantic House, Prestwick are: the Scottish Area Control Centre (SACC) and the Oceanic Area Control Centre (OACC).

SCOTTISH POLICE COLLEGE

Tullialan Castle, Kincardine, Alloa FK10 4BE
Tel: 01259-732000 Fax: 01259-732202
Director: D. Garbutt

SCOTTISH PRISONS COMPLAINTS COMMISSION

Government Buildings, Broomhouse Drive,
Edinburgh EH11 3XD
Tel: 0131-244 8423

The Commission was established in 1994. It is an independent body to which prisoners in Scottish prisons can make an application in relation to any matter where they have failed to obtain satisfaction from the Scottish Prison Service's internal grievance procedures. Clinical judgements made by medical officers, matters which are the subject of legal proceedings and matters relating to sentencing, convictions and parole decision-making are excluded from the Commission's jurisdiction. The Commissioner is appointed by the First Minister.
Commissioner: V. Barrett

SCOTTISH PRISON SERVICE

Calton House, 5 Redheughs Rigg, Edinburgh
EH12 9HW Tel: 0131-244 8745 Fax: 0131-244 8738
Email: gaolinfo@sps.gov.uk

An Executive Agency of the Justice Department and responsible for all aspects of the Prison Service.
Chief Executive: Tony Cameron

SCOTTISH PUBLIC PENSIONS AGENCY

7 Tweedside Park, Galashiels TD1 3TE

The Agency is an executive agency of the Education Department. It is responsible for the pension arrangements of some 300,000 people, mainly NHS and teaching services employees and pensioners.

Chief Executive: R. Garden
Directors: G. Mowat (Policy); M. MacDermott (Human Resources/Teachers Scheme Manager); J. Nelson (IT and Finance); G. Taylor (NHS Scheme Manager)

SCOTTISH PUBLIC SERVICES OMBUDSMAN

23 Walker Street, Edinburgh EH3 7HX
Tel: 0870-011 5378 Fax: 0870-011 5379
Email: enquiries@scottishombudsman.org.uk
Web: www.scottishombudsman.org.uk

The Scottish Public Services Ombudsman considers complaints which have not been resolved with the body concerned about devolved public services in Scotland, including the Scottish Executive and its agencies, local authorities, the NHS and housing associations. Its services are free, accessible and independent.
Ombudsman: Prof. Alice Brown
Deputy Ombudsmen: Eric Drake, Carolyn Hirst, Lewis Shand Smith

SCOTTISH QUALIFICATIONS AUTHORITY

Hanover House, 24 Douglas Street, Glasgow G2 7NQ
Tel: 0141-242 2214 Fax: 0141-242 2244

The Scottish Qualifications Authority develops and awards qualifications for the national education system and is also Scotland's national accrediting body for work-based SVQ qualifications.
Chairman: Prof. John Ward, CBE
Chief Executive: David Fraser

SCOTTISH RECORDS ADVISORY COUNCIL

HM General Register House, Edinburgh EH1 3YY
Tel: 0131-535 1314 Fax: 0131-535 1360
Email: alison.rosie@nas.gov.uk

The Council was established under the Public Records (Scotland) Act 1937. Its members are appointed by the First Minister and it may submit proposals or make representations to the First Minister, the Lord Justice-General or the Lord President of the Court of Session on questions relating to the public records of Scotland.
Chairman: Hector MacQueen
Secretary: Dr Alison Rosie

SCOTTISH SCREEN

2nd Floor, 249 West George Street, Glasgow G2 4QE
Tel: 0141-302 1700 Fax: 0141-302 1711
Email: info@scottishscreen.com
Web: www.scottishscreen.com

Scottish Screen develops, encourages and promotes every aspect of film, television and new media in Scotland through script and company development, short film production, distribution of National Lottery film production finance, training, education, exhibition funding, Film Commission Locations Support and the Scottish Screen Archive. Grant-in-aid from the Scottish Executive for 2003–4 is £2.625 million.
Chair: R. McFarlane
Chief Executive: S. McIntyre

SCOTTISH SOCIAL SERVICES COUNCIL (SSSC)

Compass House, 11 Riverside Drive, Dundee DD1 4NY
Tel: 01382-207101 Fax: 01382-207215
Email: enquiries@sssc.uk.com

Establishes registers of key groups of staff, publishes codes of practices and regulates training and education.
Convenor: Morag Alexander
Chief Executive: Carole Wilkinson

SCOTTISH WATER

Castle House, 6 Castle Drive, Carnegie Campus,
Dunfermline KY11 8GG
Tel: 01383-848240 Fax: 01383-848340
Email: customer.service@scottishwater.co.uk
Web: www.scottishwater.co.uk

Created under the Water Industry Act 2002 by combing the three previously responsible water authorities. Provides water and sewerage services throughout Scotland.
Chair: Prof. Alan Alexander
Chief Executive: Dr Jon Hargreaves

SCOTTISH SOLICITORS' DISCIPLINE TRIBUNAL

22 Rutland Square, Edinburgh EH1 2BB
Tel: 0131-229 5860

The Scottish Solicitors' Discipline Tribunal is an independent statutory body with a panel of 18 members, ten of whom are solicitors; members are appointed by the Lord President of the Court of Session. Its principal function is to consider complaints of misconduct against solicitors in Scotland.

Chairman: G. F. Ritchie
Clerk: J. V. Lea, WS

SEA FISH INDUSTRY AUTHORITY

18 Logie Mill, Logie Green Road, Edinburgh EH7 4HG
Tel: 0131-558 3331 Fax: 0131-558 1442
Email: seafish@seafish.co.uk
Web: www.seafish.co.uk

Established under the Fisheries Act 1981, Seafish works with the seafood industry to satisfy consumers, raise standards, improve efficiency and secure a sustainable future. It is sponsored by the four UK fisheries departments.
Chairman: Andrew Dewar-Durie
Chief Executive: John Rutherford

SECRETARY OF COMMISSIONS FOR SCOTLAND

1 West Rear, St Andrew's House, Regent Road,
Edinburgh EH1 3DG
Tel: 0131-244 2691 Fax: 0131-244 2623

The Secretary of Commissions deals with the appointment of justices of the peace and of general commissioners of income tax, and with lord lieutenancy business.
Secretary of Commissions for Scotland: Alan Oliver

SPECIAL COMMISSIONERS OF INCOME TAX

15–19 Bedford Avenue, London WC1B 3AS
Tel: 020-7612 9649 Fax: 020-7436 4151
Web: www.courtservice.gov.uk/tribunals/comtax

The Special Commissioners are an independent body appointed by the Lord Chancellor in conjunction with the Lord Advocate to hear complex appeals against decisions of the Board of Inland Revenue and its officials. In addition to the Presiding Special Commissioner there are several other Special Commissioners who also sit in other jurisdictions. All are legally qualified.
Presiding Special Commissioner: His Hon. Stephen Oliver, QC
Clerk: R. P. Lester

SPORTSCOTLAND

Caledonia House, South Gyle, Edinburgh EH12 9DQ
Tel: 0131-317 7200 Fax: 0131-317 7202
Email: library@sportscotland.org.uk
Web: www.sportscotland.org.uk

Sportscotland is responsible for the development of sport and physical recreation in Scotland. It aims to increase participation in sport among young people

and to provide the highest level of coaching and support for aspiring top performers. It advises the Scottish Parliament on sports matters, and it administers the Lottery Sports Fund in Scotland.
Chairman: A. Dempster
Chief Executive: I. Robson

STUDENT AWARDS AGENCY FOR SCOTLAND

Gyleview House, 3 Redheughs Rigg, Edinburgh EH12 9HH Tel: 0845-111 1711 Fax: 0131-244 5717
Email: saas.geu@scotland.gov.uk
Web: www.saas.gov.uk

The Agency administers student awards and other related services for Scottish domiciled students in full-time higher education throughout the United Kingdom.
Chief Executive: D. Stephen

TRAFFIC COMMISSIONER (SCOTLAND)

Argyle House, J Floor, 3 Lady Lawson Street, Edinburgh EH3 9SE Tel: 0131-200 4955 Fax: 0131-529 8501

The Traffic Commissioners are responsible for licensing operators of heavy goods and public service vehicles. They also have responsibility for appeals relating to the licensing of operators and for disciplinary cases involving the conduct of drivers of these vehicles. Each Traffic Commissioner constitutes a tribunal for the purposes of the Tribunals and Inquiries Act 1971.
Scottish Traffic Commissioner: J. N. Aitken

TRANSPORT TRIBUNAL

48–49 Chancery Lane, London WC2A 1JR
Tel: 020-7947 7493 Fax: 020-7947 7798
Web: www.transporttribunal.gov.uk

The Transport Tribunal hears appeals against decisions of Traffic Commissioners on passenger or goods vehicle operator licensing applications. The tribunal consists of a legally-qualified president, two legal chairmen, and five lay members. The president and legal members are appointed by the Lord Chancellor and the lay members by the Secretary of State for Transport, Local Government and the Regions.
President (part-time): H. B. H. Carlisle, QC
Legal member (part-time): His Hon. Judge Brodrick; J. Beech; F. Burton
Lay members: L. Milliken; Ms P. Steel; D. Yeomans; S. James; G. Inch
Secretary: P. J. Fisher

UK PASSPORT SERVICE

Regional Office, 3 Northgate, 96 Milton Street, Cowcaddens, Glasgow G4 0BT
Central telephone number: 0870-521 0410
Central Fax number: 020-7271 8581
Web: www.passport.gov.uk

The UK Passport Service is an executive agency of the Home Office. It is responsible for the issue of British passports. The passport offices are generally open Monday-Friday, 8.30-6.00 Saturday 9.00-3.00, but there are some regional variations. The majority of telephone calls are now handled by a call centre, but where it is essential that customers speak directly to a particular regional office calls are transferred. The call centre operates 24 hours a day.
Head of Glasgow Regional Office: R. D. Wilson

VAT AND DUTIES TRIBUNALS

44 Palmerston Place, Edinburgh EH12 5BJ
Tel: 0131-226 3551 Fax: 0131-220 6817

VAT and Duties Tribunals are administered by the First Minister in Scotland. They are independent, and decide disputes between taxpayers and Customs and Excise. Chairmen in Scotland are appointed by the Lord President of the Court of Session.
President: His Hon. Stephen Oliver, QC
Vice-President: Scotland, T. G. Coutts, QC
Registrar: R. P. Lester

VETERANS AGENCY

Norcross, Blackpool, Lancs FY5 3WP
Tel: 0800-169 2277
Email: help@veteransagency.mod.uk
Web: www.veteransagency.mod.uk

Formerly the War Pensions Agency, the Veterans Agency is an Executive Agency of the Ministry of Defence (MoD). It is responsible for the administration of the War Pensions Scheme and provides a single point of contact within the MoD to obtain information and advice on a wide range of veterans' issues. The Agency also provides welfare support to war pensioners and war widow(er)s.
Chief Executive: Alan Burnham

VISIT SCOTLAND

23 Ravelston Terrace, Edinburgh EH4 3TP
Tel: 0131-332 2433 Fax: 0131-332 1513
Thistle House, Beechwood Park North, Inverness
IV2 3ED Tel: 01463-716996 Fax: 01463-717233
Web: www.visitscotland.com

Visit Scotland is responsible for developing and marketing the tourist industry in Scotland. Visit Scotland's main objectives are to promote holidays and to encourage the provision and improvement of tourist amenities for the economic benefit of the country.
Chief Executive: Philip Riddle

WATER INDUSTRY COMMISSIONER FOR SCOTLAND

Ochil House, Sprinkerse Business Park, Stirling FK7 7XE
Tel: 01786-430200 Fax: 01786-462018
Email: enquiries@watercommissioner.co.uk
Web: www.watercommissioner.co.uk

The Water Industry Commissioner's primary role is to promote the interests of consumers of Scottish Water.
Commissioner: A. Sutherland

THE EUROPEAN PARLIAMENT

European Parliament elections take place at five-yearly intervals; the first direct elections to the Parliament were held in 1979. In mainland Britain MEPs were elected in all constituencies on a first-past-the-post basis until the elections of 10 June 1999, when a 'closed-list' regional system of proportional representation was used for the first time. Scotland constitutes a region.

Parties submitted a list of candidates for each region in their own order of preference. Voters voted for a party or an independent candidate, and the first seat in each region was allocated to the party or candidate with the highest number of votes. The rest of the seats in each region were then allocated broadly in proportion to each party's share of the vote. The Scotland region returned eight members.

British subjects and citizens of the Irish Republic are eligible for election to the European Parliament provided they are 21 or over and not subject to disqualification. Since 1994, nationals of member states of the European Union have had the right to vote in elections to the European Parliament in the UK as long as they are entered on the electoral register.

MEPs currently receive a salary from the parliaments or governments of their respective member states, set at the level of the national parliamentary salary and subject to national taxation rules (the salary of British MEPs is £56,258). If an MEP is also an MP, they receive an MP's salary plus a 'duality' rate which is equal to one-third of an MEP's salary. Thus the total salary is £75,144.

SCOTLAND REGION

at election on 10 June 1999

E. 3,979,845   T. 24.83%

Lab.	283,490	(28.68%)
SNP	268,528	(27.17%)
C.	195,296	(19.76%)
LD	96,971	(9.81%)
Green	57,142	(5.78%)
SSP	39,720	(4.02%)
Pro Euro C.	17,781	(1.80%)
UK Ind.	12,549	(1.27%)
Soc. Lab.	9,385	(0.95%)
BNP	3,729	(0.38%)
NLP	2,087	(0.21%)
Lower Tax	1,632	(0.17%)

Lab. majority 14,962
(June 1994, Lab. maj. 148,718)

SCOTTISH MEMBERS AS AT MAY 2003

Attwooll, Ms Elspeth (b. 1943), *LD, Scotland*
*Hudghton, Ian (b. 1951), *SNP, Scotland*
MacCormick, Prof. Sir D. Neil, FBA (b. 1941), *SNP, Scotland*
*Martin, David W. (b. 1954), *Lab., Scotland*
*Miller, William (Bill) (b. 1954), *Lab., Scotland*
Purvis, John R., CBE (b. 1938), *C., Scotland*
Stevenson, Struan (b. 1948), *C., Scotland*
Stihler, Ms Catherine D. (b. 1973), *Lab., Scotland*

* Member of the last European Parliament

EU INFORMATION

Relations with the European Union (EU) remain reserved to the UK government after devolution. However, since EU policies and legislation affect many of the matters for which the Scottish Parliament and Executive are responsible, both the Parliament and the Executive are involved in scrutinising EU proposals to ensure that Scotland's interests are taken into consideration.

Where national legislation is required to fulfil the UK's obligation to implement EC legislation, the Scottish Parliament and Executive may choose to use legislation in relation to devolved matters in Scotland. The Scottish Ministers will be actively involved in decision-making on EU matters.

The Scottish Executive has its own office in Brussels to help represent Scotland's interests and complement the work of the UK Permanent Representative to the EU (UKRep). The office may also gather information on behalf of the Scottish Executive and Parliament and acts as a base for visits to Brussels by Scottish Ministers and officials of the Scottish Executive.

SCOTTISH EXECUTIVE EU OFFICE

Scotland House, 6 Rond Point Schuman, B-1040 Brussels, Belgium
Tel: 00-322-282 8330 Fax: 00-322-282 8345

INFORMATION SOURCES

Information about the EU is available from a variety of sources at different levels. The European Commission has developed a decentralised information network which aims to meet both general and specialised needs. In Scotland this network is known as Scottish European Resources Network (SERN). SERN is co-ordinated by the European Commission Office in Scotland and the European Parliament Office in Scotland.

The details below represent just a selection of EU information sources that are available. Visit www.ceu.org.uk/info/sources.htm for further information.

EUROPEAN COMMISSION REPRESENTATION IN SCOTLAND
9 Alva Street, Edinburgh EH2 4PH
Tel: 0131-225 2058 Fax: 0131-226 4105
Email: janet.williamson@cec.eu.net
Web: www.europa.eu.int or
www.europe.org.uk/info/scotland

EUROPEAN PARLIAMENT OFFICE IN SCOTLAND
The Tun, 4 Jackson's Entry, Holyrood Road, Edinburgh EH8 8PJ Web: www.europarl.org.uk

EURO INFO CENTRES
The centres provide information on Europe relevant to business (particularly small and medium-sized businesses), such as company law, relevant European legislation, taxation, public contracts, opportunities and funding. They can also offer an advisory service, for which a charge may be made.

GLASGOW
Euro Info Centre Small Business Gateway,
150 Broomielaw, Atlantic Quay, Glasgow G2 8LU

INVERNESS
Highlands and Islands Enterprise, Cowan House,
Inverness Retail and Business Park, Inverness IV2 7GF
Tel: 01463-234171 Fax: 01463-244469
Email: eic@sprite.co.uk

EUROPEAN DOCUMENTATION CENTRES
These provide access to EU documentation to the academic community and promote and develop study in the field of European integration. They are based in university libraries.

EUROPEAN REFERENCE CENTRE
The reference centres keep less comprehensive collections of EU publications.

HIGHLANDS AND ISLANDS RURAL CARREFOUR CENTRE
Carrefour Highlands and Islands is part of an EU-wide network of European information providers, based in rural areas. They provide information on EU policies concerning rural areas and issues and encourage networking and transitional co-operation between different rural areas.
Cowan House, Inverness Business and Retail Park, Inverness IV3 7GF
Tel: 01463-244571 Fax: 01463-244351
Email: claire.matheson@hient.co.uk
Web: www.hie.co.uk/carrefour

EUROPEAN PUBLIC INFORMATION CENTRES

These are members of a growing network of information outlets run by UK library authorities that work together, with the support of the European Commission Representation in the UK, to provide a better European information service to their library users. EPICs aim to:

- improve access for the general public to EU information at a local level;
- answer queries by drawing on their own expertise and that of other European information providers (including the Commission's own information officers);
- provide access to official EU publications;
- carry a range of free leaflets published by the Commission.

EURODESK SCOTLAND
The European Resource Centre Scotland is part of a network set up to provide EU information to students and teachers.
Web: www.eurodesk.org.uk

EUROPE DIRECT
Europe Direct is a free telephone service providing public information on various aspects of European citizenship. Callers can order free guides and factsheets on living, working and travelling in the EU, study and training in another EU country; equal opportunities, the single market, and other subjects. The materials are published in all EU languages.
Freephone: 0800-581591

POLITICAL PARTIES

SCOTTISH CONSERVATIVE AND UNIONIST CENTRAL OFFICE
83 Princes Street, Edinburgh EH2 2ER
Tel 0131-247 6890 Fax: 0131-247 6891
Email: central.office@scottishtories.org.uk
Web: www.scottishtories.org.uk

Chairman: David W. Mitchell
Deputy Chairman: Mrs M. Goodman
Hon. Treasurer: Mrs J. Slater

SCOTTISH GREEN PARTY
PO Box 14080, Edinburgh EH10 6YG
Tel 0131-478 7896 Fax: 0131-478 7896
Email: info@scottishgreens.org.uk
Web: www.scottishgreens.org.uk

Principal Speakers: Robin Harper, MSP,
  Mrs E. Scott, MSP
Executive Convener: Gavin Corbett
Treasurer: I. Baxter

SCOTTISH LABOUR PARTY
John Smith House, 145 West Regent Street, Glasgow,
G2 4RE Tel 0141-572 6900 Fax: 0141-572 2566
Email scotland@new.labour.org.uk
Web: www.scottishlabour.org.uk

First Minister in Scotland: Jack McConnell, MSP
Chair: Carolanne Wright
Vice-chair: Pat Devine
Treasurer: Stuart Clark
General Secretary: Lesley Quinn

SCOTTISH LIBERAL DEMOCRATS
4 Clifton Terrace, Edinburgh EH12 5DR
Tel 0131-337 2314 Fax: 0131-337 3566
Email: administration@scotlibdems.org.uk
Web: www.scotlibdems.org.uk

Party President: Malcolm Bruce, MP
Party Leader: Jim Wallace, MSP
Convener: Tavish Scott, MSP
Treasurer: Douglas Herbison
Chief of Staff: Derek Barrie

SCOTTISH NATIONAL PARTY
107 McDonald Road, Edinburgh, EH7 4NW
Tel 0131-525 8900 Fax: 0131-525 8901
Email: snp.hq@snp.org
Web: www.snp.org

Parliamentary Party Leader: John Swinney, SNP
Chief Whip: Bruce Crawford, MSP
National Convener: John Swinney, MSP
Senior Vice-Convener: Roseanna Cunningham, MSP
National Treasurer: Jim Mather, MSP
National Secretary: Stewart Hosie
Chief Executive: Peter Murrell

SCOTTISH SENIOR CITIZENS UNITY PARTY
PO Box 26420, East Kilbride G75 8XS
Email: enquiries@sscup.org.uk

SCOTTISH SOCIALIST PARTY
73 Robertson Street, Glasgow G2 8QD
Tel: 0141-221 7714 Fax: 0141-221 7715
Web: www.scotsocialistparty.org

Convener: T. Sheridan
Treasurer: K. Baldasara
National Secretary: A. Green

LOCAL GOVERNMENT

The Local Government etc. (Scotland) Act 1994 abolished the two-tier structure of nine regional and 53 district councils which had existed since 1975 and replaced it, from 1 April 1996, with a single-tier structure consisting of 29 unitary authorities on the mainland; the three islands councils remain. Each unitary authority has inherited all the functions of the regional and district councils, except water and sewerage (now provided by public bodies whose members are appointed by the Scottish Ministers) and reporters panels (now a national agency).

On taking office, the Scottish Parliament assumed responsibility for legislation on local government.

REVIEW OF LOCAL GOVERNMENT

The Commission on Local Government (the McIntosh Commission), reported to the First Minister in June 1999. Subsequently the Scottish Executive established the Renewing Local Democracy working group to consider how to make council membership more attractive, make councils more representative of their communities and advise on appropriate numbers of members for each council. It also considered possible alternative electoral systems and the remuneration of councillors.

The Scottish Executive also set up the Leadership Advisory Panel in August 1999 following the recommendations of the McIntosh Report. The panel worked closely with local authorities helping them to conduct a self-review of their political management structures and to implement recommendations.

The Local Government in Scotland Bill was introduced to the Scottish Parliament in May 2002. This Bill centred on three core elements:
– a power for local authorities to promote and improve well-being of their area and/or persons in it
– statutory underpinning for community planning through the introduction of a duty on local authorities and key partners, including police, health boards and enterprise agencies
– a duty to secure best value

The overall aim of the bill was to provide a framework for more responsive public services, giving councils more flexibility and responsibility to act in the best interests of their communities.

ELECTIONS

The unitary authorities consist of directly elected councillors. Elections take place every three years, normally on the first Thursday in May. The 2003 local government elections were held on 1 May, simultaneously with the elections for the Scottish Parliament. The Scottish Local Government (Elections) Act 2002 moved elections from a three-year to a four-year cycle; the next elections will take place in May 2007.

Generally, all British subjects and citizens of the Republic of Ireland who are 18 years or over and resident on the qualifying date in the area for which the election is being held, are entitled to vote at them. A register of electors is prepared and published annually by local electoral registration officers. Candidates, who are subject to various statutory qualifications and disqualifications designed to ensure that they are suitable persons to hold office, must be nominated by electors for the electoral area concerned. The electoral roll that came into effect in 16 February 2000 showed 4,009,424 people registered to vote.

The Local Government Boundary Commission for Scotland is responsible for carrying out periodic reviews of electoral arrangements and making proposals to the Scottish Ministers for any changes found necessary.

INTERNAL ORGANISATION AND FUNCTIONS

The council as a whole is the final decision-making body within any authority. Councils are free to a great extent to make their own internal organisational arrangements. Normally, questions of policy are settled by the full council, while the administration of the various services is the responsibility of committees of councillors. Day-to-day decisions are delegated to the council's officers, who act within the policies laid down by the councillors.

The functions of the councils and islands councils are: education; social work; strategic planning; the provision of infrastructure such as roads; consumer protection; flood prevention; coast protection; valuation and rating; the police and fire services; emergency planning; electoral registration; public transport; registration of births, deaths and marriages; housing; leisure and recreation; development control and building control; environmental health; licensing; allotments; public conveniences; and the administration of district courts.

The Chairman of a local council in Scotland may be known as a Convenor; a Provost is the equivalent of a Mayor. The Chairman of the council in the cities of Aberdeen, Dundee, Edinburgh and Glasgow are Lord Provosts.

LORDS-LIEUTENANT

The Lord-Lieutenant of a county is the permanent local representative of the Crown in that county. They are appointed by the Sovereign on the recommendation of the Prime Minister. The retirement age is 75.

The office of Lord-Lieutenant dates from 1557, and its holder was originally responsible for the maintenance of order and for local defence in the county. The duties of the post include attending on royalty during official visits to the county, performing certain duties in connection with armed forces of the Crown (and in particular the reserve forces), and making presentations of honours and awards on behalf of the Crown.

LORDS-LIEUTENANT

Title	Name
Aberdeenshire	A. D. M. Farquharson, OBE
Angus	Mrs Georgiana L. Osborne
Argyll and Bute	K. A. Mackinnon, WS, Rd
Ayrshire and Arran	Maj. R. Y. Henderson, TD
Banffshire	Mrs C. N. Russell
Berwickshire	Maj. Alexander R. Trotter
Caithness	Maj. G. T. Dunnett, TD
Clackmannan	Mrs S. Cruickshank
Dumfries	Capt. R. C. Cunningham-Jardine
Dunbartonshire	Brig. D. D. G. Hardie, TD
East Lothian	W. Garth Morrison, CBE
Eilean Siar/Western Isles	Alexander Matheson
Fife	Mrs C. M. Dean
Inverness	Donald Angus Cameron of Lochiel
Kincardineshire	J. D. B. Smart
Lanarkshire	Gilbert K. Cox, MBE
Midlothian	P. R. Prenter, CBE
Moray	Air Vice-Marshal G. A. Chesworth, CB, OBE, DFC
Nairn	Ewen J. Brodie of Lethen
Orkney	G. R. Marwick
Perth and Kinross	Sir David Montgomery, Bt.
Renfrewshire	C. H. Parker, OBE
Ross and Cromarty	Capt. R. W. K. Stirling of Fairburn, TD, JP
Roxburgh, Ettrick and Lauderdale	Dr June Paterson-Brown, CBE, MBChB
Shetland	J. H. Scott
Stirling and Falkirk	Lt.-Col. J. Stirling of Garden, CBE, TD, FRICS
Sutherland	Maj.-Gen. D. Houston, CBE
The Stewartry of Kirkcudbright	Lt.-Gen. Sir Norman Arthur, KCB
Tweeddale	Capt. David Younger
West Lothian	Mrs I. G. Brydie, MBE
Wigtown	Maj. E. S. Orr Ewing

The Lord Provosts of the four city districts of Aberdeen, Dundee, Edinburgh and Glasgow are Lord-Lieutenants for those districts ex officio.

COMMUNITY COUNCILS

Unlike the parish councils and community councils in England and Wales, Scottish community councils are not local authorities. Their purpose as defined in statute is to ascertain and express the views of the communities which they represent, and to take in the interests of their communities such action as appears to be expedient or practicable. Over 1,000 community councils have been established under schemes drawn up by district and islands councils in Scotland.

Since 1996 community councils have had an enhanced role, becoming statutory consultees on local planning issues and on the decentralisation schemes which the new councils have to draw up for delivery of services.

FINANCE

Local government is financed from four sources: the council tax, non-domestic rates, government grants, and income from fees and charges for services.

COUNCIL TAX
Under the Local Government Finance Act 1992, from 1 April 1993 council tax replaced the community charge, which had been introduced in April 1989 in place of domestic rates. Council tax is a local tax levied by each local council. Liability for the council tax bill usually falls on the owner-occupier or tenant of a dwelling which is their sole or main residence.

Each island council and unitary authority sets its own rate of council tax. The tax relates to the value of the dwelling. Each dwelling is placed in one of eight valuation bands, ranging from A to H, based on the property's estimated market value as at 1 April 1991.

The valuation bands and ranges of values in Scotland are:

A	Up to £27,000
B	£27,001–£35,000
C	£35,001–£45,000
D	£45,001–£58,000
E	£58,001–£80,000
F	£80,001–£106,000
G	£106,001–£212,000
H	Over £212,000

Council tax within a local area varies between the different bands according to proportions laid down by law. The charge attributable to each band as a proportion of the Band D charge set by the council is approximately:

A	67%
B	78%
C	89%
D	100%
E	122%
F	144%
G	167%
H	200%

The Band D rate for each council is given in the individual local council entries. There may be variations from the given figure within each district council area because of different community precepts being levied.

NON-DOMESTIC RATES

Non-domestic (business) rates are collected by the billing authorities, which in Scotland are the local authorities. Rates are levied in accordance with the Local Government (Scotland) Act 1975. From 1995–6, the Secretary of State for Scotland prescribed a single non-domestic rates poundage to apply throughout the country at the same level as the uniform business rate (UBR) in England. Rate income is pooled and redistributed to local authorities on a per capita basis.

Rateable values for the current rating lists came into force on 1 April 2000. They are derived from the rental value of property as at 1 April 1998 and determined on certain statutory assumptions by Regional Assessors. New property which is added to the list, and significant changes to existing property, necessitate amendments to the rateable value on the same basis. Valuation rolls remain in force until the next general revaluation. Such

revaluations take place every five years. Certain types of property, such as places of public religious worship and agricultural land and buildings, are exempt from rates. Charities, other non-profit-making organisations, sole village shops and post offices, and certain other businesses may receive full or partial relief. Empty property is liable to pay rates at 50 per cent, except for certain specified classes which are entirely exempt.

GOVERNMENT GRANTS

In addition to specific grants in support of revenue expenditure on particular services, central government pays revenue support grant to local authorities. This grant is paid to each local authority so that if each authority budgeted at the level of its standard spending assessment, all authorities in the same class can set broadly the same council tax.

EXPENDITURE

Local authority estimated budgeted expenditure for 2002–3 was:

Service	£m
Education	3,616.7
Arts and Libraries	131.9
Social Work Services	1,473.6
Law, Order and Protective Services	1,063.7
Roads and Transport	407.6
Other Environmental Services	805.7
Tourism	9.5
Housing	4.2
Sheltered Employment	9.9
Administration of Housing Benefit	45.2
Consumer Protection	18.9
Total	7,586.8

COMPLAINTS

Commissioners for Local Administration are responsible for investigating complaints from members of the public who claim to have suffered injustice as a consequence of maladministration in local government or in certain local bodies.

Complaints are made to the relevant local authority in the first instance and are referred to the Commissioners if the complainant is not satisfied.

LOCAL AUTHORITY AREAS

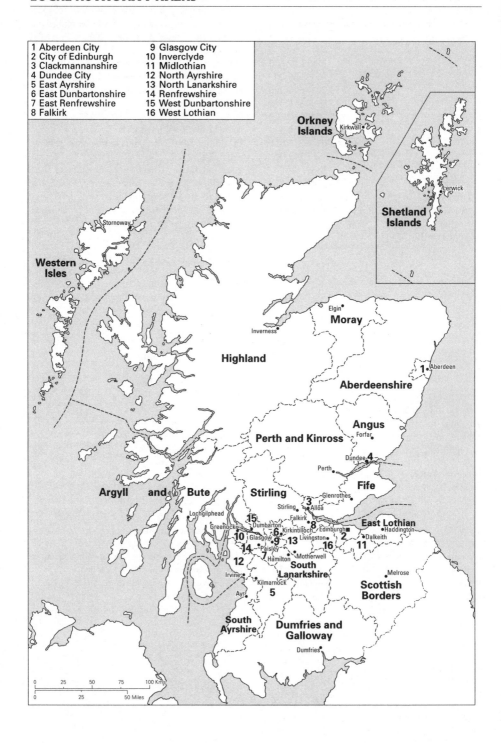

1 Aberdeen City
2 City of Edinburgh
3 Clackmannanshire
4 Dundee City
5 East Ayrshire
6 East Dunbartonshire
7 East Renfrewshire
8 Falkirk

9 Glasgow City
10 Inverclyde
11 Midlothian
12 North Ayrshire
13 North Lanarkshire
14 Renfrewshire
15 West Dunbartonshire
16 West Lothian

Orkney
Islands
Kirkwall

Lerwick

Shetland
Islands

Stornoway

Western
Isles

Elgin
Moray
Inverness

Highland

Aberdeen
1

Aberdeenshire

Angus
Forfar

Perth and Kinross
Dundee 4

Perth

Fife

Glenrothes

Stirling
Alloa
Stirling 3
Falkirk
8

Argyll and Bute
Lochgilphead
Greenock
15
Dumbarton
Kirkintilloch
10
6
Glasgow
9
14
Paisley
12
7
Hamilton
13
Livingston
16
2
Edinburgh
Dalkeith
11
Haddington
East Lothian

Motherwell
South
Lanarkshire
Irvine
Kilmarnock
5
Ayr

Melrose
Scottish
Borders

South
Ayrshire
Dumfries and
Galloway
Dumfries

0 25 50 75 100 Kms

0 25 50 Miles

COUNCIL DIRECTORY

ABERDEEN CITY COUNCIL
Town House, Broad Street, Aberdeen AB10 1FY
Tel: 01224-522000 Fax: 01224-644346
Web: www.aberdeencity.gov.uk
Chief Executive: Douglas Paterson

ABOUT THE AREA
Aberdeen is Scotland's third largest city and is northern Scotland's principal commercial and administrative area. Situated between the River Dee and the River Don and lying some 126 miles north east of Edinburgh, Aberdeen is the centre of the North Sea oil industry and is home to one of the country's largest fishing ports. There are two universities in Aberdeen: Aberdeen University and Robert Gordon University.

Area: 186 sq. km
Population (2001 census): 212,125
Council tax (average Band D) for 2003–4: £1,020.06

Political composition as at 1 May 2003:
   LD 20; Lab. 14; SNP 6; C. 3

Scottish and UK Parliamentary Constituencies: Aberdeen Central; Aberdeen North; Aberdeen South

ABERDEENSHIRE COUNCIL
Woodhill House, Westburn Road, Aberdeen AB16 5GB
Tel: 01467-620981 Fax: 01224-665444
Web: www.aberdeenshire.gov.uk
Chief Executive: Alan Campbell

ABOUT THE AREA
Aberdeenshire is situated on the north east coast of Scotland and is the country's fourth largest local authority. Aberdeenshire employs many people in the oil and gas industry and other key industries include agriculture, tourism, fishing and construction. In addition to being home to one of Scotland's largest cities, Aberdeenshire is predominantly rural. Major regions in Aberdeenshire include: Banff, Fraserburgh, Inverurie, Peterhead, Stonehaven and Westhill.

Area: 6,313 sq. km
Population (2001 census): 226,781
Council tax (average Band D) for 2003–4: £966.00

Political composition as at 1 May 2003:
   LD 28; SNP 18; C.11; Ind. 11

Scottish and UK Parliamentary Constituencies:
   Aberdeenshire West and Kincardine; Banff and Buchan; Gordon

ANGUS COUNCIL
The Cross, Forfar, Angus DD8 1BX
Tel: 01307-461460 Fax: 01307-461874
Web: www.angus.gov.uk
Chief Executive: Sandy Watson

ABOUT THE AREA
Angus lies on the Highland geological fault between the River Tay and the North Esk River. Its environment is one of contrasts from highland terrain in the north west to long, narrow coastal plains and the highly cultivated Strathmore valley. Angus is well located for businesses serving the offshore industry and key industries include agriculture, manufacturing, engineering and pharmaceuticals. Angus' main residential areas are Arbroath, Brechin, Carnoustie, Forfar, Kirriemuir, Monifieth and Montrose.

Area: 2,182 sq. km
Population (2001 census): 108,400
Council tax (average Band D) for 2003–4: £933.00

Political composition as at 1 May 2003:
   SNP 17; Ind. 6; LD 3; C.2; Lab. 1

Scottish and UK Parliamentary Constituencies: Angus; Tayside North

ARGYLL AND BUTE COUNCIL
Kilmory, Lochgilphead, Argyll PA31 8RT
Tel: 01546-602127 Fax: 01546-604349
Web: www.argyll-bute.gov.uk
Chief Executive: James McLellan

ABOUT THE AREA
Argyll and Bute combines town and village life with country and coastal living, providing magnificent scenery in the mainland and outlying islands. Industry is predominated by agriculture, forestry and fishing while other industries include call centres, construction and defence. Major regions in the area are: Argyll, Bute, Campbeltown, Dunoon, Helensburgh, Islay, Mull and Oban.

Area: 6,909 sq. km
Population (2001 census): 91,306
Council tax (average Band D) for 2003-04: £1,034.00

Political composition as at 1 May 2003:
   Ind. 22; LD. 8; C. 3; SNP 3

Scottish and UK Parliamentary Constituencies: Argyll and Bute; Dumbarton

CITY OF EDINBURGH COUNCIL

Wellington Court, 10 Waterloo Place, Edinburgh EH1 3EG Tel: 0131-200 2000 Fax: 0131-529 7477
Web: www.edinburgh.gov.uk
Chief Executive: Tom Aitchison

ABOUT THE AREA

Edinburgh is Scotland's capital city built on a number of hills and dominated by Edinburgh Castle. The city adjoins East Lothian, Midlothian, Borders and West Lothian local authorities and major sources of employment in the area include finance, business, distribution, tourism and communications. Edinburgh has one of the healthiest economic profiles in the UK and there have been high levels of investment in the city in recent years. Easily accessible by road and air, Edinburgh is a major tourist destination and in 2000, Edinburgh Castle attracted over 1 million visitors. Events that take place in the city each year include the Edinburgh Military Tattoo and the Edinburgh Festival.

Area: 264 sq. km
Population (2001 census): **448,624**
Council tax (average Band D) for 2003–4: £1,041.00

Political composition as at 1 May 2003:
   Lab. 30; LD 15; C. 13

Scottish and UK Parliamentary Constituencies:
   Edinburgh Central; Edinburgh East and
   Musselburgh; Edinburgh North and Leith;
   Edinburgh Pentlands; Edinburgh South;
   Edinburgh West

CLACKMANNANSHIRE COUNCIL

Greenfield, Alloa, Clackmannanshire FK10 2AD
Tel: 01259-450000; Fax: 01259-452230
Chief Executive: Keir Bloomer

ABOUT THE AREA

Clackmannanshire is a compact area based around the main town of Alloa and is Scotland's smallest local authority. It is situated in central Scotland and is bordered by the Firth Estuary in the south, Stirling in the west and dominated by the Ochil Hills to the north. The area has traditionally relied on mining, brewing and textiles sectors, however, in recent years it has developed growth industries such as retail, wholesale and hotels.

Area: 159 sq. km
Population (2001 census): 48,077
Council tax (average Band D) for 2003–4: £995.00

Political composition as at 1 May 2003:
   Lab. 10; SNP 6; Ind. 1; C.1

Scottish and UK Parliamentary Constituency: Ochil

DUMFRIES AND GALLOWAY COUNCIL

Council Offices, English Street, Dumfries DG1 2DD
Tel: 01387-260000 Fax: 01387-260034
Web: www.dumgal.gov.uk
Chief Executive: Philip Jones

ABOUT THE AREA

Dumfries and Galloway stretches from Langholm in the east to the Mull of Galloway in the west. While agriculture and forestry are the main industries in the area, manufacturing and service industries provide considerable employment. Much of the area is mountainous moorland and the majority of the population lives on the coastal plains and river valleys. The North Channel Ferry provides the shortest crossing from Scotland to Ireland.

Area: 6,426 sq. km
Population (2001 census): 147,765
Council tax (average Band D) for 2003–4: £931.00

Political composition as at 1 May 2003:
   Lab. 14; Ind. 12; C. 11; LD 5; SNP 5

Scottish and UK Parliament Constituencies: Dumfries;
   Galloway and Upper Nithsdale

DUNDEE CITY COUNCIL

21 City Square, Dundee DD1 3BY
Tel: 01382-434000 Fax: 01382-434666
Web: www.dundeecity.gov.uk
Chief Executive: Alex Stephen

ABOUT THE AREA

Dundee is situated at the mouth of the River Tay and has some eight miles of waterfront. The prime industry sectors in the area include biotechnology, healthcare and call centres. Known as the 'city of discovery' after Captain Scott's antarctic research ship which was built in the City, Dundee has a rich seafaring and industrial heritage. There are two universities in Dundee and places of interest include Mills Public Observatory, the Tay road and rail bridges, Dundee Contemporary Arts Centre, McManus Galleries, Claypotts Castle and Broughty Castle.

Area: 60 sq. km
Population (2001 census): 145,663
Council tax (average Band D) for 2003–4: £1,089.00

Political composition as at 1 May 2003:
SNP 11; Lab. 10; C. 5; LD 2; Ind. 1

Scottish and UK Parliamentary Constituencies: Dundee East; Dundee West

EAST AYRSHIRE COUNCIL

Council Headquarters, London Road, Kilmarnock, Ayrshire KA3 7BU
Tel: 01563-576000 Fax: 01563-576500
Web: www.east-ayrshire.gov.uk
Chief Executive: David Montgomery

ABOUT THE AREA
Located in the south west of Scotland, East Ayrshire is predominantly rural and adjoins North Ayrshire, South Ayrshire, Dumfries and Galloway, South Lanarkshire and East Renfrewshire local authorities. Industries important to the region include whisky blending, mining, engineering, textiles and agriculture. Main regions within East Ayrshire are Cumnock, Darvel, Galston, Greenholm, Kilmarnock, Newmilns and Stewarton

Area: 1,262 sq. km
Population (2001 census): 120,235
Council tax (average Band D) for 2003–4: £1,014.30

Political composition as at 1 May 2003:
Lab. 23; SNP 8; C. 1

Scottish and UK Parliamentary Constituencies: Carrick, Cumnock and Doon Valley; Kilmarnock and Loudoun

EAST DUNBARTONSHIRE COUNCIL

Tom Johnston House, Civic Way, Kirkintilloch, Glasgow G66 4TJ Tel: 0141-578 8000 Fax: 0141-777 8576
Chief Executive: Dr Vicki Nash

ABOUT THE AREA
East Dunbartonshire Council lies to the north of Glasgow and is bounded by the Campsie Fells and Kilpatrick Hills. It is one of the smallest local authority areas in Scotland and important areas include Bearsden, Bishopbriggs, Kirkintilloch and Milngavie. Largely residential, many of East Dunbartonshire's inhabitants travel to Glasgow for work, however, East Dunbartonshire Council is one of the area's largest employers.

Area: 175 sq. km
Population (2001 census): 108,243
Council tax (average Band D) for 2003–4: £996.36

Political composition as at 1 May 2003:
LD 12; Lab. 9; C. 3

Scottish and UK Parliamentary Constituencies:
Clydebank and Milngavie; Coatbridge and Chryston; Strathkelvin and Bearsden

EAST LOTHIAN COUNCIL

John Muir House, Court Street, Haddington, East Lothian EH41 3HA
Tel: 01620-827827 Fax: 01620-827888
Web: www.eastlothian.gov.uk
Chief Executive: John Lindsay

ABOUT THE AREA
Bounded on the south by the Lammermuir Hills, East Lothian stretches east to the boundary with the Scottish Borders at Cockburnspath. Haddington is the administrative centre of the region and main residential areas include Musselburgh, Prestonpans, Cockenzie and Port Seton. The region's economy was built on the farming, fishing, coalmining and manufacture industries, however, nowadays East Lothian supports industries such as electronics, chemical research, printing and tourism.

Area: 679 sq. km
Population (2001 census): 90,088
Council tax (average Band D) for 2003–4: £993.15

Political composition as at 1 May 2003:
Lab. 17; C. 4; LD 1; SNP 1

Scottish and UK Parliamentary Constituency:
East Lothian

EAST RENFREWSHIRE COUNCIL

Council Offices, Eastwood Park, Rouken Glen Road, Giffnock G46 6UG
Tel: 0141-577 3000 Fax: 0141-620 0884
Web: www.eastrenfrewshire.gov.uk
Chief Executive: Peter Daniels

ABOUT THE AREA
East Renfrewshire is comprised of 70 per cent farmland and 30 per cent residential areas. Residential areas are confined to the north east of the area and include the districts of Clarkston, Giffnock, Netherlee and Eaglesham. The region has excellent transport links with Glasgow and important industries include manufacturing, construction and service industries. East Renfrewshire adjoins the City of Glasgow, Renfrewshire, North Ayrshire, East Ayrshire and South Lanarkshire local authorities.

Area: 174 sq. km
Population (2001 census): 89,311
Council tax (average Band D) for 2003–4: £955.00

Political composition as at 1 May 2003:
  Lab. 8; C. 7; LD 3; Ind. 2

Scottish and UK Parliamentary Constituency: Eastwood

EILEAN SIAR/WESTERN ISLES COUNCIL
Council Offices, Sandwick Road, Stornoway, Isle of Lewis HS1 2BW
Tel: 01851-703773 Fax: 01851-705349
Web: www.cne-siar.gov.uk
Chief Executive: Bill Howat

ABOUT THE AREA
The Western Isles are commonly known as the Outer Hebrides and comprise 130 miles of islands stretching from the Butt of Lewis in the north to Barra Head in the south. There are four National Nature Reserves and a large number of other designated sites and a unique Gaelic culture is represented by the work of the local art community. Agriculture is the area's predominant industry although public administration is the largest employer.

Area: 3,071 sq. km
Population (2001 census): 26,502
Council tax (average Band D) for 2003–4: £867.00

Political composition as at 1 May 2003:
  Ind. 24; Lab. 4; SNP 3

Scottish and UK Parliamentary Constituency:
  Western Isles

FALKIRK COUNCIL
Municipal Buildings, West Bridge Street, Falkirk FK1 5RS Tel: 01324-506070 Fax: 01324-506071
Chief Executive: Mary Pitcaithly

ABOUT THE AREA
Falkirk is located in central Scotland between Glasgow and Edinburgh. It adjoins Clackmannanshire, North Lanarkshire, Stirling and West Lothian local auhorities and is home to the port of Grangemouth. Petrochemical and chemical industries are important to Falkirk's economy and other key employers are BT and Thomas Cook. While Falkirk has a predominantly urban population, the area is home to a number of attractive areas of natural heritage including Muiravonside Country Park and the historic estate of Kinneil at Bo'ness.

Area: 297 sq. km
Population (2001 census): 145,191
Council tax (average Band D) for 2003–4: £906.00

Political composition as at 1 May 2003:
  Lab. 14; SNP 9; Ind. 7; C. 2

Scottish and UK Parliamentary Constituencies:
  Falkirk East; Falkirk West

FIFE COUNCIL
Fife House, North Street, Glenrothes, Fife KY7 5LT
Tel: 01592-414141 Fax: 01592-414142
Web: www.fife.gov.uk
Chief Executive: Douglas Sinclair

ABOUT THE AREA
Fife is located in east central Scotland and adjoins Clackmannanshire and Perth and Kinross local authorities. It is bounded to the north by the River Tay and to the south by the River Forth.The south and west of the district are predominantly urban and the north-east is mainly agricultural. The major residential centres are Kirkcaldy, Dunfermline and Glenrothes and other main areas are Cowdenbeath, Cupar, Levenmouth and historic St Andrews.

Area: 1,325 sq. km
Population (2001 census): 349,429
Council tax (average Band D) for 2003–4: £981.00

Political composition as at 1 May 2003:
  Lab. 36; LD 23; SNP 11; Ind. 4; O. 6; C. 2

Scottish and UK Parliamentary Constituencies:
  Dunfermline East; Dunfermline West; Fife Central; Fife North East; Kirkcaldy

GLASGOW CITY COUNCIL
City Chambers, George Square, Glasgow G2 1DU
Tel: 0141-287 2000 Fax: 0141-287 5666
Web: www.glasgow.gov.uk
Chief Executive: George Black

ABOUT THE AREA
Glasgow is situated on the River Clyde in west central Scotland and adjoins West Dunbartonshire, East Dunbartonshire, North Lanarkshire, South Lanarkshire, East Renfrewshire and Renfrewshire local authorities.
  Home to many of Scotland's leading businesses, the main industry sector in Glasgow is the service sector. Glasgow is also Scotland's media capital, producing the majority of daily newspapers and housing BBC Scotland and STV. Glasgow is Scotland's largest city and, known as 'the friendly

city', is one of the UK's most popular tourist destinations.

Area: 175 sq. km
Population (2001 census): 577,869
Council tax (average Band D) for 2003–4: £1,163.00

Political composition as at 1 May 2003:
 Lab. 71; LD 3; SNP 3; C. 1; O. 1

Scottish and UK Parliamentary Constituencies:
 Glasgow Anniesland; Glasgow Baillieston;
 Glasgow Cathcart; Glasgow Govan; Glasgow
 Kelvin; Glasgow Maryhill; Glasgow Pollok;
 Glasgow Rutherglen; Glasgow Shettleston;
 Glasgow Springburn

HIGHLAND COUNCIL
Glenurquhart Road, Inverness IV3 5NX
Tel: 01463-702000 Fax: 01463-702111
Web: www.highland.gov.uk
Chief Executive: Arthur McCourt

ABOUT THE AREA
The Highland region is one of mainland Scotland's most rural areas and is home to some of the UK's most stunning scenery and landscape. In Highland the highest mountains and largest inland waters in Britain can be found, including the famous Loch Ness. The area boasts the lowest density of population in Scotland. The Highland economy is mixed, ranging from agriculture and tourism to finance and technical industries.

Area: 25,659 sq. km
Population (2001 census): 208,914
Council tax (average Band D) for 2003–4: £989.00

Political composition as at 1 May 2003:
 Ind. 57; LD 9; Lab. 8; SNP 6

Scottish and UK Parliamentary Constituencies:
 Caithness, Sutherland and Easter Ross; Inverness
 East, Nairn and Lochaber; Ross, Skye and
 Inverness West

INVERCLYDE COUNCIL
Municipal Buildings, Clyde Square, Greenock,
Renfrewshire PA15 1LY
Tel: 01475-717171 Fax: 01475-712731
Chief Executive: Robert Cleary

ABOUT THE AREA
Less than 30 minutes away from Glasgow, Inverclyde is located in west central Scotland, on the estuary of the River Clyde, and adjoins Renfrewshire and North Ayrshire local authorities. The main urban areas are Greenock, Gourock and Port Glasgow. In the last decade substantial progress has been made in attracting new industry and investment and major industries include manufacturing, tourism and the service sector.

Area: 160 sq. km
Population (2001 census): 84,203
Council tax (average Band D) for 2003–4: £1,089.00

Political composition as at 1 May 2003:
 LD 13; Lab. 6; O. 1

Scottish and UK Parliamentary Constituencies:
 Greenock and Inverclyde; West Renfrewshire

MIDLOTHIAN COUNCIL
Midlothian House, 40–46 Buccleuch Street, Dalkeith,
Midlothian EH22 1DJ
Tel: 0131-270 7500 Fax: 0131-271 3050
Web: www.midlothian.gov.uk
Chief Executive: Trevor Muir

ABOUT THE AREA
Midlothian is situated to the north of Edinburgh and the local authority is the largest employer in the area. Main regions in Midlothian include Bonnyrigg, Dalkeith, Easthouses, Gorebridge, Loanhead and Mafield. Midlothian is home to a number of conservation areas and Sites of Special Scientific Interest.

Area: 354 sq. km
Population (2001 census): 80,941
Council tax (average Band D) for 2003–4: £1,072.00

Political composition as at 1 May 2003:
 Lab. 15; LD 2; Ind. 1

Scottish and UK Parliamentary Constituencies:
 Midlothian; Tweeddale, Ettrick and Lauderdale

MORAY COUNCIL
Council Office, High Street, Elgin, Morayshire IV30 1BX
Tel: 01343-543451 Fax: 01343-540399
Web: www.moray.org
Chief Executive: Alastair Keddie

ABOUT THE AREA
Moray is situated in the north-east of Scotland the area consists of rich farmlands which are protected from the elements by the Cairngorm mountains. Moray has good road and rail links and the nearest airports are in Aberdeen and Inverness. The area is largely rural and important industries include horticulture, agriculture, fishing and whisky distilling. Moray's main regions are Buckie, Dufftown, Elgin, Forres and Lossiemouth.

Area: 2,238 sq. km
Population (2001 census): 86,940
Council tax (average Band D) for 2003–4: £907.40

Political composition as at 1 May 2003:
  Ind. 16; Lab. 5; SNP. 3; LD. 1; C. 1

Scottish and UK Parliamentary Constituencies: Gordon;
  Moray

NORTH AYRSHIRE COUNCIL
Cunninghame House, Irvine, Ayrshire KA12 8EE
Tel: 01294-324100 Fax: 01294-324144
Chief Executive: Bernard Devine

ABOUT THE AREA
North Ayrshire is situated on Scotland's scenic west
coast some 25 miles south of Glasgow. Main towns
in North Ayrshire are Irvine, Kilwinning, Ardrossan,
Saltcoats, Stevenston and Largs. The council area
also covers the islands of Arran and Cumbrae.
North Ayrshire boasts impressive road, rail, sea and
air links and the area has become one of Scotland's
key manufacturing areas.

Area: 885 sq. km
Population (2001 census): 135,817
Council tax (average Band D) for 2003–4: £977.00

Political composition as at 1 May 2003:
  Lab. 21; C. 4; SNP 3; Ind. 2

Scottish and UK Parliamentary Constituencies:
  Cunninghame North; Cunninghame South

NORTH LANARKSHIRE COUNCIL
PO Box 14, Civic Centre, Motherwell, Lanarkshire ML1
1TW Tel: 01698-302222 Fax: 01698-275125
Web: www.northlan.gov.uk
Chief Executive: Gavin Whitefield

ABOUT THE AREA
North Lanarkshire is situated in south central
Scotland, halfway between Edinburgh and Glasgow.
Important industries include manufacturing,
distribution, retail, tourism and communication and
major districts in the region include Airdrie,
Bellshill, Chryston and Muirhead, Coatbridge,
Cumbernauld, Kilsyth, Moodiesburn, Motherwell,
Newmains, Shotts and Wishaw.

Area: 470 sq. km
Population (2001 census): 321,067
Council tax (average Band D) for 2003–4: £972.00

Political composition as at 1 May 2003:
  Lab. 54; SNP 11; Ind. 5

Scottish and UK Parliamentary Constituencies:
  Airdrie and Shotts; Coatbridge and Chryston;
  Cumbernauld and Kilsyth; Hamilton North and
  Bellshill; Motherwell and Wishaw

ORKNEY ISLANDS COUNCIL
Council Offices, School Place, Kirkwall, Orkney
KW15 1NY Tel: 01856-873535 Fax: 01856-874615
Chief Executive: Alistair Buchan

ABOUT THE AREA
The Orkney Islands are the second most northerly
group of islands in the UK, being separated by
seven-mile stretch of the Pentland Firth. There are
three main island groupings, the North Isles, the
South Isles and the largest island which is known as
the Mainland. There are approximately 70 islands
in total. There are two towns, Kirkwall and
Stromness, the former being Orkney's
administrative centre. Key industries include
tourism, agriculture, fishing and food and drink
manufacture.

Area: 990 sq. km
Population (2001 census): 19,245
Council tax (average Band D) for 2003–4: £900.00

Political composition as at 1 May 2003: Ind. 21

Scottish Parliament Constituency: Orkney

UK Parliament Constituency: Orkney and Shetland

PERTH AND KINROSS COUNCIL
2 High Street, Perth PH1 5PH
Tel: 01738-475000 Fax: 01738-475710
Email: enquiries@pkc.gov.uk Web: www.pkc.gov.uk
Chief Executive: Mrs Bernadette Malone

ABOUT THE AREA
Located in the heart of Scotland, Perth and Kinross
is approximately an hour away from Edinburgh and
75 minutes from Glasgow. Perth occupies the Tay
River basin and some of Scotland's highest peaks
are located within the area, including Ben Lawers
and Schiehallion. Ninety per cent of Scotland's
population live within 90 minutes of Perth and
large employers in the area include Norwich Union
and Stagecoach. Agriculture, service sector, retail,
crafts and tourism are key industries.

Area: 5,286 sq. km
Population (2001 census): 134,949
Council tax (average Band D) for 2003–4: £983.00

Political composition as at 1 May 2003:
SNP 15; C. 10; LD 9; Lab. 5; Ind. 2

Scottish and UK Parliamentary Constituencies:
Angus; Ochil; Perth; Tayside North

RENFREWSHIRE COUNCIL
Council Headquarters, North Building, Cotton Street,
Paisley PA1 1BU
Tel: 0141-842 5000 Fax: 0141-840 3335
Web: www.renfrewshire.gov.uk
Chief Executive: Tom Scholes

ABOUT THE AREA
Renfrewshire is one of Scotland's largest local
authorities. It is situated in central Scotland and is a
largely rural district close to Loch Lomond, the
River Clyde and Burns country. It is located just
minutes from Glasgow city centre and Glasgow
International Airport is situated on the outskirts of
Paisley. In addition to Paisley, important areas in the
region include Johnstone and Renfrew.
Renfrewshire is a major industrial area, however,
agriculture still plays a vital role in the economy.

Area: 261 sq. km
Population (2001 census): 172,867
Council tax (average Band D) for 2003–4: £988.00

Political composition as at 1 May 2003:
Lab. 21; SNP 15; LD 3; C. 1

Scottish and UK Parliamentary Constituencies:
Paisley North; Paisley South; Renfrewshire West

SCOTTISH BORDERS COUNCIL
Council Headquarters, Newtown St Boswells, Melrose,
Roxburghshire TD6 0SA
Tel: 01835-824000 Fax: 01835-825142
Chief Executive: David Hume

ABOUT THE AREA
The Scottish Borders region is located in the south
east of Scotland, stretches from the outskirts of
Edinburgh to the English border and encompasses a
large part of the River Tweed area. Manufacturing is
the largest employment sector and others include
public administration, education and health,
distribution and hotels and restaurants. The main
town in the region is Melrose.

Area: 4,732 sq. km
Population (2001 census): 106,764
Council tax (average Band D) for 2003–4: £935.00

Political composition as at 1 May 2003:
Ind. 15; C. 10; LD 8; SNP 1

Scottish and UK Parliamentary Constituencies:
Roxburgh and Berwickshire; Tweeddale, Ettrick
and Lauderdale

SHETLAND ISLANDS COUNCIL
Town Hall, Hillhead, Lerwick, Shetland ZE1 0HB
Tel: 01595-693535 Fax: 01595-744509
Web: www.shetland.gov.uk
Chief Executive: Morgan Goodlad

ABOUT THE AREA
The Shetland Islands lie 204 miles north of
Aberdeen and 234 miles west of Bergen, Norway.
The Shetlands comprise over 100 islands, 15 of
which are inhabited, and local dialect retains traces
of Norse language.
   Shetland is an important part of the North Sea
oil industry, providing landfall for the Brent and
Ninian oilfield pipelines. The Sullon Voe oil facility
is the largest of its kind in Europe. Traditional
industries include tourism, knitwear, agriculture and
crafts.

Area: 1,466 sq. km
Population (2001 census): 21,988
Council tax (average Band D) for 2003–4: £873.00

Political composition as at 1 May 2003: Ind. 17; LD 5

Scottish Parliamentary Constituency: Shetland

UK Parliamentary Constituency: Orkney and Shetland

SOUTH AYRSHIRE COUNCIL
County Buildings, Wellington Square, Ayr KA7 1DR
Tel: 01292-612000 Fax: 01292-612143
Web: www.south-ayrshire.gov.uk
Chief Executive: George Thorley

ABOUT THE AREA
South Ayrshire is located in the south west of
Scotland and is the birthplace of Robert Burns and
Robert the Bruce. The area extends from Ballantrae
in the south to Troon in the north and other
districts in the area include Girvan, Prestwick and
Ayr. South Ayrshire contains a mix of rural and
urban living and is home to Burns National
Heritage Park, Ayr Race Course and Culzean
Castle.

Area: 1,222 sq. km
Population (2001 census): 112,097
Council tax (average Band D) for 2003–4: £964.00

Political composition as at 1 May 2003: Lab. 15; C. 15

Scottish and UK Parliamentary Constituencies: Ayr; Carrick, Cumnock and Doon Valley

SOUTH LANARKSHIRE COUNCIL
Council Offices, Almada Street, Hamilton, Lanarkshire ML3 0AA Tel: 01698-454444 Fax: 01698-454275
Web: www.southlanarkshire.gov.uk
Chief Executive: Michael Docherty

ABOUT THE AREA
South Lanarkshire spans central and southern Scotland and its main population centres are in the north-west and include Rutherglen, Cambuslang, East Kilbride and Hamilton. In the north, Carluke and Lanark are residential areas. The south of the region is comprised largely of farmland and is very sparsely populated. Its southern-most boundary is just over 30 minutes away from England.

Area: 1,772 sq. km
Population (2001 census): 302,216
Council tax (average Band D) for 2003–4: £971.00

Political composition as at 1 May 2003:
   Lab. 51; SNP 9; Ind. 3; C. 2; LD 2

Scottish and UK Parliamentary Constituencies:
   Clydesdale; East Kilbride; Glasgow Rutherglen; Hamilton North and Bellshill; Hamilton South

STIRLING COUNCIL
Viewforth, Stirling FK8 2ET
Tel: 0845-277700 Fax: 01786-443078
Web: www.stirling.gov.uk
Chief Executive: Keith Yates

ABOUT THE AREA
Stirling is home to outstanding natural scenery which includes the peaks of Ben Lomond, Ben More and Ben Lui. Situated at the heart of Scotland, between Edinburgh and Glasgow, Stirling straddles the highland boundary fault. South of the fault lies the Forth Valley, the principal town of Stirling and villages such as Strathblane, Drymen, Killearn and Balfron. Loch Lomond is at the western boundary. On a rocky outcrop overlooking the Forth of Firth is Stirling Castle. Callender is a main tourist centre and Stirling's areas of outstanding natural beauty include the Trossachs, home of Rob Roy and made famous by the writings of Sir Walter Scott.

Area: 2,187 sq. km
Population (2001 census): 86,212
Council tax (average Band D) for 2003–4: £1,062.00

Political composition as at 1 May 2003: Lab. 12; C. 10

Scottish and UK Parliamentary Constituencies: Ochil; Stirling

WEST DUNBARTONSHIRE COUNCIL
Garshake Road, Dumbarton G82 3PU
Tel: 01389-737000 Fax: 01389-737700
Web: www.west-dunbarton.gov.uk
Chief Executive: Tim Huntingford

ABOUT THE AREA
West Dunbartonshire is situated on the outskirts of Glasgow and is bounded by Loch Lomond in the north and to the south by the River Clyde. The economy of the area is reliant on tourism and the service industries. Towns in the area include Clydebank, Dumbarton and Alexandria.

Area: 159 sq. km hectares
Population: (2001 census): 93,378
Council tax (average Band D) for 2003–4: £1,070.00

Political composition as at 1 May 2003:
   Lab. 17; SNP 3; Ind. 1; O. 1

Scottish and UK Parliamentary Constituencies:
   Clydebank and Milngavie; Dumbarton

WEST LOTHIAN COUNCIL
West Lothian House, Almondvale Boulevard, Livingston, West Lothian EH54 6QG
Tel: 01506-777000 Fax: 01506-775099
Web: www.wlonline.org.uk
Chief Executive: Alex Linkston

ABOUT THE AREA
West Lothian is located midway between Edinburgh and Glasgow and boasts excellent communication links. The local authority area is flanked by Falkirk and North Lanarkshire to the west and Edinburgh and the Scottish Borders to the east. Attractions in the area include Hopetoun House, the Royal Palace of Linlithgow and a prehistoric burial site at Cairnpapple Hill. The main industry sector is 'high tech' manufacturing.

Area: 427 sq. km
Population (2001 census): 158,714
Council tax (average Band D) for 2003–4: £984.00

Political composition as at 1 May 2003:
   Lab. 18; SNP 12; C. 1; Ind. 1

Scottish and UK Parliamentary Constituencies:
   Linlithgow; Livingston

DEFENCE

Defence is one of the powers reserved to Westminster and the Scottish Parliament has no jurisdiction over it. However, there are a number of important armed forces installations in Scotland. In particular, all the UK's nuclear weaponry is held at the Clyde naval base.

The following gives details of the main commands and forces in Scotland.

SCOTTISH COMMANDS

FLAG OFFICER SCOTLAND, NORTHERN ENGLAND AND NORTHERN IRELAND

HM Naval Base Clyde, Helensburgh, Dunbartonshire G84 8HL Tel: 01436-674321
Flag Officer Scotland, Northern England and Northern Ireland: Rear-Adm. N. H. L. Harris, MBE

GENERAL OFFICER COMMANDING 2ND DIVISION

HQ 2nd Division, Annandale Block, Craigiehall, South Queensferry, West Lothian EH30 9TN
Tel: 0131-336 1761
General Officer Commanding 2nd Division:
  N. R. Parker, CBE
HQ 51 (Scottish) Brigade, Forthside,
Stirling FK7 7RR
HQ 52 Infantry Brigade, The Castle, Edinburgh EH1 2YT

AIR OFFICER SCOTLAND AND NORTHERN IRELAND

RAF Leuchars, St Andrews, Fife KY16 0JX
Tel: 01334-839471
Air Officer Scotland and Northern Ireland:
  Air Cdre S. Bryant

NAVAL BASE

HM NAVAL BASE CLYDE

Helensburgh, Dunbartonshire G84 8HL
Tel: 01436-674321

THE ARMY

ROYAL ARMOURED CORPS

The Royal Scots Dragoon Guards (Carabiniers and Greys)
Home HQ, The Castle, Edinburgh EH1 2YT
Tel: 0131-310 5100
Colonel-in-Chief: HM The Queen

SCOTS GUARDS

Regimental HQ, Wellington Barracks, Birdcage Walk, London SW1E 6HQ Tel: 020-7414 3324
Colonel-in-Chief: HM The Queen

SCOTTISH DIVISION

Divisional Offices, The Castle, Edinburgh EH1 2YT
Tel: 0131-310 5001
HQ Infantry, Imber Road, Warminster, Wilts BA12 0DJ
Tel: 01985-222674
Training Centre, Infantry Training Centre, Vimy Barracks, Catterick, N. Yorks DL9 4HH
Colonel Commandant: Lt.-Gen. Sir Alistair Irwin, KCB, CBE
Divisional Lieutenant-Colonel: Lt.-Col. Sir Andrew Ogilvy-Wedderburn, Bt.

THE ROYAL SCOTS (THE ROYAL REGIMENT)

Regimental HQ, The Castle, Edinburgh EH1 2YT
Tel: 0131-310 5014
Colonel-in-Chief: HRH The Princess Royal, KG, GCVO

THE ROYAL HIGHLAND FUSILIERS

Regimental HQ, 518 Sauchiehall Street, Glasgow G2 3LW Tel: 0141-332 0961/5639

THE KING'S OWN SCOTTISH BORDERERS

Regimental HQ, The Barracks, Berwick-on-Tweed TD15 1DG Tel: 01289-307426
Colonel-in-Chief: HRH Princess Alice, Duchess of Gloucester, GCB, CI, GCVO, GBE

THE BLACK WATCH (ROYAL HIGHLAND REGIMENT)

Regimental HQ, Balhousie Castle, Perth PH1 5HR
Tel: 01738-621281; 0131-310 8530

THE HIGHLANDERS (SEAFORTH, GORDONS AND CAMERONS)

Regimental HQ, Cameron Barracks, Inverness IV2 3XD
Tel: 01463-224380
Outstation, Viewfield Road, Aberdeen AB15 7XH.
Tel: 01224-318174
Colonel-in-Chief: HRH The Prince Philip, Duke of Edinburgh, KG, KT, OM, GBE, AC, QSO, PC

THE ARGYLL AND SUTHERLAND HIGHLANDERS (PRINCESS LOUISE'S)
Regimental HQ, The Castle, Stirling FK8 1EH
Tel: 01786-475165
Colonel-in-Chief: HM The Queen

ARMY PERSONNEL CENTRE
Kentigern House, 65 Brown Street, Glasgow G2 8EX
Tel: 0141-248 7890
Chief Executive: Maj.-Gen. A. P. Grant Peterkin, OBE

MAIN RAF BASES

RAF KINLOSS
Kinloss, Forres, Moray IV36 3UH Tel: 01309-672161

RAF LEUCHARS
St Andrews, Fife KY16 0JX Tel: 01334-839471

RAF LOSSIEMOUTH
Lossiemouth, Moray IV31 6SD Tel: 01343-812121

RESERVE FORCES

ROYAL NAVY RESERVES
There are two Royal Naval Reserve units in Scotland, with a total of 404 members at March 2003.

HMS DALRIADA
Navy Buildings, Eldon Street, Greenock PA16 7SL
Tel: 01475-724481

HMS SCOTIA
c/o HMS Caledonia, Hilton Road, Rosyth,
Fife KY11 2XT Tel: 01383-425794

TERRITORIAL ARMY
There are TA/reservist centres in Aberdeen, Arbroath, Cumbernauld, Cupar, Dumbarton, Dundee, Dunfermline, Dunoon, Elgin, Forfar, Glenrothes, Grangemouth, Invergowrie, Inverness, Keith, Kirkcaldy, Kirkwall, Lerwick, Leuchars, Perth, Peterhead, St Andrews, Stirling, Stornoway and Wick (Highlands), Ayr, Bathgate, Dumfries, East Kilbride, Edinburgh, Galashiels, Glasgow, Irvine, Livingston, Hamilton, Motherwell and Paisley (Lowlands).

HIGHLANDS RESERVE FORCES AND CADETS ASSOCIATION
Seathwood, 365 Perth Road, Dundee DD2 1LX
Tel: 01382-668283
Secretary: Col. J. R. Hensman, OBE

LOWLANDS RESERVE FORCES AND CADETS ASSOCIATION
Lowland House, 60 Avenuepark Street,
Glasgow G20 8LW Tel: 0141-945 4951
Secretary: Brig. C. S. Grant, OBE

ROYAL AUXILIARY AIR FORCE (RAuxAF)

There are three units of the RAuxAF in Scotland, with a total of about 280 members as at April 2001.

NO. 603 (CITY OF EDINBURGH) SQUADRON
25 Learmonth Terrace, Edinburgh EH4 1NZ
Tel: 0131-332 2333

NO. 2622 (HIGHLAND) SQUADRON, RAuxAF REGIMENT
RAF Lossiemouth, Moray IV31 6SD
Tel: 01343-812121

NO. 612 (COUNTY OF ABERDEEN) SQUADRON
RAF Leuchars, St Andrews, Fife KY16 0JY
Tel: 01334-839471

PUBLIC SERVICES SCOTLAND

EDUCATION

Overall responsibility for all aspects of education in Scotland lies with Scottish Ministers acting through the Scottish Executive Education Department and the Enterprise and Lifelong Learning Department (formerly the Scottish Office Education and Industry Department).

The main concerns of the Scottish Executive Education Department are the formulation of policy for pre-school, primary and secondary education, its administration and the maintenance of consistency in educational standards in schools. It is responsible for the broad allocation of resources for school education, the rate and distribution of educational building and the supply, training and superannuation of teachers. The Enterprise and Lifelong Learning Department is concerned with post-16 education, qualifications and student support.

EXPENDITURE

Expenditure on schools by the Scottish Executive was £141 million in 2002–3 and is a proposed £136.8 million in 2003–4. These budgets only represent a fraction of total public sector spending on school education as the main spend is channelled through local authorities who make their own expenditure decisions according to their local situations and needs. Local authority net expenditure on education for 2001–2 was £3,023 million. Provisional net expenditure for 2002–3 was £3,312.7 million.

The major elements of central government expenditure are: grant-aided special schools; curriculum development; special educational needs; school buildings; community learning; initial teacher education and professional development; research; support for higher and further education in universities and colleges (through the funding councils); and student awards and bursaries (through the Students Awards Agency for Scotland).

LOCAL EDUCATION ADMINISTRATION

The education service at present is a national service in which the provision of most school education is locally administered.

The statutory responsibility for delivering school education locally in Scotland rests with the education authorities and the schools under their management. The education authorities are responsible for the construction of buildings, the employment of teachers and other staff, and the provision of equipment and materials. Devolved School Management is in place for all primary, secondary and special schools, which means that they make their own decisions on the majority of school-level expenditure.

Education authorities are required to establish school boards consisting of parents and teachers as well as co-opted members. Boards have a duty to promote contact between parents, the school and the community and are involved, among other things, in the appointment of senior staff.

THE INSPECTORATE

HM Inspectorate of Education (HMIE) has a duty to promote improvements in standards, quality and attainment in Scottish education through independent evaluation. HM Inspectors (HMI) inspect or review and report on education in pre-school centres, nursery, primary, secondary and special schools, further education institutions (under contract to the Scottish Further Education Funding Council), initial teacher education, residential positions for pupils, and the education functions of local authorities. Independent (non-state) schools are also inspected. HMIs work in teams alongside lay members and associate assessors, who are practising teachers seconded for the inspection. The Inspectorate aims to provide a 'Generational Cycle' of school inspection where parents will be given reports as their children move through primary and secondary education. In April 2001 HMIE became an executive agency of the Scottish Executive. In 2002–3 there were 81 HMIs, five Chief Inspectors, and one Senior Chief Inspector in Scotland. All inspectors in Scotland are the responsibility of HMIE (unlike OFSTED in England and Wales which employs registered inspectors via individual contracts).

The inspection of higher education is undertaken through a service level agreement with the Scottish Further Education Funding Council. Reporting of higher education takes place every four years.

SCHOOLS AND PUPILS

Schooling is compulsory for all children between five and 16 years of age but many pupils remain at school after the minimum leaving age. No fees are charged in any publicly maintained school in Scotland.

Throughout the United Kingdom, parents have a right of choice of school for their children, within certain limits, and to appeal if dissatisfied. The policy, known as 'more open enrolment', requires schools to admit children up to the limit of their capacity if there is a demand for places, and to publish their criteria for selection if they are over-subscribed, in which case parents have a right of appeal.

The 'Parents' Charter', available free from education departments, is a booklet which tells parents about the education system. Schools are now required to make available information about themselves – their public examination results, truancy rates and destination of leavers – through the school handbook. Corporal punishment is no longer legal in publicly maintained schools in the United Kingdom.

The number of schools by sector as of September 2001 was:

Publicly maintained schools	2,855
Primary	2,271
Secondary	387
Special	197
Independent schools	155
Total	3,010

Education authority schools (known as public schools) are financed by local government, partly through revenue support grants from central government and partly from local taxation. There are nine grant-aided schools (one primary, one secondary and seven special) which are supervised by boards of managers and receive grants direct from the Scottish Executive Education Department. Under the previous government a category of self-governing schools was created. Such schools opted to be managed entirely by a board of management but remained in the public sector and were funded by direct government grants set to match the resources the school would have received under education authority management. Two schools, Dornoch Academy in Sutherland and St Mary's Primary in Dunblane, were established. Dornoch Academy has since been returned to the education authority framework.

Independent schools charge fees and receive no direct grant, but are subject to inspection and registration.

THE STATE SYSTEM

PRE-SCHOOL EDUCATION
Pre-school education is for children from two to five years and is not compulsory, but the Scottish Executive has set a target of a nursery place for every three-year-old whose parents want it. In 1997 20 per cent of Scottish three-year-olds had a free nursery place but this figure had risen to 68 per cent in 2000 and was 85 per cent for three-year-olds in 2002–3.

Pre-school education takes place in pre-school education centres, play groups, private nurseries or nursery schools (all of which may be provided either by or in partnership with the local authority, or by independent providers) or in nursery classes in primary schools.

Local authorities are responsible for the funding and management of services. All providers of pre-school education are subject to inspection.

LOCAL AUTHORITY PRE-SCHOOL EDUCATION CENTRES AND DAY CARE CENTRES AS OF JANUARY 2002

No. of pre-school and daycare centres	4,117
No. of pupils	188,408
No. of teachers (full-time equivalent)	16,796
Staff to child ratio	11.2

PRIMARY EDUCATION
Primary education begins at five years and is almost always co-educational. The primary school course lasts for seven years (from primary 1 to 7) and pupils transfer to secondary courses at about the age of 12.

Primary schools consist mainly of infant schools for children aged five to seven, junior schools for those aged seven to 12, and combined junior and infant schools for both age groups. Many primary schools provide nursery classes for children under five (see above).

PRIMARY SCHOOLS AS OF SEPTEMBER 2001

No. of schools	2,271
No. of pupils	420,523
No. of teachers (full-time)	22,289
Pupil-teacher ratio	18.9

SECONDARY EDUCATION

Secondary schools are for children aged 11 to 16 and for those who choose to stay on to 18. Most secondary schools in Scotland are co-educational. All pupils in Scottish education authority secondary schools attend schools with a comprehensive intake. Most of these schools provide a full range of courses appropriate to all levels of ability from first to sixth year.

In an attempt to encourage young people from low income households to stay on post-16, the Education Maintenance Allowance Scheme pays pupils up to £40 per week to continue their education and, in some cases, additional payments are received to contribute towards transport costs. In 2001–2 the Scottish Executive allocated £4 million to the Education Maintenance Allowance Scheme and this figure rose to £5 million in 2003–4.

SECONDARY SCHOOLS AS OF SEPTEMBER 2001

No. of schools	387
No. of pupils	316,680
No. of teachers (full-time)	24,552
Pupil-teacher ratio	12.9

SPECIAL EDUCATIONAL NEEDS

Special education is provided for children with special educational needs, usually because they have a disability which either prevents or hinders them from making use of educational facilities of a kind generally provided for children of their age in schools within the area of the local authority concerned.

It is intended that pupils with special educational needs should have access to as much of the curriculum as possible, but there is provision for them to be exempt from it or for it to be modified to suit their capabilities. In such cases the authority has always been required to open a Record of Needs describing the special education appropriate. The number of full-time pupils with Records of Need as of September 2001 was:

Under 5	5–11	12–15	16 and over
63	2,831	2,842	1,133

However, following the Scottish Executive's report *Assessing Our Children's Educational Needs: The Way Forward?* (May 2001) a draft bill has been drawn up (consultation closed in March 2003 with publication due in 2004) to change the emphasis of special needs education. The draft bill proposes a new duty on education authorities to identify and address the additional (i.e. non-educational) support needs of pupils and therefore is much a broader brief than the existing Special Education Needs framework. The draft bill also introduces a statutory Co-ordinated Support Plan (CSP) to replace the Record of Needs. The aim of the CSP is to plan long term and strategically for the achievement of learning objectives and to foster co-ordination across the range of services (multi-agency and multi-disciplinary) to support this. CSPs will be for children who face complex or multiple barriers to learning.

The school placing of children with special educational needs is a matter of agreement between education authorities and parents. Parents have the right to say which school they want their child to attend, and a right of appeal where their wishes are not being met. Legislation places a duty on education authorities, whenever possible, to educate children with special educational needs in ordinary schools (the Scottish Executive's Special Education Needs Inclusion Programme allocated £20 million in both 2002–3 and 2003–4 to assist local authorities with the additional costs of supporting children with special needs in mainstream schools). However, for those who require a different environment or specialised facilities, there are special schools, both grant-aided by central government and independent, and special classes within ordinary schools. Education authorities are required to respond to reasonable requests for attendance to independent special schools and to send children with special educational needs to schools outwith Scotland if appropriate provision is not available within the country.

The Scottish Executive funds Enquire, the national special educational needs information and advice service for parents and children on legislation, policy and provision.

SPECIAL SCHOOLS/UNITS AS OF SEPTEMBER 2001

Maintained schools	
No. of schools	197
No. of pupils (000s)	8.1
No. of teachers (full-time equivalent)	2,029
Pupil-teacher ratio	4.0
Non-maintained schools	
No. of schools	33
No. of pupils (000s)	1.0
No. of teachers (full-time equivalent)	326
Pupil-teacher ratio	3.2

ALTERNATIVE PROVISION

There is no legal obligation on parents anywhere in the United Kingdom to educate their children at school, provided that the local education authority is satisfied that the child is receiving full-time education suited to its age, abilities and aptitudes. The education authority need not be informed that a child is being educated at home unless the child is already registered at a state school, in which case the parents must arrange for the child's name to be removed from the school's register before education at home can begin. Parents educating their children at home are not required to be in possession of a teaching qualification.

Information and support on all aspects of home education can be obtained from Education Otherwise.

INDEPENDENT SCHOOLS

Independent schools receive no grants from public funds. They charge fees, and are owned and managed under special trusts, with profits being used for the benefit of the schools concerned. There is a wide variety of provision, from kindergartens to large day and boarding schools, and from experimental schools to traditional institutions. A number of independent schools have been instituted by religious and ethnic minorities. In 2001 just under 3.9 per cent of pupils in Scotland attended independent schools (around 30,400 pupils), the same proportion as in 1998.

Most independent schools offer a similar range of courses to state schools and enter pupils for the same public examinations. Those in Scotland tend to follow both the Scottish examination system and that which prevails in the rest of the United Kingdom (i.e. GCSE followed by A-levels).

Many Scottish independent schools in membership of the Headmasters' and Headmistresses' Conference, the Governing Bodies Association or the Governing Bodies of Girls' Schools Association are single-sex, but there are also many mixed schools.

Information on independent schools can be obtained from the Independent Schools Information Service or the Scottish Council of Independent Schools.

INDEPENDENT SCHOOLS AS OF SEPTEMBER 2001

No. of schools	155
No. of pupils (000s)	30.4
No. of teachers (full-time 000s)	3.2
Pupil-teacher ratio	9.3

THE CURRICULUM

The content and management of the curriculum in Scotland are not prescribed by statute but are the responsibility of education authorities and individual headteachers. Advice and guidance are provided by the Scottish Executive Education Department and Learning and Teaching Scotland, which also has a developmental role. The Scottish Executive Education Department and Learning and Teaching Scotland have produced guidelines on the structure and balance of the curriculum for the five to 14 age group as well as for each of the curriculum areas. There are also guidelines on assessment across the whole curriculum, on reporting to parents, and on standardised national tests for English language and mathematics at five levels. Testing is carried out on a voluntary basis when the teacher deems it appropriate; most pupils are expected to move from one level to the next at roughly two-year intervals. National testing is largely in place in most primary schools but secondary school participation rates are lower.

The curriculum for 14 to 16-year-olds includes study within each of eight modes: language and communication; mathematical studies and application; scientific studies and application; technological studies and application; social and environmental studies; creative and aesthetic activities; physical education; and religious and moral education. There is a recommended percentage of class time to be devoted to each area over the two years. Provision is made for teaching in Gaelic in Gaelic-speaking areas. There are 59 primary schools currently offering Gaelic-medium education in Scotland (this represents an increase of 112 pupils in the 1987–88 school year to 1,862 in 2001–2).

For 16 to 18-year-olds, National Qualifications (see below), a unified framework of courses and awards, brings together both academic and vocational courses. In these final two years of secondary education (S5 and S6) many pupils continue to study the same subjects they have studied in previous years but the level of study is higher and the number of subjects is reduced to a maximum of five or six. Several subjects will also be offered for the first time, such as additional foreign languages.

The Scottish Qualifications Authority awards the new certificates.

EXAMINATIONS AND QUALIFICATIONS

Scotland has its own system of public examinations, separate from that in England, Wales and Northern Ireland. Scottish Education aims to offer qualifications in as board a range of subjects as possible for as long as possible, with specialisation taking place at a much later point in a pupil's school and university career.

In the four years of compulsory secondary education (S1 to S4), the curriculum is usually divided into two two-year stages (S1 and S2 then S3 and S4). The first two years provide a general education following the national guidelines on five–14–year-olds. The third and fourth years have aspects of specialisation and vocational education for all. At the end of the fourth year of secondary education, at about the age of 16, pupils take examinations for the Scottish Certificate of Education (SCE). These examinations have been designed to suit every level of ability, with assessment against nationally determined standards of performance.

There are two ways to gain the Scottish Certificate of Education. Pupils can undertake to sit Standard Grade exams or they can pursue the Access and Intermediate grades that emphasise course work and continuous assessment. Whichever route is chosen, students have to study English, maths, a modern language, social studies, technological studies, creative and aesthetic arts, physical education and personal and social development. Standard grade exams are graded 1–6 and a grade 7 indicates that the course was completed but without evidence of significant attainment. For most courses there are three separate exam papers set for Credit, General and Foundation levels. Credit levels lead to awards at grades 1–2, General papers lead to awards at grades 3–4 and Foundation levels lead to awards at grades 5–6. Normally pupils will take examinations covering two pairs of grades, either grades 1–4 or grades 3–6. Most candidates take seven or eight Standard Grade examinations. For pupils who undertake to gain the SCE via the Access and Intermediate grades qualifications can be achieved at three levels. Level 1 is equivalent to Standard Grade at the General level. Intermediate courses are in two levels, Level 2 being equivalent to the Standard Grade at Credit level. Level 3 is equivalent to Standard Grade at Foundation level.

Since 1999 a new system of courses and qualifications, called National Qualifications, have been phased in for the post-16 age group. By 2004 National Qualifications will replace Highers, the one-year Certificate of Sixth Year Studies, National Certificate modules, and General Scottish Vocational Qualifications for everyone studying beyond Standard Grade in Scottish schools, and for non-advanced students in further education colleges. Standard Grade and Scottish Vocational Qualifications will remain. National Qualifications are available at five levels: Access, Intermediate 1, Intermediate 2, Higher and Advanced Higher. The Intermediate 1 and 2 levels are equivalent to the old Standard Grade General and Credit levels respectively, while the Advanced Higher qualification is equivalent to the old Certificate of Sixth Year Studies. National Qualifications courses are made up of internally assessed units, with external assessment of the full course determining the grade (A to C). The core skills of communication, numeracy, problem-solving, information technology and working with others are embedded in the National Qualifications. All these qualifications are awarded by the Scottish Qualifications Authority (SQA). In January 2003 the SQA launched the first of a cycle of major reviews of all the National Qualifications subject areas in an effort to reduce the complexity, variety and total volume of assessment in each subject. The outcomes and revisions of the first 12 subjects under review (geography, media studies, computing, information systems, craft and design, physical education, music, art and design, accounting and finance, administration, psychology, and religious, moral and philosophical studies) will be implemented in the 2004–5 school session. The second major cycle of reviews (construction, Gaelic, philosophy and sociology) commenced at the end of 2003 and any revisions deemed necessary will be implemented in 2005–6. At the end of the 2001–2 academic year 32.3 per cent of all school leavers from publicly-funded schools left at the end of compulsory education. The total number of school leavers in 2001–2 was 58,379.

THE INTERNATIONAL BACCALAUREATE

The International Baccalaureate is an internationally recognised two-year pre-university course and examination designed to facilitate the mobility of students and to promote international understanding. Candidates must offer one subject from each of six subject groups, at least three at higher level and the remainder at subsidiary level. Single subjects can be offered, for which a certificate is received. The International Baccalaureate diploma is offered by 43 schools and colleges in the United Kingdom, of which one is in Scotland (the International School of Aberdeen).

RECORDS OF ACHIEVEMENT

The Scottish Qualification Certificate replaced the National Record of Achievement from the academic year 1999–2000. It is issued by the Scottish Qualifications Authority and records all qualifications achieved at all levels. The school report card gives parents information on their child's progress in school.

TEACHERS

All teachers in publicly maintained schools must be registered with the General Teaching Council for Scotland. They are registered provisionally for a two-year probationary period, which can be extended if necessary. Only graduates are accepted as entrants to the profession; primary school teachers undertake either a four-year vocational degree course or a one-year postgraduate course, while teachers of academic subjects in secondary schools undertake the latter. Most initial teacher training is classroom-based. Colleges of education provide both in-service and pre-service training for teachers which is subject to inspection by HM Inspectorate of Education. The colleges are funded by the Scottish Higher Education Funding Council, which also sets intake levels to teacher education courses.

The Scottish Qualification for Headship is aimed at aspiring headteachers and is both a development programme and a qualification.

The General Teaching Council advises Scottish Ministers on teacher supply and the professional suitability of all teacher training courses. It is also the body responsible for disciplinary procedures in cases of professional misconduct.

TEACHERS IN PUBLICLY MAINTAINED SCHOOLS AS OF SEPTEMBER 2001
(full-time equivalent)

	Total	Male	Female
Primary			
Headteacher	2,238	469	1,769
Depute headteacher	992	85	908
Assistant headteacher	640	53	587
Senior teacher	3,087	222	2,864
Unpromoted teacher	15,332	741	14,592
Secondary			
Headteacher	382	333	49
Depute headteacher	386	287	99
Assistant headteacher	1,098	697	401
Principal teacher	7,071	4,048	3,023
Assistant principal teacher	2,970	1,202	1,769
Senior teacher	1,653	658	995
Unpromoted teacher	10,992	3,791	7,201

SALARIES

An agreement between teachers' organisations, employers and the Scottish Executive in January 2001 gave teachers a 21.5 per cent pay increase spread over three years and reduced the number of points in the pay scale to six (from a previous seven). The entry point on the pay scale depends on type of qualification, and additional allowances are payable under certain circumstances. Salaries for headteachers vary depending on various factors including the type and size of school and therefore do not appear on the same scale.

SALARIES

Scalepoint	from 1 Jan. 2003	from 1 Aug. 2003
0	£17,226	£18,000
1	£18,885	£21,588
2	£19,713	£22,875
3	£21,996	£24,174
4	£23,244	£25,578
5	£24,594	£27,198
6	£26,151	£28,707
7	£27,603	N/A
Headteacher	£36,414-£67,449	£36,414-£67,449

FURTHER EDUCATION

Further education covers all provision to people aged over 16. Responsibility for further education lies with the Scottish Executive under the Minister for Enterprise and Lifelong Learning. The Executive also liaises with the Scottish Further Education Funding Council to administer further education funding and to ensure that colleges play a full part in carrying forward Scottish Ministers' policy objectives for further education.

There are 46 further education colleges serving 514,877 students (2002 figure). Self-governing incorporated colleges, run by their own boards of management, account for 42 colleges. The boards include the principal, staff and student representatives among their members; at least half of whom must have experience of commerce, industry or professional practice. Two colleges, on Orkney and Shetland, are under Islands Council control, and two others, Sàbhal Mor Ostaig (the Gaelic college on Skye) and Newbattle Abbey College, are managed by trustees. Government grants to colleges of further education totalled £429 million in 2003–4 and are a proposed £466 million in 2004–5.

The Scottish Qualifications Authority (SQA) is the statutory awarding body for qualifications in the national education and training system in Scotland. It is both the main awarding body for qualifications for work including Scottish Vocational Qualifications (SVQs) and also their accrediting body. The SQA is by statute required to clearly separate its awarding and accrediting functions.

In further education in Scotland there are three main qualification families: National Qualifications; Higher National Qualifications (HNC and HND); and SVQs. In addition to Standard Grade qualifications, the new National Qualifications are available at five levels: Access, Intermediate 1, Intermediate 2, Higher and Advanced Higher.

Another feature of the new qualifications system is the Scottish Group Award (SGA). SGAs indicate that a learner has achieved success at particular levels of study in a range of courses or units and has a core skills profile that is complete and at a level appropriate to the SGA. SGAs are built up unit by unit and are opportunities for credit transfer from other qualifications (such as Standard Grades or SVQs), providing an additional option for learners, especially adult returners to education, training or employment.

Advanced-level courses offered by further education colleges and other institutions lead to the award of HNC and HND and, in some colleges, to degree level. HNCs and HNDs are long-established advanced level vocational qualifications covering a diverse and growing range of employment sectors.

SVQs are competence-based qualifications intended to guarantee a person's ability to do a particular job. They are suitable for workplace delivery since they are designed to national occupational standards of competence set by national training organisations. There are SVQs for almost every job and they are available at five levels; Level 1 consolidates foundation skills and basic work activities; Level 2 applies greater knowledge to a broad range of skills and responsibilities; Level 3 is apprenticeship-based (as either a craftsman or a technician); Level 4 is for managerial or specialist work; and Level 5 is aimed at professional or senior management. SVQs have mutual recognition with the National Vocational Qualifications available in the rest of the United Kingdom.

In the academic year 2001–2 there were 45,020 full-time students and 344,824 part-time students on courses of further education in further education colleges. In 2001–2 at the 42 incorporated colleges of further education there were 4,931 full-time teaching staff (comprising 4,818 permanent and 113 temporary) and 9,483 part-time teaching staff (comprising 1,459 permanent and 8,024 temporary). Salaries are determined at individual college level.

COURSE INFORMATION

Applications for further education courses are generally made directly to the colleges concerned. Information on further education courses in the UK and addresses of colleges can be found in the *Directory of Further Education* published annually by the Careers Research and Advisory Centre.

HIGHER EDUCATION

The term 'higher education' is used to describe education above Higher and Advanced Higher grade, A-level and their equivalent, which is provided in universities, colleges of higher education and some further education colleges.

The Further and Higher Education (Scotland) Act 1992 removed the distinction between higher education provided by the universities and that provided by the former central institutions and other institutions, allowing all higher education institutions which satisfy the necessary criteria to award their own taught course and research degrees and to adopt the title of university. All the central institutions, the art colleges and some colleges of higher education have since adopted the title of university. The change of name does not affect the legal constitution of the institutions.

All higher education institutions are funded by the Scottish Higher Education Funding Council. The funding allocation planned for higher education in 2003–4 was £698 million (£676 million in 2000–1).

The number of students in higher education in Scotland in 2001–2 was:

Full-time	Scottish	Other UK	Overseas	Total
Postgraduate	10,066	2,504	7,538	20,108
first degree	77,821	20,301	8,672	106,794
sub-degree	13,772	507	1,529	15,808
Part-time				
postgraduate	16,128	2,921	12,843	31,892
first degree	10,224	541	1,363	12,128
sub-degree	20,804	449	555	21,808
Total students	148,815	27,223	32,500	208,538

In the 2001–2 academic year, there were 208,538 students attending higher education courses in higher education institutes. Women made up 56 per cent of these students and 32 per cent (67,724) of all students were under 21 years of age. In 2002, 50.4 per cent of young Scots entered higher education either in Scotland or elsewhere in the United Kingdom – the first time the figure has passed 50 per cent (the highest country percentage in the UK). This trend looks set to continue as applications for 2003 were up by another 2.7 per cent (double the UK average). In 2001–2 there were 15,099 Scottish domiciled students registered with the Open University, 5,836 of whom were new entrants.

In 2001–2 students on degree courses were distributed among the subject groups as follows: business administration (39,043); multi-disciplinary studies (27,709); subjects allied to medicine (27,520); social studies (17,435); education[1] (14,825); engineering and technology (14,404); biological sciences (12,351); maths and computing (11,829); physical sciences (6,602); languages (7,187); medicine and dentistry (6,223); architecture (5,745); creative arts (6,378); humanities (5,675); agriculture (2,683); and mass communication (2,929).

[1] The education total includes students studying on teacher education courses.

UNIVERSITIES AND COLLEGES

The Scottish Higher Education Funding Council (SHEFC) funds 20 institutions of higher education, including 15 universities. Responsibility for universities in Scotland rests with Scottish Ministers. Advice to the Government on matters relating to the universities is provided by the SHEFC. The SHEFC receives a block grant from central government which it allocates to the universities and colleges.

The universities each have their own system of internal government, but most are run by two main bodies: the senate, which deals primarily with academic issues and consists of members elected from within the university; and the council, which is the supreme body and is responsible for all appointments and promotions, and bidding for and allocation of financial resources. At least half the members of the council are drawn from outwith the university. Joint committees of senate and council are common.

The institutions of higher education other than universities are managed by independent governing bodies which include representatives of industrial, commercial, professional and educational interests.

Each body appoints its own academic staff on its own conditions. The salary structure in the 'pre-1992' universities is in line with that in the rest of the United Kingdom.

The salary scales for staff in the 'post-1992' universities and colleges of higher education in Scotland are as follows:

	Until July 2003
Head of Department	£47,631–£53,761
Senior lecturer	£30,223–£43,968
Lecturer	£18,362–£36,626

Although universities and colleges are expected to look to a wider range of funding sources than before, and to generate additional revenue in collaboration with industry, they are still largely financed, directly or indirectly, from government resources.

COURSES

In the United Kingdom all universities, including the Open University, and some colleges award their own degrees and other qualifications and can act as awarding and validating bodies for neighbouring colleges which are not yet accredited.

Higher education courses last full-time for at least four weeks or, if part-time, involve more than 60 hours of instruction. Facilities exist for full-time and part-time study, day release, sandwich or block release. Most of the courses outwith the universities have a vocational orientation and a substantial number are sandwich courses.

Higher education courses comprise:

– first degree and postgraduate (including research)
– Diploma in Higher Education (Dip.HE), a two-year diploma usually intended to serve as a stepping-stone to a degree course or other further study
– Higher National Diploma (HND), awarded after two years of full-time or three years of sandwich-course or part-time study
– Higher National Certificate (HNC), awarded after two years part-time study
– preparation for professional examinations
– in-service training of teachers

In some Scottish universities the title of Master is sometimes used for a first degree in arts subjects; otherwise undergraduate courses lead to the title of Bachelor. Most undergraduate degree courses at universities and colleges of higher education take four years for Honours and three for the broad-based Ordinary degree, peculiar to the Scottish system. Professional courses in subjects such as medicine, dentistry and veterinary science take longer. Post-experience short courses are also forming an increasing part of higher education provision.

Details of courses on offer and of predicted entry requirements for the following year's intake are provided in *University and College Entrance: Official Guide,* published annually by the Universities and Colleges Admissions Service (UCAS). It includes degree, Dip.HE and HND courses at all universities (excluding the Open University) and most colleges of higher education.

Postgraduate studies vary in length, with taught courses which lead to certificates, diplomas or master's degrees usually taking less time than research degrees which lead to doctorates. Details of taught postgraduate courses and research degree opportunities can be found in the *Directory of Graduate Studies,* published annually for the Careers Research and Advisory Centre (CRAC).

ADMISSIONS

For admission to a degree, Dip.HE or HND, potential students apply through a central clearing house. All universities and most colleges providing higher education courses in the United Kingdom (except the Open University, which conducts its own admissions) are members of the Universities and Colleges Admission Service (UCAS).

Most applications for admission as a postgraduate student are made to individual institutions but there are two clearing houses of relevance. Applications for postgraduate teacher training courses are made through the Graduate Teacher Training Registry. For social work the Social Work Admissions System operates.

Details of initial teacher training courses in Scotland can be obtained from colleges of education and those universities offering such courses, and from Universities Scotland (formerly COSHEP, the Committee of Scottish Higher Education Principals).

FEES

Since September 1998, new entrants to undergraduate courses at institutions in the United Kingdom have been liable for an annual contribution to their fees (currently £1,100 a year in England but from September 2006 this figure is proposed to rise to £3,000 a year, payable after graduation), depending on their own level of income and that of their spouse or parents. In August 2000 the student liability for tuition fees was abolished for all eligible Scottish-domiciled and EU students studying on full-time higher education courses at Scottish institutions (the Student Awards Agency for Scotland pays the first £1,100 of the tuition fees and any extra payment required is met by the government, paid directly to the university or college). This move was a result of the Cubie Report (1999), which recommended that tuition fees be replaced by a Scottish Graduate Endowment Scheme whereby students (both Scottish and EU) are required to pay £2,000 (towards support for future generations of students) when their earnings reach £10,000 (which they become liable for the first April after graduation). Students from the rest of the United Kingdom must pay fees but the

tuition costs of the fourth year of a four-year degree course at a Scottish institution will be met by central government. Scottish students studying outside Scotland in England, Northern Ireland or Wales (in 2002 only around 6,000 or 5 per cent of Scottish students), have to remain under the fee system that applies wherever they study.

For postgraduate students on non loan-bearing courses, the maximum tuition fee to be reimbursed through the awards system in 2003–4 was £2,940.

STUDENT SUPPORT

Support for students on designated courses domiciled in Scotland is administered by the Student Awards Agency for Scotland (SAAS), an executive agency of the Department for Enterprise and Lifelong Learning. Designated courses are those full-time or sandwich courses leading to a degree, Dip.HE, HND, HNC, the initial teacher-training qualification, or other qualifications specifically designated as being comparable to a first degree. The schemes administered by SAAS include the Students' Allowances Scheme, the Postgraduate Students' Allowances Scheme, the Scottish Studentship Scheme, the Nursing and Midwifery Bursary Scheme and also the application process for student loans. SAAS also provides resources to the Student Loans Company, which pays student loans. Support for those students eligible for it includes the payment of loans, bursaries or grants. SAAS should be consulted for detailed information about eligibility for support and designated courses.

Students can apply to the Students Awards Agency for Scotland for a student loan of up to £3,600 a year if they live in the parental home during term time, and of £4,415 if living away from home. These amounts are made up of a Young Students' Bursary of £2,050 (for students whose parents' income is below £10,000), £510 maximum additional loan, and £1,040 or £1,855 maximum student loan, depending on where the student chooses to live during term time (2003 figures). Students may also be eligible for a loan for additional weeks (for courses over 30 weeks and three days), for payment of tuition fees (automatic for all Scottish domiciled and EU students) up to a maximum of £1,100, (this is means-tested for those studying outwith Scotland), and non-repayable supplementary grants for students who, for example, are disabled or have dependants. The student loan accrues interest linked to inflation and repayments begin from the April after graduation at 9 per cent of income exceeding £10,000 a year. Students starting their course in 2001–2 or

2002–3 can benefit from the introduction of a non-repayable Young Students' Bursary of up to a maximum of £2,050 a year for students from low-income families (of under £10,240 a year) or £1,263 (where the family income is £15,000 a year), recipients of which may also be entitled to an Additional Loan of £500 for a family income below £15,000, and the Mature Students' Bursary, which is run by individual universities and colleges who can decide to make payments to eligible students.

Scottish-domiciled students studying a full-time course of higher education at a UK institution outside Scotland are liable to contribute up to £1,100 towards the cost of tuition fees but the actual amount of contribution will depend on personal and, if appropriate, parental or spousal income. The Student Awards Agency for Scotland will pay any balance in tuition fees up to £1,100. Living cost support is provided through a loan, which is partly income–assessed. Students entering education in 2002-03 may also be entitled to the Young Students' Outside Scotland Bursary of up to a maximum of £510 a year for a family income below £15,360 a year, £70 a year for a family income of £18,000 and zero thereafter. Loans available for Scottish-domiciled students studying at a UK institution outside Scotland in 2003 were:

Living in	Students starting in 2003
College/lodgings in London area	£5,325
College/lodgings outside London area	£4,415
Parental home	£3,600

Additional (income-assessed) allowances are available if, for example, the course requires a period of study abroad (in 2003, for courses that last 30 weeks: £5,670 for Denmark, Hong Kong, Japan, Switzerland and Taiwan; £4,770 for Austria, Belgium, Finland, France, Germany, Iceland, Indonesia, Israel, Luxembourg, The Netherlands, Norway, Rep. of Ireland, Rep. of Korea, countries of the former Soviet Union and Sweden; £3,905 for all other countries). Students may also be eligible to apply for a student loan of up to £2,310. Repayment of the student loan, which is index-linked, normally begins the April after the course ends and comprises a fixed number of instalments unless income falls under 85 per cent of the national average, in which case application may be made for deferment. Means-tested non-repayable supplementary grants are available to eligible students with dependants or who are disabled.

Hardship funds are distributed by SAAS to universities and colleges and administered by the further and higher education institutions themselves. They are available to students whose access to, or continued participation in, education might otherwise be inhibited by financial considerations or where real financial difficulties are faced.

POSTGRADUATE AWARDS

Postgraduate students, with the exception of students on loan-bearing diploma courses such as teacher training, are not eligible to apply for student loans, but can apply for grants for postgraduate study. These are of two types, both discretionary: 30-week bursaries, which are means-tested and apply to certain vocational and diploma courses; and studentship awards, which depend on the class of first degree, especially for research degrees, are not means-tested, and cover students undertaking research degrees or taught master's degrees.

Postgraduate funding is provided by the Enterprise and Lifelong Learning Department through the Students Awards Agency for Scotland, the Scottish Executive Rural Affairs Department, and government research councils. An increasing number of scholarships are also available from research charities, endowments, and particular industries or companies.

The Scottish rates for 30-week bursaries for professional and vocational training in 2003–4 are:

Living in	
College/lodgings in London area	£4,125
College/lodgings outside London area	£3,255
Parental home	£2,460

Additional grants are available for school meals, lone parents, childcare, mature students, travelling expenses, disabled students and students who have to maintain two homes. Career Development loans of between £300 and £8,000 are also available. Scottish Studentship Awards are available for full-time advanced postgraduate study in Arts and Humanities subjects at universities mainly in the UK. Each year universities receive a list of courses covered by the scheme and awards are highly competitive. Studentships are generally for one-year courses. Major Scottish studentships can be held for up to three years. Studentship Awards for 2000–1 for a 44-week year were generally £6,620.

ADULT AND CONTINUING EDUCATION

The term 'adult education' covers a broad spectrum of educational activities ranging from non-vocational courses of general interest, through the acquiring of special vocational skills needed in industry or commerce, to degree-level study at the Open University.

The Scottish Executive Enterprise and Lifelong Learning Department funds adult education, including that provided by the universities and the Workers' Educational Association, at vocational further education colleges (46 in 2003) and evening centres. In addition, it provides grants to a number of voluntary organisations.

Courses are provided by the education authorities, further and higher education colleges, universities, residential colleges, the BBC, independent television and local radio stations, and several voluntary bodies.

Although the lengths of courses vary, most courses are part-time. Newbattle Abbey College, the only long-term residential adult education college in Scotland, offers one-year full-time diploma courses in European studies and Scottish studies which normally provide a university entrance qualification. Some colleges and centres offer short-term residential courses, lasting from a few days to a few weeks, in a wide range of subjects. Education authorities sponsor many of the colleges, while others are sponsored by universities or voluntary organisations.

Adult education bursaries for students at the long-term residential colleges of adult education are the responsibility of the colleges themselves. In Scotland the awards are funded by central government and administered by the education authorities. Information is available from the Scottish Executive Enterprise and Lifelong Learning Department.

The involvement of universities in adult education and continuing education has diversified considerably and is supported by a variety of administrative structures ranging from dedicated departments to a devolved approach. Membership of the Universities Association for Continuing Education is open to any university or university college in the United Kingdom. It promotes university continuing education, facilitates the interchange of information, and supports research and development work in continuing education.

Of the voluntary bodies, the biggest is the Workers' Educational Association (WEA), a charity which operates throughout the UK, offering approximately 5,000 courses via 650 voluntary centres, reaching about 150,000 adult students annually. As well as the Scottish Executive, LEAs make grants towards provision of adult education by WEA Scotland.

Advice on adult and community education, and promotion thereof, is provided by Community Learning Scotland.

LOCAL EDUCATION AUTHORITIES

ABERDEEN
Summerhill Education Centre, Stronsay Drive, Aberdeen, AB15 6JA. Tel: 01224-522000
Web: www.aberdeencity.gov.uk
Director of Education, John Stodger

ABERDEENSHIRE
Woodhill House, Westburn Road, Aberdeen, AB16 5GJ. Tel: 01224-664630
Fax: 01224-664615 Web: ww.aberdeenshire.gov.uk
Director of Education, H. Vernal

ANGUS
County Buildings, Market Street, Forfar, DD8 3WE.
Tel: 01307-461460 Web: www.angus.gov.uk
Director of Education, Jim Anderson

ARGYLL AND BUTE
Argyll House, Alexandra Parade, Dunoon, PA23 8AJ.
Tel: 01369-704000 Fax: 01639-702944
Web: www.argyll-bute.gov.uk
Strategic Director, Douglas Hendery

CITY OF EDINBURGH
Wellington Court, 10 Waterloo Place, Edinburgh, EH1 3EG. Tel: 0131-469 3000 Fax: 0131-469 3320
Email: joan.smiles@educ.edin.gov.uk
Director of Education, R. Jobson

CLACKMANNANSHIRE
Lime Tree House, Castle Street, Alloa, FK10 1EX.
Tel: 01259-452374 Fax: 01259-452440
Email: rchampion@clacks.gov.uk
Web: www.clacksweb.org.uk
Director of Education, D. Jones

DUMFRIES AND GALLOWAY
30 Edinburgh Road, Dumfries, DG1 1NW.
Tel: 01387-260427 Fax: 01387-260453
Director of Education & Community Services,
F. Sanderson

DUNDEE
Floor 8, Tayside House, Crichton Street, Dundee, DD1 3RJ. Tel: 01382-433111 Fax: 01382-433080
Email: education@dundeecity.gov.uk
Web: www.dundeecity.gov.uk
Director of Education, Mrs A. Wilson

EAST AYRSHIRE
Council Headquarters, London Road, Kilmarnock, KA3 7BU. Tel: 01563-576017 Fax: 01563-576210
Email: education@east-ayrshire.gov.uk
Web: www.east-ayrshire.gov.uk
Director, J. Mulgrew

EAST DUNBARTONSHIRE
Boclair House, 100 Milngavie Road, Bearsden, Glasgow,
G61 2TQ. Tel: 0141-578 8000 Fax: 0141-578 8653
Web: www.eastdunbarton.gov.uk
Strategic Director – Community, Ms S. Bruce

EAST LOTHIAN
John Muir House, Haddington, EH41 3HA.
Tel: 01620-827562 Fax: 01620-827291
Email: ablackie@eastlothian.gov.uk
Web: www.eastlothian.gov.uk
Director of Education & Community Services,
A. Blackie

EAST RENFREWSHIRE
Council Offices, Eastwood Park, Rouken Glen Road,
Giffnock, G46 6UG.
Tel: 0141-577 3479 Fax: 0141-577 3405
Email: john.wilson@eastrenfrewshire.gov.uk
Web: www.eastrenfrewshire.gov.uk
Director, John Wilson

EILEAN SIAR/WESTERN ISLES
Council Offices, Sandwick Road, Stornoway,
Isle of Lewis, HS1 2BW.
Tel: 01851-709530 Fax: 01851-705796
Email: murdo-macleod.el@cnesiar.gov.uk
Web: www.cne-siar.gov.uk
Director, Murdo Macleod

FALKIRK
McLaren House, Marchmont Avenue, Polmont, Falkirk,
FK2 0NZ. Tel: 01324-506600 Fax: 01324-506601
Email: director.educ@falkirk.gov.uk
Web: www.falkirk.gov.uk
Director, Dr G. Young

FIFE
Fife House, North Street, Glenrothes, KY7 5LT.
Tel: 01592-414141 Web: www.fife.gov.uk
Head of Education, Roger Stewart

GLASGOW CITY
Nye Bevan House, 20 India Street, Glasgow, G2 4PF.
Tel: 0141-287 6898 Fax: 0141-287 6786
Email: education@glasgow.gov.uk
Web: www.glasgow.gov.uk
Director, Ronnie O'Connor

HIGHLAND
Council Buildings, Glenurquhart Road, Inverness,
IV3 5NX. Tel: 01463-702802 Fax: 01463-702828
Email: ecs@highland.gov.uk
Web: www.highland.gov.uk
Director, B. Robertson

INVERCLYDE
105 Dalrymple Street, Greenock, PA15 1HT.
Tel: 01475-712824 Fax: 01475-712875
Email: ann.steele@inverclyde.gov.uk
Director, B. McLeary

MIDLOTHIAN
Fairfield House, 8 Lothian Road, Dalkeith, EH22 3ZG.
Tel: 0131-270 7500 Fax: 0131-271 3751
Email: education.services@midlothian.gov.uk
Web: www.midlothian.gov.uk
Director: D. MacKay

MORAY
Council Offices, High Street, Elgin, IV30 1BX.
Tel: 01343-563001 Web: www.moray.gov.uk
Director of Educational Services, Donald Duncan

NORTH AYRSHIRE
Cunninghame House, Irvine, KA12 8EE.
Tel: 01294-324400 Fax: 01294-324444
Email: education@north-aryshire.gov.uk
Web: www.north-ayrshire.gov.uk
Corporate Director, J. Travers

NORTH LANARKSHIRE
Municipal Buildings, Kildonan Street, Coatbridge,
ML5 3BT. Tel: 01236-812336
Web: www.northlan.gov.uk
Director of Education, Michael O'Neill

ORKNEY ISLANDS
Council Offices, Kirkwall, Orkney, KW15 1NY.
Tel: 01856-873535 Web: www.orkney.gov.uk
Director of Education, Leslie Manson

PERTH AND KINROSS
Pullar House, 35 Kinnoull Street, Perth, PH1 5GD.
Tel: 01738-476200 Fax: 01738-476210
Email: aathompson@pkc.gov.uk
Director, George Waddell

RENFREWSHIRE
Council Headquarters, South Building, Cotton Street,
Paisley, PA1 1LE.
Tel: 0141-842 5601 Fax: 0141-842 5655
Web: www.renfrewshire.gov.uk
Director, Ms S. Rae

SCOTTISH BORDERS
Council Headquarters, Newtown St Boswells, Melrose,
Roxburghshire, TD6 0SA.
Tel: 01835-824000 Fax: 01835-825091
Email: enquiries@scottishborders.gov.uk
Web: www.scottishborders.gov.uk
Director, G. Rodger

SHETLAND
Hayfield House, Hayfield Lane, Lerwick, Shetland,
ZE1 0QD. Tel: 01595-744000 Fax: 01595-692810
Web: www.shetland.gov.uk
Head of Education, Alex Jamieson

SOUTH AYRSHIRE
County Buildings, Wellington Square, Ayr, KA7 1DR.
Tel: 01292-612201
Web: www.south-ayrshire.gov.uk
Director of Education, M. McCabe

SOUTH LANARKSHIRE
Council Headquarters, Almada Street, Hamilton,
ML3 0AE. Tel: 01698-454545 Fax: 01698-454465
Email: education@southlanarkshire.gov.uk
Web: www.southlanarkshire.gov.uk
Executive Director, Ms M. Allan

STIRLING
Viewforth, Stirling, FK8 2ET. Tel: 01786-442678
Fax: 01786-442782 Email: jeyesg@stirling.gov.uk
Web: www.stirling.gov.uk
Director, Gordon Jeyes

WEST DUNBARTONSHIRE
Council Offices, Garshake Road, Dunbarton, G82 3PU.
Tel: 01389-737301 Fax: 01389-737348
Email: karen.docherty@west-dunbarton.gov.uk
Director, I. McMurdo

WEST LOTHIAN
Lindsay House, South Bridge Street, Bathgate,
EH48 1TS. Tel: 01506-776000 Fax: 01506-776378
Email: education@westlothian.gov.uk
Director of Education and Cultural Services, vacant

COLLEGES

ABERDEEN COLLEGE
Gallowgate Centre, Gallowgate, Aberdeen,
Aberdeenshire, AB25 1BN. Tel: 01224-612000
Fax: 01224-612001 Email: enquiry@abcol.ac.uk
Web: www.abcol.ac.uk

ANGUS COLLEGE
Keptie Road, Arbroath, Angus, DD11 3EA.
Tel: 01241-432600 Fax: 01241-876169
Web: www.angus.ac.uk

ANNIESLAND COLLEGE
Hatfield Campus, Hatfield Drive, Glasgow, G12 0YE.
Tel: 0141-357 3969 Fax: 0141-357 6557
Web: www.anniesland.ac.uk

AYR COLLEGE
Dam Park, Ayr, Ayrshire, KA8 0EU. Tel: 01292-265184
Fax: 01292-263889 Web: www.ayrcoll.ac.uk

BANFF AND BUCHAN COLLEGE OF FE
Henderson Road, Fraserburgh, Aberdeenshire,
AB43 9GA. Tel: 01346-586100 Fax: 01346-515370
Web: www.banff-buchan.ac.uk

BARONY COLLEGE
Parkgate, Dumfries, DG1 3NE. Tel: 01387-860251
Fax: 01387-860395
Web: www.barony.ac.uk

BELL COLLEGE OF TECHNOLOGY
Crichton University Campus, Dudgeon House,
Bankend Road, Dumfries, DG1 4SG.
Tel: 01387-702100 Fax: 01387-702111
Email: inform@bell.ac.uk
Web: www.bell.ac.uk
Principal, Dr K. MacCallum

BELL COLLEGE OF TECHNOLOGY
Hamilton Campus, Almada Street, Hamilton, ML3 0JB.
Tel: 01698-283100 Fax: 01698-282131
Email: inform@bell.ac.uk Web: www.bell.ac.uk
Principal, Dr K. MacCallum

BORDERS COLLEGE
Melrose Road, Galashiels, Borders, TD1 2AF.
Tel: 08700-505152 Fax: 01896-758179
Web: www.borderscollege.ac.uk

CARDONALD COLLEGE
690 Mosspark Drive, Glasgow, G52 3AY.
Tel: 0141-272 3333 Fax: 0141-272 3444
Web: www.cardonald.ac.uk

CLACKMANNAN COLLEGE OF FURTHER EDUCATION
Branshill Road, Alloa, Clackmannanshire, FK10 3BT.
Tel: 01259-215121 Web: www.clacks.ac.uk

CLYDEBANK COLLEGE
Kilbowie Road, Clydebank, Dumbarton and
Clydebank, G81 2AA. Web: www.clydebank.ac.uk

COATBRIDGE COLLEGE
Kildonan Street, Coatbridge, North Lanarkshire,
ML5 3LS. Tel: 01236-422316 Fax: 01236-440266
Web: www.coatbridge.ac.uk

DUMFRIES AND GALLOWAY COLLEGE
Heathhall, Dumfries, Dumfries and Galloway,
DG1 3QZ. Tel: 01387-261261 Fax: 01387-250006
Email: info@dumgal.ac.uk
Web: www.dumgal.ac.uk
Principal: T. Jakimciw

DUNDEE COLLEGE
Melrose Campus, Melrose Terrace, Dundee, DD3 7QX.
Web: www.dundeecoll.ac.uk

EDINBURGH'S TELFORD COLLEGE
Crewe Toll, Edinburgh, EH4 2NZ. Tel: 0131-332 2491
Fax: 0131-343 1218 Web: www.www.ed-coll.ac.uk

ELMWOOD COLLEGE
Cupar, Fife, KY15 4JB. Tel: 01334-658800
Web: www.elmwood.ac.uk

FALKIRK
Grangemouth Road, Falkirk, FK2 9AD.
Tel: 01324-403000 Fax: 01324-403222
Web: www.falkirkcollege.ac.uk

FIFE COLLEGE OF FURTHER AND HIGHER EDUCATION
St Brycedale Avenue, Kirkcaldy, Fife, KY1 1EX.
Tel: 0800-413280 Fax: 01592-640225
Email: enquiries@fife.ac.uk
Web: www.fife.ac.uk
Principal: Mrs J. S. R. Johnston

GLASGOW SCHOOL OF ART
167 Renfrew Street, Glasgow, G3 6RQ.
Tel: 0141-353 4500 Fax: 0141-353 4528
Web: www.gsa.ac.uk
Director: Prof. S. Reid

GLASGOW COLLEGE OF BUILDING AND PRINTING
60 North Hanover Street, Glasgow, G1 2BP.
Tel: 0141-332 9969 Fax: 0141-332 5170
Web: www.gcbp.ac.uk

GLASGOW COLLEGE OF FOOD AND TECHNOLOGY
230 Cathedral Street, Glasgow, G1 2TG.
Tel: 0141-552 3751 Fax: 0141-553 2370
Web: www.gcft.ac.uk

GLASGOW COLLEGE OF NAUTICAL STUDIES
21 Thistle Street, Glasgow, G5 9XB.
Web: www.glasgow-nautical.ac.uk

GLENROTHES COLLEGE
Stenton Road, Glenrothes, Fife, KY6 2RA.
Tel: 01592-772233 Fax: 01592-568182
Web: www.glenrothes-college.ac.uk

INVERNESS COLLEGE
3 Longman Road, Longman South, Inverness,
Highland, IV1 1SA. Web: www.inverness.uhi.ac.uk

JAMES WATT COLLEGE
Finnart Street, Greenock, Inverclyde, PA16 8HF.
Tel: 01475-724433 Fax: 01475-888079
Web: www.jameswatt.ac.uk

JOHN WHEATLEY COLLEGE
Call John Wheatley College Advice Centre
on 0141 778 2426

SHETTLESTON CAMPUS
Shettleston Campus, 1346 Shettleston Road, Glasgow,
G32 9AT. Tel: 0141-778 2426
Web: www.jwheatley.ac.uk

KILMARNOCK COLLEGE
Holehouse Road, Kilmarnock, Ayrshire, KA3 7AT.
Tel: 01563-523501 Web: www.kilmarnock.ac.uk

LAUDER COLLEGE
Halbeath, Dunfermline, Fife. Tel: 01383-845010
Fax: 01383-845001 Web: www.lauder.ac.uk

LEWS CASTLE COLLEGE
Stornoway, Isle of Lewis, HS2 0XR. Tel: 01851-770000
Fax: 01851-770001 Email: aofficele@lews.uhi.ac.uk
Web: www.lews.uhi.ac.uk
Principal: D. R. Green

MORAY COLLEGE
Moray Street, Elgin, Moray, IV30 1JJ.
Tel: 01343-576000 Fax: 01343-576001
Web: www.moray.ac.uk
Principal: Dr James Logan

NEWBATTLE ABBEY COLLEGE
Newbattle Road, Dalkeith, Midlothian, EH22 3LL.
Tel: 0131-663 1921 Fax: 0131-654 0598
Email: office@newbattleabbeycollege.ac.uk
Web: www.newbattleabbeycollege.co.uk
Principal: Ann Southwood

THE NORTH HIGHLAND COLLEGE
Ormlie Road, Thurso, Caithness, KW14 7EE.
Tel: 01847-889000 Fax: 01847-889001
Email: NorthHighlandCollege@groupwise.uhi.ac.uk
Web: www.nhcscotland.com
Principal: H. Logan

OATRIDGE AGRICULTURAL COLLEGE
Ecclesmachan, Broxburn, West Lothian, EH52 6NH.
Tel: 01506-854387 Web: www.oatridge.ac.uk

ORKNEY COLLEGE
Kirkwall, Orkney, KW15 1LX. Tel: 01856-569000
Fax: 01856-569001
Email: orkney.college@orkney.uhi.ac.uk
Principal: Dr William Ross

PERTH COLLEGE
Crieff Road, Perth, Perth and Kinross, PH1 2NX.
Tel: 01738 877000 Web: www.perth.ac.uk

QUEEN MARGARET UNIVERSITY COLLEGE
Corstorphine Campus, Clerwood Terrace, Edinburgh,
EH12 8TS. Tel: 0131-317 3000 Fax: 0131-317 3256
Email: marketing@qmuc.ac.uk
Web: www.qmuc.ac.uk
Principal: Prof. Joan Stringer, CBE

REID KERR COLLEGE
Renfrew Road, Paisley, Renfrewshire, PA3 4DR.
Web: www.reidkerr.ac.uk

ROYAL SCOTTISH ACADEMY OF MUSIC AND DRAMA
100 Renfrew Street, Glasgow, G2 3DB.
Tel: 0141-332 4101 Fax: 0141-332 8901
Email: registry@rsamd.ac.uk
Web: www.rsamd.ac.uk
Principal: John Wallace

SABHAL MÓR OSTAIG
Teangue, Isle of Skye, IV44 8RQ. Tel: 01471-888000
Fax: 01471-888001 Email: oifis@smo.uhi.ac.uk
Web: www.smo.uhi.ac.uk
College Director: Dr. Norman N. Gillies

SAC (SCOTTISH AGRICULTURAL COLLEGE)
Central Office, Kings Buildings, West Mains Road,
Edinburgh, EH9 3JG.
Tel: 0131-535 4185 Fax: 0131-535 4332
Email: information@ed.sac.ac.uk
Web: www.sac.ac.uk
Principal and Chief Executive:
   Prof. W. A. C. McKelvey

SOUTH LANARKSHIRE COLLEGE
Cambuslang Campus, Hamilton Road, Cambuslang,
Lanarkshire, G72 7NY. Tel: 0141-641 6600
Fax: 0141-641 4296
Web: www.south-lanarkshire-college.ac.uk

STEVENSON COLLEGE OF FURTHER EDUCATION
Bankhead Avenue, Edinburgh, EH11 4DE.
Tel: 0131-535 4700 Fax: 0131-535 4708
Web: www.stevenson.ac.uk

STOW COLLEGE
43 Shamrock Street, Glasgow, Strathclyde, G4 0NG.

UHI MILLENNIUM INSTITUTE
Caledonia House, 63 Academy Street, Inverness,
Highland, IV1 1LU. Tel: 01463-279000
Fax: 01463-279001 Email: EO@uhi.ac.uk
Web: www.uhi.ac.uk
Principal: Prof. Robert Cormack

WEST LOTHIAN COLLEGE
Almondvale Crescent, Livingston, West Lothian,
EH54 7EP. Tel: 01506-418181
Web: www.west-lothian.ac.uk

UNIVERSITIES

GLASGOW CALEDONIAN UNIVERSITY
70 Cowcaddens Road, Glasgow, G4 0BA.
Tel: 0141-331 3000 Fax: 0141-331 3005
Web: www.gcal.ac.uk
Full time students: 14,000
Principal and Vice-Chancellor: Dr Ian Johnston, CB

HERIOT-WATT UNIVERSITY
Edinburgh, EH14 4AS. Tel: 0131-449 5111
Fax: 0131-449 5153 Email: enquiries@hw.ac.uk
Web: www.hw.ac.uk
Full time students: 6,100
Principal and Vice-Chancellor: Prof. John Archer,
   CBE, FREng, FRSE

NAPIER UNIVERSITY
219 Colinton Road, Edinburgh, EH14 1DJ.
Tel: 0131-444 2266;
Student enquiries: 0500-353570
Fax: 0131-455 6333 Email: info@napier.ac.uk
Web: www.napier.ac.uk
Full time students: 12,000
Vice-Chancellor: Prof. Joan Stringer

ROBERT GORDON UNIVERSITY
Schoolhill, Aberdeen, AB10 1FR. Tel: 01224-262 000
Fax: 01224-263 000 Web: www.rgu.ac.uk
Full time students: 8,230
Vice-Chancellor: Prof. William S. Stevely

UNIVERSITY OF ABERDEEN
King's College, Aberdeen, AB24 3FX.
Tel: 01224-272 000 Fax: 01224-272 086
Email: pubrel@aboh.ac.uk
Web: www.abdn.ac.uk
Full time students: 10,788
Vice-Chancellor: Prof. Duncan C. Rice

UNIVERSITY OF ABERTAY DUNDEE
Bell Street, Dundee DD1 1HG. Tel: 01382-308 000
Fax: 01382-308 877 Email: sro@abertay.ac.uk
Web: www.abertay.ac.uk
Full-time students: 3,814
Vice-Chancellor: Prof. Bernard King

UNIVERSITY OF DUNDEE
Dundee, DD1 4HN. Tel: 01382-344 000
Fax: 01382-201 604 Email: secretary@dundee.ac.uk
Web: www.dundee.ac.uk
Full-time students: 12,000
Vice-Chancellor: Sir Alan Langlands

UNIVERSITY OF EDINBURGH
Old College, South Bridge, Edinburgh, EH8 9YL.
Tel: 0131-650 1000 Fax: 0131-650 2147
Email: communications.office@ed.ac.uk
Web: www.ed.ac.uk
Full-time students: 20,483
Principal and Vice-Chancellor: Prof. Tim O'Shea

UNIVERSITY OF GLASGOW
University Avenue, Glasgow, G12 8QQ.
Tel: 0141-339 8855 Fax: 0141-330 4808
Email: publicity.services@gla.ac.uk
Web: www.gla.ac.uk
Full-time students: 19,180
Vice-Chancellor: Sir Muir Russell, KCB, FRSE

UNIVERSITY OF PAISLEY
Paisley, PA1 2BE. Tel: 0141-848 3000
Web: www.paisley.ac.uk
Full-time students: 6,454
Principal and Vice-Chancellor: Prof. John Macklin

UNIVERSITY OF ST ANDREWS
College Gate, North Street, St Andrews, Fife KY16 9AJ.
Tel: 01334-476161 Fax: 01334-462570
Web: www.st-and.ac.uk
Full-time students: 6,401
Vice-Chancellor: Brian Andrew Lang, Ph.D.

UNIVERSITY OF STIRLING
Stirling, FK9 4LA. Tel: 01786-473171
Fax: 01786-463000 Email: c+d@stir.ac.uk
Web: www.stir.ac.uk
Full time students: 6,800
Principal and Vice-Chancellor: vacant

UNIVERSITY OF STRATHCLYDE
John Anderson Campus, Glasgow, G1 1XQ.
Tel: 0141-552 4400 Fax: 0141-552 0775
Web: www.strath.ac.uk
Full time students: 15,000
Vice-Chancellor: Prof. Andrew Hamnett

OTHER EDUCATION BODIES

CAREERS RESEARCH AND ADVISORY CENTRE
Sheraton House, Castle Park, Cambridge, CB3 0AX.
Tel: 01223-460277 Fax: 01223-311708
Email: enquiries@crac.org.uk Web: www.crac.org.uk
Chief Executive, D.Thomas

EDUCATION OTHERWISE
PO Box 7420, London, N9 9SG. Tel: 0870-730 0074
Web: www.education-otherwise.org

GENERAL TEACHING COUNCIL FOR SCOTLAND
Clerwood House, 96 Clermiston Road, Edinburgh,
EH12 6UT. Tel: 0131-314 6000 Fax: 0131-314 6001
Email: gtcs@gtcs.org.uk Web: www.gtcs.org.uk
Chief Executive/Registrar, Matthew M. MacIver

GRADUATE TEACHER TRAINING REGISTRY
Rosehill, New Barn Lane, Cheltenham, Glos, GL52 3LZ.
Tel: 0870-112 2205 Fax: 01242-544962
Web: www.gttr.ac.uk
Registrar, Mrs J. Pearce

INTERNATIONAL BACCALAUREATE ORGANISATION
Peterson House, Malthouse Avenue, Cardiff,
CF23 8GL. Tel: 029-2054 7777 Fax: 029-2054 7778
Email: ibca@ibo.org Web: www.ibo.org

LEARNING AND TEACHING SCOTLAND
Gardyne Road, Dundee, DD5 1NY. Tel: 01382-443600
Fax: 01382-443645 Email: enquiries@ltscotland.com
Web: www.ltscotland.com
Chief Executive, Michael Baughan

LEARNING AND TEACHING SCOTLAND
74 Victoria Crescent Road, Glasgow, G12 9JN.
Tel: 0141-337 5000 Fax: 0141-337 5050
Email: enquiries@ltscotland.com
Web: www.ltscotland.com
Chief Executive, Michael Baughan

THE OPEN UNIVERSITY IN SCOTLAND
10 Drumsheugh Gardens, Edinburgh, EH3 7QJ.
Tel: 0131-225 2889 Fax: 0131-220 6730
Email: r11@open.ac.uk Web: www.open.ac.uk
Scottish Director, Peter Syme

SCOTTISH FURTHER EDUCATION FUNDING COUNCIL
Donaldson House, 97 Haymarket Terrace, Edinburgh, EH12 5HD. Tel: 0131-313 6500 Fax: 0131-313 6501
Email: info@sfc.ac.uk Web: www.sfefc.ac.uk
Chief Executive, Roger McClure

SCOTTISH HIGHER EDUCATION FUNDING COUNCIL
Donaldson House, 97 Haymarket Terrace, Edinburgh, EH12 5HD. Tel: 0131-313 6500 Fax: 0131-313 6501
Email: info@sfc.ac.uk Web: www.shefc.ac.uk
Chief Executive, Roger McClure

SCOTTISH COUNCIL OF INDEPENDENT SCHOOLS
21 Melville Street, Edinburgh, EH3 7PE.
Tel: 0131-220 2106 Fax: 0131-225 8594
Email: admin@scis.org.uk Web: www.scis.org.uk
Director, Mrs J. Sischy

SCOTTISH QUALIFICATIONS AUTHORITY
Hanover House, 24 Douglas Street, Glasgow, G2 7NQ.
Tel: 0845-279 100 Fax: 0141-242 2244
Email: helpdesk@sqa.org.uk Web: www.sqa.org.uk
Chief Executive, David Fraser

SOCIAL WORK ADMISSIONS SYSTEM
Rosehill, New Barn Lane, Cheltenham, Glos, GL52 3LZ.
Tel: 0870-112 2207 Fax: 01242-544962
Admissions Officer, Mrs J. Pearce

STUDENT AWARDS AGENCY FOR SCOTLAND
Gyleview House, 3 Redheughs Rigg, Edinburgh, EH12 9HH. Tel: 0845-111 1777 Fax: 0131-244 5887
Email: saas.geu@scotland.gov.uk
Web: www.saas.gov.uk
Chief Executive, David Stephen

STUDENT LOANS COMPANY LTD
100 Bothwell Street, Glasgow, G2 7DJ.
Tel: 0141-306 2000 Fax: 0141-306 2006
Web: www.slc.co.uk

UNIVERSITIES AND COLLEGES ADMISSIONS SERVICE
Rosehill, New Barn Lane, Cheltenham, Glos, GL52 3LZ.
Tel: 01242-222444 Fax: 01242-544959
Email: info@ucas.ac.uk Web: www.ucas.com
Chief Executive, Tony Higgins

UNIVERSITIES ASSOCIATION FOR CONTINUING EDUCATION
University of Cambridge Board for Continuing Education, Madingley Hall, Cambridge, CB3 8AQ.
Tel: 01954-280279 Fax: 01954-280200
Email: mer1000@cam.ac.uk Web: www.uace.org.uk
Secretary, Dr Michael Richardson

UNIVERSITIES SCOTLAND
53 Hanover Street, Edinburgh, EH2 2PJ.
Tel: 0131-226 1111 Fax: 0131-226 1100
Email: d.caldwell@universities-scotland.ac.uk
Web: www.universities-scotland.ac.uk
Director, D. Caldwell

WEA SCOTLAND (WORKERS' EDUCATIONAL ASSOCIATION)
Riddle's Court, 322 Lawnmarket, Edinburgh, EH1 2PG.
Tel: 0131-226 3456 Fax: 0131-220 0306
Email: hq@weascotland.org.uk
Web: www.weascotland.org.uk
Scottish Secretary, Joyce Connor

THE ENERGY INDUSTRIES

The main primary sources of energy in Britain are oil, natural gas, coal, nuclear power and hydroelectricity. The main secondary sources (i.e. sources derived from the primary sources) are electricity, coke and smokeless fuels, and petroleum products.

Policy and legislation on the generation and supply of electricity from coal, oil and gas, and nuclear fuels, remains a matter reserved to the UK Government after devolution.

INDIGENOUS PRODUCTION OF PRIMARY FUELS (UK)

Million tonnes of oil equivalent

	2001	2002
Coal	21.7	20.5
Petroleum	127.8	127
Natural gas	106.8	104.1
Primary electricity		
Nuclear	20.77	20.32
Natural flow hydro	0.43	0.49
Total	277.6	272.5

INLAND ENERGY CONSUMPTION BY PRIMARY FUEL (UK)

Million tonnes of oil equivalent, seasonally adjusted and temperature corrected

	2001	2002
Coal	43.6	39.9
Petroleum	77.3	75.4
Natural gas	96.6	97.9
Primary electricity	22.15	21.59
Nuclear	20.82	20.34
Natural flow hydro	0.44	0.53
Net imports	0.89	0.72
Total	239.6	234.8

UK TRADE IN FUELS AND RELATED MATERIALS 2001p

	Quantity*	Value†
Imports		
Coal and other solid fuel	24.8	1,196
Crude oil	42.7	5,039
Petroleum products	22.3	3,622
Natural gas	2.3	181
Electricity	1.2	165
Total	93.0	10,202
Exports		
Coal and other solid fuel	0.7	74
Crude oil	91.4	10,177
Petroleum products	28.4	4,867
Natural gas	8.0	577
Electricity	–	5
Total	128.4	15,699

p provisional
* Million tonnes of oil equivalent
† £ million
‡ Adjusted to exclude estimated costs of insurance, freight, etc.

Source: Department of Trade and Industry (Crown copyright)

OIL AND GAS

The United Kingdom Continental Shelf (UKCS) is treated as a separate region in official economic statistics. Calculation of Scottish oil and gas outputs and revenue deriving from the UKCS is difficult and controversial. Recent research from Aberdeen University suggests that there is considerable variation from year to year in the Scottish proportion of UK tax revenue from oil and gas, depending on a number of factors, including division of the North Sea, relative expense of developing the North Sea fields, and oil price fluctuations. According to this analysis, Scotland's share of UK oil and gas revenue was 80 per cent in 1996–7, but the drop in oil prices over the last two years has reduced this to an estimated 75 per cent for 1997 and 66 per cent for 1998 (calendar years). The following table shows the total value of UKCS oil and gas production and investment in 2000–1.

	2000 £m	2001 £m
Total income	25,486	24,493
Operating costs	4,360	4,334
Gross operating surplus	21,020	20,110

OIL

Until the 1960s Britain imported almost all its oil supplies. In 1969 oil was discovered in the Arbroath field of the UKCS. The first oilfield to be brought into production was the Argyll field in 1975, and since the mid-1970s Britain has been a major producer of crude oil.

There are estimated to be reserves of 2,015 million tonnes of oil in the UKCS. Royalties are payable on fields approved before April 1982 and petroleum revenue tax is levied on fields approved between 1975 and March 1993.

Licences for exploration and production are granted to companies by the Department of Trade and Industry; the leading British oil companies are British Petroleum (BP) and Shell Transport and Trading. At the end of 2002, 1,062 Seaward Production Licences had been awarded and there were 154 offshore oilfields in production. In 2002 there were nine oil refineries and three smaller refining units processing crude and process oils.

There are four oil terminals and two refineries in Scotland.

OIL COMING ASHORE AT SCOTTISH TERMINALS 2000*
Million tonnes

Sullom Voe	28.4
Flotta, Orkney Islands	8.5
Forties Leeward	34.7
Nigg Bay, Cromarty Firth	0.2
Total	71.8

* Figures do not reflect total oil production in Scotland, because some oil produced is exported directly by tanker from offshore fields

CAPACITY OF SCOTTISH REFINERIES 2000–1
Million tonnes per annum

Grangemouth	9.4
Dundee	0.7
Total	10.1

GAS
In 1965 gas was discovered in the North Sea off the South Yorkshire coast, in the West Sole field, which became the first gasfield in production in 1967.

By the end of 1998 there were 80 offshore gasfields producing natural gas and associated gases (mainly methane). There are estimated to be 1,795,000 million cubic metres of recoverable gas reserves in existing discoveries.

There is one gas terminal in Scotland, at St Fergus, Aberdeenshire, which houses five pipelines, capable of receiving more than 40 per cent of all gas coming from the North Sea.

GAS BROUGHT ASHORE AT SCOTTISH TERMINALS 2000*
Million cubic m

Far North Liquids and Associated Gas System (FLAGS) and Fulmar	10,300
Frig and Miller Lines	10,600
Scottish Area Gas Evacuation (SAGE)	16,800
Total	37,700

* Figures do not reflect total Scottish gas production, because some gas produced is piped to terminals in England
Source: Department of Trade and Industry

Since 1986 the British gas industry, nationalised in 1949, has been progressively privatised. Competition was introduced into the industrial gas market from 1986, and supply of gas to the domestic market was opened to companies other than British Gas from April 1996 onwards. Gas companies can now also sell electricity to their customers. Similarly, electricity companies can also offer gas.

The Office of Gas and Electricity Markets is the regulatory body for the gas and electricity industries in Britain.

NATURAL GAS PRODUCTION AND SUPPLY (UK)
GWh

	2000	2001
Gross gas production	1,258,549	1,230,851
Exports	−146,342	−138,234
Imports	26,032	30,463

‡ Figures differ from gas available mainly because of stock changes

NATURAL GAS CONSUMPTION
GWh

	2000	2001
Electricity generators	312,545	311,645
Iron and steel industry	21,331	20,972
Other industries	171,016	177,329
Domestic	358,066	379,163
Public administration, commerce and agriculture	119,897	111,506
Total	982,855	1,000,615

Source: Department of Trade and Industry and DUKES Digest of UK Energy Statistics

VALUE OF UK OIL AND GAS PRODUCTION AND INVESTMENT
£ million

	2000	2001
Total income	25,518	24,493
Operating costs	4,359	4,335
Gross trading profits*	20,906	20,079
Percentage contribution to GVA	2.6	2.4
Exploration expenditure	348	411
Other Capital investment	2,748	3,509
Percentage contribution to industrial investment	12	15

* Net of stock appreciation

ELECTRICITY

In Scotland three electricity companies were formed under the Electricity Act 1989; Scottish Power plc and Scottish Hydro-Electric plc which are responsible for generation, transmission, distribution and supply; and Scottish Nuclear Ltd. Scottish Power and Scottish Hydro-Electric were floated on the stock market in 1991 (the latter merged with Southern Electric in 1998 to become Scottish and Southern Energy plc. Scottish Nuclear was incorporated into British Energy in 1995.

Scottish Power operates six power stations in Scotland. Scottish and Southern Energy operates a large power station at Peterhead, 56 hydro stations in Scotland (with two new hydro stations beginning construction in 2003) and a diesel back-up station in Lerwick, Shetland. It also operates a number of power stations in England and Wales. The Electricity Association is the electricity industry's main trade association, providing representational and professional services for the electricity companies. EA Technology Ltd provides distribution and utilisation research and development and technology transfer. The Office of Gas and Electricity Markets is the regulatory body for the electricity industry.

ELECTRICITY PRODUCTION IN SCOTLAND 2001–2
GWh

Electricity generated in Scotland	Consumed in Scotland	Transferred to England & Wales	Transferred from England & Wales
40,970	32,466	8,608	104

NUCLEAR POWER

About half of Scotland's electricity is generated by nuclear power stations. British Energy plc owns two Advanced Gas-Cooled Reactors (AGRs) at Torness and Hunterston B. British Nuclear Fuels Ltd (BNFL) owns the Magnox nuclear reactor at Chapelcross.

BNFL, which is in public ownership, provides reprocessing, waste management and effluent treatment services. The UK Atomic Energy Authority is responsible for the decommissioning of nuclear reactors and other nuclear facilities used in research and development. UK Nirex, which is owned by the nuclear generating companies and the Government, is responsible for the disposal of intermediate and some low-level nuclear waste. The Nuclear Installations Inspectorate of the Health and Safety Executive is the nuclear industry's regulator.

In 1998 the closure was announced of the nuclear reactor at Dounreay, which started up in 1956.

NUCLEAR POWER GENERATION 2001–2
Terawatt hours

Hunterston B	9.9
Torness	8.3
Total by British Energy	18.2
Chapelcross	1.04

ELECTRICITY COMPANIES

BNFL
Hinton House, Risley, Warrington, Cheshire WA3 6AS
Tel: 01925-832000 Fax: 01925-822711
Web: www.bnfl.com
Chief Executive: Norman Askew

BRITISH ENERGY PLC
3 Redwood Crescent, Peel Park, East Kilbride G74 5PR
Tel: 01355-262000 Web: www.british-energy.com
Chief Executive: Mike Alexander

EA TECHNOLOGY
Capenhurst Technology Park, Capenhurst, Chester
CH1 6ES Tel: 0151-339 4181 Fax: 0151-347 2404
Email: marketing@eatechnology.com
Web: www.eatechnology.com

ELECTRICITY ASSOCIATION LTD
30 Millbank, London SW1P 4RD
Tel: 020-7963 5700 Fax: 020-7963 5959
Email: enquiries@electricity.org.uk
Web: www.electricity.org.uk
Chief Executive: Jenny Kirkpatrick

SCOTTISH AND SOUTHERN ENERGY PLC
Inveralmond House, 200 Dunkeld Road,
Perth PH1 3AQ
Tel: 01738-456000 Web: www.scottish-southern.co.uk

SCOTTISH POWER
Spean Street, Glasgow G44 4BE
Tel: 0845-270 6543 Web: www.scottishpower.plc.uk

RENEWABLE ENERGY SOURCES

Renewable sources of energy principally include biomass, hydro, wind, waste and solar. Scotland has the greatest potential for renewable energy of any country in Europe – having 25 per cent of the wind resources, the best climate in the European Union for solar heating of buildings (thanks to the summer season's many daylight hours), and the Pentland Firth is rich in wave energy.

The UK Government intends to achieve 10 per cent of the UK's electricity needs from renewables by 2010 in order to meet the UK's international commitments to future reductions on greenhouse gases. Following the establishment of the Scottish Parliament, decisions on renewable sources of energy have been devolved.

The Scottish Executive announced in 2002 that it would work towards a figure of 18 per cent of Scotland's electricity coming from renewable energy sources by 2010 with this figure rising to 30 per cent by 2020. Scotland's existing hydro schemes and wind farms currently account for 13 per cent of Scotland's electricity (2003).

Since 1994 the Scottish Renewables Obligation Orders (SROs) have been the Government's principal mechanism for developing renewable energy sources. They were similar to the Non-Fossil Fuel Obligation Renewables Orders in England and Wales. SRO Orders required ScottishPower and Scottish and Southern Energy to buy specified amounts of electricity from specified renewable sources. Of the 109 projects awarded contracts between 1994 and March 1999 (for about 340 MW), ten projects (27 MW capacity) were commissioned. Six of these were wind schemes (combined capacity c.21.5 MW), two were hydro schemes (combined capacity c.1.5 MW), and two were waste-to-energy schemes (combined capacity c.3.8 MW).

On 1 April 2002 SROs became the Renewables Obligation Scotland (ROS), the equivalent of the Renewables Obligation in England and Wales. These obligations require energy suppliers to supply a specified and growing proportion of their electricity sales from a choice of eligible renewable sources or to demonstrate that another supplier that they have contracted has done so. Suppliers who fail to meet the Obligation will be required to pay a buy-out price per kWh shortfall. The ROS is an integral part of the Scottish Executive's Scottish Climate Change Programme and applies to all electricity suppliers in Scotland. The RSO will remain in force until 2027.

No specific mechanism to support the development of solar energy projects exists, but the Department of Trade and Industry currently funds initiatives and channels European grant funding. There are several small-scale (less than 1 MW) solar projects in operation in various places around Scotland.

Wind farms are fast becoming a feature of the Scottish landscape with 35 wind farms currently approved in Scotland and over 200 applications pending in the approvals process (2003 figure). The Scottish Executive has estimated that in order to meet the 2010 target of 18 per cent renewable energy, 10 per cent can come from existing hydro sources and the remaining 8 per cent will have to come from wind power. On this basis Scotland will need around 700-800 wind turbines to meet the 2010 target. There are currently around 200 wind turbines in Scotland at five locations:

Dun Law, Borders. Built by Renewable Energy Systems and is operated by Scottish Power. It generates enough power for 12,000 homes a year.

Beinn Ghlas, Oban. Became operational in 1999 and is owned and operated by National Wind Power. This farm has a total capacity of 8.4MW.

Novar, Evanton, Highlands. Operational since 1997, owned and operated by National Wind Power. A total capacity of 17.0MW.

Windy Standard, Galloway. In operation since 1996, owned and developed by National Wind Power and Fred Olsen Ltd. A total capacity of 21.6MW.

Hagshaw Hill, Lanarkshire. Operational since 1995 and gives a total capacity of 15.6MW. Developed by TriGen and operated by Windfarm Management Services on behalf of Scottish Power.

Together these wind farms generate 63 megawatts of electricity, enough to meet the average electricity needs of over 39,500 homes.

The massive expansion in wind power in Scotland has led Vestas, the leading Danish wind turbine manufacturer, to build a factory in Campbelltown, Kintyre, bringing 150 jobs to the area. Hostility to wind farms in other areas of the UK have led to Scotland becoming the primary destination for future wind farms – with 80 per cent of the British Wind Energy Association's proposed wind farms being targeted for Scotland. Wind farms are backed by the Scottish Executive and many members of the public but are also opposed in several locations. Plans for a wind farm on the Isle of Skye are opposed by residents who fear that the island's natural beauty will be spoiled with the building of a £330 million farm of 28 turbines. The firm involved in the Skye proposals, Amec, is also planning a 250 turbine plant on the island of Lewis that will occupy 28,000 acres. The Scottish Renewables Forum (SRF) works to facilitate links between industry, the Government and various non-governmental organisations with a view to promoting the use of sustainable energy sources in Scotland. The SRF provides a unified representation of the interests of its members, encompassing utilities, corporate bodies as well as a range of smaller companies and environmental organisations.

SCOTTISH RENEWABLES FORUM
1st Floor, The Beacon, 176 St Vincent Street, Glasgow G2 5SG. Tel: 0141-249 6705 Fax: 0141-249 6704 Web: www.scottishrenewables.com

THE WATER INDUSTRY

Overall responsibility for national water policy in Scotland rested with the Secretary of State for Scotland until July 1999, when responsibility was devolved to the Scottish Executive. Most aspects of water policy are currently administered through the Scottish Executive Rural Affairs Department.

Water supply and sewerage services were the responsibility of the local authorities and the Central Scotland Water Development Board until 1996. In April 1996 the provision of water and sewerage services became the responsibility of three public water authorities, covering the north, east and west of Scotland, under the terms of the Local Government etc. (Scotland) Act 1994. In April 2002 the three water authorities merged to form Scottish Water, thus becoming the second-largest government-owned corporation after the Royal Mail, the fourth largest water service provider in the UK and the 12th biggest business in Scotland. At the time of its creation Scottish Water employed 5,200 people but it has since shed 500 jobs and £30 million from its budget. It has plans to cut a further 900 jobs between 2002 and 2006 in a bid to cut its annual £320 million operating budget by a further £100 million over the next two-three years to bring it into line with the water industry's efficiency in England and Wales. In the company's first year it opened major new water treatment works at Inverclyde, St Andrews and Eyemouth, began a £1.8bn Capital Investment Programme (planned expenditure for 2002–6), and began laying 500 kilometres of new or refurbished water mains.

The Water Industry Commissioner for Scotland is the economic and customer service regulator of Scottish Water. This office was created by Part II of the 1999 Water Industry Act and was established on 1 November 1999. The Commissioner's duties include advising Scottish ministers on the amount of revenue that Scottish Water requires to fund its investment programme, consideration and approval of the annual charges scheme of Scottish Water, investigation of customer complaints, approval of Scottish Water's Code of Practice, and provision of advice, when requested by Scottish ministers, on a range of matters relating to the impact of Scottish Water on its customers.

The Scottish Executive is currently (2003–4) involved in the consultation process for the Water Services Bill, a proposal for a regulatory framework for public water and sewerage services to safeguard environmental and public health as the industry is opened up to competition. This bill will also prohibit anyone other than Scottish Water from providing domestic customers with water, thus protecting Scottish Water's monopoly.

The Scottish Environment Protection Agency (SEPA) is responsible for promoting the cleanliness of rivers, lochs and coastal waters, and controlling pollution. Scotland has 60 designated bathing waters, and the Scottish Executive is committed to bringing these up to European standards and to improving the quality of rivers, lochs and coastal waters. In May 2002 SEPA began a consultation process on the Water Framework Directive, a Europe-wide programme of water management. The document was a collaborative effort with Scottish Water, Scottish Natural Heritage, Fisheries Research Services, the Environment and Heritage Service of Northern Ireland and the Environment Agency of England and Wales. The document set out the guiding principles for, and implementation of, the Water Framework Directive. At present the results of the consultation are not yet published.

WATER: DEVELOPED RESOURCES IN SCOTLAND 2001–2 (EXTRACT[1])

2001 yield by Water Authority

	North	West	East	Total
Reservoirs and Lochs	325	1,372	1,380	3,077
River intakes	305	19	33	357
Boreholes	46	15	43	104
Springs	13	5	8	26
Total Supply Sources	689	1,411	1,464	3,564

[1] Extract of table. For full table with explanatory notes please see the Scottish Executive website.

Source: The Scottish Executive Water Services Unit, Crown Copyright.

WATER CONSUMPTION 2001–2

Total daily demand	2,408.7
Total potable demand	2,399.1
Unmetered	1,876.4
Metered	522.8
Non-potable[†]	9.6

† 'Non-potable' supplied for industrial purposes. Metered supplies in general relate to commercial and industrial use and unmetered to domestic use

Source: The Scottish Executive Water Services Unit, Crown Copyright

METHODS OF CHARGING

Household water and waste water charges are issued on behalf of Scottish Water by local councils. The charges are calculated according to the Council Tax property bands and are applicable to unmetered properties connected to the public water supply and public sewerage system. All household charges are regulated by the Water Industry Commissioned for Scotland. Scottish Water is required to harmonise charges across the country by April 2005 to ensure a fair and cost-effective charging structure.

WATER COMPANIES

SCOTTISH WATER
PO Box 8855, Edinburgh EH10 6YQ
Tel: 0845-601 8855 Web: www.scottishwater.co.uk
Chief Executive: Dr Jon Hargreaves

WATER INDUSTRY COMMISSIONER FOR SCOTLAND
Ochil House, Springkerse Business Park, Stirling
FK7 7XE Tel: 01786-430200 Fax 01786-462018
Email: enquiries@watercommissioner.co.uk
Web: www.watercommissioner.co.uk
Commissioner: A. Sutherland

WATER UK
1 Queen Anne's Gate, London, SW1H 9BT
Tel: 020-7344 1827
Email: info@water.org.uk
Web: www.water.org.uk
Chief Executive: Ms P. Taylor

THE FIRE SERVICE

The Scottish Executive Justice Department has overall responsibility for fire services, including the provision of training at the Scottish Fire Services College.

Each local council in Scotland is the fire authority for its area. There are six joint fire boards, comprising groups of council areas which have delegated their fire authority responsibilities to the boards. The remaining two councils, Dumfries and Galloway and Fife, each act as the fire authority for their whole council area. Membership of the joint boards comprises elected members of each of the constituent councils. The fire authorities are responsible for setting a budget, making an establishment scheme (which details fire brigade, fire stations and equipment), the 'mutual assistance' scheme for handling major incidents, and hearing disciplinary cases or appeals. Subject to the approval of the Scottish Ministers, fire authorities appoint a Firemaster, who is responsible for brigade operations.

Fire brigades are financed by local government, with the exception of some central services (e.g. the Scottish Fire Services College) which are financed by the Scottish Executive. Joint fire boards set their budgets and requisition the necessary finance from their constituent councils. The two councils that directly administer their fire brigades set budgets as for their other services. The Scottish Executive pays an annual civil defence grant to each joint board for its role in emergency planning.

HM Inspectorate of Fire Services for Scotland carries out inspections of fire brigades in order to improve the efficiency, effectiveness and standards of the fire service. HM Chief Inspector of Fire Services publishes an annual report and other reports. The interests of fire authorities and members of the fire brigades are considered by the Scottish Central Fire Brigades Advisory Council, which advises Scottish Ministers on matters affecting the service.

FIRE BOARDS

The Dumfries and Galloway council area and the Fife council area do not have joint boards as a single authority covers the whole of the fire brigade area. The chairman/convenor of the authority for these two brigades is given with the brigade's details.

CENTRAL SCOTLAND FIRE BOARD
Municipal Buildings, Falkirk, FK1 5RS
Tel: 01324-506070 Fax: 01324-506071

GRAMPIAN FIRE BOARD
Fire Brigade HQ
19 North Anderson Drive, Aberdeen AB15 6DW
Tel: 01224-696666 Fax: 01224-692224

HIGHLAND AND ISLANDS FIRE BOARD
Council Headquarters, Glenurquhart Road,
Inverness, IV3 5NX
Tel: 01463-702123 Fax: 01463-702182
Email: rhona.moir@highland.gov.uk

LOTHIAN AND BORDERS FIRE BOARD
City Chambers, High Street, Edinburgh, EH1 1YJ
Tel: 0131-529 4278 Fax: 0131-529 7607

STRATHCLYDE FIRE BOARD
Council Offices, Almada Street, Hamilton ML3 0AA
Tel: 01698-454872 Fax: 01698-454407
Email: alan.cuthbertson@southlanarkshire.gov.uk

TAYSIDE FIRE BOARD
2 High Street, Perth PH1 5PH
Tel: 01738-475102 Fax: 01738-475110
Email: j.angus@pkc.gov.uk

FIRE BRIGADES

CENTRAL SCOTLAND FIRE BRIGADE
HQ Main Street, Maddiston, Falkirk, FK2 0LG
Tel: 01324-716996 Fax: 01324-715353
Web: www.fire.org.uk/central
Divisional Officer: Thomas Mann
Divisional Officer: Malcolm Wilson

DUMFRIES AND GALLOWAY FIRE BRIGADE
Brigade HQ, Brooms Road, Dumfries, DG1 2DZ
Tel: 01387-252222 Fax: 01387-260995
Email: fmr@dumgal.gov.uk
Chairman: B. Conchie
Firemaster: L. Ibbotson

FIFE FIRE AND RESCUE SERVICE
HQ Strathore Road, Thornton, Kirkcaldy, KY1 4DF
Tel: 01592-774451 Fax: 01592-630105
Email: barbara.dunn@fife.gov.uk
Firemaster: M. J. Bitcon

GRAMPIAN FIRE BRIGADE
HQ 19 North Anderson Drive, Aberdeen, AB15 6DW
Tel: 01224-696666 Fax: 01224-692224
Email: firemaster@grampianfirebrigade.co.uk
Web: www.grampianfirebrigade.co.uk
Firemaster: J. Williams

HIGHLAND AND ISLANDS FIRE BRIGADE
HQ 16 Harbour Road, Longman West, Inverness,
IV1 1TB Tel: 01463-227000 Fax: 01463-236979
Email: firemaster@highland.fire-uk.org
Web: www.highland.fire-uk.org
Firemaster: B. A. Murray

LOTHIAN AND BORDERS FIRE BRIGADE
HQ Lauriston Place, Edinburgh, EH3 9DE
Tel: 0131-228 2401 Fax: 0131-228 6662
Email: loth00@lothian.fire-uk.org
Web: www.lothian.fire-uk.org

STRATHCLYDE FIRE BRIGADE
HQ Bothwell Road, Hamilton, ML3 0EA
Tel: 01698-300999 Fax: 01698-338444
Web: www.strathclyde.fire-uk.org
Firemaster: J. Ord, QFSM

TAYSIDE FIRE BRIGADE
Headquarters Blackness Road, Dundee DD1 5PA
Tel: 01382-322222 Fax: 01382-200791
Email: brigade@tayside.gov.uk
Web: www.taysidefire.gov.uk
Firemaster: S. Hunter

STAFF ASSOCIATIONS

SCOTTISH CENTRAL FIRE BRIGADES ADVISORY COUNCIL
Scottish Executive Justice Department, Room GW14,
St Andrews's House, Regent Road, Edinburgh,
EH1 3DG Tel: 0131-244 2166 Fax: 0131-244 2819
Email: gordon.west@scotland.gsi.gov.uk
Web: www.scotland.gov.uk
Chairman: J. Hamill
Secretary: G. A. Davidson

THE CHIEF AND ASSISTANT CHIEF FIRE OFFICERS' ASSOCIATION
10–11 Pebble Close, Amington, Tamworth B77 4RD
Tel: 01827-302300 Fax: 01827-302399
Email: info@cacfoa.fire-uk.org.uk
Web: www.fire-uk.org
President: R. Bull, QFSM
General Manager: A.S. Currey

BRIGADE STRENGTHS MARCH 2002

Wholetime uniformed personnel	4,598
Retained (uniformed on call)	2,839
Volunteer (no retainer fee)	1,270
Control room personnel	211
Non-uniformed personnel	827

SCOTLAND'S HEALTH

Public health policy is a devolved power and is now the responsibility of the Scottish Executive.

On 1 April 2003 the Health Education Board for Scotland (HEBS) and the Public Health Institute of Scotland (PHIS) merged to become NHS Health Scotland. This new body has a responsibility to provide health information and advice to the public, health professionals, and other organisations, and to advise the Government on health education needs and strategies.

HEALTH AND HEALTHCARE STATISTICS

HOSPITAL AND PRIMARY CARE SERVICES IN SCOTLAND 2001

Hospital and Primary Care Services

Medical and dental staff	
Full-time	7,250
Part-time	2,010
Nursing and midwifery	
Full-time	33,334
Part-time	29,004
Outpatients	
New cases	2,744
Total attendances	6,382
Doctors on the list	3,756
Average number of patients per doctor	1,409
Dentists on list	1,866
Prescriptions dispensed	65.56 million
Number of sight tests given	877,000

Source: Annual Abstract of Statistics 2003 (Crown Copyright)

NOTIFICATIONS OF INFECTIOUS DISEASES SCOTLAND 2001

Measles	315
Mumps	155
Rubella	234
Whooping cough	106
Scarlet fever	281
Dysentery	85
Food poisoning	8,640
Tyhoid and Paratyphoid fevers	3
Viral hepatitis	1,008
Tuberculosis	469
Malaria	24
Meningococcal infection	256
Erysipelas	39

Source: Annual Abstract of Statistics 2003 (Crown Copyright)

DEATHS IN SCOTLAND, ANALYSED BY CAUSE 2001

Total deaths	57,382
Deaths from natural causes	54,961
Intestinal infectious diseases	65
Respiratory and other tuberculosis	54
Meningococcal infection	12
Viral hepatitis	6
AIDS (HIV)	33
Malignant neoplasm of oesophagus	752
Malignant neoplasm of stomach	678
Malignant neoplasm of colon	1,062
Malignant neoplasm of rectum and anus	405
Malignant neoplasm of pancreas	595
Malignant neoplasm of trachea, bronchus, lung	3,915
Malignant neoplasm of skin	145
Malignant neoplasm of breast	1,150
Malignant neoplasm of cervix	113
Malignant neoplasm of prostate	777
Leukaemia	350
Diabetes Mellitus	695
Alcohol abuse	341
Drug dependence and abuse of drugs	238
Meningitis (including meningococcal)	16
Alzheimer's disease	324
Ischaemic heart disease	11,914
Cerebrovascular disease	6,621
Pneumonia	2,370
Asthma	101
Chronic liver disease	1,061
Diseases of the ureter and kidney	638
Sudden infant death syndrome	32
Accidents	1,350
Suicide and intentional self-harm	609
Homicide and assault	92

Source: Annual Abstract of Statistics 2003 (Crown Copyright)

HIV REPORTS BY TRANSMISSION CATEGORY
(cumulative to December 2000)

Sexual intercourse between men	1,079
Sexual intercourse between men and women	635
Injecting drug use	1,204
Other	227
All transmission categories	3,145

MENTAL ILLNESS HOSPITALS AND PSYCHIATRIC UNITS INPATIENT ADMISSIONS, BY SEX AND MAIN DIAGNOSIS

	Males	Females
All diagnoses	15,860	15,758
Dementia	2,158	3,071
Mental and behavioural disorders due to use of alcohol	2,260	1,108
Mental and behavioural disorders due to use of drugs	689	311
Schizophrenia	2,693	1,277
Mood (affective) disorders	3,416	5,418
Bipolar affective disorder	650	1,006
Depressive episode	2,102	3,377
Recurrent depressive disorder	288	626
Other psychotic disorders	1,073	875
Disorders of childhood	42	11
Neurotic, stress-related and somatotform disorders	775	1,183
Personality disorders	330	581
Mental handicap	32	23
Other conditions	2,032	1,900

Source: Scottish Health Statistics 2000 (Crown Copyright)

SELF REPORTED CIGARETTE SMOKING PREVALENCE, BY AGE AND SEX 1998

Age	Men (%)	Women (%)
16–24	38	33
25–34	39	35
35–44	35	33
45–54	33	34
55–64	32	31
65–74	20	25

Source: Scottish Health Survey 1998

WOMEN SMOKING AT THE START OF PREGNANCY 1999

Age	%
All ages	26.8
Less than 16	34.8
16–19	45.8
20–24	38.7
25–29	26.1
30–34	19.0
35–39	19.0
40–44	17.7
45 and over	11.1

Source: Scottish Health Statistics 2000 (Crown Copyright)

SUMMARY OF ADULTS' DIET 1998

Food type/Consumption frequency	Men (%)	Women (%)
Adds sugar to tea	45	25
Adds sugar to coffee	44	26
Eats chocolate, biscuits, crisps etc once a day or more	54	51
Eats fried food two or more times per week	48	28
Uses butter or margarine	44	39
Uses skimmed or semi-skimmed milk	63	69
Eats cheese two or more times per week	68	59
Eats oil-rich fish less than once a month	34	33
Eats salad or raw vegetables two times per week	45	58
Eats fresh fruit once a day or more	46	59
Eats wholemeal bread	10	16
Eats cooked vegetables five or more time a week	39	44

Source: Scottish Health Statistics 2000 (Crown Copyright)

CHANGES OVER TIME IN ADULTS' DIET 1995–8

Food type/ consumption frequency	Men (%)		Women (%)	
	1995	1998	1995	1999
Drinks soft drinks once a day or more	32	38	22	25
Uses skimmed or semi-skimmed milk	60	64	67	70
Eats wholemeal bread	14	10	21	16
Eats breakfast cereal once	68	69	71	72
Eats pasta, potatoes or rice 5 x per week or more	53	63	59	68
Eats fresh fruit once a day or more	39	45	52	58
Usually or generally adds salt to food	53	49	41	40
Eats cooked green vegetable 5 or more times a week.	40	37	45	44

Source: Scottish Health Statistics 2000 (Crown Copyright)

HEALTH TARGETS FOR SCOTLAND

A White Paper on public health in Scotland, *Towards a Healthier Scotland*, was published in February 1999. This announced initiatives to improve the health of people in Scotland, including prevention and early detection of cancer and coronary heart disease and redressing inequalities in health between richer and poorer communities in Scotland, and set targets to measure the impact of these measures by 2010. In certain fields, targets for 2000 already existed. Targets set for 2010 include:

- reducing by 20 per cent the death rate from all cancers of Scots under 75
- reducing by 50 per cent adult deaths from heart disease
- reducing by 50 per cent the death rate from cerebrovascular disease in Scots under 75
- eliminating dental disease in 60 per cent of five-year-olds
- reducing incidence of smoking by pregnant women from 29 to 20 per cent, and by young people by 20 per cent
- reducing the pregnancy rate among 13–15 year olds by 20 per cent
- reducing alcohol consumption exceeding recommended weekly limits from 33 to 29 per cent for men and from 13 to 11 per cent for women
- increasing the proportion of people taking 30 minutes of moderate exercise five or more times a week to 60 per cent of men and 50 per cent of women

Four 'demonstration projects' announced in the White Paper concentrate on child health, sexual health, cancer and coronary heart disease. These projects are: Starting Well, which promotes health and protection from harm in the period leading up to birth and throughout the first five years of childhood; Healthy Respect, which fosters responsible sexual behaviour on the part of Scotland's young people with emphasis on the avoidance of unwanted teenage pregnancies and sexually transmitted diseases; The Heart of Scotland, which focuses on the prevention of heart disease; and The Cancer Challenge, a screening programme for the early detection of colorectal cancer (to be added to existing screening programmes for breast and cervical cancer) and new measures to combat the cancer-promoting effects of tobacco smoking.

The establishment of a network of Healthy Living Centres promoting best practice in public health was launched on 29 January 1999, with £34.5 million funding over three years from the National Lottery's New Opportunities Fund.

DIET

Government plans to improve the Scottish diet were first outlined in 1991. The *Report on the Scottish Diet* (the James Report) was published in 1993 and, after further consultation, led to the announcement of the Scottish Diet Action Plan. This set targets for healthier eating among people in Scotland by 2005. These targets, incorporated into the *Towards a Healthier Scotland* programme, include:

- increasing average daily intake of non-sugar carbohydrates by 25 per cent through increased consumption of fruit, vegetables, bread (especially wholemeal and brown breads), breakfast cereals, rice, pasta and potato
- reducing average daily intake of fats to no more than 35 per cent, and of saturated fatty acids to no more than 11 per cent, of food energy
- reducing average daily sodium intake (from common salt and other sodium salts such as sodium glutamate) to 100 mm/ol
- reducing children's average daily intake of NME sugars by half to less than 10 per cent of total food energy
- doubling average weekly consumption of oil-rich fish
- increasing to over 50 per cent the proportion of mothers breastfeeding their babies for the first six weeks

THE NATIONAL HEALTH SERVICE

The National Health Service (NHS) came into being on 5 July 1948. Its function is to provide a comprehensive health service designed to secure improvement in the physical and mental health of the population and to prevent, diagnose and treat illness. It was founded on the principle that treatment should be provided according to clinical need rather than ability to pay, and should be free at the point of delivery. However, prescription charges and charges for some dental and ophthalmic treatment have been introduced over the years.

The NHS covers a comprehensive range of hospital, specialist, family practitioner (medical, dental, ophthalmic and pharmaceutical), artificial limb and appliance, ambulance, and community health services. Everyone normally resident in the UK is entitled to use any of these services.

STRUCTURE

The structure of the NHS underwent a series of reorganisations in the 1970s and, especially, the 1990s. The National Health Service and Community Care Act 1990 introduced the concept of an 'internal market' in health care provision, whereby care was provided through NHS contracts, with health authorities or boards and GP fundholders (the purchasers) being responsible for buying health care from hospitals, non-fundholding GPs, community services and ambulance services (the providers). The Act provided for the establishment of NHS Trusts. These operate as self-governing health care providers independent of health authority control and responsible to the Minister for Health. They derive their income principally from contracts to provide services to health authorities and fund-holding GPs. The community care reforms, introduced in 1993, govern the way care is administered for elderly people, the mentally ill, the physically handicapped and people with learning disabilities.

The Scottish Executive Health Department is responsible for health policy and the administration of the NHS in Scotland. The NHS in Scotland is currently administered by health boards, which are responsible for health services in their areas and also for assessing the health care needs of the local population and developing integrated strategies for meeting these needs in partnership with GPs and in consultation with the public, hospitals and others. The health boards are overseen by the Management Executive at the Scottish Executive Health Department. There are also local health councils, whose role is to represent the interests of the public to health authorities and boards.

The NHS in Scotland has around 132,000 staff, including more than 63,000 nurses, midwives and health visitors and over 8,500 doctors. There are also more than 7,000 family practitioners, including doctors, dentists, opticians and community pharmacists, who are independent contractors providing a range of services within the NHS in return for various fees and allowances.

PROPOSED REFORMS

In July 1999, responsibility for administering the NHS in Scotland was devolved from the Secretary of State for Scotland to the Scottish Executive. The White Paper *Designed to Care*, presented to Parliament by the then Secretary of State for Scotland, Donald Dewar, in 1997, laid the foundations for the work of the Scottish Parliament in developing Scotland's devolved health care service provision. The White Paper proposed several reforms, including the establishment of primary care trusts and the replacement of GP fundholding by networks of GPs organised in local health care co-operatives.

By 2003, Scotland had 26 health trusts and 15 local health boards (equivalent to English Health Authorities) responsible for the planning and provision of all primary health care, including mental health services and community hospitals.

Their role includes support to general practice in delivering integrated primary health care services, strategic planning and policy development, and promoting improvements in the quality and standards of clinical care.

However, by June 2003 the Scottish Executive had begun moves to abolish NHS Trusts in Scotland via the NHS Reform Bill. Three of Scotland's trusts (Grampian University Hospitals, Lanarkshire Acute Hospitals, and Argyll and Clyde Acute Hospital Trusts) ended the 2001–2 financial year £13.2 million in the red (despite extra funding from the Scottish Executive of £90 million), and complaints were widespread that the Trusts and Health Boards duplicated each others' work. A White Paper on Health was announced in February 2003 by the Executive's Health Minister Malcolm Chisholm. It proposed that Scotland's 26 trusts should be merged with their 15 local health boards in a bid to cut bureaucracy and that future management emphasis would be placed on integration and decentralisation in a bid to provide a greater number of services locally and to reduce waiting times (at the start of 2003 almost 2,000 patients had spent more than nine months waiting for operations and the average waiting time to see a specialist was 57 days). Other key points in the White Paper included the independent monitoring of services, the dismantling of the internal market system introduced in the 1990s, a further £26 million of investment, and a new Scottish Health Council.

FINANCE

The NHS is still funded mainly through general taxation, although in recent years greater reliance has been placed on the NHS element of National Insurance contributions, patient charges and other sources of income. Total UK expenditure on the NHS in 2001 was £73 billion, representing 7.1 per cent of GDP.

The number of people paying into private medical insurance has risen to its highest level ever, equivalent to 11.5 per cent of the UK population in 2000.

TOTAL NHS EXPENDITURE PER HEAD OF POPULATION 2000–1

	Net £	Gross £
UK	967	906
England	949	885
Wales	976	958
Northern Ireland	912	898
Scotland	1,094	1,026

EMPLOYEES
NHS WORKFORCE SUMMARY

Whole Time Equivalent	*2001*
Medical and dental	7,250
Professional and technical	11,705
Nursing and midwifery	33,334
Administrative and clerical	15,361
Domestic, Transport etc	7,625

Source: Annual Abstract of Statistics 2003 (Crown Copyright)

SALARIES

General practitioners (GPs), dentists, optometrists and pharmacists are self-employed, and work for the NHS under contract. Average salaries as at 1 April 2002 were:

Consultant	£52,640–£68,505
Specialist Registrar	£25,920–£37,775
Registrar	£25,920–£31,435
Senior House Officer	£23,190–£32,520
House Officer	£18,585–£20,975
GP	*£66,280
Nursing Grades H—I (Modern Matron) †	£25,005–£32,760
Nursing Grades G–I (Senior Ward Sister)	£22,385–£32,760
Nursing Grade F (Ward Sister)†	£18,790–£24,565
Nursing Grade E (Senior Staff Nurse)	£17,105–£20,655
Nursing Grade D (Staff Nurse)	£16,005–£17,670
Nursing Grade C (Enrolled Nurse and some Nursing auxiliary staff)	£13,040–£16,005
Nursing Grades A–B	£9,735–£13,485

*Average intended net remuneration
† including discretionary points

PRIMARY AND COMMUNITY HEALTH CARE SERVICES

Primary and community health care services comprise the family health services (i.e. the general medical, personal medical, pharmaceutical, dental, and ophthalmic services) and community services (including family planning and preventive activities such as cytology, vaccination, immunisation and fluoridation) commissioned by health boards and provided by NHS Trusts, health centres and clinics.

The primary and community nursing services include practice nurses based in general practice, district nurses and health visitors, community psychiatric nursing for mentally ill people living outside hospital, and ante- and post-natal care. Pre-school services at GP surgeries or child health clinics monitor children's physical, mental and emotional health and development, and provide advice to parents on their children's health and welfare.

The School Health Service provides for the health monitoring of schoolchildren of all ages, with a focus on prevention. The service includes medical and dental examination and advice to the local education authority, the school, the parents and the pupil of any health factors which may require special consideration during the pupil's school life.

FAMILY DOCTOR SERVICE

Any doctor may take part in the Family Doctor Service (provided the area in which he/she wishes to practise has not already an adequate number of doctors). GPs may also have private fee-paying patients.

GENERAL PRACTITIONER SERVICES 2001

Number of doctors	3,756
Average list size	1,409
Payments to doctors	£429.6m

Source: Annual Abstract of Statistics 2003 (Crown Copyright)

PHARMACEUTICAL SERVICE

Patients may obtain medicines, appliances and oral contraceptives prescribed under the NHS from any pharmacy whose owner has entered into arrangements to provide this service, and from specialist suppliers of medical appliances. In rural areas, where access to a pharmacy may be difficult, patients may be able to obtain medicines and other prescribed health care products from their doctor.

Except for contraceptives (for which there is no charge), a charge of £6.30 is payable for each item supplied unless the patient is exempt and a declaration of exemption on the prescription form is completed; booklet HC11, available from main post offices and local social security offices, shows which categories of people are exempt. Prescription charges have increased by an average of 1.64 per cent every year since 2000. Prescription charges are expected to rise up to £46 million in 2003–4 for NHS Scotland. Under the current rules for exemption and remission of charges, approximately 90 per cent of items in Scotland are supplied to patients free of charge (compared with 85 per cent in England).

GENERAL PHARMACEUTICAL SERVICES 2001

Prescriptions dispensed	65.56 million
Gross payments to Pharmacists	£788.6 million
Average gross cross per prescription	£12.03

Source: Annual Abstract of Statistics 2003 (Crown Copyright)

DENTAL SERVICE

Dentists, like doctors, may take part in the NHS and also have private patients. They are responsible to the health boards in whose areas they provide services.

Patients may go to any dentist who is taking part in the NHS and is willing to accept them. Patients are required to pay 80 per cent of the cost of NHS dental treatment. Since 1 April 2003 the maximum charge for a course of treatment has been £372. As with pharmaceutical services, certain people are exempt from dental charges or have charges remitted; full details are given in booklet HC11.

GENERAL AND COMMUNITY DENTAL SERVICES 2001

Dentists on list	1,866
Courses of treatment completed	3,390,000
Payments to dentists (gross)	£165.1 million
Payments by patients	£52.3 million
Payments by public funds	£112.9 million

Source: Annual Abstract of Statistics 2003 (Crown Copyright)

GENERAL OPHTHALMIC SERVICES

General ophthalmic services are administered by health boards. Testing of sight may be carried out by any ophthalmic medical practitioner or ophthalmic optician (optometrist). The optician must give the prescription to the patient, who can take this to any supplier of glasses to have them dispensed. Only registered opticians can supply glasses to children and to people registered as blind or partially sighted.

Those on a low income may qualify for help with the cost of NHS sight testing. Certain categories of people qualify for sight testing free of charge or are automatically entitled to help with the purchase of glasses under an NHS voucher scheme; booklet HC11 gives details.

Diagnosis and specialist treatment of eye conditions, and the provision of special glasses, are available through the Hospital Eye Service.

GENERAL OPHTHALMIC SERVICES 2001

Number of sight tests given	877,000
Number of pairs of glasses supplied	462,000
Payments out of public funds for sight testing and dispensing	£38.6 million

Source: Annual Abstract of Statistics 2003 (Crown Copyright)

HOSPITALS AND OTHER SERVICES

Hospital, medical, dental, nursing, ophthalmic and ambulance services are provided by the NHS to meet all reasonable requirements. Facilities for the care of expectant and nursing mothers and young children, and other services required for the diagnosis and treatment of illness, are also provided. Rehabilitation services (occupational therapy, physiotherapy and speech therapy) may also be provided, and surgical and medical appliances are supplied where appropriate.

Specialists and consultants who work in NHS hospitals can also engage in private practice, including the treatment of their private patients in NHS hospitals.

CHARGES

Certain hospitals have accommodation in single rooms or small wards which, if not required for patients who need privacy for medical reasons, may be made available to other patients for a small charge. These patients are still NHS patients and are treated as such.

In a number of hospitals, accommodation is available for the treatment of private in-patients who undertake to pay the full commercial-rate costs of hospital accommodation and services and (usually) separate medical fees to a specialist as well.

AMBULANCE SERVICE

The NHS provides emergency ambulance services free of charge via the 999 emergency telephone service. The Scottish Ambulance Service is responsible for all ambulance provision and operates the only integrated, publicly funded Air Ambulance service in the UK. Air Ambulance cover is provided seven days a week, twenty-four hours a day through two EC135 helicopters based in Glasgow and Inverness and four fixed-wing aircraft based in Kirkwall, Lerwick, Glasgow and Aberdeen. The Air Ambulance Service flies an average of seven missions a day. In 2001–2, 2,938 missions were flown compared with 2,156 missions in 1996–7.

The Scottish Ambulance Service covers the whole of Scotland, unlike its English counterpart which divides its fleets into smaller regions and response areas. In 2001–2 520,463 accident and emergency calls were responded to in a Scotland-wide average time of 9.5 minutes each. 2,214,101 non-emergency calls were dealt with in 2001–2.

AMBULANCE ACTIVITY
Year ending 31 March 2000

Health Board	Road Ambulance Service		Ambulance car service	
	Responses	Total mileage	Patient journeys	Mileage
Argyll and Clyde	229,594	1,689,877	226,285	371,229
Ayrshire and Arran	172,693	1,780,974	15,556	331,697
Borders	61,500	788,593	8,900	266,785
Dumfries and Galloway	74,860	1,133,023	6,688	301,193
Fife	165,633	1,372,471	25,028	427,687
Forth Valley	118,135	817,781	40,326	675,293
Grampian	221,501	1,533,833	21,642	300,500
Greater Glasgow	359,693	2,131,480	149,547	1,107,506
Highland	73,270	1,638,982	13,766	482,281
Lanarkshire	237,593	1,757,614	83,817	1,084,136
Lothian	271,961	1,996,064	51,006	640,772
Orkney	2,562	39,983	111	5,446
Shetland	6,580	57,395	—	—
Tayside	178,249	1,633,147	53,132	843,847
Western Isles	10,463	176,639	2,513	54,197
Scotland	2,184,287	18,544,057	498,317	6,892,569

HOSPICES

Hospice or palliative care for patients with life-threatening illnesses may be provided at the patient's home, in a voluntary or NHS hospice, or in hospital; it is intended to ensure the best possible quality of life for patients during their illness, and to provide help and support to both patients and their families. The Scottish Partnership for Palliative Care co-ordinates NHS and voluntary hospice services.

PATIENTS' CHARTERS

The Patient's Charter (1991) sets out the rights of patients in relation to the NHS (i.e. the standards of service which all patients will receive at all times) and patients' reasonable expectations (i.e. the standards of service that the NHS aims to provide, even if they cannot in exceptional circumstances be met). The Charter covers issues such as access to services, personal treatment of patients, the provision of information, registering with a doctor, hospital waiting times, care in hospitals, community services, ambulance waiting times, dental, optical

and pharmaceutical services, and maternity services Health boards, NHS Trusts and GP practices may also have their own local charters setting out the standard of service they aim to provide.

In December 2000 Scotland's *National Health – A Plan for Action* was launched by the Scottish Executive. The plan promises that by the end of 2003 no patient will wait longer than nine months for treatment (12 months in Scotland in 2000 and 18 months in England) and that by 2005 no patient urgently referred for cancer treatment will wait more that two months.

COMPLAINTS

The Patient's Charter includes the right to have any complaint about the service provided by the NHS dealt with quickly, with a full written reply being provided by a relevant chief executive. There are three levels to the NHS complaints procedure: first, resolution of a complaint locally, following a direct approach to the relevant service provider (e.g. a letter of complaint to the Chief Executive of a hospital or Trust or Health Board); second, an independent review procedure if the complaint is not resolved locally; third, a referral to the Health Service Ombudsman in the event that an independent review is refused or that the complainant is not satisfied with the outcome. As a final resort, patients may approach the Health Service Commissioner if they are dissatisfied with the response of the NHS to a complaint.

NHS TRIBUNALS

The National Health Service Tribunal (Scotland) considers representations that the continued inclusion of a doctor, dentist, optician or pharmacist on the list of a health authority or health board would be prejudicial to the efficiency of the service concerned.

NHS BOARDS

ARGYLL & CLYDE NHS BOARD
Ross House, Hawkhead Road, Paisley PA2 7BN
Tel: 0141-842 7200 Fax: 0141-848 1414
Web: www.show.scot.nhs.uk/achb
Chief Executive: Neil Campbell

AYRSHIRE & ARRAN NHS BOARD
Boswell House, 7–10 Arthur Street, Ayr KA7 1QJ
Tel: 01292-611040 Fax: 01292-610636
Web: www.show.scot.nhs.uk/aahb
Chief Executive: Wai-Yin Hatton

BORDERS NHS BOARD
Newstead, Melrose, Roxburghshire TD6 9BS
Tel: 01896-754333 Fax: 01896-823476
Web: www.show.scot.nhs.uk/bhb
Chief Executive: John Glennie

DUMFRIES & GALLOWAY NHS BOARD
Grierson House, The Crichton, Bankend Road,
Dumfries DG1 4ZG
Tel: 01387-272700 Fax: 01387-252375
Web: www.show.scot.nhs.uk/dghb
Chief Executive: Malcolm Wright

FIFE NHS BOARD
Springfield House, Cupar, Fife KY15 5UP
Tel: 01334-656200 Fax: 01334-652210
Web: www.show.scot.nhs.uk/fhb
Acting Chief Executive: John Wilson

FORTH VALLEY HEALTH BOARD
33 Spittal Street, Stirling FK8 1DX
Tel: 01786-463031 Fax: 01786-471337
Web: www.show.scot.nhs.uk/nhsfv
Chief Executive: Fiona Mackenzie

GRAMPIAN NHS BOARD
Summerfield House, 2 Eday Road, Aberdeen AB15 6RE
Tel: 01224-663456 Fax: 01224-404014
Web: www.show.scot.nhs.uk/ghb
Chief Executive: Neil Campbell

GREATER GLASGOW NHS BOARD
Dalian House, PO Box 15329, 350 St Vincent Street,
Charing Cross, Glasgow G3 8YZ
Tel: 0141-201 4444 Fax: 0141-201 4401
Web: www.show.scot.nhs.uk/gghb
Chief Executive: Tom Divers

HIGHLAND NHS BOARD
Assynt House, Beechwood Park, Inverness IV2 3HG
Tel: 01463-717123 Fax: 01463-235189
Web: www.show.scot.nhs.uk/hhb
Chief Executive: Dr Roger Gibbins

LANARKSHIRE NHS BOARD
14 Beckford Street, Hamilton ML3 0TA
Tel: 01698-281313 Fax: 01698-423134
Web: www.show.scot.nhs.uk/lhb
Chief Executive: David Pigott

LOTHIAN NHS BOARD
148 Pleasance, Edinburgh EH8 9RS
Tel: 0131-536 9000 Fax: 0131-536 9164
Web: www.nhslothian.scot.nhs.uk
Chief Executive: James Barbour

ORKNEY NHS BOARD
Garden House, New Scapa Road, Kirkwall KW15 1BQ
Tel: 01856-885400 Fax: 01856-885411
Web: www.show.scot.nhs.uk/ohb
Chief Executive: Judi Wellden

SHETLAND NHS BOARD
Brevik House, South Road, Lerwick, Shetland ZE1 0TG
Tel: 01595-743060 Fax: 01595-696727
Web: www.show.scot.nhs.uk/shb
Chief Executive: Sandra Laurenson

TAYSIDE NHS BOARD
King's Cross, Clepington Road, Dundee DD3 8EA
Tel: 01382-424000 Fax: 01382-424003
Web: www.show.scot.nhs.uk/thb
Chief Executive: Prof. W. J. Wells

WESTERN ISLES NHS BOARD
37 South Beach Street, Stornoway, Isle of Lewis
HS1 2BB Tel: 01851-702997 Fax: 01851-704405
Web: www.wihb.org.uk
Chief Executive: Murdo Maclennan

OTHER HEALTH ORGANISATIONS IN SCOTLAND

COMMON SERVICES AGENCY
Trinity Park House, South Trinity Road, Edinburgh
EH5 3SE Tel: 0131-552 6255 Fax: 0131-551 1392

HEALTH EDUCATION BOARD FOR SCOTLAND
Woodburn House, Canaan Lane, Edinburgh EH10 4SG
Tel: 0131-536 5500 Fax: 0131-536 5501

NHS24
Delta House, 50 West Nile Street, Glasgow G1 2NP
Tel: 08454-242424 Web: www.nhs24.com

NHS DIRECT
Tel: 0845-4647 Web: www.nhsdirect.co.uk

NHS EDUCATION FOR SCOTLAND
Hanover Buildings, 66 Rose Street, Edinburgh EH2 2NN
Tel: 0131-225 4365 Fax: 0131-225 5891
Web: www.nes.scot.nhs.uk

NHS QUALITY IMPROVEMENT SCOTLAND
Delta House, 50 West Nile Street, Glasgow G1 2NP
Tel: 0141-225 6999 Fax: 0141-248 3778

SCOTTISH AMBULANCE SERVICE
National Headquarters, Tipperlinn Road, Edinburgh
EH10 5UU
Tel: 0131-446 7000 Fax: 0131-446 7001

SCOTTISH HEALTHCARE SUPPLIES
Trinity Park House, South Trinity Road, Edinburgh
EH5 3SH Tel: 0131-552 6255 Fax: 0131-552 6535

SCOTTISH MEDICINES CONSORTIUM
Delta House, 50 West Nile Street, Glasgow G1 2NP
Tel: 0141-225 6997 Fax: 0141-248 3778

SCOTTISH NATIONAL BLOOD TRANSFUSION SERVICE
41 Lauriston Place, Edinburgh EH3 9HB
Tel: 0131-536 5360

SCOTTISH PARTNERSHIP FOR PALLIATIVE CARE
1a Cambridge Street, Edinburgh EH1 2DY
Tel: 0131-229 0538 Fax: 0131-228 2967
Web: www.palliativecarescotland.org.uk

STATE HOSPITALS BOARD FOR SCOTLAND
Carstairs Junction, Lanark ML11 8RP
Tel: 01555-840293 Fax: 01555-840024

THE POLICE SERVICE

The Scottish Executive is responsible for the organisation, administration and operation of the police service. The Scottish Executive Justice Department works in partnership with chief constables and local police to implement this responsibility, which includes the making of regulations covering matters such as police ranks, discipline, hours of duty, and pay and allowances.

Police authorities are responsible for maintaining an effective and efficient police force in their areas. There are six joint police boards made up of local councillors; the other two police authorities are councils.

Police authorities are financed by central and local government grants and a precept on the council tax. They are responsible for setting a budget, providing the resources necessary to police the area adequately, appointing officers of the rank of Assistant Chief Constable and above, and determining the number of officers and civilian staff in the force.

All police forces in the UK are subject to inspection by HM Inspectors of Constabulary, who report to the Scottish Ministers.

COMPLAINTS

Chief constables are obliged to investigate a complaint against one of their officers; if there is a suggestion of criminal activity, the complaint is investigated by an independent public prosecutor.

THE SPECIAL CONSTABULARY

Each police force has its own special constabulary, made up of volunteers who work in their spare time (usually for between 16 and 18 hours a week). Special Constables have full police powers within their force and adjoining force areas, and assist regular officers with routine policing duties.

Police Strengths (at March 2003)

Officers	15,487
men	12,590
women	2,897
Special constables	991
Support staff*	5,979

Source: Scottish Executive Justice Department
* whole time equivalent

STRENGTH BY RANK AT 31 MARCH 2002

Force	Chief Officers	Superintendents	Chief Inspectors	Inspectors	Sergeants	Constables	Total Number of Police Officers	Total Number Per 1,000 Population
Central	2	9	15	42	116	535	719	2.59
Dumfries and Galloway	2	7	7	23	73	370	482	3.20
Fife	5	14	14	37	123	710	912	2.61
Grampian	3	18	20	87	202	928	1,258	2.41
Lothian and Borders	4	32	44	142	369	2,109	2,700	3.03
Northern	2	8	13	33	122	505	683	2.46
Strathclyde	7	103	94	387	975	5,761	7,327	3.24
Tayside	3	12	17	54	157	927	1,170	3.03
Total	28	203	224	805	2,137	11,854	15,251	2.98

Source: Her Majesty's Inspectorate of Constabulary: Annual Statistical Returns.
Notes: Population as at 30 June 2000.
Figures for Chief Officers include Chief Constables, Deputy Chief Constables and Assistant Chief Constables. Figures for Superintendents include Chief Superintendents.

PAY

Basic rates of pay since 1 April 2003 are:

CHIEF CONSTABLES *(Greater Manchester, Strathclyde and West Midlands)*

Fixed term	£111,309–£125,622
No fixed term	£106,134–£119,775

*Chief Constables

Fixed term	£84,879–£121,230
No fixed term	£80,835–£115,590

Designated Deputies

Fixed term	80% of the basic salary of their chief or £81,298, whichever is higher
No fixed term	80% of the basic salary of their chief or £77,247, whichever is higher

Assistant Chief Constable

Fixed term	£70,824–£81,297
No fixed term	£67,449–£77,427
Chief Superintendent	£58,242–£61,617
Superintendent	£49,077–£57,249
Chief Inspector	£41,562–£44,052
Inspector	£37,551–£42,387
Sergeant	£29,307–£32,940
Constable	£18,666–-£29,307

Source: Home Office

The following lists are compiled from information kindly supplied by Hazell's *Police and Constabulary Almanac 2003.*

JOINT POLICE BOARDS

The Dumfries and Galloway council area and the Fife council area do not have joint boards as a single authority covers the whole of the police area.

CENTRAL SCOTLAND JOINT POLICE BOARD
Municipal Buildings, Falkirk FK1 5RS
Tel: 01324-506070 Fax: 01324-506071
Covers: Clackmannanshire, Falkirk and Stirling

GRAMPIAN JOINT POLICE BOARD
Town House, Aberdeen AB10 1AQ
Tel: 01224-523165 Fax: 01224-52293
Covers: Aberdeen City, Aberdeenshire and Moray

LOTHIAN AND BORDERS POLICE BOARD
City Chambers, High Street, Edinburgh EH1 1YJ
Tel: 0131-529 4955 Fax: 0131-529 7607
Covers: City of Edinburgh, East Lothian, Midlothian, Scottish Borders and West Lothian

NORTHERN JOINT POLICE BOARD
Council Offices, Glenurquhart Road, Inverness IV3 5NX
Tel: 01463-702012 Fax: 01463-702182
Covers: Highland, Orkney Islands, Shetland Islands and Western Isles

STRATHCLYDE JOINT POLICE BOARD
City Chambers, George Square, Glasgow G2 1DU
Tel: 0141-287 4167 Fax: 0141-287 4173
Covers: Argyll and Bute, East Ayrshire, East Dunbartonshire, East Renfrewshire, Glasgow City, Inverclyde, North Ayrshire, North Lanarkshire, Renfrewshire, South Ayrshire, South Lanarkshire and West Dunbartonshire

TAYSIDE JOINT POLICE BOARD
St James House, St James Road, Forfar DD8 2ZE
Tel: 01307-461460 Fax: 01307-464834
Covers: Angus, Dundee City, Perth and Kinross

POLICE FORCES

CENTRAL SCOTLAND POLICE HQ
Randolphfield, Stirling FK8 2HD
Tel: 01786-456000 Fax: 01786-451177
Email: mail@centralscotland.police.uk
Web: www.centralscotland.police.uk
Chief Constable: Andrew Cameron, QPM
Deputy Chief Constable: James Keenan
Strength: 730 *Civilian posts:* 319

DUMFRIES AND GALLOWAY CONSTABULARY
Cornwall Mount, Dumfries DG1 1PZ
Tel: 01387-252112 Fax: 01387-262059
Web: www.dumfriesandgalloway.police.uk
Chief Constable: D. J. R. Strang, QPM
Deputy Chief Constable: R. Ovens
Strength: 462 *Civilan posts:* 285

FIFE CONSTABULARY
Detroit Road, Glenrothes, Fife KY6 2RJ
Tel: 01592-418888 Fax: 01592-418444
Web: www.fife.police.uk
Chief Constable: Peter M. Wilson, QPM
Strength: 930 *Civilian posts:* 319

GRAMPIAN POLICE
Queen Street, Aberdeen AB10 1ZA
Tel: 01224-386000 Fax: 01224-643366
Email: mailbox@grampian.police.uk
Web: www.grampian.police.uk
Chief Constable: Andrew G. Brown
Deputy Chief Constable: Adrian J. Ward
Strength: 1,271 *Civilian posts:* 475

LOTHIAN AND BORDERS POLICE

Fettes Avenue, Edinburgh EH4 1RB
Tel: 0131-311 3131 Fax: 0131-311 3038
Chief Constable: Paddy Tompkins
Deputy Chief Constable: Thomas J. Wood
Strength: 2,602 *Civilian posts:* 1,164

NORTHERN CONSTABULARY

Old Perth Road, Inverness IV2 3SY
Tel: 01463-715555 Fax: 01463-230800
Chief Constable: Ian J. Latimer
Strength: 664 *Civilian posts:* 198

STRATHCLYDE POLICE

173 Pitt Street, Glasgow G2 4JS
Tel: 0141-532 2000 Fax: 0141-532 2475
Web: www.strathclyde.police.uk
Chief Constable: William Rae, QPM
Deputy Chief Constable: Colin McKerracher
Strength: 7,188 *Civilian posts:* 2,000

TAYSIDE POLICE

PO Box 59, West Bell Street, Dundee DD1 9JU
Tel: 01382-223200 Fax: 01382-200449
Email: mail@tayside.pnn.police.uk
Web: www.tayside.police.uk
Chief Constable: John Vine, QPM
Deputy Chief Constable: Ian A. Gordon
Strength: 1,170 *Civilian posts:* 612

OTHER POLICE FORCES

BRITISH TRANSPORT POLICE SCOTTISH AREA

90 Cowcaddens Road, Glasgow G4 0LU
Tel: 0141-332 3649 Fax: 0141-335 2155
Web: www.btp.police.uk

MINISTRY OF DEFENCE POLICE

HM Naval Base, Clyde, Helensburgh, Dunbartonshire
G48 8HL
Tel: 01436-674321 Fax: 01436-677230
Operational Commander: Chief Supt. S. R. Mason

UK ATOMIC ENERGY AUTHORITY CONSTABULARY

Building F6, Culham Science Centre, Abingdon,
Oxfordshire OX14 3DB
Tel: 01235-463760 Fax: 01235-463764
Email: constabulary@ukaea.org.uk

STAFF ASSOCIATIONS

Police officers are not permitted to join a trade union or to take strike action. All ranks have their own staff associations.

ASSOCIATION OF CHIEF POLICE OFFICERS IN SCOTLAND

173 Pitt Street, Glasgow G2 4JS
Tel: 0141-532 2052 Fax: 0141-532 2058
Email: contactus@acpos.police.uk
Hon. Secretary: William Rae, QPM

ASSOCIATION OF SCOTTISH POLICE SUPERINTENDENTS

173 Pitt Street, Glasgow G2 4JS
Tel: 0141-221 5796 Fax: 0141-221 8407
Email: secretariat@scottishpolicesupers.co.uk
Web: www.scottishpolicesupers.co.uk
President: Chief Supt. Allan Shanks

SCOTTISH POLICE FEDERATION

5 Woodside Place, Glasgow G3 7QF
Tel: 0141-332 5234 Fax: 0141-331 2436
Email: spf@scottishpolicefederation.org.uk
Web: www.spf.org.uk
General Secretary and Treasurer: Douglas J. Keil, QPM

OTHER POLICE BODIES IN SCOTLAND

SCOTTISH POLICE COLLEGE

Tulliallan Castle, Kincardine, Alloa, Clackmannanshire
FK10 4BE
Tel: 01259-732000 Fax: 01259-732100
Director: D. C. G. Garbutt, QPM, LLD, FCIPD

SCOTTISH CRIMINAL RECORD OFFICE

1 Pacific Quay, Glasgow G51 1EA
Tel: 0141-585 8400 Fax: 0141-585 8324
Director: H. W. Bell

SCOTTISH POLICE AUTHORITIES FORUM

COSLA, Rosebery House, 9 Haymarket Terrace,
Edinburgh EH12 5XZ
Tel: 0131-474 9266 Fax: 0131-474 9292
Development Officer: Robert S. Turnbull

SCOTTISH DRUG ENFORCEMENT AGENCY

Since 1 June 2000 the Scottish Drug Enforcement Agency has been mandated to drive and co-ordinate a substantially enhanced multi-agency response to combat the threat from drug trafficking and other serious and organised crime in Scotland. Figures released in June 2002 showed that the Agency had increased drug seizures by 68 per cent, arrests by 35 per cent, and had disrupted or dismantled 73 major criminal enterprises. In June 2002 134 officers were based at the Drug Enforcement Agency's Paisley headquarters with a total of 32 civilian support staff and a further 100 officers based within the eight Scottish police forces. Additional funding announced in 2001 (of £6 million) will increase the number of dedicated officers at the Agency to 200 by 2004. The Agency Headquarters also house the new (since 2002) Scottish Money Laundering Unit which uses state-of-the-art technology to help seize dealer's assets. This work will be further aided by the Proceeds of Crime Bill, which is due to come into force in 2004.

HQ, Osprey House, Inchinnan Road, Paisley PA3 2RE
Tel: 0141-302 1000 Fax: 0141-302 1099

THE PRISON SERVICE

The Scottish Prison Service is an Agency of the Scottish Executive. The chief executive is responsible for operational matters and performance.

There are 15 prison establishments in Scotland; Barlinnie in Glasgow is the largest with over 1,000 places and Porterfield in Inverness is the smallest with 108 places. A sixteenth establishment houses prisoners who present particular management problems and a National Induction Centre has been created for prisoners beginning sentences of ten years or more. The prison units in Scotland house about 6,000 prisoners in total. Four to five times this number of people pass through Scottish prisons every year. It costs approximately £204 million a year to run the Scottish Prison Service and to meet its capital spending commitments.

Convicted prisoners are classified according to their perceived security risk and are housed in establishments appropriate to that level of security. Female prisoners are housed in women's establishments or in separate wings of mixed prisons. Remand prisoners are, where possible, housed separately from convicted prisoners. Offenders under the age of 21 are usually detained in a young offenders' institution, which may be a separate establishment or part of a prison.

One prison, Kilmarnock, was built, financed (under the Private Finance Initiative) and is being run by private contractors. Kilmarnock is Scotland's newest prison (opened Spring 1999) and it provides places for 500 prisoners.

Her Majesty's Chief Inspector of Prisons is independent and reports annually to the Scottish Executive Justice Department on prison conditions and the treatment of prisoners. Every prison establishment also has an independent visiting committee made up of local volunteers appointed by the Justice Minister. Any prisoner whose complaint is not satisfied by the internal complaints procedures may complain to the Scottish Complaints Commissioner.

Women make up only 3 per cent of the Scottish prison population. Custody is less frequently used as a sanction against female offenders; in 1999, for example, only 6 per cent of women convicted of offences received a custodial sentence, whereas 14 per cent of all offenders received such a sentence.

PERSONS UNDER SENTENCE 1996–2002

1996–7	5,992
1997–8	6,059
1998–9	6,029
1999–2000	5,974
2000–1	5,883
2001–2	6,185

Source: Scottish Prison Service, Annual Report and Accounts 2001–2

AVERAGE DAILY PRISON POPULATION 2000–2 (BY TYPE OF CUSTODY)

Type of Custody	2000–1	2001–2
Remand	880	1,018
Adult prisoners	4,347	4,539
Less than 4 years[1]	2,024	2,108
4 years or over (incl. life)[2]	2,323	2,431
Young offenders	656	629
Less than 4 years	481	460
More than 4 years (incl. life)[2]	175	168
Persons under sentence: total[3]	5,003	5,168
Total[3]	5,883	6,185

[1] Includes those prisoners sentenced by court martial, civil prisoners and others
[2] Includes those persons recalled by supervision licence
[3] Components may not add to totals due to rounding

Source: Scottish Prison Service, Annual Report and Accounts 2001–2

MAIN CRIMES AND OFFENCES OF SENTENCED PRISONERS IN 2001

Main crime/offence	Sentenced total
Total crimes and offences	9,617
Non-sexual crimes of violence	1,372
Crimes of indecency	203
Crimes of dishonesty	3,963
Fire-raising, vandalism	166
Other crimes	1,233
Miscellaneous offences	1,597
Motor vehicle offences	1,009
Unknown charge	5
Other jurisdiction charge	69

Source: Scottish Prison Service, Annual Report and Accounts 2001–2 (Crown Copyright)

OPERATING COSTS OF THE SCOTTISH PRISON SERVICE FOR THE YEAR ENDING 31 MARCH 2002

Total income	£2,990,000
Total expenditure	£121,912,000
Running costs	£63,939,000
Other current expenditure	£23,363,000
Operating cost	(£206,224,000)
Cost of capital charges	(£23,264,000)
Interest payable and similar charges	(£7,000)
Interest receivable	(£68,000)
Net cost of operations after interest	£229,427,000
Cost for financial year	£229,427,000

Source: Scottish Prison Service, *Annual Report and Accounts 2002–3*

HM CHIEF INSPECTOR OF PRISONS FOR SCOTLAND

Saughton House, Broomhouse Drive, Edinburgh EH11 3XD Tel: 0131-244 8481 Fax: 0131-244 8446
HM Chief Inspector of Prisons: Dr Andrew R. C. McLellan

SCOTTISH PRISON SERVICE

Calton House, 5 Redheughs Rigg, Edinburgh EH12 9HW Tel: 0131-556 8400

SALARIES

The following pay bands have applied since 1 October 2002:

I	£48,000–£58,000
H	£38,100–£48,100
G	£30,000–£40,000

Chief Executive of Scottish Prison Service: Tony Cameron
Director, Human Resources: B. Allison
Director, Finance and Information Systems: Willie Pretswell
Director, Strategy and Business Performance: K. Thomson
Deputy Director, Rehabilitation and Care: A. Spencer
Deputy Director, Estates and Buildings: D. Williams
Head of Training, Scottish Prison Service College: W. Rattray
Head of Communications: T. Fox

PRISON ESTABLISHMENTS

*ABERDEEN
Craiginches, 4 Grampian Place, Aberdeen AB11 8FN
Tel: 01224-876868
Governor: Audrey Mooney
Prisoners as at May 2003: 201

BARLINNIE
Barlinnie, Glasgow G33 2QX
Tel: 0141-770 2000
Governor: Bill McKinlay
Prisoners as at May 2003: 1,059

CASTLE HUNTLY
Castle Huntly, Longforgan, nr Dundee DD2 5HL
Tel: 01382-360265
Governor: Ian Whitehead
Prisoners as at May 2003: 134

*† CORNTON VALE
Cornton Road, Stirling FK9 5NU
Tel: 01786-832591
Governor: Sue Brookes
Prisoners as at May 2003: 229

*† DUMFRIES
Terregles Street, Dumfries DG2 9AX
Tel: 01387-261218
Governor: Chrissie McGeever
Prisoners as at May 2003: 132

EDINBURGH
33 Stenhouse Road, Edinburgh EH11 3LN
Tel: 0131-444 3000
Governor: D. Croft
Prisoners as at May 2003: 689

†GLENOCHIL
King O'Muir Road, Tullibody, Clackmannanshire
FK10 3AD Tel: 01259-760471
Governor: Kate Donegan
Prisoners as at May: 590

GREENOCK
Gateside, Greenock PA16 9AH
Tel: 01475-787801
Governor: Stephen Swan
Prisoners as at May 2003: 312

*INVERNESS
Porterfield, Duffy Drive, Inverness IV2 3HH
Tel: 01463-229000
Governor: Alastair MacDonald
Prisoners as at May 2003: 130

KILMARNOCK
Mauchline Road, Kilmarnock KA1 5JH
Tel: 01563-548800
Governor: Nick Cameron
Prisoners as at May 2003: 533

LOW MOSS
Bishopbriggs, Glasgow G64 2QB
Tel: 0141-762 4848
Governor: E. Fairbairn
Prisoners as at May 2003: 335

NORANSIDE
Noranside, Fern, by Forfar, Angus DD8 3QY
Tel: 01356-650217
Governor: Ian Whitehead
Prisoners as at May 2003: 101

PERTH
3 Edinburgh Road, Perth PH2 8AT
Tel: 01738-622293
Governor: W. Millar
Prisoners as at May 2003: 461

PETERHEAD
Salthouse Head, Peterhead, Aberdeenshire AB42 2YY
Tel: 01779-479101
Governor: Ian Gunn
Prisoners as at May 2003: 290

†POLMONT
Brightons, Falkirk, Stirlingshire FK2 0AB
Tel: 01324-711558
Governor: Dan Gunn
Prisoners as at May 2003: 425

SHOTTS
Shotts ML7 4LE
Tel: 01501-824000
Governor: Audrey Park
Prisoners as at May 2003: 514

* Women's establishment or establishment with units for women
† Young Offender Institution or establishment with units for young offenders

SOCIAL SERVICES

Social work services became a devolved responsibility on 1 July 1999, passing into the hands of the Scottish Executive. The Scottish Executive Health Department is responsible for social work policy and in particular for community care and voluntary issues. The oversight of children and family services' functions are with the Children and Young People Group of the Education Department. Oversight of the functions of criminal justice social work services is with the Justice Department. The Social Work Services Inspectorate undertakes inspection, policy advice and programme work. Each authority has a Chief Social Work Officer, frequently known as the Director of Social Work. How each authority seeks to exercise its social work functions is a matter for the authority itself. The functions themselves cover three broad areas:

– Community Care (or adult) services;
– Children and family services;
– Criminal Justice social work services.

In 2001 the Regulation of Care (Scotland) Act brought about the creation of a new national body, the Care Commission, to regulate care services against national care standards and the Regulation of Care (Scotland) Act, and to take responsibility for the registration and inspection of social services – replacing local authorities and NHS Boards. The Care Commission came into being on 1 April 2002. The Care Commission has to keep Scottish Ministers informed about the provision and quality of care services, has to encourage improvement in the quality of services, and has to make information available to the public about the quality of care services.

The Care Commission has a Board, headed by a Convenor and Chief Executive and employs around 500 people across five regional offices throughout Scotland, with its headquarters located in Dundee. The Care Commission is a non-departmental public body which means that it operates independently of the Scottish Executive but is accountable to Ministers and the Scottish Parliament.

Over the next few years all of the following care services will be regulated by the Care Commission: support services – day care services for adults, care at home service, including domestic help (if provided or purchased by the local authority); care home services – previously residential care homes for adults and children and nursing homes; care and welfare in boarding schools and school hostels;

independent health care – independent hospitals, hospices, clinics, wholly private doctors and dentists; nurse agencies; child-care agencies; secure accommodation services for children; offender accommodation services; adoption services; adult placement services; child minding; day care and early education of children – day care of children up to 16 years, early education provision, including local authority provided nursery classes; housing support services.

FINANCE

Social work services are financed partly by central government, with decisions on expenditure allocations being made at local authority level.

NET EXPENDITURE ON SOCIAL WORK (£000S)[1,2]

	1999–2000	2000–1[3]
Children	284,457	296,536
All community care client groups	252,328	275,315
Older people	309,363	293,548
Adults with mental health problems	30,114	30,753
Substance misuse	8,340	8,975
Adults with learning disabilities	140,860	143,796
Physically disabled adults	43,087	49,139
Services for HIV/AIDS	1,767	1,868
Total community care	785,861	803,397
Adult offenders	3,892	3,713
Non specific expenditure	152,744	157,500
Total Social Work	1,226,955	1,261,146

[1] Loan charges have been excluded for all years.
[2] Figures have been adjusted to reflect current prices using GDO deflators.
[3] 2000-1 figures are provisional and may change
Source: Scottish Executive Local Government Finance Statistics 2000–1 (Crown Copyright)

STAFF OF SCOTTISH SOCIAL WORK SERVICES[1]

Client Group	2001
Children	6,420
Adults	31,641
Older people[2]	6,930
Physical disabilities[2]	519
Mental health problems[2]	297
Learning disabilities	3,975
Adults (not separately identified)[3]	19,920
Offenders	1,373
Generic provision	3,317
Management/administration	3,045
Total	45,796

[1]Staff numbers may fluctuate over time as a result of various factors, including changes in the way services are provided and changes in the number of vacancies

[2]Staff in day centres, residential establishments and special locations providing services to specific client groups

[3]Fieldwork staff providing services to adults and homecare staff

Source: Scottish Executive Staff of Scottish Local Authority Social Work Services (Crown Copyright)

OLDER PEOPLE

Services for older people are designed to enable them to remain living in their own homes for as long as possible. Local authority services include advice, domestic help, meals in the home, alterations to the home to aid mobility, emergency alarm systems, day and/or night attendants, laundry services and the provision of day centres and recreational facilities. Charges may be made for these services. Respite care may also be provided in order to allow carers temporary relief from their responsibilities.

Local authorities and the private sector also provide 'sheltered housing' for older people, sometimes with resident wardens.

The Sutherland Report, the report of the royal commission on long-term care set up by the Labour government in 1997 and headed by Sir Stewart Sutherland, Vice-Chancellor of Edinburgh University, was published in March 2000 and recommended that all elderly nursing care in the UK should be free and that personal care, such as bathing, feeding and dressing, should also be free according to assessed need. The English and Welsh parliaments rejected the Sutherland Report's findings but in September 2001 the Scottish Executive confirmed that it would comply fully with the recommendations of the Report and provide free personal care to all elderly people in

Scotland from July 2002. £125 million will be set aside annually to implement this policy, with this figure rising to £227 million in the next 20 years. The reason for this vast cost is Scotland's ageing population with the number of people over the age of 65 rising from 790,000 in 2001 to more than 1,000,000 in 2021. In 2001 average nursing homes fees were approximately £337 a week or £17,524 a year (Sutherland Report). Under the 2002 Scottish Executive plan nursing and residential home residents only have to cover their accommodation costs, estimated at £120 a week, or £6,240 a year. Since July 2002, personal care and nursing care for those with assessed need is paid up to a maximum of £90 and £65 per week respectively.

RESIDENTIAL CARE HOMES FOR OLDER PEOPLE 2001

	Local Authority	Private	Voluntary	All homes
No. homes	202	261	158	621
No. beds	6,066	5,107	3,977	15,150
No. residents	5,442	4,367	3,544	13,353

Source: Scottish Executive Health Department: Scottish Community Care Statistics 2001 (Crown Copyright)

PEOPLE WITH PHYSICAL DISABILITIES

Services for disabled people are designed to support them to lead ordinary independent lives in their own homes. Local authority services include advice, adaptations to the home, meals in the home, help with personal care, occupational therapy, educational facilities and recreational facilities. Respite care may also be provided in order to allow carers temporary relief from their responsibilities.

Special housing may be available for people with physical disabilities who can live independently, and care home accommodation for those who cannot.

RESIDENTIAL CARE HOMES FOR PEOPLE WITH PHYSICAL DISABILITIES 2001

Number of homes	57
Number of beds	699
Number of residents (including holiday/respite residents)	585

Source: Scottish Executive Health Department, Community Care Statistics 2001 (Crown Copyright)

FAMILIES AND CHILDREN

Local authorities are required to provide services aimed at safeguarding and promoting the welfare of children looked after or in need and, wherever possible, allowing them to be brought up by their families. Services include advice, counselling, help in the home and the provision of family centres. Many authorities also provide short-term refuge accommodation for women and children.

DAY CARE

In allocating day-care places to children, local authorities can, where appropriate, give priority to children with special needs, whether in terms of their health, learning abilities or social needs.

The Child Care Strategy for Scotland, under which day care and out-of-school child care facilities will be extended to match more closely the needs of working parents, was launched by Ministers in May 1998. The strategy is intended to ensure that quality, affordable childcare is available for children aged 0–14 in every neighbourhood.

As of January 2002 there were 4,117 pre-school centres or daycare centres in Scotland providing facilities for 188,408 children. Just over half of these facilities described themselves as nurseries and a further 26 per cent as playgroups. The remaining 23 per cent of centres were made up of out-of-school care clubs (11 per cent), playschemes (4 per cent), crèches (4 per cent) and family centres (4 per cent). There were just over 27,000 people working in pre-school and daycare centres of which 56 per cent worked part-time. Of the total hours worked 98 per cent were worked by female staff members.

The Scottish Childminder's Association has 6,478 childminders registered with its organisation (2003 figure).

CHILD PROTECTION

Children considered to be at risk of physical injury, neglect or sexual abuse may be the subject of a child protection conference and placed on the local authority's child protection register after a decision has been made that an inter-agency agreement is needed to protect the child. Local authority social services staff, school nurses, health visitors and other agencies work together to prevent and detect cases of abuse. In Scotland 2,018 children were on local child protection registers at 31 March 2002, an increase of eighteen on the previous year. Of these, 50.2 per cent were boys and 49.8 per cent were girls, and eight in ten were under the age of eleven. Just under 7,200 children were referred to local authorities for child protection inquiries in 2001–2 and of those children 40 per cent were the subject of an inter-agency conference. In over 75 per cent of all case conferences, the source of abuse/risk to the child was either known or thought to be the child's birth parent(s). Almost 75 per cent of children put on the child protection register were at risk of physical injury or neglect.

Source: Scottish Executive – Child Protection Statistics for 2001–2.

LOCAL AUTHORITY CARE

The Children in Care (Scotland) Act 1995 governs the provision by local authorities of accommodation for children who have no parent or guardian or whose parents or guardians are unable or unwilling to care for them. A children's hearing may impose compulsory measures of suspension where a child is being neglected or abused, or is offending, or is misusing alcohol, drugs or volatile substances, or is not attending school. The hearing must be satisfied that doing something is better than doing nothing to minimise the state's involvement in the life of the child.

Children who are being looked after by local authorities may live at home, with friends or relatives, in other community accommodation, with foster carers who receive payments to cover the expenses of caring for the child or children, or in residential care. Children's homes may be run by the local authority or by the private or voluntary sectors.

CHILDREN IN CARE/LOOKED AFTER
As at 31 March 2001

	1999	2000	2001
Boys	6,529 (58%)	6,572 (58%)	6,291
Girls	4,662 (42%)	4,737 (42%)	4,606
Total	11,191	11,309	10,897

Source: Scottish Executive (Crown copyright)

At 31 March 2002 a total of 11,200 children (1.0 per cent of all children under 18) was being looked after. Almost half of these children were living at home, less than one in seven looked after children were in residential care, 12 per cent were living with friends or relatives or in other community accommodation, and the remainder were with foster carers (*Source:* Scottish Executive, (Crown copyright)).

The number of children being looked after varies considerably from authority to authority, depending on factors such as the size of the authority, the size and age structure of the local population, and the authority's policy and resources.

The implementation of the Children in Care (Scotland) Act 1995 extended the powers and responsibilities of local authorities to look after children who would previously have left care at the age of 16. Also, a number of respite placements which were not hitherto considered as care now fall within the definition of being 'looked after'. The largest number of children being looked after is in the 12–15 age band (4,251 at 31 March 2001, 61 per cent of whom were boys). Boys outnumber girls in all age groups.

ADOPTION

Local authorities are required to provide an adoption service, either directly or via approved voluntary societies. Adoption applications can be made to any of the 49 sheriff courts in Scotland. In 2002 44 per cent of adoption applications were made through Local Authority adoption agencies (the same as in 2001). Applications made without an agency (normally by step parents) fell from 46 per cent in 2001 to 43 per cent in 2002 while applications made via a voluntary agency increased from 9 per cent in 2001 to 13 per cent in 2002. The number of adoption applications in Scotland has fallen steadily over the last two decades, with 1,081 applications being made in 1983 and only 360 applications made in 2002. The biggest increase in applications in any age group has been for 1-4 year-olds which have risen from 20 per cent in 1983 to 36 per cent in 2002. The largest age group of children for whom adoption applications are made is 5–11 years (39 per cent of applications), with the average age of children for whom applications are made being six and a half years. Less than 7 per cent of applications are made for children less than one year old. In 2002 98 per cent of applications were granted with 67 per cent of these reaching an outcome within 120 days.

PEOPLE WITH LEARNING DISABILITIES

Services for people with learning disabilities are designed to enable them to remain living in the community wherever possible. Local authority services include short breaks and respite support in the home, the provision of day services, and help with other activities outside the home.

The review of services for people with learning disabilities, *The Same As You?*, was published in May 2000 and recommended that local authorities should develop alternatives to traditional day centres in order to support people in the community through employment, lifelong learning and social involvement. Residential care may be provided for people with disabilities generally in small or group homes, but a shift in the pattern of care is occurring with most people with learning disabilities living in various forms of supported accommodation including adult placements, small group homes and supported living arrangements.

There are an estimated 120,000 people with learning disabilities in Scotland. The number of people with learning disabilities has increased by 1.2 per cent over the last 35 years but since 1965 the number of people with severe learning disabilities in Scotland has increased by 50 per cent. About £275 million is spent in Scotland on services specifically for people with learning disabilities (£115 million on health services and £160 million on social care). Average expenditure is £54 per head of the general population (compared with £59 per head in England and £63 per head in Wales).

RESIDENTIAL CARE HOMES FOR PEOPLE WITH LEARNING DISABILITIES AS AT 31 MARCH 2001 (EXTRACT[1])

	2001
Number of homes	616
Number of beds	4,526
Number of residents (including holiday/respite residents)	4,216

[1]Extract: for complete table with explanatory notes see source
Source: Scottish Executive: Residential Establishment Census Return (Crown Copyright)

PEOPLE WITH MENTAL HEALTH PROBLEMS

Under the Care Programme Approach, those with a mental illness are assessed by specialist services with the purpose of receiving a care plan reflecting their needs, and a key worker should be appointed for each patient. Regular reviews of the patient's progress should be conducted. Local authorities provide help and advice to those with a mental illness and their families, and places in day centres and social centres. In extreme cases social workers can apply for a mentally disordered person to be compulsorily detained in hospital. Where appropriate, hospital care or care in residential or nursing homes is provided.

The Millan Committee was set up in March 1999 to review the Mental Health (Scotland) Act of 1984. The Committee reported in January 2001 and the Scottish Executive began the introduction of new legislation to modernise mental health care in Scotland. The Executive has committed to increase community care, promote greater public awareness of mental health issues (particularly through the See Me advertising and education campaign of 2003), and to implement further legislative developments such as the Adults with Incapacity (Scotland) Act (2000) and the domestic application of the European Convention on Human Rights.

Mental Illness Specific Grants are paid under the National Health Service and Community Care Act (1990). It is shared 70/30 per cent between the Scottish Executive (£12.6 million in 2000-1) and local authorities (£5.4 million in 2000-1) and is intended to assist projects addressing care for people with mental health problems. These include drop-in centres, cafes to provide wholesome meals, volunteer befriending services, advocacy and support and advice day facilities.

NUMBER OF DAY CENTRES FOR PEOPLE WITH MENTAL HEALTH PROBLEMS, PLACES AND PEOPLE ATTENDING, AS OF 31 MARCH 2001

	2001–2
Number of day centres	18
Number of places	494
Number attending	463

Extract: for complete table please see source
Source: Scottish Executive: Day Care Centre Census Return D1–B (Crown Copyright)

TRANSPORT

CIVIL AVIATION

UK airlines are operated entirely by the private sector. Scottish airports are served by several major British airlines, including British Airways, Air UK, Britannia Airways, BMI British Midland, Monarch Airlines and EasyJet; by British Airways franchise Loganair (which operates several inter-island services) and franchised partner British Regional Airlines, and by other airlines such as Highland Airways, Gill-air and Business Air.

Among European airlines, SAS provides links to Scandinavia, KLM with the Netherlands and further afield, and RyanAir and Aer Lingus with Ireland. The Norwegian carrier Ugland Air provides oil industry charters from Sumburgh to Norwegian airports, and Wideroe, also Norwegian, operates scheduled flights in summer on the same route.

The Civil Aviation Authority (CAA) is responsible for the regulation of UK airlines and the larger airports, and for the safety regulation of the UK civil aviation industry. The CAA is also responsible for the provision of air traffic control services over Britain and its surrounding seas and at most major British airports. It also runs the Air Travel Organiser's Licensing (ATOL) consumer protection scheme.

The CAA advises the Government on aviation issues, represents consumer interests, conducts economic and scientific research and produces statistical data. It also provides specialist services and other training and consultancy services to clients world-wide.

AIRPORTS

Scottish Airports Ltd is a subsidiary of BAA plc, the world's leading commercial airport operator. It owns and operates Scotland's three principal airports at Glasgow, Edinburgh and Aberdeen which, together currently handle 14 million passengers annually. Some 250,000 movements of aircraft and helicopters take place each year and 29,300 metric tonnes of cargo and mail are carried through the airports.

Highlands and Islands Airports Ltd (HIAL) owns and operates ten Scottish airports and receives subsidies for providing links to remote areas of Scotland.

HIAL's airports are Barra, Benbecula, Campbeltown, Inverness, Islay, Kirkwall, Stornoway, Sumburgh, Tiree, and Wick.

A number of airports and small airfields are controlled by local authorities, including Dundee, Orkney and Shetland. Orkney Islands Council has airfields at Eday, North Ronaldsay, Papa Westray, Sanday, Stronsay and Westray. Shetland Islands Council runs Tingwall airport at Lerwick, and gives assistance to airstrips on Foula, Out Skerries and Papa Stour, which are run by local airstrip trusts. Fetlar and Whalsay have airstrips for emergency use, with only occasional other services according to need. Baltasound airstrip on Unst, currently owned by Shetland Islands Council, is maintained for emergency and ambulance use. It is available for emergency landings only. Fair Isle airfield is owned, like the whole island, by the National Trust for Scotland. Airports and airfields at Glenrothes, Cumbernauld and Perth (Scone) are privately owned. Scatsta in Shetland and Flotta in Orkney are also privately owned, principally serving the oil industry.

Airport operating hours at Barra are subject to tide variation, since aircraft land on and take off from the beach. Tiree's operating hours are also subject to the variations at Barra, as flights to and from Tiree are via Barra.

Operating hours vary seasonally at several smaller airports and airfields, including Campbeltown, Inverness, Islay and Wick.

BAA PLC
Scottish Airport Division, St Andrew's Drive, Glasgow Airport, Paisley KA9 4DG
Tel: 0141-887 1111 Fax: 0141-887 1699

HIGHLANDS AND ISLANDS AIRPORTS LTD
Head Office, Inverness Airport, Inverness IV2 7JB
Tel: 01667-462445

PASSENGER JOURNEYS
Over 19 million passenger journeys were made through Scottish airports in 2002, including terminal, transit, scheduled and charter passengers. The following list covers BAA, HIAL and local authority controlled airports:

AIR PASSENGERS 2002*

Aberdeen (BAA)	2,550,477
Barra	8,294
Benbecula (HIAL)	31,560
Campbeltown (HIAL)	8,356
Dundee	45,400
Edinburgh (BAA)	6,930,649
Glasgow (BAA)	7,803,627
Inverness (HIAL)	386,824
Islay (HIAL)	20,728
Kirkwall (HIAL)	106,271
Lerwick (Tingwall)	2,068
Prestwick	1,490,415
Stornoway (HIAL)	94,283
Sumburgh (HIAL)	133,899
Tiree (HIAL)	5,297
Unst	–
Wick (HIAL)	26,037

* Total terminal, transit, scheduled and charter passengers.
Note: passengers carried on air taxi services are excluded.
Source: Civil Aviation Authority

RAILWAYS

Responsibility for legislation on railways was not devolved to the Scottish Parliament but remains with the UK Government.

From 1994, responsibility for managing Britain's nationalised railway infrastructure rested with Railtrack, which was floated on the Stock Exchange in 1996. On 5 October 2001, Railtrack PLC was put into administration under the Railways Act 1993. Ernst and Young were appointed as Railway Administrators. On 3 October 2002 Railtrack was taken out of administration and replaced by the not for profits company Network Rail. Network Rail owns all operational track and land pertaining to the railway system, manages the track and charges for access to it, and is responsible for signalling and timetabling. It also owns the stations, and leases most of them out to the train operating companies and is also responsible for overall safety on the railways. Network Rail is run as a private organisation and operates as a commercial business, but has members instead of shareholders, who do not receive dividends or share capital, so that they do not have any financial or economic interest in Network Rail. All of Network Rail's profits are reinvested into maintaining and upgrading the rail infrastructure.

Network Rail does not operate train services. Passenger trains are operated by 26 private-sector train-operators, via a competitive tendering process overseen by the Strategic Rail Authority (SRA). The Government continues to subsidise loss-making but socially necessary rail services. The SRA is responsible for monitoring the performance of the franchisees, allocating and administering government subsidy payments, proposing closures to the Rail Regulator and designating experimental services.

Under the Railways Act 1993 and the Transport Act 2000, the Rail Regulator exercises statutory powers to regulate Network Rail Infrastructure Ltd, which owns the national rail network (track, signalling, bridges, tunnels and stations). The network is operated under a network licence, which is issued by the Government but enforced by the Regulator who is independent of the Government. The Regulator also ensures train operators are given fair access to the network and under the Competition Act 1998, prevents anti-competitive practices. Regulations, which took effect on 28 June 1998, established licensing and access arrangements for certain international train services in Great Britain. These are overseen by the International Rail Regulator. The International Rail Regulator licenses the operation of certain international rail services in the European Economic area, and access to railway infrastructure in Great Britain for the purpose of the operation of such services. The Office of the International Rail Regulator is co-located with the Office of the Rail Regulator, who fulfils both functions.

Rail Passengers Committees monitor the policies and performance of train and station operators in their area. They are statutory bodies and have a legal right to make recommendations for changes.

OFFICE OF THE RAIL REGULATOR (ORR)
1 Waterhouse Square, 138–142 Holborn, London EC1N 2TQ Tel: 020-7282 2000 Fax: 020-7282 2047
Email: rail.library@orr.gsi.gov.uk
Web: www.rail-reg.gov.uk
Rail Regulator and International Rail Regulator:
  Tom Winsor

NETWORK RAIL
40 Melton Street, London NW1 2EE
Tel: 020-7557 8000 Fax: 020-7557 9000
Web: www.networkrail.co.uk

SCOTRAIL
Caledonian Chambers, 87 Union Street,
Glasgow G1 3TA Tel: 08700-005151
Web: www.scotrail.com

RAIL PASSENGERS COMMITTEE FOR SCOTLAND
5th Floor, Corunna House, 29 Cadogan Street, Glasgow G2 7AB
Tel: 0141-221 7760 Fax: 0141-221 3393
Email: info@railpassengers.org.uk
Web: www.railpassengers.org.uk/scotland

SERVICES
Scotland is served by Great North Eastern Railway, Scotrail Railways and Virgin Trains operating companies. There are 335 stations in passenger service. Network Rail owns all of these with the exception of the station at Prestwick Airport, which is privately owned. The total route length of the railway network in Scotland is around 2,700 kilometres and the total track length is about 5,500 kilometres. Figures from the Scottish Executive (Scottish Transport Statistics: No 21) show that passenger journeys within Scotland for the period 2001 to 2002 totalled 62.7 million. Total passenger journeys, including cross-border journeys originating in Scotland totalled 65.3 million in the same year, 2.4 million fewer than in the previous year, but about 10.5 million more than ten years ago. The total revenue for internal and cross-border journeys originating in Scotland for 2002–3 was £194.6 million. (These figures exclude cross-border passenger traffic originating outside of Scotland and journeys on the Glasgow Underground.) Network Rail publishes a national timetable which contains details of rail services, coastal shipping information and connections with Ireland, the Isle of Man, the Isle of Wight, the Channel Islands and some European destinations.

The national rail enquiries service offers telephone information about train times and fares for any part of the country:

NATIONAL RAIL ENQUIRIES
Tel: 08457-484950

EUROSTAR
Tel: 08705-186186

GLASGOW UNDERGROUND RAILWAY
The Glasgow Underground railway system opened in 1896, was electrified in 1935 and reopened following modernisation in 1980. It has 15 stations and 6.55 route miles of track. Strathclyde Passenger Transport is responsible for the Underground. In 2001–2 there were 14.4 million passenger journeys. Total ticket revenue in 2001–2 was £10.5 million, an increase of 2 per cent on the previous year in cash terms, but 1 per cent less in real terms.

STRATHCLYDE PASSENGER TRANSPORT
Consort House, 12 West George Street, Glasgow G2 1HN Tel: 0141-332 6811 Fax: 0141-332 3076
Web: www.spt.co.uk

Strathclyde Passenger Transport (SPT) is Scotland's only passenger transport authority and executive, investing in rail, bus, Subway and ferry services for 42 per cent of the nation's population. SPT finances ScotRail passenger services in the west of Scotland, sets train fares and timetables and runs the SPT Subway and Renfrew-Yoker Ferry. SPT currently subsidises approximately 150 bus services in areas where local communities are not already served by commercial operators.

CHANNEL TUNNEL LINKS
Passenger services operated by Eurostar (UK) Ltd run from Waterloo station in London and Ashford, Kent, via the Channel Tunnel to Paris, Brussels, Lille and Marseilles. Connecting services from Edinburgh via London began in 1997.

ROADS

Responsibility for Scotland's road network and for policy on bus transport now rests with the Scottish Parliament and Ministers, operating through the Scottish Executive Development Department. The highway authority for non-trunk roads is, in general, the unitary authority in whose area the roads lie.

The costs of construction, improvement and maintenance are met by central government. Total expenditure on building and maintaining trunk roads in Scotland was estimated at £751.2 million in 2002–3 and projected spending for 2003–4 is £780 million (these figures include capital charges of £531.5 million and £546.6 million respectively). *Source:* Scottish Executive: *Spending Plans for Scotland 2003–4.*

FINANCE
Decisions on road transport expenditure in Scotland are devolved to the Scottish Executive. The estimated total expenditure (including the cost of capital and depreciation charges) on motorways and trunk roads in Scotland during 2002–3 was approximately £788m, based on the *Annual Expenditure Report of the Scottish Expenditure – The Scottish Budget 2003–4* published in April 2002.

PRIVATE FINANCE

The construction of the M77, Glasgow Southern Orbital Road and the M74 Extension are Public Private Partnerships.

ROAD LENGTHS
(in miles 2002)

	Miles
Total roads	33,121
Trunk roads (including motorways)	2,024
Motorways	229

MOTORWAYS

M73	Junction 4 of M74 to A80 (Mollinsburn)
M74	Glasgow to Gretna
M77	Junction 22 of M8 to Malletsheugh (Ayr Road)
M8	Edinburgh to Newhouse, Baillieston to West Ferry Interchange
M80	Junction 9 of M9 (Stirling) to Junction 4 of M80/A80 (Haggs) and M80 Stepps Bypass
M876	Kincardine Bridge to Junction 5 of M80
M989	Junction 30 of M8 to Erskine Bridge
M9	Edinburgh to Dunblane and M9 Spur to A8000
M90	Forth Road Bridge/Inverkeithing to Perth
M876	Dennyloanhead (M80) to Kincardine Bridge
A823 (M)	Junction 2 of M90 to A823 (Dunfermline)

PRINCIPAL ROAD BRIDGES

Tay Road Bridge, over Firth of Tay –
   2,245 m/7,365 ft
Forth Road Bridge, over Firth of Forth –
   1,987 m/6,156 ft
Erskine Bridge, over River Clyde –
   1,321 m/4,336 ft
Kessock Bridge, over Kessock Narrows –
   1,052 m/3,453 ft
Skye Bridge, over Kyle of Lochalsh –
   520 m/1,705 ft

ROAD PASSENGER SERVICES

There is an extensive network of bus and coach services in Scotland, particularly in rural areas. In 2001–2 there were 436 million passenger bus journeys in Scotland – an increase of 0.5 per cent on the previous year. However the 2000–1 figure was 25 per cent less than in 1990–91.

Until 1988 most road passenger transport services in Great Britain were provided by the public sector; the Scottish Bus Group was the largest operator in Scotland. Since the late 1980s almost all bus and coach services in Great Britain have been privatised; the privatisation of the Scottish Bus Group was completed in 1991. However, local authorities can subsidise the provision of socially necessary services after competitive tendering.

One of the largest bus operators in Great Britain, Stagecoach Holdings, is based in Scotland, at Perth. National Express runs a national network of coach routes, mainly operating through franchises. There are also a large number of smaller private operators.

Information on local bus routes and timetables can be obtained from bus stations and tourist board offices; telephone numbers can be found in local telephone directories.

NATIONAL EXPRESS COACH SERVICES
Tel: 08705-808080
Web: www.nationalexpress.com

SCOTTISH CITYLINK EXPRESS COACH SERVICES
Tel: 08705-505050

STAGECOACH HOLDINGS
Tel: 01738-629339

POSTBUS SERVICES

Since 1968 the Royal Mail has operated a postbus service in Scotland, providing passenger transport in rural areas. There are currently 119 postbuses covering 108 routes throughout Scotland, including the Western Isles, Orkney and Shetland and a similar network in England and Wales. Many of the services receive financial assistance from local councils. A wheelchair-accessible service in East Lothian was introduced in 1998.

The postbus service has its Scottish head office at the Royal Mail headquarters in Edinburgh but is largely administered from Inverness. Timetable information is available from the website, www.royalmail.com or from 08457-740740.

ROYAL MAIL SCOTLAND
10 Brunswick Road, Edinburgh EH7 5XX
Tel: 0131-550 8295 Web: www.royalmailgroup.com

DRIVING AND VEHICLE LICENCES
The Driver and Vehicle Licensing Agency (DVLA) is responsible for issuing driving licences, registering and licensing vehicles, and collecting excise duty in Great Britain. The Driving Standards Agency is responsible for carrying out driving tests and approving driving instructors.

A leaflet, *What You Need to Know About Driving Licences* (form D100), is available from post offices.

DRIVING LICENCE FEES
as at 1 April 2003

First provisional licence	£29.00
Changing a provisional to a full licence after passing a driving test	£12.00
Renewal of licence	£6.00
Renewal of licence including PCV or LGV entitlements	£29.00
Renewal after disqualification	£35.00
Renewal after drinking and driving disqualification	£50.00
Medical renewal	Free
Duplicate Licence	£17.00
Exchange licence	£18.00
Replacement (change of name or address)	Free

DRIVING TEST FEES
(weekday rate/evening and Saturday rate)
as at 1 April 2003

For cars	£39/£48
For motor cycles*	£48/£57
For lorries, buses	£76/£94
For cars, after disqualification†	£78/£96
For motor cycles, after disqualification†	£96/114
Written theory test (including Hazard Perception Test since November 2002)	£18.00

* Before riding on public roads, learner motor cyclists and learner moped riders are required to have completed Compulsory Basic Training, provided by DSA-approved training bodies. The CBT certificate currently costs £8.

All fees are subject to change.

†An extended driving test was introduced in 1992 for those convicted of dangerous driving.

MOTOR VEHICLE LICENCES
Registration and first licensing of vehicles is done through local Vehicle Registration Offices of the DVLA. Local facilities for relicensing are available at any post office which deals with vehicle licensing, or by postal application to the post offices shown on form V100, available at any post office. This form also provides guidance on registering and licensing vehicles.

Details of the present duties chargeable on motor vehicles are available at post offices and Vehicle Registration Offices.

VEHICLE EXCISE DUTY RATES
From 1 May 2003

	Twelve months £	Six months £
Motor Cars		
Light vans, cars, taxis, etc.		
Under 1549cc	110.00	60.50
Over 1549cc	165.00	90.75
Motor Cycles		
not over 150 cc	15.00	–
150–400 cc	30.00	–
401–600 cc	45.00	–
Others	60.00	33.00
		–
Tricycles (not over 450 kg)		
Not over 150 cc	15.00	–
Others	60.00	33.00
Buses†		
Seating 9–16 persons	165.00	90.75
	(165.00)	(90.75)
Seating 17–35 persons	220.00	121.00
	(165.00)	(90.75)
Seating 36–60 persons	330.00	181.50
	(165.00)	(90.75)
Seating over 60 persons	500.00	275.00
	(165.00)	(90.75)

† Figures in parentheses refer to reduced pollution vehicles

VEHICLE EXCISE DUTY RATES (FOR VEHICLES REGISTERED AFTER 1.3.2001)

Diesel car

Band	CO² emissions (g/km)	12 month rate £	6 month rate £
AA	Up to 120	85.00	46.75
A	121-150	115.00	63.25
B	151-165	135.00	74.25
C	166-185	155.00	85.25
D	Over 185	165.00	90.75

Petrol car		Alternative fuel car	
12 month rate £	6 month rate £	12 month rate £	6 month rate £
75.00	41.25	65.00	35.75
105.00	57.75	95.00	52.25
125.00	68.75	115.00	63.25
145.00	79.75	135.00	74.25
160.00	88.00	155.00	85.25

MOT TESTING

Cars, motor cycles, motor caravans, light goods and dual-purpose vehicles more than three years old must be covered by a current MoT test certificate, which must be renewed annually. The MoT testing scheme is administered by the Vehicle and Operator Services Agency (formerly the Vehicle Inspectorate, which merged with the Traffic Area Network on 1 April 2003).

A fee is payable to MoT testing stations, which must be authorised to carry out tests. The maximum fees (due to be revised to the figures below on 1st August 2003), which are prescribed by regulations, are:

For cars and light vans	£40.75
For solo motor cycles	£15.20
For motor cycle combinations	£24.85
For three-wheeled vehicles	£29.00
Private passenger seats and ambulances	
9-12 seats	£42.65
13-16 seats	£45.70
over 16 seats	£61.95
For light goods vehicles between	
3,000 and 3,500kg	£44.40

SHIPPING AND PORTS

Sea transport, both of passengers and freight, is important in Scotland, particularly between the many islands in the north and west and between the islands and the mainland. Major ferry operators include Stena Line (which runs a service between Stranraer and Belfast), P. & O. Scottish Ferries (serving Orkney and Shetland), and Caledonian MacBrayne (serving 22 islands and four peninsulas, mostly in the Western Isles). P. & O. Scottish Ferries are also UK agents for Smyril, running services from Lerwick to Norway, Denmark, the Faröe Islands and Iceland. Shetland Islands Council operates an inter-island service in Shetland; Orkney Ferries Ltd run seven ferries between the Orkney mainland and the 13 smaller islands.

FERRY SERVICES

Passenger ferry services within Scotland include the following:

From	To
Aberdeen	Lerwick (Shetland)
Aberdeen	Stromness
Ardrossan	Brodick (Arran)
Claonaig (Kintyre)	Lochranza (Arran)
Colintraive (Argyll)	Rhubodach (Bute)
Colonsay	Port Askaig (Islay)
Fionnphort (Mull)	Iona
Gourock	Dunoon (Cowal)
Gourock	Kilcreggan, Helensburgh
Kennacraig	Port Ellen (Islay), Port Askaig
Largs	Cumbrae Slip (Cumbrae)
Lochaline (Lochaber)	Fishnish (Mull)
Mallaig	Armadale (Skye)
Mallaig small isles service	Eigg, Muck, Rum, Canna
Oban	Castlebay (Barra)
Oban	Colonsay
Oban	Craignure (Mull)
Oban	Lismore
Oban	Lochboisdale (S. Uist)
Oban	Tobermory (Mull), Coll, Ciree
Berneray (N. Uist)	Leverburgh (Harris)
Sconser (Skye)	Raasay
Scrabster	Stromness (Orkney)
Tarbert (Kintyre)	Portavadie (Cowal)
Tayinloan	Gigha
Tobermory	Kilchoan
Uig (Skye)	Tarbert (Harris)
Uig	Lochmaddy (N. Uist)
Ullapool	Stornoway (Lewis)
Wemyss Bay	Rothesay (Bute)

FERRY OPERATORS

CALEDONIAN MACBRAYNE
Tel: 01475-650100 (general enquiries)

HEBRIDEAN CRUISES
Services to Rum, Eigg, Muck and Canna
Tel: 01687-450224

ORKNEY FERRIES LTD
Tel: 01856-811397

P. & O. STENA LINE
Web: www.posf.co.uk

SEACAT
Web: www.superseacat.co.uk

PORTS

There are many ports in Scotland and space constraints prevent the inclusion of a complete list here. Ports are owned and operated either by private companies (including shipping lines), local authorities or trusts. For further information, please contact the Transport Division of the Scottish Executive.

MARINE SAFETY

By 1 October 2002 all roll-on, roll-off ferries operating to and from the UK will be required to meet the new international safety standards on stability established by the Stockholm Agreement.

The Maritime and Coastguard Agency was established in 1998 by the merger of the Coastguard Agency and the Marine Safety Agency, and is an executive agency of the Department for Transport, Local Government and the Regions. Its aims are to develop, promote and enforce high standards of marine safety, to minimise loss of life amongst seafarers and coastal users, and to minimise pollution of the sea and coastline from ships.

HM Coastguard in Scotland is divided into two search and rescue regions, one covering the north and east of Scotland and the other covering the west of Scotland and Northern Ireland. In total the coastguard has 10,000 kilometres (6,214 miles) of coastline, 77,700 square kilometres (30,405 square miles) of land, and 790 islands to patrol.

Locations hazardous to shipping in coastal waters are marked by lighthouses and other lights and buoys. The lighthouse authority for Scotland (and the Isle of Man) is the Northern Lighthouse Board. The Board maintains 2 ships (*MV Pharos* and *MV Polestar*), 201 lighthouses, 131 buoys, 41 beacons, 3 differential global positioning system stations, 22 radar beacons and 15 fog signals. No Scottish lighthouses are now manned; the last to convert to automated operation was Fair Isle in 1998. The Board employs 200 full-time staff at their headquarters in Edinburgh and has depots in Oban and Stromness. Harbour authorities are responsible for pilotage within their harbour areas; and the Ports Act 1991 provides for the transfer of lights and buoys to harbour authorities where these are used for mainly local navigation.

LEGAL SCOTLAND

INTRODUCTION TO THE SCOTTISH LEGAL SYSTEM

COURTS AND JUDGES

LEGAL NOTES

THE SCOTTISH JUDICATURE

Scotland has a legal system separate from and differing greatly from the English legal system in enacted law, judicial procedure and the structure of courts.

The system of public prosecution is headed by the Lord Advocate and is independent of the police, who have no say in the decision to prosecute. The Lord Advocate, discharging his functions through the Crown Office in Edinburgh, is responsible for prosecutions in the High Court, sheriff courts and district courts. Prosecutions in the High Court are prepared by the Crown Office and conducted in court by one of the law officers, by an advocate-depute, or by a solicitor advocate. In the inferior courts the decision to prosecute is made and prosecution is preferred by procurators fiscal, who are lawyers and full-time civil servants subject to the directions of the Crown Office. A permanent, legally qualified civil servant known as the Crown Agent is responsible for the running of the Crown Office and the organisation of the Procurator Fiscal Service, of which he is the head.

Scotland is divided into six sheriffdoms, each with a full-time sheriff principal. The sheriffdoms are further divided into sheriff court districts, each of which has a legally qualified resident sheriff or sheriffs, who are the judges of the court.

Further information about courts in Scotland can be found at www.scotcourts.gov.uk

CRIMINAL COURTS

In criminal cases sheriffs principal and sheriffs have the same powers; sitting with a jury of 15 members, they may try more serious cases on indictment, or, sitting alone, may try lesser cases under summary procedure. Minor summary offences are dealt with in district courts, which are administered by the local government authorities of the districts and the islands and presided over by lay justices of the peace (of whom there are about 4,000) and, in Glasgow only, by stipendiary magistrates. Juvenile offenders (children under 16) may be brought before an informal children's hearing comprising three local lay people.

The superior criminal court is the High Court of Justiciary, which is both a trial and an appeal court. Cases on indictment are tried by a High Court judge, sitting with a jury of 15, in Edinburgh and on circuit in other towns. Appeals from the lower courts against conviction or sentence are heard also by the High Court, which sits as an appeal court only in Edinburgh. There is no further appeal to the House of Lords in criminal cases.

CIVIL COURTS

In civil cases the jurisdiction of the sheriff court extends to most kinds of action. Appeal against decisions of the sheriff may be made to the sheriff principal and thence to the Court of Session, or direct to the Court of Session, which sits only in Edinburgh. The Court of Session is divided into the Inner and the Outer House. The Outer House is a court of first instance in which cases are heard by judges sitting singly, sometimes with a jury of 12. The Inner House, itself subdivided into two divisions of equal status, is mainly an appeal court. Appeals may be made to the Inner House from the Outer House as well as from the sheriff court. An appeal may be made from the Inner House to the House of Lords.

COURT OF SESSION JUDGES

The judges of the Court of Session are the same as those of the High Court of Justiciary, the Lord President of the Court of Session also holding the office of Lord Justice-General in the High Court. Senators of the College of Justice are Lords Commissioners of Justiciary as well as judges of the Court of Session. On appointment, a Senator takes a judicial title, which is retained for life. Although styled 'The Hon./Rt. Hon. Lord –', the Senator is not a peer.

SUDDEN DEATHS

The office of coroner does not exist in Scotland. The local procurator fiscal inquires privately into sudden or suspicious deaths and may report findings to the Crown Agent. In some cases a fatal accident inquiry may be held before the sheriff.

COURT OF SESSION AND HIGH COURT OF JUSTICIARY

The Lord President and Lord Justice-General (£181,176)
The Rt. Hon. Lord Cullen of Whitekirk (William Cullen), *born* 1935, *apptd* 2001
Private Secretary: A. Maxwell

INNER HOUSE
LORDS OF SESSION (£166,394)

FIRST DIVISION
The Lord President
Rt. Hon. Lord Gill (Brian Gill), *born* 1942, *apptd* 2001
Rt. Hon. Lord Marnoch (Michael Bruce), *born* 1938 *apptd* 1990
Rt. Hon. Lord Penrose (George Penrose), *born* 1938, *apptd* 1990
Rt. Hon. Lord Hamilton (A. C. Hamilton), *born* 1942, *apptd* 1995
Rt. Hon. Lady Cosgrove (H. Aronson), *born* 1946, *apptd* 1996. (*She is the first woman to hold the appointment*)

SECOND DIVISION
Lord Justice Clerk, Rt. Hon. Lord Gill (Brian Gill), *born* 1942, *apptd* 2001
Rt. Hon. Lord Kirkwood (I. C. Kirkwood), *born* 1932, *apptd* 1987
Rt. Hon. Lord MacLean (R. N. M. MacLean), *born* 1938, *apptd* 1990
Rt. Hon. Lord Osborne (K. H. Osborne), *born* 1937, *apptd* 1990
Rt. Hon. Lord Macfadyen (D. J. D. Macfadyen), *born* 1945, *apptd* 1995

OUTER HOUSE
LORDS OF SESSION (£147,198)

Hon. Lord Abernethy (Alistair Cameron), *born* 1938, *apptd* 1992
Hon. Lord Johnston (Alan Johnston), *born* 1942, *apptd* 1994
Hon. Lord Dawson (Thomas Dawson), *born* 1948, *apptd* 1995
Hon. Lord Nimmo Smith (William Nimmo Smith), *born* 1942, *apptd* 1996
Hon. Lord Philip (Alexander Philip), *born* 1942, *apptd* 1996
Hon. Lord Kingarth (Derek Emslie), *born* 1949, *apptd* 1997
Hon. Lord Bonomy (Iain Bonomy), *born* 1946, *apptd* 1997
Hon. Lord Eassie (Ronald Mackay), *born* 1945, *apptd* 1997

Hon. Lord Reed (Robert Reed), *born* 1956, *apptd* 1998
Hon. Lord Wheatley (John Wheatley), *born* 1941, *apptd* 1999
Hon. Lady Paton (Ann Paton), *apptd* 2000
Hon. Lord Carloway (Colin Sutherland), *born* 1954, *apptd* 2000
Hon. Lord Clarke (Matthew Clarke), *apptd* 2000
Rt. Hon. Lord Hardie (Andrew Hardie), *born* 1946, *apptd* 2000
Rt. Hon. Lord Mackay of Drumadoon (Donald Mackay), *born* 1946, *apptd* 2000
Hon. Lord McEwan (Robin McEwan), *born* 1943, *apptd* 2000
Hon. Lord Menzies (D. A. Y. Menzies), *born* 1953, *apptd* 2001
Hon. Lord Drummond Young (J. E. Drummond Young), *born* 1950, *apptd* 2001
Hon. Lord Emslie (G. N. H. Emslie), *born* 1947, *apptd* 2001
Hon. Lady Smith (A. M. Smith), *born* 1955, *apptd* 2001
Hon. Lord Brodie (P. H. Brodie), born 1950, *apptd* 2002
Hon. Lord Bracadale (A. P. Campbell), *born* 1949, *apptd* 2003

HIGH COURT OF JUSTICIARY
Justiciary Office, Lawnmarket, Edinburgh EH1 2NS
Tel: 0131-225 2595

COURT OF SESSION
Parliament House, Parliament Square, Edinburgh EH1 1RQ Tel: 0131-225 2595

Principal Clerk of Session and Justiciary (£41,630–£67,701): J. L. Anderson
Deputy Principal Clerk of Justiciary: (£32,249–£46,766): N. J. Dowie
Deputy Principal Clerk of Session and Principal Extractor (£32,249–£46,766): R. Cockburn
Keeper of the Rolls (£23,972–£30,565): A. Moffat
Acting Depute in Charge of the Offices of Court: Miss Y. Anderson
Head of Administration (£23,972–£30,565): J. Smith
Depute Clerks of Session and Justiciary (£23,972–£30,565): M. Weir; I. F. Smith; T. B. Cruickshank; Q. A. Oliver; F. Shannly; T. Higgins; A. Finlayson; J. McLean; W. Dunn; C. C. Armstrong; R. M. Sinclair; D. W. Cullen; I. D. Martin; N. McGinley; J. Lynn; Mrs E. Dickson; R. MacPherson; G. Combe; A. Whyte; D. C. Bruton; D. MacLeod; A. Mackay; C. McGrane; L. MacLaclan; A. Thompson; J. Moyes; M. Hunter; A. Lynch

SCOTTISH COURT SERVICE

Hayweight House, 23 Lauriston Street, Edinburgh
EH3 9DQ Tel: 0131-229 9200
Email: enquiries@scotcourts.gov.uk

The Scottish Court Service is an executive agency within the Scottish Executive Justice Department. It is responsible to the Scottish Ministers for the provision of staff, court houses and associated services for the Supreme and Sheriff Courts.
Chief Executive: John Ewing

SHERIFF COURT OF CHANCERY

27 Chambers Street, Edinburgh EH1 1LB
Tel: 0131-225 2525

The Court deals with service of heirs and completion of title in relation to heritable property.
Sheriff of Chancery: I. D. McPhail

HM COMMISSARY OFFICE

27 Chambers Street, Edinburgh EH1 1LB
Tel: 0131-225 2525

The Office is responsible for issuing confirmation, a legal document entitling a person to execute a deceased person's will, and other related matters.
Commissary Clerk: G. McIlwain

SCOTTISH LAND COURT

1 Grosvenor Crescent, Edinburgh EH12 5ER
Tel: 0131-225 3595 Fax: 0131-226 4812

The court deals with disputes relating to agricultural and crofting land in Scotland.
Chairman: The Hon. Lord McGhie (James McGhie), QC
Members: D. J. Houston; D. M. Macdonald; J. Kinloch (part-time)
Principal Clerk: K. H. R. Graham, WS

SHERIFFDOMS

GRAMPIAN, HIGHLAND AND ISLANDS

Sheriff Court House, Castle Street, Aberdeen
AB10 1WP Tel: 01224-657200

Sheriff Principal: Sir Stephen S. T. Young Bt.
Area Director North: Mrs E. Laing

SHERIFFS AND SHERIFF CLERKS

Aberdeen and Stonehaven: A. S. Jessop;
G. K. Buchanan, Mrs A. M. Cowan; C. J. Harris;
K. M. Stewart; D. J. Cusine; P. P. Davies
Sheriff Clerks: Mrs E. Laing (Aberdeen);
A. Hempseed (Stonehaven)
Banff: K. A. McLernan; *Sheriff Clerk Depute:*
David Altman
Peterhead: M. Garden; *Sheriff Clerk:* B. J. McBride
Elgin: I. A. Cameron; *Sheriff Clerk:* W. Cochrane
Inverness, Lochmaddy, Portree, Stornoway, Dingwall, Tain, Wick and Dornoch: A. Pollock; D. Booker-Milburn; D. C. Sutherland; A. L. MacFadyen
Sheriff Clerks: Mrs A. Bayliss (*Inverness*);
M. McBey (*Dingwall*); *Sheriff Clerks Depute:*
Miss M. Campbell (*Lochmaddy and Portree*);
Miss S. B. Armstrong (*Stornoway*); Iain Dunbar
(*Tain*); Mrs J. McEwan (*Wick*); Len MacLachlan
(*Dornoch*)
Kirkwall and Lerwick: C. S. Mackenzie;
Sheriff Clerks Depute: Miss A. Moore (*Kirkwall*);
Barry Reid (*Lerwick*)
Fort William: W. D. Small (also *Oban*);
Sheriff Clerk Depute: Stephen McKenna

TAYSIDE, CENTRAL AND FIFE

Sheriff Court House, Tay Street, Perth PH2 8NL
Tel: 01738-620546
Sheriff Principal, R. Alastair Dunlop, QC
Area Director East: M. Bonar

SHERIFFS AND SHERIFF CLERKS

Arbroath: C. N. R. Stein; *Sheriff Clerk:*
M. Herbertson
Dundee: R. A. Davidson; A. L. Stewart, QC;
J. P. Scott; I. D. Dunbar, F. R. Crowe; L. Wood;
Sheriff Clerk: D. Nicoll
Perth: R. A. Dunlop, M. J. Fletcher; J. K. Tierney;
D. W. Pyle, L. D. R. Foulis; *Sheriff Clerk:* J. Murphy
Falkirk: A. V. Sheehan; A. J. Murphy; C. Caldwell;
Sheriff Clerk: R. McMillan
Forfar: K. A. Veal; *Sheriff Clerk:* Gordon Campbell
Stirling: R. E. G. Younger; A. W. Robertson;
Sheriff Clerk: Mrs G. McKeand
Alloa: W. M. Reid; *Sheriff Clerk:* Mrs G. McKeand
Cupar: G. J. Evans; *Sheriff Clerk:* A. Nicol
Dunfermline: R. J. MacLeod; I. G. McColl;
I. C. Simpson; D. N. Mackie;
Sheriff Clerk: J Murphy
Kirkcaldy: F. J. Keane; G. W. M. Liddle;
B. G. Donald; *Sheriff Clerk:* W. Jones

LOTHIAN AND BORDERS

Sheriff Court House, 27 Chambers Street, Edinburgh
EH1 1LB Tel: 0131-225 2525
Sheriff Principal: I. D. MacPhail, QC
Area Director East: M.G. Bonar

SHERIFFS AND SHERIFF CLERKS

Edinburgh: R. G. Craik, QC *(also Peebles)*;
 R. J. D. Scott *(also Peebles)*; Miss I. A. Poole;
 A. M. Bell; J. M. S. Horsburgh, QC;
 J. A. Farrell; A. Lothian; C. N. Stoddart;
 N. M. P. Morrison, QC; *Miss M. M. Stephen;
 Mrs M. L. E. Jarvie, QC; N. J. Mackinnon;
 Mrs K. E. C. Mackie; J. D. Allan;
 N. McPartlin; M. G. R. Edington; K. M. McIver;
 D. W. M. MacIntyre; J. C. C. McSherry;
 Sheriff Clerk: J. M. Ross
Peebles: R. G. Craik, QC (also *Edinburgh*);
 R. J. D. Scott (also *Edinburgh*);
 Sheriff Clerk: John Ross
Linlithgow: G. R. Fleming, QC; P. Gillam,
 W. D. Muirhead; M. G. R. Edington;
 Sheriff Clerk: R. D. Sinclair
Haddington: G. W. S. Presslie;
 Sheriff Clerk: J. O'Donnell
Jedburgh and Duns: T. A. K. Drummond, QC;
 Sheriff Clerk: I. W. Williamson
Selkirk: T. A. K. Drummond, QC;
 Sheriff Clerk Depute: L. McFarlane

NORTH STRATHCLYDE

Sheriff Court House, St James's Street, Paisley
PA3 2HW Tel: 0141-887 5291
Sheriff Principal: B. A. Kerr, QC
Area Director West: D. Forrester

SHERIFFS AND SHERIFF CLERKS

Oban: C. G. McKay; *Sheriff Clerk:* S. Bain
Dumbarton: J. T. Fitzsimons; T. Scott;
 S. W. H. Fraser; *Sheriff Clerk:* S. Bain
Paisley: B. A. Kerr; A. M. Cuble; S. M. Sinclair;
 J. Spy; N. Douglas; D. J. Pender; W. Dunlop (also
 Campbeltown); C. W. Pettigrew; G. C. Kavanagh;
 I. McDonald; *Sheriff Clerk:* Miss S. Hindes
Greenock: R. Swanney; J. P. Herald (also *Rothesay*);
 V. J. Canavan; *Sheriff Clerk:* A. Johnston
Kilmarnock: T. M. Croan; C. G. McKay;
 Mrs I. S. McDonald; *Sheriff Clerk:* G. Waddell
Dunoon, Mrs C. M. A. F. Gimblett;
 Sheriff Clerk: A. Johnston
Campbeltown: W. Dunlop (also *Paisley*);
 Sheriff Clerk Depute: S. Bain
Rothesay: J. Herald (also *Greenock*); *Sheriff Clerk:*
 Alan Johnston

GLASGOW AND STRATHKELVIN

Sheriff Court House, PO Box 23, 1 Carlton Place,
Glasgow G5 9DA Tel: 0141-429 8888
Sheriff Principal: E. F. Bowen, QC
Area Director West: I. Scott

SHERIFFS AND SHERIFF CLERKS

Glasgow: B. Kearney; B. A. Lockhart;
 Mrs A. L. A. Duncan; A. C. Henry; J. K. Mitchell;
 A. G. Johnston; Miss S. A. O. Raeburn, QC;
 D. Convery; I. A. S. Peebles, QC;
 C. W. McFarlane, QC; H. Matthews, QC;
 J. A. Baird; Mrs P. M. M. Bowman;
 Miss R. E. A. Rae, QC; A. W. Noble; J. D. Friel;
 Mrs D. M. MacNeill, QC; J. A. Taylor;
 C. A. L. Scott; F. L. Reith, QC; I. Miller;
 W. J. Totten; S. Cathcart; Miss L. M. Ruxton;
 M. G. O'Grady, QC; W. H. Holligan;
 A. C. Normand; S. A. Waldron;
 Sheriff Clerk: C. Binning

SOUTH STRATHCLYDE, DUMFRIES AND GALLOWAY

Sheriff Court House, Graham Street, Airdrie ML6 6EE
Tel: 01236-751121
Sheriff Principal: J. C. McInnes, QC
Area Director West: D. F. Forrester

SHERIFFS AND SHERIFF CLERKS

Hamilton: C. A. Kelly, J Montgomery, D. C. Russell;
 W. E. Gibson; J. H. Stewart; H. S. Neilson;
 S. C. Pender; Miss J. Powrie; T. Welsh;
 D. Bicket; M. Smart; H. K. Small; W. S. S. Ireland;
 Sheriff Clerk: P. Feeney
Lanark: N. C Stewart; *Sheriff Clerk:* Mrs M. McLean
Ayr: N. Gow, QC; C. B. Miller, QC; J McGowan;
 Sheriff Clerk: Miss C. D. Cockburn
Stranraer and Kirkcudbright: J. R. Smith (also
 Dumfries); *Sheriff Clerks:* B. J. Lindsay (*Stranraer*);
 P. J. McGonigle (*Kirkcudbright*)
Dumfries: K. G. Barr; K. Ross;
 Sheriff Clerk: P. J. McGonigle
Airdrie: M. M. Galbraith, R. H. Dickson;
 A. D. Vannet, J. C. Morris, QC;
 Sheriff Clerk: J. Tannahill

STIPENDIARY MAGISTRATES

GLASGOW

R. Hamilton, *apptd* 1984; J. B. C. Nisbet, *apptd*
 1984; R. B. Christie, *apptd* 1985; Mrs J. A. M.
 MacLean, *apptd* 1990

CROWN OFFICE AND PROCURATOR FISCAL SERVICE

CROWN OFFICE

25 Chambers Street, Edinburgh EH1 1LA
Tel 0131-226 2626
Crown Agent: Norman McFadyen
Deputy Crown Agent: W. A. Gilchrist

PROCURATORS FISCAL

GRAMPIAN, HIGHLANDS AND ISLANDS REGION

Regional Procurator Fiscal: John Watt (*Aberdeen*)
Procurators Fiscal: E. K. Barbour (*Stonehaven*);
A. J. M. Colley (*Banff*); A. B. Hutchinson
(*Peterhead*); D. J. Dickson (*Elgin*); J. Bamber
(*Portree, Lochmaddy*); D. S. Teale (*Stornoway*);
G. Napier (*Inverness*); Ms. S. Foard (*Kirkwall,
Lerwick*); Ms. A. E. Wyllie (*Fort William*);
A. N. MacDonald (*Tain*); R. W. Urquhart
(*Dingwall*); G. Aitkin (*Wick*)

TAYSIDE, CENTRAL AND FIFE REGION

Regional Procurator Fiscal: B. K. Heywood (*Dundee*)
Procurators Fiscal: J. I. Craigen (*Forfar*);
D. B. Griffiths (*Perth*); W. J. Gallacher (*Falkirk*);
C. Ritchie (*Stirling and Alloa*); E. B. Russell
(*Cupar*); R. G. Stott (*Dunfermline*);
Miss H. M. Clark (*Kirkcaldy*)

LOTHIAN AND BORDERS REGION

Regional Procurator Fiscal: D. Brown (*Edinburgh*)
Procurators Fiscal: Mrs C. P. Dyer (*Linlithgow*);
A. J. P. Reith (*Haddington*); A. R. G. Fraser (*Duns,
Jedburgh*); Mrs L. Thomson (*Selkirk*)

NORTH STRATHCLYDE REGION

Regional Procurator Fiscal: J. J. Miller (*Paisley*)
Procurators Fiscal: F. Redman (*Campbeltown*);
C. C. Donnelly (*Dumbarton*); W. S. Carnegie
(*Greenock, Rothesay*); D. L. Webster (*Dunoon*);
J. Watt (*Kilmarnock*); B. R. Maguire (*Oban*)

GLASGOW AND STRATHKELVIN REGION

Regional Procurator Fiscal: L. A. Higson (*Glasgow*)

SOUTH STRATHCLYDE, DUMFRIES AND GALLOWAY REGION

Regional Procurator Fiscal: D. A. Brown (*Hamilton*)
Procurators Fiscal: S. R. Houston (*Lanark*);
I. L. Murray (*Ayr*); A. S. Kennedy (*Stranraer*);
D. J. Howdle (*Dumfries, Kirkcudbright*); D. Spiers
(*Airdrie*)

Note: details of staff and departments listed correct as at June
2003

LEGAL NOTES

These notes outline certain aspects of the law in Scotland as they might affect the average person. They focus principally on those aspects of Scots law which differ from the equivalent law in England and Wales. They are intended only as a broad guideline and are by no means definitive. The information is believed to be correct at the time of going to press, but the law is constantly changing, so expert advice should always be taken. In some cases, sources of further information are given in these notes.

Timely consultation with a solicitor is always advisable. Anyone in Scotland who does not have a solicitor can contact the Citizens' Advice Bureau (addresses in the telephone directory or at any post office or town hall) or the Law Society of Scotland (26 Drumsheugh Gardens, Edinburgh EH3 7YR) for assistance in finding one.

The legal aid and legal advice and assistance schemes exist to make the help of a lawyer available to those who would not otherwise be able to afford one. Entitlement depends upon an individual's means but a solicitor or Citizens' Advice Bureau will be able to advise about this.

ADOPTION OF CHILDREN

The adoption of children is mainly governed by the Adoption (Scotland) Act 1978 (as amended by the Children (Scotland) Act 1995).

Anyone over 21 who is domiciled in the United Kingdom, the Channel Islands or the Isle of Man or has been habitually resident in any of those places throughout the year immediately preceding the date of an application, whether married, single, widowed or divorced, can apply to adopt a child.

The only organisations allowed to arrange adoptions are the adoption agencies provided by local authorities (these agencies are known collectively as the Scottish Adoption Service) or voluntary agencies approved as adoption societies.

Once an adoption has been arranged, a court order is necessary to make it legal. Petitions for adoption are made to the Sheriff Court or the Court of Session.

Each of the child's natural parents (or guardians) must consent to the adoption, unless the court dispenses with the consent or the natural parent does not have parental responsibilities or parental rights. A child of 12 years old or over must also consent although the consent will be dispensed with if the court is satisfied the child is incapable of giving consent. Once adopted, the child, for all practical purposes, has the same legal status as a child born to the adoptive parents and the natural parents cease to have any rights or responsibilities where the child is concerned. As a general rule, the adopted child ceases to have any rights to the estates of his/her natural parents.

REGISTRATION AND CERTIFICATES

All adoptions in Scotland are registered by the General Register Office for Scotland. Certificates from the registers can be obtained in a similar way to birth certificates.

Further information on qualification to adopt a child, adoption procedures, and tracing natural parents or children who have been adopted can be obtained from:

BRITISH AGENCIES FOR ADOPTION AND FOSTERING (BAAF)
Scottish Centre, 40 Shandwick Place, Edinburgh EH2 4RT Tel: 0131-225 9285

SCOTTISH ADOPTION ADVICE SERVICE
16 Sandyford Place, Glasgow G3 7NB
Tel: 0141-248 7530

BIRTHS (REGISTRATION)

The birth of a child must be registered within 21 days at the registration office of either the district in which the baby was born or the district in which the mother was resident at the time of the birth.

If the child is born, either in or out of Scotland, on a ship, aircraft or land vehicle that ends its journey at any place in Scotland, the child, in most cases, will be registered as if born in that place.

Responsibility for registering the birth rests with the parents, except where the father of the child is not married to the mother and has not been married to her since the child's conception, in which case the mother is responsible for registration. Responsibility rests firstly with the parents, but if they fail particulars may be given to the registrar by:

– a relative of the mother or father (if he is married to the mother)
– the occupier of the house in which the baby was born
– a person present at the birth
– a person having charge of the child

Failure to register the birth within 21 days without reasonable cause may lead to a court decree being granted by a sheriff.

Further information is available from local registrars, whose addresses and telephone numbers can be found in local telephone directories.

CERTIFICATES OF BIRTHS, DEATHS OR MARRIAGES

Certificates of births, deaths or marriages that have taken place in Scotland since 1855 can be obtained from the General Register Office for Scotland or from the appropriate local registrar. The General Register Office for Scotland also keeps the Register of Divorces (including decrees of declaration of nullity of marriage), and holds parish registers dating from before 1855.

Fees for certificates are:

Certificates (full or abbreviated) of birth, death, marriage or adoption, £8.50
Email application in course of Internet search, £10.00
General search in the parochial registers and indexes to the statutory registers, per day or part thereof:
Full day search (9 a.m. to 4.30 p.m.), £17.00
Afternoon (i.e. 1 p.m. to 4.30 p.m.) search, £10.00
One week search, £65.00
Four week search, £220.00
One quarter search, £500.00
One year search, £1,500.00

Further information can be obtained from:

THE GENERAL REGISTER OFFICE FOR SCOTLAND
New Register House, Edinburgh EH1 3YT
Tel: 0131-314 4452 Fax: 0131-314 4400
Web: www.gro-scotland.gov.uk

Certificate Ordering line 0131-314 4411

CONSUMER LAW

UK legislation governing the sale and supply of goods applies to Scotland as follows:

- the Sale of Goods Act 1979 applies with some modifications and has been amended by the Sale and Supply of Goods Act 1994
- the Supply of Goods (Implied Terms) Act 1973 applies
- the Supply of Goods and Services Act 1982 does not extend to Scotland but some of its provisions were introduced by the Sale and Supply of Goods Act 1994
- only Parts II and III of the Unfair Contract Terms Act 1977 apply
- the Trade Descriptions Act 1968 applies with minor modifications
- the Consumer Credit Act 1974 applies
- the Consumer Protection Act 1974 applies

- the General Product Safety Regulations 1994 apply
- the Unfair Terms in Consumer Contracts 1999 apply
- the Consumer Protection (Distance Selling) Regulations 2000 apply
- the Unfair Terms in Consumer Contracts (Amendment) Regulations 2001 apply
- The Sale and Supply of Goods to Consumers Regulations 2002 apply

DEATHS

When a death occurs, if the death was expected, the doctor who attended the deceased during their final illness should be contacted. If the death was sudden or unexpected, the family doctor (if known) and police should be contacted immediately.

If the cause of death is quite clear the doctor will either:

- issue a certificate of cause of death needed by the registrar, provided that there are no unusual circumstances. If the body is to be cremated, the doctor will arrange for the signature of the second doctor needed to complete the cremation certificate; or
- if the doctor is uncertain as to the cause of death he will report the death to the local procurator fiscal who will make enquiries.

A fatal accident inquiry will be held before a sheriff where the death has resulted from an accident during the course of the employment of the person who has died, or where the person who has died was in legal custody, or where the Lord Advocate deems it in the public interest that an inquiry be held.

A death may be registered in any registration district in which the deceased was ordinarily resident immediately before his/her death or, if different, in the registration district in which the death took place. The death must normally be registered within eight days. If the death has been referred to the local procurator fiscal it cannot be registered until the registrar has received authority from the procurator fiscal to do so. Failure to register a death may lead to a court decree being granted by a sheriff.

Whereas in most circumstances in England and Wales a certificate for burial or cremation must be obtained from the registrar before the burial or cremation can take place, in Scotland a body may be buried (but normally not cremated) before the death is registered.

Further information can be obtained from the General Register Office for Scotland (*see* above for contact details).

DIVORCE AND RELATED MATTERS

There are two main types of matrimonial action: those seeking the annulment of a marriage, and those seeking a judicial separation or divorce.

An action for 'declarator of nullity' can be brought only in the Court of Session.

An action for judicial separation or divorce may be raised in the Court of Session. It may also be raised in the Sheriff Court if either party was resident in the sheriffdom for 40 days immediately before the date of the action or for 40 days ending not more than 40 days before the date of the action. The fee for starting a divorce petition in the Sheriff Court is £81.

NULLITY OF MARRIAGE

A marriage is void (i.e. invalid) from the beginning if:

– the parties were within the prohibited degrees of consanguinity, affinity or adoption
– the parties were not male and female
– either of the parties was already married
– either of the parties was under the age of 16
– either of the parties did not truly consent to marry, e.g. in consequence of mental illness, intoxication, force or fear, or in a sham marriage where the intention was to avoid deportation
– the formalities of the marriage were defective, e.g. each of the parties did not submit a notice of intention to marry (a marriage notice) to the district registrar for the registration district in which the marriage was to be solemnised

A marriage may be voidable (i.e. a decree of nullity may be obtained but in the meantime the marriage remains valid) if either party was unable to consummate the marriage.

Where a spouse is capable of sexual intercourse but refuses to consummate the marriage, this is not a ground of nullity in Scots law, though it could be a ground for divorce.

When a marriage is void, it generally has no legal effect at all, and there is therefore no specific need to seek a declarator of nullity in the Court of Session (although it may be wise to do so, e.g. if one of the parties wishes to marry again). Nevertheless, a child conceived during a valid marriage is presumed to be the child of the 'husband'. A child's mother has parental responsibilities and parental rights in relation to the child whether or not she is or has been married to his father. A child's father has such responsibilities and rights in relation to the child only if married to the mother at the time of the child's conception or subsequently. A father is regarded as having been married to the mother at any time when he was a party to a purported marriage with her which was:
– voidable; or
– void but believed by them in good faith at that time to be valid.

When a marriage has been annulled, both parties are free to marry again.

DIVORCE

Divorce dissolves the marriage and leaves both parties at liberty to marry again. The sole ground for divorce is the irretrievable breakdown of the marriage; this must be proved on one or more of the following grounds:
– the defender has committed adultery; however the pursuer cannot rely on an act of adultery by the other party if, after discovery of the act of adultery, he or she has continued or resumed living together with the defender at any time after the end of a period of three months on which cohabitation has been continued or resumed
– the defender has behaved in such a way that the pursuer cannot reasonably be expected to continue living with him/her
– desertion, which is established by the defender having left the pursuer for a period of two years immediately preceding the action wilfully and without reasonable cause and during that 2-year period the pursuer has not refused a genuine and reasonable offer by the defender to adhere. Irretrievable breakdown is not established if, after the two year desertion period has expired, the parties resume living together at any time after the end of three months from the date when they first resumed living together
– the defender and the pursuer have lived separately for two years immediately before the raising of the action and the defender consents to the decree
– the defender and the pursuer have lived separately for five years immediately before the raising of the action

Where a divorce action has been raised, it may be sisted or put on hold for a variety of reasons, including, though rarely, enabling the parties to seek to effect a reconciliation if the court feels that there may be a reasonable prospect of such reconciliation. If the parties do cohabit during such postponement, no account is taken of the cohabitation if the action later proceeds.

A simplified procedure for 'do-it-yourself' divorce was introduced in 1983 for certain divorces. If the action is based on two or five years' separation and will not be opposed, and if there are no children under 16, no financial claims and there is no sign that the applicant's spouse is unable to manage his or her affairs because of mental illness or handicap, the applicant can write directly to the local sheriff court or to the Court of Session for the appropriate forms to enable him or her to proceed. The fee is £62, unless the applicant receives income support, family credit or legal advice and assistance, in which case there is no fee.

The extract decree will be made available fourteen days after the divorce has been granted. The extract decree brings the marriage to an end.

Further information can be obtained from any sheriff court, solicitor, Citizens' Advice Bureau, the Lord Advocate's Office or the following:

THE COURT OF SESSION
Parliament House, Parliament Square, Edinburgh
EH1 1RQ Tel: 0131-225 2595

EMPLOYMENT LAW

PAY AND CONDITIONS
Responsibility for employment legislation rests with the UK Parliament and the legislation applies to all parts of Great Britain, with the exception of some separate anti-discrimination legislation for Northern Ireland.

The Employment Rights Act 1996 consolidates the statutory provisions relating to employees' rights. It covers matters such as pay and conditions (including authorised deductions from pay, trade union membership, disputes, and the rights of part-time employees (and termination of employment including redundancy and unfair dismissal). The Working Time Regulations 1998, National Minimum Wage Act 1998 and Part-time Employees (Prevention of Less Favourable Treatment) Regulations 2000 now supplement the 1996 Act. Procedure at Employment Tribunals is governed by separate Scottish regulations.

A number of laws protect employees from discrimination in employment on the grounds of sex, race or disability:

– The Equal Pay Act 1970 (as amended)
– The Sex Discrimination Act 1975 (as amended by the Sex Discrimination Act 1986)
– The Race Relations Act 1976
– The Disability Discrimination Act 1995

The Equal Opportunities Commission and the Commission for Racial Equality have the function of eliminating such discriminations in the workplace and can provide further information and assistance. The Disability Rights Commission has

been in operation since April 2000 and aims to encourage good practice in the treatment of disabled people and can provide information and assistance.

EQUAL OPPORTUNITIES COMMISSION
St. Stephen's House, 279 Bath Street, Glasgow G2 4JL
Tel: 0141-248 5833 Fax: 0141-248 5834

COMMISSION FOR RACIAL EQUALITY
The Tun, 12 Jackson's Entry, off Holyrood Road,
Edinburgh, EH8 8PJ
Tel: 0131-524 2000 Fax: 0131-524 2001

DISABILITY RIGHTS COMMISSION
1st Floor, Riverside House, Gorgie Road, Edinburgh
EH11 3AF Tel: 08457-622 633 Fax: 08457-622 688

HOUSE PURCHASE

A contract for the sale of a house in Scotland rarely takes the form of a single document. The purchaser's solicitor issues a formal written offer to purchase. This is usually issued once a survey of the property has been carried out, but can more unusually be issued 'subject to survey'. The seller's solicitor will issue a qualified acceptance of the offer. This is then adjusted between the parties' solicitors until a final concluding letter is issued. At this point the contract is formed and both parties are contractually bound. The letters passing between the solicitors are known as 'missives'.

Some conditions contained within the missives may require the seller to provide information so that the purchaser may be satisfied that the property is unaffected by any statutory notices for repairs or by any planning proposals. Property enquiry reports are obtained by the seller's solicitor from either the local authority or private companies who provide this information. These reports disclose whether the property is adversely affected, if it is served by public water and sewage services, and whether the roads adjoining the property are maintained by the local authority.

The purchaser will also examine the title deeds for the property to make sure that there are no flaws in the title to be granted to the purchaser. Searches in the appropriate property register are made. A search is also carried out against both the purchaser and the seller to ensure there is no reason why either party cannot proceed with the transaction.

On the day of settlement the purchaser's solicitor will pass the purchase price to the seller's solicitor who in turn passes over the disposition, title deeds, an obligation to deliver a clear search brought down to disclose the recording of the purchaser's title, and keys. The disposition is the deed which transfers ownership of the property from the seller to the purchaser. This deed has to be registered in the appropriate property register in order for the purchaser to have a right to the property – either the Register of Sasines or the newer Land Register which is being phased in by county to replace the old Register of Sasines.

HUMAN RIGHTS

The Human Rights Act 1998 came into force on 2 October 2000. It incorporates into domestic UK law certain rights and freedoms set out in the articles of the European Convention on Human Rights. Rights such as Article 2 (right to life), Article 3, (prohibition of torture, an inhuman or degrading treatment), Article 4 (prohibition of slavery or forced labour), Article 6 (right to fair trial), Article 8 (right to respect for private and family life), Article 9 (freedom of thought, conscience and religion), Article 10 (freedom of expression), Article 11 (the right to freedom of association, including joining a trade union), Article 14 (freedom from discrimination in respect of convention rights).

Both the UK Parliament and the Scottish Parliament are required to legislate in a way compatible with the convention. Section 3 of the Act provides that so far as is possible to do so, primary legislation and subordinate legislation must be read and given effect to in a way which is compatible with convention rights. Section 4 provides that certain courts may make declarations of incompatibility, which may then trigger remedial action.

ILLEGITIMACY AND LEGITIMATION

Under the Legitimation (Scotland) Act 1968, which came into operation on 8 June 1968, an illegitimate person automatically becomes legitimate when his/her parents marry, even where one of the parents was married to a third person at the time of the birth.

Illegitimate and legitimate people are given, for all practical purposes, equal status under the Law Reform (Parent and Child) Scotland Act 1986.

The Children (Scotland) Act 1995 gives the mother parental responsibility for her child whether or not she is married to the child's father. The father has automatic parental rights only if he is married to the mother. An unmarried father has no automatic parental rights but can acquire parental responsibility by applying to the court or entering into an agreement with the mother. The father of

any child, regardless of parental rights, has a duty to aliment that child until he/she is 18 or 25 if he/she is still in full time education. The Child Support Agency are entitled to make an assessment if the father fails to maintain the child and the mother of the child can apply to the Child Support Agency for an assessment.

JURY SERVICE

A person charged with any serious crime is tried before a jury. Jury trials in Scottish civil cases in the Court of Session are becoming more common. In Scotland there are 12 members of a jury in a civil case in the Court of Session (the civil jury trial is confined to the Court of Session and a restricted number of actions) and 15 in a criminal trial. Jurors are expected to sit for the duration of the trial.

Every parliamentary or local government elector between the ages of 18 and 65 who has lived in the UK, the Channel Islands or the Isle of Man for any period of at least five years since reaching the age of 13 is qualified to serve on a jury in Scotland, unless ineligible or disqualified.

Those disqualified from jury service include:

- those who have at any time been sentenced by a court in the UK, the Channel Islands and the Isle of Man to a term of imprisonment or custody of five years or more
- those who have within the previous ten years served any part of a sentence of three months or more of imprisonment or detention

Members of the judiciary are ineligible whilst in post and for ten years after ceasing to hold their post, and others concerned with the administration of justice become eligible again only five years after ceasing to hold office. Members and officers of the Houses of Parliament, the Scottish Parliament and members of the Scottish Executive, representatives to the assembly of the European Parliament, full time serving members of the armed forces, registered and practising members of the medical, dental, nursing, veterinary and pharmaceutical professions, ministers of religion, persons in holy orders and those who have served on a jury in the previous five years are excusable as of right. Those who are receiving treatment for a mental disorder or are subject to guardianship under the Adults with Incapacity (Scotland) Act 2000 may also be excused.

The maximum fine for a person serving on a jury knowing himself/herself to be ineligible is £1,000. The maximum fine for failing to attend without good cause is also £1,000.

Further information can obtained from:

THE CLERK OF JUSTICIARY
High Court of Justiciary, Lawn Market, Edinburgh
EH1 2NS Tel: 0131-225 2595

LANDLORD AND TENANT

When a property is rented to a tenant, the rights and responsibilities of the landlord and the tenant are determined largely by the tenancy agreement but also the general law of Scotland. The main provisions are mentioned below, but it is advisable to contact the Citizens' Advice Bureau or the local authority housing department for detailed information.

Assured and short assured tenancies exist for lettings after 2 January 1989; the relevant legislation is the Housing (Scotland) Act 1988.

If a tenancy was granted on or after 2 January 1989, the tenant may have an assured tenancy giving that tenant greater rights. The tenant could, for example, stay in possession of the dwelling for as long as the tenant observed the terms of the tenancy. The landlord cannot obtain possession from such a tenant unless the landlord can establish a specific ground for possession (the grounds are set out in the 1988 Act) and obtains a court order. The rent payable continues throughout the period of the lease unless the rent has been fixed by the Rent Assessment Committee of the local authority. The Committee also has powers to determine other terms of the lease.

The 1988 Act also introduced short assured tenancies, which are tenancies of not less than six months where a notice has been served to the effect that the tenancy is a short assured tenancy. A landlord in a short assured tenancy has all the rights of a landlord in an ordinary assured tenancy to recover possession and also the right to regain possession on timeously giving notice to quit to the tenant, whether or not the tenant has observed the terms of the tenancy.

Most tenancies created before 2 January 1989 were regulated tenancies and the Rent (Scotland) Act 1984 still applies where these exist. The Act defines, among other things, the circumstances in which a landlord can increase the rent when improvements are made to the property. The provisions of the 1984 Act do not apply to tenancies where the landlord is the Crown, a local authority, the development corporation of a new town or a housing corporation.

The Housing (Scotland) Act 1987 and its provisions relate to local authority responsibilities for housing, the right to buy, and local authority secured tenancies.

Tenancies in agricultural properties are governed by the Agricultural Holdings (Scotland) Act 1991. The Agricultural Holdings (Scotland) Act 2003, most of which is due to come into force later this year, will run in tandem with the 1991 Act. It will establish new types of limited duration tenancies and a tenant's right to buy upon the owner proposing to transfer land. It will change the tenant's rights to use of land, deal with compensation for improvements and extend the jurisdiction of the Land Court at the expense of compulsory arbitration.

Business premises in Scotland are not controlled by statute to the same extent as in England and Wales, although the Shops (Scotland) Act 1949 gives some security to tenants of shops. Tenants of shops can apply to the sheriff for a renewal of tenancy if threatened with eviction. This application may be dismissed on various grounds, including where the landlord has offered to sell the property to the tenant at an agreed price or, in the absence of agreement as to price, at a price fixed by a single arbiter appointed by the parties or the sheriff. The Act extends to properties where the Crown or government departments are the landlords or the tenants.

Under the Leases Act 1449 the landlord's successors (either purchasers or creditors) are bound by the agreement made with any tenants so long as the following conditions are met:

– the lease, if for more than one year, must be in writing
– there must be a rent
– there must be a term of expiry
– the tenant must have entered into possession

Many leases contain references to term and quarter days.

LEGAL AID

Under the Legal Aid (Scotland) Act 1986 and subsequent Regulations, people on low or moderate incomes may qualify for help with the costs of legal advice or representation. The scheme is administered by the Scottish Legal Aid Board.

There are three types of legal aid: civil legal aid, legal advice and assistance, and criminal legal aid.

CIVIL LEGAL AID

Applications for legal aid are made through a solicitor; the Citizens' Advice Bureau will have addresses for local solicitors.

Civil legal aid is available for proceedings in the following:

- the House of Lords
- the Court of Session
- the Lands Valuation Appeal Court
- the Scottish Land Court
- Sheriff Courts
- the Lands Tribunal for Scotland
- the Employment Appeal Tribunals
- the Restrictive Practices Court

Civil legal aid is not available for defamation actions, some issues relating to bankruptcy, small claims or simplified divorce procedures.

Eligibility for civil legal aid is assessed and a civil legal aid certificate granted provided that:

- the applicant qualifies financially,
- the applicant has reasonable grounds for taking or defending the action,
- it is reasonable to grant legal aid in the circumstances of the case (for example, civil legal aid will not be granted where it appears that the applicant will gain only trivial advantage from the proceedings), and
- Financial help is not available from someone else such as a trade union, insurance company or professional body.

The financial criteria for eligibility are:

- a person is eligible if disposable income does not exceed £9,307 and disposable capital does not exceed £6,100
- if disposable income is between £2,851 and £9,307, contributions are payable
- if disposable capital exceeds £6,100, contributions are payable and legal aid may be refused if disposable capital is over £10,170
- those receiving income support or income related job seeker's allowance will qualify automatically

Emergency legal aid cover may be granted before a full application has been made and a means test has been carried out. In such cases means testing is carried out later and the applicant is required to meet the cost of any aid received which exceeded their entitlement.

A statutory charge is made if a person is awarded money or property in a case for which they have received legal aid.

LEGAL ADVICE AND ASSISTANCE

The legal advice and assistance scheme covers the costs of getting advice and help from a solicitor and, in some cases, representation in court under the 'assistance by way of representation' scheme (*see* below).

A person is eligible:
- if disposable income does not exceed £192 a week. If disposable income is between £81 and £192 a week, contributions are payable
- if disposable capital does not exceed £1,330 (£1,665 if the person has one dependant, £1,865 if two dependants, with an additional £100 for every other dependant). There are no contributions from capital

If a person is eligible, an initial amount of authorised expenditure can be incurred without the prior authority of the Scottish Legal Aid Board. The initial limit is £80 in most cases, but a higher initial limit of £150 applies in some circumstances, for example where a civil matter is only likely to be resolved in court, legal aid will be available to the client and the initial work is reasonable. Any increase in authorised expenditure must first be applied for to and granted by the Scottish Legal Aid Board.

Legal advice and assistance covers giving advice, writing letters, making an application for civil/criminal legal aid and seeking the advice of an advocate. Advice and assistance does not, in general, cover appearance before a court or tribunal other than advice by way of representation.

Assistance by way of representation is available in certain cases such as certain less serious criminal cases, some mental health proceedings and civil proceedings for fine default or breach of a court order.

CRIMINAL LEGAL AID

The procedure for application for criminal legal aid depends on the circumstances of each case. In solemn cases (more serious cases, such as murder) heard before a jury, a person is automatically entitled to criminal legal aid until they are given bail or placed in custody. Thereafter, it is for the court to decide whether to grant legal aid. The court will do this if the person accused cannot meet the expenses of the case without 'undue hardship' on him or his dependants. In less serious (or summary) cases the procedure depends on whether the person is in custody:

- anyone taken into custody has the right to free legal aid from the duty solicitor up to and including the first court appearance. Thereafter, if the person has decided to plead guilty, the duty solicitor will continue to act for him/her until the case is finished. If the person pleads not guilty to any charge, they must apply to the Scottish Legal Aid Board so that their solicitor can prepare their defence and represent them at the trial. The duty solicitor may be willing to act for the accused, or they can choose their own solicitor.

– if the person is not in custody and wishes to plead guilty, they are not entitled to criminal legal aid but may be entitled to legal advice and assistance, including assistance by way of representation. The court will not assign the person a solicitor, and they must therefore choose their own if they wish one.

– if the person is not in custody and wishes to plead not guilty, they can apply for criminal legal aid. This must be done within 14 days of the first court appearance at which they made the plea. Again, the person must choose their own solicitor.

The Scottish Legal Aid Board will grant criminal legal aid if satisfied that the applicant or their family would suffer undue hardship if they had to pay for their own defence and that it is in the interests of justice to grant legal aid (the Board will consider, for example, whether there are difficult legal points to be decided, whether the applicant's job or liberty is at risk, and whether the applicant has a realistic defence).

If criminal legal aid is awarded, no contribution from the person will be required.

Further information may be obtained from:

SCOTTISH LEGAL AID BOARD
44 Drumsheugh Gardens, Edinburgh EH3 7SW
Tel: 0131-226 7061 Fax: 0131-220 4878

MARRIAGE

REGULAR MARRIAGES

A regular marriage is one which is celebrated by a minister of religion or authorised registrar or other celebrant. Each of the parties must complete a marriage notice form and return it to the district registrar for the area in which they are to be married, irrespective of where they live, at least 15 days before the ceremony is due to take place. The district registrar must then enter the date of receipt and certain details in a marriage book kept for this purpose, and must also enter the names of the parties and the proposed date of the marriage in a list which is displayed in a conspicuous place at the registration office. This entry remains displayed until the date of the marriage has passed. All

persons wishing to enter into a regular marriage in Scotland must follow the same preliminary procedure regardless of whether they intend to have a civil or a religious ceremony.

A marriage schedule, which is prepared by the registrar, will be issued to one or both of the parties in person up to seven days before a religious marriage; for a civil marriage the schedule will be available at the ceremony. The schedule must be handed to the celebrant before the ceremony starts; it must be signed immediately after the wedding and the marriage must be registered within three days.

Civil (as opposed to religious) marriage ceremonies can be conducted by the district registrar in his office or at a location approved by the local council. Furthermore, if one of the parties cannot attend the registrar's office because of serious illness or serious bodily injury, the registrar may, on application by either party, solemnise the marriage anywhere in his registration district if delay of the wedding is undesirable.

In the case of a religious marriage, the authority to conduct a marriage is deemed to be vested in the authorised celebrant (a minister, priest or other such religious person) conducting the ceremony and the ceremony can be conducted at any time or place.

MARRIAGE BY COHABITATION WITH HABIT AND REPUTE

If two people live together constantly as husband and wife and are generally held to be such by the neighbourhood and among their friends and relations, there may arise a presumption from which marriage can be inferred. Before such a marriage can be registered, however, a decree of declarator of marriage must be obtained from the Court of Session.

CIVIL FEES

The basic statutory fee is £93.50, comprising a £20 per person fee for a statutory notice of intention to marry, a £45 fee for solemnisation of the marriage in a register office, and a fee of £8.50 for a copy of the marriage certificate.

Further information can be obtained from the General Register Office for Scotland and application forms can be downloaded from the website.

TOWN AND COUNTRY PLANNING

The principal legislation governing the development of land and buildings is the Town and Country Planning (Scotland) Act 1997. The uses of buildings are classified by the Town and Country Planning (Use Classes) (Scotland) Order 1997. The order applies to use of land as well as buildings. It is advisable in all cases to contact the planning department of the local authority to check whether planning or other permission is needed.

VOTERS' QUALIFICATIONS

All persons registered in the electoral registers (which are compiled on a local basis) and over the age of 18 are entitled to vote in Scottish Parliament, UK Parliament, European Parliament and local government elections. To qualify for registration, a person must be:

- resident in the relevant constituency or ward on 10 October in the year before the electoral register comes into effect
- over 18 years old or will attain the age of 18 during the 12 months following the publication of the annual register on 16 February
- a UK, European Union, Commonwealth or Republic of Ireland citizen

Peers registered in Scotland are entitled to vote in Scottish Parliament, European Parliament and local government elections.

Overseas electors (namely British citizens not resident in the UK on the qualifying date for the electoral register but who were registered as parliamentary electors at some point in the preceding 15 years) are only entitled to vote in UK Parliament and European Parliament elections. Similar provisions apply to enable those who were too young to be registered during the previous 20 years to register provided a parent or guardian was registered.

Peers and European Union citizens are not eligible to vote in UK Parliament elections.

Voters must be entered on an electoral register, which runs from 16 February each year to the following 15 February. Supplementary lists of electors are published throughout the duration of the register.

Further information can be obtained from the local authority's electoral registration officer (details in local telephone directories).

WILLS AND INTESTACY

WILLS

In Scotland any person over 12 and of sound mind can make a will. The person making the will can only freely dispose of the heritage and what is known as the 'dead's part' of the estate because:

- the spouse has the right to inherit one-third of the moveable estate if there are children or other descendants, and one-half of it if there are not
- children are entitled to one-third of the moveable estate if there is a surviving spouse, and one-half of it if there is not

The remaining portion is the dead's part, and legacies and bequests are payable from this. Debts are payable out of the whole estate before any division.

From August 1995, wills no longer needed to be 'holographed' and it is now only necessary to have one witness. The person making the will still needs to sign each page. It is better that the will is not witnessed by a beneficiary although the attestation would still be sound and the beneficiary would not have to relinquish the gift.

Subsequent marriage does not revoke a will but the birth of a child who is not provided for may do so. A will may be revoked by a subsequent will, either expressly or by implication, but in so far as the two can be read together both have effect. If a subsequent will is revoked, the earlier will is revived.

Wills may be registered in the sheriff court books of the Sheriffdom in which the deceased lived or in the Books of Council and Session at the Registers of Scotland. If the will has been registered in the Books of Council and Session, the original will can be inspected and a copy obtained for a small fee. On the other hand, if the will has been registered in the sheriff court books, the original would have been returned to the ingiver; however, copies may still be obtained for a small fee from the photographed copy kept in the register.

CONFIRMATION

Confirmation (the Scottish equivalent of English probate) is obtained in the sheriff court of the sheriffdom in which the deceased was resident at the time of death. Executors are either 'nominate' (named by the deceased in the will) or 'dative' (appointed by the court in cases where no executor is named in a will or in cases of intestacy). Applicants for confirmation must first provide an inventory of the deceased's estate and a schedule of debts, with a declaration or oath. In estates under

£25,000 gross, confirmation can be obtained under a simplified procedure at reduced fees with no need for a solicitor. The local sheriff clerk's office can provide assistance.

Further information can be obtained from:

REGISTERS OF SCOTLAND
Meadowbank House, 153 London Road, Edinburgh, EH8 7AU Tel: 0131-659 6111

INTESTACY

Intestacy occurs when someone dies without leaving a will or leaves a will which is invalid or which does not take effect for some reason. In such cases the person's estate (property, possessions, other assets following the payment of debts) passes to certain members of the family.

The rules of distribution are contained in the Succession (Scotland) Act 1964.

A surviving spouse is entitled to 'prior rights'. This means that the spouse has the right to inherit:

– the matrimonial home up to a value of £130,000, or one matrimonial home if there is more than one, or, in certain circumstances, the value of the matrimonial home
– the furnishings and contents of that home, up to the value of £22,000
– a cash sum of £35,000 if the deceased left children or other descendants, or £58,000 if not.

These figures are increased from time to time by regulations.

Once prior rights have been satisfied jus relicti(ae) and legitim are settled. Any remaining estate is free estate.

Jus relicti(ae) – the right of a surviving spouse to one-half of the net moveable estate, after satisfaction of prior rights, if there are no surviving children; if there are surviving children, the spouse is entitled to one-third of the net moveable estate;

Legitim – the right of surviving children to one-half of the net moveable estate if there is no surviving spouse; if there is a surviving spouse, the children are entitled to one-third of the net moveable estate after the satisfaction of prior rights.

Where there are no surviving spouse or children, half of the estate is taken by the parents and half by the brothers and sisters. Failing that, the lines of succession, in general, are:

– to descendants
– if no descendants, then to collaterals (i.e. brothers and sisters) and parents
– surviving spouse
– if no collaterals or parents or spouse, then to ascendants collaterals (i.e. aunts and uncles), and so on in an ascending scale
– if all lines of succession fail, the estate passes to the Crown

Relatives of the whole blood are preferred to relatives of the half blood. The right of representation, i.e. the right of the issue of a person who would have succeeded if he/she had survived the intestate, also applies.

CRIME AND LEGAL STATISTICS

NUMBER OF ACTIONS INITIATED IN THE COURT OF SESSION, 1991–2000

1991	5,937
1992	6,212
1993	6,182
1994	5,535
1995	5,207
1996	4,683
1997	4,513
1998	4,401
1999	4,471
2000	5,120

NUMBER OF CAUSES INITIATED AND DISPOSED OF IN THE OUTER AND INNER HOUSES ORIGINATING IN BOTH THE GENERAL PETITION DEPARTMENTS, 1991–2000

	Outer House		Inner House	
	Causes initiated	*Disposed of by final judgement*	*Causes initiated*	*Disposed of by final judgement*
1991	5,594	3,559	343	220
1992	5,860	3,820	356	212
1993	5,818	3,896	364	285
1994	5,199	3,869	336	311
1995	4,896	3,646	311	253
1996	4,390	3,619	293	164
1997	4,230	3,102	283	135
1998	4,173	2,735	228	109
1999	4,286	2,995	185	106
2000	4,918	2,993	202	98

NUMBER OF SMALL CLAIMS INITIATED 1991–2000

1991	88,512
1992	79,395
1993	72,714
1994	64,002
1995	59,710
1996	59,009
1997	56,551
1998	52,527
1999	51,096
2000	45,786

RECORDED CRIME BY TYPE OF OFFENCE 2001–2

Theft and handling stolen goods	171,000
Theft of vehicles	23,000
Theft from vehicles	40,000
Criminal damage	95,000
Burglary	45,000
Violence against the person	20,000
Fraud and forgery	21,000
Drugs offences	36,000
Robbery	4,000
Sexual offences	5,000
Rape	1,000
Other offences	25,000

Source: ONS, Social Trends 2003 (Crown copyright)

DETECTION RATES FOR RECORDED CRIME: BY TYPE OF OFFENCE, 2001–2

Drug offences	99%
Violence against the person	82%
Sexual offences	78%
of which, rape	82%
Fraud and forgery	82%
Robbery	37%
Theft and handling stolen goods	34%
of which, theft of vehicles	32%
of which, theft from vehicles	17%
Burglary	24%
Criminal damage	22%
Other crimes	96%
All recorded crime	45%

Source: ONS, Social Trends 2003 (Crown copyright)

CRIMES AND OFFENCES 2000–1

	2000	*2001*
Total Crimes and Offences	922,764	945,716
Non-sexual crimes of violence	23,349	23,751
Crimes of indecency	5,754	5,987
Crimes of dishonesty	260,936	239,892
Fire-raising, vandalism etc	83,192	94,924
Other crimes	49,941	56,539
Miscellaneous offences	153,820	162,527
Motor vehicle offences	345,772	362,096

BUSINESS SCOTLAND

THE SCOTTISH ECONOMY

BANKING

CURRENCY

LOCAL ENTERPRISE COMPANIES

PROFESSIONAL AND TRADE BODIES

TRADE UNIONS

THE VOLUNTARY SECTOR

THE SCOTTISH ECONOMY

The Scottish economy is small relative to that of the UK as a whole (under 10 per cent on most measures) and to the EU and other world economies. It is a very open economy, as reflected in the size of Scotland's trade flows with the rest of the UK, Europe and the rest of the world as a proportion of Scottish GDP, and by levels of foreign direct investment to the Scottish economy. The regional dimension is reflected in the fact that despite the devolution of significant economic powers to the Scottish Parliament, established by the 1998 Scotland Act, key policy influences on the UK economy, notably monetary and fiscal policies, are reserved to the UK Parliament. However, ultimately, the size and openness of the Scottish economy (along with that of the UK) mean that many of the major influences on its performance remain out of the control of either the Scottish or UK parliaments.

SCALE OF THE SCOTTISH ECONOMY

Many aspects of economies are thought to depend on their scale or size. The most commonly employed indicator of an economy's scale is its Gross Domestic Product (GDP), which measures the value of the goods and services produced in an economy over a particular period (usually a single year). Scotland's GDP in 1999 was £64,050 million (at 1999 basic prices), or 8.1 per cent of UK GDP (*Scottish Input-Output Tables, 1999, Regional Trends, 2001*). Note that these data exclude the oil and gas output from the UK Continental Shelf, which is treated as a separate region in the UK national accounts[1]. Other measures of scale include population and labour force. Table 1 indicates that Scotland's share of UK population and labour force in 1999 were 8.6 per cent and 8.5 per cent respectively making Scotland a comparatively small region of the UK, except where scale is measured in terms of land area. Scotland accounts for over 32 per cent of the UK's land area but has the lowest population density (average population per square kilometre) of all eleven standard regions of the UK, and just over a tenth of the density of the south-east.

Table 1. The Scale of the Scottish Region in 1999

Region	Scotland	UK	Scotland % of UK
Area (sq km)	78,133	242,910	32.2
Population (000s)	5,119	59,501	8.6
Population Density (person/sq metre)	65.5	65.5	26.7
Labour Force (000s, 1999)	2,420	28,359	8.5
GDP (1999 basic prices, £mill.)	64,050	771,849	8.3
GDP per head (£)	12,512	12,972	96.5

Source: Regional Trends, 2001

Although it is not a measure of scale, the final row of Table 1 shows GDP per head of population. This is the most commonly employed measure of the economic prosperity of regions and nations. Scottish GDP per head, at £12,512 in 1999 is 96.5 per cent of the UK average. However, Table 2 indicates that there is considerable variation in GDP per head among the sub-regions of Scotland. For example, in 1998, GDP per head in North Eastern Scotland was 27 per cent higher than in Scotland as a whole, whereas in Highlands and Islands it was 23 per cent below the Scottish average. The dominance of the south-western and eastern sub-regions of Scotland is also apparent. Combined, they account for 82 per cent of Scottish GDP (and 83 per cent of the population). However, average GDP per head of population in the western region is 5 per cent below the Scottish average, while it is 4 per cent higher in the eastern region. Smaller regions naturally show even greater variations in GDP per head, ranging from 62 per cent of the Scottish average in East Lothian and Midlothian to 152 per cent in the City of Edinburgh.

Table 2. Gross Domestic Product at Factor Cost (current prices) for Local Areas in Scotland, 1998

	£ million	% contribution to Scottish GDP	GDP per head (£)	£ per head pop (Scotland = 100)	% pop
Scotland	62,153	100.0	12,117	100	100.00
North Eastern Scotland (Aberdeen City, Aberdeenshire and North East Moray)	7,723	12.4	15,414	127	9.77
Eastern Scotland	23,870	38.4	12,576	104	37.00
Angus and Dundee City	2,929	4.7	11,387	94	5.01
Clackmannanshire and Fife	4,091	6.6	10,275	85	7.76
East Lothian and Midlothian	1,281	2.1	7,503	62	3.33
Scottish Borders	1,062	1.7	9,974	82	2.08
Edinburgh, City of	8,306	13.4	18,417	152	8.79
Falkirk	1,765	2.8	12,227	101	2.81
Perth and Kinross and Stirling	2,643	4.3	12,203	101	4.22
West Lothian	1,792	2.9	11,683	96	2.99
South Western Scotland	27,100	43.6	11,478	95	46.03
East and West Dunbartonshire, Helensburgh and Lomond	1,952	3.1	8,489	70	4.48
Dumfries and Galloway	1,633	2.6	11,063	91	2.88
East Ayrshire and North Ayrshire Mainland	2,141	3.4	8,191	68	5.10
Glasgow City	10,240	16.5	16,495	136	12.10
Inverclyde, East Renfrewshire and Renfrewshire	3,698	5.9	10,510	87	6.86
North Lanarkshire	3,133	5.0	9,573	79	6.38
South Ayrshire	1,368	2.2	11,934	98	2.23
South Lanarkshire	2,934	4.7	9,544	79	5.99
Highlands and Islands	3,461	5.6	9,369	77	7.20
Caithness and Sutherland and Ross and Cromarty	751	1.2	8,467	70	1.73
Inverness and Nairn and Moray, Badenoch and Strathspey	1,030	1.7	9,456	78	2.12
Lochaber, Skye and Lochalsh and Argyll and the Islands	873	1.4	8,630	71	1.97
Eilean Siar (Western Isles)	267	0.4	9,555	79	0.54
Orkney Islands	192	0.3	9,799	81	0.38
Shetland Islands	347	0.6	15,107	125	0.45

THE OPENNESS OF THE SCOTTISH ECONOMY

Smaller economies tend to be more open than their larger counterparts. Scotland has, like many other economies, been affected by increasing 'globalisation', with openness to international trade and capital and migration flows growing over time.

TRADE

One important feature of the scale of an economy is that smaller economies tend, in general, to be more open to trade. Both exports and imports tend to be relatively more important for small economies. The

Scottish input-output tables for 1999 (the most recent year for which these accounts are currently available) imply that Scotland's exports (excluding expenditure by tourists from the rest of the UK and the world in Scotland) amounted to £45,281 million in total. The implied export to GDP (at market prices) ratio is almost 71 per cent, whereas for the UK as a whole the export to GDP ratio for the same year was only just over 26 per cent. Note, however, that a great deal of Scotland's trade consists of exports to other regions of the UK. Scotland's exports to the rest of the World accounted for just under 35 per cent of Scottish GDP in 1999. Thus, Scotland does appear to be significantly more open than the UK as a whole (which is itself open relative to the OECD average). However, Scotland also imports more, in relative terms, than the UK as a whole. In 1999, its imports from the rest of the UK, at £32,275 million, exceeded its exports of goods and services to the other UK regions (£23,050 million), implying a large trade deficit. However, Scotland's imports from the rest of the world were only £18,708 million, while the corresponding export figure was £22,231 million, implying a trade surplus.

According to the 1999 Scottish input-output tables, which describe the structure of the economy in detail, manufacturing exports account for some 76 per cent of Scottish exports of goods and services to the rest of the world. More than half of these (52 per cent) are directly attributable to only three sub-sectors: office machinery (34.4 per cent), spirits and wines (10.3 per cent) and electronic components (7.53 per cent). However, caution is required in interpreting these figures as contributions to the nation's balance of trade since office machinery and electronic components both import a much larger proportion of their material inputs (94 per cent and 72 per cent respectively) than the spirits and wines industry (39 per cent).

A survey by the Scottish Council Development and Industry of manufactured exports for 1998 suggests that Scotland's main export markets outside of the UK remain the EU (63 per cent) and North America (11.2 per cent). The UK as a whole is less dependent on the EU (56.1 per cent) and more on North America (15.3 per cent) than Scotland. When, as has happened since the launch of the European Monetary Union, sterling increases in value against the Euro, the implication is that Scottish exporters may be more adversely affected than those in the UK as a whole.

INWARD INVESTMENT AND FOREIGN OWNERSHIP

Another important feature of the openness of the Scottish economy is levels of inward investment and foreign ownership. Over the last three decades, foreign direct investment across the global economy has grown more rapidly than international trade, partly as a result of reduced restrictions on international capital flows and the more global perspective of multinational companies. The Scottish economy has experienced relatively high levels of foreign direct/inward investment since the 1970s, particularly in the manufacturing sector. This has partly been the result of a regional policy stance that has sought to encourage inward investment, mainly through the activities of the Locate in Scotland's Enterprise Networks (Scottish Enterprise and Highlands and Islands Enterprise).

Inward investment has tended to be concentrated in the fast-growing, high-tech sectors such as electronics, producing computers and workstations or semiconductors. Foreign-owned manufacturing plants in these sectors tend to have higher productivity levels, export a higher proportion of their outputs (but import a larger proportion of inputs) and pay higher wages. Therefore, the direct and induced effects on the Scottish economy have been significant. There is also the suggestion that the Scottish economy has experienced 'spill over' benefits in terms of improved efficiency in supplier and customer firms. However, recent trends in inward investment have shown a decline over the past years. The Scottish Executive (*Scottish Economic Report, February 2003*) attribute much of the decline to the state of the international economic climate and uncertainties in market and investment intentions, particularly in the wake of the tragic events of 11 September 2001.

MIGRATION FLOWS

A further feature of the openness of the Scottish economy is the degree of integration of the Scottish and other UK regional labour markets. This is distinctly manifested in the existence of significant migration flows. While in any single year net migration flows have been of a fairly modest scale, these have cumulatively resulted in significant flows of population out of Scotland and into the rest of the UK and overseas. This has resulted in a lower population and working age population than otherwise would have been the case. While the population of the UK as a whole increased by around 20 per cent in the 1951–99 period, the Scottish population was broadly static. Over the last thirty years the population of Scotland has in fact fallen by around 1 per cent. During the 1960s net out-migration from Scotland averaged around 32,000 over the decade. However, this declined in the 1970s, and fell to around half this level in the 1980s. In the 1990s population has been fairly stable, with net out-migration to the other UK regions being balanced by net in-migration flows from overseas (which have grown significantly in recent years).

It should be noted that migration flows are an important means by which regional labour markets function, preventing even bigger rises in unemployment when there are regionally disparate changes in activity levels. For example, Scotland was less adversely affected by the 1991—92 recession than other regions of the UK, a fact that is reflected in relatively high net in-flows of population, particularly from southern English regions, in 1991 (around 9,000). Yet, in the mid-90s, when activity in the UK grew faster than in

Scotland, net-migration flows between Scotland and the rest of the UK again became negative (reaching around 4,000 in 1999).

On the other hand, while net out-migration flows may ease unemployment problems in Scotland when activity levels are subdued, they do create other problems. Loss of population from the City of Glasgow, for example, has reduced the numbers of households paying taxes to the City, thus creating funding problems.

STRUCTURE OF THE SCOTTISH ECONOMY

Table 3 reports the composition of Scottish GDP (at basic prices) in 1999 in comparison with 1989 by 10 broad industry groups[2]. The traditional notion of Scotland as being characterised by specialisation in heavy industries with shipbuilding as a key activity, as reflected in the proud 'Clyde built' label, was true of the first half of the century, but is now outdated. Service sector activities, taken here to include the 'Wholesale and Retail', 'Transport and Communication', 'Financial Intermediation and Business' and 'Other Services' sectors in Table 3, accounted for 50 per cent of Scottish GDP in 1999, while 18.5 per cent was generated in the aggregate manufacturing sector. It is interesting to note that the picture at the UK level is broadly similar, with around 54 per cent of UK GDP being accounted for by these four service sector activities, and 19 per cent by manufacturing.

The comparison of Scottish GDP in 1989 and 1999 in Table 3 shows that, while the contribution of total manufacturing has only fallen by just over 2 per cent over these ten years, the contribution of services has increased significantly, by just over 10 per cent. However, note that this increased contribution is almost entirely accounted for by growth in the 'Financial Intermediation and Business' sector.

Table 3. Composition of Scottish GDP 1989 and 1999 (basic prices) (%)

	1989	1999
Agriculture	2.2	2.0
Mining and Quarrying	1.9	2.1
Manufacturing	20.7	18.5
Elec., Gas and Water Supply	1.2	2.6
Construction	4.4	4.7
Wholesale and Retail Trade	17.0	15.5
Transport and Communication	7.7	7.6
Financial Int. and Business	11.4	22.7
Public Administration etc	30.3	20.3
Other Services	3.3	4.1

Source: Scottish Input-Output Tables, 1999

Table 4. Growth in Scottish Service Sector/ Financial Services GDP between 1997 and 2002

	All sectors	Service Sector	Financial Services
1997	100.0	100.0	100.0
1998	102.0	102.0	103.9
1999	104.3	103.6	118.2
2000	106.3	105.8	128.0
2001	107.5	112.0	142.4
2002	107.5	116.7	147.7

Source: Scottish Executive Statistics Publication Notice, July 2003

The ongoing changes in the structure of the Scottish economy are reflected in the underlying composition of GDP growth. Table 4 reports Scottish aggregate annual GDP growth for the period 1997–2002, which, while subdued has been fairly steady and following a similar trend to what is reported at the UK level. However, the increasing dominance of service sector activities is reflected in the fact that GDP growth in the aggregate services sector outpaces aggregate Scottish GDP growth.

Even more striking is the growth of the Financial Services sector (banks, building societies, insurance companies and fund managers), which has come to be of increasing importance to Scotland and, as shown in Table 4, one of the most dynamic growth areas of the Scottish economy in recent years. Edinburgh has come to be recognised as the most important UK financial centre outside of London, and is the sixth largest equity management centre in Europe and 15th in the world. In 1999 Financial Services (including auxiliary activities) directly accounted for around 5 per cent of Scottish GDP. However, if the type of growth rates shown in Figure 2 are sustained, and if the Financial Services Action Plan for Scotland, 'Investing in our Future', launched by Scottish Enterprise, the Scottish Executive and Scottish Financial Enterprise in 2001 is successful, this contribution is likely to grow in the future.

Table 5. Composition of Scottish Employment 1999 (full-time equivalents)

Agriculture	1.8
Mining and Quarrying	1.3
Manufacturing	16.4
Elec., Gas and Water Supply	0.8
Construction	6.9
Wholesale and Retail Trade	20.6
Transport and Communication	6.0
Financial Int. and Business	15.3
Public Adminstration etc	24.2
Other Services	6.7

Source: Scottish Input-Output Tables, 1999

In terms of the structure of Scottish employment, service sector activities also dominate, with the four service sector activities identified above directly accounting for just under 49 per cent of total (full-time equivalent) employment. This is reflected in Table 5, which shows that manufacturing activities account for an even smaller share of employment than GDP, with only 16.4 per cent compared to the sector's 18.5 per cent contribution to Scottish GDP. Another important sector where the contribution of activity to total employment is markedly smaller than the contribution to GDP is 'Financial Intermediation and Business', which, while directly accounting for 22.7 per cent of GDP only accounts for 15.3 per cent of Scottish employment. In terms of total service sector employment, the low employment to GDP ratio in 'Financial Intermediation and Business' is offset by the labour intensive service sectors, particularly 'Wholesale and Retail Trade', which directly accounts for 20.6 per cent of total employment. Note that the statistics in Table 5 are stated in terms of sectoral shares in full-time equivalent jobs. Due to the relatively high prevalence of part-time employment, particularly in the retail sector, this sector is likely to account for a significantly higher share of total persons employed.

LABOUR MARKET

Scotland's total working age population (men aged 16–64 and women aged 16–59) was 3.19 million in 1999. 19.7 per cent of the population were under working age, and 18 per cent were over working age. 51.9 per cent of the working age population were men and 48.1 per cent women. The Scottish labour force (those in employment plus those unemployed under the International Labour Organisation, ILO, classification) was 2.42 million. Women made up 45 per cent of the labour force, a share that has remained fairly constant throughout the last decade, with 67.4 per cent of working age women in employment compared to 74 per cent of working age men. The employment rate of working age women was very similar to that of the UK, but significantly higher than the EU average (54 per cent in 2000). The total employment rate (men and women) was 70.8 per cent, compared to 73.6 per cent in the UK.

In terms of working patterns[3], in 2000 the share of the Scottish working-age population in full-time employment was slightly lower than the UK average (49 per cent compared to 49.9 per cent), while part-time employment is slightly higher (16 per cent compared to 15.6 per cent). However, self-employment is more notably lower in Scotland (6.1 per cent of the working population, compared to 8.1 per cent in the UK). On average, the number of hours worked by Scottish full-time employees is very close to the UK average (43.4 hours per week compared to 43.6 in Spring 2000). However, the share of those employed holding a second job is significantly lower in Scotland (3.7 per cent) than the UK average (4.4 per cent). As is the case across the UK in general, a higher proportion of females in employment (4.7 per cent) hold a second job than males (2.9 per cent), a fact that is likely to be explained by the higher prevalence of part-time working among women that men.

The (ILO) rate of unemployment has fallen across the UK since the mid-90s (from 8.3 per cent in 1996 to 5.6 per cent in 2000). However the decline has been slower in Scotland (from 8.8 per cent in 1996 to 7.7 per cent in 2000). The average duration of unemployment in Scotland is still longer than the UK average and unemployment rates among those with higher education qualifications remain higher than the UK average. The redundancy rate also remains high relative to the UK average, reflecting the continuing decline in Scottish manufacturing.

As is the case across the UK in general, the structure of labour supply and demand in Scotland has changed in recent years. This is both in terms of the sectoral composition of labour demand (reflecting the changing structure of the economy discussed above) and of the skills profile of the labour force. Between 1993 and 2002, employment in highly skilled jobs[4] has grown by just under 20 per cent in Scotland. However, this growth has been less steady and has lagged behind the growth in skilled employment in the UK over the same period.

HOUSEHOLD SECTOR

Household income and expenditure is a very important part of activity in any economy, both in terms of demand for local production, but also as an indicator of the lifestyles and wealth enjoyed by local people. Over the last decade the expenditures, incomes and wealth of Scottish consumers have increased in real terms. However, Scots still earn and spend less than their counterparts south of the border. Table 6 shows total expenditure by the average household in Scotland and the UK for the period 1997–2000. This shows that for every pound spent by the average UK household, Scots spend about 91p. By examination of Table 7 it is apparent that for every £1 earned by the average UK household Scots only earn 89p. This implies that while the average Scottish household is less well off than its UK counterpart, it manages to spend a higher proportion of its weekly income. Put another way, over the period 1997–2000 household spending averaged just under 79 per cent of income in Scotland compared to 76.5 per cent for the UK.

Table 6. Average weekly household expenditure in Scotland and the UK, 1997–2000

	Scotland		UK	
	Average (£)	%	Average (£)	%
Total (per household)	317.30	100	348.10	100
Housing	46.70	14.7	55.20	15.9
Fuel, light and power	12.90	4.1	11.90	3.4
Food	57.70	18.2	58.50	16.8
Alcohol and tobacco	23.00	7.2	20.50	5.9
Clothing and footwear	21.00	6.6	21.00	6.0
Household goods and services	41.00	12.9	47.60	13.7
Motoring and fares	51.80	16.3	59.20	17.0
Leisure goods and services	51.70	16.3	59.70	17.2
Miscellaneous and personal goods and services	11.50	3.6	14.50	4.2

Source: Regional Trends, 2001

Table 7. Average weekly household income in Scotland and the UK, 1997–2000

	Scotland		UK	
	Average (£)	%	Average (£)	%
Total (per household)	403.00	100	455.00	100
Wages and salaries	274.04	68	307.93	68
Self employment	24.18	6	36.77	8
Investments	12.09	3	18.38	4
Annuities and pensions	28.21	7	32.17	7
Social Security benefits	60.45	15	55.15	12
Other income	4.03	1	4.60	1

Source: Regional Trends, 2001

Table 8. Average weekly rents (£) in Scotland and UK, by tenure, 1999–2000

Type of tenure	Scotland	Great Britain	Scotland % of UK
Private sector	71.00	86.00	82.56
Local authority	36.40	42.50	85.65
Registered social landlords	38.97	51.40	75.82

Source: Regional Trends, 2001

Table 9. Estimates of average house prices in Scotland and UK (£), 2002 Q4

	Scotland	UK	Scotland % of UK
Bank of Scotland (HBOS plc)	71,799	121,743	59.0
Nationwide	78,618	115,940	67.8
Lloyds - TSB	78,593		
Council of Mortgage Lenders	86,090	141,090	61.0
Average	78,775	126,258	62.4

Source: Scottish Economic Report, February 2003

Table 10. Estimates of house price inflation: Annual % rate to 2002 Q4

	Scotland	UK
Bank of Scotland (HBOS plc)	11.6	26.4
Nationwide	16.1	25.3
Lloyds - TSB	16.1	
Council of Mortgage Lenders	11.0	19.0
Average	14.0	24.0

Source: Scottish Economic Report, February 2003

If Scots earn and spend less than the average UK family, do they also spend their income differently? Table 6 suggests that they do. Reflecting the somewhat colder climate and darker nights north of the border, Scots spend more, in absolute terms, on fuel, light and power. However, this also equates to a larger proportion of household income, which is reflective of the fact that Scottish household earn less than their UK counterparts, and therefore have to spend proportionately more of their income on essential activities like heating and lighting. The figures in Table 6 suggest that this is also the case with regard to food, clothing and footwear. Nonetheless, the different proportionate spends of Scottish and UK households are also reflective of other factors, such as lifestyle preferences (e.g. the higher level of spending on alcohol and tobacco by the average Scottish household in both proportionate and absolute terms).

On all other categories of expenditure, the average Scottish household spends proportionately less than its UK counterpart. One important difference at the UK and Scottish levels is in terms of expenditure on housing. This partly reflects differences in the structure of the housing market in Scotland – in 2000 only 62 per cent of Scottish dwellings were owner occupied, compared with 69 per cent in the UK (though the gap has narrowed – in 1991 only 52 per cent of Scottish dwellings were owner-occupied, compared to 67 per cent in the UK). It also reflects the greater affordability of housing in Scotland. As noted above, the average household income is around 91 per cent of that in the UK. However, Table 8 shows that average weekly rents are significantly lower (between 17 per cent and 25 per cent, depending on tenure) in Scotland relative to those in Great Britain (the figures in Table 8 exclude Northern Ireland). In terms of owner-occupied dwellings, house prices are also lower in Scotland. Tables 9 and 10 are indicative of both the lower average level of house prices in Scotland and of the lower level of house price inflation. As well as spending a lower proportion of their incomes on housing, Scots also tend to be less burdened with housing debt, with average ratios of mortgage advances to the income of borrowers generally being lower in Scotland relative to the UK.

The low rate of home ownership, lower average house prices and house price inflation rates, along with a lower burden of housing debt in Scotland relative to the rest of the UK has several implications for the Scottish economy. First, the possibilities for wealth formation, particularly through house price inflation, are more limited than in other regions of the UK. (While a fuller discussion of the issue is beyond the scope of this chapter, the limited availability of housing collateral may also be an explanatory factor in terms of the low rate of new firm formation in Scotland.) However, the lower burden of housing debt implies that interest rate changes and fluctuations in UK monetary policy will on average have less impact on Scottish households than will be the case elsewhere in the country.

It is important to note though that the above discussion has been in terms of the income and expenditures of the average Scottish household. Naturally, the expenditure patterns shown in Table 6 will vary from these averages in both Scotland and the UK depending on factors such as total household income, household location and socio-economic status. One indicator of variation in the circumstances of Scottish households is the difference in average wage rates in different sub-regions of Scotland. Table 11 shows the average gross (before deductions) wage rates of workers in twenty-four Scottish local authority areas relative to the Scottish average for 2002. This shows that workers in the cities of Aberdeen and Edinburgh on average earn a significantly higher wage rate than anywhere else in Scotland, most likely due to the presence of the oil and finance industries (respectively) in these two cities. The lowest average wage rates are earned in Moray and the Scottish borders.

Table 11. Average gross weekly earnings of full-time employees on adult rates, 2002

Local Authority Areas	Average earnings (£)	Scotland = 100
(All full-time employees)		
Aberdeen City	504.5	118.1
Aberdeenshire	414.1	97.0
Angus	380.6	89.1
Argyll and Bute	390.3	91.4
Dumfries and Galloway	386.7	90.6
Dundee City	411.4	96.3
East Lothian	399.6	93.6
Edinburgh, City of	480.6	112.6
Falkirk	391.7	91.7
Fife	390.1	91.4
Glasgow City	421.4	98.7
Highland	411.8	96.4
Inverclyde	354.7	83.1
Midlothian	397.5	93.1
Moray	346.1	81.1
North Ayrshire	372.8	87.3
North Lanarkshire	413.2	96.8
Perth and Kinross	369.4	86.5
Renfrewshire	447.7	104.8
Scottish Borders	346.2	81.1
South Ayrshire	421.1	98.6
South Lanarkshire	434.2	101.7
West Dunbartonshire	387.5	90.7
West Lothian	430.1	100.7
Scotland	427.0	100.0
Great Britain	464.7	108.8

Source: Scottish Economic Statistics 2003

PUBLIC FINANCE (EXPENDITURE AND REVENUE) IN SCOTLAND

The UK government sets the total amount of government spending in Scotland, although the Scottish Parliament has full discretion over the distribution of its budgets. Funds from the Exchequer are paid into the Scottish Consolidated Fund, which was created by the Scotland Act 1998, and has two main sources of income. Firstly there is the grant from the UK exchequer, which consists of two parts: the Scottish departmental expenditure limit (DEL) and the Annually Managed Expenditure (AME). Secondly, internal revenues are raised from non-domestic rates paid in Scotland. The former operates in much the same way as the pre-devolution Scottish block grant. The AME, as its name suggests, covering demand-led expenditures such as the housing support grant, is decided on an annual basis. Changes to the Scottish departmental expenditure limits, on the other hand, are, in general, tied to changes in comparable English expenditure programmes through the 'Barnett formula', which is based on the size of the Scottish population relative to that of England.

The Scottish Parliament does have a third potential source of revenue to fund expenditures. This would arise in the form of a grant from the Inland Revenue should the Scottish Parliament move to use the tax-varying power granted to it under the Scotland Act. This allows the Parliament to raise or lower the basic rate of income tax by up to 3p from 2000–1. However, as yet the Parliament has not enacted, or announced any plans to enact this power.

Total public expenditure in Scotland is divided into three elements: identifiable (Scottish Executive spending plus social security); non-identifiable (largely public goods such as defence, foreign affairs etc); other spending (servicing of debt etc). Only the identifiable component is entirely reliably estimated, with Scotland's share of other expenditures being determined in some more or less mechanical way, normally using population shares. In 2000–1 total public expenditure in Scotland was estimated to be £36.3 billion, of which £28.4 billion was identifiable. This amounted to around 10 per cent of the UK total, well in excess of Scotland's share in population (8.6 per cent) or GDP (8.2 per cent).

The fact that many elements of government revenues and some elements of government expenditure are not directly measured at the regional level, and therefore have to be estimated somehow, has been the source of some controversy. Most commentators take the view that Scotland receives more than its population share of public expenditures while contributing roughly its population share to revenues. Accordingly, many,

including the Scottish Executive, believe that there is a public sector deficit in Scotland, with public expenditures exceeding revenues. Currently, the Scottish Executive (*GERS, 2000–1*) estimates that Scotland runs a public sector deficit equivalent to £5.4 billion net borrowing in 2000–1. This is equal to 7.1 per cent of GDP. The comparable overall figure at the UK level was a surplus equivalent to 1.2 per cent of GDP. This is an important issue in the debate over full fiscal autonomy and/or independence for Scotland, as the Maastricht requirement for EMU membership demands that net borrowing should not exceed 3 per cent of GDP.

However, on this point it is important to note the Scottish Parliament does not actually have any borrowing powers of its own. What is quoted above is UK borrowing that can be *attributed* to Scotland, and, as noted above, the whole area of public finance in the devolved regions, and in Scotland in particular, is a very controversial area. One area of debate is the attribution of tax receipts to Scotland. By recent Scottish Executive calculations (*GERS, 2000–1*), if even 66 per cent of North Sea oil revenues were attributed to Scotland the implied public sector deficit for 2000–1 would fall to £2.6 billion, or 2.8 per cent of GDP (i.e. within the boundary set by Maastricht criteria). However, it is not clear that it would be appropriate to attribute oil revenues in this way. Another area of controversy is the use of the Barnett formula in governing the allocation of expenditures to the Scottish DEL. The debate in this area centres on the fact that the allocation based on population shares is not reflective of the needs of the Scottish people, with the last 'needs assessment' exercise having been conducted in 1976. Moreover, the Barnett formula does not take into account the fact that it is more expensive to provide public services in Scotland, where the population is more geographically dispersed than in other regions of the UK.

It is outside the scope of this chapter to investigate these specific topics in any detail. The main point for the reader to take from all this is that the topic of public finance in Scotland is a very controversial one and the subject of considerable, on-going debate.

DEVOLUTION AND THE SCOTTISH ECONOMY

The Scottish Parliament's powers to affect economic policy lie mainly on the supply-side of the economy. This means that it should be possible for the Parliament to take action to influence long-term unemployment, output and productivity in Scotland. However, supply-side policy actions tend to take a lot longer to work than some of the macroeconomic (fiscal and monetary) policy instruments that are reserved to Westminster. This is likely to have been a source of frustration with some Scottish people in their expectations of the new Parliament. However, it is important to recognise that the devolution settlement is not as restrictive as it may appear in terms of meaningful economic management. Already it seems clear that devolution has led to some divergence in economic policy at the UK and Scottish levels, with the Parliament clearly seeking to satisfy particular Scottish concerns that may not have been prioritised quite as much by the old Scottish Office. For example, in the first term of the Parliament we saw the introduction of free personal care for the elderly and the abolition of up-front tuition fees in the higher education sector.

SCOTLAND'S ENTERPRISE NETWORK

The key mechanism for delivering supply-side policies in Scotland is the Enterprise Network, comprising Scottish Enterprise, the Local Enterprise Companies (LECs) and Highlands and Islands Enterprise. These bodies play quite a unique role in that they perform what could be termed as a combined Treasury and Department of Trade and Industry role in Scotland. There has been some controversy surrounding the enterprise networks and their funding (set to be £345.5 million for Scottish Enterprise and £92.5 million for Highlands and Islands Enterprise in 2003–04). However, they clearly play an important role, being charged with the development of trade/industrial/service interaction and are responsible for doing a lot more than would normally be expected of a development quango elsewhere in the UK.

The Enterprise Network was in existence prior to devolution. However, in 2001 the Scottish Executive set out its strategic direction for the Enterprise Networks in terms of delivering on the Parliament's supply-side objectives in a document entitled 'A Smart Successful Scotland'. In recognition of the point made above, regarding the time required for supply-side policies to work through the economy, a joint performance team was also established with members from the Scottish Executive and Enterprise Networks to develop measures to monitor progress towards these objectives. The first report by the joint performance team was published early in 2003.

FUTURE DEVELOPMENTS

Elections for the second term of the Scottish Parliament took place in May 2003. Given that the balance of power did not shift dramatically, with the continuation of the Labour-Liberal Democrat coalition, it can be expected that economic policies will remain on much the same path.

However, there is a feeling in the Scottish media that if voter apathy is to be overcome, the Parliament will need to try and do less, but do it better in order to win over a sceptical electorate. The political parties that are represented in the Parliament do differ in their attitudes to things like the Public Finance Initiative and business rates, as well as how Scotland should be funded. Yet given that they have to work within the confines of the powers devolved under the Scotland Act 1998, there is not a huge amount of leeway for any party. Perhaps the main area where change may be observed during the second term of the Parliament is local government. One issue is that the proposed voting reforms at local government level in Scotland are likely to make local authorities more assertive. However, it is also likely that the Scottish Executive will use the power it has to make local authorities raise more of their own revenue in order to meet the constraints imposed on total expenditure at the UK level (through the Barnett formula) without having to make service cuts.

Additional and fuller discussion of the topics covered here can be found in a recent review of the Scottish economy by Jeremy Peat and Stephen Boyle (*An Illustrated Guide to the Scottish Economy*, Duckworth, London 1999) and in the Scottish Executive's twice-yearly *Scottish Economic Report*. Further regular analysis is also available in the Fraser of Allander Institute's *Quarterly Economic Commentary*. The principal sources for the statistical information presented here are the Scottish Executive, and the UK Office for National Statistics (ONS), as published in the Scottish Executive's annual *Scottish Economic Statistics* and *Government Expenditure and Revenue in Scotland* (*GERS*) publications and *Regional Trends*, published by ONS.

[1] See the Scottish Executive's annual *Government Expenditure and Revenue in Scotland* (*GERS*) publication on the impact of allocating oil and gas revenues to Scotland. A. G. Kemp and L. Stephen – *Expenditures in and revenues from the UKCS: Estimating the Hypothetical Scottish Shares 1970–2003*, North Sea study Occasional paper No 70., Department of Economics, University of Aberdeen, January 1999 – provide more detailed research on the subject.

[2] Note that, due to changes in the Standard Industrial Classification (SIC) of production activities in 1992, some caution is required in directly comparing sectors in these two years, though this is less of a problem at the level of aggregation shown in Tables 3 and 5.

[3] All statistics quoted regarding working patterns relate to Spring 2000, as recorded in *Regional Trends, 2001*.

[4] Sections 1–3 of the Standard Occupational Classification (SOC).

BANKING

HISTORY

The history of Scottish banking dates back to the formation of the Bank of Scotland in 1695. The Bank of England was founded the previous year by a Scotsman, William Paterson. In the early part of the 18th century the Bank of Scotland's monopoly ended with the foundation of The Royal Bank of Scotland in 1727. At this time, the two banks occupied different political camps and for many years they were rivals. Elsewhere in Scotland, other banking services such as discounting and exchange were provided by merchants but as the pace of economic change gained momentum, the demand for banking services grew and other organisations developed.

Around this time, the Bank of Scotland and The Royal Bank of Scotland concentrated their credit provision in and around Edinburgh meaning that before a merchant from outside the area could borrow from one of them, he would have to be well known in the capital. Hence, only the more senior Glasgow tobacco lords found themselves creditworthy. Initially, the problem was alleviated by a growing number of small private banks that borrowed large sums from the Edinburgh banks and lent it out in smaller amounts to merchants from across Scotland. However, gradually, merchants from other cities and major towns began to set up their own banks and whereas in England, where merchants did not have the legal freedom to set up banks, there was no such restriction in Scotland.

The pioneer of branch banking was the British Linen Company. Founded in 1747 to promote the Scottish linen industry, the company later developed banking services which it offered to customers throughout Scotland. Prior to this, The Bank of Scotland had tried, unsuccessfully, to establish a branch network in the 1690s and 1730s. It was more successful at its third attempt in the 1770s, however, The Royal Bank of Scotland maintained just one branch, in Glasgow, for many years.

Cash credit was another major facet of banking to be developed in the 18th century. It was developed by The Royal Bank of Scotland early in the 18th century and was the forerunner to the modern overdraft. Another element to Scotland's emerging banking industry was the acceptance of deposits and payment of interest. This was not a new idea, however, the Scots were the first to develop it as a significant and continuing activity on a large scale.

Throughout the industrial revolution the banking system continued to grow but following the growth of the iron and railway industries, provincial banking companies and private banks ceased to be able to provide the scale of financial services required by customers. As a result, a new generation of banking organisations emerged, including the Union Bank of Scotland (1830) and the Clydesdale Bank (1838). This new generation of banks soon came to rival the Bank of Scotland and The Royal Bank of Scotland in size and by the mid-1840s, Scotland had an homogeneous banking system comprised of large-scale organisations and growing branch networks.

The first savings bank was founded in Ruthwell in Dumfries-shire in 1810 by the Revd Henry Duncan. The concept spread quickly throughout the country and to many other parts of the world, however, these were not commercial banks and they did not lend money to businesses or issue banknotes.

While the banking industry forged ahead in Scotland, London was fast developing as an international financial centre and in the 1860s Scottish banks began to open offices there, provoking a storm of protest from the English Banks. In 1874, the Clydesdale Bank opened three offices in the north of England, which lead to further outrage and resulted in the government appointing a committee of enquiry. Despite no report being published, the Scottish banks abandoned their plans to open English branch networks. At that time banking was under-developed in England and it seems that the Scots would have had the strength to stage takeover bids for many of the English banks, however, over the next 30 years, English banks, by process of merger, acquisition and takeover consolidated their position and by 1913, the Midland Bank was the largest in the world.

The attention to which Scots paid attention to the importance of education in banking was manifest in the formation of the Institute of Bankers in Scotland in 1875, the world's oldest professional body for practising bankers.

BEFORE AND AFTER WORLD WAR II

Towards the end of the First World War a number of English banks turned their attention to Scotland and began a process of acquisition of domestic banks. Four of Scotland's eight banks were taken over in this way, although they retained their own identities, note issues and boards of directors. During the Second World War more merger activity took place reducing the number of Scottish banks to six, two of which were English-owned while The Royal Bank of Scotland owned two small English Banks. Further mergers occurred in the 1960s and 1970s, reducing the number of Scottish banks to three. Only the smallest of these, the Clydesdale, remained under English control (purchased by National Australia Bank in 1987).

A more competitive banking environment in the 1970s resulted in a more diversified structure and English banks began to open branches north of the border and the Scots opened branches in England. The Scots excursion into England was a success and The Royal Bank of Scotland, renaming its English subsidiary Williams & Glyns Bank, made itself a truly UK organisation.

MERCHANT BANKS

Traditionally found only in London, merchant banks began to be formed in the 1970s and provided specialised services for corporate clients. Bank of Scotland which acquired the old British Linen Bank in 1971 launched its merchant banking arm using the old name. Overseas banks began to invest in Scotland too, mainly to Edinburgh, attracted largely by the opportunities for doing business in an oil producing country.

TODAY

Tremendous growth in competition in the 1980s coincided with great leaps forward in the development of electronic banking services. Nowadays, Scottish banks deliver quality global banking for corporate, business and personal customers. In 2001, customer deposits totalled £348,832,000 and advances to customers totalled £402,207,000. Deposit-taking institutions may be broadly divided into two sectors: the monetary sector, which is predominantly banks, and those institutions outside the monetary sector, of which the most important are the building societies and National Savings. Both sectors are supervised by the Financial Services Authority. As a result of the conversion of several building societies into banks in recent years, the size of the banking sector, which was already substantially greater than the non-bank deposit-taking sector, has increased further.

The main institutions within the British banking system are the Bank of England (the central bank), the retail banks, the merchant banks and the overseas banks. In its role as the central bank, the Bank of England acts as banker to the Government and as a note-issuing authority; it also oversees the efficient functioning of payment and settlement systems.

Since May 1997, the Bank of England has had operational responsibility for monetary policy. At monthly meetings of its monetary policy committee the Bank sets the interest rate at which it will lend to the money markets.

FINANCIAL SERVICES REGULATION

THE FINANCIAL SERVICES AUTHORITY

The Financial Services Authority (FSA) is the independent watchdog set up under the Financial Services and Markets Act 2000 (FMSA) to regulate financial services in the UK and protect the rights of retail customers. The FSA's aim is to maintain efficient, orderly and clean financial markets and help ensure customers get a fair deal. The FSA is required to pursue four statutory objectives:

– maintain market confidence
– raise public awareness
– protect consumers
– reduce financial crime

The legislation also requires the FSA to carry out its general functions whilst having regard to:

– the need to use its resources in the most efficient way
– the responsibilities of regulated firms' own management
– being proportionate in imposing burdens or restrictions on the industry
– facilitating innovation
– the international character of financial services and the competitive position of the UK
– the need to facilitate, and not have unnecessarily adverse affect, on competition

THE FSA AS AN ORGANISATION

The FSA is a company limited by guarantee, financed by levies on the industry. It receives no funds from the public purse but is accountable through the Treasury to Parliament. The FSA must report annually on the achievement of its statutory objectives and is governed by a board consisting of a chairman, three executive directors and eleven non-executives, all appointed by the Treasury. With over 2,200 staff, the FSA regulates over 11,000 institutions.

CENTRAL REGISTER/CONSUMER HELPLINE

The FSA maintains a central register of all firms that are, or were, authorised to carry on investment business and authorised deposit takers. The Consumer Helpline is available to members of the public seeking information about firms listed on the register, explains complaints procedures and provides information on what is and what is not regulated by the FSA.

Consumer Helpline: 0845-606 1234
Web: www.fsa.gov.uk

FINANCIAL SERVICES AUTHORITY

25 The North Colonnade, Canary Wharf, London
E14 5HS Tel: 020-7676 1000
Email: publicenquiries@fsa.gov.uk
Web: www.fsa.gov.uk
Chairman: Callum McCarthy
Chief Executive: John Tiner

AUTHORISED INSTITUTIONS

Banking in the UK is regulated by the Banking Act 1987, as amended by the European Community's Second Banking Co-ordination directive, which came into effect on 1 January 1993, now itself part of the Banking Consolidation Directive 2000. The Banking Act 1987 established a single category of banks eligible to take deposits from the public; these are known as authorised institutions. Authorisations under the Act has, since June 1998, been granted by the Financial Services Authority; it is an offence for anyone not on its list of authorised institutions to conduct deposits-taking business, unless they are exempt from the requirements of the Act (e.g. building societies) and certain international development bodies. The FSA is also responsible for supervision of banks and the supervision of clearing and settlement systems.

The implementation of the Second Banking Co-ordination Directive banks permits banks incorporated and authorised in one EU member state to carry on certain banking activities in other member states without the need for authorisation by that state. Consequently, the FSA no longer authorises banks incorporated in other EU states with branches in the UK; the authorisation of their home state supervisor is sufficient provided that certain notification requirements are met. UK banks, in turn, benefit from these so-called "passporting" arrangements.

FINANCIAL SERVICES COMPENSATION SCHEME (FSCS)

7th Floor, Lloyd's Chambers, 1 Portsoken Street,
London E1 8BN
Tel: 020-7892 7300 Fax: 020-7892 7301
Email: enquiries@fscs.org.uk
Web: www.fscs.org.uk

Under the FMSA the Financial Services Compensation Scheme (FSCS) provides compensation if an authorised firm is unable or unlikely to be unable to pay claims against it. This is usually when a firm stops trading or is insolvent. The FSCS covers investments, deposits and insurance.

Chairman: Nigel Hamilton

OFFICIAL INTEREST RATES 2000–3

10 February 2000	6.00%
8 February 2001	5.75%
5 April 2001	5.50%
10 May 2001	5.25%
2 August 2001	5.00%
18 September 2001	4.75%
4 October 2001	4.50%
8 November 2001	4.00%
6 February 2003	3.75%
10 July 2003	3.50%

RETAIL BANKS

The major retail banks are Abbey National, Alliance and Leicester, Bank of Scotland, Barclays (including Woolwich), Bradford and Bingley; HBOS (including Halifax and the Bank of Scotland), HSBC, Lloyds TSB, National Westminster, Northern Rock and The Royal Bank of Scotland. Clydesdale Bank is also a major retail bank in Scotland.

Retail banks offer a wide variety of financial services to companies and individuals, including current and deposit accounts, loan and overdraft facilities, automated teller (cash dispenser) machines, cheque guarantee cards, credit cards and debit cards. Most banks now offer telephone and internet banking facilities.

The Financial Services Ombudsman Service scheme provides independent and impartial arbitration in disputes between a bank and its customer.

Banking hours differ throughout the UK. Many banks now open longer hours and some at weekends, and hours vary from branch to branch. Current core opening hours in Scotland are Monday to Friday 9 a.m. to 5 p.m.

PAYMENT CLEARINGS

The Association for Payment Clearing Services (APACS) is an umbrella organisation for payment clearings in the UK. It operates three clearing companies: BACS Ltd, the Cheque and Credit Clearing Company Ltd, and CHAPS Clearing Company Ltd.

ASSOCIATION FOR PAYMENT CLEARING SERVICES (APACS)
Mercury House, Triton Court, 14 Finsbury Square,
London EC2A 1LQ Tel: 020-7711 6200
Web: www.apacs.org.uk

BACS LTD
De Havilland Road, Edgware, Middx HA8 5Q
Tel: 0870-165 0019
Bulk clearing of electronic debits and credits (e.g. direct debits and salary credits).

CHEQUE AND CREDIT CLEARING COMPANY LTD
Mercury House, Triton Court, 14 Finsbury Square,
London EC2A 1LQ Tel: 020-7711 6200
Oversees the clearing of cheque and paper credits.

CHAPS CLEARING COMPANY LTD
Mercury House, Triton Court, 14 Finsbury Square,
London EC2A 1LQ Tel: 020-7711 6200
Provides an electronic same-day value clearing for sterling and euro payments.

MAJOR RETAIL BANKS: FINANCIAL RESULTS 2002

Bank Group	Profit (loss) before taxation	Profit (loss) after taxation	Total assets
	£m	£m	£m
Abbey National	(984)	(1,136)	205,721
Alliance and Leicester	468	340	41,249
Barclays (inc. Woolwich)	3,205	2,250	403,066
Clydesdale*	146.2	99.4	7,861
HBOS (Halifax/Bank of Scotland)	2,630	1,865	312,275
HSBC	2,285	1,477	218,378
Lloyds/TSB Group	2,607	1,843	252,758
Northern Rock	3,262	2,297	41,920
Royal Bank of Scotland Group (inc. NatWest)	4,763	3,207	412,000

*2001 figures

CURRENCY

The unit of currency is the pound sterling (£) of 100 pence. The decimal system was introduced on 15 February 1971.

Since 1 January 1999, trade within the European Union has been conducted in the single European currency, the euro; euro notes and coins entered circulation on 1 January 2002 in Austria, Belgium, the Netherlands, Finland, France, Germany, Greece, Ireland, Italy, Luxembourg, Portugal and Spain.

COIN

	Metal	Standard Weight (g)	Standard diameter (mm)
Penny	Bronze	3.564	20.3
Penny	copper-plated steel	3.564	20.3
2 pence	Bronze	7.128	25.9
2 pence	copper-plated steel	7.128	25.9
5p	cupro-nickel	3.25	18.0
10p	cupro-nickel	6.5	24.5
20p	cupro-nickel	5.0	21.4
25p Crown	cupro-nickel	28.28	38.6
50p	cupro-nickel	8.00	27.3
£1	nickel-brass	9.5	22.5
†£2	nickel-brass	15.98	28.4
£2	cupro-nickel, nickel-brass	12.00	28.4
£5 Crown	cupro-nickel	28.28	38.6

† Commemorative coins; not intended for general circulation

LEGAL TENDER
Gold (dated 1838 onwards, if not below least

current weight)	to any amount
£5 (Crown since 1990)	to any amount
£2	to any amount
£1	to any amount
50p	up to £10
25p (Crown pre-1990)	up to £10
20p	up to £10
10p	up to £5
5p	up to £5
2p	up to 20p
1p	up to 20p

BANKNOTES

Bank of England notes are currently issued in denominations of £5, £10, £20 and £50 for the amount of the fiduciary note issue, and are legal tender in England and Wales. No £1 notes have been issued since 1984 and in 1998 the outstanding notes were written off.

The current E series of notes was introduced from June 1990. The predominant identifying feature of each note is the portrayal on the back of a prominent British historical figure. The figures portrayed in the current series are:

£5 June 1990–2003	George Stephenson*
£5 May 2002–	Elizabeth Fry
£10 November 2000–	Charles Darwin
£20 June 1999–	Sir Edward Elgar
£50 April 1994–	Sir John Houblon

The Bank of England stopped issuing a £1 note in 1984, although The Royal Bank of Scotland continues to be issue the Scottish £1 note, the only Scottish bank to do so.

* The £5 bank note bearing a portrait of Stephenson not legal tender from 21 November 2003.

LEGAL TENDER
Bank of England banknotes which are no longer legal tender are payable when presented at the head office of the Bank of England in London.

Scottish banknotes are not legal tender but they are an authorised currency and enjoy a status comparable to that of Bank of England notes. They are generally accepted by banks irrespective of their place of issue.

SCOTTISH BANKNOTES
The banks of issue in Scotland are Bank of Scotland, Clydesdale Bank and The Royal Bank of Scotland.

BANK OF SCOTLAND
The Mound, Edinburgh EH1 1YZ
Tel: 0131-442 7777
Web: www.bankofscotland.co.uk
Chief Executive: James Crosby
Denominations of notes issued: £5, £10, £20, £50, £100
£5 (front) Sir Walter Scott; (back) oil and energy vignette
£10 (front) Sir Walter Scott; (back) distilling and brewing vignette
£20 (front) Sir Walter Scott; (back) education and research vignette
£50 (front) Sir Walter Scott; (back) arts and culture vignette
£100 (front) Sir Walter Scott; (back) leisure and tourism vignette

CLYDESDALE BANK

30 St Vincent Place, Glasgow G1 2HL
Tel: 0141-248 7070 Web: www.cbonline.co.uk

Chief Executive: Ross Pinney
Denominations of notes issued: £5, £10, £20, £50,
    £100
£5 (front) Robert Burns; (back) fieldmouse vignette
£10 (front) Mary Slessor; (back) local map vignette
£20 (front) Robert the Bruce; (back) Robert the
    Bruce vignette
£50 (front) Adam Smith; (back) industry vignette
£100 (front) Lord Kelvin; (back) Glasgow University

THE ROYAL BANK OF SCOTLAND

PO Box 31, 42 St Andrew Square, Edinburgh EH2 2YE
Tel: 0131-556 8555 Web: www.royalbankscot.co.uk

Chief Executive: Frederick Goodwin
Denominations of notes issued: £1, £5, £10, £20,
    £100
£1 (front) Lord Ilay; (back) Edinburgh Castle
£5 (front) Lord Ilay; (back) Culzean Castle
£10 (front) Lord Ilay; (back) Glamis Castle
£20 (front) Lord Ilay; (back) Brodick Castle
£100 (front) Lord Ilay; (back) Balmoral Castle
Lord Ilay, was the first governor of the Royal Bank
    of Scotland

Note: from time to time the Scottish banks have issued notes
of varying values to commemorate special events.

LOCAL ENTERPRISE COMPANIES

Local enterprise companies operate under the aegis of either Highlands and Islands Enterprise or Scottish Enterprise. These two statutory bodies were set up in 1991 to further the development of the Scottish economy, working with the private and public sectors. Many of their functions are delegated to the local enterprise companies.

ARGYLL AND THE ISLANDS ENTERPRISE

The Enterprise Centre, Kilmory Industrial Estate, Lochgilphead, Argyll, PA31 8SH. Tel: 01546-602281 Fax: 01546-603964 Email: info@aie.co.uk Web: www.hie.co.uk

AYRSHIRE, SCOTTISH ENTERPRISE

17–19 Hill Street, Kilmarnock, KA3 1HA. Tel: 01563-526623 Fax: 01563-543636 Email: ayrshire@scotent.co.uk Web: www.scottish-enterprise.com

BORDERS, SCOTTISH ENTERPRISE

Bridge Street, Galashiels, TD1 1SW. Tel: 01896-758991 Fax: 01896-758625 Email: seb-enquiry@scotnt.co.uk Web: www.scottish-enterprise.com

CAITHNESS AND SUTHERLAND ENTERPRISE

Tollemache House, High Street, Thurso, Caithness, KW14 8AZ. Tel: 01847-896115 Fax: 01847-893383 Email: case@hient.co.uk Web: www.hie.co.uk

DUMFRIES AND GALLOWAY, SCOTTISH ENTERPRISE

Solway House, Dumfries Enterprise Park, Tinwald Downs Road, Heathhall, Dumfries, DG1 3SJ. Tel: 01387-245000 Fax: 01387-246224 Web: www.scottish-enterprise.com

DUNBARTONSHIRE SCOTTISH ENTERPRISE

Spectrum House, Clydebank Business Park, Clydebank, Glasgow, G81 2DR. Tel: 0141-951 2121 Fax: 0141-951 1907 Web: www.scottish-enterprise.com

EDINBURGH AND LOTHIAN, SCOTTISH ENTERPRISE

Apex House, 99 Haymarket Terrace, Edinburgh, EH12 5HD. Tel: 0131-313 4000 Fax: 0131-313 4231 Web: www.scottish-enterprise.com

FIFE, SCOTTISH ENTERPRISE

Kingdom House, Saltire Centre, Glenrothes, Fife, KY6 2AQ. Tel: 01592-623000 Fax: 01592-623149 Email: fife@scotnt.co.uk Web: www.scottish-enterprise.com

FORTH VALLEY ENTERPRISE, SCOTTISH ENTERPRISE

Laurel House, Laurelhill Business Park, Stirling, FK7 9JQ. Tel: 01786-451919 Fax: 01786-478123 Email: forthvalleyinfo@scotent.co.uk Web: www.scottish-enterprise.com

GLASGOW, SCOTTISH ENTERPRISE

50 Waterloo Street, Glasgow, G2 6HQ. Tel: 0141-204 1111 Fax: 0141-248 1600 Email: glasgow@scotnt.co.uk Web: www.scottish-enterprise.com

GRAMPIAN, SCOTTISH ENTERPRISE

27 Albyn Place, Aberdeen, AB10 1DB. Tel: 01224-252000 Fax: 01224-213417 Email: segrampianenquiries@scotent.co.uk Web: www.scottish-enterprise.com

INVERNESS AND NAIRN ENTERPRISE

The Green House, Beechwood Business Park North, Inverness, IV2 3BL. Tel: 01463-713504 Fax: 01463-712002 Email: ine.general@hient.co.uk Web: www.ine.co.uk

LANARKSHIRE, SCOTTISH ENTERPRISE

New Lanarkshire House, Strathclyde Business Park, Bellshill, ML4 3AD. Tel: 01698-745454 Fax: 01698-842211 Email: selenquiry@scotent.co.uk Web: www.scottish-enterprise.com

LOCHABER ENTERPRISE

St Mary's House, Gordon Square, Fort William, PH33 6DY. Tel: 01397-704326 Fax: 01397-705309 Email: lochaber@hient.co.uk Web: www.hie.co.uk

MORAY, BADENOCH AND STRATHSPEY ENTERPRISE

The Apex, Forres Enterprise Park, Forres, IV36 2AB. Tel: 01309-696000 Fax: 01309-690001 Email: mbse@hient.co.uk Web: www.scottish-enterprise.com

ORKNEY ENTERPRISE
14 Queen Street, Kirkwall, Orkney, KW15 1JE.
Tel: 01856-874638 Fax: 01856-872915
Email: oe@hient.co.uk
Web: www.scottish-enterprise.com

RENFREWSHIRE, SCOTTISH ENTERPRISE
27 Causeyside Street, Paisley, PA1 1UL.
Tel: 0141-848 0101 Fax: 0141-848 6930
Web: www.scottish-enterprise.com

ROSS AND CROMARTY ENTERPRISE
69–71 High Street, Invergordon, Ross and Cromarty,
IV18 0AA. Tel: 01349-853666 Fax: 01349-853833
Email: info@race.co.uk Web: www.race.co.uk
Chief Executive, G. Cox

SHETLAND ENTERPRISE
Toll Clock Shopping Centre, 26 North Road, Lerwick,
Shetland, ZE1 0DE. Tel: 01595-693177
Fax: 01595-693208 Email: shetland@hient.co.uk
Web: www.shetland.hie.co.uk
Chief Executive, D. Finch

SKYE AND LOCHALSH ENTERPRISE
Kings House, The Green, Portree, Isle of Skye,
IV51 9BS. Tel: 01478-612841 Fax: 01478-612164
Email: sale@hient.co.uk Web: www.sale.hie.co.uk

TAYSIDE, SCOTTISH ENTERPRISE
45 North Lindsay Street, Dundee, DD1 1HT.
Tel: 01382-223100 Fax: 01382-201319
Email: set.reception@scotent.co.uk
Web: www.scottish-enterprise.com

WESTERN ISLES ENTERPRISE
James Square, 9 James Street, Stornoway, Isle of Lewis,
HS1 2QN. Tel: 01851-703703 Fax: 01851-704130
Email: wie@hient.co.uk Web: www.hie.co.uk

PROFESSIONAL AND TRADE BODIES

The Certification Officer is responsible for receiving and scrutinising annual returns from employers' associations. Many employers' associations are members of the Confederation of British Industry (CBI).

CBI SCOTLAND

16 Robertson Street, Glasgow G2 8DS
Tel: 0141-332 8661 Fax: 0141-333 9135
Email: allan.hogarth@cbi.org.uk
Web: www.cbi.org.uk

CBI Scotland is part of the Confederation of British Industry, which was founded in 1965. CBI Scotland is an independent non-party political body financed by industry and commerce. It exists primarily to ensure that the Government and Scottish Executive understands the intentions, needs and problems of business in Scotland. It is the recognised voice of business in Scotland and is consulted as such by the Government and Scottish Executive.

CBI Scotland represents the interests of some 26,500 businesses in Scotland of all sizes and across all sectors.

The governing body of CBI Scotland is its elected Council, which meets four times a year in various parts of Scotland. The Council is assisted by eight expert Committees which advise on the main aspects of policy. The Council and the Committees establish policy in respect of matters devolved to Scotland and contribute their views to the policy formation process of the CBI as a whole on matters reserved to Westminster and in Europe. CBI Scotland has a sister office in Brussels.

Chairman: H. Currie
Director: I. McMillan
Head of Media and Public Affairs: Allan Hogarth

PROFESSIONAL AND TRADE BODIES

The following list includes the main professional institutions, employers' associations and trade associations in Scotland, and the Scottish offices of UK institutions.

ABERDEEN AND GRAMPIAN CHAMBER OF COMMERCE
213 George Street, Aberdeen, G2 8LU.
Tel: 01224-620621 Fax: 01224-645777
Chief Executive, Amanda Harvie

ABERDEEN FISH CURERS AND MERCHANTS ASSOCIATION
South Esplanade West, Aberdeen, AB11 9FJ.
Tel: 01224-897744 Fax: 01224-871405

ADVANCED CONCRETE AND MASONRY CENTRE
Department of Civil Structural and Environmental Engineering, University of Paisley, Paisley, PA1 2BE.
Tel: 0141-848 5279 Fax: 0141-848 3275
Email: peter.bartos@paisley.ac.uk
Web: www.civing.paisley.ac.uk/acm

ASSOCIATION OF CHARTERED CERTIFIED ACCOUNTANTS
83 Princes Street, Edinburgh, EH2 2ER.
Tel: 0131-247 7510 Fax: 0131-247 7514
Web: www.accaglobal.com
Head of ACCA Scotland, S. Riddell

ASSOCIATION OF SCOTTISH COLLEGES
Argyll Court, The Castle Business Park, Stirling, FK9 4TY. Tel: 01786-892100 Fax: 01786-892109
Email: enquiries@ascol.org.uk
Web: www.ascol.org.uk
Chief Officer, T. Kelly

ASSOCIATION OF SCOTTISH SHELLFISH GROWERS
Mountview, Ardvasar, Isle of Skye, IV45 8RU.
Tel: 01471-844324 Fax: 01471-844324
Email: douglasmacleod@aol.com
Chairman, D. McLeod

BOILER AND RADIATOR MANUFACTURERS ASSOCIATION
Savoy Tower, 77 Renfrew Street, Glasgow, G2 3BZ.
Tel: 0141-332 0826 Fax: 0141-332 5788
Email: barma@metcom.org.uk
Web: www.barma.co.uk
Secretary, F. Cruickshanks

BREWERS' AND LICENSED RETAILERS' ASSOCIATION OF SCOTLAND
6 St Colme Street, Edinburgh, EH3 6AD.
Tel: 0131-225 4681 Fax: 0131-220 1132
Email: Web: www.scottishpubs.co.uk
Secretary, Gordon Millar

BRITISH BOX AND PACKAGING ASSOCIATION
64 High Street, Kirkintilloch, Glasgow, G66 1PR.
Tel: 0141-777 7272 Fax: 0141-777 7747
Email: npcorg@aol.com
Web: www.boxpackaging.org.uk
President, M. Lawson

BRITISH CHRISTMAS TREE GROWERS ASSOCIATION
18 Cluny Place, Edinburgh, EH10 4RL.
Tel: 0131-447 0499 Fax: 0131-447 6443
Email: rogermhay@btinternet.com
Web: www.christmastree.org.uk
Secretary, R. M. Hay, CBE

BRITISH DISPOSABLE PRODUCTS ASSOCIATION
64 High Street, Kirkintilloch, Glasgow, G66 1PR.
Tel: 0141-777 7272 Fax: 0141-777 7747
Email: npcorg@aol.com Web: www.bdpa.co.uk
Chairman, M. Revell

BRITISH HOSPITALITY ASSOCIATION
Saltire Court, 20 Castle Terrace, Edinburgh, EH1 2EN.
Tel: 0131-200 7484 Fax: 0131-228 8888
Email: john.n.loudon@dundas.wilson.com
Web: www.bha.online.org.uk
Secretary, J. Loudon

BRITISH MARINE FEDERATION
Westgate, Toward, Dunoon, Argyll, PA23 7UA.
Tel: 01369-870251 Fax: 01369-870251
Web: www.bmif.co.uk
President, D. Wilkie

BRITISH MEDICAL ASSOCIATION
14 Queen Street, Edinburgh, EH2 1LL.
Tel: 0131-247 3000 Fax: 0131-247 3001
Email: info.edinburgh@bma.org.uk
Web: www.bma.org.uk
Scottish Secretary, Dr W. O'Neill

BRITISH POLYOLEFIN TEXTILES ASSOCIATION
Priestoun, Edzell, Angus, DD9 7UD.
Tel: 01356-648521 Fax: 01356-648521
Secretary, R. H. B. Learoyd

BRITISH VETERINARY ASSOCIATION
SAC Veterinary Science Division,
Mill of Crabstone, Aberdeen, AB21 9TB.
Tel: 01224-711177 Fax: 01224-711184

BUSINESS ENTERPRISE SCOTLAND
18 Forth Street, Edinburgh, EH1 3LH.
Tel: 0131-550 3839 Fax: 0131-550 7001
Email: bes@bes.org.uk Web: www.bes.org.uk
Chief Executive, R. Miller

CBS NETWORK
Princes House, 5 Shandwick Place, Edinburgh,
EH2 4RG. Tel: 0131-229 7257 Fax: 0131-221 9798
Email: info@cbs-network.org.uk
Web: www.cbs-network.org.uk
Development Agent, Claire Brady

CHARTERED INSTITUTE OF ARBITRATORS (ARBITERS)
Whittinghame House, 1099 Great Western Road,
Glasgow, G12 0AA.
Tel: 0141-334 7222 Fax: 0141-334 7700
Email: bruce.smith@scottish-arbitrators.org
Web: www.scottish-arbitrators.org
Hon. Secretary and Treasurer, B. L. Smith

CHARTERED INSTITUTE OF BANKERS IN SCOTLAND
Drumsheugh House, 38B Drumsheugh Gardens,
Edinburgh, EH3 7SW. Tel: 0131-473 7777
Fax: 0131-473 7788 Email: info@ciobs.org.uk
Web: www.ciobs.org.uk

CHARTERED INSTITUTE OF HOUSING IN SCOTLAND
6 Palmerston Place, Edinburgh, EH12 5AA.
Tel: 0131-255 4544 Fax: 0131-225 4566
Web: www.cih.org
Director, A. Ferguson

CHARTERED INSTITUTE OF MARKETING
3rd Floor, 100 Wellington Street, Glasgow, G2 6DH.
Tel: 0141-221 7700 Fax: 0141-221 7766
Email: glasgow@cim.co.uk Web: www.cim.co.uk
Director, Scotland, C. Gardiner

CHARTERED INSTITUTE OF PUBLIC FINANCE AND ACCOUNTANCY
CIPFA Scotland, 8 North West Circus Place, Edinburgh,
EH3 6ST. Tel: 0131-220 4316 Fax: 0131-220 4305
Email: cipfa.scotland@cipfa.org
Web: www.cipfascotland.org.uk
Director, Ian Doig

CHARTERED INSTITUTION OF WATER AND ENVIRONMENTAL MANAGEMENT
Scottish Water - Paisley Regional Office,
36–42 Underwood Road, Paisley, PA3 1TP.
Tel: 0141-271 2770
Email: colin.baillie@scottishwater.co.uk
Chief Executive, Colin Baillie

CILIPS: CHARTERED INSTITUTE OF
LIBRARY AND INFORMATION
PROFESSIONALS IN SCOTLAND
1st Floor Building C, Brandon Gate, Leechlee Road,
Hamilton, ML3 6AU. Tel: 01698-458888
Fax: 01698-283170 Email: cilips@slainte.org.uk Web:
www.slainte.org.uk
Director, Elaine Fulton

CML SCOTLAND (COUNCIL OF
MORTGAGE LENDERS)
Savile Row, London, W1S 3PB. Tel: 020-7440 2227
Fax: 020-7434 3791 Web: www.cml.org.uk
Chairman, G. Waddell

COMMITTEE OF SCOTTISH CLEARING
BANKERS
Drumsheugh House, 38 Drumsheugh Gardens,
Edinburgh, EH3 7SW. Tel: 0131-473 7770
Fax: 0131-473 7799 Email: info@scotbanks.org.uk
Web: www.scotbanks.org.uk
Chairman, Susan Rice

CONFEDERATION OF PASSENGER
TRANSPORT UK – SCOTLAND
29 Drumsheugh Gardens, Edinburgh, EH3 7RN.
Tel: 0131-272 2150 Fax: 0131-272 2152
Email: marjory@mrodger.freeserve.co.uk

COSLA (CONVENTION OF SCOTTISH
LOCAL AUTHORITIES)
Rosebery House, 9 Haymarket Terrace, Edinburgh,
EH12 5XZ. Tel: 0131-474 9200 Fax: 0131-474 9292
Email: enquiries@cosla.gov.uk
Web: www.cosla.gov.uk
President, Pat Watters

DIRECT MARKETING ASSOCIATION
(UK) LTD
41 Comely Bank, Edinburgh, EH4 1AF.
Tel: 0131-315 4422 Fax: 0131-315 4433
Web: www.dma.org.uk
Manager, J. Scobie

EDINBURGH CHAMBER OF COMMERCE
27 Melville Street, Edinburgh, EH3 7JF.
Tel: 0131-477 7000 Fax: 0131-477 7002
Email: information@ecce.org Web: www.ecce.org
Chief Executive, W. Furness

FACULTY OF ACTUARIES IN SCOTLAND
18 Dublin Street, Edinburgh, EH1 3PP.
Tel: 0131-240 1300 Fax: 0131-240 1313
Email: faculty@actuaries.org.uk
Web: www.actuaries.org.uk
Secretary, Richard Maconachie

FACULTY OF ADVOCATES
Advocates Library, Parliament House, Edinburgh,
EH1 1RF. Tel: 0131-226 5071
Dean, Colin M. Campbell, QC

FEDERATION OF MASTER BUILDERS
11 Mentone Gardens, Edinburgh, EH9 2DJ.
Tel: 0131-667 5888 Fax: 0131-667 5548
Email: grahamebarn@fmb.org.uk
Web: www.fmb.org.uk
Regional Director, G. Barn

FEDERATION OF PLASTERING AND
DRYWALL CONTRACTORS SCOTLAND
PO Box 28011, Edinburgh, EH16 6WN.
Tel: 0131-448 0266 Fax: 0131-440 4032
Email: amckinney@support-services.fsbusiness.co.uk
Web: www.fdpc.org
Secretary, A. McKinney

FEDERATION OF SMALL BUSINESSES
74 Berkeley Street, Glasgow, G3 7DS.
Tel: 0141-221 0775 Fax: 0141-221 5954
Email: scotland.policy@fsb.org.uk
Web: www.fsb.org.uk
Scottish Policy Convener, A. Willox

FOREST INDUSTRIES DEVELOPMENT
COUNCIL
53 George Street, Edinburgh, EH2 2HT.
Tel: 0131-220 9290 Fax: 0131-220 9291
Email: mail@fidc.org.uk Web: www.fidc.org.uk
Executive Director, P. Wilson

FORESTRY AND TIMBER ASSOCIATION
5 Dublin Street Lane South, Edinburgh, EH1 3PX.
Tel: 0131-538 7111 Fax: 0131-538 7222
Email: info@forestryandtimber.org
Web: www.forestryandtimber.org
Executive Director, C. J. Inglis

FORESTRY CONTRACTING ASSOCIATION
Dalfling, Blairdaff, Inverurie, Aberdeenshire, AB51 5LA.
Tel: 01467-651368 Fax: 01467-651595
Email: members@fcauk.com Web: www.fcauk.com

FREIGHT TRANSPORT ASSOCIATION LTD
Hermes House, Melville Terrace, Stirling, FK8 2ND.
Tel: 01786-457500 Fax: 01786-450412
Email: stirling@fta.co.uk Web: www.fta.co.uk
Regional Director, R. M. Armstrong

GENERAL TEACHING COUNCIL FOR SCOTLAND

Clerwood House, 96 Clermiston Road, Edinburgh, EH12 6UT. Tel: 0131-314 6000 Fax: 0131-314 6001 Email: gtcs@gtcs.org.uk Web: www.gtcs.org.uk
Chief Executive, M. McIver

GLASGOW CHAMBER OF COMMERCE AND MANUFACTURES

30 George Square, Glasgow, G2 1EQ.
Tel: 0141-572 2121 Fax: 0141-221 2336
Email: chamber@glasgowchamber.org
Web: www.glasgowchamber.org
Chief Executive, D. Tannahill

HARRIS TWEED AUTHORITY

6 Garden Road, Stornoway, Isle of Lewis, HS1 2QJ.
Tel: 01851-702269 Fax: 01851-702600
Email: enquiries@harristweed.org
Web: www.harristweed.org
Chief Executive and Secretary, I. A. Mackenzie

HEADTEACHERS' ASSOCIATION OF SCOTLAND

Jordanhill Campus, University of Strathclyde, Southbrae Drive, Glasgow, G13 1PP.
Tel: 0141-950 3298 Fax: 0141-950 3434
Email: head.teachers@strath.ac.uk
Web: www.has-scotland.co.uk
General Secretary, G. S. Ross

HEATING AND VENTILATING CONTRACTORS' ASSOCIATION

The Walled Garden, Bush Estate, Edinburgh, EH26 0SB.
Tel: 0131-445 5580 Fax: 0131-445 5548
Email: bdyer@hcva.org.uk Web: www.hvca.org.uk
Executive Officer, Bob Dyer

HOMES FOR SCOTLAND

Forsyth House, 93 George Street, Edinburgh, EH2 3ES.
Tel: 0131-243 2595 Fax: 0131-243 2596
Web: www.homesforscotland.co.uk
Chief Executive, Eileen Masterman

INDEPENDENT FEDERATION OF NURSING IN SCOTLAND

Huntershill Village, 102 Crowhill Road, Bishopbriggs, G64 1RP. Tel: 0141-772 9222 Fax: 0141-762 3776
Email: ifoninscotland@cs.com
General Secretary, Ms I. F. O'Neill

INSTITUTE OF AUCTIONEERS AND APPRAISERS IN SCOTLAND

The Rural Centre, West Mains, Ingliston, Newbridge, Midlothian, EH28 8NZ. Tel: 0131-472 4067
Fax: 0131-472 4067

INSTITUTE OF CHARTERED ACCOUNTANTS OF SCOTLAND

CA House, 21 Haymarket Yards, Edinburgh, EH12 5BH.
Tel: 0131-347 0100 Fax: 0131-347 0105
Email: enquiries@icas.org.uk Web: www.icas.org.uk
Chief Executive, D. A. Brew

INSTITUTE OF CHARTERED FORESTERS

7A St Colme Street, Edinburgh, EH3 6AA.
Tel: 0131-225 2705 Fax: 0131-220 6125
Email: icf@charteredforesters.org
Web: www.charteredforesters.org
Executive Director, Ms M. Dick, OBE

INSTITUTE OF ENVIRONMENTAL MANAGEMENT AND ASSESSMENT

St Nicholas House, 70 New Port, Lincoln, LN1 3DP.
Tel: 01522-540069 Fax: 01522-540090
Email: info@iema.net Web: www.iema.net

INSTITUTE OF FOOD SCIENCE AND TECHNOLOGY

Glasgow Caledonian University, Cowcaddens Road, Glasgow, G4 0BA. Tel: 0141-331 8514
Fax: 0141-331 3208 Email: k.aidoo@gcal.ac.uk
Hon. Secretary, Dr K. Aidoo

INSTITUTE OF FUNDRAISING

c/o Bank of Scotland, 12 Bankhead Crossway South, Edinburgh, EH11 4EN. Tel: 0131-453 6517
Email: aneem@institute-of-fundraising.org.uk
Web: www.institute-of-fundraising.org.uk
Development Officer, Ms A. Morrison

INSTITUTE OF HEALTHCARE MANAGEMENT

9 Bellevue Lane, Ayr, KA7 2DS.
Tel: 01292-280814 Fax: 01292-280814
Email: d.mcneill@ihmscotland.co.uk
Web: www.ihmscotland.co.uk
Secretary, D. McNeill

INSTITUTION OF ENGINEERS AND SHIPBUILDERS IN SCOTLAND

Clydeport Building, 16 Robertson Street, Glasgow, G2 8DS. Tel: 0141-248 3721 Fax: 0141-221 2698
Email: secretary@iesis.org
President, Prof A. Slaven

LAW SOCIETY OF SCOTLAND
26 Drumsheugh Gardens, Edinburgh, EH3 7YR.
Tel: 0131-226 7411 Fax: 0131-225 2934
Email: lawscot@lawscot.org.uk
Web: www.lawscot.org.uk
Chief Executive, Douglas Mill

MALT DISTILLERS' ASSOCIATION OF
SCOTLAND
1 North Street, Elgin, IV30 1UA. Tel: 01343-544077
Fax: 01343-548523
Email: mdas@grigor-young.co.uk
Secretary, Grigor and Young Solicitors

MINING INSTITUTE OF SCOTLAND
1/3 Russell Gardens, Edinburgh, EH12 5PG.
Tel: 0131-346 0653 Fax: 0131-346 0667
Email: d.seath@btinternet.com
Web: www.mining-scotland.org
Branch Secretary, D. Seath

NATIONAL FEDERATION OF RETAIL
NEWSAGENTS
6A Weir Street, Falkirk, FK1 1RA. Tel: 01324-625293
Fax: 01324-613128 Web: www.nfrn.org.uk
Regional Manager, David Cousins

NATIONAL FEDERATION OF ROOFING
CONTRACTORS
PO Box 28011, Edinburgh, EH16 6WN.
Tel: 0131-448 0266 Fax: 0131-440 4032
Email: amckinney@support-services.fsbusiness.co.uk
Web: www.nfrc.co.uk
Secretary, A. McKinney

NATIONAL SPECIALIST CONTRACTORS
COUNCIL
PO Box 28011, Edinburgh, EH16 6WN.
Tel: 0131-448 0266 Fax: 0131-440 4032
Email: amckinney@support-services.fsbusiness.co.uk
Web: www.scottish-trades.co.uk
Secretary, A. McKinney

NFU SCOTLAND
Rural Centre, West Mains, Ingliston, Newbridge,
Midlothian, EH28 8LT. Tel: 0131-472 4000
Fax: 0131-472 4010 Web: www.nfus.org.uk
Chief Executive, E. Rainy Brown

NHS EDUCATION FOR SCOTLAND (NES)
22 Queen Street, Edinburgh, EH2 1NT.
Tel: 0131-226 7371 Fax: 0131-225 9970
Web: www.nes.scot.nhs.uk

OFFSHORE CONTRACTORS'
ASSOCIATION
58 Queens Road, Aberdeen, AB15 4YE.
Tel: 01224-326070 Fax: 01224-326071
Email: admin@oca-online.co.uk
Web: www.oca-online.co.uk
Chief Executive, Bill Murray

PRODUCERS ALLIANCE FOR CINEMA
AND TELEVISION (PACT) SCOTLAND
249 West George Street, Glasgow, G2 4QE.
Tel: 0141-222 4880 Fax: 0141-222 4881
Web: www.pact.co.uk
Manager, Ms M. Scott

PROFESSIONAL ASSOCIATION OF
TEACHERS (SCOTLAND)
4–6 Oak Lane, Edinburgh, EH12 6XH.
Tel: 0131-317 8282 Fax: 0131-317 8111
Email: scotland@pat.org.uk Web: www.pat.org.uk
Professional Officer (Scotland), M. McA. White

PROFESSIONAL GOLFERS' ASSOCIATION
King's Lodge, Gleneagles, Auchterarder, Perthshire,
PH3 1NE. Tel: 01764-661840 Fax: 01764-661841
Email: scotland.region@pga.org.uk
Web: www.pga.org.uk

QUALITY MEAT SCOTLAND
Rural Centre, Ingliston, Newbridge, Midlothian,
EH28 8NZ. Tel: 0131-472 4040 Fax: 0131-472 4038
Email: info@qmscotland.co.uk
Web: www.speciallyselected.co.uk
Chief Executive, Jan Polley

ROAD HAULAGE ASSOCIATION LTD
Roadway House, The Rural Centre, Ingliston,
Newbridge, EH28 8NZ.
Tel: 0131-472 4180 Fax: 0131-472 4179
Email: scotland-northernireland@rha.net
Web: www.rha.net
Regional Director, P. Flanders

ROYAL COLLEGE OF GENERAL
PRACTITIONERS SCOTLAND
25 Queen Street, Edinburgh, EH2 1JX.
Tel: 0131-260 6800 Fax: 0131-260 6836
Email: scottish@rcgp.org.uk
Web: www.rcgp-scotland.org.uk

ROYAL COLLEGE OF NURSING OF THE
UNITED KINGDOM
42 South Oswald Road, Edinburgh, EH9 2HH.
Tel: 0131-662 1010 Fax: 0131-662 1032
Web: www.rcn.org.uk/scotland
Scottish Board Secretary, James Kennedy

ROYAL COLLEGE OF PHYSICIANS AND
SURGEONS OF GLASGOW
232–242 St Vincent Street, Glasgow, G2 5RJ.
Tel: 0141-221 6072 Fax: 0141-221 1804
Email: registrar@rcpsglasg.ac.uk
Web: www.rcpsglasg.ac.uk
Registrar, Mr R. K. Littlejohn

ROYAL COLLEGE OF PHYSICIANS OF
EDINBURGH
9 Queen Street, Edinburgh, EH2 1JQ.
Tel: 0131-225 7324 Fax: 0131-220 3939
Email: e.tait@rcpe.ac.uk Web: www.rcpe.ac.uk
Chief Executive, E. Tait

ROYAL COLLEGE OF SURGEONS OF
EDINBURGH
Nicolson Street, Edinburgh, EH8 9DW.
Tel: 0131-527 1600 Fax: 0131-557 6406
Email: info@rcsed.ac.uk Web: www.rcsed.ac.uk
Chief Executive, J. R. C. Foster

ROYAL ENVIRONMENTAL HEALTH
INSTITUTE OF SCOTLAND
3 Manor Place, Edinburgh, EH3 7DH.
Tel: 0131-225 6999 Fax: 0131-225 3993
Email: contact@rehis.com Web: www.rehis.org
Chief Executive, J. Frater

ROYAL INCORPORATION OF
ARCHITECTS IN SCOTLAND
15 Rutland Square, Edinburgh, EH1 2BE.
Tel: 0131-229 7545 Fax: 0131-228 2188
Email: info@rias.org.uk Web: www.rias.org.uk
Secretary, S. Tombs

ROYAL INSTITUTION OF CHARTERED
SURVEYORS IN SCOTLAND
9 Manor Place, Edinburgh, EH3 7DN.
Tel: 0131-225 7078 Fax: 0131-240 0830
Email: pmiller@rics.org.uk
Web: www.rics-scotland.org.uk
Director, Peter Miller

ROYAL PHARMACEUTICAL SOCIETY OF
GREAT BRITAIN
36 York Place, Edinburgh, EH1 3HU.
Tel: 0131-556 4386 Fax: 0131-558 8850
Email: info@rpsis.com Web: www.rpsgb.org.uk
Secretary, Dr S. Stevens

ROYAL SCOTTISH FORESTRY SOCIETY
Hagg-on-Esk, Canonbie, Dumfriesshire, DG14 0XE.
Tel: 01387-371518 Fax: 01387-371418
Email: rsfs@ednet.co.uk Web: www.rsfs.org
Director, A. G. Little

ROYAL TOWN PLANNING INSTITUTE
57 Melville Street, Edinburgh, EH3 7HL.
Tel: 0131-226 1959 Fax: 0131-226 1909
Email: scotland@rtpi.org.uk
Web: www.scotland.rtpc.org.uk
Director, G. U'ren

SCOTCH WHISKY ASSOCIATION
20 Atholl Crescent, Edinburgh, EH3 8HF.
Tel: 0131-222 9200 Fax: 0131-222 9248
Email: enquiries@swa.org.uk
Web: www.scotch-whisky.org.uk

SCOTTISH AND NORTHERN IRELAND
PLUMBING EMPLOYERS' FEDERATION
2 Walker Street, Edinburgh, EH3 7LB.
Tel: 0131-225 2255 Fax: 0131-226 7638
Email: info@snipef.org Web: www.snipef.org

SCOTTISH ASSESSORS' ASSOCIATION
Chesser House, 500 Gorgie Road, Edinburgh,
EH11 3YJ. Tel: 0131-455 7455 Fax: 0131-469 5599
Email: assessor@lothian-vjb.gov.uk

SCOTTISH ASSOCIATION OF MASTER
BAKERS
4 Torphichen Street, Edinburgh, EH3 8JQ.
Tel: 0131-229 1401 Fax: 0131-229 8239
Email: master.bakers@samb.co.uk
Web: www.samb.co.uk
Chief Executive, K. Hunter

SCOTTISH ASSOCIATION OF SIGN
LANGUAGE INTERPRETERS (SASLI)
Donaldson's College, West Coates, Edinburgh,
EH12 5JJ. Tel: 0131-347 5601 Fax: 0131-347 5628
Email: mail@sasli.org.uk Web: www.sasli.org.uk
Director, Mrs D. Mair

SCOTTISH BUILDING
Carron Grange, Carrongrange Avenue, Stenhousemuir,
FK5 3BQ. Tel: 01324-555550 Fax: 01324-555551
Email: info@scottish-building.co.uk
Web: www.scottish-building.co.uk

SCOTTISH CHAMBERS OF COMMERCE
30 George Square, Glasgow, G2 1EQ.
Tel: 0141-204 8316 Fax: 0141-221 2336
Email: admin@scottishchambers.org.uk
Web: www.scottishchambers.org.uk

SCOTTISH CHIROPRACTIC ASSOCIATION
St Boswells Chiropractic Clinic, 16 Jenny Moores Road,
St Boswells, Melrose, TD6 0AL.
Tel: 01835-824026 Fax: 01835-824046
Email: sca@scottishborders.co.uk
Web: www.sca-chiropractic.org.uk
President, Dr Dean Sluce

SCOTTISH COMMITTEE OF OPTOMETRISTS
7 Queens Buildings, Queensferry Road, Rosyth, Fife, KY11 2RA. Tel: 01383-419444 Fax: 01383-416778
Secretary, David Hutton

SCOTTISH CONTRACTORS
4 Woodside Place, Glasgow, G3 7QF.
Tel: 0141-353 5050 Fax: 0141-332 2928
Email: smith@sbca.freeserve.co.uk
Association Secretary, N. J. Smith

SCOTTISH CONVEYANCING AND EXECUTRY SERVICES BOARD
1 John's Place, Leith, Edinburgh, EH6 7EL.
Tel: 0131-555 6525 Fax: 0131-553 5011
Email: scesb@btopenworld.com
Web: www.scesb.co.uk
Secretary, E. B. Simmons

SCOTTISH COUNCIL FOR DEVELOPMENT AND INDUSTRY
23 Chester Street, Edinburgh, EH3 7ET.
Tel: 0131-225 7911 Fax: 0131-220 2116
Email: enquiries@scdi.org.uk Web: www.scdi.org.uk

SCOTTISH CROFTING FOUNDATION
The Sleading, Balmacara Square, Balmacara, IV40 8DJ.
Tel: 01520-722891 Fax: 01520-722932
Web: www.croftingfoundation.co.uk
Chief Executive, Patrick Krause

SCOTTISH DAIRY ASSOCIATION
4A Torphichen Street, Edinburgh, EH3 8JQ.
Tel: 0131-221 0109 Fax: 0131-221 0220
Email: admin@scotdairy.org.uk
Web: www.ebs.hw.ac.uk/sda
Company Secretary, K. Hunter

SCOTTISH DECORATORS FEDERATION
222 Queensferry Road, Edinburgh, EH4 2BN.
Tel: 0131-343 3300 Fax: 0131-315 2289
Chief Executive, I. Rogers

SCOTTISH ENGINEERING
105 West George Street, Glasgow, G2 1QL.
Tel: 0141-221 3181 Fax: 0141-204 1202
Email: consult@scottishengineering.org.uk
Chief Executive, P. T. Hughes, OBE, FREng.

SCOTTISH FEDERATION OF HOUSING ASSOCIATIONS
38 York Place, Edinburgh, EH1 3HU.
Tel: 0131-556 5777 Fax: 0131-557 6028
Email: sfha@sfha.co.uk Web: www.sfha.co.uk
Chief Executive, David Orr

SCOTTISH FINANCIAL ENTERPRISE
91 George Street, Edinburgh, EH2 3ES.
Tel: 0131-247 7700 Fax: 0131-247 7709
Email: info@sfe.org.uk Web: www.sfe.org.uk
Chief Executive, Amanda Harvey

SCOTTISH FISHERMEN'S ORGANISATION
601 Queensferry Road, Edinburgh, EH4 6EA.
Tel: 0131-339 7972 Fax: 0131-339 6662
Email: info@scottishfishermen.co.uk
Web: www.scottishfishermen.co.uk
Chief Executive, Iain MacSween

SCOTTISH GROCERS' FEDERATION
Federation House, 222–224 Queensferry Road, Edinburgh, EH4 2BN.
Tel: 0131-343 3300 Fax: 0131-343 6147
Email: information@scottish-grocers-federation.co.uk
Web: www.scottish-grocers-federation.co.uk
Chief Executive, L. Dewar

SCOTTISH INSTITUTE FOR WOOD TECHNOLOGY
University of Abertay Dundee, Bell Street, Dundee, DD1 1HG. Tel: 01382-308567
Fax: 01382-308663 Web: www.scieng.tay.ac.uk/siwt
Research Director, A. Bruce

SCOTTISH IPA (INSTITUTE OF PRACTITIONERS IN ADVERTISING)
25 Rutland Square, Edinburgh, EH1 2BW.
Tel: 0131-473 1576 Fax: 0131-473 1577
Web: www.scottishipa.co.uk
Chairman, G. Brooksbank

SCOTTISH IS
Livingston Software Innovation Centre, 1 Michaelson Square, Kirkton Campus, Livingston, EH54 7DP.
Tel: 01506-472200 Fax: 01506-472209
Email: info@scotlandis.com
Web: www.scotlandis.com
Chief Executive, Frank Binnie

SCOTTISH LIBRARY AND INFORMATION COUNCIL
1st Floor Building C, Brandon Gate, Leechlee Road, Hamilton, ML3 6AU. Tel: 01698-458888
Fax: 01698-283170 Email: slic@slainte.org.uk
Web: www.slainte.org.uk
Director, Elaine Fulton

SCOTTISH LOCAL GOVERNMENT INFORMATION UNIT
Room 507, Baltic Chambers, 50 Wellington Street, Glasgow, G2 6HJ. Tel: 0141-226 4636
Fax: 0141-221 8786 Email: slgiu@btinternet.com
Web: www.slgiu.gov.uk
Director, P. Vestri

SCOTTISH MOTOR TRADE ASSOCIATION LTD

3 Palmerston Place, Edinburgh, EH12 5AF.
Tel: 0131-225 3643 Fax: 0131-220 0446
Email: info@smta.co.uk Web: www.smta.co.uk
Chief Executive, D. R. W. Robertson

SCOTTISH MUSEUMS COUNCIL

20–22 Torphichen Street, Edinburgh, EH3 8JB.
Tel: 0131-229 7465 Fax: 0131-229 2728
Email: inform@scottishmuseums.org.uk
Web: www.scottishmuseums.org.uk

SCOTTISH PELAGIC FISHERMEN'S ASSOCIATION LTD

1 Frithside Street, Fraserburgh, Aberdeenshire,
AB43 9AR. Tel: 01346-510714 Fax: 01346-510614
Email: spfaltd@btinternet.com
Secretary, D. Duthie

SCOTTISH PHARMACEUTICAL FEDERATION

135 Wellington Street, Glasgow, G2 2XD.
Tel: 0141-221 1235 Fax: 0141-248 5892
Email: spf@npanet.co.uk
Secretary, F. E. J. McCrossin, CA

SCOTTISH PRINT EMPLOYERS' FEDERATION

48 Palmerston Place, Edinburgh, EH12 5DE.
Tel: 0131-220 4353 Fax: 0131-220 4344
Email: info@spef.org.uk Web: www.spef.org.uk

SCOTTISH PUBLISHERS' ASSOCIATION

Scottish Book Centre, 137 Dundee Street, Edinburgh,
EH11 1BG. Tel: 0131-228 6866 Fax: 0131-228 3220
Email: info@scottishbooks.org
Web: www.scottishbooks.org
Director, Ms L. Fannin

SCOTTISH QUALITY SALMON LTD

Durn, Isla Road, Perth, PH2 7HG.
Tel: 01738-587000 Fax: 01738-621454
Email: enquiries@scottishsalmon.co.uk
Web: www.scottishsalmon.co.uk

SCOTTISH QUALITY TROUT

Motherwell Food Park, Bellshill, Lanarkshire, ML4 3JA.
Tel: 01698-742666 Fax: 01698-742666
Email: info@sqt.org Web: www.sqt.org

SCOTTISH RENEWABLES

First Floor, The Beacon, 176 St Vincent Street,
Glasgow, G2 5SG.
Tel: 0141-249 6705 Fax: 0141-249 6704
Web: www.scottishrenewables.com
Chief Executive, R. Forrest

SCOTTISH RETAIL CONSORTIUM

222–224 Queensferry Road, Edinburgh, EH4 2BN.
Tel: 0131-332 6619 Fax: 0131-332 6597
Email: src@brc.org.uk Web: www.brc.org.uk

SCOTTISH SOCIAL SERVICES COUNCIL

Compass House, Discovery Quay, 11 Riverside Drive,
Dundee, DD1 4NY. Tel: 01382-207101
Fax: 01382-207215 Email: enquiries@sssc.uk.com
Web: www.sssc.uk.com
Chief Executive, Carole Wilkinson

SCOTTISH TIMBER TRADE ASSOCIATION

Office 14, John Player Building, Stirling Enterprise Park,
Springbank Road, Stirling, FK7 7RP.
Tel: 01786-451623 Fax: 01786-473112
Email: mail@stta.org.uk Web: www.stta.org.uk
Secretary, D. J. Sulman

SELECT

The Walles Garden, Bush Estate, Midlothian,
EH26 0SB. Tel: 0131-445 5577 Fax: 0131-445 5548
Email: admin@select.org.uk
Web: www.select.org.uk
Managing Director, M. D. Goodwin, OBE

SOCIETY OF INDEXERS

Bentfield, 3 Marine Terrace, Gullane, E. Lothian,
EH31 2AY. Tel: 01620-842247 Fax: 01620-842247
Email: annemccarthy@btinternet.com
Web: www.socind.demon.co.uk
Group Organiser, Mrs A. McCarthy

SOCIETY OF LAW ACCOUNTANTS IN SCOTLAND

Johnstone House, 52–54 Rose Street,
Aberdeen, AB10 1HA
Email: jane.macleod@ledinghamchalmers.com
Web: www.solas.co.uk
General Secretary, Mrs Jane C. MacLeod

SOCIETY OF LOCAL AUTHORITY CHIEF EXECUTIVES AND SENIOR MANAGERS

c/o Angus Council, The Cross, Forfar, Angus, DD8 1BX.
Tel: 01307-473020 Fax: 01307-461874
Email: chiefexec@angus.gov.uk
Web: www.solace.org.uk
Hon. Secretary, Sandy Watson

SOCIETY OF SCOTTISH ARTISTS

4 Barony Street, Edinburgh, EH3 6PE.
Tel: 0131-557 2354 Web: www.s-s-a.org

STONE FEDERATION GREAT BRITAIN

PO Box 28011, Edinburgh, EH16 6WN.
Tel: 0131-448 0266 Fax: 0131-440 4032
Email: amckinney@support-services.fsbusiness.co.uk
Web: www.stone-federationgb.org.uk
Secretary, A. McKinney

TIMBER FRAME INDUSTRY ASSOCIATION

The e-centre, Cooperage Way Business Village, Alloa,
FK10 3LP. Tel: 01259-272140 Fax: 01259-272141
Email: office@timber-frame.org
Web: www.timber-frame.org
Chairman, R. Macfarlane

UK FOREST PRODUCTS ASSOCIATION

John Player Building, Stirling Enterprise Park,
Springbank Road, Stirling, FK7 7RP.
Tel: 01786-449029 Fax: 01786-473112
Email: dsulman@ukfpa.co.uk
Web: www.ukfpa.co.uk

UK OFFSHORE OPERATORS ASSOCIATION LTD

9 Albyn Terrace, Aberdeen, AB10 1YP.
Tel: 01224-626652 Fax: 01224-626503
Email: info@ukooa.co.uk
Web: www.oilandgas.org.uk

TRADE UNIONS

The Certification Officer is responsible for certifying the independence of trade unions, receiving and scrutinising annual returns from trade unions, dealing with complaints about trade union elections and ensuring compliance with statutory requirements governing political funds and union mergers.

The Central Arbitration Committee determines claims for statutory recognition under the Employment Relations Act 1999 and certain issues relating to the implementation of the European Works Council Directive, the Committee also arbitrates trade disputes and adjudicates on disclosure of information complaints.

CERTIFICATION OFFICE FOR TRADE UNIONS AND EMPLOYERS' ASSOCIATIONS, SCOTLAND

58 Frederick Street, Edinburgh EH2 1LN
Tel: 0131-226 3224
Assistant Certification Officer for Scotland: J. L. J. Craig

CENTRAL ARBITRATION COMMITTEE

3rd Floor, Discovery House, 28–42 Banner Street, London EC1Y 8QE
Tel: 020-7251 9747 Fax: 020-7251 3114
Chairman: Sir Michael Burton
Secretary: Graeme Charles

SCOTTISH TRADES UNION CONGRESS

333 Woodlands Road, Glasgow G3 6NG
Tel: 0141-337 8100 Fax: 0141-337 8101
Email: info@stuc.org.uk Web: www.stuc.org.uk

The Congress was formed in 1897 and acts as a national centre for the trade union movement in Scotland. The STUC promotes the rights and welfare of those in work and helps the unemployed. It helps its member unions to promote membership in new areas and industries, and campaigns for rights at work for all employees, including part-time and temporary workers, whether union members or not. It makes representations to government and employers. In 2002, the STUC agreed a Memorandum of Understanding with the Scottish Executive, which outlines a formal mechanism for on-going dialogue on shared priorities for economic development, public sector improvement and social partnership.

As at June 2003 the STUC consisted of 46 affiliated unions with a membership of approximately 630,000.
General Secretary: B. Speirs

UNIONS AFFILIATED TO THE SCOTTISH TRADES UNION CONGRESS

ACCORD
Simmons House, 46 Old Bath Road, Charvil, Reading RG10 9QR Tel: 0118-934 1808
Fax: 0118-932 0208 Email: info@accordhq.org
General Secretary: G. Nichols

AMICUS (AEEU & MSF)
John Smith House, 145–165 West Regent Street, Glasgow G2 4RZ Tel: 0141-248 7131
Fax: 0141-221 3898 Email: glasgow@aeeu.org.uk
Scottish Regional Secretary: J. Quigley

ASSOCIATED SOCIETY OF LOCOMOTIVE ENGINEERS AND FIREMEN
70 Tantallon Garden, Muireston, Livingston EH54 9AT
Tel: 01506-419641 Fax: 01506-412239
Email: klindsay@aslef.org.uk
District Secretary: K. Lindsay

ASSOCIATION OF UNIVERSITY TEACHERS (SCOTLAND)
6 Castle Street, Edinburgh EH2 3AT
Tel: 0131-226 6694 Fax: 0131-226 2066
Email: scotland&ne@aut.org.uk
Hon. Secretary: S. Ashworth

BRITISH AIRLINE PILOTS' ASSOCIATION
81 New Road, Harlington, Hayes, Middlesex UB3 5BG
Tel: 020-8476 4000 Fax: 020-8476 4077
Email: balpa@balpa.org.uk
General Secretary: C. Darke

BRITISH DIETETIC ASSOCIATION
5th Floor, Charles House, 148–9 Great Charles Street, Queensway, Birmingham B3 3HT
Tel: 0121-200 8055 Fax: 0121-200 8081
Email: ir@bda.uk.com
National Industrial Relations Officer: D. Wood

BRITISH ORTHOPTIC SOCIETY
Tavistock House North, Tavistock Square, London WC1H 9HX
Tel: 020-7387 7992 Fax: 020-7383 2584
Regional Representative for East of Scotland: Laura McCartney

BROADCASTING, ENTERTAINMENT,
CINEMATOGRAPH AND THEATRE UNION
114 Union Street, Glasgow G1 3QQ
Tel: 0141-248 9558 Fax: 0141-248 9588
Email: pmcmanus@bectu.org.uk
Scottish Organiser: P. McManus

CHARTERED SOCIETY OF
PHYSIOTHERAPY
21 Queen Street, Edinburgh EH2 1JX
Tel: 0131-226 1441 Fax: 0131-226 1551
Email: mcnallyp@csp.org.uk
Scottish Secretary: Patricia McNally

COLLIERY OFFICIALS AND STAFF AREA
NUM
3 Elliock Place, Kirkconnell, Dumfriesshire DG4 6PW
Tel: 01659-67104 Email: rabphyll@aol.com
Contact: R. Jardine

COMMUNICATION WORKERS' UNION
2b Craigpark, Dennistoun, Glasgow G31 2NP
Tel: 0141-556 0159 Fax: 0141-554 8736
Scottish Secretary: G. Robertson

COMMUNITY AND DISTRICT NURSING
ASSOCIATION
Westel House, 32–38 Uxbridge Road, London W5 2BS
Tel: 020-8280 5342 Fax: 020-8280 5341
Email: cdna@tvu.ac.uk

CONNECT
30 St George's Road, London SW19 4BD
Tel: 020-8971 6000 Fax: 020-8971 6002
Email: union@connectuk.org
General Secretary: S. Petch

EDUCATIONAL INSTITUTE OF SCOTLAND
46 Moray Place, Edinburgh EH3 6BH
Tel: 0131-225 6244 Fax: 0131-220 3151
Email: membership@eis.org.uk
General Secretary: R. Smith

EQUITY
114 Union Street, Glasgow G1 3QQ
Tel: 0141-248 2472 Fax: 0141-248 2473
Scottish Secretary: L. Boswell

FDA
2 Caxton Street, London SW1H 0QH
Tel: 020-7343 1111 Fax: 020-7343 1145
General Secretary: J. Baume

FIRE BRIGADES UNION
4th Floor, 52 St Enoch Square, Glasgow G1 4AA
Tel: 0141-221 2309 Fax: 0141-204 4575
Scottish Regional Secretary: T. Tierney

GMB
Fountain House, 1/3 Woodside Crescent,
Glasgow G3 7YJ
Tel: 0141-332 8641 Fax: 0141-332 4491
General Secretary: J. Edmonds

GRAPHICAL, PAPER AND MEDIA UNION
Graphical House, 222 Clyde Street, Glasgow
G1 4JT Tel: 0141-221 7730 Fax: 0141-248 7085
Email: scotland@gpmu.fsnet.co.uk
Scottish Branch Secretary: D. Munro

IRON AND STEEL TRADES
CONFEDERATION
102 Hamilton Road, Motherwell ML1 3DG
Tel: 01698-304567 Fax: 01698-304568
Email: div1@istc-tu.org
Senior Organiser: S. McCool

MUSICIANS UNION
11 Sandyford Place, Sauchiehall Street, Glasgow
G3 7NB Tel: 0141-248 3723 Fax: 0141-204 3510
Email: scotland@musiciansunion.org.uk
Scotland and Northern Ireland Organiser: I. Smith

NATIONAL ASSOCIATION OF COLLIERY
OVERMEN, DEPUTIES AND SHOTFIRERS
(SCOTTISH AREA)
19 Cadzow Street, Hamilton ML3 6EE
Tel: 01698-284981 Fax: 01698-281380
Email: ross.letham@btinternet.com
Contact: R. Letham

NATIONAL ASSOCIATION OF
SCHOOLMASTERS/UNION OF WOMEN
TEACHERS (SCOTLAND)
6 Waterloo Place, Edinburgh EH1 3BG
Tel: 0131-523 110 Fax: 0131-523 1119
Email: rc-scotland@mail.nasuwt.org.uk

NATIONAL LEAGUE OF THE BLIND AND
DISABLED
43 Byron Avenue, Northfield, Aberdeen AB16 7LD
Tel: 01224-789442 Fax: 01224-696149
Regional Secretary: G. Reid

NATIONAL UNION OF JOURNALISTS
3rd Floor, 114 Union Street, Glasgow G1 3QQ
Tel: 0141-248 6648 Fax: 0141-248 2473
Web: www.nuj.org.uk
Scottish Organiser: J. Dear

NATIONAL UNION OF KNITWEAR,
FOOTWEAR AND APPAREL TRADES
Orwell, 6 London Road, Kilmarnock KA3 7AD
Tel: 01563-527476 Fax: 01563-537851
Email: general-office@kfat-scot.freeserve.co.uk
District Secretary: J. Steele

NATIONAL UNION OF MARINE, AVIATION AND SHIPPING TRANSPORT OFFICERS
Oceanair House, 750/760 High Road, London E11 3BB
Tel: 020-8989 6677 Fax: 020-8530 1015
Email: info@numast.org
General Secretary: B. Orrell

NATIONAL UNION OF MINEWORKERS: SCOTLAND AREA
30 New Street, Musselburgh, East Lothian EH21 6JP
Tel: 0131-665 4111 Fax: 0131-665 4104
Email: rose@numscotland.org.uk
General Secretary: N. Wilson

NATIONAL UNION OF RAIL, MARITIME AND TRANSPORT WORKERS
180 Hope Street, Glasgow G2 2UE
Tel: 0141-332 1117 Fax: 0141-333 9583
Divisional Organiser: P. McGarry

PRISON OFFICERS' ASSOCIATION (SCOTLAND)
21 Calder Road, Saughton, Edinburgh EH11 3PF
Tel: 0131-443 8105 Fax: 0131-444 0657
Email: adminscot@poauk.org.uk
Assistant Secretary: D. Turner

PROSPECT (IPMS & EMA)
30 New Street, Musselburgh, East Lothian EH21 6JP
Tel: 0131-665 4487 Fax: 0131-665 7513
National Secretary: Ms A. Douglas
18 Melville Terrace, Stirling FK8 2NQ
Tel: 01786-465999 Fax: 01786-465516
National Secretary: A. Denney

PUBLIC AND COMMERCIAL SERVICES UNION
6 Hillside Crescent, Edinburgh EH7 5DY
Tel: 0131-556 0407 Fax: 0131-557 5613
Scottish Secretary: E. Reilly

SCOTTISH CARPET WORKERS' UNION
62 Viewfield Road, Ayr KA8 8HH Tel/Fax: 01292-261676
General Secretary: R. Smillie

SCOTTISH FURTHER AND HIGHER EDUCATION ASSOCIATION
Suite 2C, Ingram House, 227 Ingram Street, Glasgow G1 1DA Tel: 0141-221 0118 Fax: 0141-221 2583
General Secretary: E. H. Smith

SCOTTISH SECONDARY TEACHERS' ASSOCIATION
15 Dundas Street, Edinburgh EH3 6QG
Tel: 0131-556 5919 Fax: 0131-556 1419
Email: info@ssta.org.uk
General Secretary: D. H. Eaglesham

SCOTTISH SOCIETY OF PLAYWRIGHTS
41 Nithsdale Road, Glasgow G41 2AL
Tel: 0141-423 2057
General Secretary: D. Harrower

SOCIETY OF CHIROPODISTS AND PODIATRISTS
SCP Regional Offices, 7 Maryland Drive, Craigton, Glasgow G52 1SW
Tel/Fax: 0141-883 2286 Email: gp@scpod.org
Scottish Organiser: G. Pirie

SOCIETY OF RADIOGRAPHERS
6 Victoria Road, Brookfield, Johnstone, Renfrewshire PA5 8TZ Tel/Fax: 01505-382039

TRANSPORT AND GENERAL WORKERS' UNION
290 Bath Street, Glasgow G2 4LD Tel: 0845-345 0141
Fax: 0141-332 6157 Email: abaird@tgwu.org.uk
Regional Secretary: A. Baird

TRANSPORT SALARIED STAFFS' ASSOCIATION
180 Hope Street, Glasgow G2 2UE Tel: 0141-332 4698
Fax: 0141-332 9879 Email: glasgow@tssa.org.uk
Development Manager: R. S. King

UNIFI
146 Argyle Street, Glasgow G2 8BL
Tel: 0141-221 6475 Fax: 0141-201 3315
Email: info@unifi.org.uk
Deputy General Secretary: S. Boyle

UNION OF CONSTRUCTION, ALLIED TRADES AND TECHNICIANS
53 Morrison Street, Glasgow G5 8LB
Tel: 0141-420 2880 Fax: 0141-420 2881
Scottish Secretary: A. Ritchie

UNION OF SHOP DISTRIBUTIVE AND ALLIED WORKERS
Muirfield, 342 Albert Drive, Glasgow G41 5PG
Tel: 0141-427 6561 Fax: 0141-419 1029
Email: glasgow@usdaw.org.uk
Scottish Divisional Officer: F. Whitelaw

UNISON
Unison House, 14 West Campbell Street, Glasgow G2 6RX
Tel: 0870-777 7006 Fax: 0141-331 1203
Scottish Secretary: M. Smith

THE VOLUNTARY SECTOR IN SCOTLAND

There are over 50,000 voluntary or non-profit organisations in Scotland which have a collective income of £2.08 billion. Recent research carried out by the Scottish Council for Voluntary Organisations (SCVO) into the size and characteristics of the voluntary workforce found that registered charities in Scotland in 2001 employed an estimated 107,000 paid staff (equivalent to 80,000 full-time posts), an estimated average growth from 1997–2001 of 4,000 each year, or a total of 17 per cent. Voluntary sector organisations are defined by their independence from the state and by the fact that they are run by unpaid volunteers (although they may employ paid workers), as well as by their non-profit status. However, the sector is increasingly involved in meeting needs and providing services in key areas of government policy such as social inclusion and health, housing and homelessness, and environmental protection. Other fields covered by voluntary organisations include community development; residential care, including care of elderly people; playschemes and other services for children and youth; human rights; peace issues; gender equality and women's rights; racial equality; labour and professional relations; religious interests; mental health; disabilities; racial equality and minorities issues; drugs/alcohol abuse; animal care and wildlife protection; international development and humanitarian aid; and consumers' interests. There are also many voluntary organisations promoting arts and culture, sports and outdoor activities, and informal education. The sector is very diverse, including organisations of all sizes and ranging from single-issue groups and campaigns to service provision and advocacy. Voluntary groups and organisations play a key role in the economy at the local level and in community well-being.

The fastest growth in the non-profit sector is occurring in the largest charities, with a mere 5 per cent of organisations controlling 67 per cent of the sector income. Many of these are now delivering a range of social care and health services which were previously carried out by central and local government. Nearly three-quarters of regulated voluntary organisations have an annual income of under £25,000 and only one per cent have an annual income of over £1 million. The significant role played by the voluntary sector in policy development and service provision, at the community level, and its weight as an economic sector complementary to the public and private sectors, are recognised in the Scottish Compact. Launched in 1998, the Compact sets out the principles underlying the relationship of co-operation between the Scottish government and the voluntary sector, and was drawn up by a joint working group consisting of representatives of the Scottish Office (before devolution) and the voluntary sector. As well as promoting good practice and encouraging volunteering as an expression of active citizenship, the Compact enables the voluntary sector to have a voice in policy-making through dialogue with government.

The Scottish Executive is committed to supporting the voluntary sector by creating a more stable funding environment for it, including providing core funding to national voluntary organisations and other funding packages where appropriate.

SOURCES OF FUNDING

Self-generated income is a major part of the sector's income and includes income from trading, rents and returns from investments. In 2001 it was estimated to account for approximately 39 per cent (£780 million) of the sector's income.

Funding from the Scottish Executive, NDPBs and other public sector funding sources now accounts for 38 per cent of voluntary sector income and has been slowly increasing since the late 1990s. Direct funding from the Scottish Executive has increased since devolution, with around 45 per cent of the funding coming from the Education Department and a further 20–25 per cent under Section 10 of the Social Work Services Act. A review of direct funding to the voluntary sector in 2001 clarified the role of the Scottish Executive funding and resulted in the executive committing to standardising and simplifying its funding processes. Other public sector funding includes that which comes direct from Whitehall for various activities including overseas development and employment initiatives, the most significant being through the New Deal. Communities Scotland is also a significant funder with the majority being allocated to housing associations.

Donations made by the general public through street collection, Give As you Earn, raffles and legacies remain an important source of income estimated at 12 per cent in 2001. However, a survey commissioned by SCVO in January 2000 found that although individuals were donating larger sums, the numbers of people donating had fallen by more than the donations had risen. This fall is though to be linked to the introduction of the National Lottery.

In Scotland amounts approved specifically to the voluntary sector from the National Lottery began with a high of £117 million over 1996, decreasing steadily to £64 million over 2002. The only guaranteed income from the lottery is through the Community Fund, which distributes 16.5 per cent of the total.

Private sector income was negligible at only 1 per cent in 2000, but recently there has been an interest in corporate social responsibility and a cross-sectoral forum, AGENDA, was established to promote social responsibility in Scotland. Consequently, the most recent estimates of private sector funding were placed at 3 per cent of the total sector income in 2001.

SOURCES OF INCOME TO REGULATED SECTOR 2001
Percentages

Self-generated	39%
Public sector	28%
General Public	12%
Local Authorities	10%
Lottery	5%
Charitable Trust	3%
Private Sector	3%

Source: SCVO – Funding the Scottish Voluntary Sector No. 3, April 2003

THE EUROPEAN DIMENSION

Many voluntary organisations in Scotland are involved in activities and projects implementing the European Union's national and regional Structural Fund programmes, which give financial support to measures addressing the needs of less well-off or geographically isolated regions and societal groups in Europe. The European Social Fund (ESF) is the most important Structural Fund for the voluntary sector. The ESF Objective 3 programme for the period 2000–6 makes over £320 million available for raising employability and addressing social exclusion, including promoting lifelong learning and equal opportunities, much of which will be channelled through the voluntary sector. The Programme Management Executives distribute European Structural Funds.

SCOTTISH COUNCIL FOR VOLUNTARY ORGANISATIONS

The Scottish Council for Voluntary Organisations (SCVO), established in 1936, is the umbrella body for voluntary organisations in Scotland and aims to promote and advocate the independence, interests and value of the voluntary sector among the major players in Scottish life and the wider community. The SCVO operates from offices in Edinburgh, Glasgow and Inverness. Its services to the voluntary sector include training, seminars and conferences, advice on funding, legislation and management of voluntary organisations, and research on voluntary sector issues. It has a database of sources of charitable funding, and its European Unit provides an initial point of contact for charities seeking access to European funds. It publishes a weekly newspaper, *Third Force News*, and a variety of other publications addressing practical issues of voluntary organisation management and analysing government policy and other issues affecting the sector. There is also a Parliamentary Information and Advice Service, which publishes a weekly online parliamentary newsletter, *Involve*, and provides information on the make-up and history of the Scottish Parliament and the committee system and advice on lobbying and networking. SCVO has an Equalities Policy Agenda, which aims to encourage voluntary organisations to work together towards mainstream equality across the spectrum of discrimination issues. This involves an increasing amount of policy work as SCVO seeks to keep abreast of developments in the Scottish Parliament and the Executive in relation to equalities.

COUNCILS FOR VOLUNTARY SERVICE

Councils for Voluntary Service (CVS) are a network of 60 local community development agencies across Scotland. They are co-ordinated by CVS Scotland, which operates within the SCVO and provides training, information, publications and advice to member CVS. The membership of each CVS is drawn from local voluntary and community groups. Each CVS plans its activities to meet needs identified by the local voluntary sector community. CVS develop partnerships with other local organisations (councils, health authorities, enterprise companies, etc.) and act as channels by which local groups can express their views on local policy-making.

The addresses of CVS and further information on them may be obtained from the CVS website: www.cvsscotland.org.uk or through the SCVO office in Edinburgh or from the SCVO website.

ORGANISATIONS

SCVO
Edinburgh Office, The Mansfield, Traquair Centre,
15 Mansfield Place, Edinburgh EH3 6BB
Tel: 0131-556 3882 Fax: 0131-557 6483
Glasgow Office, 3rd Floor, Centrum Building,
38 Queen Street, Glasgow G1 3DX
Tel: 0141-221 0030 Fax: 0141-248 8066
Inverness Office, 9 Ardross Terrace, Inverness, IV3 5NQ
Tel: 01463-235633 Fax: 01463-716003
Email: enquiries@scvo.org.uk
Web: www.scvo.org.uk

VOLUNTEER DEVELOPMENT SCOTLAND
Stirling Enterprise Park, Stirling FK7 7RP
Tel: 01786-479593 Fax: 01786-449285
Email: information@vds.org.uk
Web: www.vds.org.uk

SCOTTISH HUMAN RIGHTS CENTRE
146 Holland Street, Glasgow, G2 4NG
Tel: 0141-332 5960 Fax: 0141-332 5309
Email: info@scottishhumanrightscentre.org.uk
Web: www.scottishhumanrightscentre.org.uk

SCOTTISH PENSIONERS' FORUM
333 Woodlands Road, Glasgow G3 6NG
Tel: 0141-337 8100
Email: scottishpensionersforum@breathemail.net
Web: www.seniorsworld.co.uk

MEDIA SCOTLAND

TELEVISION

RADIO

THE PRESS

BOOK PUBLISHERS

INDEPENDENT PRODUCTION COMPANIES

THE MEDIA

CROSS-MEDIA OWNERSHIP

There are rules on cross-media ownership to prevent undue concentration of ownership. These were amended by the Broadcasting Act 1996. Radio companies are now permitted to own one AM, one FM and one other (AM or FM) service; ownership of the third licence is subject to a public interest test. Local newspapers with a circulation under 20 per cent in an area are also allowed to own one AM, one FM and one other service, and may control a regional Channel 3 television service subject to a public interest test. Local newspapers with a circulation between 20 and 50 per cent in an area may own one AM and one FM service, subject to a public interest test, but may not control a regional Channel 3 service. Those with a circulation over 50 per cent may own one radio service in the area (provided that more than one independent local radio service serves the area) subject to a public interest test.

Ownership controls on the number of television or radio licences have been removed; holdings are now restricted to 15 per cent of the total television audience or 15 per cent of the total points available in the radio points scheme. Ownership controls on cable operators have also been removed. National newspapers with less than 20 per cent of national circulation may apply to control any broadcasting licences, subject to a public interest test. National newspapers with more than 20 per cent of national circulation may not have more than a 20 per cent interest in a licence to provide a Channel 3 service, Channel 5 or national and local analogue radio services.

BROADCASTING

The British Broadcasting Corporation (BBC) is responsible for public service broadcasting in the UK. Its constitution and finances are governed by royal charter and agreement. On 1 May 1996 a new royal charter came into force, establishing the framework for the BBC's activities until 2006.

The Independent Television Commission and the Radio Authority were set up under the terms of the Broadcasting Act 1990. The ITC is the regulator and licensing authority for all commercially-funded television services, including cable and satellite services. The Radio Authority is the regulator and licensing authority for all independent radio services.

COMPLAINTS

The Broadcasting Standards Commission was set up in April 1997 under the Broadcasting Act 1996 and was formed from the merger of the Broadcasting Complaints Commission and the Broadcasting Standards Council. The Commisson is the statutory body for standards and fairness in broadcasting. It is the only organisation in broadcasting to cover all television and radio. This includes BBC and commercial broadcasters as well as text, cable, satellite and digital services. The Commission has three main tasks, set out in the 1996 Broadcasting Act:

– produce codes of practice relating to standards and fairness
– consider and adjudicate on complaints
– monitor, research and report on standards and fairness in broadcasting

The Broadcasting Standards Commission is to be replaced by Ofcom, the Office of Communications. Ofcom will also replace the following communications regulators: Oftel, the Independent Television Commission, the Radio Authority and the Radiocommunications Agency.

BROADCASTING STANDARDS COMMISSION

7 The Sanctuary, London SW1P 3JS
Tel: 020-7808 1000 Fax: 020-7233 0397
Email: bsc@bsc.org.uk Web: www.bsc.org.uk
Chairman: Lord Dubs of Battersea
Director: Paul Bolt

OFCOM (OFFICE OF COMMUNICATIONS)

Riverside House, 2A Southwark Bridge Road
London SE1 9HA
Tel: 020-7981 3000 Fax: 020-7981 3333
Email: www.enq@ofcom.org.uk
Web: www.ofcom.org.uk

The Office of Communications merged the functions of the Independent Television Commission, the Broadcasting Standards Commission, the Radio Authority, Oftel and the Radio Communications Agency from the end of 2003. Ofcom's remit comes from the Office of Communications Act 2002 and its general duties are:

– to further the interests of consumers
– to secure optimal use of the radio spectrum

– to ensure that a wide range of television and radio service are available in the UK, comprising high quality services of broad appeal

– to protect the public from any offensive or potentially harmful effects of broadcast media

Chief Executive: Stephen Carter

TELEVISION

All channels are broadcast in colour on 625 lines UHF from a network of transmitting stations. Transmissions are available to more than 99 per cent of the population.

The BBC broadcasts two UK-wide television services, BBC One and BBC Two; in Scotland these services are designated BBC Scotland on One and BBC Scotland on Two. The BBC's digital services include BBC One, BBC Two, BBC Three, BBC Four, BBC Knowledge, BBC News 24 and BBC Parliament. These services are funded by the licence fee.

The ITV Network Centre is wholly owned by the ITV companies and undertakes the commissioning and scheduling of those television programmes which are shown across the ITV network. Through its sister organisation, the ITV Association, it also provides a range of services to the ITV companies where a common approach is required. The total number of households with television licences in the UK at the end of December 2002 was 23,857, 341, of which, 120 were for black and white television sets. Annual television licence fees are: black and white £38.50; colour £116.00.

British Sky Broadcasting is the UK's broadband entertainment company, distributing sports, movies, entertainment and news to 6.6 million households (an estimated 15 million viewers) throughout the UK. Sky also embraces alternative platforms including interactive TV, WAP telephones, ADSL and the web. British Sky Broadcasting is one of the largest private sector employers in Scotland with more than 4000 individuals, the majority being employed at call centres in Livingston and Dunfermline. Digital television multiplex licences have been awarded, including one to SDN Ltd which guarantees space for Gaelic programmes in Scotland.

PROGRAMMING

Apart from specifically Gaelic current affairs, magazine and children's programmes (for which there was £9.5 million-worth of funding during the 1990s) independent Scottish television production seeks to create work that reflects the uniqueness of Scottish culture within the UK. This has led to a lively debate over representations of 'Scottishness' in drama, comedy and documentary output with supporters applauding national characteristics and dissenters criticising the reinforcement of stereotypes. Over the last decade Scottish independent television production has moved towards exploding the 'Scotch Myths' of old in favour of hard-hitting realism *(Taggart)*, whimsical parody *(Hamish Macbeth)*, and loutish comedy *(Rab C. Nesbitt)* which exposes the worst extremes of Scottish prejudice. This vibrant assertion of difference has been dubbed 'cultural nationalism' by some and is also evident in Scottish theatre, music, literature and film.

BBC SCOTLAND

BBC Broadcasting House, Queen Margaret Drive,
  Glasgow G12 8DG Tel: 0141-339 8844
  National Governor for Scotland: Sir Robert Smith
  Controller, BBC Scotland: J. McCormick
BBC Broadcasting House, Beechgrove Terrace,
  Aberdeen AB15 5ZT Tel: 01224-625233
BBC Broadcasting House, The Tun, 111 Holyrood Road,
  Edinburgh EH8 8PJ Tel: 0131-557 5888

INDEPENDENT TELEVISION NETWORK COMPANIES IN SCOTLAND

BORDER TELEVISION

The Television Centre, Carlisle, CA1 3NT
Tel: 01228-525101 Web: www.border–tv.com
Area covered: the Borders

GRAMPIAN TELEVISION

Craigshaw Business Park, West Tullos, Aberdeen
AB12 3QH Tel: 01224-846846
Web: www.grampiantv.co.uk
Area covered: northern Scotland

SCOTTISH TV

200 Renfield Street, Glasgow G2 3PR
Tel: 0141-300 3000 Web: www.scottishtv.co.uk
Area covered: central Scotland

OTHER INDEPENDENT TELEVISION COMPANIES

CHANNEL 5 BROADCASTING

22 Long Acre, London WC2E 9LY Tel: 020-7550 5555
Web: www.channel5.co.uk

CHANNEL 4 TELEVISION CORPORATION

124 Horseferry Road, London SW1P 2TX
Tel: 020-7396 4444 Web: www.channel4.com

INDEPENDENT TELEVISION NEWS LTD
200 Gray's Inn Road, London WC1X 8XZ
Tel: 020-7833 3000 Web: www.itn.co.uk

TELETEXT LTD
101 Farm Lane, London SW6 1QJ Tel: 020-7386 5000
Web: www.teletext.co.uk

WELSH FOURTH CHANNEL AUTHORITY
Parc Ty Glas, Llanishen, Cardiff CF4 5DU
Tel: 029-2074 7444

RADIO

UK domestic radio services are broadcast across three wavebands: FM (or VHF), medium wave (also referred to as AM) and long wave (used by BBC Radio 4). In the UK the FM waveband extends in frequency from 87.5 MHz to 108 MHz and the medium wave band extends from 531 kHz to 1602 kHz. Some radios are still calibrated in wavelengths rather than frequency. To convert frequency to wavelength, divide 300,000 by the frequency in kHz.

The frequencies allocated for terrestrial digital radio in the UK are 217.5 to 230 MHz. It is necessary to have a radio set with a digital decoder in order to receive digital radio broadcasts.

Digital radio is becoming increasingly popular although at the beginning of 2003, BBC national digital radio only covered about 60 per cent of the UK. National commercial digital radio covered 85 per cent of the UK. As at February 2003 there were 41 digital radio stations broadcasting in the UK.

BBC RADIO

BBC Radio broadcasts five network services to the UK, Isle of Man and the Channel Islands. There is also a tier of national regional services, including Scotland. The BBC World Service broadcasts over 1,000 hours of programmes a week in 42 languages including English.

BBC RADIO
Broadcasting House, Portland Place, London W1A 1AA
Tel: 020-7580 4468
Director-General: Greg Dyke

BBC WORLD SERVICE
Bush House, Strand, London WC2B 4PH.
Tel: 020-7240 3456

The BBC World Service broadcasts over 1,000 hours of programmes a week in 42 languages including English. It has a weekly audience of 150 million globally, of whom 42 million listen to English language services. Many services are also available by satellite and on the Internet.
UK frequencies: 648 MW in Southern England and on BBC Radio 4 at night.

BBC NETWORK RADIO SERVICES
RADIO 1 (Contemporary pop music, social action campaigns and entertainment news) – 24 hours a day. *Frequencies:* 97.6–99.8 FM
RADIO 2 (Popular music, entertainment, comedy and the arts) – 24 hours a day. *Frequencies:* 88–90.2 FM
RADIO 3 (Classical music, classic drama, documentaries and features) – 24 hours a day. *Frequencies:* 90.2–92.4 FM
RADIO 4 (News, documentaries, drama, entertainment, and cricket on long wave in season) – 5.55 a.m.–1.00 a.m. daily, with BBC World Service overnight. *Frequencies:* 92.4–94.6 FM and 198 LW
RADIO 5 LIVE (News and sport) – 24 hours a day. *Frequencies:* 693 and 909 MW
RADIO 6 (Digital only) (Contemporary and classic pop and rock music) – 24 hours a day. *Frequency:* 225.648 MHZ

BBC NATIONAL RADIO SERVICES IN SCOTLAND
RADIO NAN GAIDHEAL (Gaelic service) *Frequencies:* 103.5–105 FM, 990 MW in Aberdeen, coverage 90%.
RADIO SCOTLAND *Frequencies:* 810 MW plus two local fillers; 92.4–94.7 FM, coverage 99%. Local programmes on FM as above: Highlands; North-East; Borders; South-West (also 585 MW); Orkney; Shetland

INDEPENDENT RADIO
INDEPENDENT NATIONAL RADIO STATIONS
CLASSIC FM, 7 Swallow Place, London W1R 7AA.
Tel: 020-7343 9000. 24 hours a day.
Frequencies: 99.9/101.9 FM
TALK SPORT, 18 Hatfields, London SE1 8DJ.
Tel: 020-7959 7900. 24 hours a day.
Frequencies: 1053/1089 AM
VIRGIN RADIO, 1 Golden Square, London W1R 4DJ.
Tel: 020-7434 1215. 24 hours a day.
Frequencies: 1215/1197/1233/1242/1260 AM

INDEPENDENT LOCAL RADIO STATIONS
96.3 QFM, 65 Sussex St, Glasgow G41 1DX.
Tel: 0141-429 9430. *Frequency:* 96.3 FM
ARGYLL FM, 27–29 Longrow, Campbeltown, Argyll PA28 6ER. Tel: 01586-551800.
Frequency: 107.1/107.7/106.5 FM

BEAT 106, Four Winds Pavilion, Pacific Quay, Glasgow G51 1EB. Tel: 0141-566 6106. *Frequencies:* 105.7/106.1 FM

CASTLE ROCK FM, Pioneer Park Studios, Unit 3, 80 Castlegreen Street, Dumbarton G82 1JB. Tel: 01389-734422. *Frequency:* 103 FM

CENTRAL FM, 201 High Street, Falkirk FK1 1DU. Tel: 01324-611164. *Frequency:* 103.1 FM

CLAN FM, Radio House, Rowantree Avenue, Newhouse Industrial Estate, Newhouse ML1 5RX. Tel: 01689-733107. *Frequency:* 107.5/107.9 FM

CLYDE 1 (FM) AND 2 (AM), Clydebank Business Park, Clydebank, Glasgow G81 2RX. Tel: 0141-565 2200. *Frequencies:* 102.5 FM; 103.3 FM (Firth of Clyde); 97.0 FM (Vale of Leven); 1152 AM

FORTH AM AND FM, Forth House, Forth Street, Edinburgh EH1 3LE. Tel: 0131-556 9255. *Frequencies:* 1548 AM, 97.3/97.6/102.2 FM

HEARTLAND FM, Atholl Curling Rink, Lower Oakfield, Pitlochry, Perthshire PH16 5HQ. Tel: 01796-474040. *Frequency:* 97.5 FM

ISLES FM, PO Box 333, Stornoway, Isle of Lewis HS1 2PU. Tel: 01851-703333. *Frequency:* 103.0 FM

KINGDOM FM, Haig House, Haig Business Park, Markinch, Fife KY7 6AQ. Tel: 01592-753753. *Frequencies:* 95.2/96.1 FM

LOCHBROOM FM, Radio House, Mill Street, Ullapool, Ross-shire IV26 2UN. Tel: 01854-613131. *Frequency:* 102.2 FM

MORAY FIRTH RADIO, Scorguie Place, Inverness IV3 8UJ. Tel: 01463-224433. *Frequencies:* 97.4 FM, 1107 AM; local opt-outs: MFR Speysound 96.6 FM; MFR Keith Community Radio 102.8 FM; MFR Kinnaird Radio 96.7 FM; MFR Caithness 102.5 FM

NECR (NORTH-EAST COMMUNITY RADIO), The Shed, School Road, Kintore, Aberdeenshire, AB51 0UX. Tel: 01467-632909. *Frequencies:* 97.1 FM (Braemar); 102.1 FM (Meldrum and Inverurie); 102.6 FM (Kildrummy); 103.2 FM (Colpy)

NEVIS RADIO, Inverlochy, Fort William, Inverness-shire PH33 6LU. Tel: 01397-700007. *Frequencies:* 96.6 FM (Fort William); 97.0 FM (Glencoe); 102.3 FM (Skye); 102.4 FM (Loch Leven)

NORTHSOUND ONE (FM) AND TWO (AM), 45 Kings Gate, Aberdeen AB15 4EL. Tel: 01224-337000. *Frequencies:* 1035 AM, 96.9/97.6/103.0 FM

OBAN FM, 132 George Street, Oban, Argyll PA34 5NT. Tel: 01631-570057. *Frequency:* 103.3 FM

RADIO BORDERS, Tweedside Park, Galashiels TD1 3TD. Tel: 01896-759444. *Frequencies:* 96.8/97.5/103.1/103.4 FM

RADIO TAY AM AND TAY FM, 6 North Isla Street, Dundee DD3 7JQ. Tel: 01382-200800. *Frequencies:* 1161 AM, 102.8 FM (Dundee); 1584 AM, 96.4 FM (Perth)

REAL RADIO, PO Box 101 Parkway Court, Glasgow Business Park, Glasgow G69 6GA Tel: 0141-781 1011. *Frequencies:* 100-101 FM

RNA FM, Arbroath Infirmary, Rosemount Road, Arbroath, Angus DD11 2AT. Tel: 01241-879660. *Frequency:* 96.6 FM

SIBC, Market Street, Lerwick, Shetland ZE1 0JN. Tel: 01595-695299. *Frequencies:* 96.2/102.2 FM

SOUTH WEST SOUND, Unit 40, The Loreburne Centre, High St, Dumfries DG1 2BD. Tel: 01387-250999. *Frequencies:* 96.5/97.0/103.0 FM

WAVE 102, 8 South Tay Street, Dundee DD1 1PA. Tel: 01382-901000. *Frequency:* 102 FM

WAVES RADIO PETERHEAD, Unit 2, Blackhouse Industrial Estate, Peterhead AB42 1BW. Tel: 01779-491012. *Frequency:* 101.2 FM

WEST SOUND AM AND WEST FM, Radio House, 54A Holmston Road, Ayr KA7 3BE. Tel: 01292-283662. *Frequencies:* 1035 AM, 96.7 FM (Ayr); 97.5 FM (Girvan)

THE PRESS

The press is subject to the laws on publication and the Press Complaints Commission was set up by the industry as a means of self-regulation. It is not state-subsidised and receives few tax concessions. The income of most newspapers and periodicals is derived largely from sales and from advertising; the press is the largest advertising medium in Britain.

COMPLAINTS

The Press Complaints Commission was founded by the newspaper and magazine industry in January 1991 to replace the Press Council (established in 1953). It is a voluntary, non-statutory body set up to operate the press's self-regulation system following the Calcutt report in 1990 on privacy and related matters, when the industry feared that a failure to regulate itself might lead to statutory regulation of the press. The Commission is funded by the industry through the Press Standards Board of Finance.

The Commission's objects are to consider, adjudicate, conciliate, and resolve complaints of unfair treatment by the press; and to ensure that the press maintains the highest professional standards with respect for generally recognised freedoms, including freedom of expression, the public's right to know, and the right of the press to operate free from improper pressure. The Commission judges newspaper and magazine conduct by a code of practice drafted by editors, agreed by the industry and ratified by the Commission.

Seven of the Commission's members are editors of national, regional and local newspapers (including one from Scotland) and magazines, and nine, including the chairman, are drawn from other fields. One member has been appointed Privacy Commissioner with special powers to investigate complaints about invasion of privacy.

PRESS COMPLAINTS COMMISSION

1 Salisbury Square, London EC4Y 8JB
Tel: 020-7353 1248
Director: Guy Black

NEWSPAPERS

Newspapers are usually financially independent of any political party, though most adopt a political stance in their editorial comments, usually reflecting proprietorial influence. Ownership of the national and regional daily newspapers is concentrated in the hands of large corporations whose interests cover publishing and communications. The rules on cross-media ownership, as amended by the Broadcasting Act 1996, limit the extent to which newspaper organisations may become involved in broadcasting.

Scotland has a number of daily and Sunday newspapers (including Scottish editions of some of the UK national newspapers), as well as local daily and weekly newspapers. The following list shows the main editorial offices of the major newspapers in Scotland, including the Scottish editorial offices of UK national newspapers.

NATIONAL DAILY NEWSPAPERS

DAILY RECORD

One Central Quay, Glasgow G3 8DA
Tel: 0141-309 3000 Fax: 0141-309 3340
Web: www.dailyrecord.co.uk

DAILY TELEGRAPH

5 Coates Crescent, Edinburgh EH3 7AL
Tel: 0131-225 3313 Fax: 0131-225 4877

THE HERALD

200 Renfield Street, Glasgow G2 3QB
Tel: 0141-302 7000 Fax: 0141-333 1147
Web: www.theherald.co.uk

THE SCOTSMAN

Barclay House, 108 Holyrood Road, Edinburgh
EH8 8AS Tel: 0131-620 8620 Fax: 0131-620 8616
Web: www.scotsman.com

SCOTTISH DAILY MAIL

200 Renfield Street, Glasgow G2 3PZ
Tel: 0141-331 4700 Fax: 0141-331 4707

SCOTTISH MIRROR

One Central Quay, Glasgow G3 8DA
Tel: 0141-221 2121 Fax: 0141-309 3511

THE SUN

News International Newspapers Scotland,
124 Portman Street, Kinning Park, Glasgow G41 1EJ
Tel: 0141-420 5200 Fax: 0141-420 5248

REGIONAL PRINT AND ONLINE NEWSPAPERS

ABERDEEN EVENING EXPRESS

PO Box 43, Lang Stracht, Mastrick, Aberdeen
AB15 6DF Tel: 01224-690222 Fax: 01224-699575
Web: www.thisisnorthscotland.co.uk

ABERDEEN INDEPENDENT

256 Union Street, Aberdeen AB10 1TP
Tel: 01224-618316 Fax: 01224-648642

AM BRATACH

The Schoolhouse, Strathnaver KW11 6UA
Tel: 01641-561214 Fax: 01641 561211
Web: www.bratach.co.uk

BERWICK ADVERTISER AND GAZETTE

Tweedale Press, 90 Marygate,
Berwick-upon-Tweed TD15 1BW

BORDER TELEGRAPH

113 High Street, Galashiels, Selkirkshire TD1 1SB
Tel: 01896-758395 Fax: 01896-759395
Web: www.bordertelegraph.co.uk

CAITHNESS COURIER

39 Olrig Street, Thurso KW14 7HF
Tel: 01847-892015 Fax: 01847-895740

THE COURIER AND ADVERTISER

80 Kingsway East, Dundee DD4 9SL Tel: 01382-223131
Fax: 01382-454590 Web: www.thecourier.co.uk

DUNDEE EVENING TELEGRAPH AND POST

80 Kingsway East, Dundee DD4 8SL
Tel: 01382-223131 Fax: 01382-454590

DUNOON OBSERVER AND ARGYLLSHIRE STANDARD

219 Argyll Street, Dunoon PA23 7NS
Tel: 01369-703218 Fax: 01369-703458
Web: www.dunoon-observer.co.uk

EAST LOTHIAN COURIER

18 Market Street, Haddington, East Lothian EH41 3JL
Tel: 01620-822451 Fax: 01620-826143
Web: www.eastlothiancourier.com

EDINBURGH EVENING NEWS
108 Holyrood Road, Edinburgh EH8 8AS
Tel: 0131-620 8620 Fax: 0131-620 8696
Web: www.edinburghnews.com

FORRES GAZETTE
135 High Street, Forres, Moray IV36 1DX
Tel: 01309-672615 Fax: 01309-674755
Web: www.forres-gazette.co.uk

GLASGOW EVENING TIMES
200 Renfield Street, Glasgow G2 3PR
Tel: 0141-302 7000 Fax: 0141-302 6600
Web: www.eveningtimes.co.uk

GREENOCK TELEGRAPH
2 Crawfurd Street, Greenock PA15 1LH
Tel: 01475-726511 Fax: 01475 558808
Web: www.greenocktelegraph.co.uk

ILEACH
Main Street, Isle of Islay, Argyll PA43 7LA
Tel: 01496-810355 Fax: 01496-810647
Web: www.ileach.co.uk

INVERNESS COURIER
New Century House, Stadium Road, Inverness IV1 1FF
Tel: 01463-233059 Fax: 01463-238223
Web: www.inverness-courier.co.uk

JOHN O'GROATS JOURNAL
42 Union Street, Wick, Caithness KW1 5ED
Tel: 01955-602424 Fax: 01955-604822

MAIL ON SUNDAY IN SCOTLAND
200 Renfield Street, Glasgow G2 3PZ
Tel: 0141-331 4700 Fax: 0141-353 2461

THE NORTHERN SCOT
175 High Street, Elgin, Moray IV30 1DP
Tel: 01343-548777 Fax: 01343-545629
Web: www.northern-scot.co.uk

PEEBLESSHIRE NEWS
40 Northgate, Peebles EH45 8BZ
Tel: 01721-720884 Fax: 01721-721492
Web: www.peeblesshirenews.com

THE PRESS AND JOURNAL
Lang Stracht, Aberdeen AB15 6DF
Tel: 01224-690222 Fax: 01224-344114
Web: www.thisisnorthscotland.co.uk

ROSS-SHIRE JOURNAL
Dochcarty Road, Dingwall, Ross-shire IV15 9UG
Tel: 01349-863436 Fax: 01349-863456
Web: www.rsjournal.co.uk

SCOTLAND ON SUNDAY
108 Holyrood Road, Edinburgh EH8 8AS
Tel: 0131-620 8620 Fax: 0131-620 8491
Web: www.scotlandonsunday.com

SCOTTISH SUNDAY EXPRESS
Park House, Park Circus Place, Glasgow G3 6AF
Tel: 0141-352 2519 Fax: 0141-332 8538

SELKIRK WEEKEND ADVERTISER
The Hermitage, High Street, Selkirk TD7 4DA
Tel: 01750-21581

SHETLAND TIMES
Gremista, Lerwick ZE1 0PX Tel: 01595-693622
Fax: 01595-694637 Web: www.shetlandtoday.co.uk

THE SOUTHERN REPORTER
The Hermitage, High Street, Selkirk TD7 4DA
Tel: 01750-21581 Web: www.borderstoday.co.uk

SUNDAY HERALD
200 Renfield Street, Glasgow G2 3PR
Tel: 0141-302 7800 Fax: 0141-302 7809
Web: www.sundayherald.com

SUNDAY MAIL
One Central Quay, Glasgow G3 8DA
Tel: 0141-309 3000 Fax: 0141-309 3582
Web: www.dailyrecord.co.uk

SUNDAY POST
144 Port Dundas Road, Glasgow G4 0HZ
Tel: 0141-332 9933 Fax: 0141-331 1595
Web: www.sundaypost.com

WEEKLY NEWS
Courier Place, Dundee DD1 9QJ
Tel: 01382-223131 Fax: 01382-291390

WEST HIGHLAND FREE PRESS
Parc Nan Craobh, Industrial Estate, Broadford,
Isle of Skye IV49 9AP Tel: 01471-822464
Fax: 01474-822694 Web: www.whfp.com

WEST LOTHIAN HERALD AND POST
31a North Bridge Street, Bathgate, West Lothian
EH48 4PJ Tel: 01506-503406 Fax: 0131-523 0299

JOURNALS AND MAGAZINES

The following listing comprises a selection of consumer and trade periodicals published in Scotland.

ANTIQUES AND ART INDEPENDENT
PO Box 1945, Comely Bank, Edinburgh EH4 1AB
Tel: 07000-765263 Fax: 07000-268478
Email: antiquesnews@hotmail.com
Web: www.antiquesnews.co.uk

ARCHITECTURAL HERITAGE
22 George Square, Edinburgh EH8 9LF
Tel: 0131-650 6207 Fax: 0131-662 0052
Email: journals@eup.ed.ac.uk
Web: www.eup.ed.ac.uk

ARTWORK
PO Box 3, Ellon, Aberdeenshire AB41 9EA
Tel: 01651-842429 Fax: 01651-842180
Web: www.artwork.co.uk

AYRSHIRE DAIRYMAN NEWSLETTER
Ayrshire Cattle Society of Great Britain and Ireland,
1 Racecourse Road, Ayr KA7 2DE
Tel: 01292-267123 Fax: 01292-611973

THE BIG ISSUE SCOTLAND
71 Oxford Street, Glasgow G5 9EP
Tel: 0141-418 7000 Fax: 0141-418 7070
Email: editorial@bigissuescotland.com

THE BLUE BOOK
Butterworths, 4 Hill Street, Edinburgh EH2 3JZ
Tel: 0131-225 7828 Fax: 0131-220 1833
Email: scot.enquiries@lexisnexis.co.uk
Web: www.butterworthsscotland.com

BOTANICAL JOURNAL OF SCOTLAND
22 George Square, Edinburgh EH8 9LF
Tel: 0131-650 6207 Fax: 0131-662 0053
Email: journals@eup.ed.ac.uk
Web: www.eup.ed.ac.uk

THE BUSINESS
Dundee and Tayside Chamber of Commerce,
Chamber of Commerce Buildings,
Panmure Street, Dundee DD1 1ED
Tel: 01382-228545
Email: admin@dundeechamber.co.uk
Web: www.dundeechamber.co.uk

BUSINESS BULLETIN
213 George Street, Aberdeen AB25 1XA
Tel: 01224-620261 Fax: 01224-213221
Email: bulletin@agcc.co.uk Web: www.agcc.co.uk

BUSINESS SCOTLAND
Peebles Media Group, Bergius House,
Clifton Street, Glasgow G3 7LA
Tel: 0141-567 6000 Fax: 0141-331 1395

CA MAGAZINE
1a St Bernard's Row, Edinburgh EH4 1LA
Tel: 0131-343 7500 Fax: 0131-343 7505
Email: camagazine@icas.org.uk
Web: www.icas.org.uk

CALEDONIA
28 Melville Street, Edinburgh EH3 7HA
Tel: 0131-476 4670 Fax: 0131-476 4671
Email: editor@scotthouse.co.uk
Web: www.caledonia-magazine.com

CHAPMAN
4 Broughton Place, Edinburgh EH1 3RX
Tel: 0131-557 2207 Fax: 0131-556 9565
Email: editor@chapman-pub.co.uk
Web: www.chapman-pub.co.uk

CLASSIC STITCHES
80 Kingsway East, Dundee DD4 8SL
Tel: 01382-223131 Fax: 01382-452491
Email: editorial@classicstitches.com
Web: www.classicstitches.com

COMMANDO
D. C. Thomson Ltd, Albert Square, Dundee DD1 9QJ
Tel: 01382-223131 Fax: 01382-322214

DANCE RESEARCH
22 George Square, Edinburgh EH8 9LF
Tel: 0131-650 6207 Fax: 0131-662 0053
Email: journals@eup.ed.ac.uk
Web: www.eup.ed.ac.uk

THE DRUM
3 Park Street South, Glasgow G3 6BG
Tel: 0141-479 3143 Fax: 0141-332 2012
Email: info@thedrum.co.uk
Web: www.thedrum.co.uk

EAST LOTHIAN LIFE
1 Beveridge Row, Belhaven, Dunbar EH42 1TP
Tel: 01368-863593
Email: info@east-lothian-life.co.uk
Web: www.east-lothian-life.co.uk

EDINBURGH GAZETTE
73 Lothian Road, Edinburgh EH3 9AW
Tel: 0131-622 1342 Email: subscriptions@tso.co.uk
Web: www.tso.co.uk

EDINBURGH REVIEW
22 George Square, Edinburgh EH8 9LF
Tel: 0131-650 6207 Fax: 0131-662 0052
Email: journals@eup.ed.ac.uk
Web: www.eup.ed.ac.uk

THE FORTH NATURALIST AND HISTORIAN
Univerity of Stirling, Stirling FK9 4LA
Tel: 01259-215019 Fax: 01259-464994
Email: lindsay.corbett@sitr.ac.uk
Web: www.stir.ac.uk/department/naturalsciences/forth

FREELANCE PHOTOGRAPHER
Icon Publications Ltd, Maxwell Lane, Kelso,
Roxburghshire TD5 7BB
Tel: 01573-226032 Fax: 01573-226000
Web: www.freelancephotographer.co.uk

GLASGOW CHAMBER OF COMMERCE JOURNAL
30 George Square, Glasgow G2 1EQ
Tel: 0141-572 2121 Fax: 0141-221 2336

HISTORY AND COMPUTING
22 George Square, Edinburgh EH8 9LF
Tel: 0131-650 6207 Fax: 0131-662 0052
Email: journals@eup.ed.ac.uk
Web: www.eup.ed.ac.uk

THE INDEPENDENT COMMUNITY PHARMACIST
SMG Magazines, 200 Renfield Street, Glasgow G2 3PR
Tel: 0141-302 7700 Fax: 0141-302 7798
Web: www.smg.plc.uk

JOURNAL OF SCOTTISH PHILOSOPHY
22 George Square, Edinburgh EH8 9LF
Tel: 0131-650 6207 Fax: 0131-662 0052
Email: journals@eup.ed.ac.uk
Web: www.eup.ed.ac.uk

JOURNAL OF TRANSATLANTIC STUDIES
22 George Square, Edinburgh EH8 9LF
Tel: 0131-650 6207 Fax: 0131-662 0052
Email: journals@eup.ed.ac.uk
Web: www.eup.ed.ac.uk

JOURNAL OF VICTORIAN CULTURE
22 George Square, Edinburgh EH8 9LF
Tel: 0131-650 6207 Fax: 0131-662 0052
Email: journals@eup.ed.ac.uk
Web: www.eup.ed.ac.uk

LABOUR HISTORY REVIEW
22 George Square, Edinburgh EH8 9LF
Tel: 0131-650 6207 Fax: 0131-662 0052
Email: journals@eup.ed.ac.uk
Web: www.eup.ed.ac.uk

LIFE AND WORK (THE MAGAZINE OF THE CHURCH OF SCOTLAND)
121 George Street, Edinburgh EH2 4YN
Tel: 0131-225 5722 Fax: 0131-240 2207
Email: lifework@dial.pipex.com

THE LIST
14 High Street, Edinburgh EH1 1TE
Tel: 0131-550 3050 Fax: 0131-557 8500
Email: contact@list.co.uk Web: www.list.co.uk

MULTEX.COM
10–12 Young Street, Edinburgh EH2 4JB
Tel: 0131-473 7070 Fax: 0131-473 7080
Email: media@multex.com
Web: www.global-estimates.com

MY WEEKLY
D. C. Thomson & Co. Ltd, 80 Kingsway East, Dundee
DD4 8SL Tel: 01382-223131 Fax: 01382-452491
Email: myweekly@dcthomson.co.uk

NAUTICAL MAGAZINE
4–10 Darnley Street, Glasgow G41 2SD
Tel: 0141-429 1234 Fax: 0141-420 1694
Email: info@skipper.co.uk
Web: www.skipper.co.uk

ORGANIC GARDENING
Sandvoe, North Roe, Shetland ZE2 9RY
Tel: 01806-533319
Email: organicgardening@virgin.net

PACKAGING SCOTLAND
Bergius House, Clifton Street, Glasgow G3 7LA
Tel: 0141-567 6000 Fax: 0141-331 1395
Email: packagingscotland@peeblesmedia.com
Web: www.peeblesmedia.com

PARAGRAPH
22 George Square, Edinburgh EH8 9LF
Tel: 0131-650 6207 Fax: 0131-662 0052
Email: journals@eup.ed.ac.uk
Web: www.eup.ed.ac.uk

PARLIAMENTARY HISTORY
22 George Square, Edinburgh EH8 9LF
Tel: 0131-650 6207 Fax: 0131-662 0052
Email: journals@eup.ed.ac.uk
Web: www.eup.ed.ac.uk

PEOPLE'S FRIEND
80 Kingsway East, Dundee DD4 8SL
Tel: 01382-223131 Fax: 01382-452491

PORTFOLIO – THE CATALOGUE OF CONTEMPORARY PHOTOGRAPHY IN BRITAIN
43 Candlemaker Row, Edinburgh EH1 2QB
Tel: 0131-220 1911 Fax: 0131-226 4287
Email: info@portfoliocatalogue.com

ROMANTICISM
22 George Square, Edinburgh EH8 9LF
Tel: 0131-650 6207 Fax: 0131-662 0052
Email: journals@eup.ed.ac.uk
Web: www.eup.ed.ac.uk

ROYAL COLLEGE OF PHYSICIANS OF EDINBURGH
9 Queen Street, Edinburgh EH2 1JQ Tel: 0131-225 7324
Fax: 0131-220 3939 Web: www.rcpe.ac.uk

SCENES (SCOTTISH ENVIRONMENT NEWS)
Wester Lairgs, Inverarnie, Farr, Inverness IV2 6XH
Tel: 01808-521368 Email: enquiries@scenes.org.uk
Web: www.scenes.org.uk

SCOTLAND IN TRUST
28 Charlotte Square, Edinburgh EH2 4ET
Tel: 0131-243 9300 Fax: 0131-243 9301
Email: information@nts.org.uk
Web: www.nts.org.uk

SCOTLANDS
22 George Square, Edinburgh EH8 9LF
Tel: 0131-650 6207 Fax: 0131-662 0052
Email: journals@eup.ed.ac.uk
Web: www.eup.ed.ac.uk

THE SCOTS MAGAZINE
2 Albert Square, Dundee DD1 9QJ Tel: 01382-223131
Email: editor@scotsmagazine.com

SCOTTISH ARCHAEOLOGICAL JOURNAL
22 George Square, Edinburgh EH8 9LF
Tel: 0131-650 6207 Fax: 0131-662 0052
Email: journals@eup.ed.ac.uk
Web: www.eup.ed.ac.uk

SCOTTISH BEEKEEPER
Melbourne House, Regent Street, Dalmuir, Clydebank G81 3QN Tel/Fax: 0141-952 1234
Email: apisscot@aol.com

SCOTTISH BOOK COLLECTOR
c/o 8 Lauriston Street, Edinburgh EH3 9DJ
Tel: 0131-228 4837 Fax: 0131-228 3904
Web: www.scotbooksmag.demon.co.uk

SCOTTISH BUSINESS INSIDER
7 Castle Street, Edinburgh EH2 3AH
Tel: 0131-535 5555 Fax: 0131-220 1203
Email: customerservices@insider.co.uk
Web: www.insider.co.uk

SCOTTISH CATERER
Bergius House, Clifton Street, Glasgow G3 7LA
Tel: 0141-331 1022 Fax: 0141-331 1395
Web: www.peeblesmedia.com

SCOTTISH ECONOMIC AND SOCIAL HISTORY
22 George Square, Edinburgh EH8 9LF
Tel: 0131-650 6207 Fax: 0131-662 0052
Email: journals@eup.ed.ac.uk
Web: www.eup.ed.ac.uk

SCOTTISH EDUCATIONAL JOURNAL
46 Moray Place, Edinburgh EH3 6BH
Tel: 0131-225 4703 Fax: 0131-220 4260
Email: enquiries@eis.org.uk
Web: www.eis.org.uk

SCOTTISH FARMER
SMG Magazines Ltd, 200 Renfield Street, Glasgow G2 3PR Tel: 0141-302 7700 Fax: 0141-302 7799

SCOTTISH FIELD
Craigcrook Castle, Craigcrook Road, Edinburgh, EH4 3PE Tel: 0131-312 4550 Fax: 0131-312 4551
Email: editor@scottishfield.org
Web: www.scottishfield.co.uk

SCOTTISH GEOGRAPHICAL JOURNAL
22 George Square, Edinburgh EH8 9LF
Tel: 0131-650 6207 Fax: 0131-662 0052
Email: journals@eup.ed.ac.uk
Web: www.eup.ed.ac.uk

SCOTTISH HISTORICAL REVIEW
22 George Square, Edinburgh EH8 9LF
Tel: 0131-650 6207 Fax: 0131-662 0052
Email: journals@eup.ed.ac.uk
Web: www.eup.ed.ac.uk

SCOTTISH HOME AND COUNTRY
42a Heriot Row, Edinburgh EH3 6ES
Tel: 0131-225 1724 Fax: 0131-225 8129
Email: magazine@swri.org.uk
Web: www.swri.org.uk

SCOTTISH MEMORIES
Lang Syne Publishers Ltd, Strathclyde Business Centre, 120 Carstairs Street, Glasgow G40 4DJ
Tel: 0141-554 9944 Fax: 0141-554 9955

SCOTTISH WILDLIFE
Cramond House, Kirk Cramond, Cramond Glebe Road,
Edinburgh EH4 6NS Tel: 0131-312 7765
Fax: 0131-312 8705 Email: enquiries@swt.org.uk
Web: www.swt.org.uk

SHETLAND TIMES
Gremista, Lerwick, Shetland ZE1 0PX Tel: 01595-693622
Fax: 01595-694637 Web: www.shetlandtoday.co.uk

SPORTS BIOMECHANICS
22 George Square, Edinburgh EH8 9LF
Tel: 0131-650 6207 Fax: 0131-662 0052
Email: journals@eup.ed.ac.uk
Web: www.eup.ed.ac.uk

STUDIES IN WORLD CHRISTIANITY
22 George Square, Edinburgh EH8 9LF
Tel: 0131-650 6207 Fax: 0131-662 0053
Email: journals@eup.ed.ac.uk
Web: www.eup.ed.ac.uk

THE SURGEON (THE JOURNAL OF THE ROYAL COLLEGE OF SURGEONS OF EDINBURGH)
22 George Square, Edinburgh EH8 9LF
Tel: 0131-650 6207 Fax: 0131-662 0053
Email: journals@eup.ed.ac.uk
Web: www.eup.ed.ac.uk

THE TIMES EDUCATIONAL SUPPLEMENT SCOTLAND
Scott House, 10 South St Andrew Street, Edinburgh
EH2 2AZ Tel: 0131-557 1133 Fax: 0131-558 1155

THE TIMES LAW REPORTS
Butterworths Scotland, 4 Hill Street, Edinburgh
EH2 3JZ Tel: 0131-255 7828 Fax: 0131-220 1833
Email: scot.enquiries@lexisnexis.co.uk
Web: www.butterworthsscotland.com

TRANSLATION AND LITERATURE
22 George Square, Edinburgh EH8 9LF
Tel: 0131-650 4220 Fax: 0131-662 0053
Email: journals@eup.ed.ac.uk
Web: www.eup.ed.ac.uk

TRANSPORT NEWS
Wheatsheaf House, Montgomery Street,
East Kilbride, Glasgow G74 4JS
Tel: 01355-279077 Fax: 01355-279088
Email: readersletters@transportnews.co.uk
Web: www.transportnews.co.uk

UTLITAS
22 George Square, Edinburgh EH8 9LF
Tel: 0131-650 4223 Fax: 0131-662 0053
Email: journals@eup.ed.ac.uk
Web: www.eup.ed.ac.uk

YACHTING LIFE
Wheatsheaf House, Montgomery Street,
East Kilbride, Glasgow G74 4JS
Tel: 01355-279077 Fax: 01355-279088
Email: readersletters@yachtinglife.co.uk
Web: www.yachtinglife.co.uk

WEST LOTHIAN LIFE
Ballencrieff Cottage, Bathgate, West Lothian EH48 4LD
Tel: 01506-632728 Fax: 01506-635444
Email: wll@pages.clara.net

YOUNG SCOT
Rosebery House, 9 Haymarket Terrace, Edinburgh
EH12 5EZ Tel: 0131-313 2488 Fax: 0131-313 6800
Email: info@youngscot.org Web: www.youngscot.org

BOOK PUBLISHERS

Publishing in Scotland brings about £180 million per year into the Scottish economy, £26 million of which is created by independent publishing houses (as opposed to multinational concerns such as HarperCollins and Chambers Harrap). Scotland's largest independent publisher is Mainstream Publishing although Canongate Books is perhaps better known thanks to its 2002 Man Booker coup – as the publisher of Yann Martel's winning book, *Life of Pi*, Canongate became the only Scottish publishing house, as well as the only independent publishing house, ever to win the literary world's most coveted prize – and also because Canongate was awarded the title of Publisher of the Year in 2003 at the British Book Awards. Other Scottish publishers include Birlinn, promoters of new fiction and poetry in Gaelic and English, Black and White Publishing, whose Itchy Coo imprint creates original works in Scots for children and teenagers, the Tuckwell Press, which specialises in Scottish history, and Floris Books who publish works relating to the philosophy of Rudolf Steiner (70 per cent of which is exported). House of Lochar is the UK's most northerly publishing house, based on the island of Colonsay in the Western Isles.

The following list comprises details for a number of publishers in Scotland.

SCOTTISH PUBLISHERS ASSOCIATION
Scottish Book Centre, 137 Dundee Street, Edinburgh, EH11 1BG. Tel: 0131-228 6866

ACAIR LTD
7 James Street, Stornoway, Isle of Lewis, HS1 2QN.
Tel: 01851-703020 Fax: 01851-725320
Web: www.acairbooks.com

ARGYLL PUBLISHING
Glendaruel, Argyll, PA22 3AE. Tel: 01369-820229
Fax: 01369-820372 Web: www.skoobe.biz

ASSOCIATION FOR SCOTTISH LITERARY STUDIES
Department of Scottish History, University of Glasgow, 9 University Gardens, Glasgow, G12 8QH.
Tel: 0141-330 5309 Fax: 0141-330 5309
Web: www.asls.org.uk

ATELIER BOOKS
6 Dundas Street, Edinburgh, EH3 6HZ.
Tel: 0131-557 4050 Fax: 0131-557 8382
Web: www.bournefineart.co.uk

BARRINGTON STOKE LTD
10 Belford Terrace, Edinburgh, EH4 3DQ.
Tel: 0131-315 4933 Fax: 0131-315 4934
Web: www.barringtonstoke.co.uk

BIRLINN LTD
Lower Ground Floor, West Newington House, 10 Newington Road, Edinburgh, EH9 1QS.
Tel: 0131-668 4371 Fax: 0131-668 4466
Web: www.birlinn.co.uk

BLACK & WHITE PUBLISHING
99 Giles Street, Edinburgh, EH6 6BZ.
Tel: 0131-625 4500 Fax: 0131-625 4501
Web: www.blackandwhitepublishing.com

BROWN, SON & FERGUSON, LTD
4–10 Darnley Street, Glasgow, G41 2SD.
Tel: 0141-429 1234 Fax: 0141-420 1694
Web: www.skipper.co.uk

BROWN & WHITTAKER PUBLISHING
Tobermory, Isle of Mull, PA75 6PR.
Tel: 01688-302381 Fax: 01688-302454
Web: www.brown-whittaker.co.uk

CANONGATE BOOKS
14 High Street, Edinburgh, EH1 1TE.
Tel: 0131-557 5111 Fax: 0131-557 5211
Web: www.canongate.co.uk

CHAMBERS HARRAP PUBLISHERS LTD
7 Hopetoun Crescent, Edinburgh, EH7 4AY.
Tel: 0131-556 5929 Fax: 0131-556 5313
Web: www.chambersharrap.co.uk

CHARTERED INSTITUTE OF BANKERS IN SCOTLAND
38 Drumsheugh Gardens, Edinburgh, EH3 7SW.
Tel: 0131-473 7777 Fax: 0131-473 7788
Web: www.ciobs.org.uk

CHARTERED INSTITUTE OF LIBRARY AND INFORMATION PROFESSIONALS
Scottish Centre for Information and Library Services, 1 John Street, Hamilton, ML3 7EU.
Tel: 01698-458888 Fax: 01698-458899
Web: www.slainte.org.uk

CONTINUING EDUCATION GATEWAY
199 Nithsdale Road, Glasgow, G41 5EX.
Tel: 0141-422 2301 Fax: 0141-422 2006
Web: www.education-gateway.org.uk

COWAN PUBLISHING
83 Princes Street, Edinburgh, EH2 2EZ.
Tel: 0131-247 6778 Fax: 0131-247 6710
Web: www.cowanpublishing.seekbooks.co.uk

CUALANN PRESS
6 Corpach Drive, Dunfermline, Fife, KY12 7XG.
Tel: 01383-733724 Fax: 01383-733724
Web: www.cualann-scottish-books.co.uk

DUNEDIN ACADEMIC PRESS
Hudson House, 8 Albany Street, Edinburgh, EH1 3QB.
Tel: 0131-473 2397
Web: www.dunedinacademicpress.co.uk

EDINBURGH UNIVERSITY PRESS
22 George Square, Edinburgh, EH8 9LF.
Tel: 0131-650 4218 Fax: 0131-662 0053
Web: www.eup.ed.ac.uk

EDINBURGH CITY LIBRARIES
Central Library, George IV Bridge, Edinburgh, EH1 1EG.
Tel: 0131-242 8000 Fax: 0131-242 8009
Web: www.edinburgh.gov.uk

FLORIS BOOKS
15 Harrison Gardens, Edinburgh, EH11 1SH.
Tel: 0131-337 2372 Fax: 0131-346 7516

**GLASGOW CITY LIBRARIES
PUBLICATIONS BOARD**
The Mitchell Library, North Street, Glasgow, G3 7DN.
Tel: 0141-287 2846 Web: www.mitchelllibrary.co.uk

GOBLINSHEAD
130B Inveresk Road, Musselburgh, Midlothian,
EH21 7AY. Tel: 0131-665 2894 Fax: 0131-653 6566

W. GREEN
21 Alva Street, Edinburgh, EH2 4PS.
Tel: 0131-225 4879 Fax: 0131-225 2104
Web: www.wgreen.co.uk

HARPERCOLLINS PUBLISHERS
Westerhill Road, Bishopbriggs, Glasgow, G64 2QT.
Tel: 0141-772 3200 Fax: 0141-306 3119
Web: www.fireandwater.com

HODDER GIBSON
2a Paisley Street, Paisley, PA1 1NB.
Tel: 0141-848 1609 Fax: 0141-889 6315
Web: www.hodderheadline.co.uk

HOUSE OF LOCHAR
Isle of Colonsay, Argyll, PA61 7YR. Tel: 01951-200232
Fax: 01951-200232 Web: www.houseoflochar.com

INYX PUBLISHING
Countess of Moray's House, Sands Place, Aberdour,
Fife, KY3 0SZ. Tel: 01383-860100
Fax: 01383-861038 Web: www.inyx.com

KEPPEL PUBLISHING
The Grey House, Kenbridge Road, New Galloway,
Kirkcudbrightshire, DG7 3RP. Tel: 01644-420272
Fax: 01644-420277 Web: www.rorystories.com

LECKIE AND LECKIE PUBLISHERS
8 Whitehill Terrace, St Andrews, Fife, KY16 8RN.
Tel: 01334-475656 Fax: 01334-477392
Web: www.leckieandleckie.co.uk

LUATH PRESS LTD
543/2 Castlehill, The Royal Mile, Edinburgh, EH1 2ND.
Tel: 0131-225 4326 Fax: 0131-225 4324
Web: www.luath.co.uk

MAINSTREAM PUBLISHING CO.
7 Albany Street, Edinburgh, EH1 3UG.
Tel: 0131-557 2959 Fax: 0131-556 8720
Web: www.mainstreampublishing.com

MERCAT PRESS
10 Coates Crescent, Edinburgh, EH3 7AL.
Tel: 0131-225 5324 Fax: 0131-226 6632
Web: www.mercatpress.com

MERCHISTON PUBLISHING
School of Communications Arts, Napier University,
Craighouse Road, Edinburgh, EH10 5LG.
Tel: 0131-455 6150 Fax: 0131-455 6193

THE NATIONAL ARCHIVES OF SCOTLAND
HM General Register House, Edinburgh, EH1 3YY.
Tel: 0131-535 1314 Fax: 0131-535 1360
Web: www.nas.gov.uk

NATIONAL GALLERIES OF SCOTLAND
Belford Road, Edinburgh, EH4 3DS.
Tel: 0131-624 6257/6261 Fax: 0131-315 2963
Web: www.natgalscot.ac.uk

NATIONAL LIBRARY OF SCOTLAND
George IV Bridge, Edinburgh, EH1 1EW.
Tel: 0131-226 4531 Fax: 0131-622 4803
Web: www.nls.uk

**NATIONAL MUSEUMS OF SCOTLAND
PUBLISHING LIMITED**
Chambers Street, Edinburgh, EH1 1JF.
Tel: 0131-247 4026 Fax: 0131-247 4012
Web: www.nms.ac.uk

NEIL WILSON PUBLISHING LTD
Suite 303A, The Pentagon Centre,
36 Washington Street, Glasgow, G3 8AZ.
Tel: 0141-221 1117 Fax: 0141-221 5363
Web: www.nwp.co.uk

THE ORCADIAN LTD
Hell's Half Acre, Hatston, Kirkwall, Orkney,
KW15 1DW. Tel: 01856-879000 Fax: 01856-879001
Web: www.orcadian.co.uk

PASTIME PUBLICATIONS LTD
5/9 Rennie's Isle, Edinburgh, EH6 6QA.
Tel: 0131-468 2550 Fax: 0131-553 4444

POLYGON
West Newington House, 10 Newington Road,
Edinburgh, EH9 2HR. Tel: 0131-668 4371
Fax: 0131-668 4466 Web: www.eup.ed.ac.uk

RAMSAY HEAD PRESS
9 Glenisla Gardens, Edinburgh, EH9 2HR.
Tel: 0131-662 1915 Fax: 0131-662 1915

RUTLAND PRESS
15 Rutland Square, Edinburgh, EH1 2BE. Tel: 0131-229
7545 Fax: 0131-228 2188 Web: www.rcas.org.uk

ST ANDREW PRESS
121 George Street, Edinburgh, EH2 4YN.
Tel: 0131-225 5722 Fax: 0131-220 3113
Web: www.churchofscotland.org.uk

THE SALTIRE SOCIETY
9 Fountain Close, 22 High Street, Edinburgh, EH1 1TF.
Tel: 0131-556 1836 Fax: 0131-557 1675
Web: www.saltiresociety.org.uk

SARABAND (SCOTLAND) LTD
The Arthouse, 752-756 Argyle Street, Glasgow,
G3 8UJ. Tel: 0141-221 1900 Fax: 0141-221 7722
Web: www.saraband.net

SCOTTISH CHRISTIAN PRESS
21 Young Street, Edinburgh, EH2 4HU.
Tel: 0131-260 3110 Fax: 0131-260 3120
Web: www.churchofscotland.org.uk

**SCOTTISH CULTURAL RESOURCES
ACCESS NETWORK**
15 St John Street, Edinburgh, EH8 8JR.
Tel: 0131-557 2944 Fax: 0131-556 9454
Web: www.scran.ac.uk

SCOTTISH NATURAL HERITAGE
Battleby, Redgorton, Perth, PH1 3EW.
Tel: 01738-444177 Fax: 01738-827411
Web: www.snh.org.uk

SCOTTISH TEXT SOCIETY
27 George Square, Edinburgh, EH8 9LD
Web: www.scan.org.uk/scottishtextsociety.html

THE SHETLAND TIMES LTD
Prince Alfred Street, Lerwick, Shetland, ZE1 0EP.
Tel: 01595-693622 Fax: 01595-694637
Web: www.shetland-books.co.uk

SOCIETY OF ANTIQUARIES IN SCOTLAND
Royal Museum, Chambers Street, Edinburgh, EH1 1JF.
Tel: 0131-247 4115 Fax: 0131-247 4163
Web: www.socantscot.org

SPORTSCOTLAND
Caledonia House, Redheughs Rigg, South Gyle,
Edinburgh, EH12 9DQ. Tel: 0131-317 7200
Fax: 0131-317 7202
Web: www.sportscotland.org.uk

STENLAKE PUBLISHING
54-58 Mill Square, Catrine, Ayrshire, KA5 6RD.
Tel: 01290-551122

TUCKWELL PRESS LTD
The Mill House, Phantassie, East Linton, E. Lothian,
EH40 3DG. Tel: 01620-860164 Fax: 01620-860164
Web: www.tuckwellpress.co.uk

WEST DUNBARTONSHIRE LIBRARIES
Levenford House, Harbour Road, Latheronwheel,
Caithness, KW5 6DW. Tel: 01389-608045
Fax: 01389-608044

FILM, TV AND VIDEO
PRODUCTION COMPANIES

The following list comprises details for a number of
independent film, TV and video production
companies in Scotland.

1759 PRODUCTION SERVICES
2nd Floor, 3 Royal Exchange Court, Glasgow, G1 3DB
Tel: 0141-221 6069 Fax: 0141-221 6068
Email: info@1759.co.uk Web: www.1759.co.uk

ALISTAIR MILLER
Braehouse Touch, Cambusbarron, Stirling, FK8 3AH
Tel: 01786-464422 Fax: 01786-472272
Email: amtv@e-mail.msn.com
Web: www.am-tv.co.uk

BRONCO FILMS LIMITED
The Producers Centre, 61 Holland Street, Glasgow,
G2 4NJ Tel: 0141-287 6817 Fax: 0141-287 6815
Email: broncofilm@btinternet.com
Web: www.broncofilms.co.uk

CINÉCOSSE
North Meadows, Oldmeldrum, Aberdeenshire,
AB51 OGQ Tel: 01651-873311 Fax: 01651-873300
Email: admin@cinecosse.co.uk
Web: www.cinecosse.co.uk

EDINBURGH FILM PRODUCTIONS
Traquair House, Innerleithen, Peebleshire, EH44 6PP
Tel: 01896-831188

EDINBURGH FILM WORKSHOP TRUST
29 Albany Street, Edinburgh, EH1 3QN
Tel: 0131-656 9123 Fax: 0131-557 3852
Email: post@efwt.demon.co.uk
Web: www.efwt.demon.co.uk

ELECTRIC PICTURE MACHINE PRODUCTION
Paulswell, West Linton, Peeblesshire, EH46 7BH
Tel: 01968-660984 Fax: 01968-660984
Email: info@picturemachine.co.uk
Web: www.picturemachine.co.uk

FAIRLINE PRODUCTIONS
15 Royal Terrace, Kelvin Grove, Glasgow, G3 7NY
Tel: 0141-331 0077 Fax: 0141-331 0066
Email: fairprods@aol.com
Web: www.fishingontv.com

HCVF (HIGHLAND CORPORATE VIDEO FACILITIES) TV AND VIDEO
67 Kenneth Street, Inverness, IV3 5QF
Tel: 01463-224788 Fax: 01463-711460
Email: info@hcvf.co.uk Web: www.hcvf.co.uk

HAND PICT PRODUCTIONS LTD
20 Haymarket Terrace, Edinburgh, EH12 5JZ
Tel: 0131-346 1111 Fax: 0131-346 1222
Web: www.handpict.com

HOLYROOD FILM & TELEVISION PRODUCTIONS
86 Causewayside, Edinburgh, EH9 1PY
Tel: 0131-668 3366 Fax: 0131-662 4463
Email: rel@relrecords.co.uk
Web: www.relrecord.co.uk

MACTV
Unit 9 Rig Road Industrial Estate, Stornoway,
Isle of Lewis, HS1 2RF Tel: 01851-705638
Fax: 01851-706577 Email: info@mactv.co.uk
Web: www.mactv.co.uk

MEA PR
Giles St Studios, 99 Giles St, Edinburgh, EH6 6BZ
Tel: 0131-555 5995 Fax: 0131-555 0606
Email: info@mea-pr.co.uk Web: www.mea-pr.co.uk

MERMAID TALES FILM PRODUCTIONS LTD
The Mill, 72 Newhaven Road, Edinburgh, EH6 5QG
Tel: 0131-555 1177 Fax: 0131-555 3964
Email: mermaidtls@aol.com
Web: www.mermaidtls.com

MNE (MEDIA NAN EILEAN)
Pentagon Business Centre, 36 Washington Street,
Glasgow, G3 8AZ
Tel: 0141-249 9999 Fax: 0141-221 4477
Email: allan.mne@btconnect.com
Web: www.mediananeilean.co.uk

MTP
29 Lynedoch Street, Glasgow, G3 6EF
Tel: 0141-332 0589 Fax: 0141-332 6190
Email: shoot@mtp.co.uk Web: www.mtp.co.uk

NORTHLIGHT PRODUCTIONS LTD
The Media Village, Grampian Television, Queens Cross,
Aberdeen, AB15 4XJ Tel: 01224-646460
Fax: 01224-646450 Email: tv@northlight.co.uk
Web: www.northlight.co.uk

PATHWAY PRODUCTIONS
22 Colinton Road, Edinburgh, EH10 5EQ
Tel: 0131-447 3531 Fax: 0131-452 8745
Email: pathway@dial.pipex.com
Web: www.cofs.org.uk

PELICULA FILMS
59 Holland Street, Glasgow, G2 4NJ
Tel: 0141-287 9522 Fax: 0141-287 9504
Email: pelicula.films@btinternet.com

PENCIL OF LIGHT TELEVISION PRODUCTIONS
47 Newark Drive, Glasgow, G41 4QA
Tel: 0141-433 9532 Fax: 0141-433 2689
Email: kenmacgregor@penciloflight.freeserve.co.uk
Web: www.penciloflight.com

PICARDY MEDIA GROUP
1 Park Circus, Glasgow, G3 6AX Tel: 0141-333 1200
Fax: 0141-332 6002 Email: jr@picardy.co.uk
Web: www.picardy.co.uk

POSH PICTURES LTD
420 Sauchiehall Street, Glasgow, G2 3JD
Tel: 0141-353 0456 Fax: 07974-081934
Email: mail@poshpic.com Web: www.poshpic.com

SCOPE PRODUCTIONS
Keppie House, 147 Blythswood Street, Glasgow,
G2 4EN Tel: 0141-332 7720 Fax: 0141-332 1049
Web: www.scopeproductions.co.uk

SKYLINE PRODUCTIONS
10 Scotland Street, Edinburgh, EH3 6PS
Tel: 0131-557 4580 Fax: 0131-556 4377
Email: leslie@skyline.uk.com

TERN TELEVISION PRODUCTIONS LTD
73 Crown Street, Aberdeen, AB11 6EX
Tel: 01224-211123 Fax: 01224-211199
Email: office@terntv.com Web: www.terntv.com

VELOCITY OPTICS LIMITED
1/8 Waters' Close, Edinburgh, EH6 6RB
Tel 07970-571928 Fax: 0131-554 5240
Email: info@velocityoptics.com

WARK CLEMENTS COMPANY LTD
Studio 7, The Tollgate, 19 Marine Crescent, Glasgow,
G51 1HD Tel: 0141-429 1750 Fax: 0141-429 1751
Web: www.warkclements.com

LITERARY AGENTS

CURTIS BROWN GROUP LTD
37 Queensferry Street, Edinburgh EH2 4QS
Tel: 0131-225 1286/1288 Fax: 0131-225 1290

DUNCAN McARA
28 Beresford Gardens, Edinburgh EH5 3ES
Tel: 0131-552 1558 Fax: 0131-552 1558

The Great Book of Gaelic
In honour of the **Book of Kells,** the illuminated
Irish-Scottish masterpiece of the 9th century, *The
Great Book of Gaelic* was published by
Canongate in 2003. Thirty Scottish and Irish
poets have composed poems in honour of the
book and have also chosen 70 Gaelic poems from
the language's 1,500-year-old literary tradition.
One hundred Scottish and Irish artists, including
John Byrne, Alasdair Gray and Alan Davie, have
created original artworks in response to the
poems. These works range from etchings, digital
prints and oil paintings to tapestry and
photography. The art and poetry were fused into
a coherent whole by a team of calligraphers and
a master typographer who dovetailed the key
lines of poetry with the images.
The Great Book of Gaelic's launch was
accompanied by a series of radio programmes
and a TV documentary. The book has been
donated to every Gaelic-speaking school in
Scotland and Ireland along with an education
pack that discusses issues of history, geography,
art, language and culture. The artworks
themselves are currently on tour to major art
galleries in Scotland, Ireland, the UK, USA,
Canada and Europe. The tour continues until
2007 after which time the artworks will be bound
into a single volume that will alternate between
the National Libraries of Scotland and Ireland.

CULTURAL AND HERITAGE SCOTLAND

HISTORY, HERITAGE, CULTURE, LEISURE

7th–5th millennia BC: Earliest evidence of human settlement in Scotland, by Middle Stone Age hunter-gatherers and fishermen. Radiocarbon dating of large shell mounds on the island of Oronsay suggests that occupation was under way by the middle of the millennium.

4th –3rd millennia BC: New Stone Age farmers began around 4000 BC to cultivate crops and rear livestock on the western and northern coasts and islands and in Orkney. Forests began to be cleared and the making of pottery began. Apart from the Neolithic settlements at Skara Brae in Orkney and Jarlshof in Shetland, however, the principal monuments from this period, most of which date from *c.* 3000 BC, are religious. Communal burial took place in massive chambered cairns, such as those at Maeshowe and Isbister (Orkney) and Nether Largie South (Kilmartin, Argyll); while stone circles and other monuments, e.g. the Calanais (Callanish) standing stones (Lewis) and the Ring of Brodgar (Orkney), served ritual purposes.

c.2000 BC onwards: Metalworking and use of bronze artefacts began. Settlement by the Early Bronze Age 'Beaker people', so called from the distinctive style of their drinking vessels, mainly in eastern Scotland, although quantities of Beaker ware have also been found in the west, dating back perhaps to the mid-third millennium. There is evidence that the largest of the hilltop forts previously attributed to the Iron Age, such as Traprain Law (East Lothian) and Eildon Hill (Roxburghshire), may belong to the Bronze Age. Similar types of artefact found in widely separated locations are evidence of networks of exchange across Europe, in which Scotland participated.

From about 1300 BC the climate became colder and wetter, a trend which was possibly exacerbated by the effect of intense volcanic activity in Iceland (1159). Bronze Age communities gradually retreated from the uplands and marginal farming areas.

c.700 BC–AD 200: Further settlement as tribes were displaced from further south by new incursions from the Continent. This movement was accompanied by the development of Iron Age tools and weapons such as the sword and the rotary quern for grinding grain. In this period communities became more self-contained and competition and conflict between them increased. The building efforts previously put into ritual and mortuary structures was diverted into strong and imposing fortified dwellings and settlements.

Many hillforts of different types were built throughout Scotland during the first millennium BC. The huge drystone broch towers, such as those of Mousa (Shetland), Midhowe (Orkney) and Dun Carloway (Lewis), were at their peak in the latter half of the millennium and the first century AD, and other forms, such as wheelhouses, roundhouses and crannogs, were common, with regional variations. It is possible that these large buildings also reflected growing material prosperity and served a political purpose as symbols of the power of local and tribal leaders.

AD 43 onwards: Julius Agricola, the Roman governor of Britain AD 77–84, advanced deep into Caledonia, culminating with a victory at Mons Graupius in the north-east, probably in AD 84; however, he was recalled to Rome shortly afterwards and his forward policy was not pursued.

AD 122–410: Hadrian set the northern boundary of the Roman empire in Britain and ordered the construction of a wall to defend it. Hadrian's Wall marked the frontier until the Roman troops withdrew, except in AD *c.* 144–190, when the frontier moved north to the Forth-Clyde isthmus and a turf-built curtain wall, the Antonine Wall, was manned and policed. Tolls and the surrender of weapons were demanded of anyone wishing to cross. There were frequent invasions and counter-invasions by Romans and Picts in the following centuries, though the last major Roman campaign north of the Forth, carried out under the emperor Severus in 210, was a muted success and after Severus's death in 211 the Roman legions fell back to merely defending the border. The Picts, on the other hand, became much bolder in the fourth century, uniting against Rome with other peoples not only in Scotland but Ireland and the continent and at one point (AD 367) reaching as far south as London.

Although the Roman hold on the territory north of Hadrian's Wall was never more than tenuous, some Roman influence in parts of Scotland persisted until the fourth century, the legions finally being withdrawn from Britain altogether around 407 –410.

2nd–9th centuries: This period is marked by the gradual coalescing of the many small tribes existing in the Roman period into larger and more definable kingdoms, and continual warfare between them. The Picts, a loose confederation of a dozen or so tribes occupying the territory north of the Forth, appear to have dominated the north and east by the fifth century. The Scots, a Gaelic-speaking people of northern Ireland, colonised the area of Argyll and Bute from about AD 500, establishing the kingdom of Dalriada centred on Dunadd, and then expanded eastwards and northwards. The Britons, speaking a Brythonic Celtic language, colonised Scotland from the south from the first century BC; they lost control of south-eastern Scotland (incorporated into the kingdom of Northumbria) to the Angles in the early seventh century but retained south-western Scotland and Cumbria.

However, it was the arrival of the Vikings in the eighth century that constituted the next major influence on Scotland. Viking raids from the late eighth century were consolidated into a permanent Norse presence by settlement on the mainland and islands of the north and west from the early ninth century onwards.

397: First Christian church in Scotland established by St Ninian at Whithorn.

c.563: St Columba (*d.* 597) arrived from Ireland with 12 companions and established a monastery and a missionary base on Iona. Columba and his monks accomplished the conversion to Christianity of the Picts as far afield as Fife. The island became a place of pilgrimage and a centre of Christian scholarship: the eighth-century Book of Kells, now in the library of Trinity College, Dublin, was probably largely produced at the abbey of Iona and was moved to Ireland, with Columba's remains, by monks fleeing Viking raids aound 800.

612: Death of St Kentigern (also known as St Mungo), reputedly founder and first bishop of the city of Glasgow.

685: Northward incursions by the Northumbrian Angles were halted by Picts at The Battle of Nechtansmere, near Forfar. This defeat for the Northumbrians effectively checked their northward expansion into Scotland.

c.736: King Aengus of the Picts captured Dunadd, royal centre of Dalriada, thus acquiring overlordship of the Scots. In 756, in league with the Northumbrians, he defeated the north Britons at Dumbarton.

SCOTLAND'S FIRST LAW?
In 697 St Adomnn, an abbot of Iona and biographer of St Columba, drew up a *Law of the Innocents,* which aimed to protect non-combatants — women, children and members of religious communities — from violence in war. Written on Iona, the law was promulgated and enforced in Ireland, Scotland and Pictland.

---

c.794 onwards: Viking raids took place and Norse settlements were established in Argyll, Caithness and Sutherland, Orkney, Shetland, and the Western Isles. By 890 Orkney, Shetland, the Hebrides and Caithness had become part of the kingdom of Norway under Harald Fairhair and in 987 Earl Sigurd of Orkney annexed Sutherland, Ross and Moray.

843: Unification of the areas which now comprise Scotland began, when Kenneth mac Alpin, King of the Scots from *c.*834, became also King of the Picts, joining the two lands to form the kingdom of Alba (comprising Scotland north of a line between the Forth and Clyde rivers). Kenneth mac Alpin was helped in this enterprise by the severe defeat inflicted on the mainland Picts by the Danes in 839, weakening their resistance.

890: Orkney, Shetland, Caithness and the Hebrides became part of the Norwegian kingdom of Harald Fairhair.

903: St Andrews became the religious capital of Scotland after Kenneth mac Alpin's new religious centre at Dunkeld was destroyed by the Vikings.

c.973/4: Lothian, the eastern part of the area between the Forth and the Tweed was ceded or leased to Kenneth II of Alba by Edgar of England.

1010: Malcolm II defeated a Norse army at Dufftown and further secured his northern border by the marriage of his daughter to the Earl of Orkney.

c.1018: Malcolm II's victory over a Northumbrian army at Carham restored Scottish possession of Lothian, lost earlier in his reign. At about this time Malcolm placed his grandson Duncan on the throne of the British kingdom of Strathclyde, bringing under Scots rule virtually all of what is now Scotland. The hybrid name 'Scotland' began to supplant the Gaelic name 'Alba' (still the name of the country in Gaelic).

1040: Duncan I was slain in battle by Macbeth, who ruled until 1057. Macbeth fell at the battle of Lumphanan to Malcolm Canmore, who was aided by Earl Siward of Northumbria and Edward the Confessor of England.

1098: Magnus III of Norway devastated the Western Isles; but an uprising in the mid twelfth century drove the Norse from most of mainland Argyll. From then on the Norse possessions were gradually incorporated into the kingdom of Scotland.

Late 11th century onwards: Frequent conflict continued between Scotland and England over territory and the extent of England's political influence, and between the Scottish crown and rebellious Highland leaders such as Somerled, who became Lord of the Isles in 1156. At the same time Scotland was developing as a fully-fledged medieval society. Towns and burghs developed, encouraged by contact with the Normans, who brought trade and the marketplace, and by the court's increasing sophistication. David I granted the status of burgh, with special trading privileges, to numerous towns. Many had become royal burghs by the end of the 12th century. In return they paid rents and customs. As well as centres of trade and craftsmanship, royal burghs were centres of justice where the King's sheriffs held courts.

In the same period (roughly 1113–78) many of the great Scottish abbeys were founded under Alexander I, David I and William I (who founded Arbroath Abbey in 1178).

The number of burghs increased sharply during the reign of Alexander III. By 1283 most of the towns in Scotland, with exception of a few in the West Highlands and the Hebrides, had acquired the status of either royal or baronial burghs.

1237: The Treaty of York established Scotland's border with England.

1266: The Treaty of Perth was established, by which Magnus IV of Norway ceded the Hebrides and the Isle of Man to Scotland after an unsuccessful Norwegian expedition in 1263 by Haakon IV.

1296–1328: Wars of Independence. The failure of the Scottish royal line with the death of Margaret of Norway in 1290 led to disputes over the throne which were resolved by the adjudication of Edward I of England. He awarded the throne to John Balliol in 1292, but Balliol's refusal to be a puppet king led to war.

A Parliament held in Stirling in 1295 overturned Balliol's government and appointed a ruling Council, which made an alliance with Philip IV of France against England, formalising a relationship which had already existed for 200 years. (The treaty has become known as the Auld Alliance, and was the basis for Scottish military support for France in the following centuries. Scots fought in the army of Joan of Arc).

Balliol surrendered to Edward I and Edward attempted to rule Scotland himself. Resistance was led by William Wallace, who defeated the English under Hugh de Cressingham, Edward's Lord High Treasurer, at Stirling Bridge in 1297 but was later defeated by a large force under Edward himself at Falkirk the following year, and Robert Bruce, who seized the throne in 1306. Bruce had regained most of Scotland by 1311 and, famously, routed Edward II's army at Bannockburn in 1314, following up the victory by incursions deep into northern England and even into Ireland in the succeeding years.

Edward did not renounce his claim to Scotland, however, and when Bruce rejected a papal truce in 1317 Pope John XXII excommunicated him and placed Scotland under interdict. The bishops reply (also signed by eight earls and 31 barons), in a letter dated 6 April 1320 and written by Bernard of Linton, Abbot of Arbroath and Chancellor of Scotland, passionately defended Scotland's independence, and has become known as the Declaration of Arbroath or the Declaration of Independence. Former Popes had supported Scotland's independence but Pope John sided with English interests, despite the Declaration's assertion that 'for so long as a hundred of us remain alive, we will yield in no least way to English dominion. For we fight, not for glory nor for riches nor for honour, but only and alone for freedom, which no good man surrenders but with his life'.

England finally recognised Scotland's independence in the Treaty of Northampton in 1328. However, this was not the end of the story. By 1336 the forces of Edward III had penetrated Scotland again as far as Elgin; and although David II imposed a degree of stability and order in the 1360s, the conflict between Scotland and England was by no means settled when he died.

1349: Bubonic plague, the 'Black Death' which had swept through England in 1347, reached Scotland and spread throughout the country.

THE JOURNEYING STONE OF DESTINY

Reputedly brought to Scotland from Ireland by King Fergus in the sixth century, Scotland's ancient symbol of kingship graced the coronation ceremonies of generations of Scottish monarchs. The Dalriadic Kings were enthroned upon it at Iona, Dunadd and finally Scone, which became its supposedly permanent home c. 840. However, in 1296, the English King Edward I sealed his defeat of John Balliol by removing the Stone to London and placing it in Westminster Abbey, where – although the Treaty of Northampton granted its return to the Scots – it stayed for the next six-and-a-half centuries, being incorporated into the coronation ceremonies of English and then British monarchs.

In 1950 the Stone nearly succeeded in going home when a group of Nationalist students took it from Westminster Abbey early on Christmas morning; but it stayed in Scotland for only a few months, being placed symbolically in Arbroath Abbey, and was back in London for the coronation of Queen Elizabeth II. It was not until 1996, the 700th anniversary of its first removal, that the Stone was finally formally returned to Scotland.

1371 onwards: The first Stewart kings, Robert II and Robert III, were weak administrators, and the power of the barons and rivalries between them resulted in vendettas and lawlessness on which parliamentary attempts at legislation had little practical effect. In particular, the throne had little control of the Highlands or the Western Isles. Although David II had subdued the Lord of the Isles in 1369, the Western Isles were for practical purposes independent.

The Highlands and Lowlands were in many respects becoming two nations. Predating and underlying the Norman feudal system which functioned in the lowlands, the clan system was based on attachment to the land and loyalty to the clan chieftain. This continued to exist in the Highlands in an undiluted form and to pose continual challenges to the King's power in the north and west.

1390: The burning of Elgin cathedral and town by the 'Wolf of Badenoch' – Alexander Stewart, Earl of Buchan and youngest brother of Robert III took place. Though in part an act of reprisal for opposition from the Bishop of Moray, this was also part of a wider campaign of terror waged by 'the Wolf' to maintain Stewart control in the north – and to enrich himself.

1407: The city of Bruges gave Scots trading rights, opening the way for trade with the Continent; these were later suspended (1412–15) by the Hanseatic League because of Scottish piracy.

1414: Scotland's first university was founded at St Andrews. Teaching had begun in 1410 and the papal bull giving formal recognition was issued in 1414. The foundation of the universities of Glasgow and Aberdeen followed later in the century, in 1451 and 1495 respectively. Edinburgh University, founded in 1583, is Britain's oldest secular university foundation.

1411: The outbreak of open war in the Highlands. Donald, Lord of the Isles, was defeated at the Battle of Harlaw near Inverurie by the Earl of Mar (the Wolf's son) and a local army including burgesses of Aberdeen. Donald retreated to the west, but with his local power intact.

1424: James I set in motion a series of legislative reforms aimed at controlling the nobles, creating a fair and efficient judiciary, and raising national revenue. In 1426 parliament abolished all laws other than the King's. James backed this up by force in 1428 by arresting and in some cases executing about 50 Highland chiefs. Their resentment was instrumental in his death.

1468–9: Orkney and Shetland ceded to Scotland as a pledge for the unpaid dowry of Margaret of Denmark, wife of James III, though Danish claims of suzerainty persisted, to be relinquished only in 1590 with the marriage of Anne of Denmark to James VI.

1493: After continual strife in the reign of James III, James IV annexed the lands and titles of John, Lord of the Isles, to the crown, and made a series of expeditions to the west between 1493 and 1498. However, from 1504–7 he faced rebellion from John's son Donald Dubh. The integration of the west into the kingdom remained fragile, and James's granting of governorships to the Earls of Argyll and Huntly in 1500–1 bolstered the power of the Campbells and Gordons and provoked long-standing resentment from other clans.

1507: Scotland's first printing press, was licensed to Andrew Myllar and Walter Chepman by James IV, whose court promoted literature, learning and music. Their first book contained poems by William Dunbar.

1511–13: In 1511, reviving the Auld Alliance, James signed a new treaty with Louis XII of France in which Scotland pledged to make war on England if

France did so. He found himself almost at once drawn into a war of little direct relevance to Scotland, supporting the French against the Holy League of Pope Julius II, of which England, under Henry VIII, was a member. In 1513 James took on an English army at Flodden; although it was the largest and best-armed Scottish force ever to have entered England, the result was a disastrous defeat for the Scots, in which James IV, many of his nobles, and thousands of soldiers died.

1532: The Creation of the Court of Session by an Act of Parliament established a permanent 15-man College of Justice. A central criminal court, the High Court of Justiciary, was later founded. The present-day court system is based on these institutions.

1544–50: Hostilities were renewed with England. 'The Rough Wooing' was a savage campaign waged by Henry VIII on the Catholic, pro-French Scottish monarchy in retaliation for the breaking of a treaty by which Mary (later Queen of Scots) was to marry his son Edward. The whole of the south-east was ravaged and the great Border abbeys sacked.

1555–60: The doctrines of Luther and Calvin, introduced into Scotland by John Knox, a priest disaffected by the growing secularity and wealth of the Catholic church, quickly became popular among the local clergy and the lesser nobility. The outlawing of Knox and his followers in 1559 provoked riots by Protestants which flared briefly into war. The 'Reformation Parliament', held on 1 August 1560 in the name of Queen Mary but without a royal presence, abolished the Latin Mass and rejected the jurisdiction of the Pope. Only a month earlier, the Treaty of Leith effectively ended the Auld Alliance and French troops withdrew from Scotland. The Protestant majority in government was established, and was sufficiently secure to force Mary's abdication in 1567.

1603: James VI of Scotland succeeded Elizabeth I on the throne of England (his mother, Mary Queen of Scots, was the great-granddaughter of Henry VII), and from this point his successors reigned as sovereigns of Great Britain. James became an absentee monarch, and England and Scotland remained distinct in important ways, each retaining its own parliament and legal system.

The Union improved the physical links between Scotland and England and reduced much of the cross-border bickering and raiding. However, Scotland was in many respects not treated as England's equal: it could not trade with England or the colonies England later acquired without paying duties.

1608: Thousands of Border families emigrated to the province of Ulster, which James VI was colonising.

1614: The logarithmic tables of Edinburgh scholar and inventor John Napier were published.

1618: James VI attempted to bring the Church in Scotland into line with English practice in the Five Articles of Perth, passed by a General Assembly of the Church in August.

1632–40: Parliament House was built in Edinburgh, confirming its status as capital city of Scotland. Glasgow, meanwhile, was growing rapidly as a centre of industry, commerce and foreign trade. The building of a deep-water harbour at Port Glasgow began in 1667.

1638: The National Covenant was signed, overturning the Five Articles and reasserting the people's right to keep the reformed church. The Covenant overturned the Articles, sacked the Scottish bishops and proscribed the use of the Book of Common Prayer.

1666: The Pentland Rising, a popular revolt took place. Unsupported by landowners, it opposed the repression of Covenanters which followed the Restoration, and in particular the prohibition of conventicles (outdoor religious meetings). It failed when a poorly armed force of a few thousand Covenanters was defeated by government troops at Rullion Green.

1681: *Viscount of Stair* was published by James Dalrymple (1619–95). The book detailed the Institutions of the Law of Scotland and established Scots law as an independent and coherent system distinct from English law (Scots law being based on Roman law and English law being based on Greek law).

1688–9: After the abdication (by flight) in 1688 of James VII and II, the crown devolved upon William III (grandson of Charles I) and Mary II (elder daughter of James VII and II). In April 1689 the Convention of the Estates issued the Claim of Right and the Articles of Grievances, which asserted the independence of the Scottish Parliament and Presbyterianism as the established Church. William and Mary were offered the Scottish crown on condition that they accepted these proposals.

From April 1689 Graham of Claverhouse roused the Highlands on behalf of James, but died after a military success at Killiecrankie in July.

1692: The Massacre of Glencoe. The clan chiefs who had opposed William were offered pardon if they took an oath of allegiance before 1 January 1692 and threatened with persecution if they did not. The small clan of MacDonald of Glencoe missed the deadline by a few days. News that the chief had taken the oath was kept from the Privy Council, and a detachment of Campbell soldiers was sent to Glencoe and billeted with the MacDonalds with secret orders to destroy them. Thirty-eight people were killed. The violation of the tradition of hospitality and the Government's implication in the massacre turned Glencoe into a Jacobite rallying banner.

1695: The Bank of Scotland in Edinburgh, Scotland's first bank was established. It had a monopoly until around the time of the Act of Union, when the financial settlement required by the Union and the losses sustained by the collapse of the Darien scheme led to the foundation, also in Edinburgh, of the Royal Bank of Scotland in 1727. The Clydesdale Bank was founded in Glasgow in 1838, around the same time as three other Glasgow-based banks (the Union Bank of Scotland, the Western Bank of Scotland, and the City of Glasgow Bank), in a bid to challenge the financial power of Edinburgh and service the ever-growing industrial and commercial needs of Glasgow.

1698–1700: The Darien Venture. In 1695, an Act of Parliament was passed establishing the Company of Scotland Trading to Africa and the Indies, modelled on the London East India Company and intended to revive Scotland's depressed overseas trade. Darien, in Panama, was chosen as the site for a Scottish colony which would be a crossroads for world trade. Large amounts of money were invested in the scheme, but three successive attempts at settling in Darien and trading, between 1698 and 1700, failed miserably through inability to cope with the tropical climate, attacks from the Spanish, and a complete absence of trade. About 2,000 people died and the disaster not only crippled individual investors financially but dealt further blows to the already weak Scottish economy.

1701: The English parliament passed the Act of Succession. This act disputed the right of the Scottish parliament (asserted since 1689) to decide the line of succession.

1702: William, King of England and Scotland, died. The new Queen Anne (1702–14) is childless. A constitutional crisis over the line of succession becomes inevitable.

1703: The Scottish parliament passed the Act of Security to counter the Act of Succession.

1705 (February): The Westminster parliament passed The Alien Act demanding that the Scottish parliament choose the House of Hanover to succeed Queen Anne by Christmas Day. If the Scots did not reach this decision then England would treat all Scots as aliens, ban the Scottish trade to England in cattle, linen and coal, and claims of land that Scots held within England would be void. These threats had the potential to destroy the Scottish economy (by 1700 half of Scotland's export trade was to England, a figure that fell by 50 per cent between 1700 and 1704 causing ruin to many) and were nothing more than political blackmail. The reaction of the Scottish people was furious—they seized the unfortunate crew of an English ship anchored in the Firth of Forth, put them on trial for piracy, and executed three crew members.

1706: Negotiations begin on the issue of Union.

1707: The Act of Union was passed in the Scottish Parliament by a majority of 43 on 16 January, joining Scotland and England politically under one Parliament in London, in which Scotland would have 45 seats in the House of Commons and 16 seats in the House of Lords. No referendum was held to ask the Scottish people their opinion on political union and only a handful of Scottish peers voted on the transfer of power to Westminster—many of whom received cash payment for their vote, ranging from £11 (Lord Banff) to £1,104 (Earl of Marchmont). The Lords Ordinary each received £500 a year instead of £100 and all law servants of the crown received gratuities or increased salaries. When news of these arrangements became known the Scottish public rioted. Scottish taxpayers were further outraged when they discovered that they had to take on the burden of England's national debt (Scotland did not have a national debt) and increased taxes on ale, malt and salt. Scotland received compensation of £398,085 and 10 shillings (English value) for taking on this responsibility, but again this was viewed by the populace as a bribe and a limited number of people benefited from the money. Recognition of Scottish law was an integral part of the settlement, and, although certain laws have been superseded or nullified subsequently, the Scottish legal system today remains based on that in force at the time of the Union. The Scots education system and Church were also safeguarded as separate and individual from those of England and Scottish banks retained the right to print Scottish versions of the sterling currency, a duty they still perform today.

THE CLANS AND THE LAND

While political and social relations in lowland Scotland gradually became largely formalised and institutionalised during the Middle Ages, Highland society, isolated by geography and language, continued to be organised in the clan system, which originated in – and still retained many features of – the tribal organisation of early Gaelic society, based on strong but informal bonds of loyalty and trust and occupation of land. Clan members were those people, including non-relatives, living on the lands owned by the chieftain, and for whom chieftains assumed a patriarchal responsibility in return, particularly, for the loyal support of fighting men. Clan territory boundaries were broadly established by the 16th century.

Chiefs leased tracts (or tacks) of land to clan members (originally relatives) or allies to guarantee their security and also their allegiance. The traditional tack carried with it the requirement to provide military service. The tacksmen, in turn, sublet their land to tenants who worked for them on the land in return. Highland cattle were the principal source of wealth, and the tacksmen's power over the poorer tenants was potentially almost absolute.

Over time, the clan chiefs became members of the British national aristocracy; they spent time in England and became part of British society (the Scottish aristocracy had had links with Europe, particularly Rome for many centuries and could usually speak Latin and French as well as English and Gaelic). This was not the case with ordinary Highlanders, who at the beginning of the eighteenth century still spoke only Gaelic and were largely illiterate. By this time, however, some heads of clans were beginning to see themselves as landowners (and landlords) rather than chiefs. The leading chiefs were largely absentees, spending a great deal of time in England, especially after the Act of Union (1707) when many of them received English titles and estates, no doubt in recognition of their services to the Union. Chiefs were also forbidden their ancient right to private armies made up of their clansmen and with this act the clan leader suddenly had no need for his tenants, who in the past had been so vital for self defence. Clan chiefs bonds of responsibility to their tenants began to loosen as land began to signify money rather than ancestral tradition. These shifts were an important facilitator of the Highland Clearances.

1 May 1707: The union of the two parliaments comes formally into being with celebrations taking place in England and rioting taking place in Scotland. Sir John Clerk, one of the Scottish commissioners of the Act, later admits that the Articles of the Union had been carried 'contrary to the inclinations of at least three-fourths of the Kingdom'.

1714–15: After the death of Anne (younger daughter of James VII and II), the throne is devolved upon George I (great-grandson of James VI and I). In 1715, armed risings on behalf of James Stuart (the Old Pretender, son of James VII and II) led to the indecisive battle of Sheriffmuir, and the Jacobite movement died down until 1745.

1723: The Society for Improvement in the Knowledge of Agriculture was formed in Edinburgh. In 1727 the Commissioners and Trustees for Improving Manufactures and Fisheries were established. New ideas and technology were being developed by Scots farmers and manufacturers. Some heads of clans became increasingly concerned with making profit from their lands, either by selling land or by adopting the methods of improvement, which often involved turning large areas over to cattle and sheep at the expense of small tenants. The depopulation of the Highlands began.

From 1723 to 1725 there were outbreaks of protest by the Galloway Levellers, dispossessed tenants who had been evicted by lairds in Galloway in order to enclose pastures for fattening cattle.

1745: Charles Stuart (the Young Pretender) defeated the Royalist troops at Prestonpans and advanced as far as Derby (1746). From Derby, the adherents of 'James VIII and III' fell back on the defensive. The Highland army of 5,000, exhausted and outnumbered by the Duke of Cumberland's 9,000-strong force, was finally crushed catastrophically at Culloden on 16 April 1746. Prince Charles fled the country, and retaliation against the Jacobites by the victorious army was extremely savage – Cumberland's men rode through the surrounding countryside rounding up anyone they found and executing them whether they were Jacobites or not. Any wounded members of the Highland Army left on the field of battle were bayoneted or shot so that no survivors could be found, earning the Duke the title of 'Butcher Cumberland'. A systematic destruction of Scottish culture followed with the banning of tartans and bagpipes and Highlanders forced to wear trousers. Jacobite chiefs were executed or exiled, their lands confiscated by Westminster and overseen by English government officials. The clan chiefs who remained were persuaded to send their sons to school in the South of England where they lost their fluency in the Gaelic language and fully absorbed the values of the southern landowning aristocracy, thus breaking apart the clan system from within, once and for all. The Highlands were put under military occupation and the Highland regiments were established to keep the Scottish population in check. By the end of the century these regiments had been absorbed into the British army to fight battles overseas.

1745–1811: The population of the Highlands increases dramatically from 13,000 to 24,000 thanks to the introduction of the nourishing potato. This population increase was to become a factor in the Highland Clearances as landowners adopted different approaches to dealing with their enlarged communities. Some began to encourage emigration as a way of relieving the pressure on the land.

1747–8: Anxious to prevent the rise of any form of social and cultural organisation which could become a rallying point for further rebellion, the Government passed legislation intended to annihilate the clan system. The Abolition of Heritable Jurisdictions Act of 1747 confiscated the lands of those chiefs who had rebelled (the forfeited estates were later returned, in 1784), and the Disarming Act of 1748 proscribed the bearing of weapons and the playing of the Great Pipes. The wearing of Highland dress was also outlawed from 1746–82, although it made a comeback, in a somewhat romanticised form, in the early 19th century.

c.1750 onwards: Imports of tobacco and cotton were established as mainstays of the non-agrarian economy. Revenue from the processing and re-export of these commodities financed the development of Scottish merchant banking and further industry.

1754: The 'Royal and Ancient Golf Club' at St Andrews was formed.

1759: Robert Burns was born at Alloway, Ayrshire (*d.* 1796)

1767: The building of Edinburgh New Town (designed by James Craig) began, with the draining and clearing of land to the north of the Castle and the laying out of Princes Street, George Street and Queen Street. Building continued in phases until 1840.

Elsewhere, from the 1770s onward, a new model of village planning, stone-built and based on a central market square or high street, was applied by landowners, businessmen and government bodies in over a hundred villages, with the specific aim of economic development.

1770: An Act of Parliament created the Clyde Trust, authorising plans to deepen the Clyde. This initiated a process of development which led to the building of the great shipyards and docks in Glasgow in the following century.

Other technological and industrial developments around this time (e.g. the opening of the Carron Ironworks in 1759; James Watt's patenting of an improved steam engine in 1769; the introduction of large water-powered spinning mills from 1779) laid the basis for Scotland's industrial economy in the 19th and 20th centuries.

1771: Sir Walter Scott born, Edinburgh (*d.* 1832)

1776: Adam Smith (1723–90) published *The Wealth of Nations*. David Hume (*b.* 1711) died. The suspension of tobacco imports, caused by the American War of Independence, caused financial crisis in Glasgow. However, the Glasgow merchants had other commodities, including exports of their own—coal, linen and ale—which ensured their survival.

1785–1820: The first period of the Highland Clearances. As the majority of Highland estates were reorganised for sheep-farming, tens of thousands of tenants were evicted or 'cleared' from land they had farmed for generations with no security of tenure other than the unwritten contract of clan loyalty. Clearances took place across Sutherland in 1785–6, 1800, 1807, 1809, 1812–14 and 1819–20, one of the harshest being the clearance of Strathnaver on the northern coast in 1814. Some of the evicted tenants were encouraged to emigrate to the Lowlands and overseas, and a great many did so (6,000 Highlanders left for the Americas between 1800 and 1803 alone); others were evicted at gunpoint from their homes or had their homes raised to the ground and were moved forcibly to the coast where they were expected to survive as fishermen. The Clearances were the principal impetus for the mass diaspora of Scots to North America and the Antipodes.

NEW LANARK, A MODEL COMMUNITY

In 1785, David Dale, a Glasgow merchant, built a new industrial village near the old market town of Lanark. Built in a valley near the Falls of Clyde and using the river as a power source for its cotton mills, New Lanark became one of the largest cotton-manufacturing centres in Scotland, and continued in operation until 1968.

New Lanark was most renowned, however, as the place where the pioneering and enlightened ideas of Robert Owen were put into practice. Between 1800 and 1825 Owen ploughed much of the profits from the industry into improving life for the workers and their families, outlawing child labour, founding schools whose curriculum and disciplinary regime were far ahead of their time, and providing free medical care for workers and subsidised food at the village shop.

1790: The Forth–Clyde Canal, Britain's first sea-to-sea canal, was opened. The 250 miles of military road-building by General Wade in the early 18th century had improved communications in the Highlands, and from 1802 onwards Thomas Telford, engineer to the Commission for Highland Roads and Bridges, oversaw the construction of nearly 1,000 miles of roads. The Caledonian Canal was built between 1804 and 1822.

1793: The beginning of war with France and the formation of Highland regiments (e.g. Cameron Highlanders, Argyll Highlanders, Gordon Highlanders). Lairds recruited energetically in the Highlands, and the Scottish regiments played a significant part in the creation and defence of the British Empire, and in all Britain's wars of the 19th and 20th centuries.

1799: The emancipation of coal-miners and salt workers from serfdom took place. An Act of Parliament in 1606 had allowed for serfdom of these workers on the grounds that they were 'necessary servants'.

1820: Following years of economic depression and discontent among workers, exacerbated by rising grain prices after the Corn Laws of 1815, a series of riots and a widespread strike in the west culminated in a march from Glasgow to Falkirk and an attempt by a small band of radicals to seize the Carron ironworks. Both actions were crushed by government forces and the leaders executed or transported. The incidents became known as the Radical War.

1820–50: The second phase of the Highland Clearances. The people who had remained on the land after the first Clearances (mainly in Ross-shire and the Isles) were hit hard by the drop in demand for kelp and cattle, their remaining industries. Deprived of an income they quickly fell into arrears with their rents and with lower incomes from tenants chiefs began to sell their estates to non-Gaelic-speaking landlords or to clear people from the land once more to make way for yet more sheep and greater profits. The Potato Famine of 1846 sealed the Highlanders' fate and emigration became endemic, and for many, the only option. Meanwhile, in sharp contrast, the romanticisation of Scotland began with Queen Victoria's purchase of the Balmoral estate (1853), the beginnings of tourism, the revival of the tartans, and the patronage of Highland games, songs and dances.

The emotional scar left by the Clearances still resonates in modern-day Scotland and is the subject of much impassioned debate. In practical terms land reform, pertaining to access to Scotland's countryside for all and the right of crofters to buy their holdings from large landowners should the opportunity arise, has been one of the first issues the new Scottish Parliament has addressed since it came to power.

1830 onwards: New smelting processes enabled the development of the iron industry and related industries, such as coal-mining, also flourished. In the 1830s Scotland boasted the largest chemical works in the world.

1832: The First Reform Bill increased Scotland's representation at Westminster to 53 seats and extended the franchise to over 60,000 voters. The population of Scotland at the time was 2,364,000 (1831 census).

1838–9: The Scottish Chartists Organisation was formed in the wake of the Reform Bill. By 1839 there were 80 local Chartist Associations. Although their aims were modest and limited exclusively to electoral reform, they were viewed with alarm by the authorities. In 1848, 10,000 Chartists demonstrated on Calton Hill in Edinburgh and caused riots in Glasgow; but the movement became overshadowed by trade unionism.

1841: Govan shipyard was founded by Robert Napier. Aided by a fast-growing local steel industry, by the 1870s and 1880s Scotland had become the world leader in shipbuilding, particularly with the introduction of the large steel-hulled steamships that supplanted the tea clippers.

1842: The first visit to Scotland by Queen Victoria and Prince Albert. The royal family bought Balmoral Castle in 1853.

Opening of Edinburgh – Glasgow railway.

1850s onward: The development of the herring fishing industry on the east coast. New net technology and later the use of steamboats increased catches vastly, and the development of the railways enabled efficient transport of the processed fish.

1855: The United Coal and Iron Miners Association, Scotland's first effective labour organisation, was founded.

1867: The voting franchise was extended to all males and the Scottish Women's Suffrage Society was formed. In 1869 women gained the right to vote in municipal elections, but they were not to win the right to vote in parliamentary elections on the same terms as men until 1928.

1872: The Education (Scotland) Act, bringing burgh and parish schools under state control, was passed; but education was not provided free until 1892. The Scottish Leaving Certificate was introduced in 1888.

1873: The Scottish Football Association and Glasgow Rangers football club were founded. Celtic was founded in 1887.

1882: The Highland Land Leagues were formed, and the 'Battle of the Braes' in Skye, when crofters defied police and landlords in defence of their grazing rights began. Continuing trouble with crofters forced the government to set up a Royal Commission of enquiry, leading to the adoption of the Crofters (Holdings) Act in 1886, which gave crofters security of tenure, fixed rents and other rights.

1882: The Scottish Labour Party was formed, with James Keir Hardie as a founder member. Labour did not win the largest share of either votes or parliamentary seats in Scotland until 1922.

1885: The Scottish Office in Whitehall and the post of Secretary for Scotland were established. In 1928 the post was upgraded to Secretary of State for Scotland, thus reinstating a post which had been abolished in 1745.

1886: The Scottish Home Rule Association was founded, with both Labour and Liberal support. The concept of Home Rule was limited to Scotland's management of Scottish affairs, leaving wider areas such as foreign policy to Westminster, which would retain Scottish MPs.

1897: The Scottish Trades Union Congress was formed, at least partly in opposition to the British TUC, which was felt to represent the smaller Scottish unions inadequately. Organised labour was to achieve considerable strength during the Great War and its aftermath (for instance in the 1919 strike for a 40-hour working week) and was particularly militant during the inter-war period.

1909: Construction of the naval dockyard at Rosyth began.

1910: Twenty Liberal MPs set up a Scottish National Committee to promote self-government, but the issue was shelved until after World War I, when the Scottish Home Rule Association was refounded (1918) and the Scots National League, with its roots in radical politics, was formed in (1921). This was renamed the National Party of Scotland in 1927.

1924: James Ramsay MacDonald was elected Prime Minister and Secretary of State for Foreign Affairs in Britain's first Labour government. He returned as Prime Minister in 1929–31 and 1931–35 (in a coalition government with the Conservatives).

Successive draft Home Rule Bills presented to Parliament in 1924, 1926, 1927 and 1928 failed.

1934: The Scottish National Party was formed through a merger of the National Party of Scotland and the Scottish Party (formed 1932). The diverse nature of its components and their points of view, added to indifferent or unfavourable attitudes towards Home Rule on the part of government and large sections of the public, which meant that the party was slow to cohere. In 1946 it produced its statement of aims and policy, and in 1967 it won its first seat in Parliament when Winifred Ewing won the Hamilton by-election.

1930s: Scottish literary renaissance.

1937: Scottish Gaelic Text Society established.

1939–45: Industrial decline, which had already begun to worsen with the Depression (1929–31), was temporarily reversed by the need for production in the war effort. There was full employment and women workers were particularly active both in industry and on the land, as they had been in the Great War.

1948: East Kilbride and Glenrothes become Scotland's first New Towns.

1959 onwards: Large oil and gas reserves were discovered in the North Sea. In 1974 Highland One, the world's largest oil platform, was launched from Nigg on the Cromarty Firth. The first oil was pumped ashore in 1975. The oil industry has become an important, if insecure, source of revenue and employment, particularly for the north-east. In particular, the installation of the large Sullom Voe terminal in Shetland, based on agreements between the oil companies and the Island Council, has brought economic benefits to the islands.

1971 onwards: By the beginning of the 1970s the once industrially vibrant Upper Clyde was reduced to five shipyards, linked in the Upper Clyde Shipbuilders consortium. Under Edward Heath's Conservative government there was a series of sell-offs and liquidations of part of the consortium. The workers responded by organising a 'work-in' by 300 men. In February 1972 the government agreed to allow three shipyards to continue.

Nonetheless, the long, slow attrition of Scotland's industrial base was only momentarily halted, and in the next two decades mines, shipyards, iron and steel works and factories continued to be closed down and dismantled, a process accelerated with the emergence of the globalised economy. The fishing industry also contracted severely.

To some extent the heavy industries have been replaced by energy supply (oil and gas, hydroelectric power), manufacturing (computers, office machinery, television, radio and communications equipment), chemicals, tourism and related industries, and whisky. Membership of the European Union has also benefited agriculture, urban regeneration and small-scale industry in the Highlands and Islands.

1975: Major changes took place in local government introduced by the Local Government (Scotland) Act 1973. The structure was reorganised again in 1994.

1976: The Crofting Reform Act enabled crofters to buy their land.

1979: A referendum on the Scotland and Wales Act took place, which was introduced by the Labour government of James Callaghan to give some degree of devolution to Scotland and Wales. The referendum failed to reach the requisite 40 per cent of affirmative votes, partly because of a high level of abstention, and the Act was abandoned.

1988: 166 people were killed in a fire on the Piper Alpha oil rig on 6 July. On 21 December a bomb placed by Libyan terrorists caused a PanAm jumbo jet to explode over Lockerbie, killing 259 passengers and 11 townspeople.

1990: Glasgow held the title of European City of Culture.

1994 onwards: Contamination of British cattle herds by BSE (bovine spongiform encephalitis) depressed the Scottish beef industry. Confidence in British beef was not fully restored until early 2000.

1997: A referendum on the reinstatement of a separate Scottish Parliament took place. This time the people voted 'Yes', by a considerable majority, for a Scottish Parliament with powers to raise or lower taxes.

1999: The elections for Scottish Parliament took place on 6 May, carried out using a partial proportional representation system of voting for the first time in Britain. On 12 May the Parliament met for the first time since 1709. The official date of devolution was 1 July 1999.

A LOST PARLIAMENTARY MANUSCRIPT FOUND

In 1999, the year in which the Scottish Parliament was restored, a lost 17th-century manuscript, recording activities of the pre-Union Scottish government which has been missing since the council was abolished in 1708, was rediscovered. The book contains notes taken from the records of the Scottish Parliament, 1424–1621, and the Scottish privy council, 1561–1633. Written by an Edinburgh lawyer, Sir George Mackenzie of Rosehaugh, who was Lord Advocate 1677–86, the book is believed to have been lost some time after the national historian Cosmo Innes, put in a request to consult it to its owner, the Marquess of Bute, in 1842. The Manuscript has been returned to the archives of Bute House, now the official residence of the First Minister.

KINGS AND QUEENS OF SCOTS 834 TO 1603

Reign

c.834–860	Kenneth Mac Alpin, king of Scots, and also of Picts from 843; Kenneth I of Alba
860–63	Donald I
863–77	Constantine I
877–78	Aed
878–89	Giric
889–900	Donald II
900–43	Constantine II (abdicated)
944–54	Malcolm I
954–63	Indulf
963–67	Dubh (Duff)
967–71	Culain
971–95	Kenneth II
995–97	Constantine III
997	Kenneth III
997–1005	Grig
1005–34	Malcolm II (c.954–1034)

THE HOUSE OF ATHOLL

1034–40	Duncan I
1040–57	Macbeth (c.1005–57)
1057–58	Lulach (c.1032–58)
1058–93	Malcolm III (Canmore) (c.1031–93)
1093–97	Donald III Ban (c.1033–1100) Deposed May 1094, restored November 1094
1094	Duncan II (c.1060–94)
1097–1107	Edgar (c.1074–1107)
1107–24	Alexander I (The Fierce) (c.1077–1124)
1124–53	David I (The Saint) (c.1085–1153)
1153–65	Malcolm IV (The Maiden) (c.1141–65)
1165–1214	William I (The Lion) (c.1142–1214)
1214–49	Alexander II (1198–1249)
1249–86	Alexander III (1241–86)
1286–90	Margaret (The Maid of Norway) (1283–90)

First Interregnum 1290–92
Throne disputed by 13 competitors. Crown awarded to John Balliol by adjudication of Edward I of England

THE HOUSE OF BALLIOL

1292–96	John (Balliol) (c.1250–1313)

Second Interregnum 1296–1306
Edward I of England declared John Balliol to have forfeited the throne for contumacy in 1296 and took the government of Scotland into his own hands

THE HOUSE OF BRUCE

1306–29	Robert I (Bruce) (1274–1329)
1329–71	David II (1324–71)

1332 Edward Balliol, son of John Balliol, crowned King of Scots September, expelled December
1333–36 Edward Balliol restored as King of Scots

THE HOUSE OF STEWART

1371–90	Robert II (Stewart) (1316–90)
1390–1406	Robert III (c.1337–1406)
1406–37	James I (1394–1437)
1437–60	James II (1430–60)
1460–88	James III (1452–88)
1488–1513	James IV (1473–1513)
1513–42	James V (1512–42)
1542–67	Mary (1542–87)
1567–1625	James VI (and I of England) (1566–1625) Succeeded 1603 to the English throne, so joining the English and Scottish crowns

BRITISH KINGS AND QUEENS SINCE 1603

THE HOUSE OF STUART

Reign

1603–25	James I (and VI of Scotland) (1566–1625)
1625–49	Charles I (1600–49)

Commonwealth declared 19 May 1649

1649–53	Government by a council of state
1653–58	Oliver Cromwell, Lord Protector
1658–59	Richard Cromwell, Lord Protector
1660–85	Charles II (1630–85)
1685–88	James II (and VII) (1633–1701)

Interregnum 11 December 1688 to 12 February 1689

1689–1702	William III (1650–1702) and
1689–94	Mary II (1662–94)
1702–14	Anne (1665–1714)

THE HOUSE OF HANOVER

1714–27	George I (Elector of Hanover) (1660–1727)
1727–60	George II (1683–1760)
1760–1820	George III (1738–1820)

Regency 1811–20
Prince of Wales regent owing to the insanity of George III

1820–30	George IV (1762–1830)
1830–37	William IV (1765–1837)
1837–1901	Victoria (1819–1901)

THE HOUSE OF SAXE-COBURG AND GOTHA

1901–10	Edward VII (1841–1910)

THE HOUSE OF WINDSOR

1910–36	George V (1865–1936)
1936	Edward VIII (1894–1972)
1936–52	George VI (1895–1952)
1952–	Elizabeth II (1926–)

CITIES

EDINBURGH

Edinburgh is the capital of and seat of government in Scotland. The city is built on a group of hills with Edinburgh Castle at their centre, flanked by Princes Street Gardens, Princes Street (one of the most beautiful thoroughfares in the world), and the New Town on one side and the Royal Mile, Holyrood Palace and Arthur's Seat on the other. In 1995 UNESCO designated Edinburgh's Old and New Towns World Heritage Sites.

Edinburgh castle, a sprawling defensive building constructed on top of a volcanic plug, is the dramatic reason for the original settlement of the area. It is thought that the first two syllables of 'Edinburgh' probably come from *Din Eidyn*, the Gaelic words for the fort on the hill slope. Burgh means town. The importance of the castle cannot be underestimated for the town was originally nothing more than a stronghold guarding the south-east entrance to Scotland – Edinburgh began as the lion roaring at the gates of the country forbidding the passage of hostile intruders.

A bird's eye view of Edinburgh illustrates the development of the capital with a pleasing and most unusual neatness – the architectural industry and commercial, intellectual and religious concerns of each age can be easily recognised on a walk through the city.

The Royal Mile is the oldest part of Edinburgh and forms the core of the Old Town. The Mile begins at the Castle and runs for one mile downhill to Holyrood Palace. The Mile is still a partly cobbled street and is host to towering medieval tenements as well as merchants houses and a large number of 16th and 17th century houses built for the nobility who needed to be within a stone's throw of the Palace.

The plans for Edinburgh's New Town were decided upon in 1766, chosen by Provost Drummond and designed by the 22-year-old James Craig. From 1767 until the 1840s 6,000 masons built the New Town and seven water-powered sawmills were erected on the Water of Leith just to provide carcassing and joinery. The great 'Hollows ', the dips in the land that lie between Princes Street and the Old Town, were a stinking loch, commonly used as a rubbish tip, called the Nor (North) Loch. The loch was later drained to create Princes Street Gardens.

The Port of Leith sits on the shores of the Firth of Forth, the historic commercial artery for much of Edinburgh's trade and today the home to massive urban regeneration, the Royal Yacht Britannia, the new offices of the Scottish Executive, and a thriving pub and restaurant scene.

While the population of every town in Scotland has been in decline since 1974 (when the population of the country was 5.2 million; the population as of the 2001 census was 4.9 million), the population of Edinburgh (435,411) is increasing – perhaps because it has the fastest-growing economy of any city in the UK. The capital is experiencing a huge influx of people from other parts of Scotland, from England, and from outside the United Kingdom. According to the census of 2001, nearly a quarter of Edinburgh's residents were born outside Scotland (53,463 in England, 2,063 in Wales, 5,608 in Northern Ireland, 3,320 in the Irish Republic, 9,242 in EU countries and 24,988 from countries outside the EU).

Edinburgh has three universities: Edinburgh (1583), Heriot-Watt (1966), and Napier (1992).

The Edinburgh International Festival, held in August each year, is the world's largest festival of the performing arts.

The principal buildings include: the Castle, which now houses the Stone of Scone and also contains St Margaret's Chapel (12th century), the oldest building in Edinburgh, and the Scottish National War Memorial (1923); the Palace of Holyroodhouse (begun 1501 by James IV, rebuilding completed 1679); Parliament House (1632–40), the present seat of the judicature; St Giles Cathedral (15th century, but the site of a church since AD 854); St Mary's (Scottish Episcopal) Cathedral (Sir George Gilbert Scott); the General Register House (Robert Adam, 1774); the National and the Signet Libraries (founded 1682 and 1722); the National Gallery (1859); the Royal Scottish Academy; the National Portrait Gallery (1889); the Royal Museum of Scotland (1861); the New Royal Observatory (1896); St Cecilia's Hall (1762), the first purpose-built concert hall in Scotland; the Usher Hall; and the Edinburgh International Conference Centre, which opened in 1995. The Museum of Scotland opened 1998.

Other places of interest include Arthur's Seat (a volcanic hill 251 m/823 ft high overlooking the city), Calton Hill, the Royal Botanic Garden, the Physic Garden (1676), and the Firth of Forth road bridge (1964) and rail bridge (1890).

ABERDEEN

Aberdeen, 130 miles north-east of Edinburgh, received its charter as a royal burgh in 1179. Scotland's third largest city, Aberdeen is the main centre for offshore oil exploration and production – by 1981 750 oil-related firms were represented in the city and office space began growing at 6 per cent a year. Major oil firms such as Amerada Hess (1983), Britoil (1991), Conoco (1993) and Total Oil (1993) relocated their headquarters to Aberdeen bringing a boom to the housing market and a 'Klondike' reputation to Scotland's oil capital. The resulting expansion of the population and its relative affluence, brought a retail boom that saw the construction of several shopping centres – by 1994 Aberdeen was ranked seventh among 250 British shopping centres in terms of shop rents and property values – a not inconsiderable achievement considering the population stands at just over 205,000.

Aberdeen is also an ancient university town (Aberdeen University, founded 1495; Robert Gordon University, 1992) and a distinguished research centre. Other industries include engineering, fishing, food processing, textiles, paper manufacturing and chemicals.

Places of interest include: King's College (from 1500); St Machar's Cathedral (1370–1424); Brig o Balgownie (1314–18), Duthie Park (1881) and Winter Gardens (1972); Hazlehead Park; the Kirk of St Nicholas (from 12th century); the Mercat Cross (1686); Marischal College (founded 1593, present building 1891), the second largest granite building in Europe, and Marischal Museum; Provost Skene's House (from 1545); the Art Gallery (1884); Robert Gordon's College (begun by William Adam, 1731) and Robert Gordon University; the Gordon Highlanders Museum; the Satrosphere Hands-On Discovery Centre, and the Aberdeen Maritime Museum, which incorporates Provost Ross's House (1593) and the former Trinity Church.

DUNDEE

Dundee, which received its charter as a royal burgh at some point between 1153 and 1327, is thought to have existed since the second century AD. It is situated in a beautiful position on the north bank of the Tay estuary – hence its nickname 'Bonnie Dundee' – but the city itself is an obviously industrial place, a product of its manufacturing and trading history. The city has a population of approximately 160,000 and its suburbs are Baldovan, Broughty Ferry, Craigie, Invergowrie and Lochee. Dundee expanded rapidly thanks to trade by sea and by 1330 was already exporting 120 tonnes of wool a year. Dundee was one of the 'Great Towns' of Scotland known to Bruges merchants in 1348 (along with Aberdeen, Edinburgh and Perth), and throughout the 14th century royal charters were signed in the city. This prosperity was dealt a severe blow by the Black Death with only an average 96 tonnes of wool exported during the 1370s. The town revived by the 1430s with the export of cloth, particularly to the Baltic, and this trade continued to grow (along with wine making) until Dundee was manufacturing (by hand) 1.4 million metres of

coarse linen a year by the early 1700s with that figure rising to 4 million metres by 1778. Businesses of all kinds boomed at this time – James Keiller & Son founded their famous jam factory in the town in 1797 (expanding production to marmalade in 1835), whaling gained a firm foothold, with 200 whales caught and processed a year by the 1820s, four breweries were opened, and tobacco was cured locally in the 1830s. But of all the trades in Dundee, the cloth trade boomed more than any other – especially after the introduction of steam powered spinning machines. By 1838 Dundee had overtaken Leeds as the biggest centre of coarse linen manufacture in Britain and jute, imported raw from India, soon followed. This seemingly unstoppable prosperity declined, as it did throughout Britain, in the 1920s and Dundee became known for other things – such as being the home of the DC Thomson company, publishers of *The People's Friend, The Beano,* and *The Dandy.*

In the modern day, the city's port and dock installations are important to the offshore oil industry and the airport also provides servicing facilities. Principal businesses include textiles, computers and other electronic industries, lasers, printing, tyre manufacture, food processing, carpets, engineering, clothing manufacture and tourism. There are two universities, Dundee (1967) and Abertay Dundee (1994).

The unique City Churches – three churches under one roof, together with the 15th-century St Mary's Tower – are the city's most prominent architectural feature. Dundee has two historic ships: the Dundee-built RRS *Discovery* (built 1901), which took Captain Scott to the Antarctic, lies alongside Discovery Quay, and the frigate *Unicorn* (built 1825), the only British-built wooden warship still afloat, is moored in Victoria Dock. Places of interest include Mills Public Observatory, the Tay road and rail bridges, the Dundee Museum and Art Gallery (1872), McManus Galleries, the new Contemporary Arts Centre, Barrack Street Museum, Claypotts Castle (a town house built 1569–88), Broughty Castle (1454), Caledon Shipyard (1874), and Verdant Works (Textile Heritage Centre).

GLASGOW

Glasgow, a royal burgh (1611), is Scotland's principal commercial and industrial centre and the city with the biggest population (559,139).

Glasgow occupies the north and south banks of the river Clyde and has been viewed as the 'second city of the Empire' (to London's first), the 'second city of Europe', and 'the workshop of the world' for the past three centuries. We can now add the attribute of 'the first successful post-industrial city' to this range of descriptions as Glasgow has set about reinventing itself as a cultural, as opposed to an industrial, centre in the past three decades. The city staged the successful Glasgow Garden Festival in 1988 and was designated European City of Culture in 1990 and City of Architecture and Design in 1999.

The foundations of Glasgow's economic success were laid with the Act of Union (1707) and yet Glaswegians are usually reluctant to accept this fact as no other city opposed the Union with a louder voice, riots being frequent and bloody. But the Union ensured unrestricted access to the colonies for Glasgow's thriving port and waterways and by 1727, 50 ships a year sailed from Glasgow to Virginia, trading in sugar and tobacco. This figure had increased to between 300 and 400 ships by the 1770s and Glasgow merchants – soon to be known as The Tobacco Lords – controlled a bigger share of the American tobacco trade than all the other UK ports combined. This huge quantity of tobacco was re-exported to Europe, particularly France and the capital created by all this traffic was invested in items needed for the American colonies – Glasgow manufactured and transported linens, muslins, plaids, stockings, farm implements, shoes, pottery, glass, rope, furniture and ironware to America, creating a boom-town in the process. By the time demand dropped, thanks to the American War of Independence (1775–83), Britain's internal economy had grown to such an extent that Glasgow switched the destination for its goods, so beginning the expansion of trade south to London and north to the Highlands where improving landowners were attempting to farm the land more efficiently and needed Glasgow's hardy farm implements to do so.

Glasgow's next successful product would be cotton, which soon replaced tobacco as the city's principal American import. The countryside surrounding the city was appropriated for weaving, bleaching, dyeing and printing cotton and poor immigrants from Ireland (who arrived by the boatload every day) and displaced crofters from the Highlands migrated to the city to take up employment as weavers. The modern-day suburbs of Glasgow were all originally weaving communities.

Glasgow's energy seemed boundless – the port was expanded and improved, the coalfields of Monklands were exploited, an iron industry was founded, canals were built to transport yet more goods and minerals, the railway arrived and demanded yet more coal, engineering skill and construction expertise. Shipbuilding soon followed and the Clyde expanded production from 20,000 tonnes in 1850 to 50,000 by 1900 – and almost 800,000 tonnes by World War I. 100,000 people were employed in the shipyards and they represented Glaswegians self-image – powerful and successful. This image was devastated in the 20th-century with the economic slump of post-1918 Europe and America, the collapse of heavy industry in the 1960s, and the exodus of manufacturing to overseas labour markets.

The 1980s saw a concerted effort from the city council to revive the fortunes of the city. A massive advertising campaign was launched with the slogan 'Glasgow's Miles Better' and slums began to be demolished or refurbished. The Burrell Collection opened in the 1980s, new theatres were built, and the Princes Square shopping complex was opened in 1986.

Today Glasgow's main industries include engineering, electronics, finance, chemicals and printing. The city has also developed recently as a cultural, tourism and conference centre, with the Clyde Auditorium at the Scottish Exhibition Centre (affectionately called 'the Armadillo') making a playful addition to the city skyline since 1997. There are two universities: Glasgow (1451) and Strathclyde (1964). The city was raised to an archdiocese in 1492.

Among the chief buildings are the 13th-century Gothic Cathedral, the only mainland Scottish cathedral to have survived the Reformation intact; the University (Sir George Gilbert Scott); the City Chambers; the Royal Exchange (1829); the Royal Concert Hall; St Mungo Museum of Religious Life and Art, Pollok House; the Hunterian Museum (1805); the People's Palace (1898); the New Glasgow School of Art (Charles Rennie Mackintosh, 1896); Glasgow Art Gallery and Museum, Kelvingrove (1893); the Gallery of Modern Art; the Burrell Collection museum and the Mitchell Library (1911). The city is home to the Scottish National Orchestra (founded 1950), Scottish Opera (founded 1962) and Scottish Ballet (founded 1969).

INVERNESS

Inverness, a royal burgh, is the largest town in the Highlands and their administrative centre. It is situated at the northern end of the Great Glen, where the River Ness flows into the Beauly Firth, now spanned by the Kessock Bridge across to the Black Isle. Originally built on the axis between the medieval castle and the Old High Church, the town now has a population of 50,000. Inverness Castle was occupied and then destroyed by the Jacobites in 1746 and in the 19th-century was replaced by a courthouse and prison. The battlefield at Culloden, where the Jacobites were finally defeated on 16 April 1746, lies to the east of the town.

Other important buildings include the late Victorian Town House (1882), the Highland Council Buildings (1876), the episcopal St Andrew's Cathedral (1869), and the modern Eden Court Theatre (1976). Industries include light engineering, biotechnology, electronics, service industries and tourism. Nearby is the oil platform construction yard at Ardersier.

PERTH

Perth is situated in north-central Scotland, on the right bank of the River Tay. Perth is sometimes referred to as the 'Fair City', and with good reason; it has numerous parks and terraces and church spires hover above the buildings directing the eye to the surrounding unspoilt countryside. Today the city has a prosperous atmosphere and a somewhat genteel pace of life.

Perth became a burgh in 1106 and a royal burgh in 1210, and was one of the cities which fulfilled the function of Scottish capital until the mid-15th-century as a number of Parliaments and Council meetings were held there in the medieval period. The Blackfriars monastery was a favoured residence of James I, who founded Charterhouse, the last monastery to be established in Scotland, in 1425.

Little now remains to indicate Perth's former position as one of the chief towns of medieval Scotland, the ancient monasteries and castles having fallen victim to floods and conflict. The main buildings are St John's Kirk (founded by David I c.1125; Perth was also known as St John's Town until the 16th century); Perth Bridge; the King James VI Hospital; the Old Academy; the Sheriff Court buildings; Huntingtower Castle (16th-century); Scone Palace (built 1802–13 on the site of the medieval palace); and Balhousie Castle (present building, 1862). The garden of greatest note in the city is Branklyn Garden. Acquired by the National Trust for Scotland in 1967, it is often referred to as 'the finest two acres of private garden in the country'. Branklyn was the work of John and Dorothy Renton who built a house on Kinnoull Hill in 1922 and then planted their exotic garden of alpines, primulas, magnolias and mecanopsis.

The city lies between two large areas of open parkland and has a wealth of fine Georgian buildings. The principal industries are now tourism (fishing), agriculture, insurance, whisky and transport.

STIRLING

Stirling, a royal burgh since c.1124 (when this status was conferred upon it by David I), lies on the River Forth in the centre of Scotland and as such it is a mystery why it is not Scotland's modern-day capital. However, it was one of the chief cities to serve as the Scottish capital between the 13th- and the 16th-centuries, and the castle was a royal residence from c.1226. Stirling was the site of the Parliament which took over the government from John Balliol in 1295, the birthplace of James III (1451) and the site of the coronations of Mary (1543) and of James VI whose first Parliament met in the Great Hall of the castle in 1578.

Stirling's strategic situation led to its being the site of several battles. English armies led by Edward I were defeated at the Battle of Stirling Bridge in 1297 by Scots led by William Wallace and at Bannockburn in 1314 by forces led by Robert Bruce. The fact that two of Scotland's most famous patriots have victorious connections with Stirling make it a city that has a particular place in national affections – the Bannockburn monument alone is the scene of countless annual school trips and pilgrimages – and the fact that the Nationalist Covenant was launched here in 1930, rather than in Edinburgh, is significant.

The local economy comprises mainly service industries with some manufacturing. The city houses the headquarters of Scottish Amicable, the Bank of Bermuda and Scottish Natural Heritage. Stirling is also an important tourist centre with the nearby National Wallace Monument at Abbey Craig (constructed in the 1860s) a particularly popular attraction. The castle ramparts provide spectacular views. Argyll Lodging is Scotland's finest surviving Renaissance mansion – and one of the most interesting youth hostels in Scotland, located on the Castle Rock.

Places of interest include Stirling Castle; Argyll Lodgings; the National Wallace Monument; the Bannockburn Heritage Centre; Rob Roy Centre; Old Town Jail; Inchmahome Priory (1238); Cambuskenneth Abbey (1147); the Church of the Holy Rood (16th- and 17th-centuries); the Smith Art Gallery and Museum; and the Changing Room contemporary art gallery.

LANGUAGES

The main language of Scotland is English.

Gaelic and Lowland Scots are recognised minority languages and the various Scots dialects are widely spoken. Language is one of the aspects in which Orkney and Shetland are distinct from the rest of Scotland. Having been under Norse and Nordic influence and actual dominion until the fifteenth century, much longer than any other part of the country, they manifest a strong Norse influence in their place-names and dialect. Norn, an old Norse language, was commonly spoken in many of the islands until the eighteenth century, long after English had become the official language. Norse colonisation also influenced language and place-names in the Hebrides, but to a lesser extent.

GAELIC

The Gaelic language was introduced into Scotland from Ireland in the fifth century or before, and was at its strongest from the ninth to the 12th centuries. Despite the steady advance of English from the Middle Ages onwards, Gaelic remained the main language in much of rural Scotland until the early 17th century. However, in 1616 James VI and I passed an Act proscribing Gaelic, and with the suppression of Highland culture following the Jacobite rising of 1745 and the depopulation of Gaelic-speaking areas by the Highland clearances in the 19th century, the language declined.

The movement for the revival of Gaelic grew in the late 19th and early 20th centuries. A clause was inserted in the Education Act 1918 allowing Gaelic to be taught in Gaelic-speaking areas, although it was not until 1958 that a local education authority (Inverness-shire) first adopted a bilingual policy, teaching Gaelic in primary schools in Gaelic-speaking areas. Now Gaelic-only nurseries and infant schools teach in Gaelic until the age of seven and then the English language is introduced.

At the time of the 1991 census, 1.4 per cent of the population of Scotland, mainly in the Highlands and the Western Isles, were able to speak Gaelic. This represents a fall of 0.2 per cent since the 1981 census (it is estimated that for every five Gaelic speakers who die, only one new Gaelic-speaker picks up the language). The 2001 census showed that 1.9 per cent of the population of Scotland could speak, read or understand Gaelic—the rise in percentage can be attributed to the new definition of Gaelic understanding. Of the 4,968,729 people in Scotland (2001 census) 93,282 can understand, speak, read or write Gaelic with 33,746 of these aged 35–59 and only 1,934 aged 0–4. Geographically, by far the highest proportion of Gaelic speakers to total

population occurred in the Western Isles area, where over 71.6 per cent of people speak Gaelic.

The following table shows the total number of persons in each Council area and the percentage of that population aged three and over who can speak, read, write or understand Gaelic, as at the 2001 census.

Region	Total persons	% of population
Aberdeen City	205,973	1.2
Aberdeenshire	219,365	0.8
Angus	105,158	0.9
Argyll & Bute	88,676	7.3
Clackmannanshire	46,528	1.1
Dumfries & Galloway	143,546	0.7
Dundee City	141,443	0.9
East Ayrshire	116,454	0.6
East Dunbartonshire	104,973	1.4
East Lothian	86,919	0.8
East Renfrewshire	86,243	1.2
Edinburgh City	435,411	1.4
Eilean Siar	25,745	71.6
Falkirk	140,320	–
Fife	338,143	0.7
Glasgow City	559,139	1.8
Highland	202,291	9.1
Inverclyde	81,600	1.0
Midlothian	78,014	0.6
Moray	84,122	1.1
North Ayrshire	131,620	0.8
North Lanarkshire	309,773	0.7
Orkney Islands	18,698	0.9
Perth & Kinross	130,802	1.9
Renfrewshire	167,219	1.1
Scottish Borders	103,572	0.8
Shetland Islands	21,211	0.9
South Ayrshire	108,940	0.7
South Lanarkshire	292,283	0.7
Stirling	83,438	1.9
West Dunbartonshire	90,372	1.1
West Lothian	152,499	0.8
Total	4,900,492	1.9

Source: General Register Office (Scotland), 1991 and 2003 Census Monitor for Scotland (Crown copyright)

PROMOTION OF GAELIC

In recent years, more official measures have been taken to promote the revival of Gaelic, and the Scottish Executive includes a junior minister for Gaelic.

Gaelic is taught as an academic subject at universities including Aberdeen, Edinburgh and Glasgow, at numerous colleges of education, and in some schools, principally in Gaelic-speaking areas. Fifty-nine primary schools in Scotland offer Gaelic-medium education, and the Scottish Executive is committed to increasing the supply of Gaelic-medium teachers and locating training for them in the Highlands. Sàbhal Mor Ostaig is the Gaelic-medium further and higher education college.

BBC programmes in Gaelic are broadcast throughout the country. BBC Scotland delivered 116 hours of Gaelic television programmes in 1997–8 and an average of 45 hours of Gaelic radio programmes per week. The Scottish and Grampian independent stations also broadcast regular Gaelic television programmes. The Gaelic-language radio station BBC Radio nan Gaidheal is now available to 90 per cent of the audience in Scotland. There are local community radio stations in Stornoway, Ullapool, Portree and Fort William.

In 1990 the Gaelic Television Committee/ Comataidh Telebhisein Gàidhlig (now the Gaelic Broadcasting Committee/Comataidh Craolaidh Gàidhlig) was established to fund 200 hours of Gaelic television programmes a year in addition to the BBC's commitment to provide 90 hours of Gaelic programming a year and 45 hours of Gaelic radio. ITV is under no obligation to air Gaelic programmes but it does so, although output varies from year to year. The first programmes from the Committee's funded service were broadcast in 1993. Since then the Committee has funded more than 1,600 hours of Gaelic television programmes. The committee's remit was extended to radio programmes by the Broadcasting Act 1996. The Gaelic broadcasting industry now employs about 500 people in either full-or part-time work. The Committee seeks to deploy a substantial proportion of its production and development funds in the independent sector, (49 per cent in 2001), with the balance going to the broadcasters in-house production departments (28 per cent to ITV in 2001 and 23 per cent to the BBC in 2001). The Scottish Executive provides £8.5 million a year to the Committee, which is based in Stornaway. The Committee is currently in the process of lobbying the Scottish Executive to support a dedicated digital Gaelic channel.

A number of institutions for the promotion of the Gaelic language and culture exist. Comunn na Gàidhlig is the national development agency for Scottish Gaelic. It promotes the use of the Gaelic language, the continuance of Gaelic culture in education and the arts, and the integration of Gaelic into social and economic development, including the promotion of Gaelic businesses. An Comunn Gaidhealach promotes Gaelic culture through everyday use of the language and encourages the traditions of music, literature and folklore.

Fèisean nan Gàidheal, the National Association of Gaelic Arts Youth Tuition Festivals, is the independent umbrella association of the Fèis movement, which has existed since 1981, when a group on the island of Barra organised a tuition festival to begin to reverse the decline of traditional Gaelic music and dance. There are now 35 Fèisean, not only in the areas where Gaelic is still commonly spoken, but also in Edinburgh, Glasgow and Aberdeen.

LOWLAND SCOTTISH
Several dialects, known collectively as Lowland Scots, Lallans or Doric, are widely spoken in the south, east and extreme north of the country. Scots is the term commonly used in Scotland itself and in the European Charter for Minority and Regional Languages, which recognises Scots as a minority language. In the last 20 years the term Doric has come to be used locally in the north-east to refer exclusively to the group of dialects in that area.

Although the UK government ratified the European Charter in 1998, no official recognition or encouragement has yet been given to Scots. The General Register Office (Scotland) has estimated that 1.5 million, or 30 per cent of the population, are Scots speakers. Scots is vividly alive as a literary language too, appearing particularly in new drama.

PROMOTION OF SCOTS
Courses in Scots language and literature are taught at several universities, further and higher education colleges and community colleges. The Scots Language Resource Centre is the lead agency for the promotion of Scots and supports other bodies engaged in the promotion and study of Scots language and culture, including the Scottish National Dictionary Association, the Scots Language Society, the Scots Leid Associe, the Scots Speakers Curn and Scots Tung.

The Scottish Executive's National Cultural Strategy, launched in August 2000, contains a specific section on promoting Scotland's languages as cultural expressions and as means of accessing Scotland's culture and proposes a variety of actions to promote and preserve Scotland's linguistic diversity.

CHIEFS OF CLANS AND NAMES

The word 'clan', derived from the Gaelic clann, meaning children, originally referred to an extended family or tribe occupying a certain area of land. This was the early form of Gaelic society. After the Jacobean rebellion in 1745-6, the clan system was suppressed by the Government in order to forestall further rebellion, and gradually declined as an organising force in Scottish society. However, the clans continue to be one of the strongest social and emotional links between Scots in Scotland and abroad and a potent symbol of what it means to be Scottish. Their links with the land are not entirely severed either: many clan chiefs still live on the land, and in the buildings, which have been the clan seat for centuries.

The title of chief is usually hereditary, passing to the nearest heir. However, a chief may nominate a successor, subject to the confirmation of the Lord Lyon King of Arms. If a title is dormant, the Lord Lyon can award it to a person bearing the clan name, although this decision may be revoked if a proven heir is found within 20 years.

The style 'of that Ilk' began to be used by some chiefs in the late 16th century. More recently, chiefs who do not have an estate have been recognised as 'of that Ilk'. Certain chiefs use the prefix 'The'. The duplication of surnames by chiefs (e.g. Macdonald of Macdonald) is a feature that became common after the Act of Union 1707.

Only chiefs of whole names or clans are included here, except certain special instances (marked*) who, though not chiefs of a whole name, were or are for some reason (e.g. the Macdonald forfeiture) independent. Under decision (Campbell-Gray, 1950) that a bearer of a double- or triple-barrelled surname cannot be held chief of a part of such, several others cannot be included in the list at present.

STANDING COUNCIL OF SCOTTISH CHIEFS

52 Leith Walk, Edinburgh, EH6 5HW
Tel: 0131-554 6321

STYLES

There are a number of different styles for chiefs of clans and names; the appropriate use depends on the title and designation of the person, and for exact guidance a specialist source should be consulted. The following examples show the more common styles:

F—represents forename
S—represents surname
D—represents designation

EXAMPLES:
The S—
The S—of D—
F—S—of D—
Sir F—S—of D—, Bt.
F—S—of that Ilk
Madam/Mrs/Miss S—of D—(according to preference)
Dame F—S—of D—, DBE

CLAN CHIEFS

THE ROYAL HOUSE
HM The Queen

AGNEW
Sir Crispin Agnew of Lochnaw, BT, QC, 6 Palmerston Road, Edinburgh EH9 1TN

ANSTRUTHER
Sir Ian Fife Campbell Anstruther, Bt., c/o The Estate Office, Barlavington, Petworth GU28 0LG

ARBUTHNOTT
The Viscount of Arbuthnott, KT, CBE, DSC, Arbuthnott House, Laurencekirk, Kincardineshire AB30 1PA

BARCLAY
Peter C. Barclay of Towie Barclay and of that Ilk, 69 Oakwood Court, London W14 8JF

BORTHWICK
The Lord Borthwick, Crookston, Heriot, Midlothian EH38 5YS

BOYD
The Lord Kilmarnock, MBE, 194 Regent's Park Road, London NW1 8XP

BOYLE
The Earl of Glasgow, Kelburn, Fairlie, Ayrshire KA29 0BE

BRODIE
Alastair Brodie of Brodie, Brodie Castle, Forres, Morayshire IV36 0TE

BRUCE
The Earl of Elgin and Kincardine, Broomhall, Dunfermline, Fife KY11 3DU

BUCHAN
David S. Buchan of Auchmacoy, Auchmacoy House, Ellon, Aberdeenshire

BURNETT
J. C. A. Burnett of Leys, Crathes Castle, Banchory, Kincardineshire

CAMERON
Sir Donald Cameron of Lochiel, KT, CVO, TD,
Achnacarry, Spean Bridge, Inverness-shire

CAMPBELL
The Duke of Argyll, Inveraray, Argyll PA32 8XF

CARMICHAEL
Richard J. Carmichael of Carmichael, Carmichael,
Thankerton, Biggar, Lanarkshire

CARNEGIE
The Duke of Fife, Elsick House, Stonehaven,
Kincardineshire AB3 2NT

CATHCART
The Earl Cathcart, 18 Smith Terrace, London SW3 4DL

CHARTERIS
The Earl of Wemyss and March, KT, Gosford House,
Longniddry, East Lothian EH32 0PX

CLAN CHATTAN
K. Mackintosh of Clan Chattan, Fairburn, Felixburg,
Zimbabwe

CHISHOLM
Hamish Chisholm of Chisholm (The Chisholm),
Elmpine, Beck Row, Bury St Edmunds,
Suffolk IP28 8BT

COCHRANE
The Earl of Dundonald, Lochnell Castle, Ledaig,
Argyllshire

COLQUHOUN
Sir Ivar Colquhoun of Luss, Bt., Camstraddan, Luss,
Dunbartonshire G83 8NX

CRANSTOUN
David A. S. Cranstoun of that Ilk, Corehouse, Lanark

CRICHTON
Vacant

CUMMING
Sir Alastair Cumming of Altyre, Bt., Altyre, Forres,
Moray

DARROCH
Capt. Duncan Darroch of Gourock, The Red House,
Branksome Park Road, Camberley, Surrey

DAVIDSON
Alister G. Davidson of Davidson, 21 Winscombe Street,
Auckland, New Zealand

DEWAR
Michael Dewar of that Ilk and Vogrie, Rectory Farm
House, Wincanton, Somerset BA9 8ET

DRUMMOND
The Earl of Perth, Stobhall, Perth PH2 6DR

DUNBAR
Sir James Dunbar of Mochrum, Bt., 211 Gardenville
Drive, Yorktown, VA 23693, USA

DUNDAS
David D. Dundas of Dundas, 3 Crane Close, Tokai
7945, Cape Town, South Africa

DURIE
Andrew Durie of Durie, Finnich Malise, Croftamie,
Stirlingshire G63 0HA

ELIOTT
Mrs Margaret Eliott of Redheugh, Redheugh,
Newcastleton, Roxburghshire

ERSKINE
The Earl of Mar and Kellie, Erskine House, Kirk Wynd,
Alloa, Clackmannan FK10 4JF

FARQUHARSON
Capt. A. Farquharson of Invercauld, MC, Invercauld,
Braemar, Aberdeenshire AB35 5TT

FERGUSSON
Sir Charles Fergusson of Kilkerran, Bt., Kilkerran,
Maybole, Ayrshire

FORBES
The Lord Forbes, KBE, Balforbes, Alford, Aberdeenshire
AB33 8DR

FORSYTH
Alistair Forsyth of that Ilk, Ethie Castle, by Arbroath,
Angus DD11 5SP

FRASER
The Lady Saltoun, Inverey House, Braemar,
Aberdeenshire AB35 5YB

*FRASER OF LOVAT
The Lord Lovat, Beaufort Lodge, Beauly, Inver-nesshire
IV4 7AZ

GAYRE
R. Gayre of Gayre and Nigg, Minard Castle, Minard,
Inverary, Argyll PA32 8YB

GORDON
The Marquess of Huntly, Aboyne Castle, Aberdeenshire
AB34 5JP

GRAHAM
The Duke of Montrose, Buchanan Auld House,
Drymen, Stirlingshire

GRANT
The Lord Strathspey, The School House, Lochbuie,
Mull, Argyllshire PA62 6AA

GRIERSON
Sir Michael Grierson of Lag, Bt.,
40c Palace Road, London SW2 3NJ

GUTHRIE
Alexander Guthrie of Guthrie, 22 William Street,
Shenton Park, Perth, Western Australia

HAIG
The Earl Haig, OBE, Bemersyde, Melrose,
Roxburghshire TD6 9DP

HALDANE
Martin Haldane of Gleneagles, Gleneagles,
Auchterarder, Perthshire

HANNAY
David Hannay of Kirkdale and that Ilk, Cardoness
House, Gatehouse-of-Fleet, Kirkcudbrightshire

HAY
The Earl of Erroll, Woodbury Hall, Sandy, Bedfordshire

HENDERSON
John Henderson of Fordell, 7 Owen Street,
Toowoomba, Queensland, Australia

HUNTER
Pauline Hunter of Hunterston, Plovers Ridge, Lon
Crerist, Trearddur Bay, Anglesey LL65 2AZ

IRVINE OF DRUM
David C. Irvine of Drum, Holly Leaf Cottage, Banchory,
Aberdeenshire AB31 4BR

JARDINE
Sir Alexander Jardine of Applegirth, Bt., Ash House,
Thwaites, Millom, Cumbria LA18 5HY

JOHNSTONE
The Earl of Annandale and Hartfell, Raehills, Lockerbie,
Dumfriesshire

KEITH
The Earl of Kintore, The Stables, Keith Hall, Inverurie,
Aberdeenshire AB51 0LD

KENNEDY
The Marquess of Ailsa, Cassillis House, Maybole,
Ayrshire

KERR
The Marquess of Lothian, KCVO, Ferniehurst Castle,
Jedburgh, Roxburghshire TN8 6NX

KINCAID
Arabella Kincaid of Kincaid, Stoneyeld, Downton,
Ludlow, Shropshire

LAMONT
Peter N. Lamont of that Ilk, 40 Breakfast Road,
Marayong, New South Wales, Australia

LEASK
Madam Leask of Leask, 1 Vincent Road, Sheringham,
Norfolk

LENNOX
Edward J. Lennox of that Ilk, Tods Top Farm, Downton
on the Rock, Ludlow, Shropshire

LESLIE
The Earl of Rothes, Tanglewood, West Tytherley,
Salisbury, Wiltshire SP5 1LX

LINDSAY
The Earl of Crawford and Balcarres, KT, GCVO, PC,
Balcarres, Colinsburgh, Fife

LOCKHART
Angus H. Lockhart of the Lee, Newholme,
Dunsyre, Lanark

LUMSDEN
Gillem Lumsden of that Ilk and Blanerne, Stapely
Howe, Hoe Benham, Newbury, Berkshire

MACALESTER
William St. J. S. McAlester of Loup and Kennox,
27 Durnham Road, Christchurch, Dorset BH23 7ND

MACARTHUR
James MacArthur of that Ilk, 14 Hillpark Wood,
Edinburgh

MCBAIN
J. H. McBain of McBain, 7025 North Finger Rock Place,
Tucson, Arizona, USA

MACDONALD
The Lord Macdonald (The Macdonald of Macdonald),
Kinloch Lodge, Sleat, Isle of Skye

*MACDONALD OF CLANRANALD
Ranald A. Macdonald of Clanranald, Mornish House,
Killin, Perthshire FK21 8TX

*MACDONALD OF SLEAT (CLAN HUSTEIAN)
Sir Ian Macdonald of Sleat, Bt., Thorpe Hall, Rudston,
Driffield, North Humberside YO25 0JE

*MACDONELL OF GLENGARRY
Ranald MacDonell of Glengarry, Elonbank, Castle
Street, Fortrose, Ross-shire IV10 8TH

MACDOUGALL
Vacant

MACDOWALL
Fergus D. H. Macdowall of Garthland,
16 Rowe Road, Ottawa, Ontario K29 2ZS

MACGREGOR
Sir Malcolm MacGregor of MacGregor, Bt., Bannatyne,
Newtyle, Blairgowrie, Perthshire PH12 8TR

MACINTYRE
James W. MacIntyre of Glencoe, 15301 Pine Orchard
Drive, Apartment 3H, Silver Spring, Maryland, USA

MACKAY
The Lord Reay, 98 Oakley Street, London SW3

MACKENZIE
The Earl of Cromartie, Castle Leod, Strathpeffer,
Ross-shire IV14 9AA

MACKINNON
Madam Anne Mackinnon of Mackinnon, 3 Anson Way,
Bridgwater, Somerset TA6 3TB

MACKINTOSH
John Mackintosh of Mackintosh (The Mackintosh of
Mackintosh), Moy Hall, Inverness IV13 7YQ

MACLAREN
Donald MacLaren of MacLaren and Achleskine,
Achleskine, Kirkton, Balquhidder, Lochearnhead

MACLEAN
The Hon. Sir Lachlan MacLean of Duart, Bt., CVO,
Arngask House, Glenfarg, Perthshire PH2 9QA

MACLENNAN
Ruaraigh MacLennan of MacLennan, Oldmill, Dores,
Inverness-shire

MACLEOD
John MacLeod of MacLeod, Dunvegan Castle,
Isle of Skye

MACMILLAN
George Macmillan of Macmillan, Finlaystone,
Langbank, Renfrewshire

MACNAB
J. C. Macnab of Macnab (The Macnab), Leuchars
Castle Farmhouse, Leuchars, Fife KY16 0EY

MACNAUGHTEN
Sir Patrick Macnaughten of Macnaughten and
Dundarave, Bt., Dundarave, Bushmills, Co. Antrim

MACNEACAIL
Iain Macneacail of Macneacail and Scorrybreac, 12 Fox
Street, Ballina, New South Wales, Australia

MACNEIL OF BARRA
Ian R. Macneil of Barra (The Macneil of Barra),
95/6 Grange Loan, Edinburgh

MACPHERSON
The Hon. Sir William Macpherson of Cluny, TD,
Newton Castle, Blairgowrie, Perthshire

MACTAVISH
E. S. Dugald MacTavish of Dunardry, 2519 Vivaldi Lane,
Four Seasons Estates, Gambrills, MD 21054 USA

MACTHOMAS
Andrew P. C. MacThomas of Finegand, c/o Roslin
Cottage, Pitmedden, Aberdeenshire AB41 7NY

MAITLAND
The Earl of Lauderdale, 12 St Vincent Street, Edinburgh

MAKGILL
The Viscount of Oxfuird, Kemback, Stoke, Nr Andover,
Hampshire SP11 0NP

MALCOLM (MACCALLUM)
Robin N. L. Malcolm of Poltalloch, Duntrane Castle,
Lochgilphead, Argyll

MAR
The Countess of Mar, St Michael's Farm, Great Witley,
Worcestershire WR6 6JB

MARJORIBANKS
Andrew Marjoribanks of that Ilk, 10 Newark Street,
Greenock

MATHESON
Maj. Sir Fergus Matheson of Matheson, Bt., Old
Rectory, Hedenham, Bungay, Suffolk NR35 2LD

MENZIES
David R. Menzies of Menzies, 42 Panorama Drive,
Preston Beach, Western Australia

MOFFAT
Madam Moffat of that Ilk, St Jasual, Bullocks Farm
Lane, Wheeler End Common, High Wycombe

MONCRIEFFE
The Hon. Peregrine Moncrieffe of Moncrieffe, Easter
Moncrieffe, Bridge of Earn, Perthshire

MONTGOMERIE
The Earl of Eglinton and Winton, Balhomie, Cargill,
Perth PH2 6DS

MORRISON
Dr Iain M. Morrison of Ruchdi, Magnolia Cottage, The Street, Walberton, Sussex

MUNRO
Hector W. Munro of Foulis, Foulis Castle, Evanton, Ross-shire IV16 9UX

MURRAY
The Duke of Atholl, Blair Castle, Blair Atholl, Perthshire

NESBITT (OR NISBET)
Mark Nesbitt of that Ilk, 114 Cambridge Road, Teddington, Middlesex TW11 8DJ

NICOLSON
The Lord Carnock, 90 Whitehall Court, London SW1A 2EL

OGILVY
The Earl of Airlie, KT, GCVO, PC, Cortachy Castle, Kirriemuir, Angus

RAMSAY
The Earl of Dalhousie, Brechin Castle, Brechin, Angus DD7 6SH

RATTRAY
James S. Rattray of Rattray, Craighall, Rattray, Perthshire

RIDDELL
Sir John Riddell of Riddell, CB, CVO, Hepple, Morpeth, Northumberland

ROBERTSON
Alexander G. H. Robertson of Struan (Struan-Robertson), The Breach Farm, Goudhurst Road, Cranbrook, Kent

ROLLO
The Lord Rollo, Pitcairns, Dunning, Perthshire

ROSE
Miss Elizabeth Rose of Kilravock, Kilravock Castle, Croy, Inverness

ROSS
David C. Ross of that Ilk and Balnagowan, Shandwick, Perth Road, Stanley, Perthshire

RUTHVEN
The Earl of Gowrie, PC, 34 King Street, Covent Garden, London WC2

SCOTT
The Duke of Buccleuch and Queensberry, KT, VRD, Bowhill, Selkirk

SCRYMGEOUR
The Earl of Dundee, Birkhill, Cupar, Fife

SEMPILL
The Lord Sempill, 3 Vanburgh Place, Edinburgh EH6 8AE

SHAW
John Shaw of Tordarroch, East Craig an Ron, 22 Academy Mead, Fortrose IV10 8TW

SINCLAIR
The Earl of Caithness, 137 Claxton Grove, London W6 8HB

SKENE
Danus Skene of Skene, Orwell House, Manse Road, Milnathort, Fife KY13 9YQ

STIRLING
Fraser J. Stirling of Cader, 44A Oakley Street, London SW3 5HA

STRANGE
Maj. Timothy Strange of Balcaskie, Little Holme, Porton Road, Amesbury, Wiltshire

SUTHERLAND
The Countess of Sutherland, House of Tongue, Brora, Sutherland

SWINTON
John Swinton of that Ilk, 123 Superior Avenue SW, Calgary, Alberta, Canada

TROTTER
Alexander Trotter of Mortonhall, Charterhall, Duns, Berwickshire

URQUHART
Kenneth T. Urquhart of Urquhart, 507 Jefferson Park Avenue, Jefferson, New Orleans, LA 70121, USA

WALLACE
Ian F. Wallace of that Ilk, 5 Lennox Street, Edinburgh EH4 1QB

WEDDERBURN OF THAT ILK
The Master of Dundee, Birkhill, Cupar, Fife

WEMYSS
David Wemyss of that Ilk, Invermay, Forteviot, Perthshire

THE NATIONAL FLAGS

THE SCOTTISH FLAG

The flag of Scotland is known as the Saltire. It is a white diagonal cross on a blue field (saltire argent in a field azure) and symbolises St Andrew, the patron saint of Scotland.

Traditional explanation for the adoption of the St Andrew's cross as the symbol of Scotland is that the Saltire appeared in the sky to the Pictish king Hungus as an omen of victory over the Anglo-Saxons at the battle of Aethelstaneford. The Saltire was adopted as a national symbol at about the same time as St Andrew was adopted as Scotland's patron saint, and by the mid 14th century it was being used on coins. From about that time also, it has been used as a symbol of the struggle for independence.

In Scotland, HM The Queen and her representatives (The First Minister, The Lord Lyon, The Lord High Commissioner to the General Assembly and the Lord Lieutenants) use a flag called the Royal Lion Rampant (Scotland). The flag features a red lion rampant on a yellow field. George V granted permission for Scots to use the flag as a sign of loyalty.

THE NATIONAL FLAG

The national flag of the United Kingdom is the Union Flag, generally known as the Union Jack.

The Union Flag is a combination of the cross of St George, patron saint of England, the cross of St Andrew, patron saint of Scotland, and a cross similar to that of St Patrick, patron saint of Ireland.

The Union Flag was first introduced in 1606 after the union of the kingdoms of England and Scotland under one sovereign. The cross of St Patrick was added in 1801 after the union of Great Britain and Ireland.

DAYS FOR FLYING FLAGS

It is the practice to fly the Union Flag daily on some customs houses. In all other cases, flags are flown on government buildings by command of The Queen.

Days for hoisting the Union Flag are notified to the Department for Culture, Media and Sport by The Queen's command and communicated by the department to other government departments. On the days appointed, the Union Flag is flown on government buildings in the UK from 8 a.m. to sunset.

Both the Union Flag and the Saltire are flown in Scotland. The Saltire is flown from government buildings alongside, but not superior to, the Union Flag on the flag-flying days, which are the same days as those announced by the Department for Culture, Media and Sport. On Europe Day only, the EU flag flies alongside the Union Flag and the Saltire.

Birthday of the Countess of Wessex	20 January
The Queen's Accession	6 February
Birthday of The Duke of York	19 February
St David's Day (Wales)	1 March
Commonwealth Day (2004)	8 March
Birthday of The Earl of Wessex	10 March
Birthday of The Queen	21 April
St George's Day (England)	23 April
*Europe Day	9 May
Coronation Day	2 June
Birthday of The Duke of Edinburgh	10 June
The Queen's Official Birthday (2004)	12 June
Birthday of The Princess Royal	15 August
Remembrance Sunday (2004)	14 November
Birthday of The Prince Charles, (Duke of Rothesay)	14 November
The Queen's Wedding Day	20 November
St Andrew's Day (Scotland)	30 November

* The Union Flag should fly alongside the EU flag. On government buildings that have only one flagpole, the Union Flag should take precedence

FLAGS AT HALF-MAST

Flags are flown at half-mast (e.g. two-thirds up between the top and bottom of the flagstaff) on the following occasions:

(a) From the announcement of the death up to the funeral of the Sovereign, except on Proclamation Day, when flags are hoisted right up from 11a.m. to sunset

(b) The funerals of members of the royal family, subject to special commands from The Queen in each case

(c) The funerals of foreign rulers, subject to special commands from The Queen in each case

(d) The funerals of prime ministers and ex-prime ministers of the UK, subject to special commands from The Queen in each case

(e) Other occasions by special command of The Queen

On occasions when days for flying flags coincide with days for flying flags at half-mast, the following rules are observed. Flags are flown:

(a) although a member of the royal family, or a near relative of the royal family, may be lying dead, unless special commands are received from The Queen to the contrary

(b) although it may be the day of the funeral of a foreign ruler

If the body of a very distinguished subject is lying at a government office, the flag may fly at half-mast on that office until the body has left (provided it is a day on which the flag would fly) and then the flag is to be hoisted right up. On all other government buildings the flag will fly as usual.

THE ROYAL STANDARD

The Royal Standard is hoisted only when the Queen is actually present in the building, and never when Her Majesty is passing in procession.

NATIONAL ANTHEM

The official national anthem throughout the UK is God Save The Queen.

At national events and international competitions (primarily sporting), Scottish songs are sometimes used, including Scotland the Brave at the Commonwealth Games and Flower of Scotland for international rugby matches.

In 1998 the Herald newspaper ran a competition for a new Scottish anthem and the winner, announced in January 1999, was William Jackson's Land of Light.

NATIONAL DAY

The national day is 30 November, the festival of St Andrew, the patron saint of Scotland.

St Andrew, one of the apostles and brother of Simon Peter, was born at Bethsaida on the Sea of Galilee and lived at Capernaum. He preached the gospel in Asia Minor and in Scythia along the shores of the Black Sea and became the patron saint of Russia. It is believed that he suffered crucifixion at Patras in Achaea, on a crux decussata (now known as St Andrew's Cross) and that his relics were removed from Patras to Constantinople and thence to Scotland, probably in the eighth century, since which time he has been the patron saint of Scotland. The church and settlement founded at the place where the relics were brought ashore became the town of St Andrews.

THE HEAD OF STATE

ELIZABETH II, by the Grace of God, of the United Kingdom of Great Britain and Northern Ireland and of her other Realms and Territories Queen, Head of the Commonwealth, Defender of the Faith

Her Majesty Elizabeth Alexandra Mary of Windsor, elder daughter of King George VI and of HM Queen Elizabeth the Queen Mother
Born 21 April 1926, at 17 Bruton Street, London W1
Ascended the throne 6 February 1952

Crowned 2 June 1953, at Westminster Abbey
Married 20 November 1947, in Westminster Abbey, HRH The Prince Philip, Duke of Edinburgh, KG, KT, OM, GBE, AC, QSO, PC (born 10 June 1921, son of Prince and Princess Andrew of Greece and Denmark, naturalised a British subject 1947, created Duke of Edinburgh, Earl of Merioneth and Baron Greenwich 1947)
Official residences: Buckingham Palace, London SW1A 1AA; Palace of Holyroodhouse, Edinburgh; Windsor Castle, Berks
Private residences: Balmoral Castle, Aberdeenshire; Sandringham, Norfolk

THE HEIR TO THE THRONE

HRH THE PRINCE CHARLES, DUKE OF ROTHESAY

(Prince Charles Philip Arthur George), KG, KT, GCB and Great Master of the Order of the Bath, AK, QSO, PC, ADC(P)
Born: 14 November 1948, created Prince of Wales and Earl of Chester 1958, succeeded as Duke of Cornwall, Duke of Rothesay, Earl of Carrick and Baron Renfrew, Lord of the Isles and Prince and Great Steward of Scotland 1952
Married: 29 July 1981 Lady Diana Frances Spencer (Diana, Princess of Wales (1961–97), youngest daughter of the 8th Earl Spencer and the Hon. Mrs Shand Kydd), marriage dissolved 1996
Issue:
HRH Prince William of Wales (Prince William Arthur Philip Louis), born 21 June 1982
HRH Prince Henry of Wales (Prince Henry Charles Albert David), born 15 September 1984
Residences: St James's Palace, London SW1A 1BS; Highgrove, Doughton, Tetbury, Glos GL8 8TN
Office: St James's Palace, London SW1A 1BS. Tel: 020-7930 4832

ORDER OF SUCCESSION TO THE THRONE

1 HRH The Prince of Wales
2 HRH Prince William of Wales
3 HRH Prince Henry of Wales
4 HRH The Duke of York
5 HRH Princess Beatrice of York
6 HRH Princess Eugenie of York
7 HRH The Earl of Wessex
8 HRH The Princess Royal
9 Peter Phillips
10 Zara Phillips
11 Viscount Linley
12 Hon. Charles Armstrong-Jones
13 Hon. Margarita Armstrong-Jones
14 Lady Sarah Chatto

15   Samuel Chatto
16   Arthur Chatto
17   HRH The Duke of Gloucester
18   Earl of Ulster
19   Lady Davina Windsor
20   Lady Rose Windsor
21   HRH The Duke of Kent
22   Baron Downpatrick
23   Lady Marina Charlotte Windsor
24   Lady Amelia Windsor
25   Lady Helen Taylor
26   Columbus Taylor
27   Cassius Taylor
28   Eloise Taylor
29   Lord Frederick Windsor
30   Lady Gabriella Windsor
31   HRH Princess Alexandra, the Hon. Lady
      Ogilvy
32   James Ogilvy
33   Alexander Ogilvy
34   Flora Ogilvy
35   Marina, Mrs Paul Mowatt
36   Christian Mowatt
37   Zenouska Mowatt

HRH Prince Michael of Kent, and The Earl of St Andrews
both lost the right of succession to the throne through
marriage to a Roman Catholic. Lord Nicholas Windsor
renounced his right to the throne on converting to Roman
Catholicism in 2001. Their children remain in succession
provided that they are in communion with the Church of
England.

ROYAL SALUTES

Royal salutes are authorised at Edinburgh Castle and
Stirling Castle, although in practice Edinburgh
Castle is the only operating saluting station in
Scotland.

A salute of 21 guns is fired on the following
occasions:

(a) the anniversaries of the birth, accession and
    coronation of The Queen
(b) the anniversary of the birth of HRH Prince
    Philip, Duke of Edinburgh

A salute of 21 guns is fired in Edinburgh on the
occasion of the opening of the General Assembly of
the Church of Scotland.

A salute of 21 guns may also be fired in
Edinburgh on the arrival of HM The Queen or a
member of the royal family who is a Royal Highness
on an official visit.

THE MOST ANCIENT AND MOST NOBLE ORDER OF THE THISTLE

Postnominal initials, KT (Knights); LT (Ladies)
Ribbon, Green
Motto, Nemo me impune lacessit (No one provokes
   me with impunity)

The Order of the Thistle is an exclusively Scottish
order of knighthood. There is evidence of an order
of chivalry in Scotland from at least the Middle
Ages; James II created an order of knighthood in
1452, and James III (1460–88) may also have
created an order and certainly used the thistle as the
royal emblem. However, the present Order of the
Thistle was founded by James VII and II in 1687,
comprising the sovereign and eight knights.
Following James's exile, the Order fell into abeyance
until 1703 when it was revived by Queen Anne,
who increased the number of knights to 12; since
1827 the maximum number of members has been
16. Conferment of the Order also confers a
knighthood on the recipient.

The Order's motto, Nemo me impune lacessit, is
the motto of all Scottish regiments; it is usually
translated into Scots as 'Wha daur meddle wi me?'.

SOVEREIGN OF THE ORDER
The Queen

Royal Knights
HRH The Prince Philip, Duke of Edinburgh, 1952
HRH The Prince Charles, Duke of Rothesay, 1977

Lady of the Thistle
HRH The Princess Royal

Knights brethren and ladies
The Earl of Wemyss and March, 1966
Sir Donald Cameron of Lochiel, 1973
The Duke of Buccleuch and Queensberry, 1978
The Earl of Elgin and Kincardine, 1981
The Lord Thomson of Monifieth, 1981
The Earl of Airlie, 1985
Sir Iain Tennant, 1986
The Viscount of Arbuthnott, 1996
The Earl of Crawford and Balcarres, 1996
Lady Marion Fraser, 1996
The Lord Macfarlane of Bearsden, 1996
The Lord Mackay of Clashfern, 1997
The Lord Wilson of Tillyhorn, 2000
The Lord Sutherland of Houndwood, 2002
Sir Eric Anderson, 2002

Chancellor: The Duke of Buccleuch and Queensberry, KT, VRD

Dean: The Very Revd G. I. Macmillan, CVO

Secretary and Lord Lyon King of Arms: R.O. Blair, LVO, WS

Usher of the Green Rod: Rear-Adm. C. H. Layman, CB, DSO, LVO

Chapel, The Thistle Chapel: St Giles's Cathedral, Edinburgh

PRECEDENCE IN SCOTLAND

The Sovereign

The Prince Philip, Duke of Edinburgh

The Lord High Commissioner to the General Assembly of the Church of Scotland (while the Assembly is sitting)

The Duke of Rothesay (eldest son of the Sovereign)

The Sovereign's younger sons

The Sovereign's grandsons

The Sovereign's cousins

Lord-Lieutenants*

Lord Provosts of cities being *ex officio* Lord-Lieutenants of those cities*

Sheriffs Principal*

Lord Chancellor of Great Britain

Moderator of the General Assembly of the Church of Scotland

Keeper of the Great Seal (The First Minister)

Presiding Officer of the Scottish Parliament

Secretary of State for Scotland

Hereditary High Constable of Scotland

Hereditary Master of the Household

Dukes, according to their patent of creation:
 1) of England
 2) of Scotland
 3) of Great Britain
 4) of the United Kingdom
 5) those of Ireland created since the Union between Great Britain and Ireland

Eldest sons of Dukes of the Blood Royal

Marquesses, according to their patent of creation:
 1) of England
 2) of Scotland
 3) of Great Britain
 4) of the United Kingdom
 5) those of Ireland created since the Union between Great Britain and Ireland

Dukes' eldest sons

Earls, according to their patent of creation:
 1) of England
 2) of Scotland
 3) of Great Britain
 4) of the United Kingdom
 5) those of Ireland created since the Union between Great Britain and Ireland

Younger sons of Dukes of Blood Royal

Marquesses' eldest sons

Dukes' younger sons

Lord Justice-General

Lord Clerk Register

Lord Advocate

Advocate-General

Lord Justice-Clerk

Viscounts, according to their patent of creation
 1) of England
 2) of Scotland
 3) of Great Britain
 4) of the United Kingdom
 5) those of Ireland created since the Union between Great Britain and Ireland

Earls' eldest sons

Marquesses' younger sons

Lord-Barons, according to their patent of creation:
 1) of England
 2) of Scotland
 3) of Great Britain
 4) of the United Kingdom
 5) those of Ireland created since the Union between Great Britain and Ireland

Viscounts' eldest sons

Earls' younger sons

Lord-Barons' eldest sons

Knights of the Garter

Knights of the Thistle

Privy Counsellors

Senators of College of Justice (Lords of Session)

Viscounts' younger sons

Lord-Barons' younger sons

Sons of Life Peers

Baronets

Knights Grand Cross of the Order of the Bath

Knights Grand Commanders of the Order of the Star of India

Knights Grand Cross of the Order of St Michael and St George

Knights Grand Commanders of the Order of the Indian Empire

Knights Grand Cross of the Royal Victorian Order

Knights Commanders of the Order of the Bath

Knights Commanders of the Order of the Star of India

Knights Commanders of the Order of St Michael and St George

Knights Commanders of the Order of the Indian Empire

Knights Commanders of the Royal Victorian Order

Solicitor-General for Scotland

Lord Lyon King of Arms

Sheriffs Principal, except as shown above

Knights Bachelor

Sheriffs

Commanders of the Royal Victorian Order
Companions of the Order of the Bath
Companions of the Order of the Star of India
Companions of the Order of St Michael and St George
Companions of the Order of the Indian Empire
Lieutenants of the Royal Victorian Order
Officers of the British Empire
Companions of the Distinguished Service Order
Eldest sons of younger sons of Peers
Baronets' eldest sons
Knights' eldest sons, in the same order as their fathers
Members of the Royal Victorian Order
Members of the British Empire
Baronets' younger sons
Knights' younger sons, in the same order as their fathers
Esquires
Gentlemen
* During term of office and within their own counties/cities/sheriffdoms

FORMS OF ADDRESS

It is only possible to cover here the forms of address for peers, baronets and knights, their wife and children, Privy Counsellors, and holders of certain political, legal and civic posts. Greater detail should be sought in one of the publications devoted to the subject.

Both formal and social forms of address are given where usage differs; nowadays, the social form is generally preferred to the formal, which increasingly is used only for official documents and on very formal occasions.

The form of address for a woman holding office is given if different from that of a man holding the same position, but only where a woman holds or has held that particular office, as new styles tend to be adopted only when circumstances require it.

F—represents forename
S—represents surname
D—represents a designation, e.g. a title (peer) or city (convenor)

BARON
see Lord of Parliament

BARON'S WIFE
see Lord of Parliament's wife

BARON'S CHILDREN
see Lord of Parliament's children

BARONESS IN OWN RIGHT
see Lady of Parliament in own right

BARONESS (WOMAN LIFE PEER)
Envelope, may be addressed in same way as for a Lord of Parliament's wife, or, if she prefers (formal), The Right Hon. the Baroness D–; (social), The Baroness D–
Letter (formal), My Lady; (social), Dear Lady D–
Spoken, Lady D–

BARONET
Envelope, Sir F– S–, Bt.
Letter (formal), Dear Sir; (social), Dear Sir F–
Spoken, Sir F–

BARONET'S WIFE
Envelope, Lady S–
Letter (formal), Dear Madam; (social), Dear Lady S–
Spoken, Lady S–

CHAIRMAN OF SCOTTISH LAND COURT
As for Lords of Session

CONVENER OF COUNCIL
Envelope, The Convener of D—
Letter, Dear Convener
Spoken, Convener

COUNTESS IN OWN RIGHT
As for an Earl's wife

COURTESY TITLES
The heir apparent to a Duke, Marquess or Earl uses the highest of his father's other titles as a courtesy title. The holder of a courtesy title is not styled The Most Hon. or The Right Hon., and in correspondence The is omitted before the title. The heir apparent to a Scottish title may use the title Master.

DAME
Envelope, Dame F– S–, followed by appropriate post-nominal letters
Letter (formal), Dear Madam; (social), Dear Dame F–
Spoken, Dame F–

DUKE
Envelope (formal), His Grace the Duke of D–; (social), The Duke of D–
Letter (formal), My Lord Duke; (social), Dear Duke
Spoken (formal), Your Grace; (social), Duke

DUKE'S WIFE

Envelope (formal), Her Grace the Duchess of D–; (social), The Duchess of D–
Letter (formal), Dear Madam; (social), Dear Duchess
Spoken, Duchess

DUKE'S ELDEST SON

see Courtesy titles

DUKE'S YOUNGER SONS

Envelope, Lord F– S–
Letter (formal), My Lord; (social), Dear Lord F–
Spoken (formal), My Lord; (social), Lord F–

DUKE'S DAUGHTER

Envelope, Lady F– S–
Letter (formal), Dear Madam; (social), Dear Lady F–
Spoken, Lady F–

EARL

Envelope (formal), The Right Hon. the Earl (of) D–; (social), The Earl (of) D–
Letter (formal), My Lord; (social), Dear Lord D–
Spoken (formal), My Lord; (social), Lord D–

EARL'S WIFE

Envelope (formal), The Right Hon. the Countess (of) D–; (social), The Countess (of) D–
Letter (formal), Madam; (social), Lady D–
Spoken (formal), Madam; (social), Lady D–

EARL'S CHILDREN

Eldest son, see Courtesy titles
Younger sons, The Hon. F– S– (for forms of address, see Lord of Parliament's children)
Daughters, Lady F– S– (for forms of address, see Duke's daughter)

KNIGHT (BACHELOR)

Envelope, Sir F– S–
Letter (formal), Dear Sir; (social), Dear Sir F–
Spoken, Sir F–

KNIGHT (ORDERS OF CHIVALRY)

Envelope, Sir F– S–, followed by appropriate post-nominal letters. Otherwise as for Knight Bachelor

KNIGHT'S WIFE

As for Baronet's wife

LADY OF PARLIAMENT IN OWN RIGHT

As for Lord of Parliament's wife

LIFE PEER

As for Lord of Parliament/Baroness in own right

LIFE PEER'S WIFE

As for Lord of Parliament's wife

LIFE PEER'S CHILDREN

As for Lord of Parliament's children

LORD ADVOCATE

Usually admitted a member of the Privy Council on appointment.
Envelope, The Right (Rt.) Hon. the Lord Advocate, or The Right (Rt.) Hon. F– S–
Letter (formal), My Lord (if a peer), or Dear Sir; (social), Dear Lord Advocate, or Dear Lord D–/Mr S–
Spoken, Lord D–/Mr S–

LORD HIGH COMMISSIONER TO THE GENERAL ASSEMBLY

Envelope, His/Her Grace the Lord High Commissioner
Letter, Your Grace
Spoken, Your Grace

LORD JUSTICE-CLERK

Envelope, The Hon. the Lord Justice-Clerk; if a Privy Counsellor, The Right (Rt.) Hon. the Lord Justice-Clerk
Letter (formal), My Lord; (social), Dear Lord Justice-Clerk
Spoken (formal), My Lord; (social), Lord Justice-Clerk

LORD JUSTICE-GENERAL

Usually admitted a member of the Privy Council on appointment
Envelope, The Right (Rt.) Hon. the Lord Justice-General
Letter (formal), My Lord; (social), Dear Lord Justice-General
Spoken (formal), My Lord; (social), Lord Justice-General

LORD OF PARLIAMENT

Envelope (formal), The Right Hon. Lord D–; (social), The Lord D–
Letter (formal), My Lord; (social), Dear Lord D–
Spoken, Lord D–

LORD OF PARLIAMENT'S WIFE

Envelope (formal), The Right Hon. Lady D–; (social), The Lady D–
Letter (formal), My Lady; (social), Dear Lady D–
Spoken, Lady D–

LORD OF PARLIAMENT'S CHILDREN

Envelope, The Hon. F– S–

Letter, Dear Mr/Miss/Mrs S–

Spoken, Mr/Miss/Mrs S–

LORD/LADY OF SESSION

Envelope, The Hon. Lord/Lady D–; if a Privy Counsellor, The Right (Rt.) Hon. Lord/Lady D–

Letter (formal), My Lord/Lady; (social), Dear Lord/Lady D–

Spoken (formal), My Lord/Lady; (social), Lord/Lady D–

LORD OF SESSION'S WIFE

As for the wife of a Lord of Parliament, except that there is no prefix before 'Lady'

LORD PROVOSTS – ABERDEEN AND DUNDEE

Envelope, The Lord Provost of Aberdeen/Dundee

Letter (formal), My Lord Provost; (social), Dear Lord Provost

Spoken, My Lord Provost

LORD PROVOSTS – EDINBURGH AND GLASGOW

Envelope, The Right (Rt.) Hon. the Lord Provost of Edinburgh/Glasgow; or (Edinburgh only) The Right (Rt.) Hon. F– S–, Lord Provost of Edinburgh

Letter (formal), My Lord Provost; (social), Dear Lord Provost

Spoken, My Lord Provost

LORD PROVOST'S WIFE/CONSORT

Envelope, The Lady Provost of D– (may be followed by her name)

Letter (formal), My Lady Provost; (social), Dear Lady Provost

Spoken, My Lady Provost/Lady Provost

MARQUESS

Envelope (formal), The Most Hon. the Marquess of D–†; (social), The Marquess of D–

Letter (formal), My Lord; (social), Dear Lord D–

Spoken (formal), My Lord; (social), Lord D–

MARQUESS'S WIFE

Envelope (formal), The Most Hon. the Marchioness of D–; (social), The Marchioness of D–

Letter (formal), Madam; (social), Dear Lady D–

Spoken, Lady D–

MARQUESS'S CHILDREN

Eldest son, see Courtesy titles

Younger sons, Lord F– S– (for forms of address, see Duke's younger sons)

Daughters, Lady F– S– (for forms of address, see Duke's daughter)

MARQUIS

see Marquess; 'Marquis' is sometimes used for titles predating the Union

MASTER

The title is used by the heir apparent to a Scottish peerage, though usually the heir apparent to a Duke, Marquess or Earl uses his courtesy title rather than 'Master'.

Envelope, The Master of D–

Letter (formal), Dear Sir; (social), Dear Master of D–

Spoken (formal), Master, or Sir; (social), Master, or Mr S–

MASTER'S WIFE

Addressed as for the wife of the appropriate peerage style, otherwise as Mrs S–

MEMBER OF SCOTTISH PARLIAMENT

Envelope, Mr/Miss/Mrs S–, MSP

Letter, Dear Mr/Miss/Mrs S–

Spoken, Mr/Miss/Mrs S–

MODERATOR OF THE GENERAL ASSEMBLY

Envelope, The Rt. Revd the Moderator of the General Assembly of the Church of Scotland

Letter (formal), Dear Moderator/Dear Sir; (social), Dear Dr/Mr S– /Dear Moderator

Spoken, Moderator

After their year in office, former Moderators are styled The Very Reverend

PRESIDING OFFICER

Style/title used before the Scottish Parliament elections, e.g. if a minister is a privy counsellor, he is styled Rt. Hon.

Envelope (ministerial business), addressed by his appointment; (personal), Sir F–/Mr/Miss/Mrs S–, The Presiding Officer

Letter, Dear Sir F–/Mr/Miss/Mrs S–

Spoken, addressed by his appointment or name

PRIVY COUNSELLOR
Envelope, The Right (or Rt.) Hon. F– S–
Letter, Dear Mr/Miss/Mrs S–
Spoken, Mr/Miss/Mrs S–
It is incorrect to use the letters PC after the name in conjunction with the prefix The Right Hon., unless the Privy Counsellor is a peer below the rank of Marquess and so is styled The Right Hon. because of his rank. In this case only, the post-nominal letters may be used in conjunction with the prefix The Right Hon.

PROVOST
Envelope, The Provost of D–, or F– S–, Esq., Provost of D–/Mrs F– S– , Provost of D–
Letter, Dear Provost
Spoken, Provost

SCOTTISH MINISTER
Style/title used before the Scottish Parliament elections, e.g. if a minister is a privy counsellor, he/she is styled Rt. Hon.
Envelope (ministerial business), minister addressed by his/her appointment; (personal), Mr/Miss/Mrs S–, followed by the minister's appointment
Letter, Dear Mr/Miss/Mrs S–
Spoken, addressed by his/her appointment or name

SHERIFF PRINCIPAL AND SHERIFF
Envelope, Sheriff F– S–
Letter, Dear Sheriff S–
Spoken (formal), My Lord/Lady (in court); (social), Sheriff S–

VISCOUNT
Envelope (formal), The Right Hon. the Viscount D–; (social), The Viscount D–
Letter (formal), My Lord; (social), Dear Lord D–
Spoken, Lord D–

VISCOUNT'S WIFE
Envelope (formal), The Right Hon. the Viscountess D–; (social), The Viscountess D–
Letter (formal), Madam; (social), Dear Lady D–
Spoken, Lady D–

VISCOUNT'S CHILDREN
As for Lord of Parliament's children

CHIEFS OF CLANS AND NAMES
As there are a number of different styles for chiefs of clans and names, forms of address vary widely. Male chiefs are styled by their designation or estate rather than their surname; 'Esquire' is not added. A female chief is styled Madam or Mrs/Miss (according to her preference) in addition to her estate. For a list of examples, see also Chiefs of Clans and Names.
Envelope, chief's designation
Letter (formal), Dear Chief (if writer is a member of the clan or name); Dear Sir/Madam; (social), 'Dear' followed by chief's designation

CHIEF'S WIFE
As for her husband, with the addition of 'Mrs'.

CHIEF'S HEIR APPARENT
As for the chief, with the addition of 'younger' (yr), e.g.
F– S– of D–, yr
F– S– , yr. of D–

HISTORIC BUILDINGS AND MONUMENTS

Scotland is rich in buildings of historical and architectural value. They date from all periods from the Middle Ages to the 20th-century, and include castles, strongholds and keeps, palaces, tower houses, historic houses and mansions, churches, cathedrals, chapels, abbeys and priories, formal gardens, industrial buildings and military installations.

There are about 2,000 castles and towers in Scotland. Among the oldest castles still visible are Castle Sween, in Knapdale, Argyll, whose oldest parts may date from the 11th-century, and Cubbie Roo's Castle, built in 1145 by the Norseman Kolbein Hruga on the island of Wyre, Orkney, where there is also a later twelfth-century chapel. Dunvegan Castle in Skye is the oldest continuously inhabited castle in Scotland, having been occupied by the MacLeods for 700 years, although its present appearance is the result of massive 19th-century remodelling. Many castles were subject to frequent rebuilding over the centuries, and new castles were still being built as late as the nineteenth century, the most famous example being Balmoral, built in 1855 for Prince Albert. The north-east of Scotland is particularly rich in castles, and the Aberdeen and Grampian Tourist Board together with the Scottish Tourist Board promote exploration of this heritage by sign-posting a Castle Trail in the region.

Tower houses, which became popular from the 15th-century and were the major form of secular building in the sixteenth, were a peculiarly (though not exclusively) Scottish type of fortified dwelling for the local nobility. Good examples are Claypotts Castle, near Dundee, and Craigievar and Crathes Castles, Aberdeenshire.

Ecclesiastical buildings have an equally long and chequered history and many of the oldest buildings, such as St Ninian's Chapel, Isle of Whithorn, and the abbey buildings on the island of Iona, replace even earlier structures. The ruined Orphir church near Kirkwall, Orkney, is Scotland's only surviving round church, probably dating from before 1122. The monastery foundations of King Alexander I (reigned 1107–24) and his brother David I (1124–53) resulted in the building of St Margaret's Chapel in Edinburgh Castle, Inchcolm Abbey, on a small island in the Firth of Forth, and a string of great abbeys in the Borders (Dryburgh, Jedburgh, Melrose, Kelso, Sweetheart, Glenluce, etc.) in the twelfth and thirteenth centuries. The Border abbeys suffered severely in the conflicts of the 14th-century, however, and much of what is visible today reflects 15th-century rebuilding.

Scotland's built heritage from later centuries spans a wide variety of structures. From the late 17th- and 18th-centuries there are great houses such as Hopetoun House, Edinburgh, Duff House, Banff, and other buildings by William and Robert Adam, and the military bridges built by General Wade in the Highlands. The Industrial Revolution produced mills, factories, built harbours and shipyards, and the unique industrial village of New Lanark, purpose-built in 1785 as a cotton-manufacturing centre and made famous by the social ideas of Robert Owen in the 1820s. From the early 20th-century, the Hill House, Helensburgh, is a fine example of the work of Charles Rennie Mackintosh, Scotland's best-known architect. Coming almost up to the present day, a recent review of military structures by Historic Scotland has identified good survival of coastal defences in particular and this information will help to protect and preserve these structures.

Under the Planning (Listed Buildings and Conservation Areas) (Scotland) Act 1997 and the Ancient Monuments and Archaeological Areas Act 1979, the Scottish Executive is responsible for listing buildings and scheduling monuments in Scotland on the advice of Historic Scotland, the Historic Buildings Council for Scotland and the Ancient Monuments Board for Scotland.

Listed buildings are classified into Grade A, Grade B and Grade C. All buildings of interest erected before 1840 which are in use and are still largely in their original condition, are listed. More recent buildings are selected according to their individual character and quality. The main purpose of listing is to ensure that care is taken in deciding the future of a building. No changes which affect the architectural or historic character of a listed building can be made without listed building consent (in addition to planning permission where relevant). It is a criminal offence to demolish a listed building, or alter it in such a way as to affect its character, without consent. There are currently about 45,763 listed buildings in Scotland.

All monuments proposed for scheduling are considered to be of national importance. Where buildings are both scheduled and listed, ancient monuments legislation takes precedence. The main purpose of scheduling a monument is to preserve it for the future and to protect it from damage, destruction or any unnecessary interference. Once a monument has been scheduled, scheduled monument consent is required before any works are carried out. The scope of the control is more extensive and more detailed than that applied to listed buildings, but certain minor works may be carried out without consent. It is a criminal offence to carry out unauthorised work to scheduled monuments. There are currently about 7,600 scheduled monuments in Scotland, but the full number of buildings which meet scheduling standards is probably twice this. Both scheduling and listing are ongoing processes.

Whereas most listed buildings are currently in use or could be returned to use (even if it is not their original use), monuments that are scheduled have usually fallen into disuse and are unlikely to be used again in anything like their original form. In fact, a structure used as a dwelling house or in ecclesiastical use cannot be scheduled. Thus houses, bridges, factories, public buildings, war memorials and so on are more likely to be listed than scheduled, and terms of public access differ from those of access to scheduled monuments. The Forth Bridge, for instance, is a listed building – the largest in Scotland – and so are some traditional blue police boxes and red telephone boxes.

Historic Scotland, the government agency responsible for scheduling and listing, has around 330 monuments in its care. It provides financial assistance to financial assistance to private owners towards the costs of conserving and repairing important monuments and buildings. It also undertakes research into building conservation and publishes educational material on Scotland's built heritage.

The National Trust for Scotland, an independent trust, also cares for many castles, historic buildings and sites. A number of councils also care for historic buildings, while others are privately owned or cared for by independent conservation trusts.

OPENING TO THE PUBLIC

The following is a selection of the many historic buildings and monuments open to the public. Opening hours vary. Many properties are closed in winter and some are also closed in the mornings. Most properties are closed on Christmas Eve, Christmas Day, Boxing Day and New Year's Day, and many are closed on Good Friday. Information about a specific property should be checked by telephone or on the internet.

HISTORIC SCOTLAND (HS)

Longmore House, Salisbury Place, Edinburgh EH9 1SH.
Tel: 0131-668 8600 Fax: 0131-668 8669
Web: www.historic-scotland.gov.uk

NATIONAL TRUST (NTS)

Wemyss House, 28 Charlotte Square,
Edinburgh EH2 4ET
Tel: 0131-243 9300 Fax: 0131-243 9301
Web: www.nts.org.uk

ABBOT HOUSE, Dunfermline. Tel: 01383-733266.
Dates from 16th-century. Owners have included Anne of Denmark, wife of James VI

ABBOTSFORD HOUSE, Melrose, Borders.
Tel: 01896-752043. Sir Walter Scott's house

ABERDOUR CASTLE (HS), Aberdour, Burntisland, Fife.
Tel: 01383-860519. A 13th-century fortified residence extended in the 15th-, 16th- and 17th-centuries.

ABERNETHY ROUND TOWER (HS), nr Perth. One of two round towers of Irish style surviving in Scotland, dating from the 11th-century

AIKWOOD TOWER, nr Selkirk, Borders.
Tel: 01750-52253. A 16th-century fortified tower house. Home of Sir David Steel

ALLOA TOWER (NTS), Alloa. Tel: 01259-211701.
Ancestral home of Earls of Mar for 400 years

ARBROATH ABBEY (HS), Arbroath, Angus.
Tel: 01241-878756. Site of Declaration of Arbroath 1320. Founded 1178, completed 1233, granted abbey status 1285

ARDCHATTAN PRIORY (HS), Loch Etive, nr Oban.
Ruins of a Valliscaulian priory founded 1231 by Duncan MacDougall. Burnt by Cromwell's troops in 1654

ARGYLL'S LODGING (HS), Stirling. Tel: 01786-461146.
Fine example of a 17th-century town residence. Built by Sir William Alexander of Menstrie, first Earl of Stirling

ARMADALE CASTLE, Ardvasar, Skye.
Tel: 01471-844227. The seat of the Macdonalds since 1790

ARNISTON HOUSE, Gorebridge. Tel: 01875-830515.
Designed by William Adam for Robert Dundas, judge who dented the Campbell monopoly of Scottish patronage

AYTON CASTLE, Eyemouth, Berwickshire.
Tel: 01890-781212. Neo-baronial red sandstone castle built 1845–8

BALFOUR CASTLE, Shapinsay, Orkney.
Tel: 01865-711282. Completed 1848 by the Balfour family of Westray

BALGONIE CASTLE, nr Glenrothes.
Tel: 01592-750119. A 14th-century keep and courtyard. Occupied by Rob Roy and 200 clansmen in 1716

BALHOUSIE CASTLE, Perth. Tel: 01738-621281.
Neo-baronial mansion of 1862, built for the Earl of Kinnoull

BALLINDALLOCH CASTLE, Bridge of Avon, Aberlour.
Tel: 01807-500206. Begun 1546, historically a Grant seat

BALMERINO ABBEY (NTS), Balmerino, nr Leuchars.
Remains of a Cistercian abbey founded 1229 by Alexander II and built by the religious house of Melrose

BALMORAL CASTLE, nr Braemar. Tel: 01339-742534. Baronial-style castle built for Victoria and Albert. The Queen's private residence

BALVAIRD CASTLE (HS), Balvaird, Abernethy. A late 15th-century tower extended in1581 by the addition of a walled courtyard and gatehouse.

BALVENIE CASTLE (HS), Dufftown, Keith, Banffshire. Tel: 01340-820121. A 13th-century castle owned by the Comyns

BARCALDINE CASTLE, Peninsula of Benderloch. Tel: 01631-720598. Early 17th-century Campbell tower house

BARRIE'S BIRTHPLACE (NTS), Kirriemuir. Tel: 01575-572646. Birthplace of author of Peter Pan, J. M. Barrie

BEAULY PRIORY (HS), Beauly. Tel: 01667-460232. Ruins of priory founded 1230 by the Bisset family for the Valliscaulian order, later Cistercian

THE BINNS (NTS), nr Linlithgow. Castellated mansion built between 1612 and 1630. Originally property of the Livingstones of Kilsyth but sold to the Dalziels

BISHOP'S AND EARL'S PALACES (HS), Kirkwall, Orkney. Tel: 01856-871918. A 12th-century hall-house and an early 17th-century palace

BLACKHOUSE, ARNOL (HS), Lewis, Western Isles. Tel: 01851-710395. Built in the 1440s and massively strengthened in the 16th-century as an artillery fortress. Became an ammunition depot in the 1870s

BLACKNESS CASTLE (HS), nr Linlithgow, W. Lothian. Tel: 01506-834807. Following the Treaty of Union 1707, one of only four castles in Scotland to be garrisoned

BLAIR CASTLE, Blair Atholl. Tel: 01796-481207. Mid 18th-century mansion with 13th-century tower; seat of the Dukes of Atholl

BOD OF GREMISTA, Lerwick, Shetland. Birthplace of Arthur Anderson, first MP of Shetland

BONAWE IRON FURNACE (HS), Argyll and Bute. Tel: 01866-822432. Charcoal-fuelled ironworks founded in 1753

BOTHWELL CASTLE (HS), Uddingston, Glasgow. Tel: 01698-816894. Largest 13th-century castle in Scotland. Built by Moray family as protection against Edward I of England

BOWHILL, Selkirk. Tel: 01750-22204. Seat of the Dukes of Buccleuch and Queensberry; fine collection of paintings, including portrait miniatures. Includes Newark Castle, a ruined 15th-century keep and courtyard within grounds of Bowhill

BRAEMAR CASTLE, Braemar. Tel: 01339-741219. Built 1628 by John Erskine, Earl of Mar. Used as a garrison following Jacobite rising

BRECHIN CATHEDRAL (HS), Brechin. One of two remaining Irish style round towers in Scotland. Built in the late 11th-century. Stone roof added in 15th-century

BRODICK CASTLE (NTS), Isle of Arran. Tel: 01770-302202. Site of the ancient seat of the Dukes of Hamilton

BRODIE CASTLE (NTS), Forres, Moray. Tel: 01309-641371. A 16th-century castle with later additions

BROUGH OF BIRSAY (HS), Orkney. Tel: 01856-841815. Remains of Norse church and village on the tidal island of Birsay

BROUGHTON HOUSE (NTS), Kirkcudbright, Galloway. Tel: 01557-330437. Home of Edward Hornel, member of late 19th-century Scottish art establishment. Japanese garden

BROUGHTY CASTLE (HS), Broughty Ferry, Dundee. Tel: 01382-346916. Built in the late 15th-century, it was adapted over the centuries to meet the nation's changing defence needs

BURLEIGH CASTLE (HS), Milnathort. Red-sandstone tower built around 1500. Home of the Balfours of Burleigh

BURNS COTTAGE AND MUSEUM, Alloway, Ayrshire. Tel: 01292-441215. Birthplace of Robert Burns

CAERLAVEROCK CASTLE (HS), nr Dumfries. Tel: 01387-770244. Fine early classical Renaissance building. Built c.1270

CALLENDAR HOUSE, Falkirk. Tel: 01324-503770. Large ornate mansion of 1870s incorporating towers and turrets of a 15th-century castle

CAMBUSKENNETH ABBEY (HS) Stirling. Ruins of 12th-century abbey founded by David I on site of an Augustinian settlement

CARDONESS CASTLE (HS), Gatehouse of Fleet. Tel: 01557-814427. Late 15th-century stronghold

CARLYLE'S BIRTHPLACE (NTS), Ecclefechan, Lockerbie, Dumfriesshire. Tel: 01576-300666. Birthplace of Thomas Carlyle

CARNASSERIE CASTLE (HS), nr Kilmartin. Built by John Corsewell in 1560s, who published first ever book in Gaelic, Knox's Liturgy, 1567

CARRICK HOUSE, Eday, Orkney. Tel: 01857-622260. Built by Laird of Eday, 1633. Associated with pirate John Gow, on whom Sir Walter Scott's The Pirate is based

CARSLUITH CASTLE (HS), Carsluith, Creetown. A 16th-century tower house built by Richard Brown. Abandoned 1748

CASTLE CAMPBELL (HS) (NTS), Dollar Glen, nr Stirling. Tel: 01259-742408. 15th-century castle with parapet walk. John Knox preached here in 1556. Formerly known as the 'Castle of Gloom'

CASTLE FRASER (NTS), Sauchen, Inverurie, Aberdeenshire. Tel: 01330-833463. Garden and grounds open all year. Castle built between 1575 and 1636

CASTLE MENZIES, nr Aberfeldy. Tel: 01887-820982. A 16th-century tower house. Occupied by Oliver Cromwell's force in 1650s

CASTLE OF OLD WICK (HS), Wick. Tel: 01667-460232. Ruins of one of oldest castles in Scotland. Built 12th-century, when this part of Scotland was ruled from Orkney by the Norsemen

CASTLE STALKER, nr Port Appin. Tel: 01631-730234. Built on tiny rock island by the Stewarts of Appin in 16th-century and gifted to King James IV

CASTLE STUART, Petty. Tel: 01463-790745. Built between 1621–5 by James Stuart, 3rd Earl of Moray. Visited by Bonny Prince Charlie prior to Culloden

CASTLE SWEEN, (HS) Kilmichael. Ruins of 12th-century castle. Earliest stone castle in Scotland

CAWDOR CASTLE, Inverness. Tel: 01667-404615. A 14th-century keep with 15th- and 17th-century additions. Setting of Shakespeare's Macbeth

CLAYPOTTS CASTLE, (HS) Broughty Ferry. Tel: 01786-450000. Built between 1569–88. Inhabited until the 19th-century.

CORGARFF CASTLE (HS), Strathdon, Aberdeenshire. Tel: 01975-651460. Former 16th-century tower house converted into barracks

CRAIGIEVAR CASTLE (NTS), nr Alford. Tel: 01339-883635. Built by a Baltic trader, 'Willy the Merchant', in 1626

CRAIGMILLAR CASTLE (HS), Edinburgh. Tel: 0131-661 4445. Where the murder of Lord Darnley, second husband of Mary Queen of Scots, was plotted

CRAIGNETHAN CASTLE (HS), nr Lanark. Tel: 01555-860364. Castle dating from the 16th-century, with Britain's only stone vaulted artillery chamber. Last major castle built in Scotland

CRATHES CASTLE (NTS), nr Banchory. Tel: 01330-844525. A 16th-century baronial castle in woodland, fields and gardens

CRICHTON CASTLE (HS), nr Pathhead, Midlothian. Tel: 01875-320017. Erected by the Earl of Bothwell between 1581–91

CROOKSTON CASTLE (NTS), Pollok, Glasgow. Tel: 0141-226 4826. Built 12th-century by Robert de Croc. Visited by Mary, Queen of Scots. Became first property of NTS, in 1931

CROSS KIRK (HS), Peebles. Ruins of Trinitarian Friary founded 1474, dedicated to St Nicholas

CROSSRAGUEL ABBEY (HS), nr Maybole, Ayrshire. Tel: 01655-883113. Remains of 13th-century abbey

CULROSS ABBEY (HS), Culross. Remains of Cistercian abbey founded 1217 by Malcolm, Earl of Fife

CULROSS PALACE (NTS), Town House and Study, Culross, Dunfermline. Tel: 01383-880359. Refurbished 16th- and 17th-century buildings

CULZEAN CASTLE (NTS), S. Ayrshire. Tel: 01655-884455. An 18th-century Adam castle with oval staircase and circular saloon

DALMENY HOUSE, South Queensferry, Edinburgh. Seat of the Earls of Rosebery

DARNAWAY CASTLE, Darnaway, Forres. Tel: 01309-641469. Now a gothic mansion of 1802–12. Original castle acquired by the Stuarts in 1562

DEAN CASTLE, Kilmarnock. Tel: 01563-522702. Keep dates from 1350. Castle burnt 1735, now restored. Originally owned by the Boyd family

DELGATIE CASTLE, Delgatie, Turriff. Tel: 01888-562750. Original castle dates to 1030, current building 1570. Taken from Earl of Buchan 1314 and granted to the Hays

DIRLETON CASTLE (HS), Dirleton, North Berwick, E. Lothian. Tel: 01620-850330. 12th-century castle with 16th-century gardens

DORNOCH CATHEDRAL, Dornoch. Founded 1224. Cathedral of Bishops of Caithness. Restored 19th-century

DOUNE CASTLE (HS), Doune, Perthshire. Tel: 01786-841742. 14th-century castle built for the Regent Albany

DRUM CASTLE (NTS), Drumoak, by Banchory, Aberdeenshire. Tel: 01330-811204. Late 13th-century tower house

DRUMCOLTRAN TOWER (HS). Built around 1550 for the Maxwell family. Still inhabited in 1890s

DRUMLANRIG CASTLE, nr Thornhill, Dumfriesshire. Tel: 01848-330248. A 17th-century courtyard mansion. Home of Duke of Buccleuch and Queensberry

DRUMLANRIG'S TOWER, Hawick, Borders. Tel: 01450-372457. Only building left unburnt after burning of Hawick by English in 1570

DRYBURGH ABBEY (HS), Scottish Borders. Tel: 01835-822381. A 12th-century abbey containing tomb of Sir Walter Scott

DUART CASTLE, nr Craignure, Mull. Tel: 01680-812309. Headquarters of MacLean Clan from 13th-century

DUFF HOUSE (HS), Banff. Tel: 01261-818181. Georgian mansion housing part of National Galleries of Scotland collection. Built by William Adam

DUFFUS CASTLE (HS), Old Duffus, Elgin. Dates in part to 1151. Originally a royal stronghold. Abandoned in late 17th-century

DUMBARTON CASTLE (HS), Dumbarton. Tel: 01389-732167. Castle overlooking River Clyde

DUNBLANE CATHEDRAL (HS), Dunblane. Tel: 01786-823338. Dates from 13th-century, in Gothic style

DUNDONALD CASTLE (HS), Dundonald, Kilmarnock, Ayrshire. Tel: 01563-851489. Castle built by the Stewart royal dynasty

DUNDRENNAN ABBEY (HS), nr Kirkcudbright. Tel: 01557-500262. Remote 12th-century abbey. Where Mary, Queen of Scots spent her last night on Scottish soil

DUNFERMLINE PALACE AND ABBEY (HS), Dunfermline, Fife. Tel: 01383-739026. Founded by Queen Margaret in the 11th-century. Robert the Bruce is buried in the Choir.

DUNNOTTAR CASTLE, Stonehaven. Tel: 01569-762173. A 12th–17th-century fortress on a sheer cliff jutting into the sea. One of Scotland's finest ruined castles

DUNROBIN CASTLE, Golspie, Sutherland. Tel: 01408-633177. The most northerly of Scotland's great castles, seat of the Earls of Sutherland

DUNSTAFFNAGE CASTLE AND CHAPEL (HS), nr Oban. Tel: 01631-562465. Fine 13th-century castle, briefly the prison of Flora Macdonald

DUNVEGAN CASTLE, Skye. Tel: 01470-521206. A 13th-century castle with later additions; home of the chiefs of the Clan MacLeod; trips to seal colony

EARL'S PALACE (HS), Birsay, Orkney. Ruins of 16th-century courtyard castle, started by Robert Stewart, Earl of Orkney

EARL'S PALACE (HS), Kirkwall, Orkney. Tel: 01856-875461. Ruins of 17th-century palace, built by Patrick Stewart, Earl of Orkney, illegitimate half-brother of Mary, Queen of Scots

EDINBURGH CASTLE (HS). Tel: 0131-225 9846. Includes the Scottish National War Memorial, Scottish United Services Museum and historic apartments

EDZELL CASTLE (HS), nr Brechin. Tel: 01356-648631. Medieval tower house; unique walled garden. Gardens by Sir David Lindsay in 1604

EILEAN DONAN CASTLE, Wester Ross. Tel: 01599-555202. A 13th-century castle with Jacobite relics. Established by Alexander II to protect the area from the vikings

ELCHO CASTLE (HS), nr Perth. Tel: 01738-639998. 16th-century fortified mansion

ELGIN CATHEDRAL (HS), Moray. Tel: 01343-547171. A 13th-century cathedral with fine chapterhouse

FALKLAND PALACE (NTS), Falkland, Cupar, Fife. Tel: 01337-857397. Country residence of the Stewart kings and queens, built between 1502 and 1541

FASQUE HOUSE, nr Fettercairn. Tel: 01561-340202. Family home of Prime Minister William Gladstone 1789–1809

FEARN ABBEY, Fearn. A 14th-century church, one of the oldest pre-Reformation Scottish churches still used for worship

FINLAYSTONE HOUSE, nr Port Glasgow. Tel: 01475-540285. Mansion dating from 1760, incorporating 15th-century castle of the Cunningham Earls of Glencairn, where John Knox preached in 1556

FLOORS CASTLE, Kelso. Tel: 01573-223333. Largest inhabited castle in Scotland; seat of the Dukes of Roxburghe

FORT CHARLOTTE, Lerwick, Shetland. Begun by Charles II in 1665 during war against Dutch. Named in honour of George III's queen in 1780s

FORT GEORGE (HS), Highland. Tel: 01667-462800. An 18th-century fort

FYVIE CASTLE (NTS), nr Turriff, Grampian. Tel: 01651-891266. 15th-century castle with finest wheel stair in Scotland

GEORGIAN HOUSE (NTS), Edinburgh. Tel: 0131-226 3318. Fine example of 18th-century New Town architecture

GLADSTONE'S LAND (NTS), Edinburgh. Tel: 0131-226 5856. Typical 17th-century Old Town tenement building with remarkable painted ceilings

GLAMIS CASTLE, Angus. Tel: 01307-840393. Seat of the Lyon family (later Earls of Strathmore and Kinghorne) since 1372. Scene of the murder of Duncan in Shakespeare's Macbeth

GLASGOW CATHEDRAL (HS). Tel: 0141-552 6891. Built during the 13th–15th-centuries over the supposed site of the tomb of St Ketigern

GLENBUCHAT CASTLE (HS), Glenbuchat, Strathdon. Tel: 01466-793191. Ruins of tower house built 1590 by John Gordon and Helen Carnegie. Owned by Gordons until 1738

GLENFINNAN MONUMENT (NTS), Glenfinnan, Highland. Tel: 01397-722250. Monument erected by Alexander Macdonald of Glenaladale in 1815 in tribute to the clansmen who fought and died in the cause of Prince Charles Edward Stuart

GLENLUCE ABBEY (HS), Glenluce, Dumfries and Galloway. Tel: 01581-300541. Ruins of Cistercian abbey of the Blessed Virgin Mary, dating from 1192

GREENKNOWE TOWER (HS), Gordon. Tel: 0131-668 8800. Built 1581 by James Seton of Touch and Janet Edmonstone. Owned late 17th-century by Walter Pringle of Stichel, writer and Covenanter

HADDO HOUSE (NTS), nr Tarves, Ellon, Aberdeenshire.
Tel: 01651-851440. Georgian mansion house,
home to Earls of Gordon and Marquesses of
Aberdeen

HAILES CASTLE (HS), East Linton. Oldest parts date from
13th-century. Built by the Dunbars, Earls of the
March. Destroyed in 1650 by Cromwell's troops

HERMITAGE CASTLE (HS), nr Newcastleton,
Roxburghshire. Tel: 01387-376222.
A vast ruin dating to the 14th- and
15th-centuries associated with the de Soulis, the
Douglases and Mary, Queen of Scots

THE HILL HOUSE (NTS), Helensburgh.
Tel: 01436-673900. Designed by Charles Rennie
Mackintosh

HILL OF TARVIT MANSIONHOUSE (NTS), nr Cupar,
Fife. Tel: 01334-653127. Rebuilt in 1906, with
collection of paintings, furniture and Chinese
porcelain. Former home of geographer and
cartographer Sir John Scott

HOLMWOOD HOUSE (NTS), Glasgow.
Tel: 0141-637 2129. House designed by Alexander
'Greek' Thomson

HOLYROODHOUSE AND HOLYROOD ABBEY (HS)
Edinburgh. Tel: 0131-556 1096. Official residence
of monarch of Scotland. Range of buildings
dating from 16th-century. Remodelled and
extended for Charles II 1671–8

HOPETOUN HOUSE, nr Edinburgh.
Tel: 0131-331 2451. House designed by Sir
William Bruce, enlarged by William Adam

HOUSE OF DUN (NTS), nr Montrose.
Tel: 01674-810264. Georgian house with walled
garden. Built in 1730 for David Erskine, Laird of
Dun

HOUSE OF THE BINNS (NTS), nr Edinburgh.
Tel: 01506-834255. Home of Dalyell family since
1612

HUNTINGTOWER CASTLE (HS), nr Perth.
Tel: 01738-627231. Castle with painted ceilings.
James VI held captive here

HUNTLY CASTLE (HS). Tel: 01466-793191. Ruin of a
16th- and 17th-century house. Centre of the
Gordon family. Sheltered Robert the Bruce

INCHCOLM ABBEY (HS), Firth of Forth.
Tel: 01383-823332. One of the best preserved
group of monastic buildings in Scotland, founded
in 1123

INCHMAHOME PRIORY (HS), nr Aberfoyle.
Tel: 01877-385294. A 13th-century Augustinian
priory on an island in the Lake of Menteith.
Mary, Queen of Scots, as a 5-year-old, was
hidden here before being taken to France

INNERPEFFRAY CHAPEL AND LIBRARY (HS), nr Crieff.
Chapel founded by Lord Drummond 1508,
although site of a church since 1342. Adjoining
building houses the oldest library in Scotland,
founded 1691

INVERARAY CASTLE, Argyll. Tel: 01499-302203.
Gothic-style 18th-century castle; seat of the
Dukes of Argyll

INVERNESS CASTLE, Inverness. A 19th-century red-
sandstone edifice on site of earlier castles.
Currently houses the Sheriff Court

IONA ABBEY, Inner Hebrides. Tel: 01828-640411.
Monastery founded by St Columba in AD 563

ITALIAN CHAPEL, Lamb Holm, Orkney.
Tel: 01856-781268. Two Nissan huts painted in
the style of an Italian chapel

JEDBURGH ABBEY (HS), Scottish Borders.
Tel: 01835-863925. Romanesque and early Gothic
church founded c.1138

KELBURN CASTLE, Fairlie, Largs. Tel: 01475-568685.
Tower house built 1581. Home of the Boyle
family, the Earls of Glasgow from 1703

KELLIE CASTLE (NTS), nr Pittenweem, Anstruther.
Tel: 01333-720271. Restored 14th-century castle

KELSO ABBEY (HS), Scottish Borders. Remains of
great abbey church founded 1128

KILCHURN CASTLE (HS), nr Dalmally. Ruins of
15th-century castle on a rocky spit. Campbell
stronghold

KILDALTON CROSS (HS), nr Port Ellen, Islay. Ruined
12th- or 13th-century chapel dedicated to
St John the Beloved. Grounds have the finest
surviving intact High Cross in Scotland, dating
from 8th-century

KILDRUMMY CASTLE (HS), nr Alford, Aberdeenshire.
Tel: 01975-571331. A 13th-century castle, from
where the 1715 Jacobite Rising was organised

KILRAVOCK CASTLE, nr Nairn. Tel: 01667-493258.
Stately home dating from 15th-century. Bonnie
Prince Charlie was entertained here on eve of
Culloden, 1745

KINGS COLLEGE CHAPEL, Aberdeen. College
building completed 1495 in honour of James IV

KINLOCH CASTLE, Rum. Built 1900 as a base for a
few weeks each autumn for Sir George Bullough
who brought the island as a sporting estate 1888

KINNAIRD HEAD CASTLE LIGHTHOUSE AND
MUSEUM (HS), Fraserburgh, Aberdeenshire.
Tel: 01346-511022. Northern Lighthouse
Company's first lighthouse, still in working order

KISIMUL CASTLE (HS), Castlebay, Barra.
Tel: 01871-810313. Islet fortress of the MacNeil
clan. Original castle dates from 1120

LAURISTON CASTLE, Edinburgh. Tel: 0131-336 1921.
A 1590s tower house set in 30 acres of parkland

LEIGHTON LIBRARY, Dunblane. Oldest private library in Scotland, housing 4,500 books in 90 languages, printed 1500 to 1840

LEITH HALL (NTS), nr Kennethmont, Huntly. Tel: 01464-831216. Mansion house with semicircular stables, in 286-acre estate. Home of the Leith family since 1650

LENNOXLOVE HOUSE, Haddington. Tel: 01620-823720. Art collection belonging to Duke of Hamilton

LINCLUDEN COLLEGIATE CHURCH (HS), Dumfries. Nunnery founded here by Uchtred, son of Fergus, Lord of Galloway. Present ruins date from 15th-century

LINLITHGOW PALACE (HS). Tel: 01506-842896. Ruin of royal palace in park setting. Birthplace of Mary, Queen of Scots

LOCH DOON CASTLE (HS), Craigmalloch, Loch Doon. Ruins of 13th-century castle built by Earls of Carrick

LOCHLEVEN CASTLE (HS), on an island in Loch Leven. Tel: 07778-040483. Scene of Mary, Queen of Scots' imprisonment

LOCHMABEN CASTLE (HS), Castle Mains, Lochmaben. Extensive ruins. Built in the 14th-century but extensively rebuilt during the reign of James IV.

LOCHRANZA CASTLE, Isle of Arran. Acquired by the Montgomeries in 1452, lost to the Hamiltons 1705

MACLELLAN'S CASTLE (HS), Kirkcudbright, Galloway. Tel: 01557-331856. Built 1577 for Sir Thoam Maclellan of Bombie

MANDERSTON HOUSE, nr Duns, Berwickshire. Tel: 01361-883450. Edwardian country house of Miller family

MAXWELTON HOUSE, nr Moniaive, Dumfriesshire. Tel: 01848-200385. A 17th-century tower house. Home of the Laurie family

MELLERSTAIN HOUSE, nr Earlston, Borders. Tel: 01573-410225. Work of William and Robert Adam dating from 1725. Formal Edwardian gardens

MELROSE ABBEY (HS), Scottish Borders. Tel: 01896-822562. Ruin of Cistercian abbey founded c.1136. Founded by David I

MENSTRIE CASTLE, Menstrie. Tel: 01259-213131. Restored 16th-century mansion, birthplace of Sir William Alexander, first Earl of Stirling

MILLER'S BIRTHPLACE (NTS), Cromarty. Birthplace of author, geologist and folklorist Hugh Miller (1802-56)

MORTON CASTLE (HS), Morton Mains, Carronbridge. Ruins of late 13th-century castle at foot of Lowther Hills. Principal seat of the Douglas Earls of Morton

MOUNT STUART HOUSE, Isle of Bute. Tel: 01700-503877. Spectacular Victorian Gothic house with stained glass and marble.

MUNESS CASTLE (HS), Unst, Shetland. Tel: 01466-793191. Ruins of 16th-century tower house built by Lawrence Bruce of Cultmolindie, Chamberlain of the Lordship of Shetland

NEIDPATH CASTLE, nr Peebles. Tel: 01721-720333. Wall hangings depicting life of Mary, Queen of Scots

NEW ABBEY CORN MILL (HS), nr Dumfries. Tel: 01387-850260. Water-powered mill

NEW LANARK, nr Lanark. Tel: 01555-661345. Industrial village built in 1785 by David Dale for the manufacture of cotton; became famous under enlightened management (1800-25) of Robert Owen

NEWARK CASTLE (HS), Port Glasgow, Renfrewshire. Tel: 01475-741858. Virtually intact 15th-century castle

NOLTLAND CASTLE (HS), Westray, Orkney. Tel: 01856-841815. Ruined 16th-century tower house. Built by Gilbert Balfour, Master of the Household of Mary, Queen of Scots

ORCHARDTON TOWER (HS), Old Orchardton, Palnackie. Only cylindrical tower house in Scotland. Built for John Carnys around 1456

ORPHIR CHURCH, nr Kirkwall, Orkney. Ruined remains of only surviving round church in Scotland, dating from 12th-century

PAISLEY ABBEY, Paisley. Tel: 0141-889 7654. Built on site of town's original settlement, 1163 by Walter, son of Alan, Steward of Scotland. Became an abbey in 1219

PALACE OF HOLYROODHOUSE, Edinburgh. Tel: 0131-556 7371. The Queen's official Scottish residence. Main part of the palace built 1671–9

PARLIAMENT HOUSE, Edinburgh. Stronghold of the independent Scots Parliament 1639 until Treaty of Union 1707

PAXTON HOUSE, near Berwick upon Tweed, Borders. Tel: 01289-386291. A Palladian country house built in 1758

PITMEDDEN GREAT GARDEN (NTS), Pitmedden, Aberdeenshire. Tel: 01651-842352. Formal 17th-century garden

PITTENCRIEFF HOUSE, Dunfermline. Estate house, 1610. Exhibits of local history. A 76-acre park

PLUSCARDEN ABBEY, nr Elgin. Founded by Alexander II in 1230. One of only two abbeys in Scotland with permanent community of monks

POLLOK HOUSE (NTS), Glasgow. Tel: 0141-616 6410. Eighteenth-century house with collection of paintings, porcelain and furnishings, set in Pollok Country Park

PRESTON TOWER, Prestonpans. Tel: 0131-226 5922. A 15th-century tower house, enlarged in 17th-century. Residence of the Hamiltons of Preston. Burned by Cromwell in 1650

PROVOST SKENE'S HOUSE, Aberdeen. Tel: 01224-641086. A 16th-century house with period room settings. Aberdeen's oldest surviving private house, dating from 1545

QUEEN MARY'S HOUSE, Jedburgh. Tel: 01835-863331. Altered 16th-century tower house. Belonged to Scotts of Ancrum. Mary, Queen of Scots lay very ill here for many days in 1566

RAVENSCRAIG CASTLE (HS), Kirkcaldy. Ruins of 15th-century castle and courtyard. Nearby steps were the inspiration for John Buchan's novel 'The 39 Steps'

RESTENNETH PRIORY, nr Forfar. Site of 8th-century priory built by King Nechtan of the Picts; adapted as Augustinian priory in 12th-century. Remains 12th–15th-centuries

ROTHESAY CASTLE (HS), Isle of Bute. Tel: 01700-502691. A 13th-century circular castle. A favourite residence of the Stewart kings

RUTHVEN BARRACKS (HS), Kingussie. Tel: 01667-460232. Garrison built after the 1715 rebellion, taken by Jacobites 1744. Captured and burnt by Prince Charles Edward Stuart's army in 1746

SCALLOWAY CASTLE (HS), Scalloway, Shetland. Tel: 01466-793191. Ruins of 17th-century tower house built by Patrick Stewart, Earl of Orkney, 1600

SCONE PALACE, Perth. Tel: 01738-552300. House built 1802–13 on the site of a medieval palace. Once the site of the Stone of Destiny

SCOTSTARVIT TOWER (NTS), Craigrothie, Cupar. Tel: 01334-653127. Erected between 1550 and 1579 for the Inglis family

SCOTT MONUMENT, Edinburgh. Tel: 0131-529 4068. Monument affording fine views of the city

SETON COLLEGIATE CHURCH (HS), nr Tranent, East Lothian. Tel: 01875-813334. Founded 1492 by the 4th Lord Seton. Monuments survive within church

SKIPNESS CASTLE, (HS) Tarbert, Argyll. Ruins of 13th-century castle and chapel overlooking Kilbrannon Sound, probably built by the Macdonald Lord of the Isles

SMAILHOLM TOWER (HS), Scottish Borders. Tel: 01573-460365. Well-preserved tower-house

SPYNIE PALACE (HS), Elgin, Moray. Tel: 01343-546358. Residence of Bishops of Moray from 14th- to 17th-centuries

ST GILES CATHEDRAL, Edinburgh. Church on site since 854, existing building dates from 15th-century following sacking by the English in 1385

ST ANDREWS CASTLE (HS), Fife. Tel: 01334-477196 (castle). Ruins of 13th-century castle and remains of the largest cathedral in Scotland

ST BLANE'S CHURCH (HS), Kingarth, Bute. Site of Celtic community of 6th-century. In centre of site is a 12th-century chapel

ST CLEMENT'S CHURCH (HS), Rodel, Harris. A 16th-century cruciform-plan church. Built by Alasdair Crotach MacLeod

ST JOHN'S KIRK, Perth. Founded by David I, 1126. Present building dates from 15th-century. John Knox preached here

ST MACHAR'S CATHEDRAL (HS), Aberdeen. Tel: 01466-793191. Medieval cathedral of Bishops of Aberdeen. Reputedly founded in 580 by Machar, follower of Columba

ST MAGNUS CATHEDRAL, Kirkwall, Orkney. Founded 1137 by Orkney Earl Rognvald. Dedicated to St Magnus the Martyr. Completed 1500 and one of finest in Scotland

ST NINIAN'S CHAPEL (HS), Isle of Whithorn, Galloway. Ruins of 13th-century chapel on site associated with St Ninian

STIRLING CASTLE AND ARGYLL'S LODGING (HS). Tel: 01786-450000. A 17th-century town house, seat of the Campbell Earls of Argyll

STRANRAER CASTLE, Stranraer. Tel: 01776-705088. Also Known as Castle of St John. Built c.1511. Exhibitions trace history of castle

STROME CASTLE (NTS), Stromemore, Lochcarron. Tel: 01599-566325. Ruins of 15th-century castle built for Alan Macdonald Dubh, 12th chief of the Camerons. Destroyed 1602 by Colin McKenzie of Kintail

SWEETHEART ABBEY (HS), New Abbey Village, Dumfries. Tel: 01387-850397. Remains of 13th-century abbey; burial site of John Balliol's heart

TANTALLON CASTLE (HS), East Lothian. Tel: 01620-892727. Fortification with earthwork defences and a 14th-century curtain wall with towers

THIRLSTANE CASTLE, Lauder, Berwickshire. Tel: 01578-722430. One of finest castles in Scotland owned by Maitland family since 16th-century

THREAVE CASTLE (HS), Dumfries and Galloway. Tel: 07711-223191. Late 14th-century tower on an island; reached by boat, long walk to castle

TOLQUHON CASTLE (HS), nr Aberdeen. Tel: 01651-851286. Mansion house with 15th-century tower

TOROSAY CASTLE, Craignure, Mull. Tel: 01680-812421. Castellated mansion of 1858 built for the Campbells of Possel. 18th-century Venetian statues and Japanese garden

TRAQUAIR HOUSE, Innerleithen, Peeblesshire.
Tel: 01896-830323. Scotland's oldest inhabited
house. Bonnie Prince Charlie stayed here in
1745. Working 18th-century brewery. Gardens
and maze

TULLIBARDINE CHAPEL (HS), nr Crieff. Medieval
church founded 1446, rebuilt 1500. One of most
complete small collegiate churches in Scotland

URQUHART CASTLE (HS), Loch Ness. Tel: 01456-
450551. Ruins of a castle built as a base to guard
the Great Glen. Taken by Edward I of England

WALLACE MONUMENT, Stirling. Tel: 01786-472140.
Exhibitions about Sir William Wallace and others,
and a diorama showing the view from the top of
the monument

WHITHORN PRIORY (HS), nr Newton Stewart,
Dumfries and Galloway. Tel: 01988-500508. Site of
first Christian church in Scotland, dedicated to St
Ninian in 5th-century. Popular place of
pilgrimage in medieval times

ARCHAEOLOGICAL SITES AND MONUMENTS

Many visible traces remain throughout Scotland of prehistoric and early historic (to end of first millennium AD) settlement. Mesolithic sites well over 6,000 years old have been found in many parts of Scotland, generally in coastal areas and along rivers. Stone, Bronze and Iron Age settlements and the Pictish period of the early Christian era are extensively represented. Archaeological sites can be found and visited in all parts of Scotland, but the north and west and the islands are particularly rich in them, partly because the stone that was used in construction there is more durable than the wood and turf commonly used for building in the south of Scotland, and partly also because the disturbance due to modern agriculture has been less intensive in the Highlands and Islands. However, the north-east also has a good number of ancient sites.

THE NEOLITHIC PERIOD

The Neolithic period, c. 4000–2000 BC, was characterised by communal monuments serving both the living and the dead, such as stone circles, henges and domestic settlements as well as chambered cairns and other massive communal burial places. Among the best-preserved chambered cairns are the 'Tomb of the Eagles' at Isbister, South Ronaldsay, and Maes Howe on Mainland, both in Orkney. Neolithic communities include Skara Brae on Orkney and the first layers of the large Jarlshof site in Shetland. The Neolithic period also produced many of the best-known standing stones and stone circles, which had ritual and perhaps astronomical functions. Examples are the standing stone circle at Callanish (Calanais) on Lewis, the Twelve Apostles in Dumfries, Scotland's largest stone circle, and the Ring of Brodgar (Brogar) on Orkney. However, standing stones continued to be erected right through to the early Middle Ages, and can be found throughout Scotland, often in spectacular settings.

THE BRONZE AGE

During the Bronze Age, c.2000–700 BC, burial took place in individual cairns and tombs, sometimes arranged in 'cemeteries' and sometimes located within existing stone monuments, as at Cairnpapple, West Lothian. Although they are not as numerous as Iron Age settlements, traces of Bronze Age domestic settlements exist, for instance, on the island of Whalsay, Shetland, and at Lairg, Sutherland.

Towards the end of the Bronze Age the building of enclosed and fortified settlements increased.

Some of the largest hillforts in the south of Scotland show evidence of having been built in the later Bronze Age (e.g. Traprain Law, East Lothian, and Eildon Hill, Borders), and they appear to have continued in occupation for many centuries, as the important hoard of Roman silver found at Traprain Law suggests.

THE IRON AGE

The different forms of Iron Age dwelling vary widely with time and place, and include several different kinds of roundhouse of timber or stone, massive hilltop forts or enclosures sheltering a number of small roundhouses, drystone broch towers and broch villages, and crannogs – artificial islet dwellings built in lochs and joined to the shore by defended causeways. The wide regional variations are partly – but not entirely – accounted for by the geography of the country, which posed different defensive problems in different places: small dispersed settlements grew up in the broken landscapes of the north and west, where arable land was interrupted and access made difficult by deep sea-lochs and high, steep mountains, while large hillforts were more characteristic of the more open, rolling country of the east and the lowlands with its broad, flat upland summits.

Probably the best known of these structures, being the best preserved, are the brochs. These are concentrated particularly in the north and west and in Orkney and Shetland, although a group of lowland brochs was built in Angus, Perthshire and the Borders, most probably in the first century AD. Stone hut circles and roundhouses predominate in the north and east; traces of similar timber buildings are found in the lowlands; crannogs belong particularly to the Highlands and the south-west (and to Ireland). A group of Iron Age wheelhouses comprises one of the many layers of settlement at Jarlshof in Shetland.

THE ROMANS AND AFTER

While traces of the first Roman invasion of Scotland under Agricola (AD 81–83) can be seen in the remains of a string of forts thrown up to block the Forth-Clyde isthmus, and later forts, signal stations and roads built to consolidate the Roman gains, the most visible sign of the troubled Roman presence in what is now Scotland is the Antonine Wall.

From the seventh to ninth centuries – the so-called Dark Ages – symbol stones and cross-slabs were erected by the Picts, who by the seventh century had mostly been converted to Christianity. These stones occur throughout Scotland, with concentrations in the Pictish territory along the east coast and the Moray Firth and in the far north.

While there are some Pictish stones in the West Highlands, the great carved crosses characteristic of the area ruled by the Lords of the Isles until the end of the 15th-century illustrate a later artistic tradition dating from the middle ages and centred upon Iona.

The Pictish symbol stones from the seventh and early eighth centuries, usually carved only on one face and most often with the figures of animals, are probably gravestones. Examples are at Aberlemno, Forfar (Angus), Papil (Shetland), and a collection of most of the Pictish stones found in Sutherland is now in the grounds of Dunrobin Castle Museum, near Golspie.

A slightly later introduction in the eighth and ninth centuries was the more intricately carved and more obviously Christian cross-slab, in which ornamented crosses on one face are often combined with Pictish symbols on the other. The decoration of these slabs shows the influence of the Dalriadic (originally Irish) style that also produced The Book of Kells on Iona. Some of them may have served as landmarks where people might gather for worship or private prayer, or as the focus of religious processions. A battle scene on one of the stones at Aberlemno may depict the victory of the Picts over the Northumbrians at Nechtansmere (685). Other excellent examples are at Shandwick, Rosemarkie and Nigg (Ross and Cromarty); but many of the slabs are no longer in their original positions and have been re-erected (or even incorporated) inside churches and other buildings.

ABERLEMNO SCULPTURED STONES (HS), nr Forfar, Angus. Cross-slab with Pictish symbols and four other sculptured Pictish stones

ACHAVANICH STONE SETTING, nr Latheron, Caithness. Thirty-six small standing stones arranged in shape of a horseshoe. Nearby cairn dates to Neolithic period

ACHNABRECK CUP AND RING MARKS (HS), nr Lochgilphead, Kilmartin Glen, Argyll. Among the most impressive and largest ring marks in Scotland, dating over a long period of time

AIKY BRAE RECUMBENT STONE CIRCLE, Old Deer, Aberdeenshire. Hilltop circle dating from third or second millennium BC

ANTONINE WALL (HS), between the Clyde and the Forth. Adm. free. Built c. AD 142, consists of ditch, turf rampart and road, with forts every two miles

ARBORY HILL FORT, Abington, Lanarkshire. Stone fort with earlier ditches and ramparts. Includes hut circles

ARDESTIE, CARLUNGIE AND TEALING SOUTERRAINS (HS), nr Monifieth, Angus. Iron age food cellars, the first two 80 feet and 150 feet in length respectively. Probably in use between AD 150 and AD 450. Nearby stone huts. Sites approximately 1 mile apart

AUCHAGALLON CAIRN (HS), nr Blackwaterfoot, Arran. Stone cairn surrounded by stone circle

BALFARG HENGE, nr Glenrothes, Fife. Timber circle built around 3000 BC. Stone circle – only two stones remain. Possible ritual site in fourth millennium BC

BALLINABY STANDING STONES, nr Bruichladdich, Islay. Originally three standing stones of second millennium BC, two remain. The tallest at 5 metres is one of the tallest standing stones in western Scotland

BALLOCHMYLE CUP AND RING MARKS, nr Mauchline, Ayrshire. As well as cup and rings, motifs include geometric shapes. Discovered 1986. One of the largest in Britain

BALLYMEANOCH STANDING STONES, nr Kilmartin, Kilmartin Glen, Argyll. Four stones lying parallel to two others. Nearby fallen stone has a hole through it. Possibly used to seal marriage vows, hands would be joined through the hole in the stone

BARNHOUSE SETTLEMENT, nr Stromness, Orkney. Reconstructed foundations of a Neolithic village. With fifteen houses, similar to those found at Skara Brae

BARPA LANGASS CHAMBERED CAIRN, nr Lochmaddy, North Uist. Chambered burial cairn, 25 metres in diameter and 4 metres in height. Chamber has collapsed and is too dangerous to enter but can be viewed from outside

BEN FREICEADAIN, nr Dorrery, Caithness. Extensive fort of first millennium BC, known as Buaile Oscar. Occupies the summit of the hill. Within the fort is the remains of a Neolithic chambered cairn. Close-by are Neolithic and Bronze Age cairns

BENIE HOOSE, Whalsay, Shetland. Bronze Age house, over 1,800 tools discovered here. Nearby chambered tomb

BLACKHAMMER CHAMBERED CAIRN (HS), Rousay, Orkney. Chambered tomb with seven burial compartments

BROUGH OF BIRSAY (HS), Mainland, Orkney. Pictish settlement on a small tidal island. Remains of Norse church and village

BURGHEAD FORT AND WELL (HS), Burghead, Moray. Promontory fort dating from first millennium AD, one of the main centres of Pictish power

BURGI GEOS (HS), Yell, Shetland. Iron Age Fort and field system

CAIRN OF GET (HS), nr Ulbster, Caithness. Chambered cairn dating from fourth or third millennium BC. Excavations in 1866 revealed bones of at least seven people along with animal bone, flint and pottery fragments. Nearby cairn maybe a Bronze Age cairn or a Pictish grave of first millennium AD

CAIRNHOLY CHAMBERED CAIRNS (HS), nr Creetown, Dumfries and Galloway. Remains of two chambered cairns overlooking Wigtown Bay. Traces of fires and pottery suggest possible sites for ceremonies connected with burials

CAIRNBAAN CUP AND RING MARKS (HS), nr Lochgilphead, Argyll. Two rock outcrops carved with cups and rings

CAIRNPAPPLE HILL (HS), nr Bathgate, West Lothian. Tel: 01506-634622. Closed Oct.-Mar. Burial site dating from 3000 BC to 1400 BC. Three standing stones in centre surrounded by a henge. Used for burials and held sacred into the Iron Age

CAISTEAL GRUGAIG BROCH, Totaig, Inverness-shire. Late first-millennium broch on hillside overlooking the junction of Loch Alsh, Loch Duich and Loch Long

CALANAIS (CALLANISH) STANDING STONES (HS). Callanish, Lewis. Tel: 01851-621422. Visitor centred closed Sundays. Slabs of gneiss up to 4.7 metres in height, arranged in a the shape of a Celtic Cross. Transported here between 3000 BC and 1500 BC. Many stones aligned with the sun and stars; possible lunar observatory

CAPO LONG BARROW, nr Brechin, Kincardine and Deeside. Situated in clearing in Inglismaldie Forest. Neolithic earthen long mound measuring 80 metres in length and 28 metres in width. Probable burials and mortuary structures

CARN LIATH (HS), nr Golspie, Sutherland. Iron Age broch. Excavations in late 19th-century uncovered beads, rings and bangles

CASTLE HAVEN, nr Borgue, Dumfries and Galloway. Galleried dun. Restored early 20th-century

CASTLELAW HILL FORT (HS), nr Glencorse, Midlothian. Iron Age fort in Pentland Hills. Includes fenced enclosure dating to first millennium BC and 20-metre long souterrain dug into silted-up ditch of fort, probably of Roman origin

CATERTHUNS FORTS (HS), nr Menmuir, Angus. Iron Age fort and settlements sat on top of neighbouring hills, Brown Caterthun and White Caterthun. Excavations suggest dates 700 BC to 300 BC for stoneworks

CATPUND QUARRIES, nr Cunningsburgh, Shetland. In Norse times, the biggest soapstone quarry in the world

CHESTERS HILL FORT (HS), nr Drem, East Lothian. Oval Iron Age fort. Within hill fort are at least 20 hut circles

CLACH A' CHARRIDH, nr Shandwick, Ross and Cromarty. Late 8th- or early 9th-century cross-slab and one of the most impressive of all Pictish monuments standing in original position on hill overlooking Shandwick. Covered by glass for protection

CLACH AN TRUSHAL STANDING STONE, nr Barvas, Lewis. At over 6 metres in height, is one of the tallest in Scotland

CLAVA CAIRNS (NTS), nr Inverness, Highlands. Also known as Balnuaran of Clava. Burial chambers clustered on bank of River Nairn, near site of Culloden. Erected some time around 2000 BC and encircled by standing stones. Cremated remains have been found

CLEAVEN DYKE, nr Blairgowrie, Perthshire. Long bank over 2 km in length and flanked by ditches. Probably the route along which communal ritual of funerary ceremonies would have passed

CLICKHIMIN BROCH (HS), nr Lerwick, Shetland. Broch tower and Iron Age outbuildings on what was once a small island in Clickhimin Loch. Settlement began around 700 BC

CNOC FREICEADAIN CHAMBERED CAIRNS (HS), nr Thurso, Caithness. Two long cairns now covered in grass. One which measures 78 metres in length, is one of the largest in Scotland

CORRIMONY CHAMBERED CAIRN (HS), nr Drumnadrochit, Glen Urquhart, Highlands. Circular cairn similar to the Clava Cairns near Inverness dating to third millennium BC. Excavations have found that the chamber contained a crouched body

CRAIG PHADRIG FORT, nr Inverness. Dates from millennium BC with additions. Occupies summit of wooded hill owned by Forestry Commission

CULLERLIE STONE CIRCLE (HS), nr Westhill, Aberdeenshire. Circle of eight boulders surrounding eight cairns dating to second millennium BC. Excavations revealed circular pit containing cremated human bone

CULSH SOUTERRAIN (HS), nr Tarland, Aberdeenshire. Iron age underground passage and food-cellar, 12 metres long and 2 metres wide and high

CUWEEN HILL CHAMBERED CAIRN (HS), nr Finstown, Orkney. Chambered tomb which contained the skulls of 24 dogs and the skeletal remains of eight humans

DREVA CRAIG FORT, nr Biggar, Borders. Fort, hut circles and field systems dating to the late Iron Age. Round houses inside the fort

DUN-DA-LAMH FORT, nr Laggan, Inverness-shire.
Dating to first millennium AD, built on ridge
known as the Black Craig

DUN ARDTRECK, nr Corbost, Ardtreck Point, Skye.
Dun or fort. Ruins lie on stack of rock 20 metres
above the shore. Walls up to 3 metres thick with
traces of a gallery

DUN BEAG BROCH (HS), nr Dunvegan, Struanmore,
Skye. One of the best preserved brochs on Skye.
Excavations have found a variety of artefacts
including pottery, beads, rings, numerous tools
and bone and horn objects

DUN BHARPA CHAMBERED CAIRN, nr Castlebay,
Barra. Impressive chambered cairn measuring
25 metres in diameter and 5 metres in height. No
longer possible to enter cairn

DUN CHARLABHAIG (CARLOWAY) BROCH (HS),
Carloway, Lewis. One of the best preserved brochs
on Scotland's Atlantic coast. Measures up to 9
metres at its tallest point. Nearby Doune Broch
Centre

DUN DORNAIGIL BROCH (HS), nr south end of Loch
Hope, Caithness. Also known as Dun Dornadilla.
One section almost 7 metres high. Interior full of
rubble. Broch tower which may have housed
local nobility

DUN FIADHAIRT BROCH, nr Dunvegan, Skye. Also
known as Dun of Iardhard. On shores of
Camalig Bay. Excavated in 1914. Objects found
include pottery, an amber necklace and a
terracotta model of a bale of goods of Roman
origin

DUN GERASHADER FORT, Portree, Skye. A once-
powerful fort with walls 4 metres thick. Most of
the dun has gone to make dry walls on nearby
farms, but traces of walls still recognisable

DUN LAGAIDH, Loch Broom, Ross and Cromarty.
Three successive fortifications built on a ridge on
western shore of Loch Broom. Vitrified fort dates
to first millennium BC, the dun to the early
centuries AD; also medieval castle, probably built
12th-century AD

DUN MOR BROCH, Vaul, nr Scarinish, Tiree.
Constructed first century BC, continued in use
until the Norse period. Broch survives up to
2 metres in height

DUN RINGILL, Kilmarie, Skye. Galleried dun.
Foundations of two medieval buildings inside the
dun

DUN TELVE BROCH (HS), nr Glenelg, Lochalsh. One of
the best preserved Iron Age broch towers in
Scotland, although much of the wall is missing.
Built around 2000 years ago to protect
surrounding settlements from raiders. Excavations
have found pottery and stone cups which may
have been used as lamps

DUN TRODDAN BROCH (HS), nr Glenelg, Lochalsh.
Lies less than 1 mile from Dun Telve. A section of
the wall and staircase survive. Together the two
are also known as Glenelg Broch

DUN AN STICAR BROCH, nr Lochmaddy, North Uist.
One of best preserved brochs in the Western
Isles, surviving to a height of 3 metres. Medieval
rectangular house inside dun. Nearby causeway is
also medieval in date. Can only be viewed from
the outside

DUNFALLANDY STONE (HS), nr Pitlochry, Perthshire.
Pictish sculptured cross-slab, dating from
9th-century

DWARFIE STANE ROCK (HS), Hoy, Orkney.
Chambered tomb cut from a solid block of
sandstone, dating to 3000 BC. Named
'Dvergasteinn' by the Norse settlers who believed
it to be the home of dwarfs

EASTER AQUORTHIES STONE CIRCLE (HS), nr
Inverurie, Aberdeenshire. Dating from third
millennium BC. Circle measures almost 20 metres
in diameter. Raised in centre, indicative of a
burial cairn. Different stone types include pink
porphyry, red and grey granite and red jasper

EDIN'S HALL BROCH (HS), nr Preston, Borders. Oval
Iron Age fort with ditches and a broch built in a
corner of the fort. Internal diameter of 17 metres
and walls 5 metres thick

EILDON HILL FORT, nr Melrose, Borders. Summit of
Eildon Hill North. Occupied since Bronze Age.
Included some 300 houses dating to Bronze and
Iron Ages. Also traces of a Roman signal station

EILEACH AN NAOIMH (HS), island in Garvellach group,
north of Jura. Ruins of beehive cells from an early
Christian community. Small underground cell.
Supposedly traditional burial place of Eithne,
Columba's mother

EMBO CHAMBERED CAIRN, Embo, Sutherland.
Dating to between fourth and second millennium
BC. Remains of stone cairn containing two
Neolithic burial chambers and also Bronze Age
graves

FINAVON FORT, nr Forfar, Angus. Pictish or Roman
fort on the ridge of Finavon Hill. Destroyed by
fire and vitrified by the heat

GLASSEL STONE SETTING, nr Banchory,
Aberdeenshire. Oval setting of five granite pillars
dating to second millennium BC

GRAIN SOUTERRAIN (HS), Kirkwall, Orkney. Now in
centre of an industrial site. Iron Age food cellar
almost 2 metres below the ground dating to the
first millennium BC. Excavations have found a
hearth, animal bones and shells

GREY CAIRNS OF CAMSTER (HS), nr Lybster, Caithness. Burial chambers built 4000–5000 years ago. Includes a massive round cairn 18 metres in diameter and a long cairn 70 metres in length covered with two separate round cairns

GURNESS BROCH (HS), nr Evie, Orkney. Best preserved broch in the area, surrounded by a complex of later buildings. Some houses date to late Iron Age. Iron Age house has been reconstructed next to the visitors' centre

HIGH BANKS CUP AND RING MARKS, nr Kirkcudbright, Dumfries and Galloway. Over 350 cup and ring marks, some of the most impressive of south-west Scotland

HILL O' MANY STANES (HS), nr Lybster, Caithness. Also known as the Mid Clyth stone rows. Consists of 200 boulders forming 22 parallel rows down the side of the hill. Purpose unknown but possibly an astronomical observatory

HOLM OF PAPA WESTRAY CHAMBERED CAIRNS (HS), Island and Holm of Papa Westray, Orkney. Two chambered tombs, one at either end of the island, the one to the north being part of an earlier tomb

HOLYROOD PARK SETTLEMENTS (HS), Edinburgh. Natural wilderness in heart of Edinburgh containing four forts and several settlements dating from late Bronze Age and Iron Age. Forts on Arthur's Seat, above Samson's Rib and beside Dunsapie Loch. Hut circles near Hunter's Bog

IBISTER CHAMBERED CAIRN, nr St Margaret's Hope, South Ronaldsay, Orkney. Tel: 01856-831339. Also known as 'Tomb of the Eagles', as bones and talons from white-tailed sea eagles were uncovered here. Ancient chambered burial cairn. Remains of 340 people recovered during excavations in 1970s

JARLSHOF SETTLEMENT (HS), Sumburgh Head, Shetland. Tel: 01950-460112. Largest and most impressive archaeological site in Scotland. Covers three acres, with more than 4000 years of continuous occupation. Earliest buildings date to Neolithic period. Iron Age buildings include a broch, roundhouses and wheelhouses. Norse farmhouses. Latest building dates to the 17th-century laird's house

KEMP'S WALK FORT, nr Stranraer, Dumfries and Galloway. The largest of Galloway's promontory forts, overlooking Broadsea Bay and measuring 83 metres by 44 metres

KILDONAN DUN, nr Campbeltown, Kintyre. Drystone-walled dun dating to first or second century AD. Re-occupied 9th- 12th-centuries. Occupied into medieval times

KILPHEDIR BROCH AND HUT CIRCLES, Kilphedir, Sutherland. Broch and hut circles dating to the late Bronze Age. Pottery, stone and flint tools have been unearthed during excavations

KINTRAW CAIRNS AND STANDING STONE, nr Kilmartin, Argyll. Cairns excavated 1956–60 and unearthed cremated bone, shells and jet beads. Site possibly marks the sunset at mid-winter solstice as the sun set through notch in Paps of Jura

KNAP OF HOWE (HS), Papa Westray, Orkney. The island's prime prehistoric site dating from 3500 BC. Neolithic farm-building lays claims to be the oldest standing house in Europe. Bone and stone implements have been uncovered during excavations in the 1930s and 1970s

KNOCK FARRIL FORT, nr Dingwall, Ross and Cromarty. Date from late second or first millennium BC. Occupies summit of ridge overlooking Strath Peffer

KNOWE OF YARSAR, Rousay, Orkney. Chambered cairn dating to 3500 BC. Remains of 29 humans discovered here along with deer bones

LIDDLE BURNT MOUND, nr St Margaret's Hope, Orkney. Probably Bronze Age in date. One of very few to have been excavated. Consists of a central stone-built trough, surrounded by paving and a stone wall, possibly a windbreak. Served as a cooking area or sauna

LOANHEAD OF DAVIOT STONE CIRCLE (HS), nr Inverurie, Aberdeenshire. Dated to third or second millennia BC. Recumbent stone circle over 20 metres in diameter consisting of eight standing stones, the recumbent and flankers. Ring cairn later constructed within circle. Beside circle is a Bronze Age cremation cemetery. Excavations uncovered remains of 30 humans in urns and pits

LOCHBUIE STONE CIRCLE, Lochbuie, Mull. Circle containing nine stones, one replaced by a boulder, and three outliers. Possibly used for astronomical observations

LUNDIN LINKS STANDING STONES, Lundin Links golf course, Fife. Three standing stones remaining of a stone circle, the tallest 5 metres in height. According to legend the gravestones of three Danish warriors defeated by Macbeth

MACHRIE MOOR STONE CIRCLES (HS), nr Blackwaterfoot, Arran. The area of Machrie Moor contains hut circles, chambered cairns, round cairns and six Bronze Age stone circles, the most impressive has three sandstone pillars over 5 metres in height

MAES HOWE CHAMBERED CAIRN (HS), West Mainland, Orkney. Closed Thurs. afternoons, Fri. and Sun. mornings Nov.–Mar. Probably the most impressive Neolithic burial chamber in Europe dating from around 3000 BC. Original capping destroyed in 12th-century

MAIDEN STONE (HS), Chapel of Garioch, Aberdeenshire. One of the finest Pictish stones in Grampian dating from 9th-century

MEIGLE SCULPTURED STONES (HS), Meigle, Angus. Collection of 25 sculptured stones. Early Christian and Dark Age sculpture

MEMSIE ROUND CAIRN (HS), Rathen, Aberdeenshire. Dating to Bronze Age, great cairn of bare stones, 24 metres in diameter and over 4 metres in height. Only survivor of a cemetery of three large cairns on the low ridge of Cairn Muir

MIDHOWE BROCH (HS), Rousay, Orkney. Originally built as fortified family house. Continuously occupied until second century AD. A number of houses surround the broch

MIDHOWE CHAMBERED CAIRN (HS), Rousay, Orkney. 100 foot communal burial chamber dating to 3500 BC. Chamber divided into 12 compartments where remains of 25 people were found in a crouched position

MITHER TAP O BENNACHIE, nr Inverurie, Aberdeenshire. Granite tor, the summit of which is flanked by stone-walled hillfort dating to first millennium ad. Excavations in 1870s revealed ten hut foundations. Area north of Bennachie may be site of battle of Mons Graupius in AD 84

MOUSA BROCH (HS), Mousa, Shetland. The best preserved prehistoric broch in Scotland standing over 13 metres in height. Thought to be around 2000 years old. In the courtyard are remains of a wheelhouse, built around third century AD

MUTINY STONES LONG CAIRN, nr Longformacus, Borders. About 80 metres long and 20 metres wide, one of very few long cairns in the Borders

NA FIR BHREIGE, nr Lochmaddy, North Uist. Also known as the 'Three False Men'. Three standing stones which according to legend represent three spies buried alive or three men who deserted their wives and were turned to stone by a witch

NESS OF BURGI FORT (HS), nr Sumburgh, Shetland. Blockhouse positioned across the neck of the Scatness Peninsula. Access difficult and dangerous in bad weather

NETHER LARGIE CAIRNS (HS), Kilmartin, Kilmartin Glen, Argyll. Bronze Age and Neolithic cairns. Three cairns forming part of a large complex of stones and tombs in the Kilmartin Glen. Nether Largie South is a chambered cairn. Carved with cupmarks

NEW AND OLD KINORD SETTLEMENT, nr Ballater, Kincardine and Deeside. Probably dates from latter part of first millennium BC. Hut circles in an enclosure, the largest 19 metres in diameter. Settlement also contains a souterrain

ORD ARCHAEOLOGICAL TRAIL, The Ord, Lairg, Sutherland. Hill overlooking Loch Shin containing a number of structures dating from Neolithic to post-Medieval period. Two chambered cairns near summit. Hut circles date from 1500 BC

POBULL FHINN STONE CIRCLE, nr Lochmaddy, North Uist. Originally 48 stones of which 30 remain. Occupies amphitheatre cut into hillside

QUOYNESS CHAMBERED CAIRN (HS), nr Kettletoft, Sanday, Orkney. Megalithic tomb dating from around 2000 BC. Partially re-constructed. Human bones found during excavations in 1860s

RAEDYKES RING CAIRNS, nr Stonehaven, Aberdeenshire. Strung out along the crest of Campstone Hill, an important group of early ritual sites dating to the third or second millennium BC

RENNIBISTER SOUTERRAIN (HS), nr Kirkwall, Orkney. Iron Age semi-underground structure used to store grain and produce dating to first millennium BC. Excavations uncovered remains of 18 people – rare to fine human bones in an earth-house, so possibly converted to a burial vault

RING OF BRODGAR CIRCLE AND HENGE (HS), nr Stromness, Orkney. Neolithic circle and one of the largest stone circles in Scotland. Originally 60 stones of which just 36 remain. Only the ditch remains of the henge. Possibly part of a ritual complex which included Maes Howe and the Stones of Stenness

RUBH' AN DUNAIN CAIRN AND DUN, nr Glenbrittle, Skye. When cairn was excavated in 1930s pottery and flints artefacts were uncovered as well as bones of several people. Near the cairn are the remains of an Iron Age fort, one of best preserved galleried duns in Skye

SCATNESS BROCH AND SETTLEMENT, Sumburgh, Shetland. Excavations currently taking place west of the airport. Ancient broch and Iron Age village which may include Norse occupation. One of the buildings was reused by the Vikings as a smithy

ST VIGEANS SCULPTURED STONES (HS), nr Arbroath, Angus. Exhibition closed Oct.–Mar. Early Christian and Pictish stones housed in cottages

SCORD OF BROUSTER SETTLEMENT, nr Bridge of Walls, Shetland. Ruined houses and field boundaries occupied between 3000 and 1500 BC

SKARA BRAE SETTLEMENT (HS), nr Stromness, Orkney. One of the best preserved Stone Age settlements in Europe, dating back to 3000 BC. Excavated by V. G. Childe in 1920s. Reconstructed house next to visitor centre. Visitor centre displays stone and bone artefacts as well as pottery discovered during excavations

STANEYDALE SETTLEMENT (HS), nr Bridge of Walls, Shetland. Shattered Neolithic structure. Surrounding oval-shaped houses in ruins. Probably once an important community meeting-place

STONE OF SETTAR, Eday, Orkney. Orkney's most distinctive standing stone

STONES OF STENNESS AND HENGE (HS), nr Stromness, Orkney. Originally a circle of 12 rock slabs, just four remain. Dates back to the same time as the nearby Neolithic village, the Barnhouse Settlement

STRATHPEFFER SYMBOL STONE, Strathpeffer, Ross and Cromarty. Pictish symbol stone dating from 7th- or 8th-century AD. Often called The Eagle Stone

STRONTOILLER CAIRN AND STANDING STONES, nr Oban, Argyll. Standing stone stands 4 metres high. According to legend it is said to mark the grave of Diarmid, a mythical hero of Ireland. Excavations of the cairn have found cremated bone along with quartz chips and pebbles

SUENO'S STONE (HS), Forres, Moray. Probably the most remarkable sculptured stone in Scotland. Dating from 9th-century and over 22 feet in height. Protected by glass enclosure

SUNHONEY STONE CIRCLE, nr Banchory, Aberdeenshire. Consists of 11 standing stones of red granite and a recumbent stone of grey granite carved with cupmarks. Within the circle is a ring cairn

TAP O' NOTH FORT, nr Rhynie, Aberdeenshire. Timber-laced stone rampart, originally 8 metres thick, on top of a high hill. Up to 150 hut platforms within fort

TAVERSOE TUICK CHAMBERED CAIRN (HS), Rousay, Orkney. Two-storey chambered cairn dating to 3500 BC. Piles of bones found in lower chamber, cremated remains in upper chamber. Pottery bowls also recovered

TEMPLE WOOD STONE CIRCLES (HS), nr Kilmartin, Kilmartin Glen, Argyll. Stone circle 12 metres in diameter. One stone is decorated with two concentric circles and another with a double spiral. Excavations have revealed an earlier timber and stone circles

TINTO HILL CAIRN, nr Biggar, Lanarkshire. One of largest Bronze Age round cairns in Scotland, situated on top of Tinto Hill. Measures 45 metres in diameter and 6 metres in height

TIREFOUR BROCH, nr Achnacroish, Lismore. Iron Age broch. Stands up to 5 metres in height on one side

TOMNAVERIE STONE CIRCLE (HS), nr Aboyne, Aberdeenshire. Dating from third or second millennium BC. Red granite circle, 18 metres in diameter. Four uprights and the recumbent remain in place. Ring of smaller stones within the circle

TORHOUSE STONE CIRCLE (HS), nr Wigtown, Dumfries and Galloway. Circle of 19 granite boulders. Three stones in middle of the circle

TORWOODLEE FORT AND BROCH, nr Galashiels, Borders. Ruins of broch now less than 1 metre in height. Built on site of an earlier fort. Probably demolished by the Romans

TRAPRAIN LAW FORT, nr East Linton, East Lothian. Two ramparts on summit of Traprain Law. Artefacts dating back to the Neolithic period have been unearthed. Collection of late Roman silver found under floor of one of the many houses around the summit

TULLOS HILL ROUND CAIRNS, Loirston, nr Aberdeen. Four cairns, the remains of an important cairn cemetery of the Bronze Age

TWELVE APOSTLES STONE CIRCLE, nr Dumfries, Dumfries and Galloway. The largest stone circle in Scotland and one of the largest in Britain, measuring 87 metres at widest point. 11 stones remain. Originally thought to have consisted of 18 stones

TYNRON DOON, nr Moniaive, Achengibbert Hill, Dumfries and Galloway. Iron Age fort on summit of the hill. Used until relatively recently with tower house built in late 16th-century. Outlines of hut circles

UNIVAL CHAMBERED CAIRN, nr Claddach Illeray, North Uist. Square cairn now robbed of much of its stone

UNSTAN CHAMBERED CAIRN (HS), nr Stromness, Orkney. Situated on promontory in the Loch of Stenness. Concentric rings of drystone walling. Skeletal remains found in chambers along with animal and bird bones and shards of pottery known as Unstan Ware

VINQUAY CHAMBERED CAIRN, Eday, Orkney. Neolithic burial chamber dating from around 3000 BC

WAG OF FORSE BROCH AND SETTLEMENT, nr
Latheron, Caithness. Turf-walled enclosure and
remains of a number of houses including
roundhouses and brochs. Also rectangular
buildings known as 'wags'. Best preserved
dwelling is 12 metres long with two rows of
stone pillars

WIDEFORD HILL CHAMBERED CAIRN, nr Kirkwall,
Orkney. Neolithic burial chamber, similar to
chambered cairn at Maes Howe

YOXIE BIGGINS, Whalsay, Shetland. Bronze Age
house. Also known as The Standing Stones of
Yoxie as the megaliths were used to form the
walls, many still standing. Excavations have
unearthed stone tools and pottery

MUSEUMS AND GALLERIES

There are around 435 museums and galleries in Scotland, of which 270 are fully or provisionally registered with Resource: The Council for Museums, Archives and Libraries (formerly the Museums and Galleries Commission). Registration indicates that they have an appropriate constitution, are soundly financed, have satisfactory collection management standards and public services, and have access to professional curatorial advice. Museums should achieve full or provisional registration status in order to be eligible for grants from Resource and from the Scottish Museums Council.

The national collections in Scotland are the National Galleries of Scotland and the National Museums of Scotland, which are funded by direct government grant-in-aid. In 2003 Edinburgh's National Gallery of Scotland was named Gallery of the Year by the *Good Britain Guide* in recognition of the quality of its exhibitions, its collections, and its visitor relations. In line with the National Cultural Strategy, launched in August 2000, the National Museums of Scotland removed admission charges at the National Gallery of Scotland, the Royal Museum and the National Museum of Scotland, all in Edinburgh, from 1 April 2001. An online art museum (www.24hourmuseum.org.uk) has also been awarded national collection status.

Local authority museums are funded by the local authority and may also receive grants from the Museums and Galleries Commission. Independent museums and galleries mainly rely on their own resources but are also eligible for grants from the Museums and Galleries Commission.

The Scottish Museums Council is one of ten area museum councils in the UK. It is an independent charity that receives an annual grant from the Scottish Executive, and gives advice and support to museums in Scotland. It may offer improvement grants and also assists with training and marketing.

OPENING TO THE PUBLIC

The following is a selection of the museums and art galleries in Scotland. Opening hours vary. Most museums are closed on Christmas Eve, Christmas Day, Boxing Day and New Year's Day; some are closed on Good Friday or the May Day Bank Holiday. Most small museums, especially in rural areas, are closed during the winter (this can be defined as any period from October to May). Some smaller museums close at lunchtimes, on Saturday and/or Sunday mornings, or all day Sunday; others may open only on a few days each week. Information about a specific museum or gallery should be checked by telephone with the museum itself, where telephone numbers are given, or with the local tourist office.

For listings of museums, art galleries and other heritage attractions in Scotland, visit or www.24hourmuseum.org.uk. Further information can be obtained from tourist boards or local authorities.

ABBOT HOUSE HERITAGE CENTRE
Maygate, Dunfermline, KY12 7NE
Tel: 01383-733266
Web: www.abbothouse.co.uk

ABERDEEN ART GALLERY AND MUSEUM
School Hill, Aberdeen AB10 1FQ
Tel: 01224-523700
Web: www.aagm.co.uk

ABERDEEN MARITIME MUSEUM
Shiprow, Aberdeen AB11 5BY
Tel: 01224-337700
Web: www.aagm.co.uk

ABERDEEN UNIVERSITY ZOOLOGY MUSEUM
Zoology Building, Aberdeen University, Tillydrone Avenue, Aberdeen AB24 2TZ
Tel: 01224-272396
Web: www.abdu.ac.uk/zoology

ABERDEENSHIRE FARMING MUSEUM
Aden Country Park, Mintlaw, Peterhead AB42 5FQ.
Tel: 01771-622906

ABERNETHY MUSEUM
Mornington Stables, School Wynd, Abernethy, Perth PH2 9JJ
Tel: 01738-850889
Web: www.abernethymuseum.free-online.co.uk

AIKWOOD TOWER
Selkirk, TD7 5HJ
Web: www.aikwoodscottishborders.com

ALMOND VALLEY HERITAGE CENTRE
Millfield, Livingston Village, Livingston EH54 7AR.
Tel: 01506-414957
Web: www.almondvalley.co.uk

ALYTH MUSEUM
Commercial Street, Alyth PH11 8AF
Tel: 01738-632488

AN TUIREANN ARTS CENTRE
Struan Road, Portree IV51 0EG
Tel: 01478-613306

ANDREW CARNEGIE BIRTHPLACE MUSEUM
Moodie Street, Dunfermline KY12 7PL
Tel: 01383-724302
Web: www.carnegiebirthplace.co.uk

ANGUS FOLK MUSEUM
Kirkwynd, Glamis, Angus DD8 1RT
Tel: 01307-840288

ANNAN HISTORIC RESOURCES CENTRE
Bank Street, Annan DG12 6AA
Tel: 01461-201384
Web: www.dumfriesmuseum.demon.co.uk

ARBROATH ART GALLERY
Arbroath Library, Hill Terrace, Arbroath,
Angus DD11 1PU
Tel: 01241-875598

ARBROATH MUSEUM
Signal Tower, Ladyloan, Arbroath, Angus DD11 1PU
Tel: 01241-875598

ARBUTHNOT MUSEUM AND GALLERY
St Peter Street, Peterhead, Aberdeenshire AB42 1QD
Tel: 01779-477778

ARCHAEOLINK PREHISTORY PARK
Oyne, Insch AB52 6QP Tel: 01464-851500
Web: www.archaeolink.co.uk

ARRAN HERITAGE MUSEUM
Rosaburn, Brodick, Isle of Arran KA27 8DP
Tel: 01770-302636

AUCHINDRAIN MUSEUM
Auchindrain, by Inverary, Argyll PA23 8XN
Tel: 01499-500235

AULD KIRK MUSEUM
The Cross, Kirkintilloch G66 1AB
Tel: 0141-775 1185

AULD SKÖLL
Utra, Fair Isle, Shetland, ZE2 9JU
Tel: 01595-760244

BAIRD INSTITUTE
3 Lugar Street, Cumnock, Ayrshire KA18 1AD
Tel: 01290-421701

BANCHORY MUSEUM
Bridge Street, Banchory, Kincardineshire AB31 5SX
Tel: 01771-622906
Web: www.aberdeenshire.gov.uk

BANFF MUSEUM
High Street, Banff, Aberdeenshire AB45 1AE
Tel: 01771-622906

BANNOCKBURN HERITAGE CENTRE
Glasgow Road, Stirling FK7 0LJ
Tel: 01786-812664
Web: www.nts.org.uk

BARONY CHAMBERS MUSEUM
The Cross, Kirkintilloch G66 1AB
Tel: 0141-775 1185

BARRA HERITAGE AND CULTURAL CENTRE
Castlebay, Isle of Barra HS9 5XD
Tel: 01871-810413

BARRACK STREET MUSEUM
Barrack Street, Dundee DD1 1PG
Tel: 01382-432020

BARRHEAD COMMUNITY MUSEUM
128 Main Street, Barrhead G78 1SG
Tel: 0141-577 3103

BELL-PETTIGREW MUSEUM OF NATURAL HISTORY
University of St Andrews, Bute Buildings, Queen's
    Terrace, St Andrews KY16 9TS
Tel: 01334-463498

BENNIE MUSEUM
9–11 Mansefield Street, Bathgate EH48 4HN
Tel: 01506-654780
Web: www.benniemuseum.homestead.com

BERNERA MUSEUM
Bernera Museum, Bernera, Isle of Lewis HS2 9LF
Tel: 01851-612331

BLACK WATCH REGIMENTAL MUSEUM
Balhousie Castle, Hay Street, Perth PH1 5HR
Tel: 0131-310 8530

BLACKRIDGE COMMUNITY MUSEUM
Blackridge Library, Craig Inn Centre, Blackridge EH48 3RJ
Tel: 01506-776347

BLAIR'S MUSEUM
South Deeside Road, Aberdeen AB12 5YQ
Tel: 01224-869424
Web: www.blairs.net

BRANDER MUSEUM
The Square, Huntly, Aberdeenshire AB54 8AE
Tel: 01771-622906

BRECHIN MUSEUM
Brechin Library, 10 St Ninian's Square,
Brechin DD8 7AA
Tel: 01307-461460

BRITISH GOLF MUSEUM
Bruce Embankment, St Andrews KY16 9AB
Tel: 01334-460046
Web: www.britishgolfmuseum.co.uk

BROUGHTY CASTLE MUSEUM
Castle Approach, Broughty Ferry, Dundee DD5 2BE
Tel: 01382-436916
Web: www.dundeecity.gov.uk

BUCKHAVEN MUSEUM
College Street, Buckhaven, Fife KY1 1LD
Tel: 01592-712912

BUCKIE DRIFTER MARITIME HERITAGE CENTRE
Freuchny Road, Buckie, Banffshire AB56 1TT
Tel: 01542-834646

BURNS COTTAGE MUSEUM
Burns Cottage, Alloway, Ayr KA7 4PY
Tel: 01292-441215

BURNS HOUSE MUSEUM
Castle Street, Mauchline G2 5QR
Tel: 01290-550045

BURNTISLAND MUSEUM
192 High Street, Burntisland, Fife KY3 9AS
Tel: 01592-412860

BUTE MUSEUM
Stuart Street, Rothesay, Western Isles PA20 9JT
Tel: 01700-502248

CAMPBELTOWN MUSEUM
Hall Street, Campbeltown, Argyll PA28 6BS
Tel: 01586-552366
Web: www.abc-museums.demon.co.uk

CARNEGIE MUSEUM
The Square, Inverurie, Aberdeenshire AB42 6QD
Tel: 01771-622906

CASTLE DOUGLAS ART GALLERY
Market Street, Castle Douglas,
Dumfries & Galloway DG7 1BE
Tel: 01557-331643

CASTLE HOUSE MUSEUM
Castle Gardens, Dunoon PA23 7HH
Tel: 01369-701422

CENTRE OF CONTEMPORARY ART
350 Sauchiehall Street, Glasgow G2 3JD
Tel: 0141-332 7521
Web: www.cca-glasgow.com

CHAPTER HOUSE MUSEUM
The Cathedral of St Columba, Cathedral Street,
Dunkeld PH8 0AW
Tel: 01350-728732

CITY ART CENTRE
2 Market Street, Edinburgh EH1 1DE
Tel: 0131-529 3993

CLACKMANNANSHIRE MUSEUM, HERITAGE CENTRE
AND SPEIRS CENTRE
29 Primrose Street, Alloa, Clackmannanshire FK10 1JJ
Tel: 01259-216913

CLAN ARMSTRONG TRUST MUSEUM
Lodge Walk, Castleholm, Langholm DG13 0ND
Tel: 01388-517291

CLAN DONNACHAIDH MUSEUM
Bruar, Pitlochry, Perthshire PH18 5TW
Tel: 01796-483296
Web: www.donnachaidh.com

CLAN GUNN HERITAGE CENTRE AND MUSEUM
Old Parish Church, Latheron KW5 6DG
Tel: 01593-721325

CLAN MACPHERSON MUSEUM
Newtonmore, Inverness-shire PH20 1DE
Tel: 01540-673332

CLYDEBANK MUSEUM
Town Hall, Dumbarton Road, Clydebank G81 1UE
Tel: 01389-738702
Web: www.west-dumbarton.gov.uk

CLYDEBUILT – THE SCOTTISH MARITIME MUSEUM
AT BRAEHEAD
Kings Inch Road, Glasgow G51 4BN
Tel: 0141-886 1013

COATS OBSERVATORY
49 Oakshaw Street West, Paisley PA1 2DE
Tel: 0141-889 2013

COLDSTREAM MUSEUM
12 Market Square, Coldstream TD12 4BD
Tel: 01890-882630

CORRIGALL FARM MUSEUM
Corrigall, Harray, Orkney KW17 2LQ
Tel: 01856-771411

CRAIL MUSEUM AND HERITAGE CENTRE
62–64 Marketgate, Crail, Fife KY10 3TL
Tel: 01333-450869

CRAWFORD ARTS CENTRE
93 North Street, St Andrews KY16 9AL
Tel: 01334-474610
Web: www.crawfordarts.free-online.co.uk

CRAWFORDJOHN HERITAGE CENTRE
Croft Head, Crawfordjohn, Biggar ML12 6SU
Tel: 01864-504206

CREETOWN HERITAGE MUSEUM
The Exhibition Centre, 91 St Johns Street,
Creetown, Newton Stewart DG8 7JE
Tel: 01671-820343

CROMARTY COURTHOUSE MUSEUM
Church Street, Cromarty IV11 8XA
Tel: 01381-600418

CUMBERNAULD MUSEUM
Cumbernauld Library, Allender Walk, Town Centre,
Cumbernauld G67 1EE
Tel: 01236-725664

DALBEATTIE MUSEUM
Southwick Road, Dalbeattie DG5 4HA
Tel: 01556-610437

DAVID LIVINGSTON CENTRE
165 Station Road, Blantyre G72 9BT
Tel: 01698-823140

DEAN GALLERY
Belford Road, Edinburgh EH4 3DS
Tel: 0131-624 6200
Web: www.natgalscot.ac.uk

DICK INSTITUTE
Dean Castle Country Park, Dean Road,
Kilmarnock KA3 1XB
Tel: 01563-522702

DINGWALL MUSEUM
Town Hall, High Street, Dingwall IV15 9RY
Tel: 01349-865366

DISCOVERY CENTRE
Chambers Street, Edinburgh EH1 1JF
Tel: 0131-247 4199

DISCOVERY POINT
Discovery Quay, Dundee DD1 4XA
Tel: 01382-201245
Web: www.rrsdiscovery.com

DOUGLAS HERITAGE MUSEUM
Bells Wynd, Douglas, South Lanarkshire ML11 0QH
Tel: 01555-851243

DUFF HOUSE COUNTRY HOUSE GALLERY
Banff, Aberdeenshire AB45 3SX
Tel: 01261-818181 Web:

DUFFTOWN MUSEUM
The Tower, The Square, Dufftown AB55 4AD
Tel: 01309-673701

DUMFRIES MUSEUM & CAMERA OBSCURA
The Observatory, Dumfries DG2 7SW
Tel: 01387-253374
Web: www.dumgal.gov.uk/museums

DUNASKIN OPEN AIR MUSEUM
Dalmellington Road, Waterside,
Waterside by Patna KA6 7JF
Tel: 01292-531144

DUNBEATH HERITAGE CENTRE
The Old School, Dunbeath, Caithness KW6 6ED
Tel: 01593-731233

DUNBLANE MUSEUM
The Square, Dunblane FK15 0AQ
Tel: 01786-823440

DUNFERMLINE MUSEUM AND SMALL GALLERY
Viewfield Terrace, Dunfermline KY12 7HY
Tel: 01383-721814

DUNKELD CHAPTERHOUSE MUSEUM
Dunkeld Cathedral, Dunkeld, Perth and
Kinross PH8 0AW

DUNOON AND COWAL HERITAGE TRUST
Castle House, Castle Gardens, Dunoon PA23 7HH
Tel: 01369-701422

EASDALE ISLAND FOLK MUSEUM
Easdale Island, by Oban PA34 4TB
Tel: 01852-300370

EDINBURGH COLLEGE OF ART
Lauriston Place, Edinburgh EH3 9DF

EDINBURGH PRINTMAKERS WORKSHOP AND
GALLERY
23 Union Street, Edinburgh EH1 3LR
Tel: 0131-557 2479

EDINBURGH UNIVERSITY COLLECTION OF
HISTORIC MUSICAL INSTRUMENTS
Reid Concert Hall, Bristo Square, Edinburgh EH8 9AG
Tel: 0131-650 2423
Web: www.music.ed.ac.uk/euchmi

ELGIN MUSEUM
1 High Street, Elgin IV30 1EQ
Tel: 01343-543675
Web:

EYEMOUTH MUSEUM
Auld Kirk, Manse Road, Eyemouth TD14 5JE
Tel: 01890-750678

FALCONER MUSEUM
Tolbooth Street, Forres IV36 1PH
Tel: 01309-673701
Web: www.moray.org/museums/index

FERGUSSON GALLERY
Marshall Place, Perth PH2 8NU
Tel: 01738-441944

FIFE FOLK MUSEUM
High Street, Ceres, Nr Cupar KY15 5NF
Tel: 01334-828180

FORFAR MUSEUM AND ART GALLERY
The Meffan, 20 West High Street, Forfar DD8 1BB.
Tel: 01307-464123

FRASERBURGH HERITAGE CENTRE
Quarry Road, Fraserburgh, Aberdeenshire AB43 9DT
Tel: 01346-512888
Web: www.fraserburghheritage.com

FRIGATE UNICORN
Victoria Dock, Dundee DD1 3JA
Tel: 01382-200900

GAIRLOCH HERITAGE MUSEUM
Achtercairn, Gairloch IV21 2BJ
Tel: 01445-712287
Web: www.gairlochheritagemuseum.org.uk

GALLERY OF MODERN ART, GLASGOW
Queen Street, Glasgow G1 3AH
Tel: 0141-229 1996
Web: www.goma.glasgow.gov.uk

GLADSTONE COURT VICTORIAN STREET MUSEUM
Moat Park, Kirkstyre, Biggar ML12 6DT
Tel: 01899-221050
Web: www.biggar.net.co.uk

GLASGOW PRINT STUDIO
22 & 25 King Street, Glasgow G1 5QP
Tel: 0141-552 0704
Web: www.gpsart.co.uk

GLASGOW SCHOOL OF ART
167 Renfrew Street, Glasgow G3 6RQ
Tel: 0141-353 4500
Web: www.gsa.ac.uk

GLASGOW SCIENCE CENTRE
50 Pacific Quay, Glasgow G51 1EA
Tel: 0141-420 5010
Web: www.gsc.org.uk

GLENCOE AND NORTH LORN FOLK MUSEUM
Glencoe Village, Glencoe PH39 4HS
Tel: 01855-811314

GLENESK FOLK MUSEUM
The Retreat, Tarfside, Glenesk, Brechin DD9 7YT
Tel: 01356-670254

GLENFINNAN STATION MUSEUM
Glennfinnan Railway Station, Glenfinnan,
Fort William PH37 4LT
Tel: 01397-722295

GORDON HIGHLANDERS MUSEUM
St Lukes, Viewfield Road, Aberdeen AB15 7XH
Tel: 01224-311200
Web: www.gordonhighlanders.com

GRACEFIELD ARTS CENTRE
28 Edinburgh Road, Dumfries DG1 1NW
Tel: 01387-262084
Web: dumgal.gov.uk

GRAMPIAN HOSPITALS ART TRUST GALLERY
Aberdeen Royal Infirmary, Foresterhill,
Aberdeen AB25 2ZN
Tel: 01224-552429

GRAMPIAN TRANSPORT MUSEUM
Alford, AB33 8AE
Tel: 01975-562292
Web: www.gtm.org.uk

GRANTOWN MUSEUM AND HERITAGE CENTRE
Burnfield House, Burnfield Avenue,
Grantown-on-Spey PH26 3HH
Tel: 01479-872478
Web: www.grantown-on-spey.co.uk

GRANGEMOUTH HERITAGE TRUST
13A La Porte Precinct, Grangemouth FK3 8AZ
Tel: 01324-666603
Web: www.falkirkmuseums.demon.co.uk

GROAM HOUSE MUSEUM
High Street, Rosemarkie, Ross-shire IV10 8UF
Tel: 01381-621730

HALLIWELL'S HOUSE MUSEUM
Halliwell's Close, Market Place, Selkirk TD7 4BC
Tel: 01750-20096

HAWICK MUSEUM AND THE SCOTT ART GALLERY
Wilton Lodge Park, Hawick TD9 7JL
Tel: 01450-373457

HEATHERBANK MUSEUM OF SOCIAL WORK
Glasgow Caledonian University, City Campus,
Cowcaddens Road, Glasgow G4 0BA
Tel: 0141-331 8637
Web: www.lib.gcal.ac.uk/heatherbank

HIGHLAND FOLK MUSEUM, KINGUSSIE
Duke Street, Kingussie PH21 1JG
Tel: 01540-661307
Web: www.highlandfolk.com

HIGHLAND FOLK MUSEUM, NEWTONMORE
Aultlarie Croft, Newtonmore PH20 1AY
Tel: 01540-661307
Web: www.highlandfolk.com

HIGHLAND MUSEUM OF CHILDHOOD
The Old Station, Strathpeffer, Ross-shire IV14 9DH
Tel: 01997-421031
Web: www.hmoc.freeserve.co.uk

HUNTERIAN MUSEUM AND ART GALLERY
University of Glasgow, Glasgow G12 8QQ
Tel: 0141-330 4221
Web: www.gla.ac.uk/museum

HUNTLEY HOUSE MUSEUM
142 Canongate, Edinburgh EH8 8DD
Tel: 0131-529 4143

INNERLEITHEN MUSEUM
c/o Chambers Institute, High Street, Peebles EH45 8AP
Tel: 01721-724820

INVERARY MARITIME MUSEUM
The Pier, Inverary PA32 8UY
Tel: 01499-302213

INVERKEITHING MUSEUM
Queen Street, Inverkeithing KY11 1LS
Tel: 01383-313394

INVERNESS MUSEUM AND ART GALLERY
Castle Wynd, Inverness IV2 3EB
Tel: 01463-237114

IONA GALLERY
Am Fasgadh, Duke Street, Kingussie PH21 1JG
Tel: 01540-661307
Web: www.highland.gov.uk

JAMES DUN'S HOUSE
61 Schoolhill, Aberdeen AB10 1JT
Tel: 01224-646333

JAMES PATERSON MUSEUM AND HISTORICAL
SOCIETY
Meadowcroft, North Street, Thornhill DG3 4HR
Tel: 01848-200583

JEDBURGH CASTLE JAIL AND MUSEUM
Castlegate, Jedburgh TD8 6QD
Tel: 01835-863254

JOHN BUCHAN CENTRE
Broughton, Biggar ML12 6DT
Tel: 01899-830223

JOHN HASTIE MUSEUM
Threestanes Road, Strathaven ML10 6DX
Tel: 01357-521257

JOHN PAUL JONES BIRTHPLACE MUSEUM
John Paul Jones Cottage, Arbigland,
Kirkbean, Dumfries DG2 8BG
Tel: 01387-880613
Web: www.jpj.demon.co.uk

KELSO MUSEUM AND TURRET GALLERY
Turret House, Abbey Court, Kelso TD5 7JA
Tel: 01573-223464

KELVINGROVE ART GALLERY AND MUSEUM
Kelvingrove, Glasgow G3 8AG
Tel: 0141-287 2699
Web: www.glasgow.gov.uk

KILMARTIN HOUSE MUSEUM OF ANCIENT CULTURE
Kilmartin House, Kilmartin PA31 8RQ
Tel: 01546-510278
Web: www.kilmartin.org

KINNEIL MUSEUM AND ROMAN FORTLET
Duchess Anne Cottages, Kinneil Estate,
Boness EH51 0PR
Tel: 01506-778530

KIRBUSTER MUSEUM
Kirbuster, Birsay, Orkney KW15 1NY
Tel: 01856-772268
Web: www.orkney.gov.uk/heritage

KIRKCALDY MUSEUM AND ART GALLERY
War Memorial Gardens, Kirkcaldy KY1 1YJ
Tel: 01592-412860

KIRRIEMUIR GATEWAY TO THE GLENS MUSEUM
The Old Town House, 32 High Street,
Kirriemuir DD8 4EG
Tel: 01575-575479
Web: www.angus.gov.uk/history.htm

LAIDHAY CROFT MUSEUM
Laidhay, Dunbeath, Caithness KW6 6EH
Tel: 01593-731244

LAING MUSEUM
High Street, Newburgh KY14 6DX
Tel: 01337-840223

LANARK MUSEUM
8 West Port, Lanark ML11 9HD
Tel: 01555-666680

LARGS MUSEUM
Kirkgate House, Manse Court, Largs KA30 8AW
Tel: 01475-687081

LILLIE ART GALLERY
Station Road, Milngavie, Glasgow G62 8BZ
Tel: 0141-943 3247

LOCHWINNOCH COMMUNITY MUSEUM
High Street, Lochwinnoch PA12 4AB
Tel: 01505-670677

LOW PARKS MUSEUM
129 Muir Street, Hamilton ML3 6BJ
Tel: 01698-283981

MACLAURIN ART GALLERY
Rozelle Park, Monument Road, Ayr KA7 4NQ
Tel: 01292-443708

MALLAIG HERITAGE CENTRE
Station Road, Mallaig PH41 4PY
Tel: 01687-462085
Web: www.mallaigheritage.org.uk

MARISCHAL MUSEUM, UNIVERSITY OF ABERDEEN
Marischal College, Broad Street, Aberdeen AB10 1YS
Tel: 01224-274301

MARY, QUEEN OF SCOTS' HOUSE AND VISITOR
CENTRE
Queen Street, Jedburgh TD8 6EN
Tel: 01835-863331

MCDOUALL STUART MUSEUM
Rectory Lane, Dysart, Kirkcaldy KY1 2TP
Tel: 01592-412860

MCKECHNIE INSTITUTE
Dalrymple Street, Girvan, KA26 9AE
Tel: 01465 713643

MCLEAN MUSEUM AND ART GALLERY
15 Kelly Street, Greenock PA16 8JX
Tel: 01474-715624

MCLELLAN GALLERIES
270 Sauchiehall Street, Glasgow G2 3EH
Tel: 0141-331 1854

MCMANUS GALLERIES
Dundee Arts and Heritage Department,
Albert Square, Dundee DD1 1DA
Tel: 01382-432084
Web: www.dundeecity.gov.uk

MENZIES CAMPBELL DENTAL MUSEUM
9 Hill Square, Edinburgh EH8 9RU
Tel: 0131-527 1659
Web: www.rcsed.ac.uk/geninfo/museums/asp

METHIL HERITAGE CENTRE
272 High Street, Lower Methil, Fife KY8 3EQ
Tel: 01333-422100

MOAT PARK HERITAGE CENTRE
Moat Park, Kirkstyle, Biggar ML12 6DT
Tel: 01899-221050

MOFFAT MUSEUM
The Neuk, Church Gate, Moffat DG10 9EG
Tel: 01683-220868

MONTROSE AIR STATION MUSEUM
Waldron Road, Montrose DD10 9BB
Tel: 01674-673107

MONTROSE MUSEUM AND ART GALLERY
Panmure Place, Montrose DD10 8HE
Tel: 01698-673232

MOTHERWELL HERITAGE CENTRE
1 High Road, Motherwell ML1 3HU
Tel: 01698-251000

MULL MUSEUM
Columba Buildings, Main Street, Tobermory PA75 6NY
Tel: 01688-302208

MUSEUM NAN EILEAN
Francis Street, Stornaway, Western Isles HS1 2NF
Tel: 01851-703773

MUSEUM NAN EILEAN, SGOIL LIONACLEIT
Lionacliet, Benbecula, Western Isles HS7 5JP
Tel: 01870-602211

MUSEUM OF CHILDHOOD, EDINBURGH
42 High Street, Royal Mile, Edinburgh EH1 1TG
Tel: 0131-529 4142

MUSEUM OF COMMUNICATION
PO Box 12556, Boness EH51 9YX
Tel: 01506-823424
Web: www.mocft.co.uk

MUSEUM OF EDINBURGH
142 Canongate, Royal Mile, Edinburgh EH8 8DD
Tel: 0131-529 4143
Web: www.cac.org.uk

MUSEUM OF FLIGHT
East Fortune Airfield, East Fortune,
East Lothian EH39 5LF
Tel: 01620-880308
Web: www.nms.ac.uk

MUSEUM OF ISLAY LIFE
Port Charlotte, Isle of Islay PA48 7UA
Tel: 01496-850358

MUSEUM OF LEAD MINING
Wanlockhead, by Biggar, Lanarkshire ML12 6UT
Tel: 01659-74387

MUSEUM OF PIPING
The Piping Centre, 30–34 McPhater Street,
Cowcaddens, Glasgow EH1
Tel: 0141-353 0220
Web: www.nms.ac.uk

MUSEUM OF SCOTLAND
Chambers Street, Edinburgh EH1 1JF
Tel: 0131-225 7534
Web: www.nms.ac.uk

MUSEUM OF SCOTTISH COUNTRY LIFE
Wester Kittochside, East Kilbride G76 9HR
Tel: 01355-224181
Web: www.nms.ac.uk/countrylife

MUSEUM OF SCOTTISH LIGHTHOUSES
Kinnaird Head, Fraserburgh, Aberdeenshire AB43 9DU
Tel: 01346-511022

MUSEUM OF THE CUMBRAES
Garrison House, Millport, Isle of Cumbraes K28 0GD
Tel: 01475-530741

MUSEUM OF THE ISLES
Clan Donald Visitor Centre, Armadale, Ardvasar,
Isle of Skye IV45 8RS
Tel: 01471-844227

MUSEUM OF TRANSPORT
Kelvin Hall, 1 Bunhouse Road, Glasgow G3 8DP
Tel: 0141-287 2720

MUSEUM WORKSHOP AND STORES
7–11 Abbotsinch, Abbotsinch Industrial Estate,
Grangemouth FK3 9UX
Tel: 01324-504689

NAIRN FISHERTOWN MUSEUM
Laing Hall, King Street, Nairn IV12 4NZ
Tel: 01667-458531

NAIRN MUSEUM
Viewfield House, Viewfield Drive, Nairn IV12 4EE
Tel: 01667-456791

NATIONAL GALLERY OF SCOTLAND
2 The Mound, Edinburgh EH2 2EL
Tel: 0131-624 6200
Web: www.nationalgalleries.org

NATIONAL WAR MUSEUM OF SCOTLAND
Edinburgh Castle, Edinburgh EH1 2NG
Tel: 0131-225 7534

NEWHAVEN HERITAGE MUSEUM
24 Pier Place, Edinburgh EH6 4LP
Tel: 0131-529 4139

NORTH AYRSHIRE MUSEUM
Manse Street, Saltcoats KA21 5AA
Tel: 01294-464174

NORTH BERWICK MUSEUM
School Road, North Berwick EH39 4JU
Tel: 01620-895457
Web: www.elothian-museums.demon.co.uk

NORTHLANDS VIKING CENTRE
The Old School, Auckengill, by Wick KW14 4XP
Tel: 01955-603761

OLD BRIDGE HOUSE MUSEUM
Old Bridge House Museum, Mill Road,
Dumfries DG2 7BE
Tel: 01387-656904
Web: www.dumgal.gov.uk/museums

OLD GALA HOUSE MUSEUM
Scott Crescent, Galashiels TD1 3JS
Tel: 01750-720096

OLD HAA TRUST
Altona, Mid Yell, Shetland ZE2 9BN
Tel: 01957-702037

ORKNEY MUSEUM
Tankerness House, Broad Street, Kirkwall KW15 1DH
Tel: 01856-873191
Web: www.orkney.com

ORKNEY WIRELESS MUSEUM
Kiln Corner, Kirkwall KW15 1LB
Tel: 01856-871400

PAISLEY MUSEUM AND ART GALLERY
High Street, Paisley PA1 2BA
Tel: 0141-889 3151

PALACERIGG HOUSE MUSEUM
Palacerigg, Cumbernauld G67 3HU
Tel: 01236-735077

PEACOCK GALLERY AND STUDIOS
21 Castle Street, Castlegate, Aberdeen AB1 1AJ
Tel: 01224-639539

PEOPLE'S PALACE MUSEUM
Glasgow Green, Glasgow G40 1AT
Tel: 0141-554 0223

PEOPLE'S STORY MUSEUM
Canongate Tolbooth, 163 Canongate,
Edinburgh EH8 8BN
Tel: 0131-529 4057

PERTH MUSEUM AND ART GALLERY
George Street, Perth PH1 5LB
Tel: 01738-632488

PETER ANSON GALLERY
Town House West, Cluny Place, Buckie AB5 1HB
Tel: 01309-673701

PETERHEAD MARITIME HERITAGE
South Road, Peterhead AB42 2YP
Tel: 01779-473000

PIER ARTS CENTRE
Victoria Street, Stromness KW16 3AA
Tel: 01856-850209

PITTENCRIEFF HOUSE MUSEUM
Pittencrieff Park, Dunfermline KY12 8QH
Tel: 01383-722935

PLAYFAIR HALL MUSEUM OF PATHOLOGY
Royal College of Surgeons, 18 Nicholson Street,
Edinburgh EH8 9DW
Tel: 0131-527 1649
Web: www.rcsed.ac.uk/geninfo/museums.asp

PRESTONGRANGE INDUSTRIAL HERITAGE MUSEUM
Morison's Haven, Prestonpans EH32 9RX
Tel: 0131-653 2904
Web: www.elothian-museums.demon.co.uk

QUEENSFERRY MUSEUM
53 High Street, South Queensferry EH30 9HP
Tel: 0131-331 5545

REGIMENTAL MUSEUM OF THE ARGYLL AND
SUTHERLAND HIGHLANDERS
The Castle, Stirling FK8 1EH
Tel: 01786-475165
Web: www.argylls.co.uk

REGIMENTAL MUSEUM OF THE CAMERONIANS
129 Muir Street, Hamilton ML3 6BJ
Tel: 01698-283981

REGIMENTAL MUSEUM OF THE QUEEN'S OWN
HIGHLANDERS
Regimental HQ, The Highlanders, Cameron Barracks,
Inverness IV2 3XD
Tel: 01463-224380

REGIMENTAL MUSEUM OF THE ROYAL SCOTS
DRAGOON GUARDS
The Castle, Edinburgh EH1 2YT
Tel: 0131-220 4387

ROBERT BURNS CENTRE
Mill Road, Dumfries DG2 7BE
Tel: 01387-264808
Web: www.dumgal.gov.uk/museums

ROBERT BURNS HOUSE
Burns Street, Dumfries DG1 2PS
Tel: 01387-255197
Web: www.dumgal.gov.uk/museums

ROYAL HIGHLAND FUSILIERS REGIMENTAL MUSEUM
518 Sauchiehall Street, Glasgow G2 3LW
Tel: 0141-332 0961

ROYAL MUSEUM
National Museums of Scotland, Chambers Street,
Edinburgh EH1 1JF
Tel: 0131-225 7534
Web: www.nms.ac.uk

SANQUHAR TOLBOOTH MUSEUM
High Street, Sanquhar DG4 6BN
Tel: 01659-50186
Web: www.dumgal.gov.uk/museums

SATROSPHERE
The Tramsheds, 179 Constitution Street,
Aberdeen AB24 5TU
Tel: 01224-640340
Web: www.satrosphere.net

SAVINGS BANKS MUSEUMS
Ruthwell, Dumfries DG1 4NN
Tel: 01387-870640
Web: www.savingsbanksmuseum.co.uk

SCAPA FLOW VISITOR CENTRE
Lyness, Hoy, Kirkwall, Orkney Islands KW16 3NU
Tel: 01856-791300
Web: www.orkneyislands.com

SCOTLAND STREET SCHOOL MUSEUM
225 Scotland Street, Glasgow G5 8QB
Tel: 0141-287 0500

SCOTLAND'S LIGHTHOUSE MUSEUM
Kinnaird Head Lighthouse, Fraserburgh AB43 5DU
Tel: 01346-511022

SCOTLAND'S SECRET BUNKER
Crown Buildings, Troywood, Nr St Andrews KY16 8QH
Tel: 01333-310101
Web: www.secretbunker.co.uk

SCOTTISH AGRICULTURAL MUSEUM
Ingliston, Newbridge EH28 8NB
Tel: 0131-333 2674
Web: www.nms.ac.uk

SCOTTISH FISHERIES MUSEUM
St Ayles, Harbourhead, Anstruther KY10 3AB
Tel: 01333-310628
Web: www.scottish-fisheries-museums.org

SCOTTISH FOOTBALL MUSEUM
The National Stadium, Hampden Park, Glasgow
Tel: 0141-616 6100
Web: www.scottishfootballmuseum.org.uk

SCOTTISH JEWISH ARCHIVES CENTRE
Garnethill Synagogue, 127 Hill Street,
Glasgow G3 6UB
Tel: 0141-332 4911

SCOTTISH MARITIME MUSEUM
Laird Forge, Gottries Road, Irvine KA12 8QE
Tel: 01294-278283

SCOTTISH MINING MUSEUM
Lady Victoria Colliery, Newton Grange EH22 4QN
Tel: 0131-663 7519
Web: www.scottishminingmuseum.com

SCOTTISH NATIONAL GALLERY OF MODERN ART
Bedford Road, Edinburgh E4 3DR
Tel: 0131-624 6200
Web: www.nationalgalleries.org

SCOTTISH NATIONAL PORTRAIT GALLERY
1 Queen Street, Edinburgh EH2 1JO
Tel: 0131-332 2266
Web: www.natgalscot.ac.uk

SCOTTISH RUGBY UNION LIBRARY AND MUSEUM
Murrayfield, Edinburgh EH12 5PJ
Tel: 0131-346 5073

SCOTTISH TARTANS MUSEUM
The Institute Hall, Mid Street, Keith AB55 5BJ
Tel: 01542-888419

SHAMBELLIE HOUSE MUSEUM OF COSTUME
New Abbey, Dumfries DG2 8HQ
Tel: 01387-850375
Web: www.nms.ac.uk

SHETLAND CROFTHOUSE MUSEUM
Voe, Boddam, Dunrossness, Lerwick ZE2 9JG
Tel: 01595-695057

SHETLAND MUSEUM
Lower Hillhead, Lerwick ZE1 0EL
Tel: 01595-695057

SHETLAND TEXTILE WORKING MUSEUM
Weisdale Mill, Weisdale ZE2 9LW
Tel: 01595-830419

SHOTTS HERITAGE CENTRE
Benhar Road, Shotts ML7 5EN
Tel: 01501-821556

SMITH ART GALLERY AND MUSEUM
Dumbarton Road, Stirling FK8 2RQ
Tel: 01786-471917

SPRINGBURN MUSEUM
Atlas Square, Ayr Street, Glasgow G21 4BW
Tel: 0141-557 1405

ST ANDREWS MUSEUM
Kinburn House, Kinburn Park, Doubledykes Road,
St Andrews KY16 9DF
Tel: 01334-412690

ST ANDREWS PRESERVATION TRUST MUSEUM
12 North Street, St Andrews KY16 9PW
Tel: 01334-477629

ST MUNGO MUSEUM OF RELIGIOUS LIFE AND ART
2 Castle Street, Glasgow G4 0RH
Tel: 0141-553 2557

STEWARTRY MUSEUM
St Mary Street, Kirkcudbright DG6 4AQ
Tel: 01557-331643

STIRLING SMITH ART GALLERY AND MUSEUM
Dumbarton Road, Stirling FK8 2RQ
Tel: 01786-471917
Web: www.smithartgallery.demon.co.uk

STRANRAER MUSEUM
The Old Town Hall, 55 George Street,
Stranraer DG9 7JP
Tel: 01776-705088
Web: www.dumgal.gov.uk/museums

STRATHNAVER MUSEUM
Clachan, Bettyhill KW14 7SS
Tel: 01641-521418

STROMNESS MUSEUM
52 Alfred Street, Stromness KW16 3DF
Tel: 01856-850025

SUMMERLEE HERITAGE PARK
Heritage Way, Coatbridge, Glasgow ML5 1QD
Tel: 01236-431261

TAIN AND DISTRICT MUSEUM
Tower Street, Tain IV19 1DY
Tel: 01862-894089

TALBOT RICE GALLERY
The University of Edinburgh, Old College,
South Bridge, Edinburgh EH8 9YL
Tel: 0131-650 2211
Web: www.trg.ed.ac.uk

THE FRUITMARKET GALLERY
45 Market Street, Edinburgh EH1 1DF
Tel: 0131-225 2383
Web: www.fruitmarket.co.uk

THE QUEEN'S GALLERY
The Palace of Holyrood House, Edinburgh EH8 8DX
Tel: 0131-556 5100
Web: www.the-royal-collection.com

THE TALL SHIP AT GLASGOW HARBOUR
100 Stobcross Road, Glasgow G3 8QQ
Tel: 0141-339 0631
Web: www.thetallship.com

TIMESPAN HERITAGE CENTRE AND ART GALLERY
Dunrobin Street, Helmsdale KW8 6JX
Tel: 01431-821327
Web: www.timespan.org.uk

TOLBOOTH ART CENTRE
High Street, Kirkcudbright DG6 4JL
Tel: 01557-331556

TOLBOOTH MUSEUM
Old Pier, The Harbour, Stonehaven AB39 2JU
Tel: 01771-622906

TOY MUSEUM
Glendale, Isle of Skye IV55 8WS
Tel: 01470-511240
Web: www.toy-museum.co.uk

TWEEDDALE MUSEUM
c/o Chambers Institute, High Street, Peebles EH45 8AP
Tel: 01721-724820

ULLAPOOL MUSEUM AND VISITOR CENTRE
7–8 West Argyle Street, Ullapool IV26 2TY
Tel: 01854-612987

VENNEL GALLERY
10 Glasgow Vennel, Irvine KA12 0BD
Tel: 01294-275059

VERDANT WORKS
West Henderson's Wynd, Dundee DD1 5BT
Tel: 01382-225282

WEST HIGHLAND MUSEUM
Cameron Square, Fort William PH33 6AJ
Tel: 01397-702169

WEST KILBRIDE MUSEUM TRUST
Public Hall, 1 Arthur Street, West Kilbride KA23 9EN
Tel: 01294-822987

WHITBURN COMMUNITY MUSEUM
Whitburn Library, Union Road, Whitburn EH47 0AR
Tel: 01506-776347

WRITER'S MUSEUM
Lady Stair's House, Lady Stair's Close,
Lawnmarket, Edinburgh EH1 2PA
Tel: 0131-529 4901

GARDENS

Scotland's varied climate allows for a very wide range of plants to be grown. Particularly on the west coast and in the islands of the west and southwest, mild weather caused by the Gulf Stream makes it possible to grow palms, tender perennials, and plants from the southern hemisphere; while acid, peaty soil and the frequency of rain and low cloud provide a suitable climate for plants usually thought of as typically Scottish, such as rhododendrons and heathers. Several national collections of plants are housed in Scotland.

The National Trust for Scotland is the country's largest garden owner, with just over 700 acres under intensive cultivation supporting over 13,500 different sorts of plants. The Trust acquired its first garden in 1945 when it accepted Culzean Castle. Several years later Inverewe, Brodik, Falkland Palace and Pitmedden Gardens were added. It plays an important role in promoting the conservation of the art and craft of horticulture, through its School of Practical Gardening at Threave.

Each year a large number of Scottish gardens, most privately owned, open their gates to the public for one or more weekends under the banner of Scotland's Gardens Scheme. Founded in 1931, the Scheme is an independent charity and the money raised from garden visitors supports the Queen's Nursing Institute (Scotland) and the gardens fund of the National Trust for Scotland. In addition garden owners may donate up to 40 per cent of their takings to a charity of their choice. The National Scotland's Gardens Scheme Handbook is available from any National Trust for Scotland shop or by post from the Trust's headquarters.

Historic Scotland and Scottish Natural Heritage jointly maintain an Inventory of Gardens and Designed Landscapes in Scotland. The Inventory provides a representative sample of historic gardens and landscapes of special interest, and includes botanic gardens, parks, private gardens and policies in country estates. The Inventory is currently being extended.

The following is a list of gardens in Scotland which are regularly open to the public, including botanic gardens and historical gardens. Also included are gardens in the grounds of castles and houses which are open to public, and in some cases gardens which are open to the public although the buildings are not.

ACHAMORE, Isle of Gigha, Argyll and Bute. Tel: 01583-505254. Established by Sir James Horlick of the hot drink fame. Rhododendrons and azaleas

ACHNACLOICH, Connel, Oban, Argyll and Bute. Tel: 01631-710221. Spring bulbs, azaleas, Japanese maples

AN CALA, Easdale, Isle of Seil, Argyll. Tel: 01852-300237. Created in 1930s. Water features

ARBUTHNOTT HOUSE, Laurencekirk, Kincardineshire. Tel: 01561-361226. Late 17th-century herbaceous borders, roses, rhododendrons, hostas

ARDENCRAIG, Rothesay, Isle of Bute. Tel: 01700-504644. Victorian hothouses

ARDKINGLAS WOODLAND GARDEN, Cairndow, Loch Fyne. Rhododendrons, azaleas, conifers

ARDTORNISH, Lochaline, Morvern, Oban, Highland. Tel: 01967-421288. Shrubs, deciduous trees, conifers, rhododendrons

ARDUAINE, Oban, Argyll and Bute. Tel: 01852-200366. Originally planted early 1900s. Restored after 1971. 20 acres. Lawns, lily ponds, mature woods, rhododendrons and magnolias

ARMADALE CASTLE AND MUSEUM OF THE ISLES. Armadale, Sleat, Isle of Skye. Tel: 01471-844305. Pond gardens, herbaceous border, lawns and ornamental trees

ASCOG HALL FERNERY AND GARDEN, nr Rothesay, Bute. Tel: 01700-504555. Victorian fernery. Boasts a fern reputed to be 1,000 years old

ATTADALE, Strathcarron, Highland. Tel: 01520-722217. Water features, rhododendron walk, herb plot

BALLINDALLOCH CASTLE, Grantown-on-Spey, Highland. Tel: 01807-500206. A 1937 rock garden, rose and fountain garden

BALMORAL CASTLE, Ballater, Aberdeenshire. Tel: 01339-742334. A 3-acre garden; rare coniferous forest trees, sunken rose garden, water garden

BELL'S CHERRYBANK GARDENS, Cherrybank, Perth. Tel: 01738-621111. Two 18-acre gardens; includes 830 varieties of heather, largest collection of heathers in Britain

BOLFRACKS, Aberfeldy, Perth and Kinross. Tel: 01887-820207. A 3-acre garden. Spring bulbs, shrub roses, gentians

BRANKLYN, 116 Dundee Road, Perth. Tel: 01738-625535. Alpine plants and rhododendrons on 2-acre hillside

BRODICK CASTLE, Isle of Arran, North Ayrshire. Tel: 01770-302202. Plants from Himalayas, China and South America, bog garden

BROUGHTON HOUSE, 12 High Street, Kirkcudbright, Dumfries and Galloway. Tel: 01557-330437. Created by artist E. A. Hornel. Sunken courtyard, Japanese garden, rose parterre

BROUGHTON PLACE, Broughton, Biggar, Scottish Borders. Tel: 01899-830234. An 18th-century beech avenue. National collections of thalictrums and tropaeolums

CAMBO, Kingsbarns, St. Andrews, Fife.
Tel: 01333-450054. Walled garden. Ornamental garden, lilac walk

CANDACRAIG, Dinnet, Aberdeenshire.
Tel: 01975-651226. An 1820s garden, cottage-garden flowers, mecanopsis, primulas

CASTLE FRASER, Sauchen, Inverurie, Aberdeenshire.
Tel: 01330-833463. A 17th- to 18th-century designed landscape, herbaceous border, walled garden

CASTLE KENNEDY, Stranraer, Wigtownshire, Dumfries and Galloway. Tel: 01776-702024. Laid out 1730. A 75-acre garden noted for monkey-puzzle trees, magnolias, rhododendrons, spring bulbs

CAWDOR CASTLE, Cawdor, Nairn, Highland.
Tel: 01667-404615. Herbaceous borders, peony border, rose tunnel, thistle garden, holly maze

CLUNY HOUSE, Aberfeldy, Perth and Kinross.
Tel: 01887-820795. Wild garden. National Collection of Asiatic primulas; meconopsis, rhododendrons

CRARAE, Minard, Inveraray, Argyll and Bute.
Tel: 01546-886614. Laid out early 20th-century as a 'Himalayan ravine' with 400 rhododendrons, azaleas, eucalyptus and conifers

CRATHES CASTLE, Banchory, Aberdeenshire.
Tel: 01330-844525. Eight themed gardens, rare shrubs, herbaceous borders. National Collection of Malmaison carnations

CRUICKSHANK BOTANIC GARDEN, University of Aberdeen, St. Machar Drive, Aberdeen.
Tel: 01224-272704. Eleven acres; arboretum, rose garden, water gardens. Essentially for research

CULZEAN CASTLE MAYBOLE, South Ayrshire.
Tel: 01655-884400. Camelia house and orangery, 563-acre country park, 30-acre garden, walled garden, herbaceous borders

DAWYCK BOTANIC, Stobo, Peebleshire, Scottish Borders. Tel: 01721-760254. Branch of Royal Botanic Garden Edinburgh. 300 years of tree-planting. Fine arboretum, beech walk, azalea terrace

DRUM CASTLE, Drumoak by Banchory, Aberdeenshire.
Tel: 01330-811204. Garden of historic roses. Herbaceous borders, plants from 17th- to 20th-centuries

DRUMMOND CASTLE, Muthill, Crieff, Perth and Kinross. Tel: 01764-681257. Laid out by John Drummond, 2nd Earl of Perth, 1630. French and Italian influence. A 17th-century Scottish garden

DUNROBIN CASTLE, Golspie, Sutherland, Highlands.
Tel: 01408-633177. Victorian formal gardens in French style, laid out 1850. Water features, roses, clematis, sweet peas

DUNVEGAN CASTLE, Isle of Skye. Tel: 01470-521206.
Box-wood parterre, mixed borders, fern houses, woodland waterfall dell, walled garden

EDZELL CASTLE, Edzell, Brechin, Angus.
Tel: 01356-648631.Walled garden dating from 1930s but laid out as it may have looked in early 1600s

FALKLAND PALACE, Falkland, Fife. Tel: 01337-857397.
Shrub island borders, herbaceous borders, delphiniums, orchard

FINLAYSTONE, Langbank, Renfrewshire.
Tel: 01475-540285. A ten-acre garden and 70-acre woodland laid out 1900. Herbaceous borders, copper beeches, Celtic paving maze, bog garden

FLOORS CASTLE, Kelso, Roxburghshire.
Tel: 01573-223333. Herbaceous borders, walled kitchen garden

GLAMIS CASTLE, Glamis, Forfar, Angus.
Tel: 01307-840393. Landscaped 1790s by designer influenced by Capability Brown. Two-acre Italian garden, herbaceous borders, gazebos

GLASGOW BOTANIC GARDENS, 730 Great Western Road, Glasgow. Tel: 0141-334 2422. Glasshouses contain orchids, cacti and ferns. Paths alongside wooded banks of River Kelvin

GLENARN, Rhu, Dunbartonshire. Tel: 01436-820493.
Woodland garden established 1920s. Rhododendrons, magnolias, olearias, pieris

GLENWHAN, Dunragit, Stranraer, Dumfries and Galloway. Tel: 01581-400222. A twelve-acre hillside garden laid out 1979. Exotic plants, trees and shrubs, lakes and bog gardens, rhododendrons, primulas

GREENBANK, Flenders Road, Clarkston, Glasgow.
Tel: 0141-639 3281. Walled garden, water features, woodland walks, herb garden

HADDO HOUSE, nr Tarves, Ellon, Aberdeenshire.
Tel: 01651-851440. With 177 acres of woodland, lakes and ponds, home to otters, red squirrels, pheasants and deer

HILL OF TARVIT, Cupar, Fife. Tel: 01334-653127. Rose garden, perennials and annuals, ornamental trees

HIRSEL, Coldstream, Berwickshire. Tel: 01890-882834.
Spring bulbs, rhododendrons, rose beds, herbaceous borders

HOUSE OF PITMUIES, Guthrie, by Forfar, Angus.
Tel: 01241-828245. Walled gardens, rhododendrons, semi-formal gardens with old fashioned roses and delphiniums

INVERESK LODGE, Musselburgh, East Lothian.
Tel: 01721-722502. Semi-formal gardens, shrub roses, conservatory

INVEREWE, Poolewe, Highlands. Tel: 01445-781200.
Brainchild of Osgood Mackenzie; created from 1865 covering the Am Ploc Ard peninsula. Wild garden, rock gardens, rhododendrons, vegetable garden and orchard. Species from around the world. National collections of olearias and ourisias

JURA HOUSE, Ardfin, Isle of Jura, Argyll and Bute. Tel: 01496-820315. Walled garden. Fuchsias, ferns and lichens. Antipodean plants. Organic walled garden

KAILZIE, Peebles, Peebleshire, Scottish Borders. Tel: 01721-720007. A 17-acre walled-garden. Spring bulbs, secret gardens, laburnum, rhododendrons, azaleas, mecanopsis, primulas. Trout pond

KELLIE CASTLE, Pittenweem, Fife. Tel: 01333-720271. Lawn edged with box-hedges and borders, roses, vegetable garden, woodland walks

KILDRUMMY CASTLE, Alford, Aberdeenshire. Tel: 01975-571203. Rock garden, water garden, Japanese garden, maples, rhododendrons, acers, mecanopsis

KILMORY WOODLAND PARK, nr Lochgilphead. Gardens laid out in 1830 around Kilmory Castle

KINROSS HOUSE, Kinross, Perth and Kinross. A four-acre formal walled garden designed 1680s. Herbaceous borders, rose borders, ornamental yew hedges

LECKMELM SHRUBBERY AND ARBORETUM, Little Leckmelm House, Lochbroom, Ullapool, Highland. A ten-acre arboretum

LEITH HALL, Huntly, Aberdeenshire. Tel: 01464-831216. Rock garden, perennial borders, catmint border, water features

LOGAN BOTANIC GARDEN, Port Logan, Stranraer, Dumfries and Galloway. Tel: 01776-860231. Outpost of Edinburgh's Royal Botanic Garden. Exotic plants from around the world. Excellent collection of Scottish tender perennials. A one hundred year old walled garden. Water garden, palms and ferns. Eucalyptus, magnolias

MALLENY, Balerno, Edinburgh. Tel: 0131-449 2283. Three-acre walled garden with Deodar cedar. With 17th-century clipped yews. Herbaceous borders, herb and ornamental vegetable garden. National Collection of 19th-century shrub roses

MANDERSTON, Duns, Scottish Borders. Tel: 01361-883450. With 56 acres including formal terraces, woodland garden, formal walled garden, water features

MEGGINCH CASTLE, Errol, Perthshire. Tel: 01821-642222. Gardens and Gothic courtyard of 1806. Yew and holly topiary, 1,000 year old yews, 18th-century walled garden and annual border

MELLERSTAIN HOUSE, nr Earlston, Borders. Tel: 01573-410225. Parkland and formal Edwardian gardens, rose garden laid out by Sarah, 12th Countess of Haddington

MERTOUN, St Boswell's, Roxburghshire, Scottish Borders. A 26-acre flower garden beside the Tweed. Azaleas, herbaceous border, ornamental pond. 3-acre walled garden

MONTEVIOT, Jedburgh, Scottish Borders. River garden with herbaceous perennials and shrubs. Rose gardens, water garden

MOUNT STUART HOUSE, Rothesay, Isle of Bute. With 300-acres of designed landscape. A mature pinetum, lime tree avenue, conifers, rock gardens, kitchen and herb garden, exotic southern hemisphere plants

PITMEDDEN, Pitmedden, Ellon, Aberdeenshire. Tel: 01651-842352. A 17th-century patterned garden, box hedging and annuals. Herbaceous borders

PRIORWOOD GARDEN, Melrose. Orchard; flowers suitable for drying

ROYAL BOTANIC GARDEN, EDINBURGH. Inverleith Row, Edinburgh. Tel: 0131-552 7171. Established 17th-century, now a 75-acre site. Noted for rhododendrons and azaleas. Rock garden, peat and woodland gardens, herbaceous borders. Arboretum. Glasshouses display orchids, giant water-lilies and 200-year-old West Indian palm tree. Chinese Garden

ST ANDREWS BOTANIC GARDEN, Canongate, St. Andrews. Tel: 01334-477178. Peat, rock and water gardens

SEA VIEW, Durnamuck, Dundonnell, Highland. Tel: 01854-633317. Began 1990 on shores of Little Loch Broom. Heather bed, rock garden, orchard, bog garden

TEVIOT WATER GARDEN, Kirkbank House, Eckford, Kelso, Scottish Borders. Tel: 01835-850734. Waterfalls, aquatic plants, perennials, grasses, ferns, bamboos

THREAVE, Stewartry, Castle Douglas, Dumfries and Galloway. Tel: 01556-502575. A 65-acre garden used as a school of horticulture since 1960. Perennials and annuals. Walled garden, vegetable garden and orchard. Woodland and rock gardens. Specialty rose garden and rhododendrons. Arboretum

TOROSAY CASTLE, Craignure, Isle of Mull, Argyll and Bute. Tel: 01680-812421. Formal Italian garden with Italian rococo statues. Water garden, Japanese garden, rhododendrons, azaleas. Australian and New Zealand trees and shrubs

UNIVERSITY OF DUNDEE BOTANIC GARDEN, Riverside Drive, Dundee. Tel: 01382-566939. A 23-acre garden, glasshouses

YOUNGER BOTANIC GARDENS, Dunoon, Argyll and Bute. Tel: 01369-706261. Offshoot of Edinburgh's Royal Botanic Gardens. Flowering trees and shrubs. With 250 species of rhododendrons and Great Redwoods planted in 1863; magnolias; arboretum

THE ARTS IN SCOTLAND

The distinctive character of the arts in Scotland is recognised worldwide. While the country is perhaps most widely known for the works of certain writers (Scott, Burns, MacGonagall) and for its traditional music and dance, and the popular concepts of 'Scottishness', Scotland has produced, and continues to produce, internationally important works of art, architecture, literature, classical music, and cinema. Scotland has over 150 art galleries and 180 performing arts venues. In the performing arts, Scottish musicians and actors are outstanding in many fields.

Crafts, too, are thriving. A significant percentage (14 per cent) of the total population involved in crafts in Britain work in Scotland, a proportion which rose sharply during the 1980s, possibly under the influence of rapidly expanding tourism.

Around 50,000 people in Scotland work in the cultural sector, and the creative industries (including architecture, arts and cultural industries, advertising, design, film, interactive leisure software, music, new media, publishing, radio and television) are worth an estimated £5 billion to the Scottish economy annually. Glasgow's designation as European City of Culture in 1990 is widely held to have given a big stimulus to its wider regeneration in the 1990s, and this was boosted by it being City of Architecture and Design in 1999.

NATIONAL CULTURAL STRATEGY

In August 2000 the Scottish Executive released its National Cultural Strategy for Scotland, a new policy framework to guide the work of national and local government and cultural bodies in planning, promoting and resourcing cultural activity. The Strategy sets out the Scottish Executive's objectives regarding promoting creativity, celebrating Scotland's diverse cultural heritage, realising the potential contribution of culture to education at all stages, and ensuring an effective national framework of support to all aspects of culture in national life. It calls for a holistic approach to the arts within the departments of the Scottish Executive itself, especially those concerned with education, tourism and the creative industries. The Executive announced the allocation of an additional £7.25 million to kick-start the Strategy. The Strategy's priorities include:
- developing a political and economic climate supportive to people working in the arts
- enhancing Scotland's creative industries
- celebrating excellence in the arts, including recognising the importance of Scottish traditional arts

- supporting companies with national scope beyond the existing companies generally thought of as 'national companies' (Scottish Opera, Scottish Ballet, the Royal Scottish National Orchestra and the Scottish Chamber Orchestra)
- promoting all the languages of Scotland, including non-European languages spoken as well as Gaelic and Scots
- conserving, presenting and promoting Scotland's cultural heritage
- promoting international cultural exchange
- promoting and enhancing the arts in education and lifelong learning, with an emphasis on the importance of equal access to learning and tuition, especially for schoolchildren
- developing wider opportunities for cultural access, overcoming perceptions of the arts as a preserve of the elite
- maximising the social benefits of culture to both individuals and communities

Among the activities under way or contemplated are the development of a national architecture strategy, the development of a policy on contemporary popular music, and the formation of a ministerial task force to carry forward the work of promoting the arts as an important strand of cultural tourism. Delivering the priorities outlined in the Strategy is a commitment of the Scottish Executive's budget spending in financial year 2002–2003.

ANNUAL PLANNED SCOTTISH EXECUTIVE BUDGET EXPENDITURE ON TOURISM, CULTURE AND SPORTS (£M)

2003–4	2004–5	2005–6
209	235	254

Source: Scottish Executive, The Scottish Budget annual expenditure report of the Scottish Executive

ARTS FESTIVALS IN SCOTLAND

Founded in 1947, the Edinburgh International Festival (EIF) was the first major festival of the arts to be established in Europe as it recovered from the cataclysm of World War II. It was the initiative of Rudolph Byng, director of the Glyndebourne Festival Opera. Ironically, London, Oxford and Cambridge all turned down Byng's proposals for a festival in the style of Salzburg or Bayreuth, and the Edinburgh Festival quickly expanded to become one of the world's major festivals of the arts, attracting world-class performers in music, opera and drama each

August, surrounded by a flotilla of other events. In 2003 an estimated 400,000 people attended Festival events. Simultaneously with the EIF, the Festival Fringe and the Edinburgh International Film, Jazz and Book Festivals are held. The Fringe in particular has grown exponentially in recent years and now features thousands of events at hundreds of venues. In 1998 it decided to shift its dates to a week before the opening of the EIF; the decision proved controversial but has been sustained. In 2000 the Edinburgh Military Tattoo which always accompanies the Festival celebrated its 50th anniversary.

Edinburgh is the largest but by no means the only arts festival held regularly in Scotland. The annual St Magnus Festival in Orkney (June) is an important event, particularly for classical music, with a strong focus on new music and on involving the local community. There are big festivals at Glasgow (Celtic Connections, January; Glasgow International Jazz Festival, July; World Pipe Band Championship, August); Aberdeen (Aberdeen International Youth Festival, July; Aberdeen Alternative Festival, October; Bon Accord Festival, June), Perth (Perth Festival of the Arts, May), Dundee (Dundee City Festival, June), Caithness (Northlands Festival, September, an annual celebration of Scottish and Nordic cultures in the north of Scotland), and many other places. There is even an annual Mendelssohn festival on the Isle of Mull.

Festivals focusing chiefly on traditional music and jazz are held in many towns and regions throughout the country. A large pop music festival, 'T in the Park', is held annually in Balado, Kinross, Fife, in July. T in the Park is now one of the UK's biggest music festivals with over 100 bands appearing over a two-day period, on seven sound stages. An average of 52,000 people attend the festival on each day and acts for 2003 included REM, The Polyphonic Spree, Coldplay, Supergrass, Turin Brakes, The Coral and Sugababes.

Detailed information on festivals can be obtained from the Scottish Arts Council, tourist boards, and the Scottish Music Information Centre.

THE SCOTTISH ARTS COUNCIL

The Scottish Arts Council (SAC) is the principal channel for government funding of the contemporary arts and crafts in Scotland and a key actor in the development of Scotland's arts and cultural policy. It receives an annual grant from the Scottish Executive, most of which is distributed to arts organisations and individual artists and craftspeople across Scotland, and is the channel for distributing National Lottery funds to the arts in Scotland. It also does important work in the promotion of arts education in schools.

However, despite the support of the SAC, arts funding is a perennial problem, particularly for many of the larger institutions. Because Scotland has a small population relative to its size, expected audiences outwith the Edinburgh–Glasgow central belt and the major arts festivals are inevitably lower than in, for instance, the south-east of England, and it is not always easy to attract funding or sponsorship, particularly for permanent entities such as galleries and performance spaces or the national performing companies. Scottish Opera, for instance, has suffered periodic funding crises almost since its foundation, and a lively debate surrounds its current funding and the balance between its roles of promoting and commissioning new indigenous opera (such as James MacMillan's *Inés de Castro*, premièred in 1996) and presenting high-quality and high-profile productions of well-known works (such as the current productions of Wagner's Ring cycle).

SUMMARY OF SAC BUDGET, 2002/03 AND 2003/04: GRANT ALLOCATION, LOTTERY AND GENERAL FUND COMBINED

Budget item	2003/4 £	2002/3 £
Arts Development		
Crafts	577,509	641,531
Dance	1,500,677	1,234,092
Drama	8,829,900	7,774,926
Literature	1,916,285	2,086,785
Music	2,511,618	2,316,618
Visual Arts	3,129,408	3,131,408
National Companies	14,503,088	15,488,088
Policy and Research	220,000	220,000
Multi Arts Organisations	2,005,500	1,854,000
International Fund	500,000	500,000
Digital Media	125,000	125,000
Burns Theme Activities	150,000	125,000
Arts Development	5,220,000	6,849,000
Total	41,188,985	42,346,448
Strategic Development		
Organisations	1,674,015	1,582,552
Professional Support	850,000	1,600,000
Audience Development	820,000	720,000
Cultural Diversity	380,000	480,000
Arts and Disability	350,000	200,000
Area Development	140,000	155,000
Education	1,103,000	1,323,000
Arts and Tourism	25,000	25,000
Voluntary and Community Arts	30,000	30,000
Capital	9,000,000	9,500,000
TOTAL	14,372,015	15,615,552
Total Direct Services and Administration	4,600,000	4,600,000
TOTAL GRANTS ALLOCATED	60,161,000	62,562,000

Source: Scottish Arts Council.

ARTS COUNCIL GRANTS

Annual grant to SAC from Scottish Executive:

2003–4:   £36.9 million
2004–5:   £38.8 million
2005–6:   £40.1 million

LOTTERY FUNDING TO THE ARTS

The SAC has distributed over £190 million in National Lottery funds to Scottish artists and arts organisations since 1995. As elsewhere in Britain, the bulk of Lottery funding tends to go to building projects, and some of these have been impressive, e.g. The Hub, Edinburgh (an all-year-round base for the Edinburgh Festival, opened in June 1999, containing an auditorium, rehearsal space, café-bar, and ticket office); Dundee Contemporary Arts Centre (opened in March 1999, containing two art cinema screens, galleries, a printmaking studio, and a café-bar); An Tuireann Arts Centre in Portree, Skye; refurbishment of the Tron Theatre, Glasgow; and the proposed upgrading of Edinburgh's Usher Hall to turn it into a world-class concert venue by 2010.

RESEARCH AND POLICY DEVELOPMENT

As part of an ongoing research programme, the SAC has initiated several pieces of research on the impact of the arts in Scotland, including a two-year study of the impact of lottery-funded arts buildings. The Scottish Executive has taken up the SAC's recommendation, made in a recent study on cultural statistics, that it play a central co-ordinating role in gathering and disseminating statistics on cultural activity, as an aid to planning.

The SAC has followed the National Cultural Strategy process closely and has published a comprehensive response to the strategy. It is the principal channel for additional or specific funding to initiatives under the strategy.

AWARDS

The SAC issues a number of awards for excellence in the different arts. A new set of awards, started in 2000 are the Creative Scotland Awards, 10 of which, each worth £30,000, are awarded annually to established artists living in Scotland and working in architecture, crafts, dance, design, digital media, drama/theatre, film/video, literature, music, photography, visual arts, and other art forms. The substantial size of the awards reflects their purpose in enabling artists to undertake new projects of significant scope. The 2003 award winners were:

Jim Buckley, visual artist/sculptor: to create light sculptures in Clydebank and Aberdeen.
Malcolm Fraser, architect: to create an outdoor dance studio/exhibition space in Edinburgh's Grassmarket

that will convert into an ice rink during the winter months.
Ian Hamilton Finlay, visual artist and poet: to create a 'grove of tree shadows' in his Little Sparta Garden, Dunsyre.
Brian Kellock, jazz pianist: for new compositions.
Frank Kuppner, writer: to investigate the work of the poet Thomas Campbell and produce new writings based on his life.
Nicola McCartney, writer: to write the first draft of a novel, *Ice Angel.*
Bernard MacLaverty, writer: to write and direct a short film based on *Bye Child,* a poem by Seamus Heaney.
Gordon MacPherson, composer: to create a multimedia piece exploring paranormal phenomena.
Mark O'Keeffe, musician: to develop a multi-disciplinary work, based on the trumpet.
Colette Sadler, choreographer: to explore and redefine the boundaries of visual art and dance.

COUNCIL MEETINGS

All SAC Council meetings are public and are held at different venues around the country.

Information on the Scottish Arts Council, its funding policies, and the arts in Scotland can be obtained from the SAC Helpdesk Tel: 0845-603 6000.

LITERATURE

It is impossible here to survey the whole wealth of Scottish literature; but we can mention a few of the best-known authors, beginning with William Dunbar and Robert Henryson, two of the 'Scottish Chaucerians' of the 15th- and 16th-centuries. These poets were all clearly influenced by Chaucer, but were by no means imitators of him. Writing in Scots, Dunbar, court poet to James IV, wrote celebratory poetry for the king but also mordant satire with equal virtuosity. Henryson returned several times to classical themes such as the tales of Orpheus and Eurydice, Troilus and Cressida (his most overt reference to Chaucer, but with an alternative ending), and his *Morall Fabillis,* which look back to Aesop. Sir David Lindsay's great morality play, *Ane Pleasant Satyre of the Thrie Estaitis,* is the first surviving play in Scottish literature (1540).

The 18th- and early 19th-centuries produced the two most famous figures in Scottish literature: Robert Burns and Sir Walter Scott. The immense popularity of both authors has turned them into icons of 'Scottishness', though from very different perspectives. Both were immensely prolific, and both confronted the enormous changes taking place in Scottish society and governance after the suppression of Jacobitisim. But whereas Burns, the son of an Ayrshire tenant farmer, is loved for his celebration of ordinary people and democratic values and for his ability to express personal feelings, particularly love, in vivid and apparently simple verse and song, the novels and poems of Scott (who came from a more prosperous farming family in the Borders and had a successful career as a lawyer) reflect a vision of history that, while romantic and mythologising, also helped to revive and sustain an idea of Scottish identity and nation.

From the late Victorian era and the turn of the 20th-century come several well-known authors such as Robert Louis Stevenson, J. M. Barrie, and John Buchan. Then, from the 1920s onward, there was a fresh flowering of Scottish literature which has become known as the 'Scottish Renaissance'. One of its instigators, and its main poet, was Hugh McDiarmid, possibly most famous for *A drunk man looks at the thistle* (1926). The novels of Neil M. Gunn, Sir Compton Mackenzie, Lewis Grassic Gibbon, Jessie Kesson and others deal in different ways with social change and social conditions of the time – and, in the case of Gunn in particular, of other times in Scotland's history. The poems and novels of George Mackay Brown are also steeped in history, landscape and lore; that of his native Orkney.

The last two decades have seen a new generation of Scottish novelists and a shift of attention towards often uncompromising realism and urban themes. These writers include James Kelman, Janice Galloway, Candia McWilliam and Irvine Welsh. Since early 2000 the Edinburgh-based children's author J. K. Rowling has achieved great celebrity – and become one of the world's most highly-paid authors – through the runaway success of her series of *Harry Potter* novels.

LEWIS GRASSIC GIBBON

February 2001 marks the centenary of the birth of Lewis Grassic Gibbon (pseudonym of James Leslie Mitchell, 1901–35), novelist, short-story writer, and journalist. Born near Kirktown of Auchterless, Aberdeenshire, Gibbon lived and worked as a journalist in Aberdeen, Glasgow and London before moving to Welwyn Garden City, Hertfordshire. It was there he wrote his best-known work, the novel trilogy *A Scots Quair* (for which he adopted his mother's name as a pseudonym), set in the rural society of the Mearns where he spent his formative years. An extremely prolific writer considering his short life, he wrote 17 books in seven years, including, as well as the Quair (1932–4), *Stained Radiance* (1930), *The Thirteenth Disciple* (1931) *Three Go*

Back (1932), and *Gay Hunter* (1934). He was of socialist opinions and wide-ranging interests; his short stories appeared in *Scottish Scene*, a miscellany co-written with Hugh MacDiarmid, and he also wrote on the great explorers, human prehistory and history, and Mesoamerican archaeology. His last, unfinished novel, *The Speak of the Mearns*, was posthumously published in 1982.

NIGEL TRANTER

Nigel Tranter (1909–2000), novelist and historian was born in Glasgow. He published over 140 books, including the many historical novels for which he is best known, children's fiction, and non-fiction works chiefly on the history, lore and landscape of Scotland. Under the pseudonym Nye Tredgold, he also published a series of novels set in the American West. His novels on Scottish themes include: *Trespass* (1937), *Margaret the Queen* (1979), *Columba* (1987), *Highness in Hiding* (1995), and the quadrilogy *Sword of State*, the last volume of which was published in 2000. Non-fiction includes: *The fortified house in Scotland* (6 vols, 1962–6),

GAELIC LITERATURE

Alongside literature in English and Scots stands a strong tradition of poetry and prose in Gaelic reaching back to at least the early Middle Ages and encompassing heroic ballads narrating the deeds of legendary figures; an oral tradition of prose sagas; poems of praise written by professional bards in the services of clan chiefs and the nobility; songs and love poems, many of them anonymous, from the 16th- and 17th-centuries; poems of satire and nostalgia expressing a specifically Gaelic consciousness in response to the slow disintegration of Highland culture after the Jacobite rebellion and, later, the Clearances; and religious prose works. Much of the oral tradition in both prose and poetry was collected and written down in the 18th- and 19th-centuries. An Comunn Gaidhealach, founded in 1891 to promote Gaelic language and culture, increased interest in Gaelic writing in Gaelic-language periodicals which published stories and essays. Contemporary issues began to be written about in Gaelic.

Iain Crichton Smith (1928–98) was among those instrumental in maintaining and enriching the tradition of Gaelic prose writing after World War II, with novels and collections of stories. Sorley Maclean (1911–96) is a seminal figure in 20th-century Gaelic poetry; and he has been followed by a generation of young writers, particularly poets, carrying writing in Gaelic strongly into the new millennium.

CURRENT INSTITUTIONS

Several organisations of different kinds exist for the promotion of Scottish literature. The Association for Scottish Literary Studies, based at the University of Glasgow, promotes the study, teaching and writing of Scotland's literature and languages. Founded in 1970, it is now an international organisation with members in over 20 countries. It publishes a variety of periodicals (e.g. *Scottish Studies Review*), and in addition publishes each year an edition of a Scottish work which has either gone out of print or needs to be reintroduced to a contemporary readership, and an anthology of new writing.

The Scottish Poetry Library is a reference and lending library promoting Scottish and other poetry. Among other services, it has a computerised index to its collection called INSPIRE (International and Scottish Poetry Information Resource). The Society of Authors in Scotland is an independent trade union representing writers' interests in all areas of the profession.

The literary journal and magazine scene in Scotland is also lively, with old and new periodicals including the *Edinburgh Review*, *Cencrastus* (Edinburgh), *Cutting Teeth* (Glasgow), *Dark Horse* (Glasgow), *Inscotland* (Edinburgh, formerly *Books in Scotland*), *Markings* (Kirkcudbright), *Northwords* (Inverness), *Poetry Scotland* (Edinburgh), and *Scottish Studies* (Edinburgh). *Gairm*, the only all-Gaelic quarterly in existence, has been published since 1952; *Lallans*, the journal of the Scots Language Society, publishes work in Scots.

In addition, many of the major Scottish publishers specialise in Scottish literature, e.g. Canongate, Polygon, Chapman, and a number of small and locally focused presses.

In February 2001 the first Literature Forum for Scotland was inaugurated, bringing together representatives of literature organisations, writers, publishers, and the Literature Department and Literature Committee of the SAC. It was established in response to an audit of Scottish literature organisations commissioned in 2000 by the SAC, and examined the formulation of a national policy for literature and publishing in Scotland.

EVENTS AND AWARDS

Coinciding with the Edinburgh International Festival, the annual Edinburgh International Book Festival holds readings, meetings and interviews with writers and publishers, and sells a wide range of books. The Book Festival is annually attended by 100,000 people and hundreds of authors, with over 600 author events taking place in 2002.

The Scottish Arts Council issues Spring and Autumn Book Awards and has recently instituted annual Children's Book Awards. Other awards include the Dundee Book Prize (University of Dundee), the Fidler Award for children's literature (c/o Scottish Book Trust), the James Tait Black Memorial Prize (Department of English Literature at the University of Edinburgh), the Macallan/ *Scotland on Sunday* Short Story Competition, the RLS Memorial Award (National Library of Scotland), the Scottish International Open Poetry Competition, the Saltire Society Scottish Literary Awards, and the Scottish Writer of the Year (c/o Scottish Book Trust).

In 2001–2 the SAC instituted a New Writers' Bursaries Scheme, offering eight bursaries to writers with few or no previous publications.

THEATRE

The development of a Scottish theatre tradition can be effectively dated only to the late 19th-century. In the early 16th-century, mystery and morality plays such as Sir David Lindsay's *Ane Pleasant Satyre of the Thrie Estaitis*, were performed in a theatrical context very similar to that of England at the time. However, under the pressure of the Reformation, theatre then virtually disappeared in Scotland. The removal of the artistic patronage of the court which moved to London in 1603 and the 1737 Licensing Act, directed at political satire all had an impact. When theatrical performance did surface again it was often in the form of music hall, which began in the early 19th-century, nurtured performers such as Harry Lauder, Harry Gordon and, later, comedy actors such as Jimmy Logan and Stanley Baxter, and declined in popularity only in the 1950s and 1960s.

The 20th-century saw the development of a distinct Scottish voice in the theatre and at the same time the establishment of many theatres and theatre companies presenting a broader repertoire. Several of the existing repertory companies were founded between 1935 and 1965. Companies concentrating on plays by Scottish authors, such as the Scottish National Players, were founded in the early 20th-century but have disappeared. However, the promotion of indigenous talent has been taken up by others, often by touring companies, for instance 7:84 Scotland, formed in 1973. In the late 1990s, the Traverse Theatre, an important arena for new work, has increasingly featured work by Scottish playwrights, both established dramatists such as Liz Lochhead and Edwin Morgan and a new generation including Mike Cullen, David Greig, Stephen Greenhorn, Zinnie Harris, and Nicola McCartney. The Traverse in Edinburgh and the Tron Theatre in Glasgow both have annual showcase festivals of new writing.

In the National Cultural Strategy (August 2000) the Scottish Executive expressed the view that the time is right to begin working towards the establishment of a national theatre for Scotland. However, in 2003 the Executive stated that the £1 million that had originally been set aside in 2003 to develop this project had been given over to the support of theatre infrastructure instead of the proposed national theatre. While the Scottish Arts Council welcomed the proposal, the debate about whether Scotland should have a national theatre analogous to existing national companies such as Scottish Opera or Scottish Ballet is long-running and unresolved. Key figures in the Scottish Arts scene, such as Liz Lochhead and Janice Galloway, have criticised the Executive's slowness to support the project in financial terms. The Federation of Scottish Theatre proposed a Scottish national theatre which would be a commissioning institution, without a specific building or a permanent company, under which existing companies and artists would present new work as national theatre productions. But the potential constraints on artistic freedom implied in a high degree of public funding are of concern to many practitioners in the Scottish theatre.

Sir James (Jimmy) Shand (1908–2000), musician. Born East Wemyss, Fife. One of Scotland's best-known country dance musicians and band leaders, as popular in the countries of the Scottish diaspora as in Scotland itself, particularly in the 1950s and 1960s. He made many appearances on television, for instance in Andy's Stewart's *White Heather Club*. Awarded MBE 1962; knighted 1999.

Jimmy Logan (James Short, 1928–2001), actor and entertainer. Born Glasgow. Awarded OBE 1996 and elected a Fellow of the RSAMD in 1998. He began working in the theatre at 14 and by 1944 was in pantomime, in which he acted for many years. His 'straight' acting debut was in 1949, in a film, *Floodtide*. He had dramatic roles in many plays, including *The Mating Game* (1973), *The Entertainer* (1984), *The Comedians* (1991), and *Death of a Salesman* (1992), and is also remembered for his show based on the life of Scottish music-hall entertainer Sir Harry Lauder (1870–1950). In 1964 he bought and refurbished the Glasgow Metropole Theatre, but the Glasgow authorities blocked any further development of it.

CURRENT INSTITUTIONS

While Scotland may not yet have a single 'national' company, it has a large number of theatre companies and venues great and small. While the Edinburgh Festival Theatre boasts the largest stage in Britain; the Mull Theatre at Dervaig, Isle of Mull, is one of the smallest professional theatres in the world. The Perth Theatre is the oldest continuously producing rep in Scotland and in 2000 celebrated its 100th birthday and its 65th year as a repertory theatre. The Traverse, formed in 1963, was Scotland's first studio theatre company and has always focused on new productions from within and outside of Scotland. In the early 1990s it moved into new premises next to the Usher Hall in Edinburgh. In Glasgow, the Citizens' Theatre is known for productions of European drama. Other important repertory theatres are the Dundee Rep, the Pitlochry Festival Theatre, and the Byre (St Andrews). Other major theatre buildings range from the Edwardian splendour of His Majesty's Theatre at Aberdeen (1904–6) and the spare lines of the Traverse in Edinburgh (1992) to imaginative conversions of other buildings, such as the Byre Theatre at St Andrews, a former cowshed which opened as a theatre in 1933 and has reopened in June 2001 after rebuilding.

Several touring companies are active, some attached to larger institutions. Touring theatre, dance and opera companies are extremely important in Scotland given the low population density and widely-spaced communities outside the central belt.

A number of projects also recognise the social benefits of participation in theatre for communities and individuals. Dundee Rep's Theatre Community Department includes a community drama outreach team, a specialist drama therapy service, and an arts advocacy project. Citizens' Theatre, located in the Gorbals in Glasgow – still one of Scotland's poorest areas – has long been committed to work involving the local community, and holds its Community Performance project twice a year, one in the spring and one in the autumn. The autumn project is specifically a Culturally Diverse Project with people whose first language is not English. At Theatre Workshop Edinburgh disabled performers work alongside able-bodied.

Educational institutions for theatre include the Royal Scottish Academy of Music and Drama, to which the drama school was added in 1945, and Scottish Youth Theatre. The Federation of Scottish Theatre is a professional association of Scottish theatre companies, the voice of Scottish theatre to funding bodies and the public, and the umbrella organisation for anyone professionally involved in theatre in Scotland.

MUSIC

CLASSICAL MUSIC

There is archaeological evidence of music-making in Scotland as far back as the eighth century BC, in finds such as a fragment of a bronze horn of that date, a carnyx (a long bronze war trumpet) from about 200 BC–AD 200, and representations of musical instruments on Pictish stone carvings of the eighth to tenth centuries AD.

The first music manuscripts containing Scottish music date from the 13th-century, although some of the music in them, such as the chants for St Columba, may be older. They bear witness to a highly developed tradition of church music in Scotland, which seems to have reached its peak in the early 16th-century with the work of Robert Carver, Scotland's greatest pre-Reformation composer and one of its greatest of any period. The manuscript containing all his extant work is one of the few music books to have survived the destruction wrought by the Reformation. Choral music from the late 16th-century shows how radically the style of music permitted in church changed from the complex polyphony of Carver to unornamented hymn tunes and psalm settings, in Scots rather than Latin. Instrumental music, such as the keyboard works of William Kinloche, dating from c.1610, shows a continuing secular tradition with some distinct echoes of contemporary French styles. However, the Union of the Crowns in 1603 and the removal of the court to London and its patronage of the arts was a severe blow to classical musicians.

From the late 17th-century a flow of composers and performers between Scotland and Italy began, stimulated in part by the fast-growing popularity of the violin in Scotland. One of the first to travel was John Clerk of Penicuik, who studied with Corelli. Among his many cantatas was one celebrating the ill-fated Darien venture of 1689; like its subject, it was abandoned unfinished. William McGibbon (1695–1756) was a leading Scottish composer of the late Baroque period, writing sonatas for violin and flute, trio sonatas and variations on Scottish folk tunes.

In the late 18th- and the 19th- centuries, political and social turbulence and a shortage of resources limited the production of composed music. Sir Alexander Campbell Mackenzie (1947–1935), although based chiefly in London and Germany, produced several works on Scottish themes; his *Scottish Concerto* was made famous by the pianist Paderewski.

In the late 20th-century, after the foundation of the Edinburgh International Festival and the establishment of the major orchestras and Scottish Opera and Ballet, a new wave of outstanding composers based in Scotland arose. These include Sally Beamish, James MacMillan, Sir Peter Maxwell Davies, Thea Musgrave, Ronald Stevenson, William Sweeney and Judith Weir. The new generation currently active includes Stuart Macrae, Magnus Robb and Marc Yeats.

TRADITIONAL MUSIC

Alongside – and intertwined with – the history of composed classical music runs a strong double strand of Gaelic and Scots traditional music, unbroken for centuries. It is an essentially oral tradition, and although many of the old songs and tunes have been written down since the 17th-century and have been the subject for much scholarship, the tradition is passionately alive today and continually developing. The Gaelic tradition is the oldest of all, and was probably brought to Scotland with the early settlers from Ireland. Its characteristic instrument is the clàrsach, or Celtic harp. A well-known form of Gaelic song is the *waulking song*, a strongly rhythmic work song which accompanied the hand-treatment of linen or tweed cloth. The tradition of Scots-language songs and ballads began later, in about the 13th-century, and included epic narrative ballads as well as work songs and dance forms. The industrial revolution, the Clearances, and emigration were later ballad themes.

The 17th-century, while something of a fallow period for large-scale classical compositions, was one of the richest times for the ballad tradition and especially for Gaelic music. It was in this period that the music of the pipes and the uniquely Scottish *piobaireachd* or *pibroch* form were developed. Similarly, in the 19th-century, perhaps the strongest area of musical activity, in part inspired by romantic views of Scottish history, was the collection, notation and arrangement of folk-songs, ballads and fiddle tunes. In fact, people had been writing ballads down since the 16th-century, and Robert Burns was an avid collector and writer of songs (many of which were recorded by the traditional singer Jean Redpath in the 1970s). The National Mod, an annual, competitive festival of performing arts in Gaelic, was instituted in 1892 and remains an important instrument for the promotion of Gaelic culture.

The last 20 years have seen a big upsurge in traditional music and popular music with strong folk elements, building upon the pioneering work of Ewan McColl and his recordings of Scottish popular ballads in the 1950s and 1960s. A few key figures of the many musicians in this movement are the Boys of the Lough with the Shetland fiddle player Aly Bain, the Whistlebinkies, fiddler Alasdair

Fraser, singers Cathy-Ann McPhee and Sheena Wellington, and bands singing in Gaelic such as Runrig and Capercaillie.

A POLICY FOR CONTEMPORARY POPULAR MUSIC

In March 2001 the SAC issued a policy statement on support for contemporary popular music, in line with its response to the National Cultural Strategy and after a two-year consultation process. This is the first time a British arts council has proposed a policy on pop music. The policy statement covers a wide range of current music styles and recommends actions including encouragement for the development of a national showcase event for new talent, support for training young promoters, agents and managers, and support for pilot touring projects.

CURRENT MUSICAL INSTITUTIONS

Scotland's contemporary musical life is underpinned by several national performing companies: the Royal Scottish National Orchestra (RNSO; founded 1890), Scottish Opera (founded 1962 under Alexander Gibson), and the Scottish Chamber Orchestra (SCO; founded 1974). Each of these has an associated chorus, and there is also an Edinburgh Festival Chorus which performs specifically for the Festival. The BBC Scottish Symphony Orchestra is based in Glasgow. There are also a number of smaller professional orchestras and vocal groups of international status, such as the BT Scottish Ensemble, the Paragon Ensemble and Cappella Nova.

The National Youth Orchestras of Scotland (NYOS), formed in 1979, comprises four orchestras: the National Youth Orchestra of Scotland (symphony orchestra), Camerata Scotland (a pre-professional chamber orchestra), the National Children's Orchestra of Scotland, and the National Youth Jazz Orchestra of Scotland. Together, they aim to provide a continuous sequence of practical music education and playing experience from nursery-school age to the professional level.

St Mary's Music School in Edinburgh is Scotland's only independent school for gifted young musicians. It has just 65 pupils aged between 9 and 19 and students must prove their talents in any number of musical fields, including singing, composing, and playing. All places are grant-aided through the Scottish Executive and as well as talent children have to show real dedication to music. The school's academic results are the highest in Scotland (hardly surprising considering the teacher/pupil ratio is in excess of one to one). By 2006 every pupil in Scotland's State education system will be given the opportunity to take a year of free music lessons before they reach primary six. The Scottish Executive earmarked £17.5 million for this project in February 2003. The Royal Scottish Academy of Music and Drama, in Glasgow, is the chief higher education institution for music, theatre and opera. It began in 1928 as the Scottish National Academy of Music, becoming the Royal Scottish Academy of Music in 1944 and adding the drama school the following year.

For traditional music, the Traditional Music and Song Association of Scotland, founded in 1966, is a valuable resource centre. Also in Glasgow, the Piping Centre is a national centre for the promotion of the bagpipes and their music.

DANCE

CLASSICAL DANCE

Scottish Ballet is Scotland's national classical dance company. Originally formed in Bristol in 1957 as Western Theatre Ballet, it moved to Glasgow in 1969, and on 3 May that year had a famous debut together with Scottish Opera in Berlioz's *The Trojans*. The company's arrival to take on the role of Scotland's national ballet company followed a series of unsuccessful attempts to establish such a company from about 1940 onwards, one candidate for which had been the Glasgow-based Celtic Ballet Company run by Margaret Morris, wife of the Colourist painter J. D. Fergusson.

Scottish Ballet performs both large-scale classics with a full dance company and orchestra in major theatres such as the Edinburgh Festival Theatre and chamber works for much smaller forces in spaces as small as a village hall or school gym. Its Education Unit carries out an extensive programme of education and outreach work in schools from nursery to secondary level (both mainstream and special education), universities and colleges of further education, community groups and hospitals, and with senior citizens groups and sight- and hearing-impaired adults. It organises summer schools and courses, and can tailor projects to meet the needs of specific groups.

DanceBase in Edinburgh's Grassmarket area is the National Centre for Dance and holds classes for the general public in everything from Highland dancing, ballet and ballroom to Nepalese dance, Bhangra, pink mambo, South African gumboot and hip hop.

In recent years Dundee has become a focus for dance and dance education, with its own full-time professional dance company, Scottish Dance Theatre, based at the Dundee Repertory Theatre, and Scotland's only contemporary dance school,

Scottish School of Contemporary Dance, which was founded in 1999 and is based at Dundee College. An aim of the school was to enable students to pursue their three-year training for the profession in Scotland rather than having to travel elsewhere. The College's new multi-purpose, £5 million venue, The Space, accommodates dance and drama classes, workshops and master classes for the local community and college students, and other facilities for the community and business.

The Dance School of Scotland, at Knightswood Secondary School in Glasgow, is Scotland's first full-time dance course for secondary-level students offering dance, singing and drama training within the state comprehensive school system.

TRADITIONAL DANCE

Traditional Scottish dance encompasses various forms: sets or dances for groups of four of more people, dances for couples, and solo dances. Strictly speaking, 'Highland dancing' refers to the dancing which has its roots in the creation of the Highland regiments in the 18th- and 19th- centuries and the development of Highland Games, which always included dancing. The solo Sword Dance, for instance, is certainly as old as the 18th-century and possibly older. In that context the pipes would have provided the music, but as Highland dancing became fashionable with Queen Victoria's patronage of Highland Games, other instruments, especially the violin, became associated with dancing. Dances for couples became popular in the 19th-century under the influence of dances from England and further afield. Scottish country dancing seems always to have been a democratic affair; much the same dances were performed at balls and at village gatherings. No doubt the steps were familiar to most people; in the 19th-century dances would often be taught by dancing masters at village schools and today Scottish country dancing is taught in primary and secondary schools across the whole spectrum of independent and state education.

Modern Scottish country dancing or 'ceilidh dancing' generally means set dancing. The term 'country dance' is a corruption of the French 'contredanse', referring to the fact that in these dances two lines of dancers typically stand facing ('opposite') each other. Ceilidhs (literally, the Gaelic word *céilidh* means 'visit') were (and still are) an essential feature of social life in the Highlands, accompanying most celebrations, particularly weddings. Dancing is still a standard ingredient of weddings today, as well as Christmas and other celebrations, in both the Highlands and the Lowlands. However, ceilidh dancing nowadays is most often performed by non-experts. As dancing has become more popular among people who are not necessarily skilled at it, the practice of having a caller to call out the steps has been adopted. Formal Scottish country dances are also still held, where the dancers are expected to know the steps.

From quite early in the 20th-century a movement to record and preserve traditional dances arose. The Scottish Country Dance Society was formed in 1923 (later adding 'Royal' to its title); it has published a large amount of dance music. Thirty years later, the Scottish Official Board of Highland Dancing was founded to preserve the traditional forms. Also concerned with researching and conserving Scotland's dance traditions is the Scottish Traditions of Dance Trust.

Traditional dance has a competitive as well as a social side, and several Highland dancing competitions are held each year. Dunoon hosts the World Highland Dancing championships, attracting competitors not only from Scotland but also from around the world.

FILM

Until the 1990s, the film industry in Scotland was small. Scottish directors and actors tended to migrate to London or Hollywood and few feature directors derived their thematic material from their own country and culture before the 1980s, when Bill Douglas and Bill Forsyth began to make feature films showing a picture of Scotland that reached beyond the folkloric to address issues such as city life, poverty, or growing up. Yet Scots have been involved in moving pictures for many decades, ever since Queen Victoria was filmed at Balmoral in 1895. Among the most notable figures is John Grierson, founding father of the British documentary.

Scotland's roll-call of well-known and highly regarded film actors is long. Current stars such as Ewan McGregor, Robert Carlyle, John Hannah, Peter Mullan, Alan Cumming, Douglas Henshall, and others are just the latest in a long line – many of them also well known for their stage work – including James Robertson Justice (1905–75), Deborah Kerr CBE (1921–), Gordon Jackson (1923–90), Ian Bannen (1928–99), Sir Sean Connery (1930–), Phyllida Law (1932–), Tom Conti (1941–), Bill Paterson (1946–), Billy Connolly (1942–), and Phyllis Logan (1956–).

But it is since 1994, the year in which Danny Boyle's *Shallow Grave* appeared, that the film industry in Scotland has been experiencing a boom. The unexpected success of that film, the immense popularity of Mel Gibson's *Braveheart* (1995), and particularly the runaway success in 1996 of Boyle's next film, *Trainspotting*, made the mid-1990s a watershed for Scottish film. Since then a stream of successful and well-received Scottish features has appeared, including *Small Faces* (Gillies MacKinnon, 1996), *Mrs Brown* (John Madden, 1997), *Carla's song* and *My Name is Joe* (Ken Loach, 1995 and 1998), *Orphans* (Peter Mullan, 1999), *Ratcatcher* (Lynne Ramsay, 1999), *Women Talking Dirty* (Coky Giedroyc, 1999), *Complicity* (Gavin Millar, 2000), *Morven Callar* (Lynne Ramsay, 2002), *Sweet Sixteen* (Ken Loach, 2002), and *The Magdalene Sisters* (Peter Mullen, 2003).

On the small screen, whereas representations of Scotland once tended to be synonymous with *Dr Finlay's Casebook*, Scottish themes as well as Scottish locations, from the gritty (*Roughnecks, Rebus*) to the whimsical (*Monarch of the Glen, Hamish MacBeth*), are now more and more frequently seen on British television. Scottish actors known for their television work include Siobhan Redmond (also a renowned theatre actor, especially through her collaboration with Liz Lochhead), Richard Wilson, Annette Crosbie, Daniela Nardini, Gregor Fisher, and Stanley Baxter. The Edinburgh Television Festival, held each year immediately after the Edinburgh International Film Festival, has become an important fixture for television professionals throughout the UK. Conceived as a Scottish millennium project, the *Castaways* television series, filmed on the Hebridean island of Taransay, was the first real-life drama of its type to be made in the UK.

Much of this growth in the film and television industry is due to the development of an institutional infrastructure and the increased availability of funding from the SAC (particularly via the National Lottery), Scottish Screen, Channel 4, the BBC, and the Glasgow Film Fund.

SCOTLAND THE PHOTOGENIC

Interest in Scotland's potential as a source of film locations has been recognised in recent years. Over 40 feature films – 14 of them in 1999 alone – were shot entirely or partly in Scotland in the 1990s by directors as varied as Franco Zeffirelli, Brian de Palma, Ken Loach, Lars von Trier and Mel Gibson, as well as by Scottish directors. Even 'Bollywood', the Indian commercial film industry, seeking ever more exotic locations for its popular spectaculars, has used Scottish castles as a backdrop. In 2002 revenue from film and television location fees brought £1.4 million to the city of Edinburgh alone. Edinburgh Film Focus promotes Edinburgh as a location and reported that demand went up by 10 per cent in 2002 with enquiries for 2003 and

2004 from countries as far flung as China and New Zealand. The films *Young Adam*, starring Ewan McGregor and Tilda Swinton, *16 Years of Alcohol*, starring Kevin McKidd and Ewan Bremner and the BBC television series *Daniel Deronda*, were all filmed in Edinburgh in 2002.

The connection between more Scottish locations appearing on screen and more tourists appearing in Scotland has not passed unnoticed, either. In April 2000 Scottish Screen joined forces with the Scottish Tourist Board, Scottish Trade International and Historic Scotland to promote Scottish film locations to the industry.

FILM EXHIBITION

Developments in commercial distribution and exhibition in Scotland parallel those elsewhere in Britain, with a trend towards big-chain multiplexes and a corresponding reduction in other cinemas. The principal chains operating in Scotland are UCI, Odeon, Virgin, ABC, Warner Village and Showcase. There are still some cinemas in smaller communities run by the Scottish chain Caledonian Cinemas, and a few family-run enterprises such the Pavilion, Galashiels, and the Dominion in Edinburgh.

Outside the major conurbations, however, permanent commercial cinemas are rare. The SAC has identified a cinema shortage, and National Lottery funding has recently been awarded to cinema development projects in Newton Stewart, Thurso, Portree, Stornoway, and Stranraer, and to Britain's first mobile cinema. The Screen Machine, a lorry trailer which converts to a 110-seat cinema, tours the Highlands and Islands showing mainstream and other films. It is administratively based in Inverness.

The Edinburgh International Film Festival (EIFF) is Scotland's largest annual film event and the world's longest continuously running film festival (founded 1947). The EIFF is a world-class festival, premiering both British and international films. Scotland also hosts annual French and Italian film festivals with showings in Glasgow, Edinburgh and Aberdeen, often showing British premieres of French and Italian films.

A PIONEER OF TELEVISION

The inventor John Logie Baird (1888–1946), a pioneer of television and radio, was a native of Helensburgh. His achievements in sending images by telephone wire from London to Glasgow and then across the Atlantic enabled the BBC to show its first television picture in 1929. However, his technological innovations were overtaken by those of IBM in the mid-1930s, although he continued to experiment with colour, 3-D and radar.

SCOTTISH SCREEN

Scottish Screen is the public body responsible for promoting and developing all aspects of film, television and multimedia in Scotland, through the support of industrial and cultural initiatives. It took over the Scottish Film Production Fund in 1996 and is a major financer of films in Scotland. In 2000 it took over from the Scottish Arts Council the role of distributing body for National Lottery funding for film. For the financial year 2002–3 it received £2.625 million from the Scottish Executive and for 2003–4 grant-in-aid from the Scottish Executive was £2.625 million. Scottish Screen supports and facilitates the production of films by Scottish film-makers, the use of Scottish locations by national and international film-makers, the preservation of Scotland's film heritage, and increased cinema-going and understanding of film in Scotland. Its large information service, which houses the Shiach Library of film scripts and other materials and holds a wide range of trade directories and periodicals related to film and television, is a free public reference facility. It runs a variety of long and short training courses, industry-related initiatives and educational activities, and is a first port of call for both Scottish film-makers developing a project and foreign film-makers looking for locations and facilities. It is a member of the Cinema Exhibitors' Association, the trade association for the cinema industry, and works with the commercial sector where appropriate.

The Scottish Film and Television Archive, set up in 1976, preserves Scotland's heritage of films from the past, both professional and amateur. It holds some 20,000 reels of film from 1897 onwards, largely on 16 and 35 mm with some acquisitions of 9.5mm and 8mm film and videotape. The collection is mostly non-fiction, including thousands of old feature films, home movies, newsreels, government information films and early advertisements for local businesses, unearthed and donated by members of the public. The television archive includes Gaelic broadcast material from 1993 onwards. The archive can be browsed online through the website of the Performing Arts Data Service (PADS).

Scottish Screen provides support to ten art cinemas:

Filmhouse, Edinburgh
Glasgow Film Theatre, Glasgow
MacRoberts Arts Centre, Stirling
Eden Court Theatre, Inverness
Steps Theatre, Dundee
Robert Burns Centre Theatre, Dumfries
The Belmont, Aberdeen
Dundee Contemporary Arts, Dundee

Screen Machine, Inverness
Adam Smith Theatre, Kirkcaldy

OSCAR-WINNING TARTAN SHORTS

Seawards the Great Ships was made for Films of Scotland and the Clyde Shipbuilders Association in 1960. An evocative testimony to the achievements of the shipbuilders on the Clyde and to the men of the "black squads", it was directed by Hilary Harris from a treatment by John Grierson. It won an Oscar for best live-action short film 1961.

Thirty-five years later, the 1995 Oscar for best live-action short film went to Peter Capaldi's *Franz Kafka's It's a Wonderful Life*.

BAFTA SCOTLAND

The Scottish branch of BAFTA, the British Film and Television Awards, held its first awards ceremony in 1991 and has been an annual event since then, alternating awards in the 'mainstream' film and television industry with New Talent awards.

VISUAL ARTS

ART IN EARLY SCOTLAND

Evidence of artistic skill in Scotland from the earliest times survives in finely wrought gold jewellery and bronze weapons; in the bronze boar's head from the Deskford carnyx (*see* Classical Music); in the early Christian stones and slabs which combine Pictish spirals and stylised animal motifs with ornamented crosses and other motifs of Irish origin, visible also in the great illuminated books such as that of Kells. The seventh to ninth centuries were a high point for Celtic art.

Though the arrival of the Vikings is often thought of merely as a time of destruction, their long occupation of parts of Scotland did make a cultural contribution, reflected most strongly in the 12th-century Lewis chess pieces, whether these were locally made or imported from Norway.

REFORMATION AND RECOVERY

The double blow of the Reformation and the departure of the court to London in 1603 was devastating to the field of visual art. Only a few tantalising fragments – remnants of wall paintings (Dunkeld cathedral), textile fragments, maps – give clues to the flourishing visual culture under James IV and James V that was lost in this period and the mid-17th-century Bishops' Wars.

It was not until the 1640s that Scottish artists appeared again in their own country. The portraits painted by George Jameson of Aberdeen, including his self-portrait against a background of other paintings, establish him as the first Scottish painter in the modern sense. The Scottish School of Portraiture was to find its highest expression in the works of Allan Ramsay and Henry Raeburn in the following century. But before them came a series of painters including John Michael Wright, Jameson's most distinguished pupil. Wright's portrait of Lord Mungo Murray in Highland dress, echoed both in costume and pose by Raeburn's famous picture of Alasdair Macdonell of Glengarry over a century later, created an image of 'Scottishness' that was to become persistent.

THE SCOTTISH ENLIGHTENMENT

The neoclassicism of the 18th-century was mainly expressed through architecture, but as the century progressed landscape paintings began to be produced which show the influence of Continental neoclassicists such as Claude Lorrain. A circle of intellectuals and artists grew up in Edinburgh, and Scotland's first art school, the Academy of St Luke, was established in 1729. Portraitists like William Aikman (1682–1731) found it easier to get commissions in London than in Scotland, though some, such as Aberdonians John Alexander (c. 1690–1757) and William Mosman (1700–71), spent most of their careers in Scotland after studying in Rome.

The second half of the 18th-century was marked by the interaction of art and philosophy – Allan Ramsay, together with his friends the philosopher David Hume and the economist Adam Smith, formed the Select Society – and further development of art training institutions, such as the Foulis Academy in Glasgow (1754) and the Trustees' Academy in Edinburgh (1766). Ramsay is the outstanding figure of this period. His genius lay in his empathetic interpretation of the sitter in either formal or intimate portraits, and in his delicate luminosity of style.

Alongside the classical themes favoured by several painters of this period (e.g. the six huge canvases by Gavin Hamilton (1723–98)) depicting scenes from Homer's *Iliad*, there grew up a romantic interest in the Celtic past, a pioneer in this respect being Alexander Runciman (1736–85), who chose the harper Ossian and other themes from Celtic legend for his etchings and some sketches for a set of murals (now lost) for the house of Sir James Clerk of Penicuik. This began a process of Celtic revival and reclamation of the Scottish past which in some respects is still going on, and a duality between classicism and Celticism that was to continue throughout the century.

Henry Raeburn was the second great portraitist of the Scottish Enlightenment, and probably the best-known painter of the century, not least because of his famous *Rev. Robert Walker Skating* in Edinburgh's National Gallery. His major portraits date from the early 1790s and are works of great humanity and perception as well as masterly essays in the study of light.

After its zenith with Raeburn, portraiture became less central to Scottish painting (although an active school of portrait sculpture developed in the early 19th-century), and landscape and genre painting came to the fore. Alexander Nasmyth was the seminal figure in landscape painting. To the usual art education in London and Rome he added an acquaintance with northern European – particularly Dutch – landscape painting and an interest in the relationship between human beings and landscape, nature and culture; this can be seen in his two canvases of Edinburgh, which juxtapose the wild natural forms of Calton Hill and Arthur's Seat with the perspectives of human construction. Nasmyth was also an influential teacher.

In genre painting, David Wilkie became the master of paintings depicting daily life. His paintings 'tell a story' and assert the dignity of ordinary people; some of them implicitly comment on the social and economic reality of the time.

WILDERNESS AND DISPOSSESSION

In 1826 a group of 11 artists formed themselves into the Scottish Academy as a representative body for Scottish artists. The academy was modelled loosely on the Royal Academy in London. It obtained its royal charter in 1837, and its members were instrumental in founding the National Gallery of Scotland, which opened in 1859.

As the 19th-century progressed, a school of painting emerged which could lay claim to be distinctively Scottish. Many of its members had studied at the Trustees' Academy, which became the principal art school in the country under Robert Scott Lauder (1803–61). Lauder painted scenes from Scott's Waverley novels, among other subjects, and was one of a diverse circle including David Octavius Hill (1802–70), also a pioneering photographer, Horatio McCulloch (1805–67), Thomas Faed (1826–1900) and William Dyce (1806–64). These artists painted the Highlands as uninhabited wilderness and spectacle, while at the same time depicting themes of emigration and exile from the land, for instance in Faed's *Highland Mary* (1857) and his famous *The Last of the Clan* (1865), or McCulloch's *The Emigrant's Dream of his Highland Home* (1860).

At this time there was a vogue for large public sculptures of important Scottish and British figures. Outstanding here is John Steell (1804–91), whose figure of Sir Walter Scott forms the central element of the Scott Memorial in East Princes Street Garden, Edinburgh.

THE RISE OF GLASGOW AS AN ART CENTRE

Toward the end of the century, a new approach to landscape painting was introduced by William McTaggart, who used an almost impressionist technique, particularly noticeable in his coastal scenes and seascapes. He too took up the theme of the Highland Clearances and emigration in a series of Emigrant Ship canvases of the 1890s.

In the 1880s Glasgow took over from Edinburgh as the epicentre of Scottish painting. The Glasgow Institute of the Fine Arts had been set up in 1861 as a counterpart – and in part a challenge – to Edinburgh's Royal Scottish Academy, and a sizeable group of artists, nicknamed the 'Glasgow Boys' (although four at least were women) coalesced around a reaction to the Victorian concept of landscape and a tendency to look to France for inspiration. Following McTaggart's lead, this as the first group of Scottish painters who regularly painted in the open air, and this led to a change in landscape subject matter from mountain and moor to rivers, coasts and villages. The 'Boys' also returned to subjects from ordinary life, such as John Lavery's *Tennis party* of 1885 or James Guthrie's more down-to-earth *A Hind's Daughter* (1883), with hints of Cézanne in its brushwork. It is possible to discern a line of descent from these works, via the jewel-like watercolours of Arthur Melville (1855–1904), to the treatment of colour and paint characteristic of the Colourists a few decades later.

Also in the early 1890s, Charles Rennie Mackintosh was at the centre of a group of artists, fellow-students at the Glasgow School of Art: Margaret Macdonald (1863-1933), who became Mackintosh's wife, her sister Frances (1874–1921), and Herbert MacNair (1868–1955). The decorative style they developed, close to Art Nouveau but identifiably their own, has become very famous, and inspired the work of a wider circle of graphic and applied artists. Mackintosh's own landscape paintings, however, overshadowed by the popularity of his design, have not fully received the appreciation they deserve. In Edinburgh, the clear thematic and stylistic links between the Arts and Crafts movement and the Celtic Revival are illustrated in the work of Phoebe Anna Traquair (1852–1936), which encompasses a vast range of crafts from metalwork to murals. Her murals for the Catholic Apostolic Church are an impressive example.

THE 20TH CENTURY

The four Colourists – Samuel Peploe, J. D. Fergusson, F. C. B. Cadell and G. L. Hunter – are distinguished by their freshness and spontaneity and the brilliance of light and colour in their paintings. All four spent considerable time in France and it is likely the Fauves were an influence on them and, later, Matisse.

By the 1930s, Modernism was firmly established in Scottish painting in the works of William Crozier (1897–1930), Anne Redpath (1895–1965), William Johnstone (1897–1981), James Cowie (1880–1956) and others. The continental influence (Matisse, Klee, Cubism) remained strong, but landscape continued to be a principal source of subject matter. The influence of the Colourists continued to be felt after World War II and to show up in Scottish interpretations of newer styles. But great diversity characterises artists of the 1950s and after, such as Robert MacBryde (1913–66), Robert Colquhoun (1914–62), Joan Eardley (1921–63), and the sculptors Eduardo Paolozzi (1924–) and Ian Hamilton Finlay. Among yet more recent work are large projects working in the landscape by George Wyllie, Kate Whiteford and Will Maclean; Maclean's three large works on Lewis (1996), commemorating the struggle between landlords and tenants at the turn of the 20th-century, raise again questions of national history and identity. Calum Colvin, a winner of one of the SAC's Creative Scotland Awards, is taking up the Celtic thread with an exhibition of digital and analogue photographic works based on James Macpherson's *The Poems of Ossian and Related Works*. A resurgence of figurative art has informed the work of the new generation of Glasgow painters such as Alexander Moffat; and the opening of the Glasgow Gallery of Modern Art in 1996 has made a new space available for the work of Scotland's new generation of artists.

PHOTOGRAPHY

The origins of modern photography date from 1839 when the Frenchman Louis Jaques Mandes Daguerre (1787–1851) announced his discovery of the daguerreotype process in Paris on 7 January. Daguerre's discovery was the catalyst the Englishman William Henry Fox Talbot (1800–77) needed to present the results of his negative/positive process, which he described as 'photogenic drawing', to the Royal Institution in London on 25 January. Early in February 1839 Talbot sent examples of his work to Sir David Brewster, who was later to become the first President of the Photographic Society of Scotland (founded 1856) and an Honorary Member of the Edinburgh Photographic Society (founded 1861).

The discovery of photography held immediate interest for the citizens of Edinburgh with arts and science societies holding meetings to discuss the latest developments and public lectures playing to packed houses. In December 1839 the Exhibition of Arts, Manufacturers and Practical Science was held at the Assembly Rooms on George Street and exhibited 20 photographs by Talbot. The exhibition attracted over 50,000 visitors.

Robert Adamson and David Octavius Hill set up their famous Rock House Studio on Calton Hill in Edinburgh in 1843. Their work over the next four years was to be seminal in the development of early Scottish photography. 1843 also saw the founding of the Edinburgh Calotype Club, thought to be the earliest photographic society in the world. In the wake of Hill and Adamson several other professional photographers set up shop in Princes Street in the 1840s.

Elsewhere in Scotland photographers were setting up studios to capitalise on the patronage of Queen Victoria and Prince Albert (Prince Albert became the first Patron of the Photographic Society of Scotland). The royal couple's enthusiasm for the photographic process guaranteed its fashionable status and their love of all things Scottish ensured a steady stream of tourists from across the border. It was these tourists who fuelled the explosion in Scottish photography with major tourist sites offering photographic souvenirs, albums and keepsakes. James Valentine learned the Daguerreotype process in the late 1840s in Paris then returned to his native Dundee in 1856 to establish a portrait studio. Valentine's empire grew and by the 1870s his company was one of the two largest photographic publishers in Scotland – the other was operated by George Washington Wilson, a photographer who had direct links with the royal family. Both Valentine and Wilson introduced systems of mass production in their factory-like studios to cope with demand and they are thought to be amongst the first commercial photographers in Britain to do so.

Photography continues to have great importance for Scotland's tourist economy with lavishly-produced books of photographs of the dramatic Scottish landscape sold in huge quantities all over the world.

CURRENT INSTITUTIONS
Most of the art institutions set up in the last century continue in existence, though they have all undergone changes and sometimes crisis over the years. Bodies existing today include the following.

The Royal Scottish Academy (RSA) is the main exhibiting body promoting the works of living Scottish professional artists. It has about 40 full members and 50 associate members, elected from the disciplines of architecture, painting, printmaking and sculpture, and holds a large annual exhibition.

The Royal Glasgow Institute of the Fine Arts, established in 1861 also has a gallery and exhibition space, and holds lectures.

The Royal Society of Painters in Watercolours promotes the status of watercolour as a major art form. It holds an annual exhibition at the RSA galleries, and also issues financial awards.

The principal remit of the Royal Fine Art Commission for Scotland is to advise government on the visual impact of new constructions.

Among institutions for art education and training, many are part of universities. Glasgow School of Art is one of the very few remaining independent art schools in the United Kingdom. It was founded in 1845 as a Government School of Design and added the study and practice of the fine arts and architecture to its curriculum in the late 19th-century. The present building, commissioned in 1896, is one of Charles Rennie Mackintosh's masterpieces. The School's degrees are accredited by the University of Glasgow.

At Aberdeen, Gray's School of Art, which is part of the Robert Gordon University, has almost as long a history as the Glasgow School of Art. It was founded in 1850, gifted to Robert Gordon's College by John Gray, an engineer and philanthropist. A new Gray's School was built at its current location in 1966.

Other art schools include the Edinburgh College of Art and the Duncan of Jordanstone College of Art in Dundee.

ARCHITECTURE

A HERITAGE IN STONE
Stone has always been a characteristic material of Scottish architecture, and this has ensured a very large and varied built heritage from all periods, with buildings more likely to have been destroyed by conflict than to have fallen into decay. The prevailing styles of the Middle Ages, except in the Highlands and Islands, were very similar to those found in England and France, since it was to these countries that the kings responsible for the upsurge in building from the 12th-century onwards looked. Norman-style churches such as Dalmeny church, near South Queensferry, and Dunfermline Abbey date from the early part of this period. The Gothic style which followed can be seen at its best in what survives of the Border abbeys, of which Melrose is both one of the latest (having been completely

destroyed in the 14th-century and rebuilt in the 15th) and most elaborate.

Over the medieval period, the typical form of the castle settled into that of a keep with a courtyard defended by a heavy curtain wall. Many castles dating from the 14th- and 15th- centuries survive: some well-known examples are Glamis, Dunvegan and the much-photographed Eilean Donan. Smaller castles of the period, such as Smailholm (Borders), show the features that were to evolve into the tower house, the typical dwelling of the Scottish lairds from the 15th- to the 17th-centuries. Here the jewel in the crown is widely held to be Craigievar Castle (Aberdeenshire), largely because its elegant original lines escaped Victorian remodelling. Meanwhile, beauty as much as strength was the principle governing the creation of the great palaces of the Stewart kings, such as Linlithgow, Falkland and Stirling, which show strong French Renaissance influences; while in the crowded city of Edinburgh (now the Old Town), confined within the city wall, a jigsaw of closes and wynds with six- and seven-storey tenements proliferated, becoming ever more cramped and jumbled.

CLASSICISM AND ROMANTICISM

The first Scottish buildings whose architects are known, date from the early 17th-century. The names of William Wallace, William Ayton, and John and Robert Mylne are associated with the building of George Heriot's Hospital (now a school) in Edinburgh, begun in 1628, while the palace of Holyroodhouse was rebuilt, after a fire in 1650, to a design by Sir William Bruce, assisted by Robert Mylne (1633–1710). Mylne was one of a dynasty of master masons and architects, spanning 200 years from the late 16th-century and based in Dundee.

In the late 18th-century, a more flourishing economy fuelled a boom in building and a flowering of the English Classical style, which is best illustrated by Edinburgh's New Town, designed by James Craig in 1767 and with later contributions by Robert Adam (Charlotte Square, 1791). Robert and his father William Adam, probably Scotland's greatest classicists, designed Mellerstain House (Borders), and were responsible for both the interior and exterior of a large extension to Hopetoun House (South Queensferry), originally built by William Bruce. This was also the period of construction of new towns and villages, part of the Policy of Improvement.

Victorian architecture was heavily influenced by retrospection and a romantic idea of Scotland, but innovative in its eclectic borrowing from any and every style of the past. In a revival of the Scottish baronial style, the turrets and crenellations of 16th-century tower houses reappeared not only on country mansions but suburban villas. As the cities mushroomed, the tenement, at varying levels of luxury, became the typical urban dwelling. Church-building took off again and neo-Gothic churches are to be seen in every Scottish town. Gilbert Scott's Glasgow University Building of 1867 is a fine example of this style, as is St John's Tolbooth on the High Street, Edinburgh, originally built as General Assembly Rooms by James Gillespie Graham in 1842, later transformed by Augustus Pugin, and converted in 1999 to a new administrative and social centre for the Edinburgh Festival, the Hub.

Looking even further back to classical models, but also forward in his use of them, was Alexander 'Greek' Thomson in Glasgow. His churches at St Vincent Street (1859), and Caledonian Road (1856) are particularly important examples of neoclassical architecture; while in his use of Egyptian-inspired decoration and severely horizontal composition, for instance in the Egyptian Halls, Union Street (1871–3), he was well ahead of his time. A major exhibition of his work as part of Glasgow's year as City of Architecture and Design (1999) has contributed to a revaluation of Thomson.

MACKINTOSH AND AFTER

Glasgow's other major architect, and probably Scotland's best known architect and designer ever, is Charles Rennie Mackintosh, whose greatest work was carried out at the turn of the 20th-century. One of the greatest exponents of the British Arts and Crafts movement, Mackintosh was also a designer of furniture and textiles and a painter, and his elegant Art Nouveau decoration, which has been overly imitated in recent years, has perhaps distracted attention from his architecture such as the Glasgow School of Art (1897), his most famous building, the Willow Tea Rooms in Sauchiehall Street, and Hill House (Helensburgh, 1902), a Scottish tower house for the 20th-century with an exquisitely detailed interior.

Glasgow continues to produce innovative buildings at the end of the 20th-century, such as Sir Norman Foster's Clyde Auditorium, nicknamed 'the Armadillo' because of its use of overlapping shells reminiscent of the Sydney Opera House. In Dundee, Richard Murphy's Contemporary Arts Centre, converted from a former garage and car showroom, combines a spacious, clean-lined interior with a sweeping, curvilinear frontage.

Meanwhile, in Edinburgh, the new National Museum of Scotland (1996–8), built mostly of sandstone, has been widely acclaimed. At the time of writing, the most controversial architectural project in Scotland is the new Scottish Parliament Building in Edinburgh. An architectural competition in 1997 awarded the design contract to the Catalan architect Enric Miralles in 1999, who submitted an imaginative and elegant design; but progress has been dogged by budget problems – the original budget for the project was £50 million but the cost, as of 2003, was £345 million with no scheduled completion date and continuing scandals regarding the cost of interior fittings (such as £80,000 for a reception desk). The project was dealt a further blow by Miralles untimely death, at the age of 45, in July 2000.

HOUSE FOR AN ART LOVER

In 1901 Charles Rennie Mackintosh and his wife Margaret Macdonald entered a German competition to design a house for an art lover. The couple were disqualified because they didn't present the correct number of interior drawings but they were awarded a special prize of 600 Deutsche marks in recognition of their outstanding design. Mackintosh saw the brief as a modern living space for someone who loved to be surrounded by art all the time. His design rejected traditional Greek, Roman, Renaissance and Gothic styles and opted for a significant Japanese influence.

In 1995, nearly a century after he first designed it, Glasgow City Council and the Glasgow School of Art collaborated to build Mackintosh's House for an Art Lover. Visitors can now experience Mackintosh and Macdonald's stunning house at first hand. Mackintosh envisioned a grand house built for entertaining with art integrated throughout the design in the form of paintings, specially-designed furniture, gesso work, stained glass, panelling, textiles and metal work.

The entrance is deliberately small and enclosed so that the full impact of the dramatic open space of the ground floor can be felt as visitors walk from a dark, confined room into one filled with light, height and space. The bedrooms are situated off an upper gallery and are very obviously private, but the residents of the house can walk out of their rooms to peer over their suspended walkway to see what is going on in the public area.

Mackintosh's House for an Art Lover is open to the public from 10am-4pm every day except Fridays. The House also has a gift shop and the Art Lover's Cafè.

HOUSE FOR AN ART LOVER

Bellahouston Park, 10 Drumbreck Road,
Glasgow G41 5BW
Tel: 0141-353 4770 Fax: 0141-353 4771
Web: www.houseforanartlover.co.uk

SOME KEY FIGURES IN THE ARTS

WRITERS, POETS AND DRAMATISTS

Atkinson, Kate (1951–), novelist and short-story writer, born York, England. Studied English Literature at Dundee University and later taught at the university. Atkinson began writing short stories in 1981 and won an Ian St James Award in 1993 for her short story *Karmic Mothers*, which she later adapted for BBC television as part of its Tartan Shorts series. Her first novel, *Behind the Scenes at the Museum* (1995), won the Whitbread Book of the Year Award. Atkinson has published two other novels: *Human Croquet* (1997) and *Emotionally Weird* (2000). She has written two plays for the Traverse Theatre in Edinburgh: *Nice* (1996) and *Abandonment* (2000). Her latest published work is a collection of short stories, *Not the End of the World* (2002).

Ballantyne, R.M. (1825–94), children's writer, born Edinburgh. After working for Hudson's Bay Company in Canada, 1841–47, published *Hudson's Bay, Everyday Life in the Wilds of North America* (1848). Wrote over 90 books, mainly children's adventure stories, the best-known being *The Coral Island* (1857). Autobiography: *Personal Reminiscences in Book-making* (1893).

Banks, Iain (1958–), novelist, born Fife. Banks writes innovative and sometimes disturbing fiction under the name of Iain Banks. Works include *The Wasp Factory* (1984), *Walking on Glass* (1985), *The Crow Road* (1992), *Complicity* (1993), *Whit* (1995) and *The Business* (1999). Every other year Banks writes science fiction under the name of Iain M. Banks. Works include *Consider Phlebas* (1987), *Feersum Endjinn* (1994) and *Inversions* (1998). *The Crow Road* was made into a television series and *Complicity* is currently being filmed.

Barrie, Sir James M. (1860–1937), playwright and novelist, born Kirriemuir, Angus. Beginning his career with magazine articles and novels (e.g. *The Little Minister*, 1891, later dramatised), he became a successful playwright. Best known for *Peter Pan* (1904); other work includes *Quality Street* (1902), *The Admirable Crichton* (1902), *The Boy David* (1936).

Boswell, James (1740–95), biographer and travel writer, born Edinburgh. With Samuel Johnson, undertook extensive tour of Scotland in 1773. Account of journey written by Johnson but Boswell published *Journal of a Tour to the Hebrides* (1785). Contributed over 40 articles to *London Magazine* (1777–83). Published biography of Johnson in 1791. Other work includes *An Account of Corsica* (1768).

Bridie, James (1888–1951), playwright, born in Glasgow as Osborne Henry Mavor, Bridie is widely acknowledged as the father of modern Scottish theatre with over 40 plays to his name. Bridie trained as a doctor, qualifying in 1913. He served in the Middle East in the RAMC during the 1914–18 war and returned home to pursue a medical career – only to be overtaken by his passion for the theatre. Bridie's best-known play is *The Anatomist* (1930) the story of Dr Robert Knox, the 19th-century Edinburgh anatomist who was supplied with bodies by Burke and Hare. In addition to his work as a playwright Bridie was one of the founders of Glasgow's Citizen's Theatre in 1943 and of the first College of Drama in Scotland in 1950.

Brown, George Douglas (1869–1902), novelist, born Ochiltree, Ayrshire. Douglas Brown made his living by teaching and journalism and published his first novel, *Love and a Sword*, in 1899. In 1900 he began work on *The House with the Green Shutters* (1901), the novel for which he is famous. *The House with the Green Shutters* is an unsentimental, some would say brutal, portrayal of Scottish rural life. The Scottish Modernists, Hugh MacDiarmid, Lewis Grassic Gibbon and Neil Gunn, embraced the fluent Scots of the book's prose and welcomed its realistic tone.

Brown, George Mackay (1921–1996), poet, novelist and short-story writer, born Stromness. Orkney forms the subject and backdrop of most of his work. Work includes: poetry: *Loaves and Fishes* (1959), *Fishermen with Ploughs* (1971), *Stone: Poems* (1987); novels: *Greenvoe* (1972), *Magnus* (1973), *Beside the Ocean of Time* (1994; Scottish Book of the Year); short stories: *A Calendar of Love* (1967), *The Masked Fisherman and Other Stories* (1989). Collaborated with or inspired Peter Maxwell Davies in several works.

Buchan, John (1875–1940), novelist, biographer, historian, essayist, journalist, editor, poet and publisher, born Perth. As well as pursuing a varied career as diplomat (from 1901), war correspondent (*c*. 1915) and MP (1927–35), he wrote 100 books, including *The Thirty-Nine Steps* (1915), *Greenmantle* (1916), *Witch Wood* (1927), *Castle Gay* (1930), and biographies of Montrose, Cromwell, and Scott.

Burns, Robert (1759–96), poet and songwriter, born Alloway, Ayrshire. Regarded as Scotland's national poet, and its chief writer and collector of ballads and songs. Inspired by his travels round Scotland, from 1788 onwards he contributed hundreds of songs to collections edited by James Johnson and George Thomson. Published his first collection of poems, *Poems Chiefly in the Scottish Dialect*, in 1786; Among his most famous poems are 'Auld lang syne', 'O' my luve is like a red, red rose', 'Ae fond kiss', 'Tam O Shanter' (1790), 'Is there for honest poverty' (1793).

Boyd, William (1952–), novelist, screenwriter, born Ghana. Boyd's first novel, *A Good Man in Africa* (1982) was a comic work following a drunken diplomat who was being blackmailed by a local politician while the country falls into chaos. His second novel, *An Ice Cream War* (1983) was shortlisted for the Booker Prize. *Brazzaville Beach* (1991) won the James Tait Black Memorial Prize, *The Blue Afternoon* (1994) won The Los Angeles Times Book Award for Fiction in 1995 and *Any Human Heart* (2002) was nominated for the Man-Booker Prize.

Byrne, John (1940–), dramatist and artist, born Paisley. Byrne's first stage work, *The Slab Boys* (1978), was based on the writer's experience of working in a carpet factory. This play set the pattern for Byrne's concerns as a dramatist – he is always exploring the conflict between Scottish provincialism and the mass culture of the wider (usually American) world. Byrne is best known for his television series *Tutti Frutti* (1987) and *Your Cheatin' Heart* (1989). Byrne also works as an artist and illustrator. Awarded MBE in 2001.

Carlyle, Thomas (1795–1881), essayist, historian and critic, born Ecclefechan, Dumfriesshire. Very highly regarded during his own day, his works are idiosyncratic and difficult to classify today. They include *Sartor Resartus* (1835), *The French Revolution* (1837), *On Heroes, Hero-worship and the Heroic in History* (1841), *Past and Present* (1843), *Oliver Cromwell's Letters and Speeches* (1845), *The History of Frederick the Great* (1858–65).

Corrie, Joe (1894–1968), playwright, poet, journalist and short story writer, born Slamannan. Corrie left school in 1908 and went to work in the coal pits of Fife. His work is heavily influenced by these experiences and the poverty he experienced, especially after the General Strike of 1929. Corrie's *In Time o' Strife* (1927) was his first full-length play and *The Image o' God and Other Poems*, his first volume of poetry (1928). Corrie's work was rejected by Scotland's theatre establishment because of its obvious Socialism; instead he made a living by writing lighthearted one-act plays for performance by amateur theatre groups belonging to the Scottish Community Drama Association.

Cronin, A. J. (1896–1981), novelist, born Cardross, Dunbartonshire. His works, based on his own experiences as a doctor, include *Hatter's Castle* (1931), *The Keys of the Kingdom* (1942) and *The Green Years* (1945); the latter two were filmed. *The Citadel* (1937), based on the practices of Harley Street doctors, led indirectly to creation of the National Health Service. The 1960s television and radio series *Dr Finlay's Casebook* were based on Cronin's experiences.

Doyle, Sir Arthur Conan (1859–1930), author, born Edinburgh. The novella *A Study in Scarlet* (1887) introduced his most famous characters, Sherlock Holmes and Dr Watson. Published two series of Sherlock Holmes tales in the *Strand Magazine* (1891–93 and from 1903), and a novel, *The Hound of the Baskervilles* (1902). Other works include adventure novels *The Lost World* (1912) and *The Poison Belt* (1913), historical romances, and two propagandist works justifying Britain's involvement in the Boer War in South Africa.

Dunbar, William (1460–*c.*1513), poet. Court poet to James IV, writing both eulogism and works of social and moral criticism. Works include *Lament for the Makaris* ('makar', or maker, is the old Scots word Dunbar used to describe his contemporary poets), *The Thrissil and the Rois* (nuptial song for marriage of James IV and Margaret Tudor in 1503), *The Flyting of Dunbar and Kennedie, Dance of the Sevin Deidly Synnes.*

Dunn, Douglas (1942–), poet and teacher, born Inchinnan, Renfrewshire. Appointed Professor of English Language and Literature at St Andrews University in 1991. His poetry in deeply personal although his first collection, *Terry Street* (1969) also demonstrated his social and political concerns. His seventh collection of poetry, *Elegies* 1985, is expressive of his love for his wife who died of cancer. *Elegies* won the Whitbread Book of the Year Award. Dunn's eleventh book of poetry, *The Year's Afternoon*, was published in 2000 to great acclaim. His latest work is *The Donkey's Ears* (2002), a 170-page poem about the voyage of the Russian Imperial Fleet bound for the Straits of Tsushima and battle with the Japanese.

Dunnett, Dorothy (1923–2001), novelist, born Dunfermline, Fife. Dunnett is a novelist who has followed in the footsteps of Scott and Stevenson by writing Scottish historical romance. Dunnett's most famous character is the 16th-century Scots mercenary Francis Crawford of Lymond and Sevigny. The six Crawford novels are: *Game of Kings* (1961), *Queen's Play* (1964), *Disorderly Knights* (1966), *Pawn in Frankincense* (1969), *The Ringed Castle* (1971) and *Checkmate* (1975). Dorothy Dunnett was awarded an OBE in 1992.

Fraser, George MacDonald (1925–), journalist, novelist, born Carlisle. MacDonald Fraser's most infamous creation is that of Flashman, a bully, soldier, womaniser, adventurer and coward, originally taken from Thomas Hughes' (1822–96) *Tom Brown's Schooldays*. MacDonald Fraser's other popular invention is Private McAuslan. As well as works of fiction the author has also written *Quartered Safe Out Here* (1992), an account of the Burma campaign seen through the eyes of Fraser's platoon, and *The Steel Bonnets* (1971) a factual account of the border wars between England and Scotland.

Galloway, Janice (1956–), novelist and short-story writer, born Ayrshire. Work includes several prizewinning novels: *The Trick is to Keep Breathing* (1989), *Blood* (1992), *Foreign Parts* (1994). Her most recent novel, *Clara* (2002), won the Scottish Saltire Book of the Year Award. Galloway has also written a play, *Fall* (1997–8), collaborated with Sally Beamish and Alasdair Nicolson on three song cycles, and worked with Beamish on an opera libretto, *Monster*, which was performed in 2002.

Gibbon, Lewis Grassic (James Leslie Mitchell, 1901–35), novelist, journalist, and historian, born Aberdeenshire. Works include: *A Scots Quair* (trilogy, 1932–4), *Stained Radiance* (1930), *Scots Scene: or, The Intelligent Man's Guide to Albyn* (1934, with Hugh MacDiarmid); *Speak of the Mearns* (unfinished, published 1982).

Grahame, Kenneth (1859–1932), essayist and children's writer, born Edinburgh. Grahame's first published work was *By a Northern Furrow* (1888) and he followed this with short stories and articles published in a variety of journals such as *The Yellow Book*, and the *National Observer*. *The Golden Age* (1895) was Grahame's first critical success and is the story of a fictional Victorian family that the author invented during his own difficult childhood. Grahame married in 1899 and his only child, Alastair, was born in 1900. It was for Alastair that Grahame wrote the *Wind in the Willows* (1908), his most famous work.

Gray, Alasdair (1934–), novelist, playwright, painter and book designer, born Glasgow. His first and largest novel, *Lanark*, was begun in the 1950s but not published until 1981. Other works include: *Janine* (1982), *Poor Things* (1992), *Printer's Devil* (1995), *The Book of Prefaces* (2000). *Why Scots Should Rule Scotland* (1992, 2nd edn 1997) argues for Scottish independence.

Gunn, Neil M. (1891–1973), novelist, born Dunbeath, Caithness. After meeting Hugh MacDiarmid in the 1920s, became involved both in political nationalism and the literary renaissance. His novels are imbued with a deep sense of history and place. Works include: *The Grey Coast* (1926), *Morning Tide* (1930), *Highland River* (1937), *The Silver Darlings* (1941), *The Serpent* (1943).

Henryson, Robert (*c.*1420–*c.*1490), poet. Probably a schoolmaster at Dunfermline Abbey school. One of the Scottish 'Chaucerians'. Extant works include: *The Testament of Cresseid, The Morall Fabillis of Esope the Phrygian, Robene and Makyne*.

Hogg, James (1770–1835), poet and novelist, born Ettrick, Borders. Known as 'the Ettrick Shepherd'. His first published work was a volume of ballads, *The Mountain Bard* (1807). *The Queen's Wake* (1813) made him famous, relating a poetic contest at the court of Queen Mary. Other works include: *The Poetic Mirror* (1816), *The Three Perils of Man* (1822), *The Three Perils of Women* (1823), *Tales of the Wars of Montrose* (1835), and *The Shepherd's Calendar* (1829), written for *Blackwood's Magazine*. But Hogg is best known for *The Private Memoirs and Confessions of a Justified Sinner* (1824) which many critics consider to be the greatest Scottish novel ever.

Home, John (1722–1808), dramatist, born Leith. After studying divinity at Edinburgh University Home took up the position of Minister at a church in East Lothian. It was while he was administering to his flock that he wrote his first work, *Agis* (1749), which was unsuccessful. His second play *The Douglas* (1750) was performed in Edinburgh in 1756 to huge acclaim and went on to Covent Garden in 1757. The success of *The Douglas* forced Home to resign his parish, so outraged was the

church establishment by his association with such a disreputable profession. Home wrote six tragedies in all, most of which were performed at Drury Lane, as well as *The History of the Rebellion in Scotland, 1745–6* (1802) which he had fought in as a young man.

Kelman, James (1946–), novelist and short-story writer, born Glasgow. The social realism and social analysis of his work has influenced the younger generation of Scottish writers. Works include: *Greyhound for Breakfast* (1987), *A Disaffection* (1989), *How Late It Was, How Late* (1994, Booker Prize), short stories, *The Good Times* (1998), *Translated Accounts: A Novel* (2001).

Kennedy, A. L. (Alison Louise) (1965–), novelist and short story writer, born Dundee. Kennedy first came to public attention with her first collection of short stories, *Night Geometry and the Garscadden Trains* (1991). Since then there have been four novels: *Looking for the Possible Dance* (1993), *So I am Glad* (1995), *Original Bliss* (1997), and *Everything You Need* (1999), another collection of stories, *Now That You're Back* (1994) and a non-fiction monograph, *The Life and Death of Colonel Blimp* (1997). Kennedy also writes for the stage and screen.

Kesson, Jessie (1916–94), novelist and playwright, born Jessie Grant Macdonald in Inverness. Kesson's childhood experiences of workhouse and orphanage formed the basis for her first novel *The White Bird Passes* (1958), later dramatised by the BBC. Other works include *Glitter of Mica* (1963) and *Another Time, Another Place* (1983) (made into a film). As well as writing novels, Kesson also produced Women's Hour and wrote over 90 plays for radio and television.

Lang, Andrew (1844–1912), scholar and man of letters, born Selkirk. A man of wide-ranging interests, Lang is best remembered for his translations of the *Odyssey* (1879) and the *Iliad* (1882), and his retelling of popular fairy tales in the *Blue Fairy Book* (1900–7).

Lindsay, Sir David (1486–1555), poet and playwright, usher to Prince James (later James V). His first poem *The Dreme* was written in 1528 but, significantly, not published until after his death, and was an allegorical comment on the mismanagement of the kingdom. *His Testament and Complaynt, of our Soverane Lordis Papyngo* (finished 1530, published 1538) was a poem of advice to the king put into the mouth of his parrot. The parrot dies when interrogated by the Church, a measure of Lindsay's low regard for the Church. But his most famous work is his *Ane Pleasant Satyre of the Thrie Estaitis* (produced 1540), which was performed in front of the king.

Linklater, Eric (1899–1974), novelist, born Penarth, Wales but spent his childhood in Orkney and considered himself an Orcadian. Served as a sniper in the Black Watch during the 1914–18 war then became the Assistant Editor of the *Times of India*, followed by two years in the USA which inspired his first novel *Juan in America* (1931) a satire on Prohibition. Linklater went on to write 23 novels, around 30 short stories, several prose poems, three volumes of autobiography and stage and radio plays.

Lochhead, Liz (1947–), poet and playwright, born Motherwell. Poetry includes: *Memo for Spring* (1972), *The Grimm Sisters* (1981), *True Confessions and New Clichés* (1985); plays include: *Blood and Ice* (1982), *Mary Queen of Scots Got Her Head Chopped Off* (1989), *Perfect Days* (2000), *Medea* (2000).

McCabe, Brian (1951–), poet and novelist, born Bonnyrigg. McCabe's poetry has a dark Surrealist edge and often ventures into satire – particularly of human relationships. But McCabe's sense of humour also wins through and is obvious in his short stories and his novel *The Other McCoy* (1990), an account of a young man's alcohol-fuelled journey through Hogmanay (New Year).

MacCaig, Norman (1910–96), poet, born Edinburgh. MacCaig's early work, *Far Cry* (1943), was part of the Apocalyse Movement but by 1955 he demonstrated that he had moved away from this influence with the publication of *Riding Lights*, the first of his many collections of highly observant, metaphysical and descriptive poetry. MacCaig's major poem is *'A Man in Assynt'*, first published in *A Man in My Position* (1969) and originally commissioned by the BBC. Awarded the Queen's Medal for Poetry in 1986.

MacDonald, Sharman (1951–), playwright and novelist, born Glasgow. MacDonald's first play, *When I Was a Girl I Used to Scream and Shout* (1984) was an instant success when it was first performed in London at the Bush Theatre and she went on to win the Evening Standard Most Promising Playwright award for that year. Other successes have included *The Brave* (1988) and *When We Were Women* (1989). MacDonald's novels, *The Beast* (1986), and *Night Night* (1988) have not been as successful.

McGrath, Tom (1940–), poet and dramatist, born Rutherglen. McGrath's early poetry was first performed in London in the 1960s but he returned to Scotland in 1969 to pursue his career as a writer full-time and to complete his first play *Laurel and Hardy* (later *Mr Laurel and Mr Hardy*), first produced in 1976. *The Hard Man* followed in 1977 and is based on the life of convicted murderer Jimmy Boyle (and was written in co-operation with him). *The Hard Man* caused great controversy at the time because of its portrayal of violence, both in society and within the prison system.

McIlvanney, William Angus (1936–), novelist, journalist, short story writer, poet, born Kilmarnock. McIlvanney explored working class themes and the erosion of working class values in his first novel *Remedy is None* (1966), *Docherty* (1975) and *The Big Man* (1985, made into a film). McIlvanney has also successfully written crime fiction set in Glasgow and played out through the character of Detective Jack Laidlaw. The most popular Laidlaw novel is *Strange Loyalties* (1991).

MacLaverty, Bernard (1942–), novelist, journalist, playwright, children's author, short story writer, born Belfast. MacLaverty came to Scotland in 1975 and currently lives in Glasgow. He has published four collections of short stories and four novels. His novel *Grace Notes* (1997) was given the Saltire Scottish Book of the Year Award and was shortlisted for the Booker Prize. In 2003 MacLaverty won a £30,000 Creative Scotland Award to write and direct a short film based on the Seamus Heaney poem *Bye Child*.

McLellan, Robert (1907–1985), playwright, poet and short story writer, born Kirkfieldbank, Lanarkshire. McLellan wrote almost exclusively in Scots and his play *The Flouers o' Edinburgh* (1948) is a debate between 18th-century Edinburgh gentlemen on the use of Scots or English in everyday life. McLellan's best-known play is *Jamie the Saxt* (1937) a study of James IV and I and his ascension to the thrones of both England and Scotland.

MacDiarmid, Hugh (Christopher Murray Grieve, 1892–1978), born Langholm, Dumfriesshire. Poet, critic and journalist. Key figure of Scottish 20th-century literary renaissance, writing chiefly in Scots. Works include: *Sangschaw* (1925), *A Drunk Man Looks at the Thistle* (1926), *In Memoriam James Joyce* (1954), *On a raised beach* (1934).

MacGonagall, William (1825/1830–1902), affectionately hailed as the 'world's worst poet'. Born Edinburgh. A weaver by trade, he became an amateur actor in Dundee and later published verse in broadsheet and book forms. Works include '*Railway bridge of the silv'ry Tay*' (1877), '*The Tay Bridge Disaster*', '*The death of Lord and Lady Dalhousie*'; a selection was published as *Poetic Gems* (1890).

Mackenzie, Sir Compton (1883–1972), novelist, playwright, journalist and broadcaster, born West Hartlepool of Scottish ancestry. Works include *Sinister Street* (1918); *Gallipoli Memories* (1929), based on his experiences in the first world war; *The Four Winds of Love* (6 vols., 1937–45); and *Whisky Galore* (1947), made famous as a film. Awarded OBE 1919, knighted 1952.

MacLean, Sorley (1911–96), English name of Somhairle MacGill-Eain, Gaelic poet, born Osgaig, Island of Raasay. MacLean worked as a teacher all his life (apart from service in North Africa during World War II). MacLean's first poems were published in 1940 but his most important work is *Dain do Eimhir agus Dain Eile* (1943), a selection of love poems and elegies which had a huge effect on modern Scottish Gaelic poetry. The series of love poems at the core of this book are intensely personal and passionate and yet are also fused with deep political conviction, specifically MacLean's rage at the triumph of the fascism in Spain. MacLean is also important for his experimental use of language and his exploration of the themes of family, Ireland, and the devastation of Gaelic Scotland.

Maclean, Alistair (1982–1987), novelist, born Glasgow. Wrote 30 popular novels of which 28 sold over a million copies in the UK, including *HMS Ulysses* (1955), based on his own wartime experiences, and *The Guns of Navarone* (1957).

McWilliam, Candia (1955–), novelist and short-story writer, born Edinburgh. Works include: *A Case of Knives* (1988), *A Little Stranger* (1989), *Debatable Land* (1994; Guardian Fiction Prize); short stories, *Wait Till I Tell You* (1997); editor, *Shorts II: The Macallan/Scotland on Sunday Short Story Collection.*

Massie, Allan (1938–), novelist and critic, born Singapore, educated Aberdeenshire. Massie is a writer of wide-ranging interests. His first novel, *Change and Decay in All Around I See* (1978) was an exploration of the decay in contemporary social and spiritual life. This was followed by *The Last Peacock* (1980) a gentle comedy of manners set amongst the Scottish gentry. *The Death of Men* (1981) is a chilling book about terrorism in Italy, partly based on the murder of the Italian politician Aldo Moro in 1978. More recent work has focused on the Roman Emperor *Tiberius* (1991) and the inherent dangers of leadership.

Maxwell, Gavin (1914–69), novelist, born Galloway. Maxwell is primarily a novelist of locations – his evocative descriptions go beyond the mundane to reveal the spirit of the place. Maxwell's first book, *Harpoon at a Venture* (1952), describes his failed attempt to commercially hunt sharks from Soay in Skye. His second book, *A Reed Shaken by the Wind* (1957), is a masterpiece of travel writing, which describes the journey he made with Ernest Thesiger to the Marsh Arabs of Iraq. But Maxwell's most famous work is *Ring of Bright Water* (1960), a brilliant evocation of Sandaig and Maxwell's otter Edal.

Mitchison, Naomi (1897–1999), novelist, journalist, short story writer, poet, biographer, born Edinburgh. Wrote over 70 books, including science fiction, children's novels, poetry, memoir and biography. Mitchison was active in the local politics of her Kintyre home as well as being connected to national politics through her husband, a Labour MP (and later peer). Mitchison was also interested in global politics and her lifelong friendship with the Bakgatha tribe of Botswana led to her adoption by the tribe as advisor and Mmarona (mother) during the 1960s. Mitchison's feminism is evident throughout her work, one of her central themes being the reality of life for women when a man-made world falls apart.

Muir, Edwin (1887–1959), novelist and poet, born Orkney, Argyll. Muir's work is suffused with longing for 'Eden' a place he geographically associated with Orkney, his childhood home until the age of 14. At 14 the family moved to Glasgow. Within four years two of his five siblings and both his mother and father were dead. Muir spent his adult life trying to come to terms with this loss of childhood. Muir published seven collections of poetry between 1925 and 1956 and three novels. He translated Kafka with his wife, Willa Anderson, and taught in Europe before finally ridding himself of his demons and settling down as Warden of Newbattle Abbey. Muir published his *Autobiography* in 1954.

Munro, Neil (1864–1930), novelist, journalist and poet, born Inverary, Argyll. Editor of *Glasgow Evening News* 1918–27. Early works include *The*

Last Pibroch (1896), a collection of Celtic tales and *Gilean the Dreamer* (1899), a story of 19th-century Scottish life. Best known today for collections of stories of 'Para Handy', beginning with *The Vital Spark* (1906). He also wrote a number of historical novels and some poetry.

Oliphant, Margaret (1828–1897), novelist, born Wallyford, near Edinburgh. Wrote over 100 novels as well as non-fiction and articles for *Blackwood's Magazine*. Novels include: *Passages in the Life of Mrs Margaret Maitland* (1849); *Caleb Field* (1851); *Katie Stewart* (1853, serialised in *Blackwood's*); *A Quiet Heart* (1854). Between 1861 and 1876, wrote a seven-volume series of novels on English country life, *The Chronicles of Carlingford*.

Ramsay, Allan (1684–1758), poet and editor, born Leadhills, Lanarkshire. Wrote collections of verse in Scots and English, 1721, 1728; editor of *The Ever Green* (anthology of Middle Scots poetry) and *Tea-Table Miscellany* (traditional songs and ballads plus some compositions of his own). His pastoral *The Gentle Shepherd* (1725) was later made into a ballad opera. Father of the painter Allan Ramsay.

Rankin, Ian (1960–), novelist, born Fife. Rankin is one of the most successful authors in Scotland today with his Edinburgh-based Inspector Rebus detective series having sold more than 100,000 copies each. The Rebus novels have been translated into several languages and Rankin has had up to six of his novels in the Scottish Top Ten list at any time in the last three years. The first Rebus novel, *Knots and Crosses* (1987) was followed by eleven others with *Black and Blue* (1997) winning the Crime Writers Association Gold Dagger. The Rebus novels not only provide a fascinating insight into the mind of their central character, each one also examines an aspect of modern Scotland, such as the impact of devolved government.

Rowling, J. K. (Joanne Kathleen) (1965–), children's writer, born Chipping Sodbury, Gloucestershire, England. Possibly the most famous modern-day children's writer in the world. J. K. Rowling wrote her first book – *Harry Potter and the Philosopher's Stone* (1997) whilst living on benefits in an unheated Edinburgh flat with her baby daughter. The Scottish Arts Council gave her a grant to finish the book, Bloomsbury published the book, and the rest is history – the five Harry Potter books (*Harry Potter and the Chamber of Secrets*, 1998, *Harry Potter and the Prisoner of Azkaban*, 1999 and *Harry Potter and the Goblet of Fire*, 2000, *Harry Potter and the Order of the Phoenix*, 2003) have sold well over 30 million copies worldwide, have been translated into 35 languages and made into two films. J. K. Rowling lives and works in Edinburgh and Perthshire.

Scott, Sir Walter (1771–1832), novelist, poet, editor and critic, born Edinburgh. Regarded as a great author even in his own lifetime, he, produced over 25 novels as well as poetry, *Lives and Works of Dryden* (18 vols, 1808) and *Swift* (19 vols, 1814), and contemporary history, such as a nine-volume life of Napoleon Bonaparte. Poetry includes: *The Lay of the Last Minstrel* (1805), *The Lady of the Lake* (1810), and a ballad collection, *Minstrelsy of the Scottish Border* (1802–3); novels include: *Waverley* (1814), *Rob Roy* (1817), *The Heart of Midlothian* (1818), *Ivanhoe* (1819), *Kenilworth* (1821), and *St Ronan's Well* (1823).

Smith, Iain Crichton (1928–98), English name of Iain MacGhobhainn, poet, short story writer and novelist, born Isle of Lewis. Smith wrote in Gaelic and English and explored the themes of religion and island life. His first collection of poems, *The Long River* (1955), was followed in 1960 by a book of Gaelic stories and poems, *Burn is Aran*. Smith's most famous novel is *Consider the Lillies* (1968), which examines the effect of the Highland Clearances on an old woman and her betrayal by the Free Church. Other works include *My Last Duchess* (1971), *An End to Autumn* (1978) and *Murdo and Other Stories* (1981).

Smollett, Tobias (1721–71), novelist, historian and travel writer. Born Dumbarton. First publication, *The Tears of Scotland* (1746) centred on the Jacobite Rising of 1745. Novels include: *The Adventures of Roderick Random* (1748), *The Adventures of Peregrine Pickle* (1751), and *The Adventures of Ferdinand Count Fathom* (1753); travel writing includes: *A Compendium of Authentic and Entertaining Voyages* (7 vols, 1756). His final work, *The Expedition of Humphrey Clinker* (1771), was considered his finest.

Soutar, William (1898–1943), poet, born Perth. Soutar wrote in both English and Scots and published his first work of poetry in 1923. Soutar is known for his 'bairn-rhymes' (children-rhymes), first seen in *Seeds in the Wind: poems in Scots for children* (1933), dedicated to his adopted daughter, Evelyn. But Soutar's 'whigmaleeries 'are considered his most original invention. These poems are written in Scots and are short, to the point and highly comic. The poet published 11 volumes of poetry in all and left 34 diaries, called 'Dream Books' to the National Library of Scotland.

Spark, Dame Muriel (1918–), novelist, short-story writer, biographer and poet. Born Edinburgh. Her 1961 novel *The Prime of Miss Jean Brodie*, has become her best-known work through its adaptation as a play and film. Other works include *The Comforters* (1957, her first novel), *The Ballad of Peckham Rye* (1960), *Loitering with Intent* (1995), *Curriculum Vitae: A Volume of Autobiography* (1993), and *Aiding and Abetting* (2000), her most recent novel. Awarded OBE in 1967, Dame of British Empire 1993.

Stevenson, Robert Louis (1850–94), novelist, poet, playwright, essayist, travel writer. Born Edinburgh. Despite suffering from tuberculosis for most of his life, he travelled widely, gathering material for books such as *Travels with a Donkey in the Cevennes* (1879), and, much later, *In the South Seas*. Novels include *Treasure Island* (1883), *The Strange Case of Dr Jekyll and Mr Hyde* (1886), *Kidnapped* (1886); *The Master of Ballantrae* (1889). Short stories include 'Thrawn Janet' and 'The beach at Falesa'. Poetry includes *A Child's Garden of Verses* (1885), recalling his own childhood.

Warner, Alan (1964–), novelist, born Argyll. A prominent Scottish member (along with Irvine Welsh) of the Chemical Generation of writers whose work is just as comfortably read out in clubs as in bookshops. Warner's first novel, *Morven Callar* (1995), was as much an anthem to dance culture as it was a reaction against Scottish small-town attitudes. Warner's second book, *The Sopranos* (1998), confirmed his ability to speak convincingly in a female voice. *Morven Callar* was made into a film in 2002 and *The Sopranos* is currently in production. Warner's most recent novel is *The Man Who Walks* (2002).

Welsh, Irvine (1961–), novelist and short-story writer, born Edinburgh. His stories, rooted in young urban working-class life, are characterised by *noir* humour and first-person narratives. Works include: short stories: *The Acid House* (1994); novels: *Trainspotting* (1994), *Marabou Stork Nightmares* (1996), *Filth* (1998), *Glue* (2001), *Porno* (2002).

COMPOSERS

Beamish, Sally (1956–), composer and viola player, born London. Played viola with the Raphael Ensemble, recording four discs of string sextets. Received an Arts Council Composer's Bursary in 1989 and moved to Scotland where she and her husband, cellist Robert Irvine, founded the Chamber Group of Scotland, with co-director James MacMillan. In 1993 Beamish received the

Paul Hamlyn Foundation Award for outstanding achievement in composition. She has written two symphonies, concertos for violin, viola, cello, oboe and saxophone. Her trumpet concerto for Hakan Hardenberger, commissioned by the National Youth Orchestra of Scotland, was performed in 2003 at the BBC Proms. Beamish won a BAFTA award for best composer for her score for the film *The Practicality of Magnolia* (2003).

Carver, Robert (1487–1566), Scotland's greatest 16th-century composer. Studied at the Flemish University of Leuven 1503–4 and was a canon of the Augustinian abbey of Scone from 1508. His 19 surviving works include: motets *O bone Jesu* (19 parts), *Gaude flore virginali*; 5 masses including the 10-part *Missa Dum sacrum mysterium* (1506), which was sung at the coronation of James V in 1513.

Clarke (or Clerk), Sir John of Penicuik (1676–1755), studied at Glasgow and Leiden. Works include: cantatas: *Leo Scotiae irritatus, Dic mihi, saeve puer* (1690s); violin sonata (*c.*1705). Also an architect.

Davies, Sir Peter Maxwell (1934–), born Manchester. has lived and worked in Orkney since 1970. Founder of St Magnus festival in 1977. His over 200 published works include: *Job; The Doctor of Myddfai; The martyrdom of St Magnus; Eight songs for a mad king; Orkney Wedding with Sunrise; 10 Strathclyde Concertos*, 8 symphonies. Awarded CBE 1981, knighted 1987.

MacMillan, James (1959–), born Kilwinning, Ayrshire. Works include: *The Tryst* (1984), setting of text by William Soutar; *The confession of Isabel Gowdie* (1990), *Veni, veni Emmanuel* (1992), percussion concerto for Evelyn Glennie and SCO; *Seven last words from the Cross* (1993); cello concerto for Mstislav Rostropovich; *Inés de Castro* (opera, 1996); *Parthenogenesis* (2001).

McGuire, Edward (1948–), born Glasgow. Works include: operas *Calgacus* (1997) and *The Loving of Etain* (1990); *A Glasgow Symphony* (1990); *Celtic Epic* (1997), orchestra and traditional musicians; several new works 2000–1. Also a performer and composer of traditional music associated since the early 1970s with the traditional music group the Whistlebinkies.

Macrae, Stuart (1976–), born Inverness. His first major work, *Boreraig* (1996), was performed by the BBC Philharmonia, who also performed *The Witch's Kiss* (1997). Other works include: *Landscape*

and the Mind: Distance, Refuge (1997); *Elemental* (1999); *Sinfonia* for chamber orchestra (2000).

Musgrave, Thea (1928–), born Edinburgh. Works include: *Journey through a Japanese landscape* (marimba and wind orchestra, 1994); *Helios* (oboe concerto, 1995); *Autumn Sonata* (A concerto for bass clarinet and orchestra); *Simón Bolívar* (opera, 1995).

Peebles, David (c.1510–79), a canon at the Augustinian priory of St Andrews whose four-part harmonisations of metrical psalm tunes from *The Scottish Psalter*, produced under the supervision of Thomas Wode, vicar of St Andrews, were collected in the *Wode Part-Books*. Other extant works include: *Si quis diligit me; Quam multi, Domine*

Robb, Magnus (1970–), composer, born Edinburgh. Began composing at the age of sixteen and studied music at the University of York. While there he composed *Lios Mor* for nine players which was later played by the Nash Ensemble in the Barbican Hall when he was a finalist in the BBC Young Musicians of the Year Lloyds Bank Composer Award, and *Delphi* for chamber orchestra which was performed in Amsterdam by the Netherlands Radio Chamber Orchestra. After leaving York, Robb went to the Guildhall School of Music and Drama in London and in 2003 he was based in Holland on a Sir James Cairdis Travelling Scholarship where he is studying with Louis Andriessen.

Stevenson, Ronald (1928–), born Lancashire, now based in the Borders. Best known for his piano works, especially *Passacaglia on DSCH* (1963), based on the composer Shostakovich's musical initials, and *Barra Flyting Toccata*. Other works include: violin concerto 1992; cello concerto *In memoriam Jacqueline du Pré*; song cycles *A Child's Garden of Verses, Nine Haiku, Border Boyhood*; over 200 songs.

Sweeney, William (1950–), born Glasgow. Strongly influenced by traditional Gaelic music and jazz; has made several settings of work by Scottish poets in Gaelic and Scots. Works include: *An Turus* (1997), collaboration with poet Aonghas MacNeacail; *Salm an fhearainn/Psalm of the land* (1987), also to Gaelic text by MacNeacail; *An rathad ur/The new road* (1988), *Coilltean Ratharsair/The woods of Raasay* (1993), setting of poem by Sorley Maclean.

Weir, Judith (1954–), born Cambridge of Scottish parents. Has worked at Glasgow University (1979–82) and RSAMD (1988–91). Artistic director of Spitalfields Festival, London, 1995–2000. Works include: operas: *A night at the Chinese opera* (1987), *The vanishing bridegroom*

(1990); *Blond Eckbert* (1994); *Moon and star* (chorus/orchestra, 1995), written for the 1995 Proms.

Yeats, Marc (1962–), composer, born London, lives Isle of Skye. Began composing in 1994 after participating in the Hoy Summer School. His compositions take visual art, particularly abstract art, as their starting point and try to bring to life their language of colour, texture and form. Recent commissions include a new work for the London Sinfonietta and a work for Kathryn Stott and the BBC Philharmonic premiered in February 2000.

DANCERS

Clark, Michael (1962–), dancer and choreographer, born Aberdeen. Formed his own company at the age of 22. Works include: *I Am Curious, Orange* (1988), *Mmm* (1993), *O* (1994). Also appeared as Caliban in Peter Greenaway's film *Prospero's Books*.

Darrell, Peter (1929–87), dancer, choreographer, director, born Richmond, Surrey. Trained at Sadler's Wells Ballet School then remained with the company as a dancer. Darrell went on to become the co-founder of Western Theatre ballet in Bristol in 1957 where he made the first ballet to the music of the Beatles. Most of his Bristol company moved with him when he came to Glasgow in 1969 and created the Scottish Ballet – a company he led until his death in 1987. Awarded a CBE in 1984.

Kemp, Lindsay (1939–), dancer, choreographer and mime artist. Formed Lindsay Kemp Company 1973. Works include *Flowers, Salomé, Duende, Alice, Onnagata, Dreamdances* (1998). Has appeared in films, including *Sebastiane* (Derek Jarman, 1975) and *Savage Messiah* (Ken Russell, 1972).

MacMillan, Sir Kenneth (1929–92), choreographer, born Dunfermline. In 1946 became a founder member of Sadler's Wells Theatre Ballet. Principal choreographer, Royal Ballet, 1977–92. A leading figure in contemporary ballet. Works include: *Danses Concertantes* (1955), *The Invitation* (1960), *Romeo and Juliet, Anastasia, The Prince of the Pagodas, The Judas Tree* (Olivier Award,1992). Knighted 1983.

Morris, Margaret (1891–1980), dancer and dance teacher. Developed a dance method and notation system and a system of movement therapy which have influenced many later dance teachers. Founder of Celtic Ballet Company and Celtic Ballet Theatre, Glasgow, in 1940.

FILM-MAKERS AND ACTORS

Bannen, Ian (1928–99), actor, born Airdrie, Lanarkshire. Bannen established himself as a theatre actor at the beginning of his career, making his debut at Dublin's Gate Theatre in *Armlet of Jade* in 1947, eventually going on to the Royal Shakespeare Company in 1961. Bannen's first film role was in *Private's Progress* (1956) and he went on to play many distinguished supporting roles, including *The Flight of the Phoenix* (1965) for which he received an Academy Award nomination. Bannen continued to work in films, including *Bite the Bullet* (1975), *Hope and Glory* (1987) and *Waking Ned Devine* (1998) until his death in a car crash in 1999.

Baxter, Stanley (1926–), comic actor, born Glasgow. Baxter began his career in radio and moved on to the theatre after the War, making his debut as Correction's Varlet at the Edinburgh Festival production of *The Thrie Estates* in 1948. He made his first appearance on television in *Shop Window* (1951) and had his first film outing in *Geordie* (1956). But it is for his roles in pantomime and for his television series *Stanley Baxter On . . .* (1960–4), *The Stanley Baxter Show* (1967–71) and his annual Christmas shows that Baxter is most fondly remembered.

Boyle, Danny (1956–), director, born Manchester. Began his career in theatre, and has also directed many television features, including *Mr Wroe's Virgins* and episodes of *Inspector Morse*. Films include: *Shallow Grave* (1994), *Trainspotting* (1996), *The Beach* (2000), and *28 Days Later* (2002).

Carlyle, Robert (1961–), actor and theatre director, born Glasgow. Graduated in 1986 from the Royal Scottish Academy of Music and Drama. Worked extensively in theatre but first came to public attention through his role as Hamish MacBeth, a Glasgow policeman posted to the small fictional Highland village of Lochdubh in *Hamish MacBeth* (1995–7). His reputation was further enhanced by his performance as Begbie in *Trainspotting* (1996), Gaz in *The Full Monty* (1997), the villain Renard in the James Bond movie *The World is Not Enough* (1999), and as Malachy McCourt Sr. in *Angela's Ashes* (2000). Awarded an OBE in 1999 for his services to drama.

Coltrane, Robbie (1950–), comedian, actor, born Rutherglen. After art college Coltrane began his career as a comedian in the BBC's *Blackadder* and *Comic Strip* series. His serious acting roles include a Bond villain in *Goldeneye* (1995) and *The World is Not Enough* (1999) and Hagrid in *Harry Potter and the Philosopher's Stone* (2001) and *Harry Potter and*

the *Chamber of Secrets* (2002). In Britain his most famous role is that of the TV forensic psychologist Fitz in the series *Cracker*, which won him BAFTA's best TV actor award three years running.

Connery, Sir Sean Thomas (1930–), actor, born Edinburgh. Connery got his first break as a member of the chorus of *South Pacific* (1951–2) after being talent spotted in a Mr Universe competition. Occasional film work followed and notable television roles in *Requiem for a Heavyweight* (1956) and *Anna Karenina* (1957). Chosen for the role of James Bond in the 1962 film *Dr. No*, Connery went on to play the part seven more times, until 1983. He won a Best Actor BAFTA for his performance as a monk in *The Name of the Rose* (1986), and an Oscar for his portrayal of an Irish policeman in *The Untouchables* (1987). Connery is one of the most famous film stars in the world, an obsessive golfer, and a supporter of Scottish Independence. He received a knighthood in July 2000.

Connolly, Billy (1942–), comedian, actor, born Glasgow. Connolly started life as a welder in the shipyards of Clydebank and played the banjo at night in folk clubs and bars. He turned professional in 1965 and became part of a group called the Humblebums. Striking out on his own as a comedian, he starred in *The Great Northern Welly Boot Show* at the 1972 Edinburgh Festival and his success was instant. It was here that he acquired the affectionate title 'The Big Yin'. Connolly now divides his time between his homes in Scotland and the USA and works as an actor as well as a comedian. His most famous film role to date is as Queen Victoria's faithful Scottish servant, John Brown, in *Mrs Brown* (1997).

Conti, Tom (1941–), actor, born in Paisley. Studied acting at Glasgow's Royal Scottish Academy of Music and Drama but did not find success quickly and supported himself by being a part-time tour guide and a singing waiter. Finally found theatrical success in *The Black and White Minstrels* (1972) and *Savages* (1973) before going onto television recognition with *The Glittering Prizes* (1976). Praised for his depiction of a paraplegic in *Whose Life Is It Anyway?* (1978), a play which he then took to Broadway. Nominated for an Academy Award in 1983 for his lead role in *Reuben, Reuben*.

Cox, Brian (1946–), actor, teacher and director, born Dundee. First appeared on stage in London as Orlando in *As You Like It* (1967). More West End performances followed with Alan Bennett's *Getting On* (1971) and Eugene O'Neill's *Strange Interlude* (1984). After a distinguished career in the theatre, where he worked at the Royal Court in London, the National Theatre, and the Royal Shakespeare Company, Cox went on to a successful Hollywood career, starring in films such as *Manhunter* (1986), *Rushmore* (1998), *Murder by Numbers* (2001), *The Ring* (2002) and *X Men 2* (2003). He was awarded a CBE in 2002.

Crosbie, Annette (1934–), actor, born Gorebridge. This television, stage and screen actress is most famous for her portrayal of Victor Meldrew's wife, Margaret, in the BBC-TV comedy *One Foot in the Grave* (1990–2000). Other television roles have included *The Six Wives of Henry VIII* (1971), *Edward the Seventh* (1975), *Dr Finlay's Casebook* (1993), and *Oliver Twist* (1999). Films have included *Nervous Energy* (1995), *Shooting Fish* (1997) and *The Debt Collector* (1999). Awarded an OBE in 1998.

Cumming, Alan (1965–), actor, born Perthshire. Attended the Royal Scottish Academy of Music and Drama and met Forbes Masson, one half of the comedy duo that they later formed, called Victor and Barry. They later wrote and starred in the BBC TV sitcom *The High Life.* After three years of television and theatre work in Scotland, Cumming made his West End debut in 1989 at the Royal Court Theatre in *The Conquest of the South Pole.* In 1998 Cumming accompanied the transfer of *Cabaret* to Broadway with Sam Mendes. He won a Tony Award for Best Actor in a Featured Role in 1998 for his performance as the Emcee in Cabaret. Cumming also has a successful film career and has appeared in films such as *Circle of Friends* (1995), *Goldeneye* (1995), *Emma* (1996), *Spice World* (1998), *Eyes Wide Shut* (1999), *Titus* (2000), *Get Carter* (2000), *Spy Kids* (2001) and *Josie and the Pussycats* (2001).

Douglas, Bill (1937–91), film-maker, born Newcraighall. His autobiographical trilogy – *My Childhood* (1972), *My Ain Folk* (1973), *My Way Home* (1978) – describes growing up in a Scottish mining community.

Fisher, Gregor (1953–), actor and comedian, born Glasgow. Went to the Royal School of Music and Drama in Glasgow but left before completing his studies. Best known for his portrayal of Rab C. Nesbitt, a string-vested Glaswegian philosopher in the series of the same name. Other television work includes *The Tales of Para Handy* (1994), *The Baldy Man* (1995) and *The Railway Children* (2000).

Forsyth, Bill (1946–), director, writer and producer, born Glasgow. Known for small-scale, quiet comedies. Works include: *That Sinking Feeling* (1979), *Gregory's Girl* (1981), *Local Hero* (1983), *Being Human* (1993), *Gregory's Two Girls* (1999).

Glen, Iain (1961–), actor, born Edinburgh. A graduate of Aberdeen University, Glen won the Bancroft Gold Medal at RADA and went on to gain public attention as a ruthless gang leader in the television series *The Fear* (1988). In 1990 Glen won the Best Actor Award at the Berlin Film Festival for his performance as the Scottish prisoner Larry Winters in *Silent Scream.* He has also starred in popular mainstream films such as *Tomb Raider* (2001). His most recent film is *Darkness* (2002). Glen has extensive stage appearances including *The Blue Room,* with Nicole Kidman (1998) at the Donmar Warehouse in London.

Grierson, John (1898–1972), pioneer documentary film-maker and producer, born Deanston. He produced a vast number of documentaries but directed relatively few. They include: *Drifters* (1929), made for the Empire Marketing Board Film Unit, which he founded in 1928; *Industrial Britain* (1933), *Song of Ceylon* (1934), *Night Mail* (1936). Founder of the National Film Board of Canada in 1939. Coined the word 'documentary' in 1925.

Hannah, John (1962–), actor, born East Kilbride. Hannah's acting aspirations began with the East Kilbride Rep Theatre Club. Eventually he gave up his apprenticeship (as an electrician) and attended the Royal Scottish Academy of Music and Drama. After graduation he gained small parts in theatre productions before his big break came in the film *Four Weddings and a Funeral* (1994). Hollywood soon beckoned and he took a part in *The Mummy* (1999) and *The Mummy Returns* (2001). In 1997 Hannah established a production company, Clerkenwell Films, which has undertaken production of Ian Rankin's highly successful series of Inspector Rebus detective novels.

Hardy, Forsyth (1910–94), writer and producer. Founded Edinburgh Film Guild, Scottish Film Council and the Edinburgh International Film Festival.

Henshall, Douglas (1967–), actor, born Glasgow. A member of the Glasgow Youth Theatre before he went to London to train at the Mountview Theatre School. Upon completing his training Henshall moved back to Glasgow and joined the 7:84 theatre company. Eventually Henshall returned to London and received great critical acclaim for his theatre work, notably *Life of Stuff* (1993) at the Donmar Warehouse and *American Buffalo* (1997) at the Young Vic. One of his first successful film roles was in *Angels and Insects* (1995), followed by *Orphans* (1997). Television appearances include *Psychos* (1999) and *Kid in the Corner* (1999).

Jackson, Gordon Cameron (1923–90), actor, born Glasgow. Performed in radio plays as a child before leaving school at 15 to become a draughtsman with Rolls Royce. First film performance came in 1941 in *The Foreman Went to France*, where he was cast, inevitably, as a young Scottish soldier. Similar roles followed but his stage career was more varied and distinguished as he played Ishmael in Orson Welles's production of *Moby Dick* (1955) and Banquo to Alec Guinness's Macbeth in *Macbeth* (1966). Films included *Whisky Galore* (1948), *The Great Escape* (1963), *The Prime of Miss Jean Brodie* (1969) and *The Shooting Party* (1984). But it was television that brought him to mass public attention in the roles of the butler, Hudson, in *Upstairs, Downstairs* (1970–5) and a CI5 boss in *The Professionals* (1977–81).

Kerr, Deborah (1921–), actor, born Helensburgh, Dumbartonshire. Trained as a ballet dancer and performed as part of the corps-de-ballet at Sadler's Wells. Kerr then turned to acting, appearing in repertory in Oxford before making her screen debut in *Contraband* (1940). She starred in *The Life and Death of Colonel Blimp* (1943) and *Black Narcissus* (1947) before moving to Hollywood where she tended to be typecast in upper class roles except, sensationally, in *From Here to Eternity* (1953). During her career she was nominated for an Academy Award six times and was given a CBE in 1998.

Kissling, Werner (1885–1988), photographer, born Germany. His film Eriskay, a *Poem of Remote Lives* (1935) was the first ever film in which the Gaelic language was spoken.

Law, Phyllida (1932–), actor, born Glasgow. Now just as famous for being Emma Thompson's mother as she is for her acting roles. Law established her career as a character actor on the stage, playing in everything from *The Merry Wives of Windsor* to *La Cage Aux Folles* to *Noises Off*. She first appeared in films in 1968 in *Otley* but didn t really pursue the screen until the 1990s when she featured in *Peter's Friends* (1992), *Much Ado About Nothing* (1993), *The Winter Guest* (1997) and *Saving Grace* (2000), amongst others.

Lawson, Denis (1947–), actor and director, born Glasgow. Attended the Royal Scottish Academy of Music and Drama in Glasgow then began a career in theatre, acting in everything from *Hair* to Shakespeare. Lawson's film debut was in *Dinosaur* (1976), followed by his famous role as Wedge Antilles, an X-wing fighter, in *Star Wars* (1976) and *Local Hero* (1983). Lawson has continued to work in theatre and television with appearances in *Hornblower* (1998), *Cold Feet* (1998) and *Holby City* (2002). He recently directed his nephew Ewan McGregor in a short film, *Solid Geometry* (2002).

Logan, Phyllis (1956–), actor, born Glasgow. has performed extensively on the stage, small screen and big screen. Is particularly remembered for her performance in Mike Leigh's *Secrets and Lies* (1996) and for her comedic roles in *Scotch and Wry* (1986).

McGregor, Ewan (1971–), actor, born Crieff. McGregor left school at the age of 16 to follow his uncle, Denis Lawson (see above) into acting. Attended the Guildhall School of Music and Drama but left before the end of his course in order to take up a part in the Dennis Potter television series *Lipstick on Your Collar*. The following year MacGreggor took the lead in the BBC production of *Scarlet and Black*. Danny Boyle's *Shallow Grave* in 1994 was the actor's big screen break and was quickly followed by *Trainspotting* (1996) and *A Life Less Ordinary* (1997). But the films that MacGreggor is best known for internationally are undoubtedly *Moulin Rouge* (2001), and the first three episodes of George Lucas' *Star Wars* series of films (2001, 2002, 2003), where he plays the young Obi Wan Kenobi.

Mackendrick, Alexander (1912–93), animator, screenwriter, and director, born Boston of Scottish parents. Works include: *Whisky Galore* (1949), *The Maggie* (1954), *The Ladykillers* (1955), *The Man in the White Suit* (1951).

MacKinnon, Gillies (1948–), director and writer, born Glasgow. Works include: *Small Faces* (1996), *Regeneration* (1997), *Hideous Kinky* (1998).

Mullan, Peter, director/writer and actor, born Glasgow. Works include: *Good Day for the Bad Guys* (1995), *Fridge* (1996), *Orphans* (1997) and *The Magdalene Sisters* (2003). Acting credits include: *My Name is Joe* (Ken Loach, 1998), *The Claim* (Michael Winterbottom, 2000).

Nardini, Daniela (1967–), actor, born Largs. Has appeared mostly in television and is best known for her portrayal of Anna Forbes in the series *This Life*

(1989–96), a performance which won her a BAFTA (1989). More recent television work includes *Rough Treatment* (2000), *Table 12* (2001), *Outside the Rules* (2002) and *Sirens* (2002). Her only big screen performance to date was in *Elephant Juice* (1999).

Niven, David (1909–83), actor, born Kirriemuir. Following several years in the Highland Light Infantry, Niven resigned his commission and moved to the USA where he began a career in the movies as an extra in 1935. More major roles began appearing, starting with *The Charge of the Light Brigade* (1936), *The Dawn Patrol* (1938) and *Raffles* (1940). With the outbreak of World War II Niven joined the British Army becoming a Lieutenant Colonel in the Commandos. After the war Niven returned to Hollywood and his life as an actor, performing in nearly 100 films, including *Around the World in 80 Days* (1956), *The Guns of Navarone* (1961), *The Pink Panther* (1964) and *The Sea Wolves* (1980).

Ramsay, Lynne (1969–), director and writer, born Glasgow. Her first feature-length film, *Ratcatcher* (1999), set in a Glasgow tenement in the 1970s, won many awards, including a BAFTA award for best newcomer in British Film (2000), the Guardian New Director Award at the 1999 Edinburgh Film Festival, the Sutherland Award for first feature films at the 1999 London Film Festival, and the Grand Prix at the Bratislava Film Festival 1999. Two of her short films, *Small Deaths* (1995) and *Gasman* (1998), won Grand Jury prizes at Cannes.

Robertson-Justice, James (1905–75), actor, born Wigtownshire. Initially a journalist with Reuters, Robertson-Justice served with the International Brigade in the Spanish Civil War (1936–9) and then as an officer in the Royal Navy during World War II before finally turning to acting in 1944, when he appeared in the film *Fiddlers Three*. Other films include *Whisky Galore* (1948), *Moby Dick* (1956) and *Mayerling* (1968). He is most famous for his role as Sir Lancelot Sprat in the series of 'Doctor' comedies that began in 1953. Robertson-Justice retired from acting in 1970 after *Doctor in Trouble*.

Swinton, Tilda (1960–), actor, born London to Scottish parents. Swinton has concentrated on appearing in off-beat productions and experimental films that very often explore gender identity. Films include: *Caravaggio* (1986), *Orlando* (1992), *The War Zone* (1999) and *Adaptation* (2002). She is married to Scottish playwright and artist John Byrne and lives in Tain.

Wilson, Richard (1936–), actor and director, born Greenock. Worked as a research scientist before becoming an actor. Wilson landed his first acting job at the age of 29 when he played a stonemason in the original *Dr Finlay's Casebook*. He has worked extensively in theatre and TV since then. The television role he is most famous for is Victor Meldrew in *One Foot in the Grave* (1990–2000, a role he won three BAFTAs and one British Comedy Award for). Wilson has also been heavily involved in the theatre, which he has directed for over three decades. Awarded the OBE in 1994.

VISUAL ARTISTS

Aikman, William (1682–1731), born Cairney, Forfarshire. Was pupil to Sir John Medina (1659–1719), the leading painter of the day in Scotland. Travelled to Italy between 1706 and 1711 or 1712. On his return to Edinburgh he set up as a portrait painter and quickly became the outstanding portraitist of his generation. Moved to London in 1723 and became fashionable, obtaining many important commissions, including portraits of the poets John Gay (1685–1732), Alexander Pope (1688–1744), and Allan Ramsay (1686–1758).

Bellany, John, (1942–), painter and printmaker, born Port Seton. Works inspired by religion and by the sea and the life of east-coast fishing communities. Works include: *Allegory* (1964), *Homage to John Knox* (1969), *The Old Man and the Sea, Celtic Sacrifice, The Sea People, Odyssey: Elegy for Alexander Kasser* (1998). Awarded CBE.

Blackadder, Elizabeth, (1931–), born Falkirk. Early works were landscapes, inspired by travels in Mediterranean Europe (e.g. *Church in Salonika,* 1954; *Façade, Mistra,* 1963) and Scotland (*Wall Town,* 1961; *Beach, Elgol,* 1965); more recently she has concentrated on still life and images of flowers and cats, in oils, watercolour and prints (e.g. *Chinese Still-Life with Fan,* 1982; *Still-Life with Cats,* 1991–4; *Shop Window, Kyoto,* 1998). First Scottish woman painter to become an academician of both the Royal Scottish Academy and the Royal Academy. Awarded OBE in 1982. Large retrospective exhibition held 2000.

Colquhoun, Robert (1914–62), artist, lithographer, theatrical designer and graphic artist, born Kilmarnock. Won a scholarship to Glasgow School of Art (1933–8) where he met his life-long companion Robert MacBryde (see below). The 'two Roberts', as they were known, visited Paris and Italy 1938–9 on a travelling scholarship. Colquhoun served in the RAMC 1940–1 until he was invalided out. In 1941 he settled in London with MacBryde. The two Roberts exhibited together in 1942 and Colquhoun had his first one-man show in 1943. He continued to exhibit regularly up until 1950, but his 1947 exhibition was the highpoint of his career.

Conroy, Stephen (1964–), painter, born Helensburgh, Dumbartonshire. Spotted very early on in his career, Conroy was a postgraduate student at Glasgow School of Art (1982–7) when he won the First Prize for Painting at the Royal Academy's British Institute Fund Awards (1986). He was included in the exhibition *The Vigorous Imagination* (1987) at the Scottish National Gallery of Modern Art and has been successful ever since, exhibiting regularly in London and New York. His work is classical in style and is carefully planned with each painting undergoing several stages of preparatory drawings and compositional sketches. Enigmatic figures populate his work and his painting technique is sometimes reminiscent of the Impressionist, Edgar Degas.

Cowie, James (1880–1956), artist and teacher, born Monquhitter, Aberdeenshire. Art master at Bellshill Academy from 1914, painted several pictures of schoolgirls. Works include: *Two Schoolgirls* (c. 1937), *Falling Leaves* (1934), *Self-portrait: The Blue Shirt* (1945–50).

Crozier, William (1897–1930), landscape painter, born Edinburgh. A member of the Edinburgh School; not widely known today, he was once thought the most original of the group. Works include: *Buildings, Trees and River* (1920), *Red Roofs, Pennan* (1924), *Edinburgh from Salisbury Crags* (1927), *Tuscan Landscape* (1927).

Currie, Ken (1960–), painter, born North Shields to Scottish parents, moved with his family to Glasgow when he was three months old. Currie studied social science at Paisley College of Technology (1977–8) and then painting at Glasgow School of Art (1978–83). He intended to follow a career in film, believing that it to be a more accessible medium than art but he returned to painting in 1985 after becoming disillusioned with the cost of film-making. He was quickly commissioned to paint a series of eight murals depicting Scottish labour history for the People's Palace in Glasgow (1986–7). Since this time Currie has become one of Scotland's foremost painters, known especially for his Socialist-Realist influenced works. He has exhibited internationally and contributed to the regeneration of the Gorbals through his art (2003).

Davie, Alan (1920–), born Grangemouth. Abstract expressionist painter, with an interest also in ancient Scotland. Works include: *Playing card adventure no. 4* (1964), *Jingling space* (1950).

Demarco, Richard (1930–), artist, broadcaster, teacher, curator, born Edinburgh. Studied at Edinburgh College of Art (1949–53) and still practises as an artist but is known for the championing of artists such as Joseph Beuys in Scotland. Awarded an OBE in 1985.

Dyce, William (1806–1864), born Aberdeen. Influenced by Italian Renaissance painting and later Pre-Raphaelitism. Advised on murals for new House of Lords building. Works include: *Titian's first essay in colour* (1857), *Christ as the Man of Sorrows* (1860), *Pegwell Bay, Kent – a Recollection of October 5th, 1858.*

Eardley, Joan (1921–63), painter, born Warnham, Sussex. Began her studies at Goldsmith's College of Art in London but moved to Glasgow School of Art in 1940. In 1949 Eardley took a studio in Cochrane Street in Glasgow and started painting the children of the nearby tenements. In 1950 she visited Catterline, a small fishing village on the north-east coast of Scotland and this location inspired her seascapes and landscapes. Eardley lived and worked in Catterline from 1951 until her death from cancer.

Faed, Thomas (1826–1900), painter, born Gatehouse, Galloway. Thomas' brother, John, was also a painter and Thomas found his way to John's studio in Edinburgh at the age of 15, where he studied and enrolled in the city's art school. He was so successful that by the age of 23 he was elected an associate of the Royal Scottish Academy. In 1852 Faed's popularity led him to move to London, a city that he remained in for the rest of his life, rising through the ranks of the Royal Academy while painting pictures with distinctly Scottish themes and subjects, such as *The Mitherless Bairn* (1855) and *The Last of the Clan* (1865).

Finlay, Ian Hamilton (1925–), poet, sculptor and landscape artist. A trademark is the inclusion of printed or incised words in his work. Since the 1960s he has created a garden with sculpture and installations called 'Little Sparta', at his home, Stonypath, in Dunsyre, Lanarkshire.

Goldsworthy, Andy (1956–), sculptor, born Cheshire, moved to Scotland 1985. A sculptor who works mostly in the open air and with natural materials that are often allowed to decay after the work has been completed. Goldsworthy has worked at the North Pole and in Japan, the Australian Outback and the Northern Territories of Canada. He has gained enormous success in Britain through the many publications illustrating his work but has greater establishment recognition in the USA where, in March 2003, he was awarded a $1 million commission to design a 'garden of stones' for the Museum of Jewish Heritage – A Living Memorial to the Holocaust in New York.

Guthrie, Sir James (1859–1930), painter, born Greenock. Attended the University of Glasgow to read law but gave up in 1877 to become an artist. One of the Glasgow Boys, he was mostly self-taught and heavily influenced by the French school of Realism. He went on to become one of the most progressive of Scottish 19th-century painters, preferring to choose his subjects from every day life. Guthrie settled in Cockburnspath (in the Borders) in 1883 and was elected to the Royal Scottish Academy in 1888, becoming its President in 1902. His masterpiece is *Highland Funeral* (1881) and it can be seen at Glasgow Art Gallery.

Hamilton, Gavin (1723–98), painter, picture dealer and archaeologist. Hamilton settled permanently in Rome in 1766 and became a leading member of the Neoclassical school there. His work as an archaeologist on sites near Rome contributed a great deal to contemporary collections and had an influence on artists such as Antonio Canova (1757–1822). His business as a dealer in Classical antiquities and Old Masters had a decisive effect on the development of Neoclassicism and history painting in Britain and on the Continent but his own history paintings are not thought of as important works.

Harvey, Jake (1948–), sculptor, born Langholm, Borders. Works include: Hugh MacDiarmid memorial near Langholm (1984), *Cup Stones* (1993), inspired by prehistoric Scottish art.

Howson, Peter (1958–), painter, born London. Howson moved to Scotland in 1962 and attended Glasgow School of Art from 1975–7 and 1979–81. Howson's paintings, drawings and prints debate class structures and often depict thug-like men that exude physical strength but seem directionless and confused. Howson was chosen as Britain's official war artist during the Bosnian War and the uncompromising images of rape, murder and torture that came out of his experience cost the artist his marriage and led to a nervous breakdown. The artist's recent work has reflected his return to Christianity and his portraiture continues to be

controversial – the pop star Madonna's rejection of his rather brutal portrait of her being the most famous example.

Jameson, George (c.1589–1644), born Aberdeen. Influenced by contemporary painters of the Low Countries, he is considered the founder of Scottish portraiture. Works include: portraits of Mary Erskine, Countess Marischal (1626), self-portrait (*c.* 1637–40).

Johnstone, William (1897–1981). Studied in Paris and the USA; his works reflect Cubist and Surrealist influences and inner landscapes of the unconscious. Works include: *A point in time* (1929–38), *Ode to the North Wind, Celebration of Earth, Air, Fire and Water* (1974).

Lauder, Robert Scott (1893–69), painter and teacher, born Silvermills, Edinburgh. Lauder was one of the first 24 artists to be admitted to the newly founded Royal Scottish Academy in 1829. In 1852 he was made Master of the Trustee's Academy in Edinburgh, ultimately becoming one of their greatest teachers and a pioneer of innovative teaching methods – but this success reduced his artistic output and achievements.

Lavery, Sir John (1856–1941), painter, born Belfast. Studied in Glasgow and Paris and became a member of the Glasgow School before settling in London in 1895. Enjoyed a successful career as a portraitist.

MacBryde, Robert (1913–66), painter, born Ayr. Worked in industry for five years before studying at the Glasgow School of Art, where he met Robert Colquhoun (see above). Heavily influenced by Cubism and Expressionism.

MacDonald, Margaret (1864–1933), designer, born Tipton, Wolverhampton, England. MacDonald first came to Glasgow with her parents in 1890. She attended the Glasgow School of Art (1890–4) where she met Charles Rennie Macintosh. They married in 1900. MacDonald was a highly successful and versatile artist who turned her hand to metalwork, painting, embroidery, architectural design, textiles and furniture design. Between 1895 and 1924 MacDonald contributed to more than 40 exhibitions throughout Europe and America and was widely collected, written about and commissioned.

MacDonald, Frances (1873–1921), designer, metalworker, water colourist, and embroiderer, born Tipton, Wolverhampton, England. Sister of

Margaret MacDonald and one of the Glasgow Four (along with Charles Rennie Macintosh, Margaret MacDonald and Herbert MacNair). The two sisters collaborated a great deal in their early work and much of it has been given joint attribution. Frances' work was less popular than her sister's (as it was thought to be less feminine) but equally skilled and influential with other artists. Frances MacDonald married Herbert MacNair in 1899.

Mach, David (1956–), sculptor, born Methil, Fife. Studied at Duncan of Jordanstone College of Art, Dundee (1974–79) and then at the RCA, London (1979–82). He works on a colossal scale, producing contemporary and permanent installations using waste products, consumer durables and multiples such as newspapers, bricks, toys and tyres. His first public work, *Rolls Royce,* was created from thousands of old books. He has exhibited work in Britain, Europe and the USA and is represented in major international collections. Since 2000 he has been Professor of Sculpture at the Royal Academy of Arts, London.

Maclean, Will (1941–), painter and sculptor, born Inverness. Studied at Gray's School of Art, Aberdeen (1961–7) and won a scholarship to the British School in Rome in 1967 before working as a ring-net fisherman off the coasts of Scotland. He exhibited his paintings throughout the 1960s and 1970s. From 1974 onwards Maclean has concentrated on sculptures constructed of driftwood and found objects with sculpted elements. His work is heavily influenced by traditional Scottish fishing techniques and cultures. Maclean's three large works on Lewis (1996), commemorating the struggle between landlords and tenants at the turn of the 20th-century, raise questions of national history and identity.

McCulloch, Horatio (1805–67), painter, born Glasgow. McCulloch began his artistic career as a painter of snuff boxes, then he moved to Edinburgh and became an engraver and then a painter. He was recognised in his day as a master of Scottish landscapes and his work had a great influence on the generation of Scottish painters that followed him.

Mackintosh, Charles Rennie (1868–1928), architect, water colourist, designer, born Glasgow. Despite his enormous influence as an architect, Macintosh found little recognition in Britain during his lifetime. The Mackintoshes moved away from Glasgow in 1914, first to Chelsea, then to Port Vendres in the South of France (1923–7). It was here that Mackintosh concentrated on watercolour painting, especially landscapes and flower studies.

MacNair, Herbert (1868–1955), designer, furniture designer, illustrator, water colourist, and graphic artist, born Glasgow. The least well-known of the 'Glasgow Four', the other members of the group being Charles Rennie Mackintosh, Margaret MacDonald and Frances MacDonald (whom he married in 1899). He was a draughtsman with Honeyman and Keppie, a prominent Glasgow architectural practice, where he met Rennie Mackintosh. He attended the Glasgow School of Art at night and then set up his own business in 1895. In 1897 he left Glasgow to take up a position as Instructor in Design at the School of Architecture at University College, Liverpool. Whilst in Liverpool MacNair carried out a number of decorative schemes but fell into financial difficulties whereupon he returned to Glasgow and a succession of menial jobs.

Melville, Arthur (1855–1904), painter, born East Linton (East Lothian). Trained at the Royal Scottish Academy before travelling to Paris in 1878. Initially worked in watercolour and became influential within the Glasgow Boys. Melville spent two years in the Middle East (1881–3) and some time in Spain (1892) and became known for his watercolours of exotic locations. His work can be seen in the National Gallery of Scotland, Edinburgh, and the Victoria & Albert Museum, London.

McTaggart, William (1835–1910), landscape painter, born Macrihanish, Kintyre. His land and seascapes are grounded in the social reality of rural and coastal Scotland. Works include: *A Ground Swell, Carradale* (1883), *Sailing of the Emigrant Ship* (1895), *The Coming of St Columba* (1895).

Moffat, Alexander (1943–), painter, born Dunfermline. Studied at Edinburgh Art College (1960–4) then worked in an engineering factory and as a photographer. Moffat is principally known as a portraitist and since 1979 he has lectured at Glasgow School of Art where his style and teaching methods have been very influential on the new wave of Scottish painters.

Nasmyth, Alexander (1758–1840), painter, builder and architect. Known as 'the father of Scottish landscape'. Works include: *Edinburgh from Calton Hill* (1825), *Princes Street with the Commencement of the Building of the Royal Institution* (1825); portrait of his friend Robert Burns (1787).

Paolozzi, Sir Eduardo (1924–), sculptor, born Leith. Pioneer of Pop Art in Europe, interested in Surrealism and in the iconography of machines. Has created much public sculpture. Works include: *Icarus* (1957), *Master of the Universe* (1989), *Newton After Blake* (1997, for the new British Library), *London–Paris* (2000). Designed mosaics for Tottenham Court Road underground station, London. Also made collages such as *Bunk* (1947). In 1986, appointed Her Majesty's Sculptor-in-Ordinary for Scotland by the Queen. Awarded CBE 1968; knighted 1988.

Raeburn, Henry (1756–1823), born Edinburgh. Foremost portrait painter of his day, he painted many of his contemporary politicians, scientists and philosophers, including Scott, Hume, Boswell, the fiddler Niel Gow (1793), Colonel Alasdair Macdonell of Glengarry (1811); Sir John and Lady Clerk of Penicuik (1792); *The Rev. Robert Walker Skating.* Admired for the confidence and ease of his style and for his sense of his sitters' personalities.

Ramsay, Allan (1713–84), born Edinburgh. Son of the poet. After studies in Italy, settled in London, becoming portrait painter to George III (e.g. portraits of George III as Prince of Wales, 1737, Queen Charlotte, 1763). Also painted eminent Scots (e.g. John Stuart, 3rd Earl of Bute, Flora Macdonald), philosophers Hume and Rousseau (1766), and his two wives Anne Bayne (1740) and Margaret Lindsay (early 1760s).

Read, Catherine (1723–78), portraitist and pastellist. One of the earliest Scottish women artists, but based for much of her life in London, she specialised in portraits of women. Works include portrait of Frances Moore Brooke (d. 1789), Canada's first novelist who emigrated from England.

Redpath, Anne (1895–1965), painter, born Galashiels. A member of the Edinburgh School, strongly influenced by French painting, in particular Matisse. Still-lifes and interiors include *The Indian rug* (c. 1942), *The white cyclamen, The mantelpiece.* Elected to RSA 1951.

Runciman, Alexander (1736–85) and John (1744–68), painters, born Edinburgh. Both of these brothers painted religious, literary and historical subjects although John is believed to be the more talented of the two; his masterpiece, *King Lear in the Storm* (1767) hangs in Edinburgh's National Gallery and lives and breathes in its own right, rather than as a frozen scene from a stage play. Unfortunately, Alexander's finest work – the decoration of

Penicuik House near Edinburgh – was destroyed by fire in 1899 but is generally acknowledged to have been the most ambitious decorative arts scheme of its time, Alexander having stated that he wished it to rival the Sistine Chapel Ceiling.

Steell, Sir John (1804–91), sculptor, born Aberdeen. Was Queen Victoria's Sculptor in Scotland. Works include most of Edinburgh's major public statues, e.g. Scott (1845), Queen Victoria, Prince Albert, Wellington, and Burns (in Thames Embankment Gardens); and a bust of Florence Nightingale (1862).

Traquair, Phoebe Anna (1852–1936), muralist, embroiderer, bookbinder, illuminator and illustrator, jeweller. A key figure in the late Arts and Crafts movement in Edinburgh. Painted murals for a mortuary for the Royal Hospital for Sick Children (1885), the Song School of St Mary's Cathedral, Edinburgh (1888-92) and the Catholic Apostolic Church, Mansfield Place, Edinburgh. In 1920, elected first honorary woman member of RSA.

Vettriano, Jack (1954–), painter, born Fife. Began life as a miner but was given a box of watercolours by his girlfriend for his 21st birthday and began painting in his spare time. Exhibited for the first time at the age of 35 and has gone on to become hugely successful with millions of posters of his work sold worldwide. Vettriano offered his most famous painting, *The Singing Butler,* to the Scottish Arts Council in 1990 for £2,000. The SAC refused the offer and the work now brings the artist over £250,000 a year in royalties alone. Vettriano has been snubbed by the arts establishment but has been recognised by the public as the most popular artist in the UK with his *Singing Butler* and *The Billy Boys* paintings ranking as the two best-selling fine arts prints in Britain.

Whiteford, Kate (1952–), painter, born Glasgow. Studied drawing and painting at Glasgow School of Art (1969–73) then studied History of Art at Glasgow University (1974–6). Whiteford won a British Council scholarship in 1977 that allowed her to travel to Rome, Herculaneum and Pompeii, an experience that greatly influenced her work. Her first solo exhibition took place in 1978. Whiteford's work is minimal in palette and non-figurative but since 1980 has featured recognisable symbols from the Celtic and Classical cultures.

Wilkie, David (1785–1841), painter, born Fife. Founder of Scottish 19th-century school of genre painting, influencing many painters of his own and succeeding generations. His scenes of village life and Scottish history contain not only social commentary but a philosophical Enlightenment interpretation of Scottish history. Works include: *The village politicians* (1806), *The Blind Fiddler* (1806), *Distraining for Rent* (1815); *The Cottars' Saturday Night* (1837).

Wiszniewski, Adrian (1958–), painter, born Glasgow. Studied at the Mackintosh School of Architecture (1979–83) then won a series of scholarships. Held his first one-man show in 1984 and by 1985 his work had been bought by the Tate Gallery, London, and the Museum of Modern Art, New York. His early work was executed in charcoal on paper but since 1985–6 he has concentrated on large-scale oil paintings. Many of his works contain self-portraits. The surface of his canvases tend to be heavily worked and to contain melancholy young men in confusing, Surrealist landscapes.

Wright, John Michael (1617–94), born London of Scottish parentage, returned to Scotland in 1630s to become pupil of George Jameson, and spent much of 1640s in Rome. As a Jacobite, lost favour after the accession of William of Orange. Works include portraits of the architect Sir William Bruce (1664), Lord Mungo Murray (c.1680).

Wyllie, George (1921–), sculptor, born Glasgow. Inspired by Italian metal sculpture he joined welding classes at the Royal Technical College (now Strathclyde University) and studied part-time at the Glasgow School of Art. Became a full-time artist in 1979. Specialises in mixed media, kinetic, installation and performance art. Has exhibited throughout the UK since the 1960s. His giant *Crystal Ship* (2000) is a permanent feature of the rejuvenated Govan dry dock in Glasgow.

THE SCOTTISH COLOURISTS

The group of four painters known as the Scottish Colourists can be seen as the heirs to the Glasgow Boys. All four studied in Paris, were clearly influenced by developments in French art at the turn of the 20th-century, from Cézanne and Gauguin to Matisse and Derain, and found thematic inspiration equally in Scotland and France. However, they never formally constituted a group and exhibited jointly only three times in their lifetimes. Fergusson moved to France permanently in 1909, while the other three remained based in Scotland.

A major exhibition of the Colourists work, organised by the Scottish National Gallery of Modern Art, was held in 2000 in Scotland and at the Royal Academy, London, and revived a keen interest in the work of this evocative and influential group of Scottish painters.

Cadell, Francis Campbell Boileau (1883–1937), born Edinburgh. Works include: *Afternoon* (1913), *Lunga from Iona, Still Life (The Grey Fan)* (c.1920-5), *The Blue Jug* (c.1922), *The Black Hat* (1914), *The Orange Blind* (c.1927).

Fergusson, John Duncan (1874–1961), born Perthshire. Works include: *Rhythm* (1911), *Les Eus* (c.1910–13), *In the Sunlight.* Fergusson was also an influential sculptor.

Hunter, G. Leslie (1877–1931), born Rothesay. Works include: *Houseboats, Balloch* (c.1924), *Provençal Landscape* (1929), *Reflections, Balloch* (c.1930). *Village in Fife.*

Peploe, Samuel John (1871–1935), born Edinburgh. Works include: *Ben More from Iona* (1925), *Palm Trees, Antibes* (1928), *Portrait of Peggy MacRae; Still Life with Roses.*

PHOTOGRAPHERS

Adamson, Robert (1821–1848), chemist and photographer, Edinburgh. Adamson had to give up his proposed career of engineering due to ill health (ill health that would kill him by the age of 27). He set up a partnership with David Octavius Hill, an academic painter, and their earliest dated photograph is from 1843. Of the calotypes that Hill and Adamson exhibited at the Royal Scottish Academy Adamson was credited with the photography and Hill with the artistic genius. Their collaboration only lasted four years but produced superb portraits, landscapes and social commentary that are a priceless record of Scotland at the time and masterpieces of early photography. Much of their work is now stored at the Victorian & Albert Museum, London.

Brewster, Sir David (1781–1868), scholar, scientist, teacher and preacher, born Jedburgh. Brilliant scholar who attended Edinburgh University at the age of eleven. Elected a Fellow of the Royal Society in 1815. Founder of the British Association for the Advancement of Science. Worked primarily on the properties of light and optics and invented the kaleidoscope and various scientific instruments. Corresponded with William Henry Fox Talbot and invented the stereoscope (1849), a viewer for stereoscopic prints.

Colvin, Calum (1961–), artist, born Glasgow. Colvin explores Scottish identity through sculpture and photography, bringing both medias together to form 'constructed photography'. He lectures at Dundee University, has exhibited widely and has illustrated Robert Burns' selected poems.

Gardner, Alexander (1821–82), photographer, born Paisley, Renfrew. Emigrated to the United States and was hired to photograph the American Civil (1861–5). His two-volume study of the war was published in 1866 and is unflinchingly graphic in detail and content. In 1867 he recorded the building of the Union Pacific Railroad. He also documented the execution of the conspirators against Abraham Lincoln and Lincoln's funeral. Worked extensively in stereoscopic photographs. Opened his own gallery in Washington after the Civil War.

Hill, David Octavius (1802–70), painter and photographer, born Perth. Hill gave up his profession for four years to work with Robert Adamson (*see* above). In 1843 Sir David Brewster (*see* above) suggested to Hill that he should approach Adamson to photograph all 470 members of the newly-formed Free Church of Scotland. Hill and Adamson took portraits of each of the members of the new church and were paid £1,500 for the work. A painting was created from the portraits but the photographs are much more famous. In the four years of their partnership Hill and Adamson created 1,500 calotypes. After Adamson's death Hill returned to painting but he is remembered principally for his photography.

Marzaroli, Oscar (1933–88), photographer and film-maker, born La Spezia, Italy, came to Glasgow aged two. Worked as a freelance journalist in Europe from 1955–9 before returning to Glasgow where, in 1967, he co-founded Ogam Films which specialised in high-quality short films about Scottish artists, life in the Highlands and Islands and in the city of Glasgow. Marzaroli spent 39 years walking across Scotland taking powerful pictures of ordinary people engaged in their everyday lives but his photographs are anything but ordinary and are a fascinating account of life in Scotland between the 1950s and the 1980s.

Valentine, James (1815–80), photographer and publisher, born Dundee. The son of a printer, Valentine trained as an engraver and designer of illustrated envelopes. After learning the Daguerreotype process in the late 1840s in Paris Valentine opened a portrait studio in Dundee in 1856, specialising in *cartes de visite.* In the 1850s the Valentine company began photographic publishing. By the 1870s Valentine's was one of the two largest photographic publishers in Scotland (the other being George Washington Wilson's establishment, see below). Valentine covered the whole of Britain and was a pioneer in the mass production of photographs.

Wilson, George Washington (1823–93), artist and photographer, born near Banff. Set up business as a portrait miniaturist in 1849. In 1855 he established a photographic portrait studio. Queen Victoria and Prince Albert commissioned Hay and Wilson to record the construction of Balmoral from 1853 onwards. This was the beginning of Wilson's long association with the royal family. In 1868 he illustrated some of the Queen's *Leaves from the Journal of our Life in the Highlands* and in 1873 he was awarded a royal warrant. Wilson was very successful as a commercial photographer and had sold over half a million prints by 1864. In 1876 Wilson built new offices and mass produced photographs – by the 1880s he was one of the largest photographic publishers in the world, employing more than 30 assistants at his Aberdeen headquarters.

ARCHITECTS

Adam, Robert (1728–1792), born Kirkcaldy. Led Classical revival in England in both architecture and decoration, using and adapting Greco-Roman (e.g. Etruscan vase decoration), Italian and French Renaissance elements. Works in Scotland include: Register House, Charlotte Square (Edinburgh, 1791), Culzean Castle (Ayrshire, from 1777).

Adam, William (1684–1748), father of Robert and James, both also architects. A signatory of the 1729 charter establishing the Academy of St Luke in Edinburgh, Scotland's first art school. Designed the Roman Baroque front of Hopetoun House (South Queensferry, Edinburgh, from 1721); Duff House (Banff, 1735); Robert Gordon's College, Aberdeen (1739).

Bruce, Sir William (c.1630–1710), born Blairhall, West Fife. As Surveyor and Master of Works to Charles II from 1671, rebuilt and extended the Palace of Holyroodhouse, Edinburgh, in the Palladian style (1671–9). Also responsible for original design of Hopetoun House (1699–1702), Kinross House (1685–93), and other great houses for Scottish lairds.

Cameron, Charles (1740–1812), architect, born in London to Scottish parents. Little is known of his early life other than the fact that he was at first apprenticed to his father and then to the architect Isaac Ware. He studied architecture in Rome and produced a book of drawings of the baths of the Romans in 1772. By 1779 Cameron had travelled to Russia to become Catherine the Great's architect – how he secured this position is unknown. Cameron worked at the Russian court for the rest of his life designing public and private buildings for the Russian aristocracy. His major works were his extensive additions to the Palace of Tsarskow Selo near St Petersburg, from 1779 onwards (for fifteen years) and the design and construction of the Palace of Pavlovsk for the Grand Duke Paul (1782–5). He was acclaimed for his use of interior colour schemes and, like Adam (see above), he believed in designing all the interior details of his buildings. Most of his drawings are housed in the Hermitage State Museum, Russia.

Chambers, Sir William (1726–96), architect, born Stockholm to Scottish parents. Studied in Italy and France as a draftsman and architect then returned to London to become the drawing teacher of the Prince of Wales. Along with Robert Adam (*see* above) he became the architect of the King's works. Persuaded the king to help set up and fund the Royal Academy – he went on to be Treasurer of this organisation from 1769 until his death in 1796. His most important buildings are Somerset House in London, the Pagoda in Kew Gardens and King's College.

Craig, James (1744–95), architect, born Edinburgh. Nothing is known of Craig's life before he achieved fame in 1766 by winning the competition to design a plan for Edinburgh's New Town. Craig received a gold medal and the freedom of the city. He was the architect of St James Square (1773), the Physician's Hall (1775) in George Street and the Old Observatory (now Observatory House) on Calton Hill (1876–92). Despite his early success he never developed a thriving practice and he died in poverty.

Graham, James Gillespie (1776–1855), born Dunblane. Designed churches and large country houses in the Neo-Gothic style. Works include: St John's Tolbooth (Edinburgh, 1842), St Mary's Roman Catholic Cathedral (Edinburgh, 1813–14), Armadale Castle, Isle of Skye (1815), extensions to Brodick Castle, Arran (1844). Also designed interiors, such as the State Dining Room at Hopetoun House.

Lorimer, Sir Robert (1864–1929), architect, born Edinburgh. Architect known for his restoration of castles and his promotion of the Arts and Crafts movement in Scotland. Began his own practice in 1892 and went on to build or remodel a large number of country houses and public buildings. He was the architect of the Scottish War memorial at Edinburgh Castle and the Thistle Chapel at St Giles Cathedral, Edinburgh.

Mackintosh, Charles Rennie (1868–1928), born Glasgow. With his wife, Margaret Macdonald, her sister Frances, and Herbert MacNair, a principal figure of the Scottish Arts and Crafts movement, and creator of 'the Glasgow Style'. As famed for his furniture and textile designs as for his buildings, he also produced landscape and flower paintings. His architecture is anti-Classical and often (e.g. in the Hill House) looks back to the Scottish baronial style of late medieval tower-houses. Works include: Glasgow School of Art (1897–99, 1907–09), Hill House, Helensburgh (1902), Willow Tea Rooms, Glasgow (1904). He designed few religious buildings.

Matthew, Sir Robert (1906–75), architect, born Edinburgh. The son of John Matthew, the partner of Sir Robert Lorimer (*see* above). Apprenticed to his father's firm in the 1930s, Matthew joined the Scottish Department of Health in 1936 and had become its chief architect by 1945. In 1946 he was made Architect to London County Council but returned to Scotland to become the first Professor of Architecture at Edinburgh University (1953–68). He established the architectural practice of Robert Matthew Johnson Marshall in Edinburgh and London in 1956 and the company is now the UK's biggest architectural firm with more than 400 employees. Matthew is best known as the designer of London's Festival Hall and Pakistan's new capital of Islamabad.

Playfair, William (1790–1857), architect, born London to Scottish parents, came to Edinburgh as a young boy to live with an uncle. Playfair is the architect credited with earning Edinburgh the title 'The Athens of the North' – his Classical buildings dominate the city, many from dramatic, dominant sites, and significantly contribute to the capital's unique character. Major works include the Royal Terrace (1820), Carlton Terrace (1820), Regent Terrace (1820), the National Gallery (1850), the Surgeons' Hall, (1832) and the Royal Scottish Academy, (1818–26).

Thomson, Alexander 'Greek' (1817–75), born Balfron, Stirlingshire, but identified with Glasgow, where most of his work is to be found. Designed churches, warehouses, tenements, villas, and (in the 1850s) several mansion houses in the fashionable village of Cove on the Rosneath peninsula. Despite his nickname, Italian, Scottish Baronial, Gothic and even Egyptian elements are found in his style. His use of glass and iron in buildings was revolutionary. Works include: Moray Place, Strathbungo (1859); United Presbyterian Churches at Caledonian Road (1856) and St Vincent Street (1857–59); Egyptian Halls, Union Street (1871–73).

ARTS ORGANISATIONS

The following list of arts organisations includes those organisations and institutions which are in receipt of revenue grants or three-year funding from the Scottish Arts Council.

7:84 THEATRE COMPANY
2nd Floor, 333 Woodlands Road, Glasgow, G3 6NG.
Tel: 0141-334 6686 Fax: 0141-334 3369
Email: admin@784theatre.com
Web: www.784theatre.com

AN LANNTAIR
Town Hall, South Beach, Stornoway, Isle of Lewis, HS1 2BX. Tel: 01851-703307
Email: lanntair@sol.co.uk Web: www.lanntair.com
Director, R. Murray

AN TUIREANN
Arts Centre, Struan Road, Portree, Isle of Skye, IV51 9EG. Tel: 01478-613306 Fax: 01478-613156
Email: exhibitions@anttuireann.org.uk
Web: www.antuireann.org.uk
Director, Norah Campbell

THE ARCHES THEATRE COMPANY
253 Argyle Street, Glasgow, G2 8DL.
Tel: 0901-022 0300 Web: www.thearches.co.uk

ART.TM (HIGHLAND PRINTMAKERS WORKSHOP)
20 Bank Street, Inverness, IV1 1QU.
Tel: 01463-712240 Fax: 01463-239991
Email: info@arttm.org.uk Web: www.arttm.org.uk
Interim Manager, Astrid Shearer

ARTLINK (EDINBURGH AND THE LOTHIANS)
13a Spittal Street, Edinburgh, EH3 9DY.
Tel: 0131-229 3555 Fax: 0131-228 5257
Email: info@artlinkedinburgh.co.uk
Web: www.artlinkedinburgh.co.uk
Director, J-B van den Berg

ART IN PARTNERSHIP
233 Cowgate, Edinburgh, EH1 1JQ.
Tel: 0131-225 4463 Fax: 0131-225 6879
Email: info@art-in-partnership.org.uk
Web: www.art-in-partnership.org.uk
Executive Director, R. Breen

ASSEMBLY DIRECT
89 Giles Street, Edinburgh, EH6 6BZ.
Tel: 0131-553 4000 Fax: 0131-554 0454
Email: info@assemblydirect.ednet.co.uk
Web: www.jazzmusic.co.uk
Directors, F. Aleaxander, R. Spence

ASSOCIATION FOR SCOTTISH LITERARY STUDIES
Department of Scottish History, University of Glasgow, 9 University Gardens, Glasgow, G12 8QH.
Tel: 0141-330 5309 Fax: 0141-330 5309
Email: d.jones@scothist.arts.gla.ac.uk
Web: www.asls.org.uk
General Manager, Duncan Jones

BENCHTOURS
Bonnington Mill, 72 Newhaven Road, Edinburgh, EH6 5QG. Tel: 0131-555 3585 Fax: 0131-555 1595
Email: info@benchtours.com Web: benchtours.com

BOILERHOUSE THEATRE COMPANY
Arts Quarter, Gateway Theatre, Elm Row, Edinburgh, EH7 4AH. Tel: 0131-556 5644 Fax: 0131-556 5516
Email: info@boilerhouse.org.uk
Web: www.boilerhouse.org.uk
Artistic Director, Paul Pinson

BYRE THEATRE
Abbey Street, St Andrews, KY16 9LA.
Tel: 01334-47500 Fax: 01334-475370
Email: enquiries@byretheatre.com
Managing Director, Tom Gardner

CAPPELLA NOVA
172 Hyndland Road, Glasgow, G12 9HZ.
Tel: 0141-552 0634 Fax: 0141-552 4053
Email: rebecca@cappella-nova.com
Web: www.cappella-nova.com
Chief Executive, Ms R. Tavener

CENTRE FOR CONTEMPORARY ARTS
350 Sauchiehall Street, Glasgow, G2 3JD.
Tel: 0141-332 7521 Fax: 0141-332 3226
Email: gen@cca-glasgow.com
Web: www.cca-glasgow.com
Director, G. McKenzie

CITIZENS' THEATRE
Gorbals, Glasgow, G5 9DS.
Tel: 0141-429 0022 Fax: 0141-429 7374
Email: info@citz.co.uk
Web: www.citz.co.uk
General Manager, Ms A. Stapleton

COLLECTIVE GALLERY
22–28 Cockburn Street, Edinburgh, EH1 1NY.
Tel: 0131-220 1260 Fax: 0131-220 5585
Email: collgall@aol.com

CRAWFORD ARTS CENTRE
93 North Street, St Andrews, KY16 9AD.
Tel: 01334-474610 Fax: 01334-479880
Email: crawfordarts@crawfordarts.free-online.co.uk
Web: www.crawfordarts.free-online.co.uk
Director, D. Sykes

CUMBERNAULD THEATRE
Kildrum, Cumbernauld, G67 2BN.
Tel: 01236-737235 Fax: 01236-738408
Artistic Director, S. Sharkey

DUMFRIES AND GALLOWAY ARTS ASSOCIATION
Gracefield Arts Centre, 28 Edinburgh Road, Dumfries,
DG1 1JQ. Tel: 01387-262084 Fax: 01387-255173

DUNDEE CONTEMPORARY ARTS
152 Nethergate, Dundee, DD1 4DY.
Tel: 01382-909900 Fax: 01382-909221
Email: dca@dundeecity.gov.uk
Web: www.dca.org.uk
Head of Communication, Jeni Iannetta

EDEN COURT THEATRE
Bishop's Road, Inverness, IV3 5SA. Tel: 01463-239841
Fax: 01463-713810 Email: admin@eden-court.co.uk
Web: www.eden-court.co.uk
Director, C. Marr

EDINBURGH INTERNATIONAL BOOK FESTIVAL
Scottish Book Centre, 137 Dundee Street, Edinburgh,
EH11 1BG. Tel: 0131-228 5444 Fax: 0131-228 4333
Email: admin@edbookfest.co.uk
Web: www.edbookfest.co.uk
Director, Ms C. Lockerbie

EDINBURGH CONTEMPORARY ARTS TRUST (ECAT)
16 Clerwood Gardens, Edinburgh, EH12 8PT.
Tel: 0131-539 8877 Fax: 0131-539 2211
Email: info@ecat.org.uk Web: www.ecat.org.uk

EDINBURGH FESTIVAL FRINGE SOCIETY
The Fringe Office, 180 High Office, Edinburgh,
EH1 1QS. Tel: 0131-226 0026
Email: admin@edfringe.com Web: www.edfringe.com
Director, P. Gudgin

EDINBURGH INTERNATIONAL FESTIVAL
The Hub, Castlehill, Edinburgh, EH1 2NE.
Tel: 0131-473 2000 Fax: 0131-473 2002
Email: info@eif.co.uk Web: www.eif.co.uk
Administrative Director, Adrian Trickey

EDINBURGH PRINTMAKERS
23 Union Street, Edinburgh, EH1 3LR.
Tel: 0131-557 2479 Fax: 0131-558 8418
Email: printmakers@ednet.co.uk
Web: www.edinburgh-printmakers.co.uk
Director, D. Watt

EDINBURGH SCULPTURE WORKSHOP
25 Hawthornvale, Edinburgh, EH6 4JT.
Tel: 0131-551 4490 Fax: 0131-551 4491
Email: admin@edinburgh-sculpture.org.uk
Web: www.edinburgh-sculpture.org.uk
Chairman, Prof. Bill Scott

ENTERPRISE MUSIC SCOTLAND
37 Dee Street, Aberdeen, AB11 6DY.
Tel: 01224-574422 Fax: 01224-572315
Email: info@musicscotland.co.uk
Web: www.musicscotland.co.uk
Executive Director, R. Rae

FABLEVISION
7 Water Row, Glasgow, G51 3UW.
Tel: 0141-425 2020 Fax: 0141-425 2020
Email: info@fablevision.org Web: www.fablevision.org

FACTIONAL PRODUCTIONS
10 Dalcross Street, Glasgow, G11 5RF
Email: info@factional.co.uk Web: www.factional.co.uk

FEDERATION OF SCOTTISH THEATRE
25 Ainslie Place, Edinburgh, EH3 6AJ.
Tel: 0131-467 2525 Email: fst@blueyonder.co.uk Web:
www.scottishtheatre.org

FRUITMARKET GALLERY
45 Market Street, Edinburgh, EH1 1DF.
Tel: 0131-225 2383 Fax: 0131-220 3130
Email: info@fruitmarket.co.uk
Web: www.fruitmarket.co.uk
Director, G. Murray

THE GAELIC BOOKS COUNCIL/ COMHAIRLE NAN LEABHRAICHEAN
22 Mansfield Street, Glasgow, G11 5QP.
Tel: 0141-337 6211 Fax: 0141-341 0515
Email: fios@gaelicbooks.net
Web: www.gaelicbooks.net
Director, I. MacDonald

GREY COAST THEATRE COMAPANY
Traill House, Olrig Street, Thurso, Caithness, KW14 7BJ.
Tel: 01847-890840 Fax: 01847-890840
Email: info@greycoast.org.uk
Web: www.greycoast.org.uk
Artistic Director, G. Gunn

GLASGOW PRINT STUDIO
22 King Street, Glasgow, G1 5QP.
Tel: 0141-552 0704 Fax: 0141-552 2919
Email: gallery@gpsart.co.uk Web: www.gpsart.co.uk
Director, J. MacKechnie

GREENOCK ARTS GUILD
Campbell Street, Greenock, PA16 8AP.
Tel: 01475-723038 Fax: 01475-721811
Web: www.geocities.com/broadway/orchestra/9054/

GRID IRON THEATRE COMPANY
85 East Claremont Street, Edinburgh, EH7 4HU.
Tel: 0131-558 1879 Fax: 0131-558 8048
Email: jude@gridiron.org.uk
Web: www.gridiron.org.uk
Producer, J. Doherty

HEBRIDES ENSEMBLE
28 Elm Row, Edinburgh, EH7 4RR.
Tel: 0131-476 2816 Fax: 0131-557 8676
Email: hebridesensemble@blueyonder.co.uk
Web: www.hebridesensemble.co.uk
Chairman, Sir Russel Hillhouse

HI ARTS
Suites 4 and 5 Ballantyne House, 84 Academy Street,
Inverness, IV1 1LU.
Tel: 01463-717091 Fax: 01463-720895
Email: robert@hi-arts.co.uk Web: www.hi-arts.co.uk
Director, R. Livingston

THE LEMON TREE TRUST
5 West North Street, Aberdeen, AB24 5AT.
Tel: 01224-642230 Fax: 01224-630888
Email: info@lemontree.org Web: www.lemontree.org
Director, K. McArdle

LUNG HA'S THEATRE COMPANY
Central Hall, West Tolcross, Edinburgh, EH3 9BP.
Tel: 0131-228 8998 Fax: 0131-229 8965
Email: info@lunghas.co.uk Web: www.lunghas.co.uk

MACROBERT ARTS CENTRE
University of Stirling, Stirling, FK9 4LA.
Tel: 01786-467155 Fax: 01786-466600
Email: macrobert-arts@stir.ac.uk
Web: www.macrobert.org
Director, Liz Moran

MAGNETIC NORTH THEATRE PRODUCTIONS LTD
18 Brandon Terrace, Edinburgh, EH3 5DZ.
Tel: 0131-556 3299 Email: mail@magneticnorth.org.uk
Web: www.magneticnorth.fsnet.co.uk
Artistic Director, N. Bone

MONIACK MHOR
Teavarran, Kiltarlity, Beauly, Inverness-shire, IV4 7HT.
Tel: 01463-741675 Fax: 01463-741733
Email: m-mhor@arvonfoundation.org
Web: www.arvonfoundation.org
Director, Chris Aldridge

MULL THEATRE/TAIGH-CLUICHE MHUILE
Royal Buildings, Tobermory, Isle of Mull, Argyll,
PA75 6NU. Tel: 01688-302828
Email: mulltheatre@aol.com
Web: www.mulltheatre.com
Chairman, Gillian King

MAKING MUSIC SCOTLAND (THE NATIONAL FEDERATION OF MUSIC SOCIETIES)
8c Cowal View, Duncan Street, Clydebank,
Dunbartonshire, G81 3DF. Tel: 0141-952 6979
Email: l.young@makingmusic.org.uk
Web: www.makingmusic.org.uk/scotland
Secretary, Ms L. Young

NEW STAGE THEATRE
c/o Steve Brown, 42 Herriot St, Glasgow, G41 2JY.
Tel: 0141-423 9024 Fax: 0141-423 9648
Email: steve.brown@easynet.co.uk

OUT OF THE DARKNESS THEATRE COMPANY
The Flat, Elgin Town Hall, Elgin, Moray, IV30 1UD.
Tel: 01343-543500 Email: enquiries@odtheatre.org.uk
Web: www.odtheatre.org.uk

PARAGON ENSEMBLE
1 Bowmont Gardens, Glasgow, G12 9LR.
Tel: 0141-342 4242 Fax: 0141-342 4442
Email: mail@paragon.sol.co.uk
Web: www.paragonensemble.org.uk

PEACOCK VISUAL ARTS
21 Castle Street, Aberdeen, AB11 5BQ.
Tel: 01224-639539 Fax: 01224-627094
Email: info@peacockvisualarts.co.uk
Web: www.peacockvisualarts.co.uk

PERTH THEATRE
185 High Street, Perth, PH1 5UW. Tel: 01738-472700
Fax: 01738-624576 Email: info@perththeatre.co.uk
Web: www.perththeatre.co.uk
General Manager, P. Hackett

PIER ARTS CENTRE
Victoria Street, Stromness, Orkney, KW16 3AA.
Tel: 01856-850209 Fax: 01856-851462
Email: info@pierartscentre.com
Director, Neil Firth

PITLOCHRY FESTIVAL THEATRE
Pitlochry, PH16 5DR. Tel: 01796-484600
Fax: 01796-484616 Email: admin@pitlochry.org.uk
Web: www.pitlochry.org.uk
Chief Executive, Nikki Axford

PORTFOLIO GALLERY
43 Candlemaker Row, Edinburgh, EH1 3LR.
Tel: 0131-220 1911 Fax: 0131-226 4287
Email: info@portfoliocatalogue.com
Web: www.portfoliocatalogue.com
G. Chalmers

PROISEACT NAN EALAN/THE GAELIC
ARTS AGENCY
10 Shell Street, Stornoway, HS1 2BS.
Tel: 01851-704493 Fax: 01851-704734
Email: pne@gaelic-arts.com
Web: www.gaelic-arts.com
Director, M. MacLean

PROJECT ABILITY
Centre for Developmental Arts, 18 Albion Street,
Glasgow, G1 1LH.
Tel: 0141-552 2822 Fax: 0141-552 3490
Email: info@project-ability.co.uk
Web: www.project-ability.co.uk
General Manager, Ms A. Knowles

THE PUPPET AND ANIMATION FESTIVAL
MacRobert Arts Centre, University of Stirling, Stirling,
FK9 4LA.
Tel: 01786-467155 Fax: 01786-466600
Email: puppetanimation@stir.ac.uk
Director, S. Hart

RAINDOG
5 Park Circus Place, Glasgow, G3 6AH.
Email: info@raindog.org.uk
Web: www.raindog.org.uk

ROYAL LYCEUM THEATRE COMPANY
30b Grindlay Street, Edinburgh, EH3 9AX.
Tel: 0131-248 4800 Fax: 0131-228 3955
Web: www.lyceum.org.uk
Artistic Director, David Mark Thomson

ROYAL SCOTTISH NATIONAL ORCHESTRA
73 Claremont Street, Glasgow, G3 7JB.
Tel: 0141-226 3868 Fax: 0141-221 4317
Email: admin@rsno.org.uk Web: www.rsno.org.uk
Chief Executive, Simon Crookall

ST MAGNUS FESTIVAL
60 Victoria Street, Kirkwall, Orkney, KW15 1DN.
Tel: 01856-871445
Email: info@stmagnusfestival.com
Web: www.stmagnusfestival.com
Festival Administrator, Angela Henderson

SCOTTISH ACADEMY OF ASIAN ARTS
Govanhill Neighbourhood Centre, 6–8 Daisy Street,
Govanhill, Glasgow, G42 8JL. Tel: 0141-423 2210 Fax:
0141-423 2294 Email: info@saaa.org.uk
Web: www.saaa.org.uk

SCOTTISH BALLET
261 West Princes Street, Glasgow, G4 9EE.
Tel: 0141-331 2931 Fax: 0141-331 2629
Email: promo@scottishballet.co.uk
Web: www.scottishballet.co.uk
Chairman, D. C. McGhie

SCOTTISH CHAMBER ORCHESTRA
4 Royal Terrace, Edinburgh, EH7 5AB.
Tel: 0131-557 6800 Fax: 0131-557 6933
Email: info@sco.org.uk Web: www.sco.org.uk
Managing Director, R. McEwan

SCOTTISH DANCE THEATRE
Dundee Repertory Theatre, Tay Square, Dundee,
DD1 1PB. Tel: 01382-342600 Fax: 01382-228609
Email: sdt@dundeereptheatre.co.uk
Web: www.scottishdancetheatre.com
Senior Administrator, Amanda Chinn

SCOTTISH ENSEMBLE
CCA, 350 Sauchiehall Street, Glasgow, G2 3JD.
Tel: 0141-332 4747 Fax: 0141-332 3555
Email: scottishensemble@yahoo.com
General Manager, Ms H. Duncan

SCOTTISH INTERNATIONAL CHILDREN'S
FESTIVAL
45A George Street, Edinburgh, EH2 2HT.
Tel: 0131-225 8050 Fax: 0131-225 6440
Email: info@imaginate.org.uk
Web: www.imaginate.org.uk
Director, T. Reekie

SCOTTISH MUSIC INFORMATION
CENTRE
1 Bowmont Gardens, Glasgow, G12 9LR.
Tel: 0141-334 6393 Fax: 0141-337 1161
Email: info@smic.org.uk Web: www.smic.org.uk
Chief Executive, Andrew Logan

SCOTTISH OPERA
39 Elmbank Crescent, Glasgow, G2 4PT.
Tel: 0141-248 4567 Fax: 0141-221 8812
Web: www.scottishopera.org.uk
Chief Executive, Christopher Barron

THE SCOTTISH POETRY LIBRARY
5 Crichton's Close, Edinburgh, EH8 8DT.
Tel: 0131-557 2876 Fax: 0131-557 8393
Email: inquiries@spl.org.uk Web: www.spl.org.uk
Chief Executive, Dr Robyn Marsack

SCOTTISH SCULPTURE WORKSHOP
1 Main Street, Lumsden, Huntly, Aberdeenshire,
AB54 4JN. Tel: 01464-861372 Fax: 01464-861550
Email: admin@ssw.org.uk Web: www.ssw.org.uk

SCOTTISH STORYTELLING CENTRE
The Netherbow Arts Centre, 43-45 High Street,
Edinburgh, EH1 1SR.
Tel: 0131-556 9579 Fax: 0131-557 5224
Email: netherbow-storytelling@dial.pipex.com
Web: www.scottishstorytellingcentre.co.uk
Co-ordinator, J. Bremner

SCOTTISH COMMUNITY DRAMA
ASSOCIATION
5 York Place, Edinburgh, EH1 3EB.
Tel: 0131-557 5552
Email: headquarters@scda.org.uk
Web: www.scda.org.uk

SCOTTISH YOUTH THEATRE
3rd Floor, Forsyth House, 111 Union Street, Glasgow,
G1 3TA.
Tel: 0141-221 5127 Fax: 0141-221 9123
Email: info@scottishyouththeatre.org
Web: www.scottishyouththeatre.org
Artistic Director, Mary McCluskey

SCOTTISH YOUTH DANCE
Unit 5, Ladywell Business Centre, 94 Duke Street,
Glasgow, G4 0UW. Tel: 0141-552 7712
Fax: 0141-552 9118 Web: www.ydance.org
Artistic Director, A. Howitt

SHETLAND ARTS TRUST
Pitt Lane, Lerwick, Shetland, ZE1 0DW.
Tel: 01595-694001 Fax: 01595-692941
Email: admin@shetland-arts-trust.co.uk
Web: www.shetland-music.com
General Manager, A. Watt

STELLAR QUINES THEATRE COMPANY
c/o Royal Lyceum Theatre, 30b Grindlay Street,
Edinburgh, EH3 9AX. Tel: 0131-248 4847
Email: stephanie@stellarquines.co.uk

STILLS GALLERY
23 Cockburn Street, Edinburgh, EH1 1BP.
Tel: 0131-622 6200 Fax: 0131-622 6201
Email: info@stills.org Web: www.stills.org

STREET LEVEL PHOTOWORKS
26 King Street, Glasgow, G1 5QP.
Tel: 0141-552 2151 Fax: 0141-552 2323
Email: info@sl-photoworks.demon.co.uk
Web: www.sl-photoworks.demon.co.uk
Director, M. Dickson

SUSPECT CULTURE
CCA, 350 Sauchiehall Street, Glasgow, G2 3JD.
Tel: 0141-332 9775 Fax: 0141-332 8823
Email: info@suspectculture.co.uk
Web: www.suspectculture.co.uk
Artistic Director, G. Eatough

TAG THEATRE COMPANY
Floor 2, 18 Albion Street, Glasgow, G1 1LH.
Tel: 0141-552 4949 Fax: 0141-552 0666
Email: info@tag-theatre.co.uk
Web: www.tag-theatre.co.uk
Artistic Director, J. Brining

TALBOT RICE GALLERY
University of Edinburgh, Old College, South Bridge,
Edinburgh, EH8 9YL.
Tel: 0131-650 2211 Fax: 0131-650 2213
Email: info.talbotrice@ed.ac.uk
Web: www.trg.ed.ac.uk
Curator, Prof. D. Macmillan

THEATRE BABEL
11 Sandyford Place, Sauchiehall Street, Glasgow,
G3 7NB. Tel: 0141-226 8806 Fax: 0141-249 9900
Email: enquiries@theatrebabel.co.uk
Web: www.theatrebabel.co.uk
General Manager, Katen Bowen

THEATRE CRYPTIC
350 Sauchiehall Street, Glasgow, G2 3JD.
Tel: 0141-354 0544 Fax: 0141-354 0545
Email: enquiries@cryptic.org.uk
Web: www.cryptic.org.uk

THEATRE WORKSHOP EDINBURGH
34 Hamilton Place, Stockbridge, Edinburgh, EH3 5AX.
Tel: 0131-225 7942 Fax: 0131-220 0112

THEATRE ALBA
52c Mansfield Avenue, Musselburgh, EH21 7DP.
Tel: 0131-665 9742
Email: admin@theatrealba.ukvintage.co.uk
Artistic Director, Charles Nowosielski

TOSG THEATRE COMPANY
Sàbhal Mor Ostaig, Sleat, Isle of Skye, IV44 8RQ.
Tel: 01471-888542 Fax: 01471-888541
Email: tosg@tosg.org Web: www.smo.uhi.ac.uk/tosg
Director, Sìm Mac Coinnich

**THE TRADITIONAL MUSIC AND SONG
ASSOCIATION OF SCOTLAND**
95–97 St Leonard's Street, Edinburgh, EH8 9QY.
Tel: 0131-667 5587 Fax: 0131-441 3189
Web: www.tmsa.info

TRAMWAY
25 Albert Drive, Glasgow, G41 2PE.
Tel: 0141-422 2023 Fax: 0141-423 1194
Email: info@tramway.org Web: www.tramway.org

TRANSMISSION GALLERY
28 King Street, Glasgow, G1 5QP.
Tel: 0141-552 4813 Fax: 0141-552 1577
Email: info@transmissiongallery.org
Web: www.transmissiongallery.org

TRAVERSE THEATRE
Cambridge Street, Edinburgh, EH1 2ED.
Tel: 0131-228 3223 Fax: 0131-229 8443
Web: www.traverse.co.uk
Chief Executive, P. Howard

TRAVELLING GALLERY
City Arts Centre, 2 Market Street, Edinburgh, EH1 1DE.
Tel: 0131-529 3930 Fax: 0131-529 8977
Email: alison.chisholm@edinburgh.gov.uk
Web: www.cac.org.uk/venues/travel.htm
Chief Executive, Alison Chisholm

TRON THEATRE
63 Trongate, Glasgow, G1 5HB.
Tel: 0141-552 3748 Fax: 0141-552 6657
Email: admin@tron.co.uk
Web: www.tron.co.uk
Director, Neil Murray

VANISHING POINT THEATRE COMPANY
CCA, 350 Sauchiehall Street, Glasgow, G2 3JD.
Tel: 0141-353 1315 Fax: 0141-332 5792
Email: info@vanishing-point.org
Web: www.vanishing-point.org
Artistic Director, Matthew Lenton

VISIBLE FICTIONS
Paisley Arts Centre, New Street, Paisley, PA1 1EZ.
Tel: 0141-887 2986 Fax: 0141-887 6300
Email: info@visiblefictions.co.uk
Web: www.visiblefictions.co.uk
Artistic Co-Directors, Kate Brailsford and Douglas
  Irvine

WASPS
256 Alexandra Parade, Glasgow, G31 3AJ.
Tel: 0141-554 8299 Fax: 0141-554 7330
Email: info@waspsstudios.org.uk
Web: www.waspsstudios.org.uk
Director, D. Cook

FAIRS

HISTORY OF FAIRS IN SCOTLAND
Many of the agricultural shows that are now a regular feature of Scottish life can be traced back to mediaeval and later fairs. Originally licensed under royal charter, and later under the jurisdiction of the local laird or trades guilds, fairs of different kinds were important centres for buying and selling goods and hiring agricultural and domestic labour, as well as for social interaction and entertainment. There was considerable specialisation in the products traded at different fairs, and taxes were levied on every item sold at a fair, often by the local laird, at some places until quite late in the 19th-century.

Fairs usually took place in market squares or on moors, links or other open ground close to towns, and could last for up to two weeks. They were the occasion for large movements of people and livestock about the country; for tradesmen such as packmen or pedlars, travelling from town to town and fair to fair with their horse-drawn carts or caravans laden with goods was their whole livelihood. In the west, boats would bring traders from the Western Isles to fairs such as that at Greenock. Some fairs even attracted merchants from the Continent.

Many of the traditional dates of fairs correspond with key dates in the religious calendar. Fairs were often held on the quarter days – Candlemas (2 February), Whitsun (25 May), Lammas (1 August) and Martinmas (11 November) – or on the feast day of the saint to which the local church was dedicated. Important saints' days were also popular dates, and fairs held on these days reflected the names of the saints celebrated: for instance Andermas Fairs, held on St Andrew's Day, 30 November, and Marymas Fairs, those held on 15 August, the feast of the Assumption of the Virgin Mary. These fairs had a more overt religious aspect and included the saying of Mass; but there was also generally plenty of drinking, dancing and sports, including horse-races. Fortune-telling was common, although it was strictly speaking illegal. The Church of Scotland considered fairs immoral, and James VI abolished the holding of fairs and feasts on saints days. In contrast, Holy Fairs were sacred – days of worship, fasting and no work. Usually held during the spring and autumn, these survive today in the annual spring and autumn holiday weekends, which are still held on different dates in different parts of Scotland.

Lammas Fairs were held in many towns across Scotland, but the biggest and most famous was that at St Andrews. It is still held in the streets in early August and is Scotland's oldest surviving market fair. Originally a feeing fair, it was established in 1620 by Charter from James VI. Another popular Lammas Fair was held in Kirkwall on the first Tuesday after 11 August. Hallowmas Fairs were held in autumn to celebrate the feast of All Saints Day, the 1st November. The most famous, at its peak during the 18th-century, was held in Edinburgh.

FAIRS AS LABOUR MARKETS

Feeing fairs were held every six months, usually at the Whitsun and Martinmas terms, which were the times of year when farm workers would be paid their wages and would either renew their hire or move to a different farm. Other feeing fairs were held at Candlemas and Lammas, the latter being a labour market for shearers and reapers for the harvest season. In Aberdeen, Feeing Day was known as Muckle Friday. Foys were feasts and entertainments given to bid farewell to departing workers and welcome new workers to a farm. Anster Fair, held at Anstruther in Fife, was a foy held for those leaving for Great Yarmouth to work in the gutting and packing of herring. The Johnmas Foy held each June at Lerwick celebrated the arrival in Shetland of the Dutch herring fleet.

LIVESTOCK TRADING

Many fairs became renowned for the trade of livestock. Following the Union of the Crowns in 1603, cattle fairs and cross-border trade between England and Scotland grew in importance, and the Crieff Tryst became an important cattle fair to which both English and Scottish drovers would bring their cattle. The main centre moved to Falkirk in 1777, which became the site of the largest livestock tryst in Scotland. During the mid 19th century about 300,000 cattle were sold at the three great cattle fairs held in August, September and October. Other centres included Brechin, Pennymuir, the Gorgie Market in Edinburgh, which remained a major meeting for livestock owners up to the mid 19th-century, and the Ellon Fair, near Aberdeen, which was an important north-eastern cattle trading centre before the advent of the railway.

Other fairs, particularly in the Borders, specialised in sheep and lambs. These included Stirling, and Ettrick in the former county of Selkirkshire. Langholm in Dumfriesshire, just eight miles from the English border, became a major centre of cross-border trade; while Lockerbie's Lammas fair became the largest Scottish centre of all and was renowned for its August lamb sale, held on Lamb Hill.

Pigs were sold at Dunfermline's Pudding Fairs, held in November and December and named after the white puddings made from the slaughtered animals. Horse fairs such as the Keltonhill Fair, held at Rhonehouse in Galloway on St John's Day, 24 June, developed from gypsy gatherings. At Whitesands in Dumfriesshire there was an annual fair devoted to the sale of hare-skins; while the Cardross Whelk Fair was held on the shores of the Clyde from 1822 onward. At the Kipper Fair, which marked the end of the salmon fishing season at Ayr until the 1830s, smoked salmon was distributed free to all the public houses.

THE ROYAL HIGHLAND SHOW

The Royal Highland Show is organised each June by the Royal Highland and Agricultural Society of Scotland (RHASS). This four-day event, held at Ingliston, near Edinburgh airport, is Scotland's national showcase for the land-based and allied industries, and is attended by an annual average of 150,000 people. As well as its famous livestock parade and show, it includes sheepdog trials, show jumping, exhibitions on forestry, the countryside, Scottish food, around 1,000 trade stands, craft and flower pavilions, and a variety of entertainments. It is also the largest trade exhibition of agricultural machinery in Britain. Around 4,000 livestock compete in 400 categories. The 2003 event took place from 9–22 June. Visitor numbers were up on the 2002 figure of over 134,000.

The RHASS has promoted agriculture in Scotland since its foundation in 1784, when it was established with the aim of improvement of the Highlands and Islands and the conditions of their people. The Chair of Agriculture at the University of Edinburgh was established on the Society's initiative in 1790. It supports education in agriculture-related subjects, giving financial support to courses in agriculture, veterinary science and forestry at universities and colleges, and issues awards in recognition of excellence in various aspects of agriculture such as technical innovation, food, and forest management.

CLOTH AND SEED FAIRS

A number of fairs specialised in the trade of certain items. During the spring many towns held Seed Fairs, where flax, corn, oats, wheat and seed potatoes were sold. In Edinburgh, Grassmarket was the corn and livestock market of the city. In 1560 the market was moved to the foot of the West Bow and in 1587 to a site behind St Giles but in 1716 it returned to Grassmarket, where the Corn Exchange was erected in 1849.

Amongst the more famous of the cloth fairs were the Links Market at Linkstown in Fife and the Lawnmarket in Edinburgh. The cloth market at Edinburgh's Lawnmarket was established by James III in 1477. At Linkstown, two fairs a year took place, the spring fair specialising in lintseed and linen goods. Although the original form of the fair has declined, the Links Market is still held each year along the promenade of Kirkcaldy, a burgh formed from Linkstown and nearby Abbotshall. Other towns also dealt in cloth: at Kirkintilloch, Dunbartonshire, there were Lintseed Saturdays in spring for the sale of this commodity. Kirkmadrine in Galloway had an annual Sooty Poke Fair, named after the weavers' custom of carrying their wares in bags stained with soot. Other fairs included St Conan's Fair, Glenorchy, and Shott's Yarn Fair, Lanarkshire, held each August until the early 19th century. Wool was also traded at a number of towns, and linen and sheets at Aberdeen's Muckle Paise Market.

Yet other fairs were places for trade in domestic and agricultural implements, such as wrought iron goods, dairy utensils, spinning wheels and cooper's barrels, knives and weapons, certain towns being renowned for each commodity. One fair, the Old Cumnock Scythe Fair, even specialised in sand, sold as a sharpening agent for knife and weapon blades.

By the 20th century most Scottish fairs were degenerating into funfairs. The Industrial Revolution had brought about a fundamental change in their role as centres of rural trade and social contact, as towns grew rapidly and became more accessible and shops became the main theatre of local commerce. However, many towns and villages across Scotland now hold an annual agricultural show, and these events have taken over from the fairs as meeting places for farmers and livestock traders.

THE GLASGOW FAIR

Of all the summer fairs held across Scotland, that of Glasgow is the largest and most famous. Originating in 1190, when King William I granted the Bishop of Glasgow the right to hold an annual fair beginning on 7th July, the fair was held at a variety of locations around the city. By the end of the 18th century it had moved to the Saltmarket, around Jail Square; but the development of the retail trade led to the decline of the fair as a market and its transformation into a place of popular entertainment. In the mid 19th century it began to sprawl into the neighbouring Glasgow Green, and, following protest from the local residents, a new site for the Fair was found in 1871 at Vinegar Hill near Camlachie. However, the Fair returned to Glasgow Green in the 20th century.

In the 19th century the Glasgow Fair marked the closure of most industries for an annual trade holiday, which became known as the Fair Week and later Fair Fortnight, beginning the second Friday in July. At one time huge spectacles were displayed in annual competition, including such things as waterfalls and re-enactments of the battles of the Boer War. Today the Fair is an extremely popular annual festival of entertainment, but it now consists of standard fairground attractions, although in 1990, when Glasgow held the title of European City of Culture, there were attempts to revive more traditional fair entertainments such as juggling, dancing, music and theatre.

GAMES AND GATHERINGS

Highland games and gatherings are held in most towns and districts in the Highlands, and also in other parts of Scotland, in the summer, including Aberlour, Aboyne, Alva, Argyllshire, Ballater, Beauly, Blair Atholl, Blairgowrie, Blairmore, Braemar, City of Aberdeen, Cowal, Crieff, Drumtochty, Dufftown, Forfar, Forres, Glenisla, Glen Moray and Elgin, Helmsdale and District, Lochearnhead, Balquhidder and Strathyre, Lonach, Oldmeldrum, Stirling, Stonehaven, Tomintoul and Strathavon. Annual agricultural shows are also held in many places. Further details can be obtained from the Scottish Games Association (Tel: 01738-627782) and the various local tourist boards.

RIDINGS

Ridings of the Marches and Common Ridings are held in the Borders region between June and August in: Annan, Biggar, Galashiels, Hawick, Linlithgow, Lockerbie, Selkirk, Lauder, Langholm, Sanquhar and other places. Of some antiquity, they symbolise the people's patrolling of the disputed borderlands, or Marches, between England and Scotland, and the laying of claim to common lands.

Festivals of arts and music are organised in a large number of places. The larger festivals are included in the list below, but there are many others, for instance those of: Banchory, Kirkcudbright, Inverclyde and Renfrew, Gatehouse of Fleet, Harris, Islay, Langholm and Eskdale, Peebles, Mallaig (Fèis Na Mara).

Folk festivals include: Inverness, Islay, Isle of Arran, Isle of Skye, Penicuik, Stonehaven, Stromness, and Shetland.

The dates on which these events are held and other information about them, can be obtained from the Scottish Tourist Board, regional/local tourist boards, or the relevant local authorities.

Many events, particularly local ones, are not planned very far in advance or may be subject to alteration. For up-to-date information, contact the local tourist board.

TRADITIONAL/FOLKLORIC EVENTS

Fèisean (festivals), as outlined below, are held at different times and various locations throughout the year. All are tuition based, and in most cases prior notification has to be given if you are considering taking part. Many of the fèisean are exclusively for children, although some accommodate a wider participation. The fèis organiser will be able to tell you what is on offer e.g. dancing, learning an instrument, singing, etc. Each fèis celebrates their talent in a concert or cèilidh on the final night. This is open to all.

Fèis Obar Dheathain (Aberdeen)
Tel 01224-846846

Fèis Dhun Eideann (Edinburgh)
Tel 0131-447 1252

Fèis Oigridh Ile (Isle of Islay)
Tel 01496-302059

Fèis an Earraich (Portree)
Tel 01478-612386

Fèis Rois Oigridh (Ullapool)
Tel 01349-862600

Fèis Asainte (Lochinver)
Tel 01571-844262

Fèis Lochabair Bheò (Fort William)
Tel 01397-702090

Fèis Latharna (Oban)
Tel 01631-566135

Fèis Rois Inbhich (Dingwall)
Tel 01349-862600

Fèis Tìr an Eòrna (North Uist)
Tel 01876-580630

Fèis Eige (Isle of Eigg)
Tel 01687-482410

Fèis Chataibh (Golspie)
Tel 01408-621924

Fèis Bharraigh (Isle of Barra)
Tel 01871-810562

Fèis Tìr a Mhurain (South Uist)
Tel 01878-710341

Fèis Thiriodh (Isle of Tiree)
Tel 01879-220323

Fèis Eilean na Hearadh (Isle of Harris)
Tel 01859-502050

Fèis nan Garbh Chriochan (Acharachle)
Tel 01687-470261

Fèis Eilean an Fhraoich (Isle of Lewis)
Tel 01851-870264

Fèis Srath Fharragaig (Gorthleck)
Tel 01456-486641

Fèis na h-Oige (Inverness)
Tel 01463-223860

Fèis a Bhaile (Inverness)
Tel 01463-230141

Fèis Rois nan Deugairean (Gairloch)
Tel 01349-862600

Fèis Spè (Nethybridge)
Tel 01540-661141

Fèis Mhuile (Isle of Mull)
Tel 01681-700431

HOGMANAY
(NEW YEAR CELEBRATIONS)

Hogmanay has always been taken very seriously in Scotland – it was only relatively recently that Christmas and New Year were awarded the same number of days off (two), until the 1970s Christmas was a public holiday of one day and Hogmanay was a public holiday lasting two days. Even though Scotland has entered a less pagan age, Hogmanay celebrations can still last several days and most towns, cities and villages will host traditional cèilidhs or discos as well as marathon parties in people's homes, pubs or community halls. The City of Edinburgh plays host to the largest of Scotland's Hogmanay festivities with a wealth of events ushering in the New Year. Regular Highlights include: a Winter Wonderland in Princes Street Gardens featuring food from around the world, an outdoor ice rink, and fairground rides; a charity Torchlight Procession – hundreds of revellers buy torches and process through the city from Parliament Square to Calton Hill where live music finishes the night; massed pipe bands on the Royal Mile; street theatre on George Street; a classical candlelit concert in St Giles cathedral; a New Year Ball in the Assembly Rooms; and a massive street party of 100,000 people on Princes Street which is closed to traffic and home to several stages of live music and spectacular midnight fireworks. New Year's Day (called Ne' er Day) sees other kinds of madness as people take part in the One O' Clock Run from Edinburgh Castle to Holyrood Palace, the Edinburgh Bicycle Triathlon and the Loony Dook, where anyone who feels up to it can jump into the Firth of Forth at Queensferry, near the Forth Rail Bridge and receive a free hot toddy and soup for their troubles.

TOURIST BOARDS

ABERDEEN AND GRAMPIAN
Exchange House, 26-28 Exchange Street
Tel: 01224-288828 Fax: 01224-581367
Email: info@castlesandwhisky.org
Web: www.agtb.org

ANGUS AND DUNDEE
21 Castle Street, Dundee DD1 3AA
Tel: 01382-527527 Fax: 01382-527551
Email: enquiries@angusanddundee.co.uk
Web: www.angusanddundee.co.uk

ARGYLL, THE ISLES, LOCH LOMOND, STIRLING AND THE TROSSACHS
41 Dumbarton Road, Stirling FK8 2QQ
Tel: 08707-200620 Fax: 01786-450039
Web: www.visitscotlandheartlands.com
(this tourist board has other offices in addition to
   Stirling. Please check the web for details.)

AYRSHIRE AND ARRAN
Unit 2, 15 Skye Road, Prestwick, Ayrshire KA9 2TA
Tel: 01292-678100 Fax: 01292-471832
Email: info@ayrshire-owan.com
Web: www.ayrshire-arran.com

DUMFRIES AND GALLOWAY
64 Whitesands, Dumfries DG1 2RS
Tel: 01387-253862 Fax: 01387-245551
Web: www.visit-dumfries-and-galloway.co.uk

EDINBURGH AND LOTHIANS
4 Rothesay Terrace, Edinburgh EH3 7RY
Tel: 0845-225121 Fax: 01506-832222
Email: info@visitscotland.com
Web: www.edinburgh.org

FIFE
Haig Business Park, Balgonie Road, Markinch KY7 6AQ
Tel: 01592-611180 Fax: 01334-472021
Web: www.standrews.com/file

GREATER GLASGOW AND CLYDE VALLEY
11 George Square, Glasgow G2 1DY
Tel: 0141-204 4480 Fax: 0141-204 4074
Email: corporate@seeglasgow.com
Web: www.seeglasgow.com

HIGHLANDS OF SCOTLAND
Castle Wynd, Inverness IV2 3BJ
Tel: 01463-234353 Fax: 01463-710609
Web: www.extranet.host.co.uk
(this tourist board has other offices in addition to
Inverness. Please check the web for details.)

ORKNEY
6 Broad Street, Kirkwell, Orkwell KW15 1NX
Tel: 01856-872856 Fax: 01856-875056
Email: info@otb.com.net
Web: www.visitorkney.com

PERTHSHIRE
Lower City Mills, West Mill Street, Perth PH3 1LQ
Tel: 01738-450600 Fax: 01738-444863
Web: www.perthsire.co.uk

SCOTTISH BORDERS
Shepherd's Mill, Whinfield Road, Selkirk TD7 5DT
Tel: 0870-608 0404 Fax: 01750-21886
Email: info@scot-borders.co.uk
Web: www.scot-borders.co.uk

SHETLAND ISLANDS
Market Cross, Lerwick, Shetland ZE1 0LU
Tel: 01595-693434 Fax: 01595-695807
Email: shetland.tourism@zetnet.co.uk
Web: www.shetland-tourism.co.uk

STIRLING
Castle Esplanade, Stirling FK8 1EH
Tel: 01786-479901 Fax: 01786-451881
Email: info@scottish.heartlands.org
Web: www.scottish.heartlands.org

WESTERN ISLES
26 Cromwell Street, Stornorway, Isle of Lewis HS1 2DD
Tel: 01851-703088 Fax 01851-705244
Email: stornowaytic@visitthehebrides.co.uk
Web: witb.co.uk

SPORT AND PHYSICAL RECREATION

AMERICAN FOOTBALL

Britain's only professional American Football team is the Scottish Claymores, a team established in 1995 and named after the two-edged sword formerly used by warriors of the Scottish clans. They play their games at Murrayfield and Hampden Park.

The team competes in a six-team NFL Europe League in an annual 11-week season from April to June. Each NFL Europe League season culminates in the World Bowl. The NFL Europe League is allied to the National Football League, America's biggest sports league and is a joint venture between NFL and Fox Sports, a division of News Corporation. All six NFL League teams (Scotland, Amsterdam, Barcelona, Berlin, Dusseldorf and Frankfurt) are owned by the joint venture partners.

The Scottish Claymores hosted the World Bowl in 1996, defeating Frankfurt Galaxy 32-27 in front of a large crowd of 38,982 at Murrayfield. The Claymores won through to the finals of the World Bowl 2000, held in Frankfurt but lost 13-10 to Rhein Fire. In 2002 the Claymores won five matches and lost five matches.

ANGLING

Fishing as a sport can be dated to the early 17th-century. Rod fishing for food probably existed in the Highlands much earlier, but most of the clan chiefs and tacksmen (leaseholders or tenants) would have had ghillies (gamekeepers) to provide them with fish. By the latter half of the 18th-century the Duke of Gordon was letting salmon fishing for sport on the Spey; and with the arrival of railways and the building of new roads and bridges, parts of Scotland hitherto practically inaccessible were opened up for field sports. By then, much of Scotland, especially the Highlands, had already become a playground for the rich; sporting estates and hunting and fishing lodges sprang up across the country.

Scotland's oldest angling club is the Ellem Fishing Club, founded in 1829 by gentlemen from Edinburgh and Berwickshire. The influential sporting writer William Scrope, who also popularised deerstalking, helped to boost interest in fly-fishing in the late 1800s. Victorian anglers fished with huge 18-foot rods of split cane and green heart wood imported from the colonies.

The protection of salmon was the subject of legislation probably before the eleventh century and was first recorded by the Scottish Parliament in 1318. In 1862 Scotland was divided into 101 salmon fishery districts, each with a catchment area consisting of a river or a system of rivers. District Salmon Fishery Boards were created by the owners of the salmon rivers fishings, and they form the basis of the present-day organisation of the sport. Almost all river fishings are in private ownership and the fishing policy is determined by the owner.

Today, salmon and trout fishing in Scotland is enormously popular. Arrangements for fishing by time-share even developed in the 1980s. Thousands of anglers compete in annual events such as the Worldwide Trout Open fly-fishing competition. However, the industry, estimated at a value of £140 million a year, is now threatened by shrinking numbers of salmon and sea trout in the rivers and increased danger of disease spread by fish escaping from salmon farms.

The largest authenticated salmon ever caught by rod and line in Scotland was a huge fish weighing 29kg (64lbs) caught on the Tay by Miss G. W. Ballantine in 1922. The sea trout record was set in 1989 by Mr S. Burgoyne's catch of a 10kg (22½ lb) fish on the River Leven, which flows out of Loch Lomond.

BOXING

The rules of boxing were first drawn up by Sir John Sholto Douglas, 8th Marquess of Queensberry (1844–1900). In 1866 he published a code of 12 rules, the first being that gloves had to be worn. There has been a gradual modification of the rules over the years, but the Queensberry Rules laid the foundations of modern boxing.

Amateur boxing in Scotland is administered by the Scottish Amateur Boxing Association, founded in 1909. There are 86 directly affiliated clubs. Tournaments are regularly held with England, Wales and Ireland and the Commonwealth Games and Olympics are contested every four years. The best Scottish performance was by Dick McTaggart, gold medallist at the 1956 Melbourne Olympic Games.

Scotland has produced six world champions at the professional level: four at flyweight, Benny Lynch (1935), Jackie Paterson (1943), Walter

McGowan (1966) and Clinton, and two at lightweight, Kenny Buchanan (1970) and Jim Watt (1979).

The record attendance for a Scottish boxing match was 32,000, for the fight between Tommy Milligan and Frank Moody at the Carntyne Stadium in 1928. Milligan was the welterweight champion of Great Britain and Europe in 1924.

CRICKET

Cricket was introduced to Scotland by English soldiers garrisoned in the country in the years following the Jacobite rising of 1745 and by immigrant English workers in the paper, textile and iron industries. But it was developed and codified by Richard Nairn, a Jacobite who had settled in Hampshire after the rising. Nairn also introduced the middle stump. Records exist of Scottish immigrants playing cricket at Savannah, Georgia, in the United States, in the 1730s. A match involving English officers is believed to have been played at Perth as early as 1750, but the first cricket match in Scotland for which records are extant was played in September 1785 at Shaw Park, Alloa, between the Duke of Atholl's XI and a Colonel Talbot's team.

The oldest known cricket club in Scotland is that of Kelso, in the Borders, dating back to 1820, when Kelso was a garrison town; but the Perthshire club claims the longest continuous existence from 1826. Teams representing Scotland have played matches since 1865. The governing body for cricket in Scotland is the Scottish Cricket Union (SCU). It was originally set up in 1879 but then disbanded in 1883. Grange Club in Edinburgh acted as the Scottish equivalent of the MCC until the SCU was re-formed in 1908. The Western Division Union and Border Leagues date from the 1890s and the county championship from 1902. Scotland's only victory over a Test-playing nation took place on 29 July 1882, when Australia were defeated in a one-day match at Raeburn Place, Edinburgh.

Scottish players have often appeared in English county teams, but more rarely at test-match level. Douglas Jardine, born of Scottish parents in India, captained England during the famous 'Bodyline' tour of Australia in 1932–33. J. D. F. Larter, born in Inverness, played 10 tests for England between 1962 and 1965. Mike Denness, born in Bellshill, Lanarkshire, captained England from1973 to 1975.

Since 1980, Scotland have taken part, by invitation, in England's Benson and Hedges Cup and NatWest Trophy one-day competitions. There are annual three-day matches against Ireland and the MCC with regular games against overseas touring sides. The Triple Crown Tournament, inaugurated in 1993 and involving the England

Amateur XI, Wales, Ireland and Scotland, was won by Scotland in 1994 and 1995. In 1992 Scotland resigned from the UK Cricket Council and in 1994 it was elected to associate membership of the International Cricket Council (ICC). This gave Scotland autonomy in world cricket, and the Scottish team competed for the first time in the ICC Trophy in Kuala Lumpur in March/April 1997, reaching the semi-finals. The national side also won through to the final stages of the 1999 Cricket World Cup. Although they reached only the first stage, top scorer Gavin Hamilton has since represented England in a test match.

As of 2000, 150 local cricket clubs are affiliated to the SCU, but there are estimated to be well over 200 clubs existing in Scotland. The most famous win at this level by a Scottish club was by Freuchie over Rowledge at Lords in the final of the national Village Cup competition in 1985.

CURLING

Curling is a traditional winter sport which has been played in Scotland for over 450 years. Often described as a sort of 'bowls on ice', it is still occasionally played on a frozen outdoor rink, but is usually played on an indoor ice-rink. The game involves sliding smooth-bottomed 18kg discs of granite, called 'stones', across the ice towards a target circle, known as the 'house'. Each team consists of four players, and the 'skip', or captain, standing behind the house, nominates the shot required. Once the shot has been made, two players accompany the stone along the ice with brooms, sweeping the ice in front of the stone according to instructions from the skip. Sweeping, originally intended to remove twigs and leaves from the path of the stone when the game was played on a frozen loch, pond or river, influences the speed and distance the stone travels across the ice.

Rival claims to the origins of curling have been made by Scotland and the Netherlands. The Dutch claim that 16th-century paintings by Pieter Bruegel the elder (1530–69) show a game similar to curling being played on frozen canals. Claims by Scotland are based on a varied collection of old stones which have been salvaged from lochs and ponds over the centuries (the earliest one dates from 1511) and on written reports of curling matches that have been traced to Paisley Abbey and date from 1541. While the controversy about origins goes on, what is certain is that the Scots have nurtured the game, provided the rules of play and exported it throughout the world.

The early curling stones were called 'loofies' (*lof* being the old Scots world for the palm of the hand) because they resembled this shape. They had grooves for fingers and thumb and were thrown with a quoiting action. Over 300 years ago strong-arm curling was introduced. 'Channel' stones were used: they were given this name because they were taken from the channels of rivers and had been worn smooth by the water. The stones had rough handles inserted in them, and over time bigger and bigger stones became used. The object was to hurl them into the house where it would be difficult to dislodge them.

Spherical stones replaced rough and irregularly shaped stones towards the end of the 18th century, and with the introduction of these stones came a whole new aspect to curling. Skill and accuracy took over from brute strength, and with the turning of the hand on delivery, the round stones 'curled' consistently on the ice. Solid iron crampits were used as footholds during delivery, thus replacing the old 'cramps' and 'tramps' (iron or steel pads) with prongs underneath, which were attached to the boots with straps. Nowadays the modern hack is used throughout the curling world.

The earliest curling club was probably formed in Stirlingshire in 1716, followed by Muthill, Tayside in 1739. The famous Duddingston Club in Edinburgh, founded in 1795, formulated the first curling rules in 1804 and 12 of the Duddingston regulations for play for the basis of the much-enlarged modern rulebook.

The Grand Caledonian Curling Club was established in Edinburgh in 1838 and became the Royal Caledonian Curling Club (RCCC) in 1843 after a visit by Queen Victoria to Scone Palace, where the Earl of Mansfield demonstrated the game to her on a polished ballroom floor. The Club's first president was the sports greatest innovator, John Cairnie of Largs.

The Scots made their first tour to Canada in 1902-3 with a team of 28 members, who toured the country for three months. The first indoor game to be held in Scotland was at Glasgow in 1907. In 1909 the Canadians first toured in Scotland and 500 curlers attended a welcoming banquet in Edinburgh. As a result of these tours came the Strathcona Cup (first presented by RCCC president Lord Strathcona and Mount Royal), which is played every five years on a home-and-away basis. Curling was taken to Canada by Scottish settlers and Canada is today the game's most enthusiastic supporter, with 90 per cent of the world's 1.5 million playing population hailing from this country. Scotland has around 10,000 players.

Scottish women began touring with the men in the 1950s on exchange tours to Canada and the USA and play against European countries was arranged on a regular basis.

The most prestigious tournament is the World Championship (known as the Scotch Cup from 1959 to 1967 and the Silver Broom from 1968 to 1985), which was launched in Scotland in 1959, and is sponsored by the Scotch Whisky Association. It was originally played between the champion teams from Scotland and Canada, but the competition quickly grew into the men's World Championship.

The formation of the International Curling Federation (ICF) was initiated by the RCCC in 1965 during the World Championship for the Scotch Cup. A meeting was attended by office-bearers and representatives from Scotland, Canada, the USA, Norway, Sweden and Switzerland to consider setting up an international committee. The following year the Scotch Cup was held in Canada, at Vancouver, and the six countries that attended the previous meeting met again, along with a representative from France. The International Curling Federation was officially established on 1 April 1966. Major Allan Cameron, President of the RCCC was its first president. The Federation became independent in 1973 and in 1982 was recognised as the governing body of world curling. In 1991 the ICF became the World Curling Federation (WCF).

The Ladies World Championship was established in Scotland in 1979 and sponsored by the Royal Bank of Scotland. For the first three years this tournament was played in Scotland, but it is now played in a different country each year. Scotland were the winners of the World Junior Curling Championships in 1991. In February/March 2000 the world championships were held at Glasgow, with the Canadian men and women both receiving top honours.

The first Olympic Gold Medal to be awarded in the sport was won by a British team in Chamonix in 1924. All the members of the team were Scots. The second Olympic Gold medal to be won in the sport was in 2002 at the Winter Olympics in Salt Lake City in the USA. On 21st February an estimated 5.6 million people in Britain tuned in to watch Rhona Martin (Skip), Debbie Knox, Fiona MacDonald, Janice Rankin and Margaret Morton curl their way to Olympic gold – giving Britain its first Olympic gold in 20 years. All the members of the team were Scots.

The outdoor game has now all but disappeared. The greatest outdoor curling match, the 'Bonspiel', now only takes place in exceptionally severe winters and has occurred just 33 times in the last 150 years or so. It is traditionally held on the Lake of Menteith, Perthshire, between teams representing the North and the South of Scotland. The match is announced only when the ice on the lake is 10 inches (253 mm) thick. This depth was increased from the previous limit of 8 inches (203 mm) after the last Bonspiel, held on 7 February 1979, when the rarity of the occasion attracted a crowd of 10,000 onto the ice, threatening the safety of all concerned.

DEERSTALKING

Deerstalking became established in the Highlands during the 19th century, and marked a change in practice from earlier methods of hunting deer, in which deer were driven into an enclosed space, either a natural pass or a built enclosure, and shot by waiting riflemen. The new sport was based on approaching the deer as closely as possible, and killing it with a single shot. In the early days deerhounds were used as a back-up to the rifle, which often wounded the deer without killing it outright. The introduction of telescopic sights in the 1880s was at first considered unsporting, as it gave the stalker an unfair advantage.

The 19th-century fashion for deerstalking, fuelled by the creation of deer forests, lodges, bothies and improved access into the hills, was even further promoted when Queen Victoria and Prince Albert took a long lease on the Balmoral estate in 1848. Deerstalking inspired the work of Sir Edwin Landseer, painter of the famous *Monarch of the Glen* and himself a keen stalker. The growth of the sport gave rise to the professional stalker, or gamekeeper. The gamekeeper looked after the sporting estate all year round and acted as a guide to stalkers in the open season.

Paradoxically, the organised pursuit of deer helped to increase their chances of survival, by reducing poaching, and the numbers of deer steadily increased through the 19th century. By the end of the century over seven million acres were given over to deer forest.

Today deer face competition from many sources – hikers, climbers, skiers and tourists, as well as foresters. New forestry plantations deny the deer low ground. Poaching has made a comeback. Nonetheless, deer and the sport of deerstalking continues to flourish.

EQUESTRIAN SPORTS

In the 12th century, William the Lion organised a horse race, known as the Lanark Silver Bell, on Lanark Moor, making Scotland the birthplace of British horse racing. Scotland once boasted 15 racecourses. Lanark, the oldest, closed in 1977, and today just five survive: Ayr, Edinburgh, Hamilton Park, Kelso and Perth.

The Scottish Grand National is held at Ayr. It moved from Belleisle, where racing had taken place since 1576, to today's site in 1907. The largest crowd for a race meeting in Scotland was 20,000, on Scottish Grand National Day 1969. Ayr is also the home of the September Gold Cup. Edinburgh racecourse was founded in 1816 as Musselburgh Race Course, and the current course opened in 1978. Evening race meetings were first held in Scotland at Hamilton Park, near Glasgow, which was also the first course to install plastic safety racing barriers comprehensively. Crowds exceeding 7,000 regularly attend the 'Saints and Sinners' evening meeting, a charity fundraising event.

Scotland has produced a number of racing celebrities over the years. Matt Dawson was a trainer who won the Derby in 1860 and on five subsequent occasions, as well as 23 other major classics. Charlie Cunningham rode and trained his own horses at Wooden, Kelso, with great success between 1865 and 1891. Despite his great height (6 feet 3 inches), he was champion amateur jockey in 1852. In the 1950s George Boyd produced 700 winners from his east coast stables. Willie Carson is the most successful Scottish jockey, being five times champion jockey and having ridden almost 4,000 winners in Great Britain during his career.

Scotland's most famous horse, Peaty Sandy, was the first Scottish horse to win the Coral Welsh National, which he did in 1981. He won 20 of his 74 jumping races, never falling until the last fence of his last race, and earning £100,000 in total.

Pony trekking as an organised leisure activity originated in Scotland. It was introduced to encourage people to explore the country via its old drover roads, by the late Lieutenant Commander Jock Kerr Hunter, who opened Scotland's first riding school in the 1940s. Since then, riding centres have increased to around 60 across Scotland. All are approved by either the Trekking and Riding Society of Scotland (TRSS) or the British Horse Society (BHS).

FOOTBALL

Association football (also, but less commonly, known as 'soccer' in Scotland) shares its early history with rugby, both having a common origin in early ball games of the Roman era.

Rapid growth and regulation of the game began in the second half of the 19th century, as the cities grew more populated and the introduction of Saturday afternoons created a demand for public entertainment. The Queen's Park Football Club was founded in Glasgow in 1867 and the first recognised match took place in 1868. However, as most of Scotland's population became centred in

Glasgow, Edinburgh and one or two smaller cities, football clubs in more isolated and less populated areas found it hard to arrange fixtures with other clubs. With no formal structure, matches were often irregular and organised in a casual manner. It was not unusual to find, when a fixture had been arranged between clubs, that the two teams were playing to different sets of rules.

The Scottish Football Association (SFA) is the second oldest football association in the world. It came into being after a meeting in Glasgow on 13 March 1873 to establish an annual cup competition, proposed by Queen's Park FC and attended by the teams that played Scottish Club Association rules. The original eight clubs belonging to the SFA were Queen's Park, Clydesdale, Vale of Leven, Dumbreck, Third Lanarkshire Rifle Volunteers, Eastern, Granville and Rovers. Queens Park were the first winners, in 1873–74, of the cup competition which later became the Scottish FA Cup. However, Queens Park's amateur status, which it still maintains to this day, contributed to its decline as the trend towards professionalism grew. The Glasgow clubs, Rangers (founded 1873) and Celtic (1888), went on to dominate Scottish football. It was the Scottish Cup that produced what is still regarded as the world's highest ever football score, the 36–0 victory of Arbroath over Bon Accord of Aberdeen in 1885. Bon Accord were in fact a cricket club and had been mistakenly sent an invitation to play in the Cup. The SFA continues to be the governing body of football in Scotland and has ultimate responsibility for the regulation and development of the game. Junior football is administered by the Scottish Junior Football Association, founded in Glasgow in 1886.

The Scottish Football League (SFL) was founded in 1890 of which only a handful of the original member clubs are still in existence, namely Celtic, Dumbarton, Hearts, Partick Thistle, Rangers and St Mirren. The inaugural championship of 1890–91 was shared by Dumbarton and Rangers. Regional associations include The Highland Football League, founded 1893 and The East of Scotland League, founded in 1930. All these leagues are administered by the SFA.

The Scottish Women's Football Association was founded in 1974. It now has over 900 registered players, 28 senior clubs and 16 under-sixteen sides playing in the National Leagues in Scotland. It is the fastest growing sport for women in the country. Scottish women's football was given a boost in 2000 with the news that the national squad was to receive £66,000 of National Lottery funding. This would allow 22 members of the team, through the Talented Athlete programme, to develop their sporting skills and also compete in tournaments such as the Pacific Cup in Australia.

The national stadium for Scotland games is Hampden Park. It officially opened in 1903 and recent development has made it into one of the finest stadiums in the world, capable of holding 52,000 spectators. A British record crowd of 149,547 watched a Scotland v England international at Hampden Park in 1937 and just eight days later a crowd of 147,365 watched Celtic v Aberdeen there in the Scottish Cup Final. The highest attendance at a league match in Britain was 118,567 for Rangers v Celtic match at Ibrox in 1939. These attendance levels are no longer attainable because of safety regulations limiting crowd numbers, among other factors.

Scotland's worst sporting disaster occurred at Ibrox Stadium, home of Rangers, where 66 spectators lost their lives on 2 January 1971 when some spectators lost their footing on a stairway while leaving the stadium at the end of the traditional New Year match between Rangers and Celtic.

The first ever live TV coverage of league football in Scotland was for an Aberdeen v Hearts match in 1986.

THE INTERNATIONAL DIMENSION

The first official international football match in history was played on 30 November 1872 at the West of Scotland cricket ground in Partick, Glasgow, between England and Scotland, in front of about 4,000 spectators.

In 1886 the football associations from Scotland, England, Wales and Ireland set up the International Football Association Board to control the rules of the game. The SFA joined the Fédération Internationale de Football Association (FIFA), football's world governing body, in 1910 and was a founding member of the Union des Associations Européennes de Football (UEFA) in 1954.

The first official international match against a continental team was in 1929, when Scotland beat Norway 7–3 in Oslo. Scotland's international teams lost only 3 of their first 43 international matches and first participated in the World Cup in 1954, having previously turned down a chance to appear in 1950. Scotland have reached the World Cup final stages on seven other occasions, namely 1958, 1974, 1978, 1982, 1986, 1990 and 1998. The five consecutive appearances 1974–1990 constitute a record for the competition for a team qualifying solely through its efforts on the field and not through special circumstances such as automatic qualification as hosts or cup holders.

PREMIER DIVISION TEAMS FOR SEASON 2002–3

ABERDEEN FOOTBALL CLUB
Founded 1903; entered League 1904
Pittodrie Stadium, Pittodrie Street, Aberdeen
AB24 5QH Tel: 01224-650400 Fax: 01224-644173
Web: www.afc.co.uk
Manager: Steve Paterson

CELTIC FOOTBALL CLUB
Founded 1888; entered League 1890
Celtic Park, 95 Kerrydale Street, Glasgow G40 3RE
Tel: 0141-556 2611 Fax: 0141-551 8106
Ticket Office: 0141-551 8653
Email: visitorexperience@celticfc.co.uk
Web: www.celticfc.co.uk
Manager: Martin O'Neill

DUNDEE FOOTBALL CLUB
Founded 1893; entered League 1893
Dens Park stadium, Sandeman Street, Dundee DD3 7JY
Tel: 01382-889966 Fax: 01382-832284
Email: dundeefc@dfc.co.uk
Web: www.dundeefc.co.uk
Manager: Jim Duffy

DUNDEE UNITED FOOTBALL CLUB
Founded 1909; entered League 1910
Tannadice Park, Tannadice Street, Dundee DD3 7JW
Tel: 01382-833166 Fax: 01382-889398
Ticket Office: 01382-833166
Email: dundee.united.fc@blueyonder.co.uk
Web: www.dundeeunitedfc.co.uk
Manager: Ian McCall

DUNFERMLINE ATHLETIC FOOTBALL CLUB
Founded 1885; entered League 1921
East End Park, Halbeath Road, Dunfermline KY12 7RB
Tel: 01383-724295 Fax: 01383-723468
Ticket Office: 01383-724295
Email: pars@dunfermline-athletic.com
Web: www.dunfermline-athletic.com
Manager: Jimmy Calderwood

HEART OF MIDLOTHIAN FOOTBALL CLUB
Founded 1874; entered League 1890
Tynecastle Stadium, Gorgie Road, Edinburgh EH11 2NL
Tel: 0131-200 7200 Fax: 0131-200 7222
Ticket Office: 0131-200 7201
Web: www.heartsfc.co.uk
Manager: Craig Levein

HIBERNIAN FOOTBALL CLUB
Founded 1875; entered League 1893
Easter Road Stadium, 12 Albion Place, Edinburgh
EH7 5QG Tel: 0131-661 2159 Fax: 0131-659 6488

Ticket Office: 0131-661 1875
Web: www.hibs.co.uk
Manager: Alex McLeish

KILMARNOCK FOOTBALL CLUB
Founded 1869; entered League 1896
Rugby Park, Rugby Road, Kilmarnock KA1 2DP
Tel: 01563-545300 Fax: 01563-522181
Web: www.kilmarnockfc.co.uk
Manager: Tim Jeffries

LIVINGSTON FOOTBALL CLUB
Founded 1943; entered League 1974
Almondvale Stadium, Almondvale Stadium Road,
Livingston EH54 7DN Tel: 01506-417000
Fax: 01506-418888 Email: info@livingstonfc.co.uk
Web: www.livingstonfc.co.uk
Manager: Jim Leishman

MOTHERWELL FOOTBALL CLUB
Founded 1886; entered League 1893
The Chapman Building, Firpark Street, Motherwell
ML1 2QN Tel: 01698-333333 Fax: 01698-338001
Ticket Office: 01698-333033
Email: mfc@motherwellfc.co.uk
Web: www.motherwellfc.co.uk
Manager: Terry Butcher

RANGERS FOOTBALL CLUB
Founded 1873; entered League 1890
Ibrox Stadium, 150 Edmiston Drive, Glasgow G51 2XD
Tel: 0870-600 1972 Fax: 0870-600 1978
Ticket Office: 0870-600 1993
Web: www.rangers.co.uk
Manager: Alex McLeish

ST JOHNSTONE FOOTBALL CLUB
Founded 1884; entered League 1911
McDiarmid Park, Crieff Road, Perth PH1 2SJ
Tel: 01738-459090 Fax: 01738-625771
Ticket Office: 01738-455000
Email:enquiries@saints.co.uk
Web: www.stjohnstonefc.co.uk
Manager: Billy Stark

FOOTBALL ASSOCIATIONS

SCOTTISH FOOTBALL ASSOCIATION
Hampden Park, Glasgow G42 9AY Tel: 0141-616 6000
Fax: 0141-616 6001 Email: info@scottishfa.co.uk
Web: www.scottishfa.co.uk

SCOTTISH FOOTBALL LEAGUE
National Stadium, Hampden Park, Glasgow G42 9EB
Tel: 0141-620 4160 Fax 0141-620 4161
Email: info@sfl.scottishfootball.com
Web: www.scottishfootball.com

GOLF

Golf is commonly regarded as the quintessentially Scottish game, but there is some evidence that it may have originated in Holland. The most likely derivation, however, is the Scots verb 'gowf', meaning to cuff or strike hard.

In 1457 a Scottish Act of Parliament by James II banned both golf and football because they interfered with his subjects' archery practice. James III in 1471 and James IV in 1491 also adopted this Act. It was not until 1502 that Scots were able to indulge in their national pastime. During the Stewart era, the links of Leith and St. Andrews were the chief centres of golf. When James VI acquired the English throne, he introduced golf south of the border. At this time it was the local bowmakers who were called upon to manufacture clubs and balls.

The modern history of golf began with the formation of clubs in the 18th century. The Gentlemen Golfers of Edinburgh (now the Honourable Company of Edinburgh Golfers) was founded in 1744 and is generally considered to be the first golf club, with Edinburgh Town Council granting a Silver Cup to the 'Gentlemen', which became the first golf trophy. The first competition for the Silver Cup was played on the Links of Leith on 7 March 1744 and from this event sprang the first known rules of golf.

The club played at Musselburgh from 1836 to 1891, and their present home is Muirfield. Musselburgh Golf Club came into being in 1744, although golf had probably already been played there for as many as 300 years. In the mid 19th-century Musselburgh became the focus of Scottish golf, not only as the home of the Gentlemen Golfers of Edinburgh but also the home of the Edinburgh Burgess Golfing Society, founded 1773 and the Bruntsfield Links Golf Club, founded 1761. The first women's golf tournament, for the town's fishwives, was held at the Musselburgh Golf Club in 1811. The town was also the centre of golf ball and club manufacturing and it was here that a tool to cut the standard 4¼-inch hole was introduced in 1829.

The Society of St Andrews Golfers was formed on the 14 May 1754 and drew up a set of 13 rules for their annual golfing competition. In 1834 the name was changed to The Royal and Ancient Golf Club of St Andrews (R & A) after the society received royal patronage from William IV. Although the R & A has the function of lawgiver in golf, the parchment on which the original 13 rules of golf were drafted is in the possession of the Honourable Company of Edinburgh Golfers and a copy hangs in the Muirfield clubhouse. The standard round of golf at St Andrews was 22 holes (11 holes to the shoreline and 11 back), but in 1764 this was reduced to 18 holes, bringing St Andrews into line with other clubs.

The first known professional tournament was played at St Andrews in 1819. In 1821 James Cheape, Laird of Strathtyrum, purchased the St Andrews Links to preserve it for the game of golf. The Links were re-purchased by St Andrews Town Council in 1894 for £5,000 and were run by the Green Committee of St Andrews Link. The first clubhouse at St Andrews was built in 1835 by the Union Club offering facilities to sportsmen. By 1854 a new clubhouse was opened behind the first tee on the Old Course.

At Prestwick Golf Club, founded in 1851, the first Open Championship was held in 1860. The winner, Willie Park Snr, received the Challenge Belt, and the runner-up was the local favourite, 'Old Tom' Morris from St Andrews. In 1870 the Challenge Belt would become the property of the player who won the Open three years in succession. This was achieved by 'Young Tom' Morris, whose father had become keeper of the green at St Andrews in 1864.

The first 12 Open Championships, 1860-72, were played at Prestwick over three rounds of the 12-hole links. There was no championship in 1871. The R & A and the Honourable Company of Edinburgh Golfers then joined with Prestwick in contributing towards the Silver Claret Jug, which became the permanent trophy for the Open. The competition was played in rotation at Prestwick, St Andrews and Musselburgh, and this began a tradition of rotating the venue for the Open among several courses which has been maintained up to the present. The last Open to be played at Prestwick was in 1925. The R & A removed it from the rota after the crowd engulfed the Scottish American Macdonald Smith of Carnoustie in that year. Musselburgh hosted the Open on six occasions between 1874 and 1889, the Scot Willie Auchterlonie winning the 1883 tournament, but when the Honourable Company moved to Muirfield in 1891, they took the competition with them. Muirfield have since staged the competition 15 times between 1892 and 2002.

The Open was first played at St Andrews in 1873 and was won by the local Tom Kidd. In 1919 the R & A took over responsibility for organising the Open. The holding of the 129th Open there in July 2000 brought St Andrews' total of Opens to 26, one more than that of Prestwick, the original venue.

Spectators were charged gate money for the first time at the 1926 Open, and as the popularity of the championship grew, the ability to accommodate spectators influenced the selection of venues, which by then included places both north and south of the border. Other British Open Championship courses in Scotland include Troon, where more golf is probably played than in any other town in Scotland, and where the Open was first played in 1923. It has been played there several times between 1950 and 1997. Turnberry, founded 1902, has hosted three Open Championships, in 1977, 1986 and 1994, replacing Carnoustie on the rota.

Golf is first recorded at Carnoustie as long ago as 1650, but a club was not formed until 1842. The first Open to be played there was in 1931 and was won by Edinburgh-born Tommy Armour, who had emigrated to the United States in the 1920s. The competition has been held at Carnoustie at irregular intervals but returned to a revamped course in 1999 following a 24-year absence. It was won in a dramatic play-off by Paul Lawrie of Aberdeen. The only other modern Scottish winner of the Open is Sandy Lyle, who won in 1985.

The Scottish PGA Championship is staged at the Monarch's Course, Gleneagles, during August. The most successful Scottish golfer of the modern era is Colin Montgomerie, who in May 2000 won the Benson & Hedges Tournament at Wentworth for a record-breaking third consecutive year. In 2002 Mongomerie played outstandingly at the De Vere Belfry and was the top points scorer, thus maintaining his position at the top of the European order of merit.

In 1897 Britain's leading golf clubs asked the R & A to take charge of setting up and administering a universal code of rules for golf, and since then every new golfing nation with connections to the R & A has agreed to abide by them. The rules set up by the R & A were freely available to all by 1908 and a sponsorship deal was struck with Royal Insurance for the publication of all English-language copies. The United States, however, set their own rules, and these were used until 1952 for contests inside that country. In at least one case the United States led the way: in 1938 the United States Golf Association (USGA) limited the number of clubs a golfer can carry to 14, and in the following year the R & A followed suit.

The R & A and USGA have worked together since 1952 to create a common international set of rules. These supreme authorities of the game meet every four years to agree any revisions that are required.

Several Scots have won tournaments outside of Britain. Gordon Brand Jnr has won the Scandinavian Open, Bernard Gallacher both the Spanish and French Opens, Sam Torrance the Zambian Open in 1975 and Spanish Open in 1982, Sandy Lyle the US Masters in 1988. Scotswomen have won their share of UK and overseas tournaments as well: Jessie Valentine won the New Zealand Ladies in 1935 and the French Ladies in 1936, Cathy Panton the British Ladies Open in 1976, Gillian Stewart the European Open in 1984, and Dale Reid the European Open in 1988.

Television coverage of golf was provided live from St Andrews for the first time in 1955.

The Amateur Championships were played at Royal Dornoch, Sutherland, for the first time in 1985. The British Golf Museum opened at St Andrews in 1990.

There are currently over 400 golf courses in Scotland, and Scotland boasts the highest course in Britain, Leadhills in Strathclyde, which is 1,500 feet (457 metres) above sea level.

Championship courses
St Andrews – Tel 01334-475757.
Carnoustie – Tel 01241-853789.
Gleneagles – Tel 01764-663543.
Turnberry – Tel 01655-331000.
Muirfield – Tel 01620-842255.
Royal Dornoch – Tel 01862-810219.

BRITISH GOLF MUSEUM
Bruce Embankment, St Andrews, Fife KY16 9AB
Tel: 01334-478880 Fax: 01334-473306
Web: www.britishgolfmuseum.co.uk

HIGHLAND AND BORDER GAMES

The origins of Highland and Border games lie in competitions arranged by ancient kings and clan chiefs to help them select the strongest men as their champions, the fastest cross-country runners as their couriers, and the best pipers and dancers to entertain both themselves and their guests. The earliest organised games probably date back to the eleventh century, when Malcolm Canmore held contests to find the best soldiers for the struggles against the Normans. Games took place in Ceres, Fife, in 1314, when victorious soldiers returning from the Battle of Bannockburn discovered an outlet for their high spirits by taking part in athletic competitions. However, the holding of games was prohibited following the suppression of the Jacobite Rising in 1746, when large gatherings, the wearing of the kilt and the playing of the bagpipes – in fact any expression of Scottish culture – were forbidden.

Highland games began to be formally organised again in the 1820s as part of a romantic revival of Highland culture and traditions, encouraged by Sir Walter Scott and King George IV, and became an annual occurrence across Scotland. The first 'modern' Highland games took place in 1819 at St Fillians, Perthshire, organised by the Highland Society. Events at the Invergarry games in the 1820s included twisting the four legs from a cow, for which a fat sheep was offered as the prize. Queen Victoria's love for Scottish things and her patronage of the Braemar Gathering from 1848 contributed to this revival of interest and involvement in the games.

HIGHLAND GAMES TODAY

Highland games today are organised and run by their own committees under the rules of the Scottish Games Association (SGA), which was established in 1946. The objectives of the SGA are to encourage and foster the highest standards of ethics and performance, lay down and enforce rules and regulations covering all aspects of traditional Highland Games activities and to assist committees in the improvement of their events. All competitors must register with the SGA prior to participating in any events.

Highland and Border games are held annually between May and September. In spite of their name, they are held all over Scotland. The events cover a full range of running and cycle track events, light field and heavy field events, along with Highland dancing and piping. The Border Games have more emphasis on track competitions.

The most distinctive events are known as the 'heavies'. Weights of 28lbs and 56lbs are thrown for distance, with that of 56lbs thrown for height over a bar. The famous Scottish caber events have athletes running while carrying an entire tree trunk, some over 20ft in length, and then tossing it end over end.

All competitors in heavy field events must wear a kilt. Some Games use stones in the putting events and the Scottish hammer has a rigid wooden or bamboo handle, with the throwers wearing special boots with an extended sole beyond the toe so that they can 'dig in' and throw without turning their whole body.

Tug-of-war takes place at the more traditional Highland Games and involves teams of five or eight men plus a coach. Draws take place before the competition starts, the judge tossing a coin to decide the direction of the pull. The length of the pull is 12 feet and the team with the best of three pulls is declared the winner.

Just as important as the sporting events are the piping competitions for both individuals and bands, as well as the dancing competitions, where girls and boys, some as young as three years old, perform the intricate steps of dances such as the Highland Fling, the Sword Dance and the *Seann Triubhas*.

The most famous Highland games are the Braemar Gathering, which have been attended regularly by successive generations of the Royal Family since the days of Queen Victoria, and the Cowal Highland Gathering, the largest of its kind in the world, which ends with the massed pipes and drums of over 150 bands marching through the streets of Dunoon, Argyll.

As Scots have moved and settled throughout the world they have taken with them their love of the Games, and today there are events in Europe, America, Asia and to Australia. Many of the overseas venues have attracted large numbers of exiled Scots, their descendants and friends.

For more information about the Highland Games, contact the local Tourist Board in the area concerned.

MOTOR RALLYING AND RACING

Scotland's terrain has made it a favourite location for motor rallying ever since a Glasgow-built car finished in second place in a 500-mile trial organised by the Automobile Club of Britain in 1901. Scotland's principal annual motor sports event, the international RSAC Scottish Rally, was established in 1932 but was born out of a series of reliability trials begun in 1903 by the Scottish Automobile Club, formed in 1899 and the forerunner of the Royal Scottish Automobile Club (RSAC). The rally is held in June and covers 700 miles. At the UK level, the RAC Lombard Rally includes some Scottish stages. The first Scot to win the RAC Rally was Colin MacRae in 1994. He also won in 1995 and 1997, and was the first Briton to become World Rally Champion in 1995.

Scots have made a major contribution to motor-racing since the 1950s. Ecurie Ecosse was formed in 1952 as a non-profit-making syndicate of Scottish racing enthusiasts. In 1956 and 1957 the team won the Le Mans 24-hour race. One of Scotland's famous Grand Prix drivers, Jim Clark, began his career with the Border Reivers, a Berwickshire team formed in the 1950s. In 1961, Innes Ireland became the first Scot to win a major Grand Prix, in the USA, and in his wake Jim Clark won 25 Grand Prix races and twice became World Champion, in 1963 and 1965. Jackie Stewart topped this by winning three World Championships (1969, 1971 and 1973). In the late 1990s Stewart attempted to boost Scottish interest in motor-racing by forming a Grand Prix team under his own name, but met with little success. David Coulthard won several Grand Prix races during the latter part of the 1990s but has yet to be crowned World Champion.

RUGBY

A game similar to rugby, called *harpastum*, was played in Scotland during the time of the Romans. It involved two teams running, passing and throwing a small round ball, the aim being to cross the opponents' line at the far end of a rectangular field. This game still lives on in certain street games in Hawick and Jedburgh.

During the 15th- and 16th-centuries, football (which bore more resemblance to rugby in those days) was banned by royal edict on the grounds that it interfered with archery practice. The first recorded match between teams representing Scotland and England took place in 1599. The venue was Bewcastle in Cumbria, and resulted in a number of English being taken prisoner and one man disembowelled.

By the mid 19th-century some private schools, colleges and universities in Scotland played a game that involved kicking and handling of the ball. H. H. Almond of Merchiston School, Edinburgh, is generally credited with popularising rugby among schools. In 1846 rules were formally introduced, which brought some consistency to this new sport. However, the first senior game in Scotland took place in 1858 and was played between Edinburgh Academicals and a University team. It was spread out over four successive Saturdays and involved around 50 players. As a result, in 1868, a number of Scottish clubs formulated a book of rules called the 'Green Book'.

Captains from five Scottish rugby clubs got together in 1870 and discussed challenging English clubs to represent their respective countries to the first international rugby match. The game took place on 27 March 1871 at Raeburn Place (a cricket field) at Edinburgh Academy, with Scotland winning. This gave Scotland the distinction of being both the first hosts and first winners ever in an international rugby match. The match initiated the fixture which has since become a highlight of the rugby calendar and which since 1879 has been known as the Calcutta Cup. Scotland has won the cup 41 times compared to England's 58, and there have been 17 drawn matches.

The Scottish Football Union (SFU) was formed on 3 March 1873, comprising eight clubs, soon to be joined by six others from the Borders. One of its main objectives was to find a pitch for international matches. The first few international fixtures had been played at Old Hampden Park in Glasgow, Powderhall in Edinburgh and the West of Scotland Cricket Club's ground in Hamilton. The SFU purchased a ground at Inverleith in Edinburgh, thus becoming the first Home Union to own and run its own rugby ground. The first international match at the new location was in 1899 against Ireland.

On 25 April 1883 the first seven-a-side tournament took place at The Greenyards after Ned Haig, a butcher by trade, suggested a tournament in order to raise cash for his club, Melrose. Melrose defeated their close neighbours and rivals, Gala, in the final. Most clubs now organise sevens tournaments at the end of the season, but the Melrose Sevens continues to be the top tournament of its class.

Rugby's popularity continued to grow after World War I, but Inverleith could no longer hold the large crowds that flocked to see Scottish games. In 1922 the SFU purchased 19 acres of land at Murrayfield, which had previously been the home of the Edinburgh Polo Club. Funds were raised for the new stadium by an issue of debentures and on 21 March 1925 it officially opened with an international match against England and 70,000 spectators cheering throughout the immensely exciting game. Scotland once again defeated England by a score of 14-11.

The year 1925 saw changes at the administration level with the SFU becoming the Scottish Rugby Union (SRU). Most of the rugby club grounds were used to grow potatoes during World War II and the armed forces arranged a game between England and Scotland Services Internationals, which took place at Inverleith, as Murrayfield was being used as a supply depot.

In 1955 Scotland's defeat of Wales at Murrayfield ended a 17-game winless streak, which started when the Fourth Springboks from South Africa visited the UK in 1950–1. In 1960 Scotland became the first of the home unions to tour foreign countries when they went to South Africa – a tradition that continues to this day. The highest attendance for a rugby match in Scotland is 104,000 for Scotland's 12-10 win over Wales at Murrayfield in 1975.

In 1986 HRH the Princess Royal accepted an invitation to become patron of the SRU. A year later Scotland reached the quarter-finals of the first Rugby World Cup in New Zealand, but lost to the mighty All Blacks, who became the eventual winners.

In 1990 Scotland won their third Grand Slam (the first one was in 1925 and the second in 1984) by defeating Wales, Ireland and France, finally beating England at Murrayfield 13-7.

The 125th anniversary of the first international rugby match was celebrated in 1996, followed by the 125th anniversary of the SFU (SRU) in 1998 and Murrayfield celebrated its 75th birthday in March 2000.

Approximately 300 clubs belong to the SRU and there are 200 affiliated schools. Member clubs account for some 13,500 people currently playing the game and around 32,000 are non-playing members of clubs. From the 1975–76 season onwards club rugby was standardised as seven divisions, with district divisions beneath.

DIVISION 1 RUGBY CLUBS 2002–3

ABERDEEN GSFP RFC
Club founded 1893
Rubislaw Playing Fields, 86 Queens Road,
Aberdeen AB10 6XA Tel: 01224-316827
E-mail: derek@derekyounger.freeserve.co.uk

BOROUGHMUIR RFC
Club founded 1919
Meggetland, Colinton Road, Edinburgh
EH14 1AS Tel: 0131-443 7571
Email: admin@boroughmuirfc.co.uk
Web: www.boroughmuirfc.co.uk

CURRIE RFC
Club founded 1970
5 Malleny, Malleny Park, Balerno, Midlothian EH14 7AF
Tel: 0131-449 2432 Fax: 0131-449 7688
Web: www.currierfc.freeserve.co.uk

GLASGOW HAWKS RFC
Club founded 1997 on merger of Glasgow Accies & GHK
The Pavilion, Old Anniesland, 689 Crow Road,
Glasgow G13 1LQ
Tel: 0141-950 1222 Fax: 0141-959 9972
E-mail: hugh.barrow@ntlworld.com
Web: www.glasgowhawks.com

HAWICK RUGBY FOOTBALL CLUB
Club founded 1873
Mansfield Park, Hawick TD9 8AL
Tel: 01450- 370687 or 374216 Fax 01450-373619
Emails: enquiries@hawickrfc.co.uk
Web: www.hawickrfc.co.uk

HERIOTS FP RFC
Club founded 1890
52 Netherbank, Edinburgh EH16 6YR
Tel: 0131-552 5925 Fax: 0131-551 4519
Email: douglas_bruce@talk21.com
Web: www.george-heriots.com

JED-FOREST RFC
Club founded 1885
Riverside Park, Jedburgh TD8 6UE
Tel: 01835-862232
Web: www.jedforestrfc.com

MELROSE RFC
Club founded 1877
The Greenyards, Melrose TD6 9SA
Tel: 01896-822993
Email: mrfc@melrose.bordernet.co.uk
Web: www.melroserugby.bordernet.co.uk

PEEBLES RFC
Club founded 1894
The Gytes, Peebles EH45 8GL Tel: 01721-720020
Web: www.peeblesrugbclub.org.uk

STIRLING COUNTY
Club founded 1904
Bridgehaugh Park, Causewayhead Road, Stirling
FK9 5AP Tel: 01786-478866 Fax: 01786-447767
Web: www.stirlingcountyrfc.co.uk

SHINTY

The Gaelic name for shinty, *camanachd*, identifies the sport as possibly the oldest organised team game in western Europe. Many of the ancient Irish heroes were said to have played shinty. Cu Chulainn, the hero of the Ulster cycle of tales, is said to have attended an ancient training school for young heroes, where *camanachd* was part of the curriculum. In 563 Columba left Ireland for Scotland because of a quarrel that had supposedly broken out during a game of *camanachd*, so tradition says the game was brought to Scotland in that year, if not before. Its roots were shared with Irish hurling until the mid 14th-century.

The first written records mentioning shinty date from the 14th- and 15th-centuries. A 15th-century memorial stone on the island of Iona depicts not only the owner's broadsword beneath his name in the old Lombard script, but also a caman (stick) with a ball beside it. The following description of the game is from Jamieson's *Dictionary of the Scottish Language* (1821): "A game in which bats, somewhat resembling a golf-club, are used. At every fair or meeting of the country people, there were contests at racing, wrestling, putting the stone, etc., and on holidays all the males of the district, young and old, met to play at football, but oftener at shinty. Shinty is a game played with sticks, crooked at the end, and balls of wood".

Shinty has remained popular in the Highlands, although Lowland law against it and the enforced observation of the Sabbath in many places affected the game, as it was customarily played on Sundays. The custom of playing on Sundays eventually faded away, but the game survived Culloden, the Highland Clearances, and later waves of migration out of the Highlands, and is still played according to virtually the same rules as it was centuries ago.

By the mid 19th-century the popularity of the game had declined until it was played only in the glens of Lochaber, Strathglass and Badenoch. Captain Chisholm of Glassburn published a code of rules for the Strathglass Club in 1880 and in February 1887 Strathglass (led by Chisholm) played against Glen-Urquhart in a 15-a-side game at Inverness. Strathglass won the game, but the following year they were defeated. Following the loss, Chisholm revised the rules he had published earlier.

Celtic Club rules drawn up in Glasgow were played in the south of the country. The lack of set rules prompted a meeting of representatives from all the leading clubs on 10 October 1893 at Kingussie, which led to the formation of the Camanachd Association. This became the governing body of the game and drew up rules to control play and competitions which are still followed today.

The Challenge Trophy was set up in 1895 and Kingussie defeated Glasgow Cowal 2-0 at Inverness in 1896 in the first final. The trophy has been contested annually, except during the two world wars. Shinty's premier competition is now known as the Glenmorangie Camanachd Cup and is played each year at one of five regular venues – An Aird, Fort William; Bught Park, Inverness; Mossfield Park, Oban; The Dell, Kingussie; and a venue in Glasgow. The cup final attracts shinty's biggest crowd of the season, usually 3,000 to 5,000, and is normally played on the first Saturday in June. The biggest crowd ever to watch a shinty match is believed to have been at Murrayfield in Edinburgh, now home of Scotland's rugby team. The occasion was the 1948 Edinburgh Highland Games. The teams were Newtonmore and Ballachulish and instead of a trophy the prize for this game were sets of pots and pans! The Sutherland Cup began in 1918 to provide a competition for junior clubs.

THE MODERN GAME

Shinty is played by teams of 12, each player armed with a curved stick known as a *caman*. The caman used to be made from a piece of ash or hickory cut from a tree with a natural bend in it; modern shinty sticks are manufactured using strips of wood glued together or from fibre-glass and aluminium. The ball is more or less the same size as a tennis ball, but the interior is made of cork and woollen fabric and the ball is covered in leather. The game is similar to hockey but there are significant differences. In shinty, the feet can be used to stop the ball and the ball may be carried on the caman, which can be swung above shoulder level.

There are currently 38 shinty clubs in Scotland competing in leagues and a variety of cup competitions, often dominated by Speyside rivals Kingussie and Newtonmore. Although, in the past it was usual in the Highlands to hold the principal games at New Year (1 January) or Old New Year (12 or 13 January), shinty is nowadays played virtually all year round. In the old contests, there was no limit to the numbers taking part. Players arrived and departed at will, and often play continued from the morning until darkness fell. New Year matches are still held in Skye, Lewis, Fort William and Inverness.

There are no international matches apart from play against Irish hurling teams, which has happened sporadically since 1897. The first of these meetings took place in Glasgow, where Scotland won 11-2, and was followed by a return match in Dublin, also won by Scotland 2-0. Subsequent matches were played in the 1920s and 1932. The series resumed in the 1970s, when the Irish had the better of the exchanges, and again in the late 1980s. The challenges have been held annually since 1993 and are played alternately in Scotland and Ireland, usually in October.

On 3 October 1993, the Camanachd Association began a year-long series of special events marking its centenary as shinty's ruling body. In a reconstruction of the 1893 match between Kingussie and Cowal at The Dell, the players and spectators were led to the field in procession, with pipers at the head.

SKIING

Compared with other sports, skiing in Scotland is a relatively recent introduction. It dates back to 1890, when W. W. Naismith, founder of the Scottish Mountaineering Club, ventured into the hills on wooden Nordic-style skis to test the efficacy of skis as a form of cross-country transport. However, Nordic skiing did not catch on in Scotland because snow conditions were – as they remain – too unpredictable, there were few dependable routes, and the equipment was heavy and cumbersome.

Scotland offered more potential for the development of Alpine, or downhill skiing, and the Scottish Ski Club was founded in 1907, shortly after the Ski Club of Great Britain (founded 1903). The founder members of the Club were all mountaineers and included Naismith.

Alpine skiing was just becoming popular in Scotland when World War I broke out. The Scottish Ski Club did not reconvene until 1929. By that time equipment had improved, and this, plus easier access to the hills and a string of cold, snowy winters, all generated a surge in popularity of skiing in the 1930s and 1940s. Powered ski-tows were introduced on Ben Lawers, Glen Clunie and Glenshee in the late 1940s, and the first permanent ski-lift in Scotland was installed at Glencoe in

1956. The development of Aviemore as Scotland's first snow sports centre began in the early 1960s and it is still Scotland's principal centre for snow sports.

Skiing and snowboarding now take place at five major resorts: Glenshee, The Lecht and Cairngorm (near Aviemore) and Glencoe and Aonach Mor in the Nevis range. National and international events are staged, weather permitting. The uncertainty of weather conditions is the greatest obstacle faced by snow sports and the resort facilities that depend on them. A succession of mild winters in the 1990s, for instance, has seriously threatened the viability of the companies who run the resorts.

However, there are artificial slopes at some of the major resorts and elsewhere in Scotland. The biggest dry ski slope in Europe is at Edinburgh's Hillend Park.

The Scottish National Ski Council (SNSC) was formed in 1963. It was renamed Snowsport Scotland in 1998 and is the national governing body for all sports that take place on snow and artificial slopes in Scotland. At January 2003, 36 clubs were affiliated to Snowsport Scotland; many of them were involved in setting up the SNSC in 1963 and are still actively involved in running its successor.

WALKING AND MOUNTAINEERING

Scotland is a walker's paradise. It has thousands of walks and climbs on coastal footpaths, nature trails, woodland trails, long-distance footpaths and hundreds of mountain peaks. It is known worldwide for its rock climbs.

The earliest recorded rock climb in the UK took place in 1698, on Stac na Biorrach, St Kilda, by Sir Robert Murray. The first recorded ascent of Ben Nevis was that of James Robertson in 1771; Ben MacDui and Braeriach were both climbed in 1810 by the Revd George Keith.

Scotland has 284 mountains over 3,000 feet (914 metres) high, and these have become known as Munros, after Sir Hugh Munro, who first listed them in 1891. Sir Hugh's list has undergone several revisions over the years, most recently in 1998, when the number of peaks increased from 277 to 284. Munro himself died in 1909 just before climbing the last of the 238 summits he had identified; however, they had already been conquered by the Revd A. E. Robertson in 1901, who achieved the feat over a period of 10 years. In 1974, Hamish Brown completed the challenge of 277 Munros, covering 1639 miles and 449,000 feet (136,855 metres) of ascent in just 112 days. Kathy Murgatroyd repeated this feat for the women

in 1982. George Keeping was the first to complete the entire round on foot in 1984. Hugh Symonds climbed all the Munros in 66 days and 22 hours in 1990. Munro-bagging, as it has become known, is a popular pastime, especially since most of the Munros are reasonably accessible and within easy reach of public roads.

Peaks between 2,500 and 3,000 feet (762–914 metres) in height, with a drop of at least 500 feet (152.4 metres) between each listed hill and any adjacent higher one, are called Corbetts. They are named after J. Rooke Corbett, who listed them in 1930. Currently 222 mountains are classed as Corbetts. The current record for completing all the Munros and Corbetts was set by Craig Caldwell in 1985-86 when he achieved the feat in 377 days. A further list of hills in the Lowlands of 2,000-2,500 feet (609-762 metres) was produced by Percy Donald, giving these hills the nickname of Donalds. In 1992, the popular walking magazine *The Great Outdoors* published a list of 244 hills compiled by Fiona Graham. The list included every hill between 2,000 feet and 2,500 feet in the Highlands. A Graham must have a descent all round of 150 metres, or be the highest point for two miles all round.

The principal hill-walking and climbing areas are in the Highlands, include Glencoe, Lochaber, the Cairngorms, the Monadhliath, Kintail, Wester Ross, Torridon, and Skye. The accepted freedom to roam allows extensive walking and climbing, although access may be restricted during the lambing season (April and May) and the deerstalking season (mid-August to around 20 October). Rules regarding access to land were further formalised recently when the Land Reform Bill passed through the Scottish Parliament and was given the Royal Assent in March 2003. The Land Reform Bill will not come into force until Scottish ministers have approved the Scottish Outdoors Access Code (SOAC), likely to come into law, at time of writing, in November 2003. The new SOAC will, amongst other things, confer rights of access to all classes of users, such as cyclists, horseriders, canoeists and the disabled, as well as walkers and climbers.

Scotland has several long-distance footpaths (LDFs). By far the longest is the Southern Upland Way, which crosses the country from coast to coast, is 212 miles. The best known is the West Highland Way, which runs for 95 miles from Milngavie on the outskirts of Glasgow to Fort William at the southern end of the Great Glen. This is eventually expected to link up with the Great Glen Way which, when completed, will run from Fort William to Inverness. The final section of the Speyside Way, Ballindalloch to Aviemore, was officially opened on 8 April 2000. The route now stretches for some 65 to 80 miles, including all the spurs, from Buckie on the Moray coast to Aviemore. St Cuthbert's Way spans the border, stretching 60 miles from Melrose to Lindisfarne in Northumberland. Many other cross-country routes include drove roads, the long-established paths through the hills along which clansmen once led their cattle to or from markets held in the larger settlements.

SCOTTISH RIGHTS OF WAY SOCIETY
John Cotton Business Centre, 10–12 Sunnyside, Edinburgh EH7 5RA Tel: 0131-652-2937

The hillphones service has been organised by the Mountaineering Council of Scotland and Scottish Natural Heritage with aims of improving communications between deerstalking and hillwalking. The Hillphones scheme runs for three complete months each year from 1 August to 31 October. The official dates for the stag stalking season are July 1st to October 20th, although most estates don't start until late August and some start in late September. A number of estates do not stalk on Saturdays, but it is against the law to stalk on Sundays. The hillphone messages give an indication of the whereabouts of stalking over the following few days as well as giving a more detailed report on the location of stalking for that day. Walkers who are planning to go to the hills for the weekend often call the Hillphone on the Thursday or Friday to see if there is a forecast for the Saturday. Weather information for walkers and climbers is provided by the Met. Office. All map numbers given are in the Ordnance Survey Landranger Map (OSLM) series.

Hillphones: Grey Corries and Mamore, including Sgurr Eilde Mor and Stob Coire Easain (Tel: 01855-831511). Map 41

Glen Dochart and Glen Lochay, including Meall Glas and Sgiath Chuil (Tel: 01567-820886). Map 51.

North Arran Hills, covering the northern half of the island (Tel: 01770-302363). Map 69.

South Glen Shiel, including The Saddle and the South Cluanie Ridge (Tel: 01599-511425). Map 33.

Drumochter, including Geal Charn and A'Bhuidheanach Bheag (Tel: 01528-522200). Map 43.

Glenshee, including Carn a'Gheoidh and Creag, Leacach (Tel: 01250-885288). Map 43.

Callater and Clunie, including Carn an t-Sagairt Mor and Carn an Tuirc (Tel: 01339-741997). Map 43 and 44.

Invercauld, including Ben Avon and Beinn a'Bhuird (Tel: 01339-741911). Map 36 and 43.

Balmoral and Lochnagar, including White Mounth (Tel: 01339-755532). Map 44.

Glen Clova, including Driesh and Tom Buidhe (Tel: 01575-550335). Map 44.

Paps of Jura, including Beinn Chaolais, Beinn an Oir and Beinn Shiantaidh (Tel: 01496-820151). Map 61.

Atholl and Lude, including Beinn a'Ghlo and Beinn Dearg (Tel: 01796-481740). Map 43.

MUNROS
The 284 Munros in Scotland are listed below with their heights given in metres and feet. All map numbers given are in the Ordnance Survey Landranger Map (OSLM) series.

Ben Nevis, 1,344m, 4,409f, map 41.
Ben Macdui, 1,309m, 4,295f, map 36.
Braeriach, 1,296m, 4,252f, map 36.
Cairn Toul, 1,292m, 4,236f, map 36.
Sgor an Lochain Uaine, 1,258m, 4,127f, map 36.
Cairn Gorm 1,245m, 4,085f, map 36.
Aonach Beag (Lochaber), 1,234m, 4,049f, map 41.
Aonach Mor, 1,221m, 4,006f, map 41.
Carn Mor Dearg, 1,220m, 4,003f, map 41.
Ben Lawyers, 1,214m, 3,983f, map 51.
Beinn a'Bhuird, – North Top 1,197m, 3927f, map 36.
Carn Eige, 1,183m, 3,881f, map 25.
Beinn Mheadhoin, 1,182m, 3,878f, map 36.
Mam Sodhail, 1,181m, 3,875f, map 25.
Stob Choire Claurigh, 1,177m, 3,862f, map 41.
Ben More, (Crianlarich), 1,174m, 3,852f, map 51.
Ben Avon – Leabaidh an Daimh Bhuidhe, 1,171m, 3,842f, map 36.
Stob Binnein, 1,165m, 3,822f, map 51.
Beinn Bhrotain, 1,157m, 3,796f, map 43.
Derry Cairngorm, 1,155m, 3,789f, map 36.
Lochnagar – Cac Carn Beag, 1,155m, 3,789f, map 44.
Sgurr nan Ceathreamhnan, 1,151m, 3,776f, map 25.
Bidean nam Bian, 1,150m, 3,773f, map 41.
Sgurr na Lapaich, 1,150m, 3,773f, map 25.
Ben Alder, 1,148m, 3,766f, map 42.
Geal-charn (Loch Pattack), 1,132m, 3,714f, map 42.
Creag Meagaidh, 1,130m, 3,707f, map 34.
Ben Lui, 1,130m, 3,707f, map 50.

Binnein Mor, 1,230m, 3,707f, map 41.
An Riabhachan, 1,129m, 3,704f, map 25.
Ben Cruachan, 1,126m, 3,694f, map 50.
Beinn a'Ghlo – Carn nan Gabhar, 1121m, 3678f, map 43.
A'Chralaig, 1,120m, 3,674f, map 33.
Sgor Gaoith, 1,118m, 3,668f, map 36.
Meall Garbh (Lawers), 1,118m, 3,668f, map 51.
An Stuc, 1,118m, 3,668f, map 51.
Aonach Beag (Badenoch), 1,116m, 3,661f, map 42.
Stob Coire an Laoigh, 1,116m, 3,661f, map 41.
Stob Coire Easain, 1,115m, 3,658f, map 41.
Monadh Mor, 1,113m, 3,652f, map 43.
Tom a'Choinich, 1,112m, 3,648f, map 25.
White Mounth, – Carn a'Coire Bhaidheach 1,110m, 3,642f, map 44.
Sgurr Mor (Fannichs), 1,110m, 3,642f, map 20.
Sgurr nan Conbhairean, 1,109m, 3,638f, map 34.
Meall a'Bhuiridh, 1,108m, 3,635f, map 41.
Stob a'Choire Mheadhoin, 1,105m, 3,625f, map 41.
Beinn Ghlas, 1,103m, 3,619f, map 51.
Beinn Eibhinn, 1,102m, 3,615f, map 42.
Mullach Fraoch-choire, 1,102m, 3,615f, map 33.
Creise, 1,100m, 3,609f, map 41.
Sgurr d'Mhaim, 1,099m, 3,606f, map 41.
Sgurr Choinnich Mor, 1,094m, 3,589f, map 41.
Sgurr nan Clach Geala, 1,093m, 3,586f, map 20.
Bynack More, 1,090m, 3,576f, map 36.
Stob Ghabhar, 1,093m, 3,576f, map 50.
Beinn a'Chlachair, 1,087m, 3,566f, map 42.
Beinn Dearg (Ross-shire), 1,084m, 2,556f, map 20.
Schiehallion, 1,083m, 3,553f, map 51.
Sgurr a'Choire Ghlais, 1,083m, 3,553f, map 25.
Beinn a'Chaorainn, (Cairngorms), 1,082m, 3,550f, map 36.
Beinn a'Chreachain, 1,081m, 3,547f, map 50.
Beinn Heasgarnich, 1,078m, 3,537f, map 51.
Ben Starav, 1,087m, 3,537f, map 50.
Beinn Dorain, 1,076m, 3,530f, map 50.
Stob Coire Sgreamhach, 1,072m, 3,517f, map 41.
Braigh Coire Chruinn-bhalgain, 1,070m, 3,510f, map 43.
Meall Corranaich, 1,069m, 3,507f, map 51.
An Socach, (Glen Cannich), 1,069m, 3,507f, map 25.
Glas Maol, 1,068m, 3,504f, map 43.
Sgurr Fhuaran, 1,067m, 3,501f, map 33.
Cairn of Claise, 1,064m, 3,491f, map 43.
An Teallach – Bidein a'Ghlas Thuill, 1,062m, 3,484f, map 19.
An Teallach – Sgurr Fiona, 1,060m, 3,478f, map 19.
Na Gruagauichean, 1,055m, 2,461f, map 41.
Liathach – Spidean a'Choire Leith, 1,055m, 3,461f, map 25.
Stob Poite Coire Ardair, 1,053m, 3,455f, map 34.
Toll Creagach, 1,053m, 3,455f, map 25.
Sgurr a'Chaorachain, 1,053m, 3,448f, map 25.

Glas Tulaichean, 1,051m, 3,445f, map 43.
Beinn a'Chaorainn (Glen Spean), 1,050m, 3,442f, map 34.
Geal Charn (Loch Laggan), 1,049m, 3,442f, map 42.
Sgurr Fhuar-thuill, 1,049m, 3,435f, map 25.
Carn an t-Sagairt Mor, 1,047m, 3,435f, map 44.
Creag Mhor (Glen Lochay), 1,047m, 3,435f, map 50.
Cruach Ardrain, 1,046m, 3,432f, map 51.
Chno Dearg, 1,046m, 3,432f, map 41.
Ben Wyvis – Glas Leathad Mor, 1,046m, 3,432f, map 20.
Beinn Lutharn Mhor, 1,045m, 3,428f, map 43.
Stob Coir'an Albannaich, 1,044m, 3,425f, map 50.
Meall nan Tarmachan, 1,044m, 3,425f, map 51.
Carn Mairg, 1,042m, 3,419f, map 51.
Sgurr na Ciche, 1,040m, 3,412f, map 33.
Meall Ghaordaidh, 1,039m, 3,409f, map 51.
Beinn Achaladair, 1,038m, 3,405f, map 50.
Carn a'Mhaim, 1,037m, 3,402f, map 36.
Sgurr d'Bhealaich Dheirg, 1,036m, 3,399f, map 33.
Gleouraich, 1,035m, 3,396f, map 33.
Carn Dearg (Loch Pattack), 1,034m, 3,392f, map 42.
Am Bodach, 1,032m, 3,386f, map 41.
Beinn Fhada, 1,032m, 3,386f, map 33.
Carn an Righ, 1,029m, 3,376f, map 43.
Ben Oss, 1,029m, 3,376f, map 50.
Carn Gorm, 1,028m, 3,373f, map 51.
Sgurr d'Mhaoraich, 1,027m, 3,369f, map 33.
Sgurr na Ciste Duibhe, 1,027m, 3,369f, map 33.
Ben Challum, 1,025m, 3,363f, map 50.
Beinn a'Bheithir – Sgorr Dhearg, 1,024m, 3,360f, map 41.
Liathach – Mullach an Rathain, 1,023m, 3,356f, map 25.
Buachaille Etive Mor – Stob Dearg, 1,022m, 3,353f, map 41.
Aonach air Chrith, 1,021m, 3,350f, map 33.
Ladhar Bheinn, 1,020m, 3,346f, map 33.
Beinn Bheoil, 1,019m, 3,343f, map 42.
Carn an Tuirc, 1,019m, 3,343f, map 43.
Mullach Clach a'Bhlair, 1,019m, 3,343f, map 35.
Mullach Coire Mhic Fhearchair, 1,019m, 3,343f, map 19.
Garbh Choich Mhor, 1,013m, 3,323f, map 33.
Cairn Bannoch, 1,012m, 3,320f, map 44.
Beinn Udlamain, 1,011m, 3,317f, map 42.
Beinn Ime, 1,011m, 3,317f, map 56.
Sgurr an Doire Leathain, 1,010m, 3,314f, map 33.
The Saddle, 1,010m, 3,314f, map 33.
Beinn Eighe – Ruadh-stac Mor, 1,010m, 3,314f, map 19.
Sgurr Eilde Mor, 1,010m, 3,314f, map 41.
Beinn Dearg (Atholl), 1,008m, 3,307f, map 43.
Maoile Lunndaidh, 1,007m, 3,304f, map 25.
An Sgarsoch, 1,006m, 3,300f, map 43.
Carn Liath (Loch Laggan), 1,006m, 3,300f, map 34.

Beinn Fhionnlaidh (Glen Cannich), 1,005m, 3297f, map 25.

Beinn an Dothaidh, 1,004m, 3,294f, map 50.

The Devil's Point, 1,004m, 3,294f, map 43.

Sgurr an Lochain, 1,004m, 3,294f, map 33.

Sgurr Mor (Loch Quoich), 1,003m, 3,291f, map 33.

Sail Chaorainn, 1,002m, 3,287f, map 34.

Sgurr na Carnach, 1,002m, 3,287f, map 33.

Aonach Meadhoin, 1,001m, 3,284f, map 33.

Meall Greigh, 1,001m, 3,284f, map 51.

Beinn a'Bheithir – Sgorr Dhonuill, 1,001m, 3,284f, map 41.

Stob Ban (Mamores), 999m, 3,278f, map 41.

Sgurr Choinnich, 999m, 3,278f, map 25.

Sgurr Breac, 999m, 3,278f, map 20.

Broad Cairn, 998m, 3,274f, map 44.

Stob Diamh, 998m, 3,274f, map 50.

Ben More Assynt, 998m, 3,274f, map 15.

Glas Beinn Mhor, 997m, 3,271f, map 50.

A'Chailleach (Fannichs), 997m, 3,271f, map 19.

Spidean Mialach, 996m, 3,268f, map 33.

An Caisteal, 995m, 3,264f, map 50.

Sgor na h-Ulaidh, 994m, 3,261f, map 41.

Carn an Fhidhlier (Carn Eelar), 994m, 3,261f, map 43.

Sgurr na Ruaidhe, 993m, 3,258f, map 25.

Beinn Eighe – Spidean Coire nan Clach, 993m, 3,258f, map 25.

Carn nan Gobhar (Glen Strathfarrar), 992m, 3,255f, map 25.

Carn nan Gobhar (Glen Cannich), 992m, 3,255f, map 25.

Sgurr Alasdair, 992m, 3,255f, map 32.

Sgairneach Mhor, 991m, 3,251f, map 42.

Beinn Eunaich, 989m, 3,254f, map 50.

Sgurr Ban, 989m, 3245f, map 19.

Conival, 987m, 3,238f, map 15.

Creag Leachach, 987m, 3,238f, map 43.

Druim Shionnach, 987m, 3,238f, map 33.

Gaor Bheinn (Gulvain), 987m, 3,238f, map 41.

Sgurr Dearg – Inaccessible Pinnacle, 986m, 3,235f, map 32.

Lurg Mhor, 986m, 3,235f, map 25.

Beinn Alligin – Sgurr Mhor, 986m, 3,235f, map 19.

Ben Vorlich (Loch Earn), 985m, 3,232f, map 57.

An Gearanach, 982m, 3,222f, map 41.

Mullach na Dheiragain, 982m, 3,222f, map 25.

Creag Mhor (Glen Lyon), 981m, 3,218f, map 51.

Stob Coire a'Chairn, 981m, 3,218f, map 41.

Maol Chinn-dearg, 981m, 3,218f, map 33.

Slioch, 981m, 3218f, map 19.

Beinn a'Chochuill, 980m, 3,215f, map 50.

Cona'Mheall, 980m, 3,215f, map 20.

Stob Coire Sgriodain, 979m, 3,212f, map 41.

Ciste Dhubh, 979m, 3,212f, map 33.

Beinn Dubhchraig, 978m, 3,209f, map 50.

Meall nan Ceapraichean, 977m, 3,205f, map 20.

Stob ban (Grey Corries), 977m, 3,205f, map 41.

Carn a'Gheoidh, 975m, 3,199f, map 43.

Carn Liath (Beinn a'Ghlo), 975m, 3,199f, map 43.

A'Mharconaich, 975m, 3,199f, map 42.

Stuc a'Chroin, 975m, 3,199f, map 57.

Ben Lomond, 974m, 3,195f, map 56.

Beinn Sgritheall, 974m, 3,195f, map 33.

Sgurr a'Ghreadaidh, 973m, 3,192m, map 32.

Meall Garbh (Glen Lyon), 968m, 3,176f, map 51.

Aonach Eagach – Sgor nam Fiannaidh, 967m, 3,173f, map 41.

A'Mhaighdean, 967m, 3,173f, map 19.

Ben More (Mull), 966m, 3,169f, map 48.

Sgurr na Banachdich – North Peak, 965m, 3,166f, map 32.

Sgurr nan Gillean, 964m, 3,163f, map 32.

Carn a'Chlamain, 963m, 3,159f, map 43.

Sgurr Thuilm, 963m, 3,159f, map 40.

Sgorr Ruadh, 962m, 3,156f, map 25.

Ben Klibreack – Meall nan Con, 961m, 3,153f, map 16.

Stuchd an Lochain, 960m, 3,150f, map 51.

Meall Glas, 959m, 3,146f, map 51.

Beinn Fhionnlaidh (Appin), 959m, 3,146f, map 50.

Buachaille Etive Beag – Stob Dubh, 958m, 3,143f, map 41.

Tolmount, 958m, 3,143f, map 44.

Bruach na Frithe, 958m, 3,143f, map 32.

Beinn nan Aighenan, 957m, 3,140f, map 50.

Tom Buidhe, 957m, 3,140f, map 44.

Carn Ghluasaid, 957m, 3,140f, map 34.

Sgurr nan Coireachan (Glen Finnan), 956m, 3,136f, map 40.

Saileag, 956m, 3,136f, map 33.

Buachaille Etive Mor – Stob na Broige, 956m, 3,136f, map 41.

Sgor Gaibhre, 955m, 3,133f, map 42.

Beinn Liath Mhor Fannaich, 954m, 3,130f, map 20.

Am faochagach, 954m, 3,130f, map 20.

Sgurr nan Coireachan (Glen Dessarry), 953m, 3,127f, map 33.

Beinn Mhanach, 953m, 3,127f, map 50.

Meall Dearg, 953m, 3,127f, map 41.

Meall Chuaich, 951m, 3,120f, map 42.

Meall Gorm, 949m, 3,113f, map 20.

Beinn Bhuidhe, 948m, 3,110f, map 56.

Sgurr Mhic Choinnich, 948m, 3,110f, map 32.

Driesh, 947m, 3,107f, map 44.

Creag a'Mhaim, 947m, 3,107f, map 33.

Beinn Tulaichean, 946m, 3,104f, map 56.

Carn Bhac, 946m, 3,104f, map 43.

Meall Buidhe (Knoydart), 946m, 3,104f, map 33.

Stob a'Choire Odhair, 945m, 3,100f, map 50.

Bidein a'Choire Sheasgaich, 945m, 3,100f, map 25.

Varn Dearg (Monadh Liath), 945m, 3,100f, map 35.

Sgurr na Sgine, 945m, 3,100f, map 33.

An Socach (Glen Ey) – West Summit, 944m, 3,097f, map 43.

Sgurr Dubh Mor, 944m, 3,097f, map 32.

Ben Vorlich (Loch Lomond), 943m, 3,094f, map 56.
Binnein Beag, 943m, 3,094f, map 41.
Carn na Caim, 941m, 3,087f, map 42.
Carn Dearg (Loch Ossian), 941m, 3,087f, map 42.
Beinn d'Chroin, 940m, 3,084f, map 50.
Mullach nan Coirean, 939m, 3,081f, map 41.
Mount Keen, 939m, 3,081f, map 44.
Luinne Bheinn, 939m, 3,081f, map 33.
Beinn Sgulaird, 937m, 3,074f, map 50.
Beinn na Lap, 937m, 3,074f, map 41.
Beinn tarsuinn, 937m, 3,074f, map 19.
A'Bhuidheanach Bheag, 936m, 3,071f, map 42.
Sron a'Choire Ghairbh, 935m, 3,068f, map 34.
Meall a'Chrasgaidh, 934m, 3,064f, map 20.
Am Basteir, 934m, 3064f, map 32.
Beinn Chabhair, 933m, 3,061f, map 50.
The Cairnwell, 933m, 3,061f, map 43.
Maol Chean-dearg, 933m, 3,061f, map 25.
Fionn Bheinn, 933m, 3,061f, map 20.
Meall Buidhe (Glen Lyon), 932m, 3,058f, map 51.
Ben Chonzie, 931m, 3,054f, map 51.
Beinn Bhreac, 931m, 3,054f, map 43.
A'Chailleach (Monadh Liath), 930m, 3,051f, map 35.
Meall nan Eun, 928m, 3,045f, map 50.
Mayar, 928m, 3,045f, map 44.
Moruisg, 928m, 3,045f, map 25.
Bla Bheinn (Blaven), 928m, 3,045f, map 32.
Eididh nan Clach Geala, 928m, 3,045f, map 20.
Ben Hope, 927m, 3,041f, map 9.
Seana Bhraigh, 927m, 3,041f, map 20.
Meall a'Choire Leith, 926m, 3,038f, map 51.
Geal Charn (Monadh Liath), 926m, 3,038f, map 35.
Beinn Narnain, 926m, 3,038f, map 56.
Beinn Liath Mhor, 926m, 3,038f, map 25.
Buachille Etive Beag – Stob Coire Raineach, 925m, 3,035f, map 41.
Creag Pitridh, 924m, 3,031f, map 42.
Sgurr nan Eag, 924m, 3,031f, map 32.
Sgurr nan each, 923m, 3,028f, map 20.
An Coileachan, 923m, 3,028f, map 20.
Beinn Alligin – Tom na Gruagaich, 922m, 3,025f, map 19.
Sgiath Chuil, 921m, 3,022f, map 51.
An Socach (Glen Affric), 921m, 3,022f, map 25.
Carn Sgulain, 920m, 3,018f, map 35.
Gairich, 919m, 3,015f, map 33.
Ruadh Stac Mor, 918m, 3,012f, map 19.
Sgurr a'Mhadidh – Southwest Peak, 918m, 3,012f, map 32.
A'Ghlas-bheinn, 918m, 3,012f, map 25.
Creag nan Damh, 918m, 3,012f, map 33.
Meall na Teanga, 917m, 3,008f, map 34.
Carn Aosda, 917m, 3,008f, map 43.
Geal-charn (Drumochter), 917m, 3,008f, map 42.
Beinn a'Chleibh, 916m, 3,005f, map 50.
Beinn a'Chlaidheimh, 916m, 2,005f, map 19.

Ben Vane, 916m, 3,005f, map 56.
Sgurr nan Ceannaichean, 915m, 3,002f, map 25.
Beinn Teallach, 915m, 3,002f, map 34.

WRESTLING

Scottish wrestling is known as 'backhold' and has a style and rules that are different from those of standard wrestling. The Scottish Amateur Wrestling Association organises and registers wrestlers. The sport is still quite widespread in Scotland, and is most commonly practised at Highland Games. In backhold, the wrestlers take hold of each other's waist with the right hand under the left arm. Both men then close their hands and when the referee shouts 'Hold', the bout commences. If any part of a wrestler's body, except the soles of his feet, touches the ground, he loses the bout. The wrestlers are not permitted to break their grip until the opponent is on the ground. Bouts are normally the best of three or five.

The earliest depiction of wrestling in Scotland is to be found on two carved Pictish stones dating from the 6th- and 7th-centuries, which are housed in the National Museum of Antiquities in Edinburgh.

In the Western Isles, wrestling was made popular by the men of a Highland regiment known as the Lovat Scouts, formed in 1900. The Highlanders practised two forms of wrestling, one using the same rules as the rest of Scotland and an alternative form which did not allow tripping of opponents, which developed in Europe into the 'classical' style of wrestling. An ancient Norse style of wrestling known as Hryggspenna is still practised in the Hebrides.

YACHTING

Pioneered in the Netherlands during the 17th-century, boats offered practical ways and means of travelling along the waterways throughout the country. Modern yachting was introduced to Britain by Charles II, who was given a Dutch pleasure boat named Mary shortly after his return from exile in the Low Countries in 1660 and went on to build a fleet of pleasure craft. The word 'yacht' comes from the Dutch word jaght, which means a small cargo or passenger carrier. In the early 18th-century yachting was considered a rather eccentric occupation because of the discomforts associated with it.

However, sailing off the west coast of Scotland and among the western and northern islands is now a very popular pastime and sport, although the weather and currents can be tricky. Several yachting events take place each year, generally during the summer. Yacht races of the famous Scottish Series off the west coast and the Round Mull Three-Day Yacht Race, held in June, are the largest events. During May there is also an annual race between Bergen in Norway and Shetland. The Scottish Hebridean Islands Peak Race is the biggest combined sailing and fell-running competition in the world.

OTHER SPORTS IN BRIEF

The first *skating* club in Britain was the Edinburgh Ice Skating Society, formed in 1778.

The first *lacrosse* club in Britain was the Glasgow Lacrosse Club founded in 1867.

Orienteering in the UK was inaugurated by the Scottish Council of Physical Recreation at the 1962 Championships held at Dunkeld in Perthshire.

The oldest *rowing* club in Scotland is the St Andrews Boat Club, Edinburgh, formed in 1850.

The oldest *archery* club is the Society of Kilwinning Archers. They have contested the Papingo Shoot since 1488.

The oldest surviving *Royal (Real) tennis* court in Britain and still in use is at Falkland Palace, built for James V in 1539.

SCOTTISH SPORTSMEN & SPORTSWOMEN

SCOTLAND'S OLYMPIC MEDALLISTS, SYDNEY 2000

In the Olympic games held in Sydney in September 2000, Scotland's athletes won a total of nine medals (three gold and six silver), a number not equalled since the 1912 Stockholm Games, when Scottish athletes carried off seven gold, one silver and one bronze medals. The 2000 games also gave Scotland's participants their first gold medals since the 1988 Seoul games, and represented a huge improvement on the 1996 Atlanta Games, where Scottish competitors, participating as always as part of the UK team, won a solitary bronze medal.

Stephanie Cook (1972–). Athlete, born Irvine. Gold, women's modern pentathlon. This was the first time the event had been included in the Olympics. She received an OBE in 2001.

Mark Covell (1967–). Yachtsman, born Glasgow. Covell was the crewman and Ian Walker was at the helm when they won silver in the two-man star yachting event. They teamed up in 1999 after two tragedies: Walker had lost his partner in a car crash in 1997 and Covell's helm Glynn Charles perished in the storm-ravaged 1999 Sydney–Hobart race.

Covell also won gold at the 1997 and 1998 world championships, in the 5.5 metre class.

Katherine Grainger (1975–). Rower, born Glasgow. Silver, quadruple sculls, with fellow Scot Gillian Lindsay and Guin and Miriam Batten; they were the first British women ever to win an Olympic medal for rowing. Grainger also won gold at the 1996 Henley Regatta coxless pairs, the 1997 world junior championships coxless pairs, and the 1998 British championships single sculls.

Chris Hoy (1976–). Cyclist, born Edinburgh. Silver, as member of Olympic sprint cycle team. Also won gold at 1998 British championships Olympic sprint and 1999 European championships Olympic sprint, and silver at 1999 and 2000 world championships Olympic sprint. Represented Scotland at the 1987 BMX world championships. Won a Gold medal in the 1km time trial at the 2002 Commonwealth Games in Manchester.

Andrew Lindsay (1977–). Rower, born in Portree, Skye. Gold, men's eight. Lindsay rowed in the key position of bow to help Great Britain win in this blue riband event – the first time Britain had won the men's eight since the 1912 Olympics in Stockholm, which had also included two Scots, Philip Fleming and Angus Gillan. Lindsay also won gold at the 2000 World Cup overall eights and bronze at the 1994 World Junior Championship eights.

Gillian Lindsay (1973–). Rower, born Paisley. Silver, quadruple sculls, with Katherine Grainger and Guin and Miriam Batten. Together with Miriam Batten, she won the scull pairs at the World Championships in 1998, the pair becoming the first British women to win a World Rowing Championship gold.

Craig MacLean (1971–). Cyclist, born Grantown-on-Spey. Silver, as member of Olympic sprint cycle team. Also won gold at 1998 British championships (1 km and sprint) and 1999 European Championships (Olympic sprint), and silver at 1999 and 2000 world championships (Olympic sprint). Represented Scotland at 1986 BMX world championships.

Shirley Robertson (1968–). Sailor, born Dundee. Gold, Europe class dinghy sailing; this made her the first Scottish woman to win an Olympic gold medal since 1912 and also Britain's first female Olympic sailing medallist. Won 4th place in 1996 Atlanta Olympics in this class. Awarded OBE in 2001.

Ian Stark (1954–). Badminton; born Galashiels. Became Scotland's most prolific Olympian by winning his fourth silver medal in the three-day team event at the Sydney 2000 Olympics. He also won silver medals for the same discipline in 1984 and 1988 Olympics, and silver for the three-day individual event in 1988. Also won gold medals at the 1991 European Championships (team and individual events), the 1997 European championships (team), and the 1999 Badminton International three-day event. Awarded OBE.

SCOTLAND'S PARALYMPIC MEDALLISTS, SYDNEY 2000

Great Britain finished second in the medal table with 41 gold, 43 silver and 47 bronze medals. The Scots in the British team won 8 gold, 14 silver and 10 bronze medals. At the 1996 Paralympic games in Atlanta, Scots won 9 gold, 11 silver and 7 bronze medals. The success of British athletes at the Sydney Paralympics was recognised with MBEs for Caroline Innes, who won two gold medals in the 200m and 400m, Kenny Cairns, who won silver in the 200m freestyle swimming, and Isabel Newstead, who won gold in the 10m air pistol and has amassed 14 medals in competition since the 1980 games, in a variety of disciplines including swimming, discus, shot, javelin and air pistol.

James Anderson (1963–) Swimming. 50m freestyle silver; 100m freestyle silver; 200m freestyle silver. Broke world records in all four of his events at the 1999 European Championships. Won two gold medals at 1996 Paralympics and three silvers in 1992 Paralympics.

Kenneth Cairns (1957–) Swimming. 100m freestyle gold; 50m freestyle silver; 200 metre freestyle silver (Paralympic Games record); 4 x 50m freestyle relay bronze. Gold winner European Championships 1997, 1999), World Championship 1998, Nordic Open 2000. Awarded MBE 2000.

Lara Ferguson (1980–) Swimming. 4 x 100m medley relay silver; 100m breaststroke bronze. Two golds in 1997 European Championships.

Kay Gebbie (1955–) Equestrianism. Freestyle gold; Team gold; set test bronze. Won gold medals at British Championships 2000 and 1998.

Caroline Innes (1974–) Athletics. 400m gold; 200m gold; 100m silver. Also won gold for 100m in 1996 Paralympics, and six gold medals in British and World Championships 1996–99. Awarded MBE 2000.

Paul Johnston (1974–) Swimming. 4 x 50m freestyle relay bronze. Won five golds in 1997 World Championships.

Pauline Latto (1975–) Athletics. Javelin silver. At 1998 British Championships, won four golds and was British record-holder in her class in 100m, 200m, 400m and javelin. Broke the world record in Class 7 javelin (23.5 m) at the CP-ISRA World Games in Nottingham in July 2001.

Janice Lawton (1948–) Athletics. Discus silver. Won gold at 1994 World Championships in javelin, and has garnered many silvers in javelin, discus and shot in various paralympic championships since 1994.

Andrew Lindsay (1979–) Swimming. 100m backstroke gold. Has also won gold in European Championships 1995, 1997, 1998, 1999 and 2000, and silver in 1996 Paralympics and 1997 European Championships.

Margaret McEleny (1965–) Swimming. 50m breaststroke gold; 150m individual medley bronze; 4 x 50m medley bronze. Also won two gold medals at European Championships 1999, two at World Championships 1998, and one at 1996 Paralympics. Awarded MBE 2000.

Isabel Newstead (1955–) Air pistol. 10m gold. Since 1988 has won paralympic gold medals in three sports – swimming (1980, 1984), shooting (2000), and discus (1988) – and many bronze and silver medals in other paralympic championships. Finished 6th overall in 1996 Paralympics. Awarded MBE 2000.

Paul Noble (1965–) Swimming. 4 x 100m medley relay silver. Golds at 1997 European Championships, 1992 and 1988 Paralympic Games.

Stephen Payton (1977–) Athletics. 400m silver; 4 x 100m relay silver; 100m bronze; 200m bronze. Has many golds to his credit: 2000 Australian Open, 2000 French Indoor Open, 1999 European Championships, 1998 World Championships (4), 1996 and 1994 Paralympic Games (3 each).

Allan Stuart (1981–) Athletics. 400m silver. Won gold at 2000 Cyprus Junior International, 2000 West of Scotland Championship – both able-bodied competitions. First athlete with a disability to represent a Scotland able-bodied team.

Tracy Wiscombe (1979–) Swimming. 200m freestyle silver; 50m freestyle bronze; 100m freestyle bronze. Won six golds in European Championships 1999, two in 1998 World Championship, and two at 1996 Paralympic Games.

SCOTLAND'S OLYMPIC MEDALLISTS, SALT LAKE CITY 2002

In the Olympic games held in Salt Lake City, USA, in February 2002, Scotland's athletes won one medal (gold), the first gold medal for Scotland, or Britain, in almost 20 years.

Rhona Martin (1966–). Curler. Won a silver medal at the 1998 European Championships and was named Scottish Ladies Champion in 2000. Skip of the 2002 Olympic team that won gold at Salt Lake City. Awarded OBE.

Margaret Morton (1968–). Curler. Morton took fourth place at the European Championships in 1999 and the World Championships in 2000. Second in command to Rhona Martin at the Salt Lake City Olympics but took on the role of fifth player in the round robin. Awarded OBE.

Fiona MacDonald (1974–). Curler. A former World Junior Champion (1993), MacDonald only made her senior competitive debut in 1999 and was the youngest member of the gold-winning British team. Awarded OBE.

Janice Rankin (1972–). Curler. Former World Junior Champion (1992). Silver medal winner at senior level in the World Championships ladies event in 1994 and the European Championships in 1998. Awarded OBE.

Debbie Knox (1968–). Curler. Has won gold medals at the 1992 and 1999 Scottish Ladies events and was a semifinalist at the 2000 World Championships, finishing fourth with Rhona Martin, fifth in 1992 and tenth in 1999. Third Player and deputy skip at Salt Lake City. Awarded OBE.

SCOTTISH SPORTING PERSONALITIES

ALL-ROUNDERS

Sir Thomas Lipton (1850–1931). Grocer and entrepreneur, born in Glasgow, who became a millionaire through his tea plantations in Sri Lanka. Started the World Cup in football in 1910. He also unsuccessfully challenged for the Americas Cup in yachting several times.

Leslie Balfour Melville (1854–1937). Possibly Scotland's greatest ever sportsman. His sports included golf, cricket, rugby union and tennis. He won the Scottish Lawn Tennis Championships in 1879 and the British Amateur Golf Championship in 1895. At one time he was captain of the Royal and Ancient Golf Club. He represented his country in rugby union against England in 1872. He is best remembered as a cricketer representing Scotland 1876–1910; in 1882, as captain, opening batsman and wicket-keeper, he led Scotland to victory over Australia.

ATHLETICS

Walter Menzies Campbell (1941–). Now a Liberal Democrat politician, and MP for North-east Fife since 1987, he was formerly a successful athlete and competed in the 1964 Olympic games in Tokyo and the 1966 Commonwealth Games in Jamaica. He held the British 100m record 1967–1974. He was awarded the CBE in 1987.

Eric Henry Liddell (1902-45). Born in Tientsin, China. At the 1924 Paris Olympics, owing to his religious principles, he refused to run in the 100m heats because they were held on a Sunday. However, he went on to win two medals at the Games, a bronze in the 200m and a gold in the 400m. His achievements are remembered in the 1981 film *Chariots of Fire*.

Liz McColgan (1964–). Long-distance runner, born in Dundee. She won the gold medal for the 10,000m at the 1986 and 1990 Commonwealth Games, silver for the same distance at the 1988 Olympic Games (Seoul) and bronze for the 3,000m in the 1990 Commonwealth Games. She was the 1990 world 10,000m champion and gained the UK women's record for the 10,000m in 1991. She had the fastest marathon debut, 2 hours 27.32 minutes, in the New York marathon and also won the London Marathon in 1996.

Tom McKean (1963–). Born in Bellshill. In his specialist distance, 800m, he won the European Cup in 1985, 1987 and 1989, the World Cup in 1989, and the European championships in 1990. He also won silver medals in the 1986 Commonwealth Games (Edinburgh) for the 800m and the 4 x 100m relay.

Duncan McLean (1884–1980). Had the longest career in the world in athletics. Having broken the record for the 100 yards sprint in 9.9 seconds in 1904, he set another world record for men of his age group, of 21.7 seconds for the same event 73 years later, in 1977, at the age of 92.

Yvonne Murray (1964–). Born in Edinburgh. Her specialist distance was 3,000m, in which she won bronze medals at the 1986 Commonwealth Games and the 1988 Olympics and silver at the 1986 European Championship and the 1990 Commonwealth Games. Gold medals, 3,000m, European Championships, 1990; 10,000m, Commonwealth Games, 1994. At various times during her career she held the Scottish women's record for 1,500m, 1 mile, 2,000m, 3,000m and 5,000m. Awarded th MBE in 1990.

Cameron Sharp (1960–). Gold medal, 4 x 100m relay, Commonwealth Games, Edmonton, 1978. Silver medal, 200m, European Championship, 1982. Bronze medals, 100m, 200m, and 4 x 100m relay, Commonwealth Games, Brisbane, 1982; 4 x 100m relay, Commonwealth Games, Edinburgh, 1986. He was involved in a serious car accident in 1991 which left him physically and mentally disabled.

Dougie Walker (1973–). Born in Inverness. Represented Scotland in the 1994 Commonwealth Games. Became the Commonwealth and European 300m record holder and won gold medals for the 200m and 4 x 100m relay in the 1998 European Championships.

Alan Wells (1952–). Born in Edinburgh. He won a gold medal in the 100m and a silver medal at the 200m at the 1978 Commonwealth Games. At the 1980 Olympics he won gold for the 100m and silver for the 200m, becoming the oldest-ever winner in the history of the Olympic 100m. He also won gold medals for the 100m and 200m at the 1982 Commonwealth Games in Brisbane.

BOXING

Ken Buchanan (1945–). Born in Edinburgh. Probably Scotland's greatest ever boxer. Became

world lightweight champion in 1970 and successfully defended the title before being beaten in 1972. In 1970 a New York journalists' poll declared him the best in the world, relegating Muhammad Ali to third place. He won back the European Lightweight Championship in 1972.

Sir John Sholto Douglas (1844–1900). Succeeded to the Queensberry title in 1858, becoming the 8th Marquis of Queensberry and Viscount Drumlanrig. Best known for devising the Queensberry Rules for boxing in 1867, and for his instrumental part in the trial and imprisonment of the playwright Oscar Wilde.

Benny Lynch (1913–1946). Born in Glasgow. As the first world flyweight champion, he also became the first Scot to hold a world boxing title, capturing both the world title in 1935, defending it successfully for three years, and then winning the American title in 1937. Also won the British and European flyweight titles. However, he died in poverty aged only 33.

Walter McGowan (1942–). Born in Burnbank, near Hamilton. He won the world flyweight championship in 1966, but lost that title in 1968, after fighting at bantamweight.

Jackie Paterson (1920–1966). Born in Springside, Ayrshire. Came to prominence by winning the World Flyweight Championship at Hampden in 1943. However, it was a title he was unable to defend, owing to the war and ill health, and he lost the title in 1948.

Alex 'Bud' Watson (1914–). Born in Leith. Has held the most titles in a boxing career, 10 in all, including the Scottish heavyweight title in 1938, and 1942–43, the lightweight championship 1937–39, 1943–45 and 1947, and the ABA (Amateur Boxing Association) light-heavyweight title in 1945 and 1947.

Jim Watt (1948–). Born in Glasgow. Became a professional boxer in 1968. British lightweight champion on two occasions; European lightweight champion 1977–79; world lightweight champion 1979–81, successfully defending his title on four occasions. Awarded the MBE in 1980.

CLIMBING & MOUNTAINEERING

James Robertson. Appointed by the Commissioners of the Forfeited Estates to carry out a botanical and mineralogical survey of the Highlands in the years after the 1745 rebellion, he made the first recorded ascents of several mountains over 3,000 feet, including Ben Hope, Ben Wyvis and Ben Kilbreck in 1767 and Ben Nevis in 1771.

Alexander Nicolson (1827–1893), born Huabost, Skye. Scotland's first mountaineer in the modern sense. At different times in his life a journalist, academic and sheriff-substitute, in 1865 he began exploring the Cuillin peaks, then still largely unknown to mountaineers. His four ascents of Sgurr nan Gillean are commemorated in the naming of a steep cleft leading to the summit as Nicolson's Chimney. He also made the first recorded ascents of Sgurr Alasdair (named after him, in the Gaelic form of his name) and Sgurr Dubh.

W. W. Naismith. A pioneer of Scottish mountaineering and a founder of the Scottish Mountaineering Club, 1889. Accomplished first recorded ascent of Crowberry Ridge in 1895/6 and a solo ascent of the Eiger in the 1880s. Also made first recorded use of skis in Scotland, 1890. In 1892 he developed a formula for estimating route times in the Scottish Highlands.

Dougal Haston (1940–1977). Born in Currie. Among other achievements, he was a member of the British team which conquered the south face of Annapurna in 1970, and later (1975) took part in the first ascent of the south-west face of Mount Everest and the first ascent of Mount McKinley in Alaska. He was also the first British mountaineer to climb the north face of the Eiger. Died in an avalanche in the Alps.

Hamish Brown (1934–). Born in Colombo. Has climbed and travelled widely in Scotland, the Alps, the Himalayas, the Andes, and the Atlas Mountains in Morocco, and has published over 20 books specialising in mountaineering and travel subjects. Completed all the Munros in a single 112-day trip (involving 449,000 feet of ascent), and has trekked the Atlas Mountains from end to end. Awarded the MBE in 2000.

Tom Patey (1934–1970). Rock-climber. Achieved unprecedented output of new rock- and ice-climbing routes in the 1950s and 1960s, among them winter routes on Lochnagar and Creag Meagaidh and a number of summer routes in the Northern Highlands. Together with Hamish MacInnes and Graeme Nicol, made first winter ascent of Zero Gully on Ben Nevis. In February 1965 he participated in the first winter traverse of the Cuillin Ridge by two ropes. Died in a fall from the Maiden seastack.

Hamish McInnes (1930–) Mountaineer and innovator in climbing and mountain rescue equipment. Has climbed Everest, many Alpine peaks, and the peak of Roraima in Brazil. Leader of Glencoe Mountain Rescue team and an international authority on mountain rescue. In 1957 he participated, with Tom Patey and Graeme Nicol, in the first winter ascent of Zero Gully on Ben Nevis. His designs for winter climbing tools culminated in the development, in 1970, together with Yvon Chouinard, of a curved ice axe pick which enabled standards in ice climbing to rise rapidly. Awarded OBE.

David Cuthbertson (1961–). A key member of a group of Scottish climbers who have pushed standards of rock and ice climbing forward from the late 1970s. He made new routes of extreme technical difficulty on outcrops and mountains in various Scottish locations, including the north peak of the Cobbler, in 1979 (with R. Kerr), Sron na Ciche in Skye (with Gary Latter), and Dumbarton Rock.

CRICKET

Mike Denness (1940–). Born in Bellshill, Lanarkshire. Scorer of 25,886 first-class runs between 1959 and 1980. Represented Scotland before captaining England 1973–1975. He was also a successful captain of Kent and Essex CCCs.

Gavin Hamilton (1974–). Born in Broxburn. An all-rounder who has represented both Scotland and England at international level. Since 1994 he has played his county cricket for Yorkshire. In the 1999 World Cup, playing for Scotland, he scored two fifties against strong opposition. Selected to tour South Africa with the England team in 1999–2000.

Brian Hardie (1950–). Born in Stenhousemuir. An all-rounder who has represented Scotland as well as Essex, for whom he won four championship medals in a 17-year career in English county cricket.

Douglas Jardine (1900–1958). Born in Bombay, of Scottish parents. He followed his father into the Oxford University team and made his debut with Surrey in 1923, becoming captain of Surrey in 1932 and, shortly after, of England. A controversial figure, he is mostly remembered as the captain of England in the 'bodyline' series of 1932–33 against Australia, where he directed his bowlers to aim short-pitched deliveries at the batsmen, a tactic used successfully against Don Bradman. Jardine left cricket after 1934.

Richard Nairn (*Nyren*) (*c.*1734–1797). A Jacobite who settled in Hampshire after the 1745 Rising. He introduced certain laws to the game of cricket, including the use of the middle stump.

CYCLING

Robert Millar. The only Scot to have won a stage in the Tour de France, capturing the 'King of the Mountains' stage in 1984 and finishing overall fourth in the tournament.

Graeme Obree (1965–). The most influential figure in bicycle dynamics for most of the 1990s. Developed the 'Superman' position in cycling, which has since been banned. Pursuit Olympic champion 1992. Won the 4,000m individual pursuit world title 1993–96. Also in 1993, he won the 1-hour cycling record with a distance of 51.6km, on a bicycle costing just £100 and incorporating a part from a washing-machine.

DARTS

Jocky Wilson (1951–). Born in Kirkcaldy. Scotland's most successful darts player. While unemployed he won the Butlin's Grand Masters competition in 1979. By 1980 he had become one of the world's top eight darts players. In 1982 he won the Embassy World Professional Championship trophy, the first Scot to gain the title. He became World Champion again in 1989.

FOOTBALL

Jim Baxter (1939–2001). Born in Hill o' Beath. Known as 'Slim Jim', he played for Raith Rovers before moving to Rangers. A midfielder, he scored 24 goals in 254 games for Rangers between 1960 and 1970. He was a member of the 1961 Rangers team which was the first Scottish side to reach the final of a European tournament. He won three championships, 1960–61, 1962–63 and 1963–64, as well as three Scottish Cups, 1963, 1964 and 1965, and 34 full international caps for Scotland.

Billy Bremner (1942–1997). Born in Glasgow, spent most of his playing career at Leeds United, where he was possibly the most revered of all Leeds United players, as a half-back, 1959–76. He won 54 full international caps for Scotland, and captained the national team at the 1974 World Cup Finals.

Sir Matt Busby (1909–1994). Son of a Scottish miner. Played half-back with Manchester City and Liverpool before World War II. Won only one full cap for Scotland but captained his country in several wartime internationals. Manchester United manager

1945–69 and briefly 1970–71. Rebuilt the team to win the FA Cup in 1963, the League Championship in 1965 and 1967, and the European Cup 1967. He was knighted after this last triumph, and was elected a vice-president of the Football League in 1982. Awarded CBE.

Kenny Dalglish (1951–). Born in Glasgow, he played for Celtic 1968–77 before signing for Liverpool. Became player-manager of Liverpool in 1985 and managed Blackburn Rovers 1991–95, before returning briefly to Celtic. Won a total of 102 full international caps for Scotland, which remains a record for any player, scoring 30 international goals. Awarded an MBE in 1985.

Tommy Docherty (1928–). One of the most controversial characters in football. Won 25 caps for Scotland. Began his playing career for Celtic, before making 324 appearances for Preston North End. He also played for Arsenal and Chelsea and has managed a host of clubs in England, Scotland and Australia, including Queens Park Rangers. Under his guidance Scotland qualified for the 1974 World Cup Finals.

Sir Alex Ferguson (1941–). Began playing career in 1957 for Stranraer. Went on to play for Queens Park, St Johnstone, Dunfermline, Rangers, Falkirk and finally Ayr United in 1973. His career as manager began at East Stirling in 1974, followed by St Mirren. He became the most successful manager for Aberdeen, 1978–86, where he won three league titles, four Scottish Cups and the European Cup Winners Cup. Briefly took over as manager of the Scottish national team in 1986 following the death of Jock Stein. Since November 1986 he has been at Manchester United, which has become the top English team under his guidance. Awarded CBE in 1995, knighted 1999.

Archie Gemmill (1947–). Born in Paisley and began playing career for St Mirren. he went on to play for a number of English clubs, including Preston North End, Derby County and Nottingham Forest. Capped by Scotland 43 times, scoring eight goals, which included the most memorable goal scored in the World Cup Finals of 1978, when Scotland beat Holland.

Denis Law (1940–). Born in Aberdeen but spent more than half of his playing career at Manchester United, 1962–73. Also played for Huddersfield, Manchester City and Turin. Played inside forward, winning 55 full international caps for Scotland.

Jim Leighton (1958–). The most-capped Scottish goalkeeper, with 91 appearances for Scotland. Played in four World Cups. Apart from a few seasons in the 1990s with Hibernian, much of his career has been with Aberdeen, where he has made over 900 appearances since 1978.

Ally McCoist (1962–). Born in Glasgow. Played for St Johnstone and Sunderland before joining Rangers in 1983. In 15 years he scored more than 300 goals in over 500 appearances in all competitions, and he remains the top scorer in Rangers' history. Won 59 full international caps for Scotland. In 1998 he left Rangers for Kilmarnock. He is better known nowadays for his appearances on television.

Jimmy McCrory. One of the greatest Celtic players. During his career with Celtic 1922–38 he scored 550 goals, once scoring eight goals in a single game against Dunfermline. He is the only British player to have averaged a goal a game during his career. However, despite this record he won only seven international caps for Scotland. Manager of Celtic 1945–65.

Bobby Murdoch (1944–2001). Joined Celtic in 1959 aged 15. In 1967 he played a major part in the goal that helped Celtic become the first to lift the European Cup. Scottish Football Writers' player of the year 1969; scored a memorable goal for Scotland in a 1-1 World Cup qualifier against West Germany. Won 12 international caps for Scotland. In 1973 left Celtic for Middlesbrough.

Rose Reilly (1960–). The first Scot to captain an Italian first division women's team, where she has won eight championships and five cup-winners' medals. In 1987 she was the first Scot to win the Women's World Cup, playing for Italy.

Bill Shankly (1913–1981). Born in Glenbuck, Ayrshire. He became a professional footballer in 1932, signing first for Carlisle and then Preston North End. During his playing career he won seven caps for Scotland. After World War II he turned to management, managing several English teams and becoming Liverpool's most revered manager (1959–74). He won eight league titles and number of FA Cup successes and in 1973 the UEFA Cup.

Jock Stein (1922–1985). The most successful football manager ever in Scotland. His playing career began at Albion Rovers, and he was signed up by Celtic in 1951. After managing Dunfermline Athletic and Hibernian, he became Celtic's most successful manager, 1965–78. During this time Celtic won nine consecutive League Championships, seven Scottish Cups and, in 1967, the European Cup. After managing Leeds United for a short while, he took over the Scottish national team. He died on 10 September 1985, just as Scotland qualified for the 1986 World Cup Finals. Awarded CBE.

GOLF

Tommy Armour (1895–1968). Born in Edinburgh. Successful amateur golfer, although partially losing his sight in World War I. Turned professional 1924 and became one of the many Scottish golfers who emigrated to the USA to capitalise on the early American golfing boom. He won the US PGA title in 1924 and 1930 and won three of the four Grand Slams but never the US Masters. Won the first British Open to be played at Carnoustie, in 1931.

James Braid (1870–1950). Born in Elie but moved to England in 1893, becoming a golf-club maker. He became a professional golfer and was a founder member of the Professional Golfers' Association (PGA). Won five British Open Championships over a 10 year period between 1901–10, including Muirfield (1901), Prestwick (1908) and St Andrews (1910).

Paul Lawrie (1969–). Winner of 1992 UAP Under-25s Championship, 6th in 1993 British Open Championship. Trailing by 10 strokes he came from behind to win the 1999 British Open Championship at Carnoustie following a play-off against Frenchman Jean Van de Velde and American Justin Leonard. He won the Dunhill Links in 2001. Awarded MBE in 2000.

Sandy Lyle (1958–). Made his international amateur debut at 14 and was a prolific winner before turning professional in 1977. Has won a total of 17 European Tour events, including the 1985 British Open Championship (becoming the first Briton since 1969 to win this trophy). First British golfer to win the US Masters (1988). His last title was the Volvo Masters in 1992.

Catriona Matthew (1969–). Born in Edinburgh. She enjoyed a successful amateur career and was the 1986 Scottish Girls champion and the 1988 and 1989 Scottish Under-21 Stroke Play champion. Won the Scottish amateur title 1991, 1993 and 1994. She won the 1993 British Amateur title and was a member of the 1990, 1992 and 1994 Curtis Cup teams. When she turned professional she made her Solheim Cup debut as a member of the 1998 European team. She became WPGA champion for

1998. Winner of the Hawaiian Ladies Classic in 2001.

Colin Montgomerie (1963–). Scotland's top golfer. Won seven successive titles on the European Circuit, an unprecedented track record, finally lost his place as top player on that circuit in 2000. Runner-up in US Open in 1994 and 1997 and US PGA in 1997. Winner of the PGA title in 1998 and World Match Play title in 1999. Won the Ericsson Masters at the beginning of 2001 to capture his first title Down Under, shared the 2002 Volvo Masters Andalucia with Bernhard Langer. Awarded MBE in 1998.

Tom Morris ('Old Tom') (1821–1908). Born in St Andrews. He competed in every Open championship up to and including 1896. He won the Open four times, including 1867, when he was 46, and remains the oldest ever winner. In 1851 he created the first purpose-built golf course in Scotland, at Prestwick. He is commemorated in the name of the final hole at the Royal and Ancient at St Andrews.

Tom Morris ('Young Tom') (1851–1875). Born in St Andrews. Along with his father he has passed into the folklore of golf. In 1868, at the age of 17, he became the youngest ever Open champion. He recorded his first championship hole-in-one at Prestwick, where he registered the first of four consecutive Open titles, a feat still unequalled. He died in his sleep on Christmas Day 1875, aged just 24.

Andrew Oldcorn (1960–). Born in Bolton, Lancashire but raised in Edinburgh. Won the English Amateur Championship but after many years living in Scotland was eventually given status as a Scot. Won all four of his matches in the 1983 Walker Cup. Produced his best ever golf to win the 2001 Volvo PGA Championship.

Willie Park Snr (1834–1903). Born in Musselburgh. Winner of the first professional golf tournament, the Open, held at Prestwick in 1860. He went on to win three more Opens, in 1863, 1866 and 1875. His brother Mungo Park won in 1874 and his son Willie Jnr won in 1887 and 1889.

Dale Reid (1959–). Born in Ladybank. As an amateur she represented Scotland internationally in 1978. She turned professional in 1979 and has achieved 24 victories, including the European Open in 1988. She finished first on the Women's Professional Order of Merit in 1984 and 1987, and represented Europe in the 1990, 1992, 1994 and 1996 Solheim Cup matches.

Isabella Robertson (1936–). Winner of the British Ladies' Open Amateur Golf Championship at the age of 45 in 1981.

Sam Torrance (1953–). Became a professional golfer at the age of 16 and has won several events over the last 30 years including the 1982 Spanish Open. The most recent of his 21 titles is the Peugeot Open de France in 1998. He was an early pioneer of the broom handle putter. Awarded MBE in 1996 for services to golf and an OBE in 2003 for his inspired captaincy of Europe's Ryder Cup Team in 2002, leading them to victory over the USA at Muirfield.

HORSE-RACING
Willie Carson (1942–). Born in Stirling, he became one of Britain's most successful jockeys. He was champion jockey on five occasions and the first 'Jockey to the Queen' in 1977. He retired in 1997 with 3,838 winners during his career, which included a record 14 British classics, among them the Derby at Epsom, which he won on four occasions, 1979, 1980, 1989 and 1994.

MOTOR SPORTS
Jim Clark (1936–1968). Formula 1 racing driver; his racing career included 25 Grand Prix wins. Drove for the Ecurie Ecosse team. Formula 1 world champion 1963 and 1965, driving for Lotus. Won the Indy 500 at Indianapolis in 1965. Awarded an OBE in 1964. Killed in a Formula 2 race at Hockenheim, Germany, in 1968.

David Coulthard (1971–). Formula 1 racing driver. Began his career in Scottish Junior Karting; champion 1983, 1984 and 1985. Scottish open cart champion 1986, 1987 and 1988; British Super Kart 1 champion 1986 and 1987. Moved to Formula Ford racing 1989, winning the Dunlop/Autosport Championship, the P&O Ferries Junior Championship, and the McLaren/Autosport Young Driver of the Year award. In 1992, won the Le Mans 24 hours (GT class). Switched to Formula 1 racing in 1994. His first Grand Prix win was in Portugal in 1995, and he has had several more wins, the most recent being the Brazilian Grand Prix 2001. He has finished third in the championship 1995, 1997 and 1998.

Bob McGregor McIntyre (1928–1962). Born in Glasgow. Motorcycle racer, known as 'The Flying Scotsman'. He began off-road racing in 1948 but soon turned to track racing. He won his very first competition at Balado Airfield, Kinross. He made his name with the Isle of Man TT race, where he recorded the first-ever 100mph lap. He was killed while competing at Oulton Park in 1962.

Colin McRae (1968–) Rally driver; made his debut in 1986, winning his first world rally the following year. British Rally Champion 1991, 1992 and 1998. In 1994 he became the first Scot to win an RAC rally. Between 1991 and 1998 he drove for the 555 Subaru World Rally Team. Has won many individual rallies, becoming overall World Rally Champion in 1995. In 1999 switched to the Ford Martini World Rally Team.

Sir Jackie Stewart (1939–). Formula 1 racing driver; launched his racing career in 1961, switching to Formula 1 racing in 1965 and winning his first race that year for BRM at Monza. In 1968 he joined the Tyrell team. Formula 1 world champion 1969, 1971 and 1973. Won 27 Grand Prix races in his career. In 1996, together with his son Paul, he formed the Stewart Grand Prix team. In 1999, having achieved fourth place in the constructors championship, he sold the company to Ford. Awarded OBE 1972; knighted 16 June 2001.

Richard Noble (1946–). Born in Edinburgh. He broke the land speed record in 1983, clocking up 1,012 km/hour (633 mph) in the Nevada Desert, USA. He regained the title in 1997 with the Thrust SSC team, which broke the sound barrier, reaching 1,220 km/hour (763 mph).

RUGBY
Gordon Lamont Brown (1947–2001). Born in Troon. Scotland's greatest rugby forward. Capped 30 times for Scotland, touring Argentina in 1969 and Australia in 1970. Played nine times for the British Lions. Following a brawl, he stopped playing for Scotland, but continued to play for the victorious Lions in New Zealand in 1971 and South Africa in 1974. He holds the world record of eight tries scored by a forward on an international tour.

Gavin Hastings (1962–). Born in Edinburgh. Capped for Scotland 61 times, 20 times as captain of his country. He also played in three World Cups for Scotland between 1987 and 1995. He holds records for the most points scored for Scotland in a rugby international (44 against Ivory Coast in 1995) and the most points scored for Scotland in an international career, 676 in total.

Scott Hastings (1964–). Born in Edinburgh. With 66 internationals to his name, he remains Scotland's most capped rugby international.

SAILING, YACHTING, CANOEING
Sir Chay Blyth (1940–). Born in Hawick. In 1966, with John Ridgeway, rowed across the Atlantic from Cape Cod to the Aran isles on a 20-foot dory. They completed the crossing in 90 days setting the record for the fastest modern-day double-handed crossing. In 1971, on the ketch *British Steel*, he became the first person to sail non-stop westwards around the world against prevailing winds and currents, completing the journey in 292 days. He has accumulated a long list of racing successes and in 1986 co-skippered the successful Blue Riband transatlantic attempt on *Virgin Atlantic Challenger III*. Awarded CBE, BEM.

Peter Haining. World sculling champion for 1993, 1994 and 1995. He was also Scottish champion and along with George P. Parsonage held the double-scull record for rowing the length of Loch Ness. George Parsonage also held the single-scull record for rowing the length of Loch Ness.

Rodney Pattison (1943–). Born in Campbeltown. At the 1968 Olympics in Mexico, on *Super...docious*, he and Iain Macdonald Smith won five first places and a second, with three penalty points, the lowest ever penalty score in an Olympic regatta, winning the gold in the Flying Dutchman class. In 1972 Munich Olympics, his yacht was called *Superdoso* and again he won gold in the Flying Dutchman class. Four years later at the 1976 Montreal games he won silver for the same event.

Jock Wishart (1955–). Born in Dumfries. International adventurer and yachtsman. Captain of the *Cable & Wireless Adventurer* on the record-breaking fastest circumnavigation of the globe (26,000 miles) in 1998. He raised money for this by rowing across the Atlantic Ocean in a 3,000-mile race in 1997. He was project leader of the team that broke the 1989 Round Britain Powerboat record. He was also a member of the first team to walk unsupported to the geomagnetic North Pole in 1992 and organised the first ever televised trek to the magnetic North Pole in 1996.

SNOOKER
Stephen Hendry (1969–). Born in Edinburgh. Turned professional in 1985 at 16 and dominated the game during the 1990s. Has won the World Snooker Championship seven times between 1990, when he became the youngest world champion, and 1999. He holds the record for the most titles won in a single season, nine in 1991–92, and has gathered a total of 72 major titles worldwide. Awarded MBE in 1999.

John Higgins (1975–). Turned professional in 1992 but came to prominence in 1994–5. His most successful year was 1999, when he rose to no.1 in the world rankings having won the German and British Opens as well as the Embassy World Championship in 1998.

SQUASH

Peter Nicol (1973–). Born in Inverurie, son of the Scottish national squash team coach. First came to prominence at the British Open Junior Championships, and by 1992 had entered the world rankings. He won the British National title in 1996 and became world no. 2 in 1997. By 1998 he was world no. 1, the first Briton for 25 years to win the British Open. He took the gold medal for Scotland at the 1998 Commonwealth Games in Kuala Lumpur. Awarded MBE in 1999.

SWIMMING

Isabella Moore. Until the 2000 Sydney Olympics she was the only Scottish woman to have won an Olympic gold medal, which she achieved as a member of the 100m freestyle swimming team at the 1912 Olympic games held in Stockholm.

David Wilkie (1954–). Born in Edinburgh. Won silver medal in the 200m breaststroke at the 1972 Olympics in Munich. He went on to win gold medal for the same event at the 1974 Commonwealth Games and the 1976 Olympics in Montreal, winning with a world-record time. He also won a silver medal for the 100 metre breaststroke at the Montreal Olympics.

WRESTLING

George Kidd (1925–1998). Born in Dundee. Scotland's top wrestler. By 1947 he was Scottish lightweight champion, by 1948 British champion, by 1949 European champion and by 1950 world champion. Over the next 20 years he successfully defended his world lightweight title 49 times. When he retired undefeated as world lightweight champion in 1976, he had lost only 19 of the 1,800 bouts in his 30-year career.

SPORTS BODIES

The following list includes the main organisations concerned with sports and physical recreation in Scotland.

SPORTSCOTLAND
Caledonia House, South Gyle, Edinburgh, EH12 9DQ.
Tel: 0131-317 7200 Fax: 0131-317 7202
Email: library@sportscotland.org.uk
Web: www.sportscotland.org.uk

SCOTTISH NATIONAL CENTRES
Inverclyde, Burnside Road, Ayrshire, KA30 8RW.
Tel: 01475-674666 Fax: 01475-674720
Glenmore Lodge, Aviemore, Inverness-shire,
PH22 1QU. Tel 01479-861256 Fax: 01479-861212
Millport, Isle of Cumbrae, KA28 0HQ.
Tel 01475-530013

SCOTTISH DISABILITY SPORT
Fife Institute of Physical and Recreational Education,
Viewfield Road, Glenrothes, Fife, KY6 2RB.
Tel: 01592-415700 Fax: 01592-415710
Email: ssadsds@aol.com
Web: www.scottishdisabilitysport.com

Aeromodelling
SCOTTISH AEROMODELLERS ASSOCIATION
50 Leinster Crescent, Howwood, Renfrewshire,
PA5 8PE. Tel: 01505-706300

Angling
SALMON AND TROUT ASSOCIATION SCOTLAND
National Game Angling Centre, The Pier, Loch Leven,
KY13 8UF. Tel: 01577-861116 Fax: 01577-864769

SCOTTISH ANGLERS NATIONAL ASSOCIATION
The National Game Angling Academy, The Pier,
Loch Leven, Kinross, KY13 8UF. Tel: 01577-861116
Fax: 01577-864769 Email: admin@sana.org.uk
Web: www.sana.org.uk

Association Football
SCOTTISH AMATEUR FOOTBALL ASSOCIATION
Hampden Park, Glasgow, G42 9DB.
Tel: 0141-620 4550

SCOTTISH FOOTBALL ASSOCIATION
Hampden Park, Glasgow, G42 9AY.
Tel: 0141-616 6000 Fax: 0141-616 6001
Email: info@scottishfa.co.uk
Web: www.scottishfa.co.uk

SCOTTISH FOOTBALL LEAGUE
Hampden Park, Glasgow, G42 9EB.
Tel: 0141-620 4160 Fax: 0141-620 4161
Email: info@scottishfootballleague.com
Web: www.scottishfootballleague.com

SCOTTISH WOMEN'S FOOTBALL ASSOCIATION
Hampden Park, Glasgow, G42 9DF.
Tel: 0141-620 4580 Fax: 0141-620 4581
Web: www.scottishwomensfootball.com

Athletics
SCOTTISH ATHLETICS
Caledonia House, South Gyle, Edinburgh, EH12 9EB.
Tel: 0131-539 7320
Email: admin@scottishathletics.org.uk
Web: www.scottishathletics.org.uk

Badminton
BADMINTON SCOTLAND
Cockburn Centre, 40 Bogmoor Place, Glasgow,
G51 4TQ. Tel: 0141-445 1218 Fax: 0141-425 1218
Email: enquiries@badmintonscotland.org.uk
Web: www.badmintonscotland.org.uk

SCOTTISH BADMINTON UNION
Cockburn Centre, 40 Bogmoor Place, Glasgow,
G51 4TQ. Tel: 0141-445 1218 Fax: 0141-425 1218
Email: name@scotbadminton.demon.co.uk
Web: www.scotbadminton.demon.co.uk

SCOTTISH SCHOOLS BADMINTON UNION
The Sheiling, Browsburn Road, Airdrie, ML6 9QG.
Tel: 01236-760943 Fax: 01236-621320
Email: h.ainsley@blueyonder.co.uk

Basketball
BASKETBALL SCOTLAND
Caledonia House, South Gyle, Edinburgh, EH12 9DQ.
Tel: 0131-317 7260 Fax: 0131-317 7489
Email: enquiries@basketball-scotland.com
Web: www.basketball-scotland.com

SCOTTISH SCHOOLS BASKETBALL ASSOCIATION
Caledonia House, South Gyle, Edinburgh, EH12 9DQ.
Tel: 0131-317 7260 Fax: 0131-317 7489

Billiards
SCOTTISH SNOOKER LTD
PO Box 147, Dunfermline, KY12 8ZB.
Tel: 01383-625373 Fax: 01383-626373

Bowling
SCOTTISH BOWLING ASSOCIATION
50 Wellington Street, Glasgow, G2 6EF.
Tel: 0141-221 8999/2004 Fax: 0141-221 8999
Email: scottishbowling@aol.com

SCOTTISH WOMEN'S BOWLING ASSOCIATION
Kingston House, 3 Jamaica Street, Greenock,
PA15 1XX. Tel: 01475-724676 Fax: 01475-724676

SCOTTISH WOMEN'S INDOOR BOWLING
ASSOCIATION
Watson Street, Letham, Forfar, DD8 2QB.
Tel: 01307-818238

Boxing
BRITISH AMATEUR BOXING ASSOCIATION
136 Fountainbleu Drive, Dundee, DD4 8BL.
Tel: 01382-508261 Fax: 01382-509425
Email: frankhendry@accnet.zzn.com

Canoeing
SCOTTISH CANOE ASSOCIATION
Caledonia House, South Gyle, Edinburgh, EH12 9DQ.
Tel: 0131-317 7314 Fax: 0131-317 7319
Email: enquiry@scot-canoe.org
Web: www.scot-canoe.org

Caving
GRAMPIAN SPELEOLOGICAL GROUP
8 Scone Gardens, Edinburgh, EH8 7DQ

Cricket
SCOTTISH CRICKET LTD
National Cricket Academy, Ravelston, Edinburgh,
EH4 3NT. Tel: 0131-313 7420 Fax: 0131-313 7430
Email: admin@scottishcricket.co.uk
Web: www.cricketeurope.org

Croquet
SCOTTISH CROQUET ASSOCIATION
2 Rannoch Drive, Crossford, Dunfermline.
Tel: 01383-729289

Curling
ROYAL CALEDONIAN CURLING CLUB
Cairnie House, Ingliston Showground, Newbridge,
Midlothian, EH28 8NB.
Tel: 0131-333 3003 Fax: 0131-333 3323
Email: office@royalcaledoniancurlingclub.org
Web: www.royalcaledoniancurlingclub.org

Cycling
CTC SCOTLAND
4 Mansionhouse Road, Camelon, Falkirk, FK1 4PS
Web: www.ctcscotland.org

SCOTTISH CYCLISTS UNION
The Velodrome, Meadow Bank Stadium, London Road,
Edinburgh, EH7 6AD. Tel: 0131-652 0187
Fax: 0131-652 0187 Web: www.scuweb.com

Dance and Fitness
BRITISH ASSOCIATION OF TEACHERS OF DANCING
23 Marywood Square, Glasgow, G41 2BP.
Tel: 0141-423 4029 Fax: 0141-423 0677
Email: enquiries@batd.co.uk Web: www.batd.co.uk

FITNESS SCOTLAND
Caledonia House, South Gyle, Edinburgh, EH12 9DQ.
Tel: 0131-317 7243 Fax: 0131-317 1998
Email: fitscot@talk21.com
Web: www.fitness-scotland.com

SCOTTISH DANCESPORT
Caledonia House, South Gyle, Edinburgh, EH12 9DQ.
Tel: 0131-339 8785 Fax: 0131-339 5168

SCOTTISH OFFICIAL BOARD OF HIGHLAND DANCING
32 Grange Loan, Edinburgh, EH9 2NR.
Tel: 0131-668 3965 Fax: 0131-662 0404
Email: admin@scottishhighlanddancing.org
Web: www.scottishhighlanddancing.org

Equestrianism
SCOTTISH EQUESTRIAN ASSOCIATION
c/o Grange Cottage, Station Road, Langbank,
Renfrewshire, PA14 6YB. Tel: 01475-540687

TREKKING AND RIDING SOCIETY OF SCOTLAND
Bruaich-na-h'abhainne, Maragowan, Killin,
Perthshire, FK21 8TN. Tel: 01567-820909
Web: www.ridinginscotland.com

Fencing
SCOTTISH FENCING
Cockburn Centre, 40 Bogmoor Place, Glasgow,
G51 4TQ. Tel: 0141-453 9074 Fax: 0141-453 9079
Email: scottishfencing@aol.com
Web: www.scottish-fencing.com

Field Sports
SCOTTISH COUNTRYSIDE ALLIANCE
Royal Highland Showground, Ingliston, Edinburgh,
EH28 8NF. Tel: 0131-335 0200 Fax: 0131-335 0201
Email: info@scottishcountrysidealliance.org
Web: www.scottishcountrysidealliance.org

Gliding
SCOTTISH GLIDING CENTRE
Portmoak Airfield, Scotlandwell, Nr Kinross, KY13 9JJ.
Tel: 01592-840543 Web: www.portmoak.force9.co.uk

Golf
GOLF FOUNDATION
Foundation House, The Spinney, Hoddesdon Road,
Stanstead Abbotts, Ware, Herts, SG12 8GF.
Tel: 01920-876200 Fax: 01920-876211
Email: info@golf-foundation.org
Web: www.golf-foundation.org

LADIES' GOLF UNION
The Scores, St Andrews, Fife, KY16 9AT.
Tel: 01334-475811 Fax: 01334-472818
Email: info@lgu.org Web: www.lgu.org

ROYAL AND ANCIENT GOLF CLUB OF ST ANDREWS
Golf Place, St Andrews, Fife, KY16 9JD.
Tel: 01334-460000 Fax: 01334-460001
Email: thesecretary@randagc.org
Web: www.opengolf.com

SCOTTISH GOLF UNION
Scottish National Golf Centre, Drumoig, Leuchars,
St Andrews, KY16 0DW.
Tel: 01382-549500 Fax: 01382-549510
Email: sgu@scottishgolf.com
Web: www.scottishgolf.com

SCOTTISH LADIES GOLFING ASSOCIATION
Scottish National Golf Centre, Drumoig, Leuchars,
St Andrews, Fife, KY16 0DW. Tel: 01382-549502
Fax: 01382-549512 Email: slga@scottishgolf.com
Web: www.slga.scottishgolf.com

SCOTTISH SCHOOLS GOLF ASSOCIATION
16 Windsor Gardens, St Andrews, Fife, KY16 8XL.
Tel: 01334-475681 Email: sandot.scott@tiscali.co.uk

Gymnastics
SCOTTISH GYMNASTICS
Woodhall Mill, Lanark Road, Edinburgh, EH14 5DL.
Tel: 01324-886505 Fax: 01324-886507
Email: info@scottishgymnastics.com
Web: www.scottishgymnastics.com

Handball
SCOTTISH HANDBALL ASSOCIATION
10a Main Road, Condorrat, Cumbernauld, G67 4BJ
Email: info@scottishhandball.com
Web: www.scottishhandball.com

Hang Gliding
SCOTTISH HANG GLIDING AND PARAGLIDING
ASSOCIATION
16 Johnston Street, Menstrie, Clackmannanshire,
FK11 7DB. Tel: 01259-762055
Web: www.flyingscot@f9.co.uk

Highland Games
SCOTTISH GAMES ASSOCIATION
10 Jamie Anderson Place, St Andrews, KY16 8YG.
Tel: 01334-476413
Email: andrew@highlandgames.org.uk
Web: www.highlandgames-sga.com

Hockey
SCOTTISH HOCKEY UNION
589 Lanark Road, Edinburgh, EH14 5DA.
Tel: 0131-453 9070 Fax: 0131-653 9079
Email: info@scottish-hockey.org.uk
Web: www.scottish-hockey.org.uk

Ice Hockey and Ice Skating
SCOTTISH ICE HOCKEY ASSOCIATION
7 Prestwick Road, Ayr, KA8 8LQ. Tel: 01292-284053
Web: www.siha.net

SCOTTISH ICE SKATING ASSOCIATION
The Ice Sports Centre, Riversdale Crescent, Edinburgh,
EH12 5XN. Tel: 0131-337 3976 Fax: 0131-337 9239
Web: www.sisa.org

Ju-jitsu
SCOTTISH JU-JITSU ASSOCIATION
3 Dens Street, Dundee, DD4 6BU. Tel: 01382-534672
Fax: 01382-458262 Email: scottishjujitsu@aol.com
Web: www.scottish-jujitsu.com

Judo
JUDO SCOTLAND
Caledonia House, South Gyle, Edinburgh, EH12 9DQ.
Tel: 0131-317 7270 Fax: 0131-317 7050
Email: info@judoscotland.com
Web: www.judoscotland.com

Karate
SCOTTISH KARATE BOARD
2 Strathdee Road, Netherlee, Glasgow, G44 3TJ.
Tel: 0141-633 1116 Fax: 0141-633 1116
Email: scottishkarateboard@btinternet.com

Lacrosse
SCOTTISH LACROSSE ASSOCIATION
Fa'Side House, Ayr Road, Newton Mearns, Glasgow,
G77 6RT. Tel: 0141-639 1246
Email: stleonards@fife.org

Lawn Tennis
TENNIS SCOTLAND LTD
Craiglockhart Tennis and Sports Centre,
177 Colinton Road, Edinburgh, EH14 1BZ.
Tel: 0131-444 1984 Fax: 0131-444 1973
Email: gduncan@slta.org.uk

Modern Pentathlon
SCOTTISH MODERN PENTATHLON ASSOCIATION
16 Plewlands Terrace, Edinburgh, EH10 5JZ.
Tel: 0131-447 7427 Fax: 0131-229 2088

Motor Sport

SCOTTISH AUTO CYCLE UNION LTD
28 West Main Street, Uphall, West Lothian,
EH52 5DW. Tel: 01506-858354 Fax: 01506-855792
Email: office@sacu.co.uk Web: www.sacu.co.uk

RSAC MOTORSPORT LTD
St. James Business Centre, Linwood Road, Paisley,
PA3 3AT. Tel: 0141-887 9905 Fax: 0141-887 9906
Email: rsac_motorsport@compuserve.com
Web: www.rsacmotorsport.co.uk

Mountaineering

MOUNTAIN BOTHIES ASSOCIATION
1/4 Turnhouse Farm, Edinburgh, EH12 0AT.
Tel: 0131-339 0165
Web: www.mountainbothies.org.uk

MOUNTAINEERING COUNCIL OF SCOTLAND
Ground Floor, The Old Granary, West Mill Street, Perth,
PH1 5QP. Tel: 01738-638227 Fax: 01738-442095
Email: info@mountaineering-scotland.org.uk
Web: www.mountaineering-scotland.org.uk

MOUNTAIN LEADER TRAINING SCOTLAND
Glenmore, Aviemore, Inverness-shire, PH22 1QU.
Tel: 01479-861248 Fax: 01479-861249
Email: smltb@aol.com

Netball

NETBALL SCOTLAND
2nd Floor Central Chambers, 93 Hope Street, Glasgow,
G2 6LD. Tel: 0141-572 0114 Fax: 0141-572 0052
Email: netballscotland@btinternet.com
Web: www.netballscotland.com

Orienteering

SCOTTISH ORIENTEERING ASSOCIATION
10 Neuk Crescent, Houston, Johnstone, PA6 7DW.
Tel: 01505-613094
Email: donald@scottish-orienteering.org
Web: www.scottish-orienteering.org

Parachuting

SCOTTISH SPORT PARACHUTE ASSOCIATION
Strathallan Airfield, Auchterarder, Perthshire, PH3 1LA.
Tel: 01764-662572 Email: info@sspa.co.uk
Web: www.sspa.co.uk

Petanque

SCOTTISH PETANQUE ASSOCIATION
62 Palmerston Place, Edinburgh, EH12 5AY
Email: spa@scottishpetanque.org
Web: www.scottishpetanque.org

Polo

SCOTTISH BICYCLE POLO ASSOCIATION
16 Edmiston Drive, Linwood, Paisley, PA3 3TD.
Tel: 01505-328105 Web: www.scotpolo.org.uk

SCOTTISH POLO ASSOCIATION
c/o Iona Designs, 4 High Street, Auchterarder.
Tel: 01382-330234 Fax: 01382-223135
Email: ionadesign@aol.com
Web: www.scottishpolo.com

Rowing

SCOTTISH AMATEUR ROWING ASSOCIATION
39 Polton Road, Lasswade, Midlothian, EH18 1AF.
Tel: 0131-663 8949
Web: www.scottish-rowing.org.uk

SCOTTISH SCHOOLS ROWING COUNCIL
1 Kirkhill Gardens, Edinburgh, EH16 5DF.
Tel: 0131-229 7263 Fax: 0131-229 6363

Rugby

SCOTTISH RUGBY UNION
Murrayfield, Edinburgh, EH12 5PJ. Tel: 0131-346 5000
Fax: 0131-346 5001 Email: feedback@sru.org.uk
Web: www.sru.org.uk

SCOTTISH WOMEN'S RUGBY UNION
Murrayfield, Edinburgh, EH10 5QL.
Tel: 0131-346 5163 Fax: 0131-346 5001

Shinty

THE CAMANACHD ASSOCIATION
11 High Street, Fort William, Inverness-shire,
PH33 6DG. Tel: 01397-703903
Web: www.shinty.com

Shooting

SCOTTISH AIR RIFLE AND PISTOL ASSOCIATION
45 Glenartney Court, Glenrothes, Fife, KY7 6YF.
Tel: 01592-743929
Email: ericwallace.erane@btopenworld.com
Web: www.sarpa.org.uk

SCOTTISH ASSOCIATION FOR COUNTRY SPORTS
River Lodge, Trochry, Dunkeld, PH8 0DY.
Tel: 01350-723259 Fax: 01350-723259
Web: www.sacs.org.uk

SCOTTISH PISTOL ASSOCIATION
Sandhole, Furness, by Inverary, Argyll, PA32 8XU.
Tel: 01499-500640 Fax: 01499-500640

SCOTTISH SMALL-BORE RIFLE ASSOCIATION
Tel: 01324-720440 Fax: 01324-711747
Email: secretary@ssra.co.uk
Web: www.ssra.co.uk

Skiing

BRITISH ASSOCIATION OF SNOWSPORT
INSTRUCTORS
Glenmore, Aviemore, Inverness-shire, PH22 1QU.
Tel: 01479-861717 Fax: 01479-861718
Email: basi@basi.org.uk Web: www.basi.org.uk

SCOTTISH SCHOOL SKI ASSOCIATION
Dollar Academy, Dollar, FK14 7DU. Tel: 01259-742511
Fax: 01259-742867
Email: lhh@dollaracademy.org.uk

SNOWSPORT SCOTLAND
Hillend, Biggar Road, Midlothian, EH10 7EF.
Tel: 0131-445 4151 Fax: 0131-445 4949
Email: info@snowsportscotland.org
Web: www.snowsportscotland.org

Squash

SCOTTISH SQUASH
Caledonia House, South Gyle, Edinburgh, EH12 9DQ.
Tel: 0131-317 7343 Fax: 0131-317 7734
Email: scottishsquash@aol.com
Web: www.scottishsquash.com

Sub Aqua

SCOTTISH SUB AQUA CLUB
Cockburn Centre, 40 Bogmoor Place, Glasgow,
G51 4TQ. Tel: 0141-425 1021 Fax: 0141-425 1021
Email: ab@hqssac.demon.co.uk
Web: www.scotsac.com

Surfing

SCOTTISH SURFING FEDERATION
Mybster Croft, Spitall, Caithness, KW1 5XR.
Tel: 01847-841300

Swimming

SCOTTISH SWIMMING
National Swimming Academy, University of Stirling,
Stirling, FK9 4LA.
Tel: 01786-466520 Fax: 01786-466521
Email: info@scottishswimming.com
Web: www.scottishswimming.com

Table Tennis

TABLE TENNIS SCOTLAND
Caledonia House, South Gyle, Edinburgh, EH12 9DQ.
Tel: 0131-317 8077 Fax: 0131-317 8224
Web: www.tabletennisscotland.com

Triathlon

SCOTTISH TRIATHLON ASSOCIATION
Glenearn Cottage, Edinburgh Road, Port Seton,
E. Lothian, EH32 0HQ.
Tel: 01875-811344 Fax: 01875-811344
Email: jacqui.dunlop@btinternet.com
Web: www.tri-scotland.org

Tug-of-War

SCOTTISH TUG-OF-WAR ASSOCIATION
47 Finlay Avenue, East Calder, West Lothian, EH53 0RP.
Tel: 01506-881650 Fax: 01506-881650

Volleyball

SCOTTISH VOLLEYBALL ASSOCIATION
48 The Pleasance, Edinburgh, EH8 9TJ.
Tel: 0131-556 4633 Fax: 0131-557 4314
Email: info@scottishvolleyball.org
Web: www.scottishvolleyball.org

Walking

RAMBLERS' ASSOCIATION SCOTLAND
Kingfisher House, Auld Mart Business Park, Milnathort,
Kinross, KY13 9DA.
Tel: 01577-861222 Fax: 01577-861333
Email: enquiries@scotland.ramblers.org.uk
Web: www.ramblers.org.uk

Wrestling

SCOTTISH AMATEUR WRESTLING ASSOCIATION
Kelvinhall International Sports Arena, Argyle Street,
Glasgow, G3 8AW. Tel: 0141-334 3843
Fax: 0141-334 3843 Web: www.britishwrestling.org

Yachting

ROYAL YACHTING ASSOCIATION SCOTLAND
Caledonia House, South Gyle, Edinburgh, EH12 9DQ.
Tel: 0131-317 7388 Fax: 0131-317 8566
Web: www.ryascotland.org.uk

CLUBS

AYR COUNTY CLUB
Savoy Park Hotel:, Racecourse Road, Ayr, KA7 2UT.
Tel: 01292-266112

EAST LOTHIAN YACHT CLUB
The Harbour, North Berwick, East Lothian, EH39 4QG.
Tel: 01620-892698 Web: www.elyc.org.uk

GLASGOW ART CLUB
185 Bath Street, Glasgow, G2 4HU.
Tel: 0141-248 5210

NEW CLUB
86 Princes Street, Edinburgh, EH2 2BB.
Tel: 0131-226 4481 Fax: 0131-225 9649
Email: info@newclub.co.uk Web: www.newclub.co.uk

ROYAL FORTH YACHT CLUB
Middle Pier, Granton Harbour, Edinburgh, EH5 1HF.
Tel: 0131-552 8560 Fax: 0131-552 8560
Email: info@royalforth.mariner.co.uk
Web: www.rfyc.org

ROYAL GOUROCK YACHT CLUB
The Clubhouse, Ashton, Gourock, Renfrewshire,
PA19 1DA. Tel: 01475-632983 Fax: 01475-637192
Web: www.rgyc.org.uk

ROYAL HIGHLAND YACHT CLUB
Raslie House, Slockavullin, Argyll, PA31 8QG.
Tel: 01546-510261 Fax: 01546-510261
Email: rhyctr@rhyc.org.uk Web: www.rhyc.org.uk

**ROYAL NORTHERN AND CLYDE YACHT
CLUB**
Rhu, By Helensburgh, Argyll and Bute, G84 8NG.
Tel: 01436-820322 Fax: 01439-821296
Email: mail@rncyc.com Web: www.rncyc.com

**ROYAL NORTHERN AND UNIVERSITY
CLUB**
9 Albyn Place, Aberdeen, AB10 1YE.
Tel: 01224-583292 Fax: 01224-571082
Email: secretary@rnuc.org.uk
Web: www.rnuc.org.uk

ROYAL SCOTTISH AUTOMOBILE CLUB
11 Blythswood Square, Glasgow, G2 4AG.
Tel: 0141-221 3850 Fax: 0141-221 3805
Email: club@rsac.co.uk Web: www.rsac.co.uk

ROYAL TAY YACHT CLUB
Fort William House, 34 Dundee Road, West Ferry,
Dundee, DD5 1LX. Tel: 01382-477516
Email: rtyc@royaltay.org Web: www.royaltay.org

ROYAL WESTERN YACHT CLUB
Braidhurst Cottage, Shandon, Helensburgh,
Argyll and Bute, G84 8NP. Tel: 01436-820256

WESTERN CLUB
32 Royal Exchange Square, Glasgow, G1 3AB.
Tel: 0141-221 2016 Fax: 0141-248 6630
Email: secretary@westernclub.co.uk
Web: www.westernclub.co.uk

FOOD AND DRINK

Scottish food is different from food in the rest of the British Isles because the Scottish landscape demands it – there is very little good farming land so game, birds and fish traditionally provide sustenance. Scottish history also plays a part – Scotland was poorer than other areas of Britain for a lot longer and so a limited number of inexpensive foodstuffs had to suffice. Simple ingredients dominate the history of Scottish food and it is only in recent times that these basics have reinvented themselves as luxury commodities – oysters are a prime example of this shift in values. During the 19th-century individual taverns in Edinburgh sold upwards of 10,000 oysters a week each along with their beverages, in some parts of the Highlands and Islands oysters were viewed as the food of the most poverty-stricken and were only eaten by the poorest families. Throughout Scotland soups routinely contained upwards of 60 oysters a pot, added for their flavour and cheapness, while roast turkey, called 'roastit bubbly-jock', was often stuffed with oysters due to their plentiful supply – a stuffing which would be considered prohibitively expensive today.

Scottish food and drink is found all over the world – shortbread and scones are beloved of high teas everywhere; marmalade, created in 1797 by Mrs Janet Keiller when her husband bought a cheap cargo of Seville oranges off a Spanish ship that had been forced into Dundee harbour after a storm, graces breakfast tables on every continent; fudge is consumed in huge quantities every year; smoked salmon is one of the world's favourite foods and whisky is one of Scotland's major exports. Scotland's most famous dish is the haggis, made from sheep's offal boiled inside the lining of a sheep's stomach, eaten every year on Burns Night and traditionally served with tatties (potatoes) and neeps (turnip) to the accompaniment of bagpipes and poetry. Scotland's second most famous food is, like the haggis, a source of some amusement: deep-fried Mars bar or 'Bounty Breakfast', both of which are dipped in batter, flash-fried in oil and served, upon request, with fish and chips. Scotland's number one selling non-alcoholic drink is Irn Bru (not Coca-Cola as in most European countries), an orange fizzy drink reputedly 'made from girders'. Preconceptions about Scottish food haven't moved much beyond these infamous examples and yet new Scottish cuisine rivals the finest food of any country by embracing Scottish products – which are amongst the most sought-after in the world: fresh lobsters, crab, oysters and hand-dived scallops daily wing their way to the finest tables in France, Tokyo and New York; Arbroath Smokies are exported as far afield as Australia and Scottish beef, pork, lamb and game all have large export markets.

After a tour of Scotland H. V. Morton wrote 'if a man has an honest appetite sharpened by the open air, he will satisfy it with less risk to his mechanism more speedily in a Scottish kitchen than elsewhere', adding that France is all very well for the man who has to be 'led gently to his food'. Not much has changed today, apart from the usual invasions of fast and convenience foods that are now common to the high streets and diets of all European countries. Restaurants in Scotland range from the large hotel:s and expensive venues in major cities to small, informal family establishments in the remotest areas of the Highlands and Islands (many of which are only open during the tourist season, typically from Easter to October). Local delicacies and organic foods can be found at any of 46 farmers' markets, usually held on Saturday mornings (call 01738-449430 or visit www.scottishfarmersmarkets.co.uk for more information) and at roadside stalls and shops throughout the year. The food on offer ranges from the simple and hearty, full of strong flavours using only a few excellent ingredients, to ornate and delicate dishes heavily influenced by international cuisine.

SOME SCOTTISH DISHES

Arbroath Smokies: haddock, smoked in wood, produced in small, individual family smoke houses in the east coast fishing town of Arbroath.

Black Bun: fruit cake made with raisins, currants, finely-chopped peel, chopped almonds, and brown sugar, cinnamon and ginger. Very rich. Very dark in colour.

Clapshot: a potato and turnip dish from Orkney served with haggis, stews or fried meat.

Clootie Dumpling: a spiced fruit dumpling made with wholemeal flour, suet, cinnamon, ginger, nutmeg, cumin, sultanas, currants, black treacle, apples, a lemon, fresh orange juice and eggs – all wrapped up in a linen cloth and boiled.

Cock a Leekie soup: served throughout the winter and often at Burns' Suppers. Recipes vary but usually include chicken, rice, sugar, bay leaf, parsley, thyme, various vegetables and, sometimes, prunes.

Colcannon: from the Western Islands of Scotland (originally from Ireland). Also called Rumplethumps: 'rumbled' means 'mixed together' and thumped means 'bashed together'. Made from boiled cabbage, carrots, turnip and potatoes, drained and stewed for about 20 minutes in a pan with butter, salt, pepper. Served piping hot.

Cranachan: a soft fruit dessert, known as a 'brose', created specially for celebrations. Toasted oatmeal is added to whipped cream, honey and whisky, and then layered with fresh raspberries. Traditionally Cranachan was a communal dish – the oatmeal, fruit and cream were put onto the table and everyone made his/her own mix, lubricating it with whisky and honey according to personal taste.

Crowdie: white cheese made from the whey of slightly soured milk seasoned with salt and pepper. The seasoned cheese is squeezed in a muslin bag to get rid of water and then left for two days before being rolled in oats.

Cullen Skink: a fisherman's soup made from Finnan haddock and potatoes. From Cullen, a small town on the Moray Firth Coast.

Drop Scones: a pancake-like mixture is traditionally 'dropped' by the tablespoonful onto a hot gridle to produce a scone (that looks and tastes more like a pancake) that is smooth on one side and bubbled on the other. A frying pan is now more commonly used.

Dundee Cake: a rich fruit cake popular from the 19th-century onwards. Made with whisky, milk, sugar, lemon, mixed peel, currants, raisins, sultanas, flour and butter.

Forfar Bridies: an oval pastry stuffed with minced beef, suet (now usually substituted with butter) and onion.

Haggis: Scotland's national dish, made from sheep's offal (also called 'pluck') – the windpipe, lungs, heart and liver of the sheep are boiled and then minced. This mixture is then mixed with beef suet and lightly toasted oatmeal. All of this is then placed inside the lining of a sheep's stomach and sewn closed before being boiled (for up to three hours).

Oatcakes: hard biscuits made from oatmeal and beef dripping, bacon fat or vegetable oil. Called 'breed' in the north east of Scotland, where bread is called loaf. Oatcakes are cooked on a griddle and are served with haggis, stovies or cheese.

Partan Bree: a traditional crab soup. 'Partan' is the Scots word for crab and 'bree' is a liquid in which something edible has been boiled or left to soak.

Porridge: boiled oatmeal cooked with salt, thick in consistency, eaten hot for breakfast with a further sprinkling of salt or, if you are not a true Scotsman, sugar. In the past Highlanders would make a large quantity of porridge at the beginning of every week (sometimes poured into a drawer in a chest of drawers or a large tray) and would cut a cold slice of it every day to take to work for their lunch.

Scones: the word 'scones' comes from the gaelic word 'sgoon' which rhymed with 'gone', thus giving a pointer to the correct modern-day pronunciation. There are many kinds of scones, including treacle, cheese and fruit.

Scotch broth: a thick soup designed to keep out the cold on a winter's night. A mutton-stock base is freely populated with vegetables such as carrots, garden peas, leeks, cabbage and turnips, and a handful of barley.

Selkirk Bannock: a bannock is an oatcake but a Selkirk bannock is more like a fruitcake and was originally only made for great occasions such as weddings.

Shortbread: a simple biscuit made with plain flour, butter and sugar. Eaten all over the world at New Year and all year round in Scotland.

Skirlie: oatmeal and onions served with mashed potatoes or used as a stuffing for any kind of game bird or poultry. Also an accompaniment to rich meaty and gamey stews.

Stovies: a dish created to use up leftovers much in the same way as Shepherd's Pie uses up leftovers in England. Diced onions are fried in beef dripping and anything that comes to hand, such as meat and vegetables, are added to the mixture. Next, peeled and chopped potatoes are added to the pan containing the meat and onion mixture and about 4 centimetres of water. The pot is then put on to boil until the potatoes are cooked, further water only being added if the potatoes require it. The stovies are then served hot in bowls with bread and tea.

Tablet: tablet looks and tastes like fudge but is hard in consistency.

Tipsy Laird: 'laird' is the Scottish word for lord. This is a dessert made of sherry or Madeira, sugar, greengage jam, apricot jam, raspberry jam, almonds, eggs, lemon and cream.

SOME SCOTTISH PRODUCE

Cheeses: including the Orkney, Islay and Galloway cheeses.

Game birds: such as grouse, pheasant, partridge and wood pigeon.

Heather honey: produced anywhere there are heather moors (a great many places!).

Oats: the basis for many dishes and the traditional foodstuff of the entire population. Scots still eat more oats than any other nation in Europe and, correspondingly, consume fewer breakfast cereals that anyone else. There are many varieties of oats and all are widely available in supermarkets. Some of the best oatmeal is Oatmeal of Alford from Montgarrie Mill, Alford, Aberdeenshire. This oatmeal is made with methods in use since Jacobean times – it is slowly toasted on a flat kiln and turned twice with a wooden shovel in a process taking 20 days – supermarket oatmeals tend to take only a couple of hours to toast.

Scottish beef: rich and tasty meat, excellent for steaks. Aberdeen Angus beef descends from cattle found in the north east of Scotland from the 12th-century onwards.

Seafood: there are major commercial salmon farms in the sea lochs of the West coast of Scotland. The Rivers Tay and Tweed are the main fisheries for fresh-caught salmon (which is acknowledged to have a superior taste and a firmer meat). Sole, cod, herring, plaice, mussels, scallops, shrimp, Dublin Bay oysters, lobster, crab, haddock, mackerel and halibut are all fished in Scotland.

Soft fruit such as raspberries, strawberries, tayberries and brambles from the Carse of Gowrie. Excellent raspberries are grown in the Nairn Valley (near Inverness) and in the northeast.

Venison: from the great Highland estates, found in local butchers made into sausages, cuts of meat and ready-for-the oven casseroles.

Whisky: also known as Uisge Beatha, Gaelic for 'the water of life'. Produced in some of the most beautiful places in the world, adding to its romantic appeal. Famous Highland malts include Glen Grant, Macallan, Glenfarclas, Knockando, Cardhu, Glenfiddich, Strathisla and Tamnavullin. Famous island malts include Highland Park and Scapa from Orkney, Talisker from the misty Isle of Skye, Jura and the Islay malts which include Laphroig, Bowmore and Bruichladdich.

ENVIRONMENTAL SCOTLAND

THE LAND

AREA

	Scotland	UK
	sq. km	sq. km
Land	77,925	242,513

Source: The Stationery Office, Annual Abstract of Statistics 2003 (Crown Copyright)

GEOGRAPHY

Scotland occupies the northern portion of the main island of Great Britain and includes the Inner and Outer Hebrides, and the Orkney, Shetland, and many other islands. It lies between 60° 51′ 30″ and 54° 38; N. latitude and between 1° 45′ 32 and 6° 14″ W. longitude, with England to the south, the Atlantic Ocean on the north and west, and the North Sea on the east.

The greatest length of the mainland (Cape Wrath to the Mull of Galloway) is 274 miles, and the greatest breadth (Buchan Ness to Applecross) is 154 miles. The customary measurement of the island of Great Britain is from the site of John o' Groats house, near Duncansby Head, Caithness, to Land's End, Cornwall, a total distance of 603 miles (965 km) in a straight line and approximately 900 miles (1,440km) by road.

RELIEF

The highest parts of the United Kingdom lie in Scotland. As part of Highland Britain, 65 per cent of Scottish landscape lies above 120m (400ft), of which 6 per cent is above 600m (2,000ft), while 20 per cent lies below 60m (200ft).

There are three natural orographic divisions of mainland Scotland. The southern uplands have their highest points in Merrick (2,764ft/814m), Rhinns of Kells (2,669ft/814m), and Cairnsmuir of Carsphairn (2,614ft/796m), in the west; and the Tweedsmuir Hills in the east (Broad Law 2,756ft/830m, Dollar Law 2,682ft/817m, Hartfell 2,651ft/808m).

The central lowlands, formed by the valleys of the Clyde, Forth and Tay, divide the southern uplands from the northern Highlands, which extend almost from the extreme north of the mainland to the central lowlands, and are divided into a northern and a southern system by the Great Glen.

The Grampian Mountains, which entirely cover the southern Highland area, include in the west Ben Nevis (4,406ft/1,343m), the highest point in the British Isles, and in the east the Cairngorm

Mountains (Ben Macdui 4,296ft/1,309m, Braeriach 4,248ft/1,295m, Cairn Gorm 4,084ft/1,246m). The north-western Highland area contains the mountains of Wester and Easter Ross (Carn Eighe 3,880ft/1,183m, Sgurr na Lapaich 3,775ft/1,150m).

Created, like the central lowlands, by a major geological fault, the Great Glen (60 miles/96km long) runs between Inverness and Fort William, and contains Loch Ness, Loch Oich and Loch Lochy. These are linked to each other and to the north-east and south-west coasts of Scotland by the Caledonian Canal, the River Lochy and the long sea-loch Loch Linnhe, providing a navigable passage between the Moray Firth and the Inner Hebrides.

HYDROGRAPHY

The western coast is fragmented by peninsulas and islands and deeply indented by sea-lochs (fjords), the longest of which is Loch Fyne (42 miles long) in Argyll. Although the east coast tends to be less fractured and lower, there are several great drowned inlets (firths), for instance the Firth of Forth, the Firth of Tay and the Moray Firth. The Firth of Clyde is the chief example of this feature in the west.

The lochs are the principal hydrographic feature. The largest in Scotland and in Britain is Loch Lomond (27.46sq. miles/71.12sq. km), in the Grampian valleys; the longest and deepest is Loch Ness (24 miles/38km long and 800ft/244m deep), in the Great Glen. Loch Shin (20 miles/32km long) and Loch Maree in the Highlands are the longest lochs in the north-west Highlands

The longest river is the Tay (117 miles/188km), noted for its salmon. It flows into the North Sea, with Dundee on the estuary, which is spanned by the Tay Bridge (10,289ft/3,137m), opened in 1887, and the Tay Road Bridge (7,365ft/2,245m), opened in 1966. The present Tay rail bridge is the second to have been built; the original collapsed in 1879, only a year after completion, with the loss of 150 lives.

Other noted salmon rivers are the Dee (90 miles/144km) which flows into the North Sea at Aberdeen, and the Spey (110 miles/172km), the swiftest flowing river in the British Isles, which flows into the Moray Firth. The Tweed, which gave its name to the woollen cloth produced along its banks, marks in the lower stretches of its 96-mile (155km) course the border between Scotland and England.

The most important river commercially is the Clyde (106 miles/171m), formed by the junction of the Daer and Portrail water, which flows through the city of Glasgow to the Firth of Clyde. During its course it passes over the picturesque Falls of Clyde, Bonnington Linn (30ft/9m), Corra Linn (84ft/26m), Dundaff Linn (10ft/3m) and Stonebyres Linn (80ft/24m), above and below Lanark. The Forth (66 miles/106km), upon which stands Edinburgh, is spanned by the Forth (Railway) Bridge (1890), which is 5,330 feet (1,625m) long, and the Forth (Road) Bridge (1964), which has a total length of 6,156 feet (1,987m) (over water) and a single span of 3,300 feet (1,006m).

On 26 May 2001 the Forth and Clyde canal, linking the North Sea and the Atlantic via the firths of Forth and Clyde, was reopened after decades of closure.

The highest waterfall in Scotland, and the British Isles, is Eas a'Chùal Aluinn with a total height of 658 feet (200m), which falls from Glas Bheinn in Sutherland. The Falls of Glomach, on a head-stream of the Elchaig in Wester Ross, have a drop of 370 feet (113m).

THE ISLANDS

Scotland's northern and western coasts are fringed by 790 islands and islets, products of the same geological forces that have shaped its deeply indented coastlines. They fall into four main groups: Orkney, Shetland, and the Inner and Outer Hebrides. There are also some offshore islands, which lie in the North Atlantic well outwith the main Outer Hebrides group but are still part of the Outer Hebrides. Rockall, 184 miles west of St Kilda, was annexed in 1955 and added to the territories of the UK by an Act of Parliament in 1972.

Only 130 of the islands are inhabited today, although some of them became uninhabited only in the last century or so, some after many centuries of habitation, such as Mousa, site of one of the major Iron Age brochs but uninhabited since the mid 19th-century. The last families to leave the St Kilda group were evacuated in 1930 (a military base and missile-tracking station were installed on Hirta in 1957, but the island is not permanently occupied). A number of the uninhabited islands are, or contain, nature reserves, principally for the protection of birds.

ORKNEY
The Orkney Islands lie about six miles north of the mainland, separated from it by the Pentland Firth. Of the 90 islands and islets (holms and skerries) in the group, about one-third are inhabited.

The principal islands and their areas are:

Mainland (with Burray, South Ronaldsay and Hunda) acres	58,308 ha/144,079 acres
Hoy	14,381 ha/35,380
Graemsay	409 ha/1,011 acres
Flotta	876 ha/2,165 acres
Rousay	4,860 ha/12,009 acres
Shapinsay	2,948 ha/7,285 acres
Stronsay	3,275 ha/8,093 acres
Eday	2,745 ha/6,783 acres
Sanday	5,043 ha/12,461 acres
Westray	4,713 ha/11,646 acres
Papa Westray	918 ha/2,268 acres
North Ronaldsay	690 ha/1,705 acres

Most of the inhabited islands are low-lying and fertile owing to the geological underlay of Old Red Sandstone, and farming, principally of beef cattle, is the main economic activity. Flotta is the site of a large oil terminal.

Hoy is the highest of the islands (highest point Ward Hill, 479m/1,571ft) and has the most dramatic landscape. Although most of the Orkney Islands are low-lying, St John's Head on Hoy (350m/1,148ft) is one of the highest sea-cliffs in the British Isles.

Several of the islands contain rare flora – e.g. Hoy, where rare alpine plants are to be found – and several contain nature reserves specialising in birds. The mainland boasts over 600 species of flowering plant, some of which are extremely rare.

North Ronaldsay, the northernmost island, is very isolated but also sufficiently fertile to support a small farming population. It has been continuously populated since prehistoric times. A species of small sheep, descendants of the original Orkney sheep, is unique to the island.

SHETLAND
The Shetland Islands lie about 50 miles north of Orkney, with Fair Isle about half-way between the two groups. Out Stack, off Muckle Flugga, one mile north of Unst, is the most northerly point in the British Isles (60° 51′ 30″ N. lat.). Lerwick, the capital, is in fact almost equidistant from Aberdeen and Bergen in Norway. Foula, the most westerly of the Shetland Islands, is the most isolated inhabited island in the British Isles. The group contains over 100 islands, of which 16 are populated.

The principal islands and their areas are:

Mainland (with Muckle Roe, West and East Burra and Trondra)	100,230 ha/247,668 acres
Bressay	2,805 ha/6,932 acres
Fair Isle	768 ha/1,898 acres
Fetlar	4,078 ha/10,077 acres

Foula	1,265 ha/3,126 acres
Housay (with Bruray and Grunay)	218 ha/539 acres
Unst	12,068 ha/29,820 acres
Whalsay	1,970 ha/4,868 acres
Yell	21,211 ha/52,412 acres

Shetland's geology is different from that of Orkney, resulting in a harsher, more dramatic landscape, with impressive sea cliffs (e.g. the Kame of Foula, 376m/1,233ft) and also in poorer soil, which has made fishing traditionally more important than agriculture as a livelihood. The islands are largely treeless, and peat bog, grass and heather moorland are characteristic. The North Atlantic Drift, an extension of the Gulf Stream, keeps Shetland's climate milder than its northern latitude would suggest.

THE HEBRIDES

The Inner and Outer Hebrides, stretching from Lewis, the most northerly island, to Ailsa Craig, the most southerly, comprise over 500 islands and islets, of which about 100 are inhabited, although mountainous terrain and extensive peat bogs and heather mean that only a fraction of the total land area is under cultivation.

THE INNER HEBRIDES

The Inner Hebrides lie off the west coast of Scotland, relatively close to the mainland. The largest and best known of the islands is Skye (1,648 sq. km/ 643sq. m), which contains the spectacular Cuillin Hills (highest peak Sgurr Alasdair 993m/3,257ft), the more smoothly shaped Red Cuillin (highest peak Beinn na Caillich, 732m/2,403ft), Bla Bheinn (928m/3,046ft), and, in the north of the island, the strange formations of the Quiraing and the Storr (719m/2,358ft). Skye is itself surrounded by several small islands, and not far to the south-west are the Small Isles, Rum, Eigg, Muck, and Canna. Muck is low-lying and is the most fertile of the Small Isles; Eigg and Rum are craggier. Some of the rock formations on Rum are geologically unique. Further north, off the north-west coast, lie a few small islands of which the principal group is the Summer Isles, about a dozen islands lying off the Coigach peninsula. Tanera Mór, the largest of the group, has tourist facilities. Still further north, Handa is famous for its rich bird life.

Major islands in the southern Inner Hebridean islands include:

- Arran–area 43.201 ha/106,750 acres; highest points Goat Fell (874m/2,868ft) Caisteal Abhail (834m/2,735ft); geologically very

complex, it was described by Scottish geologist Sir Archibald Geikie (1835–1924) as 'a complete synopsis of Scottish geology';

- Bute–area 12,217 ha/30,188 acres; undulating and relatively fertile, hence much of its land is cultivated, with some woodland, although it is today chiefly geared up for tourism;
- Colonsay and Oronsay–area 4,617 ha/11,409 acres; a wide stretch of shell sand between them may be crossed on foot at low tide;
- Islay–61,956 ha/151,093 acres; its large peat deposits colour the water used in its famous whiskies;
- Jura–36,692 ha/90,666 acres; highest points the picturesque Paps of Jura (Beinn an Oir, 785m/2,575ft, Beinn Shiantaidh, 755m/2,476ft, and Beinn a' Chaolais, 734m/2,408ft); poor soils mean that much of the land is now used only for deerstalking;
- Mull–area 941 sq. km/367 sq. m; highest point Ben More, 966m/3,168ft, the highest example of volcanic tertiary basalt in Britain; some natural woodland remains and there is relatively little heather; sea lochs cut deeply into the coastline;
- Iona–area 877 ha/2,167 acres; best known for its religious aspects, it attracts visitors from all over the world;
- Coll and Tiree–areas 7,685 ha/18,989 acres and 7,834 ha/19,358 acres respectively; a single island until relatively recently in geological time, they are flattish in profile; their rock contains quartz and marble (which was briefly mined at Tiree in the late eighteenth century); the coasts are fringed with dunes and machair, and on Tiree are favourable for surfing and windsurfing. Tiree is also much more fertile than Coll and supports crofting.

THE OUTER HEBRIDES

The Outer Hebrides are separated from the mainland by the Minch. The main islands are:

- Lewis and Harris with Great Bernera–total area 220,020 ha/5,389,369 acres; highest point Clisham, 799m/2,621ft; Great Bernera is joined to Lewis by a bridge; much of Lewis is ancient, deep peat bog, while its south-western end and Harris are more mountainous;
- Barra with Vatersay–area 6,385 ha/16,889 acres; highest point Heaval (383m/ 1,256ft); the two islands are linked by a causeway completed in 1990;
- North and South Uist with Benbecula, Baleshare, Grimsay, Vallay, Kirkibost, and Oronsay–total area 72,827 ha/179,956 acres;

highest point Beinn Mhór (620m/2,034ft), on South Uist; North Uist is very low-lying, with half its total area under water; all one long island until the Ice Age; Vallay, Kirkibost and Oronsay are now uninhabited;

- Berneray–located in the Sound of Harris, this island is now joined to North Uist by a causeway built in 1999;
- Eriskay–area 703 ha/1,737 acres; famed as the spot where, in 1745, Bonnie Prince Charlie first set foot in Scotland, and for its traditional music; however, the island itself is rather barren;
- Scalpay–now part of Lewis and Harris, joined to Harris by a bridge completed in 1998.

THE OFFSHORE ISLANDS

The offshore Hebridean islands are:

- Flannan Isles (seven islands known as the Seven Hunters), 21 miles west of Butt of Lewis;
- Sula Sgeir, 41 miles north of Butt of Lewis;
- Rona, 10 miles east of Sula Sgeir;
- St Kilda archipelago, 100 miles WSW of Butt of Lewis, consisting of Hirta (main island), Soay, Boreray and Dun.

GEOLOGY

The geology of Scotland is extremely complex. Its rugged mountains, hundreds of rocky islands, fjord-like lochs, moorlands and glens are the result of a gradual modification by weather, erosion, the work of ice and water and, most recently, human intervention. The British Geological Survey (BGS) is the nation's laboratory concerned with understanding onshore and offshore geology, geochemistry and groundwater. Its activities cover geological resources such as minerals and oil, environmental pollution and hazards from abandoned mines, waste, landslips, earthquakes and magnetic storms.

BRITISH GEOLOGICAL SURVEY (SCOTLAND)

Murchison House, West Mains Road, Edinburgh EH9 3LA Tel: 0131-667 1000 Fax: 0131-667 1877
Email: c.browitt@bgs.ac.uk
Web: www.bgs.ac.uk
Director, BGS Scotland: Dr Chris Browitt
Onshore Geology: Dr Martin Smith
Offshore Geology: Dr Nigel Fannin
Earthquakes and Geomagnetism: Dr David Kerridge

YEARS BP	EVENT
c. 2,500-3,000 million	Metamorphic Lewisian gneiss, found in north-western Scotland and the Outer Hebrides, is formed.
c. 1,000 million	These rocks uplifted to form the mountain ranges of north-west Scotland, at the time linked to what are now Greenland and Canada. In the Inner Hebrides, Coll and Tiree form part of the Lewisian landform of the far north-west.
c. 900 million	Torridonian sandstone, the oldest sedimentary rock in Britain, is deposited by rivers from Greenland in north-west Scotland, forming Torridonian mountains, e.g. Liathach (1,054m/3,436ft) and An Teallach (1,062m/3,484ft), once over 10,000 feet high. Further north, sand fills an old valley in Assynt, leaving relict mountains, e.g. Suilven (731m/2,399ft), rising abruptly from barren moorland
From c. 800 million	The formation of the rocks that make up most of the Highlands we now see begins, when the area is an ocean trough. River deposits pour into this trough for some 400-500 million years.
c. 670 million	Scotland (at the time 30° south of the Equator) is covered by huge ice-sheet, resulting in glacial deposits which form Inner Hebrides south of Coll and Tiree.
c. 500 million	Caledonian Mountains are thrust up and folded as the American and European tectonic plates start to converge. Subsequent glaciation and weathering mould the rocks into what are now the Grampians and Cairngorms. These rocks, mostly granites, lavas and schists, make up the largest outcrop of granite in the United Kingdom, covering 410sq. km (160sq. miles) and its most extensive area above 3,000 feet, including Britain's highest mountain, Ben Nevis (1,343m /4,406ft).

c. 400 million Scotland lies 20° south of the Equator. Collisions of the crustal plates cause cracks or fault lines (e.g. the Great Glen). Highland Boundary Fault (Firth of Clyde to Stonehaven) and Southern Upland Fault (Stranraer to Dunbar) form boundaries of a great central rift valley into which Old Red Sandstone, debris from Caledonian Mountains to the north, pours for 50 million years. Widespread volcanic activity, especially in what is now Central Lowlands, producing the Ochil Hills, the Pentland Hills and also Glencoe.

340 million Arthur's Seat (251m/833ft), in Edinburgh, Scotland's best-preserved extinct volcano; active. The igneous rocks of this area, a mixture of lavas and granite, extend to the Cheviot Hills on the English border.

350-300 million Carboniferous period: Scotland lies at Equator. Volcanic activity ceases; warm seawater floods central rift valley. Tropical swamps and deltas result, laying down rock types which give rise to limestone, coal, oil-shale and ironstone. East and north of the Caledonian Mountains, sedimentary Old Red Sandstone, deposited in shallow seas, is eventually uplifted, producing the sandstone lowlands of the Moray Firth area, Caithness and Orkney. Erosion after this uplift can now be seen in cliffs and sea stacks, e.g. the Old Man of Hoy.

300-200 million Permian and Triassic periods: New Red Sandstone formed. Much of this is now under water, notably under the North Sea, providing the basis for North Sea oil reserves.

70-50 million Jurassic period: American and European continents begin to pull apart; faults develop, forming the North Atlantic. Major volcanic upheaval affects Inner Hebrides, parts of Argyll and Arran. Extensive lava flows from massive volcanoes bury the older rocks; there is further faulting and uplift. Ben More

(966m/3,169ft), the highest mountain on Mull, consists entirely of lava. Lava flows result in the contorted landscape of northern Skye. Erosion of these volcanic rocks produces the gabbro of the Cuillin ridge, Skye. Small Isles also a product of volcanic activity.

from 50 million Scotland gradually attains its present shape.

from 3 million Three periods of glaciation occur, each lasting thousands of years. Scotland's ice-cap is centred in the Grampians. Intense glaciation produces the characteristic U-shaped valleys, some filled with water (e.g. Loch Lomond). Glacial erosion can also be seen in the mountain areas as corries and troughs, and in the lowlands and plateaux. Large areas of Lewis and Sutherland are moulded down into the characteristic knob and lochan terrain. Lowland areas accumulate layers of glacial deposits, such as those on which Glasgow is built.

c. 10,000 End of the Ice Age: glacial deposits result in the white sands found on Barra, the Uists and parts of the west coast. As the ice recedes, the sea-level rises, leading to formation of the fjord-like coastline of western Scotland; post-glacial drowning in Shetland produces a similar effect.

8,000 to present Human activity, e.g. deforestation, mining, quarrying, dumping, is the greatest cause of change in the shape and structure of the land.

CLIMATE

Scotland's temperate climate owes much to the warm ocean current known as the Gulf Stream. In the same latitude in the northern hemisphere, only the west coast of Canada, close to the border of Alaska, enjoys a similar climate. Pressure systems rolling in off the Atlantic control Scotland's climate, especially on the west coast, which is significantly wetter than the rest of the country, but milder in winter, due to the influence of the Gulf Stream. The climate of some of the Western Isles is sufficiently mild to allow introduced subtropical plant species to grow.

RAINFALL

Rainfall varies markedly from west to east across Scotland. The rugged scenic areas are very wet: the Western Highlands, especially around Loch Quoich, average 4,000mm (157 inches) a year, falling on average over 250 days per annum. By contrast the east coast averages less than 800mm (31 inches) falling on an average of 175 days per annum, with Dunbar, at 555mm (22 inches), being the driest. It is the heavy rainfall that provides the natural resource for the generation of hydro-electricity. There is a marked seasonal variation in average monthly rainfall in the west of Scotland, the wettest months being September to January; this seasonal variation is less marked in the east. There is a much greater chance of enjoying dry, settled weather in spring and early summer.

The wettest day on record was 17 January 1974, when 238.4mm (9.39 inches) fell at Sloy Main Adit on Loch Lomond. A local storm produced 254mm (10 inches) in just over 24 hours at Cruadach on Loch Quoich in December 1954.

The most damaging floods in the last 200 years include the Moray floods of August 1829, when record levels were reached on the Spey and Dee. Massive floods occurred on 5–6 February 1989 in widespread storms from Loch Shin to Loch Lomond. Kinlochhourn registered 306mm (12.05 inches), the highest two-day total ever recorded in Britain. The floods of April 2000 and 2001 caused millions of pounds of damage to parts of eastern Scotland, and more especially central Scotland and Edinburgh.

SUNSHINE

Monthly averages of mean daily sunshine show a strong bias in favour of late spring and early summer, especially on the west coast and the Western Isles, where May is the sunniest month of the year, closely followed by June. April on the west coast is often more sunny than July or August. The sunniest parts of Scotland are in Angus, Fife, the Lothians, Ayrshire, Dumfries and Galloway, and the western coastal fringes from the Uists to the Firth of Clyde and the Solway Firth. In any given year, Dunbar, on average, is the sunniest place in Scotland with 1,523 hours. The dullest parts of Scotland are the mountain regions of the Highlands, with an average of less than 1,100 hours of sunshine a year. The sunniest months on record were May 1946 and May 1975, when 329 hours of bright sunshine were registered at Tiree. Conversely, the dullest month on record was January 1983 with just 0.6 hours (36 minutes) recorded at Cape Wrath.

Scotland's relatively high latitude means that winter days are very short, but in compensation, summer days are long with extended twilight. Around the longest day of the year darkness is never complete in the north of Scotland. In Shetland this is called the 'simmer dim'. Lerwick has about four hours more daylight, including twilight, at mid-summer than London. The least sunshine in Britain is at Lochhranza on the Isle of Arran, where the south-east end of the village is in continuous shadow from 18 November to 8 February each year.

TEMPERATURE

In winter the temperature in Scotland is influenced by the surface temperature of the surrounding sea. The North Sea is cooler than the waters off the west coast, thus the temperature decrease across the country is from west to east. The average winter daytime maximum varies from 6.5 to 7.5 Celsius on the west coast to 5.5 to 6.0 Celsius on the east coast. At night, the average minimum temperature ranges from 1.5 to 2.5 Celsius on the west coast to a little below 0 Celsius over low ground in Central Scotland. The coldest nights occur when skies are clear, winds are light and there is a covering of snow on the ground. The lowest temperature reading recorded in Britain was −27.2 Celsius at Braemar in upper Deeside on 11 February 1895, repeated on 10 January 1982.

In spring, summer and autumn the effect of latitude on the heat received from the sun is a dominant factor; hence Scotland is cooler than England, with the greatest difference in the summer. The mid-summer daily maximum varies from 16 to 18 Celsius on the west coast to 19 Celsius in the east central highlands. The night minimum averages out at around 10–10.5 Celsius across the bulk of Scotland. The extreme south-west, Arran, southern Kintyre peninsula, and Mull and Islay, as well as the Berwick-on-Tweed area, are all about a degree warmer. There are few excessively hot days or nights. The hottest day in Scotland was at Dumfries on 2 July 1908, when the temperature soared to 32.8 Celsius. This temperature was equalled on a few other occasions between 1868 and 1908, namely at Selkirk, Swinton in Berwickshire and Stenton near Dunbar.

Warm or even hot weather can occur in inland Scotland, but it is often accompanied by a large daily range of temperature in the glens, especially in spring and early summer. Occasionally the temperature will fall below freezing at night and rise to the mid-twenties during the day. The greatest range of temperature in one day occurred at Tummel Bridge, Tayside on 9 May 1978. At night the temperature dipped to −7 Celsius, the following afternoon soaring to 22 Celsius giving a range of 29 degrees.

WIND

Many of the major Atlantic depressions pass close to or over Scotland, making strong winds and gales frequent. The windiest areas are the Western Isles, the north-west coast, Orkney and Shetland. Even in these extreme western and northern parts of Scotland the highest frequency of gales occurs during the winter months and prolonged spells of strong winds are unusual between May and August. An exceptional storm occurring during the second week of June 2000 gave the strongest summer winds for more than 30 years over much of the country.

A day with a gale is defined as one on which the mean wind speed at the standard measuring height of 10 metres above ground reaches a value of 34 knots (39 mph) or more over any period of 10 minutes during the 24 hours. The frequency of gales in a year varies from 4 at Glasgow to 47 in Lerwick. The gale of January 1968 was probably the most destructive, causing extensive damage especially to forestry plantations in west and central Scotland. The strongest gust recorded at a low-level site is 123 knots (142 mph) at Fraserburgh, Grampian on 13 February 1989. The strongest gust recorded at high-level is 150 knots (173 mph) at Cairngorm Automatic Weather Station on 20 March 1986.

The frequency of winds from different directions also varies with the seasons. Winds with an easterly component are much more frequent from April through to early June than they are during the autumn and winter, when westerlies are predominant. The lowest barometric pressure measured in Britain is 925.5 millibars (27.33 inches) at Ochtertyre on 26 January 1884.

SNOW

The frequency of snow cover varies considerably from place to place and year to year. On low ground in the Western Isles and in most coastal areas of Scotland, snow lies on average for less than 10 days in a year. This increases to around 20 days in the north and north-east and up to 70 days inland at Braemar. Temperature generally falls with height, and rain which reaches the ground at low levels may fall as snow over high ground. As a result there is a marked increase with height in the number of days with snow falling and lying. Snow cover can exceed 100 days in the Cairngorm mountains.

The windiness of Scotland's winter months determines the pattern of snow cover. When snowfall is accompanied by strong winds the snow is mostly deposited on leeward slopes, exposed areas often being left bare. Natural hollows become filled to a considerable depth. It is the existence of these high-level corries which has enabled the development of the skiing industry in Scotland. It is rare for complete snow cover to persist for long except near the summits of the highest mountains. On average snow lies for six to seven months on the tops of Ben Nevis and Ben Macdui, but snow beds are even more persistent and

many survive well into the summer, some being semi-permanent and only disappearing in very occasional summers. The oldest snow bed in Britain has persisted for 50 years, and is on Braeriach, the third highest mountain in Scotland.

VISIBILITY

In contrast to popular clichés about Scotland's mistiness, the general visibility over Scotland is very good. The greater part of the country is remote from the industrial and populous areas of Britain and continental Europe. Smoke fogs are now rare even in industrial areas of central Scotland, and the growing obsolescence of open fires for domestic heating has greatly reduced pollution.

Inland fogs on calm, clear nights usually clear quickly the following morning except possibly in the glens. When poor visibility occurs on or near the east coast or in the Northern Isles the cause is, more often than not, a sea fog from the North Sea known locally as haar. Haar occurs from time to time, mainly from April to September, often accompanied by glorious sunshine just a few miles inland. It is caused by warmer air flowing over colder sea, which causes evaporation from the sea surface.

Moist south-west winds can result in very low cloud which can be quite dense and reduce visibility to under 100 metres. The west is more prone to this type of fog, which tends to shroud all high ground in cloud and is a potential hazard to hillwalkers. One of the longest-lasting fogs in the world is at the summit of Ben Nevis, which is cloaked in low cloud for around 300 days a year.

THE HISTORICAL PERSPECTIVE

At a time when global warming is high on climatologists' agendas, there is ample historical and archaeological evidence that the changes in Scotland's climate observable today are not unique. Scotland has undergone, and is still undergoing, considerable climate change and variability.

There was a significant increase in warmth, for instance, from c. AD 800 to 1300, when the treeline and limits of cultivation were higher compared to today. Climatic upheavals towards the end of this period, including severe storms, flooding along low coasts, and droughts, affected vegetation and animals, and therefore also the lives of the people of Scotland. A protracted run of wet summers between 1313 and 1320 resulted in crop failure, starvation and disease.

A period of gradual cooling set in from the 14th-century onward. The 1430s especially were noted for a series of extremely severe winters. The history of clan raids and cattle stealing from the Lowlands shows the impact of a deteriorating climate. During the 'Little Ice Age' of the 16th- to

18th-centuries, sea temperatures off the north and east coasts of Scotland were some 5°C cooler than today, and snow was permanent on the Cairngorms. Frosts, a short growing season and low summer temperatures resulted repeatedly in famine and loss of livestock, occurring with increasing frequency and severity. The 1740s witnessed probably the most severe winter weather on record.

The 19th- and 20th-centuries have seen a gradual improvement in Scotland's climate, although with occasional regressions. The last decade of the 20th-century witnessed a significant rise in average temperature and weather events, especially storms and flooding which have become more extreme.

THE FUTURE
What will be the impact and consequences of global warming on the climate of Scotland? In short, the climate is likely to become warmer, wetter and windier. An overall increase in world temperature would mean more moisture. Storms thrive on available moisture, hence Atlantic storms would become even more frequent and destructive. Increased storminess is likely to be accompanied by increased rainfall and the melting of the polar ice-cap will result in a rise in sea-level. As a result, flooding, including flooding of coastal areas, has been identified as one of the main impacts of climate change for Scotland. This has implications for the design standards of existing river flood prevention schemes.

LAND USE

USES OF LAND

AREA UNDER AGRICULTURE (THOUSAND HECTARES)

	1982	1990	1995	1998	1999	2000
Grazing	4,533	4,286	4,159	4,055	4,013	3,978
Grass	1,104	1,130	1,159	1,153	1,176	1,188
Crops, fallow and set-aside	641	644	643	660	656	652
Woodland and other	114	153	213	246	256	261
Total land[6]	6,392	6,213	6,174	6,113	6,101	6,078
Set-aside land[7]	n/a	17.9	80.2	42.9	76.8	76.1

Source: *Agricultural Census, SEERAD*

[6]. Figures may not sum to total due to rounding.

[7]. Set aside figures from SEERAD payments to the one-year and five year set aside schemes and the AAPs.

Broad Habitat	area '000 ha	%
Improved Grass	1050.8	13.1
Arable and horticultural	639.5	8.0
Neutral Grass	168.4	2.1
Broadleaf, mixed and yew woodland	300.3	3.7
Conifer woodland	993.5	12.4
Bog	2038.5	25.4
Dwarf shrub heath	1002.2	12.5
Acid Grass	748.2	9.3
Fen, marsh and swamp	337.0	4.2
Bracken	165.9	2.1
Calcareous Grass	26.8	0.3
Inland rock	38.4	0.5
Montane	48.2	0.6
Standing open water and canals	84.8	1.0
Rivers and streams	20.9	0.3
Littoral rock	0.1	0.001
Littoral sediment	2.1	0.02
Supra-littoral rock	57.4	0.7
Supra-littoral sediment	22.6	0.3
Built up and gardens	150.7	1.9
Boundary and linear features	86.9	1.1
Unclassified	1.7	0.02
Sea	172.0	2.2

Source: *Countryside Survey, 2000*

Much of Scotland is open hill and moorland; less than 40 per cent is developed farmland or woodland and less than 3 per cent is urban land (1998 figures). Of particular note are the Caithness and Sutherland peatlands. These lands constitute Europe's largest area of blanket bog, extending over about 400,000 hectares.

In the period between 1990 and 1998, the largest change in land cover in Scotland has been a decline in the amount of semi-natural habitats by about 90,000 hectares (222,390 acres).

FORESTS AND FORESTRY

Forests and woodlands cover about 16 per cent of Scotland, and nearly half of these are less than 30 years old. While very little remains of Scotland's old native woodland (about 0.15 million hectares remain), large tracts of land have been taken over by productive and commercial forestry. One of the most visible, and most debated, current features of the Scottish landscape, particularly – but not exclusively – in the Highlands, is the presence of large swathes of non-native species of conifer. Although the practice of planting exotic conifer species had been pioneered in the 19th-century by some landowners, much of this planting was introduced after the Second World War. In particular it was encouraged by the Dedication Scheme which was introduced in the late 1940s and allowed private landowners tax exemptions for timber production. More recently, in the 1980s, individual buyers from business and media circles acquired big tracts of northern Scotland and began planting conifers there, the choice of tree depending more on quick returns on investment than on use of native tree species. This loophole was closed by the 1988 Finance Act, and although quite a number of individuals and companies still invest heavily in forestry in Scotland, production-oriented forestry is now balanced by a policy driven by the twin concerns of conservation and access. This change followed the recognition that the forest industry was providing poor economic returns to the community and pressure from environmentalists.

Recently there has been additional pressure from environmental groups for more to be done to improve and expand Scotland's native woodlands, while in 1999 a new voluntary certification scheme for timber products was introduced to give consumers more information about which forest products are produced in a sustainable manner. In 2000, the Scottish Forestry Strategy, *Forests for Scotland*, was launched. This sets out an integrated framework for the long-term development of the country's forestry sector and prioritises environmental conservation and the enhancement of native woodlands through the development of a forest habitat network.

Scotland's state-owned forests are managed by the Forestry Commission, which is responsible for their production and amenities and also acts as an advisory and implementing body for UK government forestry policy towards both public and private sectors. The Commission manages about 40 per cent of all Scotland's forests. Although its remit is UK-wide, the Commission is based in Edinburgh in recognition of the fact that Scotland accounts for about half the nation's publicly-owned forestry.

Privately-owned forestry also owes much to Forestry Commission expertise and financial assistance in the form of grants and tax incentives. Forestry is a major source of rural employment providing over 10,000 jobs.

LAND OWNERSHIP

About three per cent of Scotland's land area is covered by cities and towns. Approximately 12 per cent is owned by public bodies, such as the Forestry Commission. Ownership of the rest of the country is dominated by a relatively small number of institutional and private landowners. Recent figures indicate that of the 6,558,978 hectares (16,207,236 acres) in private ownership:

One quarter is owned by 66 landowners in estates of 30,700 acres and larger

One third is owned by 120 landowners in estates of 21,000 acres and larger

One half is owned by 343 landowners in estates of 7,500 acres and larger

Two thirds is owned by 1,252 landowners in estates of 1,200 acres and larger

Source: *The Pattern of Landownership in Scotland*
Derived from Wightman (1996), Wightman (1998) and other unpublished data.

Estates are owned by individuals and entities other than individuals – joint owners, trusts, non-governmental organisations (NGOs) and companies, including investment forestry companies. Some owners are resident all year round and make a living from their estates; some use them as holiday homes; others, particularly owners of land under forestry, exploit them commercially but live elsewhere. Recent figures produced by Highland Council show that foreign owners now control 365,000 hectares (about 900,000 acres) in the Highlands, while other research suggests that overseas buyers now control as much as 18 per cent of all land in Scotland.

THE TOP FIVE NON-PUBLIC LANDOWNERS IN SCOTLAND

- Buccleuch Estates Ltd
- National Trust for Scotland
- Blair Trust and Sarah Broughton
- Invercauld and Torloisk Trusts
- Alcan Highland Estates Ltd

Land changes hands faster in the Highlands than elsewhere in Scotland. Research carried out in 1983 showed that about 6 per cent of Highland estates changed hands every year compared with 2 per cent for the rest of Scotland, and only four estates had remained in the same hands for over a century.

The agility of turnover has also been beneficial for the non-profit sector, whose holdings in Scotland have more than doubled in size since 1980 and are expected to double again by 2010. About 45 not-for-profit organisations, including 'green charities' such as the National Trust for Scotland (NTS), the John Muir Trust (JMT), the Royal Society for the Protection of Birds (RSPB) and the Scottish Wildlife Trust, own or lease about 266,413 hectares (about 658,000) acres in the Highlands. The RSPB now holds some 35,630 hectares (88,041 acres) in the Highlands and the island of Skye, compared to 16,000 hectares (nearly 40,000 acres) some 10 years ago; while the John Muir Trust owns and manages seven sites around Scotland, totalling some 20,000 hectares (50,000 acres). In spring 2000, JMT purchased 1,694 hectares (4,185 acres) including the southern parts of Ben Nevis, together with two neighbouring mountains and the upper Glen Nevis nature reserve, from the Fairfax-Lucy family, who had owned the land for the past 150 years.

In the past ten years, crofting communities have started to acquire the land on which they live and work. In 1993, the Assynt Crofters' Trust accomplished the first ever community buy-out of estate land in Scotland, and are now developing projects there to strengthen the local economy and conserve the environment. Following this pioneering example, Eigg, one of the small isles south of Skye, was sold in 1997 for £1.5 million to the Isle of Eigg Heritage Trust, which is jointly controlled by the island's 75 residents, Highland Council and Scottish Wildlife Trust. (Two other islands of the group, Rum and Canna, already belong to national conservation agencies.) In Knoydart, one of Scotland's most isolated inhabited peninsulas, crofters won control over the land they lived on in a community buy-out in 1998. This was followed by the community purchase of the 3,500 acre island of Gigha in 2001 and the purchase of 55,000 acres of the North Harris Estate by residents in 2003.

New land reform legislation gives crofters the right to acquire their croft land and communities a right to buy land when it changes hands. The Scottish Land Fund, administered by Highlands and Islands Enterprise in partnership with Scottish Enterprise, will also make over £10 million available to help communities buy, develop and manage local land and land assets.

This tranche of legislation opens the door for more local land takeovers or buy-outs and there are a number in preparation during 2003, most notably a proposed community purchase of the Galston Estate in Lewis,

ACCESS

With the growth in large-scale, mechanised agriculture and forestry, tourism, and the popularity of outdoor pursuits, public access to the countryside has become an increasingly fraught question in Scotland, especially in the Highlands and other areas of great natural beauty. In recent years, changes in the pattern of land ownership have also generated many challenges to the long-standing but contested 'right to roam'.

In response to this problem legislation granting a right of responsible access to land for the purposes of informal recreation and passage has been incorporated into the new Land Reform (Scotland) Bill that received Royal Assent in February 2003.

The government's commitment to access legislation followed publication in November 1998 of recommendations by the Access Forum and their endorsement by Scottish Natural Heritage. The January 1999 conclusions of the Land Reform Policy Group recognised the importance of public access to the countryside as part of the wider land reform agenda and the need for change in the existing access arrangements in Scotland.

The access legislation itself was developed with the input of many stakeholders, including a multi-sectoral access forum that included groups such as the Scottish Rights of Way Society, the Scottish Landowners' Federation and the Scottish Tourism Board.

The new access law applies not only to walkers, but also to cyclists, horseriders, canoeists and the disabled.

To ensure that access rights are exercised fairly, Scottish Natural Heritage worked with other stakeholders to draw up the Scottish Outdoors Access Code (SOAC) which defines what constitutes responsible behaviour by the public and land managers in relation to access rights.

THE SCOTTISH RIGHTS OF WAY SOCIETY

The Scottish Rights of Way Society is the successor of the Scottish Rights of Way and Recreation Society Ltd, formed in 1845 for the preservation, maintenance and defence of public rights of way in Scotland. It gives advice on matters relating to rights of way and, where practicable, seeks to secure the recognition of rights of way by agreement. It also signposts the major rights of way in Scotland and maintains a national Catalogue of Rights of Way.

LAND REFORM

The Land Reform (Scotland) Bill received Royal Assent on 25 February 2003, after completing the Parliamentary Process in January 2003. The Bill represents a milestone in the often-heated debate on land ownership and access that has been part of Scottish politics for hundreds of years. The bill has three main aims:

1. to establish the principle of a rights of responsible access to the countryside (land and inland water) for recreation and passage;
2. to give communities the right to buy land as and when it changes hands;
3. to give all crofting communities a right to acquire their croft land.

It is expected that implementation of the bill will be completed by mid-2004. The bill is just part of a raft of new land reform legislation that has been passed since 2000 or is due to be introduced in coming months and years.

Land reform in Scotland has been regarded as a high priority for the Scottish government since well before devolution. In preparation for the advent of the Scottish Parliament, a Land Reform Policy Group was set up in October 1997 to identify and assess proposals for reform in rural Scotland. The Group issued two consultation papers in 1998 and published its final recommendations in January 1999, setting out a comprehensive Land Reform Action Plan, covering ownership, tenure and access, which was adopted by the Scottish Executive. This was followed by a White Paper in July 1999.

The Action Plan contained an integrated package of legislative and non-legislative measures, which included:

A Legislation to reform and modernise existing property laws, including legislation to abolish the feudal system and to replace it with a system of outright ownership of land;
B Legislation on land reform, including legislation to allow time to assess the public interest when major properties change hands, giving a community the right to buy such land when it changes hands, and increasing powers of compulsory purchase in the public interest;
C Legislation on the countryside and natural heritage, including reform of access arrangements and the revision of the SSSI habitat protection system;
D Legislation on agricultural holdings, including provisions for more flexible tenancy arrangements, extension of the role of the Scottish Land Court and greater protection for tenants against eviction, legislation to permit wider diversification and part-time farming by farm tenants;
E Legislation on crofting, including legislation to give all crofting communities the right to buy their croft land, to allow the creation of new crofts and the extension of crofting to new areas, to devolve regulatory decisions to local bodies, to remove the link between crofting grants and agricultural production, and to clarify the law on crofter forestry;
F Non-legislative changes, e.g. increasing the involvement of local communities in the management of publicly-owned land, developing codes of good practice for rural land ownership and land use, and setting up a substantially enhanced lottery-funded Scottish Land Fund.

Key developments in the implementation of this legislation since July 2000 include:

- The Abolition of Feudal Tenure (Scotland) Act (section A) was passed on 3 May 2000 (Royal Assent 9 June 2000) and was enacted early in 2002.

- The Title Conditions (Scotland) Bill, which follows the Abolition of Feudal Tenure (Scotland) Act 2000, passed Stage 3 of the Parliamentary process on 26 February 2003. This Bill is intended to reform, modernise and simplify the law relating to all conditions and burdens on land contained in title deeds.

- The Bill to reform leasehold casualties, introduced to Parliament on 11 May 2000; obtained Royal Assent on 12 April 2001.

- The National Parks (Scotland) Act was passed by the Scottish Parliament on 5 July 2000 (Royal Assent 9 August 2000). The boundaries of the first National Park, Loch Lomond and Trossachs, were formally defined in June 2001 (see National Parks, p381).

- Detailed proposals for reform of the SSSI system were published on 7 March 2001 by the Environment Minister Sam Galbraith in "The Nature of Scotland."

- The Agricultural Holdings (Scotland) Bill was introduced to the Scottish Parliament on 19 December 2002, Stage 2 consideration was completed in February 2003.

- The Draft Land Reform (Scotland) Bill (section B) was launched for consultation on 22 February 2001, with the intention of introducing the Bill to Parliament in September. The consultation period for the Bill was extended to 30 June 2001, owing in part to the difficulties created by the foot-and-mouth disease outbreak which began in late February.

- Simultaneously with the Draft Land Reform Bill, the Draft Scottish Outdoor Access Code – Public access to the outdoors: rights and responsibilities, was drawn up by Scottish Natural Heritage in consultation with the Access Forum. It was published for consultation in parallel with the Bill.

PROGRESS ON NON-LEGISLATIVE MEASURES

A number of the non-legislative measures included in section F of the Land Reform Action Plan have now been achieved. Among them is the setting up of the Scottish New Opportunities Land Fund of £10.78 million to assist communities' right to buy. Community Land Units of Scottish Enterprise and Highlands & Islands Enterprise will administer this in 2001–2. The Fund was formally launched on 26 February 2001.

Commitments have also been forthcoming from a number of public bodies with landholdings to increasing local community involvement in the management of their land, and guidance on the use of existing compulsory purchase powers has been issued.

THE ENVIRONMENT

The UK government is committed to sustainable development under the terms of the 1992 Rio Declaration, and to meeting internationally agreed targets with regard to the reduction of greenhouse gases, improving air and water quality, protecting the sea, increasing and protecting forest and woodland areas, making energy savings, reducing and recycling waste, reducing empty housing, and so on. While these targets apply to Scotland as part of the UK,

policy on sustainable development and the environment has been devolved to the Scottish Parliament and Executive, which is free to adopt a separate approach to sustainable development in accordance with Scottish circumstances and priorities.

SUSTAINABLE DEVELOPMENT

A series of policy documents dating from before devolution outline the Scottish government's approach to sustainable development. *Down to Earth: A Scottish perspective on sustainable development* (February 1999) covers planning for sustainability in energy, industry, waste management, housing, transport, and other areas. Two strategic documents under the general title *Scotland the Sustainable?*, published by the Secretary of State for Scotland's Advisory Group on Sustainable Development (March 1999) recommended the setting of objectives, activities, targets, and timescales, the establishment of a Sustainable Development Commission, and support for innovation in sustainable development initiatives, and laid out an action plan for the Scottish Parliament and Executive.

Since devolution, the Scottish Parliament and Executive have frequently reiterated this commitment to sustainable development. In its first Programme for Government, '*Making it Work Together*', Scottish Ministers committed themselves to working to integrate the principles of environmentally and socially sustainable development into all Government policies. The second Programme for Government, '*Working Together for Scotland*', reinforced this message.

To guide its work on sustainable development the Scottish Executive has adopted three groups of priority issues: waste/resource use, energy and travel (the three pillar approach). Although adopted in 1999, these priorities accord well with the European Union sustainable development strategy agreed in June 2001.

Waste minimisation and recycling are key priorities. The National Waste Plan 2003, launched in February 2003, sets out objectives for the sustainable management of Scotland's waste. Built around a major funding commitment by the Scottish Executive it sets a target of 55 per cent recycling and composting of all municipal waste by 2020.

Rural Scotland is another priority area. The rural areas of the country constitute 89 per cent of its landmass and are home to 29 per cent of the population, and, despite a low population density of 0.21 persons per hectare, 29 per cent of employment. Twelve per cent of all rural Scottish employees are engaged in agriculture.

AVERAGE POPULATION DENSITY IN RURAL
SCOTLAND, SCOTLAND AND THE EUROPEAN UNION

Rural Scotland	All Scotland	EU
0.21	0.66	1.1

Source: *Scottish Executive, Rural Scotland: A new approach*

There have been a number of important schemes in recent years to encourage environmentally-friendly farming practices. Examples include the Environmentally Sensitive Areas Schemes, introduced in 1987, the Organic Aid Scheme, introduced in 1994, and the Countryside Premium Scheme, introduced in 1997. Rural Scotland: A new approach (May 2000) sets out the Scottish Executive's commitments as regards support for rural life and the natural environment and the promotion of their sustainability. The Rural Stewardship Scheme, launched in 2000, aims to promote a viable and environmentally friendly farming industry and support farmers' management of natural resources by making payments to farmers who manage their land in accordance with specific environmental conditions and requirements – it supersedes the Environmentally Sensitive Areas and Countryside Premium Schemes.

RESOURCES TO BE DEVOTED BY SCOTTISH
EXECUTIVE TO AGRI-ENVIRONMENT SCHEMES,
1999–2002

1999–2000	2000–2001	2001–2002
£18.9m	£20.2m	£21.5m

Source: *Scottish Executive, Rural Scotland: A new approach, chap.5, 'Sustaining and making the most of its natural and cultural heritage'.*

Scottish Natural Heritage (SNH) and the Scottish Environment Protection Agency (SEPA) have a statutory duty to take sustainable development into account in all their overall environmental functions. SNH's budget has been increased from £39 million in 1999–2000 to £46.5 million in 2001–2

More generally, the Executive established in February 2000 a Ministerial Group on Sustainable Scotland, chaired by Sarah Boyack, the then Environment Minister, which would work with representatives of the business and environment sectors to identify practical ways of integrating sustainability considerations into areas such as waste, energy and transport.

In the European context, the Scottish Executive is committed, like the UK as a whole, to sustainable development as a principle underpinning its overall policies and programmes in the environmental, social and economic areas. A long-term strategic view is seen as vital, and sustainability is defined as being not only about the environment but also about social and economic progress. In line with the definition of sustainable development in the Treaty of Amsterdam (1997), the Scottish Executive's approach links the promotion of environmental sustainability firmly with its existing commitments to economic growth with social cohesion and inclusion. Environmental sustainability is being included together with economic growth and social cohesion in the ambit of European Structural Funds programmes for the period 2000–6.

LOCAL AGENDA 21

As elsewhere in the world, local government and organisations seek to promote sustainable development through the Local Agenda 21 programme, under which local authorities draw up a sustainable development strategy for their area, to protect and enhance the local environment while meeting social needs and promoting economic success. The programme is managed by the Local Agenda 21 Steering Group, made up of representatives from the Local Government Association, the Convention of Scottish Local Authorities, the Association of Local Authorities of Northern Ireland, the TUC, the Advisory Committee on Business and the Environment, the World-Wide Fund for Nature, and other organisations.

Although local authorities are under no statutory obligation to take part in Local Agenda 21, most local authorities are engaged in or committed to the programme, and have a Local Agenda 21 officer or responsible staff member. They can contribute to a wide variety of activities related to planning, transport, waste management and pollution control, and so on, depending on local circumstances and needs. There is also LA21 involvement in Local Biodiversity Action Plans, which aim to contribute to local public awareness of issues such as biodiversity and the contribution local action can make to preserving biodiversity at the national and global levels.

The government web-site about sustainable development in Scotland is at www.sustainable.scotland.gov.uk

ENVIRONMENTAL PROTECTION AND CONSERVATION

THE CHANGING COUNTRYSIDE

Particularly in the Highlands, changes in land ownership and use over the past 50 years have been far-reaching. Among the factors involved are grazing pressure from greatly increased numbers of sheep and deer, the loss of land around lochs and rivers to hydro-electric schemes, the rapid expansion of commercial forestry, and a growing tendency for land to be purchased by new owners who are not experienced in the sustainable management of rural and forested estates. The process of change on the land in Scotland is practically as old as its human habitation. There is evidence that much forest was cleared in prehistoric times as the first farming communities became established. Up to the early 18th-century, agricultural life was dominated by seasonal farming cycles. Change accelerated sharply particularly after the suppression of the Jacobite rebellion of 1745, with the disintegration of the old clan society, a marked growth in population (not fully offset at first by emigration), and most of all by agricultural improvement and the introduction of sheep farming into the Highlands, aimed at pacifying the Highlands and exploiting them economically. Also, throughout the late 18th-, 19th-, and early 20th-centuries, much of the Highlands was developed and managed by large landowners as productive forests and sporting estates, including deer forests[1], grouse moors, and angling reaches.

Later, the development of hydro-electric schemes from the 1930s required the damming of rivers, resulting in an increase in the area of lochs and a reduction in the area of grazing land available to both domestic animals and deer.

The Hill Farming Act of 1946 and subsequent legislation on agriculture put in place subsidies that underpinned the hill farming sector until the UK joined the European Economic Community (now the European Union) in 1973. Since then British agriculture of all kinds became subject to the European Common Agricultural Policy. These developments have further shaped patterns of land use across Scotland. Now, the new land reform legislation is set to become the next landmark in the shaping of Scotland's countryside.

[1] Since the Middle Ages, the word 'forest' has been used in Scotland to describe a hunting reserve, especially of deer. A deer forest does not necessarily contain trees.

SCOTTISH NATURAL HERITAGE

Scottish Natural Heritage (SNH) is the government's statutory adviser on the conservation and enhancement of Scotland's natural heritage and on its enjoyment and understanding by the public. It was formed in 1992 under the Natural Heritage (Scotland) Act of 1991, through a merger of the Countryside Commission for Scotland with the Nature Conservancy Council for Scotland. As well as its advisory function to government and others, it carries out certain executive tasks on behalf of government, for example, implementing the EU Directives on Habitats and Birds, collectively known as the Natura 2000 programme. SNH works in partnership with a range of other bodies and land owners on conservation and sustainable management projects in environmentally fragile areas of Scotland, particularly focusing on Sites of Special Scientific Interest (SSSIs), National Nature Reserves and National Scenic Areas. SNH also takes direct action to conserve threatened wildlife through the Species Action Programme. It also engages extensively in environmental education activities.

NATURAL HERITAGE DESIGNATIONS

Natural heritage designations are given to areas of land or water that are considered important to preserve or manage sensitively in the interests of scientific knowledge, the preservation of flora or fauna, or the enhancement of the natural landscape. The system of designations has evolved over about 50 years according to perceived need and they cover a very wide variety of landscape and conservation scenarios. Designated areas can be of many different sizes, again according to the situation they address. Nowadays designated land is being managed more frequently in the context of a working countryside, laying emphasis on sustainability and a harmonious interaction between human intervention and natural processes rather than on preservation for its own sake.

Some, but by no means all, designations are supported by Acts of Parliament: this is the case, for instance, with the new Scottish National Parks. Since designations tend to respond to particular conservation needs, such as the protection of a specific kind of landscape or of particular flora or fauna, a single area of land or water may have more than one designation. National designations can also overlap with European designations or those emanating from international conventions. For example, recent European Directives on wild birds, and on habitats and species, now provide strong protection for a selection of important conservation sites in Scotland, under the Natura network.

Scottish Natural Heritage is the principal body responsible for implementing the provisions of different natural heritage designations. However several other public and non-governmental bodies also own, lease or manage extensive areas in the interests of conserving and promoting Scotland's natural or cultural heritage. These groups include local authorities, the Forestry Commission, the National Trust for Scotland, Historic Scotland, the Royal Society for the Protection of Birds and other wildlife protection organisations, and the John Muir Trust.

NATIONAL PARKS

Scotland's first National Park was formally inaugurated on 24 July 2002. The Loch Lomond and Trossachs park covers 1,650 square kilometres of countryside and includes the Argyll Forest Park, the Lake of Menteith, Ben Vorlich, Glen Ogle, Loch Earn, Ben More and the communities of Tyndrum, Crianlarich and Killin.

The development of Scotland's second National Park – the Cairngorms National Park – is underway. Despite controversy about the park's area, the park authority was established in March 2003 and took up its operational powers in September 2003. The establishment of these two parks follows many years of debate and discussion: legislation setting the framework for National Parks in Scotland was introduced to the Scottish Parliament on 27 March 2000. The National Parks (Scotland) Act was passed by the Scottish Parliament on 5 July 2000 and received Royal assent on 9 August 2000. It sets out the framework for all future National Parks in Scotland. It identifies the aims of National Parks to:

- conserve and enhance the natural and cultural heritage of the area
- promote sustainable use of the natural resources of the area
- promote understanding and enjoyment (including enjoyment in the form of recreation) of the special qualities of the area by the public
- promote sustainable economic and social development of the area's communities

On 19 September 2000 Scottish ministers made a formal proposal under the National Parks (Scotland) Act 2000 to establish parks in the Loch Lomond and Trossachs area and the Cairngorms. The initial consultation on the Loch Lomond and Trossachs National Park closed on 9 February 2001 and a series of public meetings followed. To aid the process a consultation document was produced which outlined the whole process as well as offering options for the development of the park. On 11 June

2001 the extent of the park and its management were announced.

Public consultation concerning the Cairngorms National Park took place until 30th April 2001. Scottish Natural Heritage (SNH), as reporter to Government, then embarked on a consultation exercise designed to discover the public's views on key issues including the area the designation should cover, the make-up of the governing board, its powers and the Park's name.

SITES OF SPECIAL SCIENTIFIC INTEREST (SSSIS)

As of 31 March 2002 there were 1,447 SSSIs in Scotland with an area of 1,007,260ha/2,488,939 acres, approximately 13 per cent of the country. These sites range in size from 0.1 ha (0.24 acres) to almost 30,000 ha (74,130 acres). Many large sites are in the north and west of the country, with the largest complex, in the Flow Country of Caithness and Sutherland, totalling over 150,000 hectares (370,650 acres).

Site of Special Scientific Interest (SSSI) is the main nature conservation designation in Great Britain. In Scotland it is a legal notification applied to land that Scottish Natural Heritage (SNH) identifies as being of special interest because of its flora, fauna, geological or physiographical features. As well as land, SSSIs include rivers, freshwater areas, and inter-tidal areas, including mudflats, as far as the mean low water of spring tides.

Most SSSIs are in private ownership and the management and protection of these sites therefore depends on the co-operation of individual landowners and occupiers. Owner/occupiers must consult SNH and gain written consent before they can undertake certain listed activities on the site.

SNH must notify the designation of a SSSI to the local planning authority, every owner/occupier of the land, and the Scottish Executive. Forestry and agricultural departments and a number of other bodies are also informed of this notification.

Objections to the notification of a SSSI are dealt with by the appropriate regional board or the main board of SNH, depending on the nature of the objection. Unresolved objections on scientific grounds must be referred to the Advisory Committee for SSSI. The SNH encourages positive management on SSSIs by their owners through grants from a range of sources, the most important of which is the SNH's Natural Care programme of management schemes and agreements. This programme was launched in October 2001 in response to the Scottish Executive's 'Nature of Scotland' proposals. These were launched in March 2001 by the Environment Minister, Sam Galbraith, and included proposals to improve the management and effectiveness of SSSIs and to combat 'wildlife crime' by giving Scottish police the power of arrest in cases of suspected wildlife crime and allowing courts the discretion to impose jail sentences in such cases. These proposals have since been incorporated into draft legislation on countryside and heritage issues as part of the on-going land reform legislation process. They are due to be debated in 2003.

NATIONAL NATURE RESERVES (NNRs)

National Nature Reserves are defined in the National Parks and Access to the Countryside Act 1949 and the Wildlife and Countryside Act 1981 as land designated for the study and preservation of flora and fauna, or of geological or physiographical features.

Scotland's NNRs include some of the country's best known natural assets such as Beinn Eighe, the Cairngorms and the island of St Kilda, as well as less familiar yet equally spectacular reserves like Tentsmuir Point in Fife or Silver Flowe in Dumfries and Galloway.

Scotland was the first part of Britain to acquire an NNR, with the designation of Beinn Eighe (4,758 ha/11,757 acres) in Wester Ross in 1951. The largest NNR in Scotland and indeed the whole of Britain is the Cairngorms National Nature Reserve (25,949ha/64,120 acres). Other well-known NNRs are Ben Lawers, Isle of Rum, Creag Meagaidh, Spey Valley, Loch Lomond, Inverpolly (north of Ullapool), and Sands of Forvie (north of Aberdeen). NNR designation has four main functions:

- Safeguarding the natural heritage for which the reserve was identified.
- Raising national awareness by providing opportunities for people to visit these special sites.
- Providing specialised management to safeguard the conservation interests of the sites.
- Encouraging research and habitat management demonstration projects.

SNH allows access to all reserves provided this is compatible with the wildlife conservation interests of the area. In practice this means that there is open public access to most NNRs.

Most NNRs are either managed by SNH, under lease or ownership, or are privately owned and managed in collaboration with the owner under a Nature Reserve Agreement (NRA). Three NNRs, covering 14,645ha/36,187 acres, are managed on an approved body basis.

As of 31 March 2002 there are 73 NNRs in Scotland, occupying 130,904 hectares/323,463 acres, about 1.7 per cent of the country. All NNRs are supported by or form part of a notified SSSIs. They cover a wide range of habitats:

Habitat	Percentage of total NNRs
Uplands	68
Coastlands	12
Woodlands	10
Peatlands	6
Open water	3
Lowlands	1

NATIONAL NATURE RESERVES

National Nature Reserve	SSSI within which the Nature Reserve lies	Local Authority	Area (ha)
Abernethy Forest	Abernethy (inc. Dell Woods)	Highland	2,296
Achanarras Quarry	Achanarras Quarry	Highland	43
Allt nan Carnan	Allt nan Carnan	Highland	7
Ariundle Oakwood	Ariundle	Highland	70
Beinn Eighe	Beinn Eighe	Highland	4,758
Ben Lawers	Ben Lawers	Perth and Kinross	4,060
Ben Lui	Ben Lui	Argyll and Bute/Stirling	2,104
Ben Wyvis	Ben Wyvis	Highland	5,673
Blar Nam Faoileag	Blar Nam Faoileag	Highland	2,126
Blawhorn Moss	Blawhorn Moss	West Lothian	69
Braehead Moss	Braehead Moss	South Lanarkshire	87
Caenlochan	Caenlochan	Angus	3,714
Caerlaverock	Upper Solway Flats & Marshes	Dumfries and Galloway	7,706
Cairngorms	Cairngorms	Highland/Aberdeenshire/Moray	25,949
Cairnsmore of Fleet	Cairnsmore of Fleet	Dumfries and Galloway	1,922
Claish Moss	Claish Moss	Highland	563
Clyde Valley Woodlands	Cartland Craigs	South Lanarkshire	51
	Cleghorn Glen	South Lanarkshire	
Corrieshalloch Gorge	Corrieshalloch Gorge	Highland	5

Cragbank Wood	Cragbank & Wolfhopelee Woods	Scottish Borders	9
Craigellachie	Craigellachie	Highland	257
Creag Meagaidh	Creag Meagaidh	Highland	3,948
Den of Airlie	Den of Airlie	Perth and Kinross/Angus	87
Dinnet Oakwood	Dinnet Oakwood	Aberdeenshire	13
Dunnet Links	Dunnet Links	Highland	465
Eilean na Muice Duibhe	Eilean na Muice Duibhe	Argyll and Bute	360
Flanders Moss	Flanders Moss	Stirling	210
Forvie	Sands of Forvie & Ythan Estuary	Aberdeenshire	973
Glasdrum Wood	Glasdrum	Argyll and Bute	169
Glen Affric	Glean Affric	Highland	14,537
Glen Diomhan	Arran Northern Mountains	North Ayrshire	10
Glen Nant	Glen Nant	Argyll and Bute	59
Glen Roy	Parallel Roads of Lochaber	Highland	1,168
Glen Tanar	Glen Tanar	Aberdeenshire	4,185
Glencripesdale	Glencripesdale	Highland	609
Gualin	Foinaven	Highland	2,522
Hermaness	Hermaness	Shetland Islands	964
Inchnadamph	Ben More Assynt	Highland	1,295
Invernaver	Invernaver	Highland	552
Inverpolly	Inverpolly	Highland	10,857
Isle of May	Isle of May	Fife	57
Keen of Hamar	Keen of Hamar	Shetland Islands	30
Kirkconnell Flow	Kirkconnell Flow	Dumfries and Galloway	142
Loch a'Mhuilinn	Loch a'Mhuilinn	Highland	67
Loch Druidibeg	Loch Druidibeg	Western Isles	1,677
Loch Fleet	Loch Fleet	Highland	1,058
Loch Leven	Loch Leven	Perth and Kinross	1,597
Loch Lomond	Aber Bog, Gartocharn Bog & Bell Moss	Stirling/West Dunbartonshire	428
	Endrick Mouth & Islands	West Dunbartonshire	
Loch Maree Islands	Loch Maree	Highland	200
Mealdarroch	Tarbert to Skipness Coast	Argyll and Bute	205
Milton Wood	Milton Wood	Perth and Kinross	24
Moine Mhor	Moine Mhor	Argyll and Bute	493
Monach Isles	Monach Isles	Western Isles	577
Morrone Birkwood	Morrone Birkwood	Aberdeenshire	225
Morton Lochs	Morton Lochs	Fife	24
Mound Alderwoods	Mound Alderwoods	Highland	267
Muir of Dinnet	Muir of Dinnet	Aberdeenshire	1,415
Nigg and Udale Bays	Cromarty Firth	Highland	640
North Rona and Sula Sgeir	North Rona and Sula Sgeir	Western Isles	130
Noss	Noss	Shetland Islands	313
Rannoch Moor	Rannoch Moor	Perth and Kinross	1,499
Rassal Ashwood	Rassal	Highland	85
Rum	Rum	Highland	10,684
Staffa	Staffa	Argyll and Butte	31
St Abb's Head	St Abb's Head to Fast Castle Head	Scottish Borders	77
St Cyrus	St Cyrus & Kinnaber Links	Aberdeenshire	92
St Kilda	St Kilda	Western Isles	853
Silver Flowe	Merrick Kells	Dumfries and Galloway	191
Strathfarrar	Glen Strathfarrar	Highland	2,189
Strathy Bogs	Strathy Bogs	Highland	281
Taynish	Taynish Woods	Argyll and Bute	362
Tentsmuir Point	Tayport Tentsmuir Coast	Fife	515
Tynron Juniper Wood	Tynron Juniper Wood	Dumfries and Galloway	5
Whitlaw Mosses	Whitlaw Mosses	Scottish Borders	19
		TOTAL:	130,904

NATIONAL SCENIC AREAS (NSAS)

National Scenic Areas have a broadly equivalent status to the Areas of Outstanding Natural Beauty in England and Wales. They were identified by the Countryside Commission for Scotland (now part of SNH) and introduced by the government under town and country planning legislation in 1980. NSAs encompass some of the finest landscape in Scotland and represent nationally important areas of outstanding natural beauty. The designation is unique to Scotland. As of 31 March 2002 there were 40 NSAs covering a total area of 1,001,800 hectares (2,475,448 acres), extending from the Solway Firth to Shetland.

Development within National Scenic Areas is dealt with by the local planning authority, which is required to consult Scottish Natural Heritage concerning certain categories of development. Land management uses can also be modified in the interest of scenic conservation.

A review of the NSA designation was conducted in 1997 and SNH made suggestions to the Government about how it could be made more effective. These are being assessed. The SNH also conducted pilot projects to develop management strategies for NSAs in Wester Ross and on the Solway coast. It is expected that NSAs within the new National Parks will be subsumed into that designation.

NATIONAL SCENIC AREAS

Assynt-Coigach (Highland), 90,200 ha/222,884 acres
Ben Nevis and Glen Coe (Highland/Argyll and Bute/Perth and Kinross), 101,600 ha/251,053 acres
Cairngorm Mountains Highland/Aberdeenshire/Moray), 67,200 ha/166,051 acres
Cuillin Hills (Highland), 21,900 ha/54,115 acres
Deeside and Lochnagar (Aberdeenshire/Angus), 40,000 ha/98,840 acres
Dornoch Firth (Highland), 7,500 ha/18,532 acres
East Stewartry Coast (Dumfries and Galloway), 4,500 ha/11,119 acres
Eildon and Leaderfoot (Scottish Borders), 3,600 ha/8,896 acres
Fleet Valley (Dumfries and Galloway), 5,300 ha/13,096 acres
Glen Affric (Highland), 19,300 ha/47,690 acres
Glen Strathfarrar (Highland), 3,800 ha/9,390 acres
Hoy and West Mainland (Orkney Islands), 14,800 ha/36,571 acres
Jura (Argyll and Bute), 21,800 ha/53,868 acres
Kintail (Highland), 15,500 ha/38,300 acres
Knapdale (Argyll and Bute), 19,800 ha/48,926 acres

Knoydart (Highland), 39,500 ha/97,604 acres
Kyle of Tongue (Highland), 18,500 ha/45,713 acres
Kyles of Bute (Argyll and Bute), 4,400 ha/10,872 acres
Loch Lomond (Argyll and Bute/Stirling/West Dunbartonshire), 27,400 ha/67,705 acres
Loch na Keal, Isle of Mull (Argyll and Bute), 12,700 ha/31,382 acres
Loch Rannoch and Glen Lyon (Perth and Kinross/Stirling), 48,400 ha/119,596 acres
Loch Shiel (Highland), 13,400 ha/33,111 acres
Loch Tummel (Perth and Kinross), 9,200 ha/22,733 acres
Lynn of Lorn (Argyll and Bute), 4,800 ha/11,861 acres
Morar, Moidart and Ardnamurchan (Highland), 13,500 ha/33,358 acres
North-west Sutherland (Highland), 20,500 ha/50,655 acres
Nith Estuary (Dumfries and Galloway), 9,300 ha/22,980 acres
North Arran (North Ayrshire), 23,800 ha/58,810 acres
River Earn (Comrie to St. Fillans) (Perth and Kinross), 3,000 ha/7,413 acres
River Tay (Dunkeld) (Perth and Kinross), 5,600 ha/13,838 acres
St Kilda (Western Isles), 900 ha/2,224 acres
Scarba, Lunga and the Garvellachs (Argyll and Bute), 1,900 ha/4,695 acres
Shetland (Shetland Islands), 11,600 ha/28,664 acres
Small Isles (Highland), 15,500 ha/38,300 acres
South Lewis, Harris and North Uist (Western Isles), 109,600 ha/270,822 acres
South Uist Machair (Western Isles), 6,100 ha/15,073 acres
The Trossachs (Stirling), 4,600 ha/11,367 acres
Trotternish (Highland), 5,000 ha/12,355 acres
Upper Tweeddale (Scottish Borders), 10,500 ha/25,945 acres
Wester Ross (Highland), 145,300 ha/359,036 acres

LOCAL NATURE RESERVES (LNRs)

The 1949 National Parks and Access to the Countryside Act gives local authorities the power to designate local nature reserves, where they own or lease the land and have an agreement with the landowner. They are managed in consultation with SNH. Conservation trusts can also own and manage non-statutory LNRs. LNRs have an educational as well as a conservation purpose and should have facilities to enable people both to enjoy and to understand them.

As of 31 March 2002 there are 34 LNRs in Scotland, covering 9,382 ha (23,183 acres). Many LNRs are located in or on the edge of cities, for instance Kincorth Hill, Aberdeen, and Corstorphine Hill, Edinburgh; but large areas of countryside such as Findhorn Bay in Moray, Wigtown Bay, Dumfries and

Galloway, and Montrose Basin, Angus, are also LNRs.

Other designations which local authorities can make are:

- Regional Parks: large areas, principally in private ownership and not dedicated exclusively to conservation, landscape or heritage purposes, but where initatives can be taken by local authorities to increase informal recreation land uses. There are four Regional Parks in Scotland, of between 6,500 and 44,000 hectares: Clyde-

Muirsheil, Fife, the Pentland Hills and Loch Lomond. In total they cover an area of 86,160 ha (212,901 acres).

- Country Parks: also in multiple use, though here recreation is the main use of the land. Close to, or within, urban areas and smaller than Regional Parks (40-600 hectares), they are mostly owned and managed by local authorities. There are 36 in Scotland, covering a total area of 6,481 ha (16,014 acres).

LOCAL NATURE RESERVES

Local Nature Reserve	Unitary Authority	Area (ha)
Aberlady Bay	East Lothian	582.0
Arnhall Moss	Aberdeenshire	9.6
Balquidderock Wood	Stirling	6.0
Birnie and Gaddon Lochs	Fife	28.2
Bishop Loch	Glasgow City	24.3
Broughty Ferry	Dundee City	3.9
Castle & Hightae Lochs	Dumfries & Galloway	137.0
Corstophine Hill	City of Edinburgh	67.3
Coul Den	Fife	10.7
Coves Community Park	Inverclyde	44.0
Den of Maidencraig	Aberdeen City	15.0
Donmouth	Aberdeen City	36.0
Duchess Wood	Argyll & Bute	22.0
Dumbreck Marsh	North Lanarkshire	18.6
Eden Estuary	Fife	891.0
Findhorn Bay	Moray	1,200.0
Gartmorn Dam	Clackmannanshire	44.0
Hermitage of Braid/Blackford Hill	City of Edinburgh	59.4
Hogganfield Park	Glasgow City	46.0
Inner Tay Estuary	Dundee City/Perth and Kinross	1,176.0
Jenny's Well	Renfrewshire	6.0
Kincorth Hill	Aberdeen City	41.0
Langlands Moss	South Lanarkshire	20.0
Montrose Basin	Angus	1,024.0
Mull Head	Orkney Islands	243.5
Paisley Moss	Renfrewshire	4.0
Perchy Pond	North Lanarkshire	40.7
Scotstown Moor	Aberdeen City	34.0
Stevenston Beach	North Ayrshire	12.0
Straiton Pond	Midlothian	5.2
Torry Bay	Fife	683.0
Trottick Mill Ponds	Dundee City	3.0
Waters of Philorth	Aberdeenshire	0.3
Wigtown Bay	Dumfries & Galloway	2,844.7
	TOTAL	9,382.4

FORESTRY AREAS

Forest Enterprise (an executive agency of the Forestry Commission) is responsible for the environmental management of the Commission's forests. There are about 300 SSSIs on the Forestry Commission's estates, some of which are also Nature Reserves. There are also a number of other different designations for forestry areas that are of particular importance to wildlife and in which the conservation of natural habitats, flora and fauna is given a particular priority. These include:

- SSSIs.

- Forest Parks: large tracts of Forestry Commission land, often containing areas of scenic importance, and managed as multi-purpose forestry. The first Forest Park in Britain was in Scotland, Argyll Forest Park (established in 1935). The parks are:
  - Glenmore Forest Park; 3,500 hectares around Loch Morlich. Caledonian Forest Reserve, contains some of the country's most important remnants of ancient Caledonian pinewood.
  - Queen's View Forest Park – Perthshire; 17,000 hectares. Some spectacular white water rivers draw canoeists from across the country.
  - Queen Elizabeth Forest Park; 20,000 hectares. Beautiful mixed woodlands in the famous Trossachs area.
  - Argyll Forest Park; 21,000 hectares. Mixed oakwoods and spruce forest.
  - Galloway Forest Park; 77,000 hectares. Britain's biggest forest park. Boasts Britain's largest network of off-road horse riding routes.
  - Tweed Valley Forest Park; 6,000 hectares.

- Caledonian Forest Reserves: like FNRs, established by Forestry Enterprise as representing the best of the Forestry Commission's conservation areas. These cover about 18,000 hectares of native oak and pine woods in the Highlands;

- Woodland Parks: smaller versions of Forest Parks, usually located nearer to population centres. All woodland Parks are relatively small in area, ranging between 10-150 hectares. Typical examples are Magbie Woodland Park near Dumfries, and Quarrel Wood, near Elgin.

Forest Nature Reserves. There are 46 forest nature reserves that extend in size from under 50 hectares (124 acres) to over 500 hectares (1,236 acres).

Several of the largest are in Scotland, including the Black Wood of Rannoch, by Loch Rannoch; Culbin Forest, near Forres; Glen Affric, near Fort Augustus; Kylerhea, Isle of Skye; and Starr Forest, in Galloway Forest Park.

MARINE RESERVES

There is statutory provision for Marine Nature Reserves analogous to NNRs, covering the management of marine sites in British waters, but it is has never been used in Scotland.

However, SNH has identified 29 coastal marine areas in Scotland that have particular conservation importance. The areas, which cover 111,895 ha (276,492 acres) and include the Firth of Lorn in Argyll and Bute and St. Kilda in the Western Isles, have no statutory focus, but are made known to bodies with which SNH consults on marine issues.

EUROPEAN UNION NATURAL HERITAGE DESIGNATIONS

Two pieces of EU legislation in particular apply to the conservation of the natural environment in Scotland:

- Council Directive 92/43/EEC on the conservation of natural habitats and of wild fauna and flora, commonly known as the EC Habitats Directive (1992);
- Council Directive 79/409/EEC on the conservation of wild birds, commonly known as the EC Birds Directive (1979).

The implementation of these two Directives was brought into UK law by the Conservation (Natural Habitats, etc.) Regulations (1994).

SPECIAL AREAS OF CONSERVATION (SACs)

SACs are areas designated to safeguard rare or endangered fauna and flora under the terms of the EC Habitats Directive. SACs on land are normally also SSSIs. Together with Special Protection Areas, SACs form the Natura 2000 network of sites.

The preliminary list of 90 possible SAC sites was announced in June 2000 by the then Scottish Environment Minister, Sarah Boyack. As of 31 March 2001, a total of 222 sites in Scotland, covering a total area of 839,739 hectares (2,074,995 acres), had been submitted to the European Commission as candidate SACs (CSACs). These include Cape Wrath, Fair Isle, the Monadhliath mountains, and the Solway Firth, along with a number of areas in the Cairngorms.

These areas contain a high diversity of habits and species of European importance, including high-altitude plant communities, bog woodland, alpine and boreal heaths and native Scots pine forests. The area is also important to the Scottish otter population. The area of the CSAC coincides to a considerable extent with that of the proposed Cairngorms National Park.

SPECIAL PROTECTION AREAS (SPAs)
SPAs are land and marine sites devoted to the protection of birds under the terms of the EC Wild Birds Directive. Following the publication in July 1999 of selection guidelines for SPAs by the Joint Nature Conservation Committees, the Scottish Executive has developed a programme to classify appropriate sites as SPAs. SPAs on land are normally also SSSIs. As of 31 March 2002 there were 132 sites in Scotland classified as SPAs. These covered an area of 520,026 hecatres (1,284,984 acres). These include areas providing habitat for some of Scotland's most important birds such as the Glenmore Forest in the Cairngorms (Scottish crossbill, capercaillie); Fiacaill a' Choire Chais, to the west of the Cairn Gorm summit (dotterel and various raptors); and Loch Urigill and six other lochs around Inverpolly NNR in south-west Sutherland (black-throated diver).

NATURA 2000
The Habitats Directive introduced the idea of 'Natura 2000', symbolising the conservation of precious natural resources into the new millennium; and this name has been given to a European network consisting of SACs and SPAs, that is designed to maintain rare, endangered or vulnerable species and conserve their habitats throughout Europe.

In Great Britain the designation is generally operated through the SSSI mechanism for terrestrial sites and protected via the Conservation (Natural Habitats etc.) Regulations 1994.

INTERNATIONAL CONVENTIONS
The UK is party to a number of international conventions protecting wildlife and its habitats including:

- the Ramsar Convention on Wetlands of International Importance (ratified 1976). As of 31 March 2002 there are a total of 51 Ramsar sites in Scotland (total area 313,668 hecatres (775,074 acres)) designated as being of international importance as waterfowl habitats.
- the Bonn Convention on the Conservation of Migratory Species of Wild Animals (ratified 1979).
- the Bern Convention on the Conservation of European Wildlife and Natural Habitats (ratified 1972).

- the Convention on Trade in Endangered Species of Wild Fauna and Flora (CITES) (ratified 1975).

WORLD HERITAGE SITES
These are areas of outstanding natural or cultural value identified and listed by the World Heritage Committee of UNESCO under the Convention on World Cultural and Natural Heritage (1972). They may be urban or rural.

St Kilda is listed as a World Heritage Site. It was the first such site awarded in Scotland and the first for a wildlife area in Britain. The Cairngorm Mountains and the Flow Country have been proposed as future sites and their status is under review.

Edinburgh Old and New Towns were accorded World Heritage Site status in 1995 due to their cultural heritage value. The Heart of Neolithic Orkney and New Lanark are also designated as World Heritage Sites for this reason.

WILDLIFE CONSERVATION
The Wildlife and Countryside Act 1981 gives legal protection to a wide range of wild animals and plants. Subject to parliamentary approval, the Secretary of State responsible for the Environment may vary the animals and plants given legal protection. The most recent review of Schedules 5 and 8 was published by the Joint Nature Conservation Committee in September 2002. It recommended increased protection for one species (Water Vole, to become fully protected), partial protection for one species (Roman Snail), and full protection for seven marine fish (two Seahorses and five elasmobranchs) and two Burnet moths (the Narrow-bordered Five-spot Burnet (or Talisker Burnet) and the Slender Scotch Burnet). During 2003 a public consultation took place under the Quinquennial review and revisions will be made to the Schedules in 2004 by secondary legislation.

Under Section 9 and Schedule 5 of the Act it is illegal without a licence to kill, injure, take, possess or sell any of the listed animals (whether alive or dead) and to disturb its place of shelter and protection or to destroy that place.

Under Section 13 and Schedule 8 of the Act it is illegal without a licence to pick, uproot, sell or destroy any of the listed plants and, unless authorised, to uproot any wild plant.

The Act lays down a close season for wild birds (other than game birds) from 1 February to 31 August inclusive, each year. Exceptions to these dates are made for:

Capercaillie - 1 February to 30 September
Snipe - 1 February to 11 August
Wild Duck and Wild Goose (below high water mark) - 21 February to 31 August

Birds which may be killed or taken in Scotland outside the close season (except on Sundays and on Christmas Day) are the above-named, plus coot, certain wild duck (gadwall, goldeneye, mallard, pintail, pochard, shoveler, teal, tufted duck, wigeon), certain wild geese (Canada, greylag, pink-footed), moorhen, golden plover and woodcock.

Certain wild birds may be killed or taken subject to the conditions of a general licence at any time by authorised persons: crow, collared dove, gull (great and lesser black-backed or herring), jackdaw, jay, magpie, pigeon (feral or wood), rook, sparrow (house) and starling. Conditions usually apply where the birds pose a threat to agriculture, public health, air safety, other bird species, and to prevent the spread of disease.

All other British birds are fully protected by law throughout the year.

The Protection of Wild Mammals (Scotland) Act 2002 was passed by the Parliament on 13 February 2002 and received Royal Assent on 15 March 2002. This act aims to protect wild mammals and makes it an offence for a person to deliberately hunt a wild mammal with a dog.

PROTECTED SPECIES

The lists below contain details of protected species of animal and plant in the UK. Degrees of protection for certain species are determined statutorily. For further information please contact Scottish Natural Heritage.

ANIMALS PROTECTED BY SCHEDULE 5

Common name	Scientific name
Adder	Vipera berus
Allis shad	Alosa alosa
Anemone, Ivell's Sea	Edwardsia ivelli
Anemone, Startlet Sea	Nematosella vectensis
Apus	Triops cancriformis
Bat, Horseshoe (all species)	Rhinolophidae
Bat, Typical (all species)	Vespertilionidae
Beetle	Graphoderus zonatus
Beetle	Hypebaeus flavipes
Beetle, Lesser Silver Water	Hydrochara caraboides
Beetle, Mire Pill	Curimopsis nigrita
Beetle, Rainbow Leaf	Chrysolina cerealis
Beetle, Stag	Lucanus cervus
Beetle, Violet Click	Limoniscus violaceus
Beetle, Water	Paracymus aeneus
Burbot	Lota lota
Butterfly, Adonis Blue	Lysandra bellargus
Butterfly, Black Hairstreak	Strymonidia pruni
Butterfly, Brown Hairstreak	Thecla betulae
Butterfly, Chalkhill Blue	Lysandra coridon

Butterfly, Chequered Skipper	Carterocephalus palaemon
Butterfly, Duke of Burgundy Fritillary	Hamearis lucina
Butterfly, Glanville Fritillary	Melitaea cinxia
Butterfly, Heath Fritillary	Mellicta athalia (otherwise known as Melitaea athalia)
Butterfly, High Brown Fritillary	Argynnis adippe
Butterfly, Large Blue	Maculinea arion
Butterfly, Large Copper	Lycaena dispar
Butterfly, Large Heath	Coenonympha tullia
Butterfly, Large Tortoiseshell	Nymphalis polychloros
Butterfly, Lulworth Skipper	Thymelicus acteon
Butterfly, Marsh Fritillary	Eurodryas aurinia
Butterfly, Mountain Ringlet	Erebia epiphron
Butterfly, Northern Brown Argus	Aricia artaxerxes
Butterfly, Pearl-bordered Fritillary	Boloria euphrosyne
Butterfly, Purple Emperor	Apatura iris
Butterfly, Silver Spotted Skipper	Hesperia comma
Butterfly, Silver-studded Blue	Plebejus argus
Butterfly, Small Blue	Cupido minimus
Butterfly, Swallowtail	Papilio machaon
Butterfly, White Letter Hairstreak	Stymonida w-album
Butterfly, Wood White	Leptidea sinapis
Cat, Wild	Felis silvestris
Cicada, New Forest	Cicadetta montana
Crayfish, Atlantic Stream	Austropotamobius pallipes
Cricket, Field	Gryllus campestris
Cricket, Mole	Gryllotalpa gryllotalpa
Damselfly, Southern	Coenagrion mercuriale
Dolphin (all species)	Cetacea
Dormouse	Muscardinus avellanarius
Dragonfly, Norfolk Aeshna	Aeshna isosceles
Frog, Common	Rana temporaria
Goby, Couch's	Gobius couchii
Goby, Giant	Gobius cobitis
Grasshopper, Wart-biter	Decticus verrucivorus
Hatchet Shell, Northern	Thyasira gouldi
Hydroid, Marine	Clavopsella navis
Lagoon Snail	Paludinella littorina
Lagoon Snail, De Folin's	Caecum armoricum
Lagoon Worm, Tentacled	Alkmaria romijni
Leech, Medicinal	Hirudo medicinalis
Lizard, Sand	Lacerta agilis
Lizard, Viviparous	Lacerta vivipara
Marten, Pine	Martes martes

Moth, Barberry Carpet	*Pareulype berberata*
Moth, Black-veined	*Siona lineata (otherwise known as Idaea lineata)*
Moth, Essex Emerald	*Thetidia smaragdaria*
Moth, Fiery Clearwing	*Bembecia chrysidiformis*
Moth, Fisher's Estuarine	*Gortyna borelii*
Moth, New Forest Burnet	*Zygaena viciae*
Moth, Reddish Buff	*Acosmetia caliginosa*
Moth, Sussex Emerald	*Thalera fimbrialis*
Mussel, Fan	*Atrina fragilis*
Mussel, Freshwater Pearl	*Margaritifera margaritifera*
Newt, Great Crested (otherwise known as Warty newt)	*Triturus cristatus*
Newt, Palmate	*Triturus helveticus*
Newt, Smooth	*Triturus vulgaris*
Otter, Common	*Lutra lutra*
Porpoise (all species)	*Cetacea*
Sandworm, Lagoon	*Armandia cirrhosa*
Sea Fan, Pink	*Eunicella verrucosa*
Sea Slug, Lagoon	*Tenellia adspersa*
Shad, Allis	*Alosa alosa*
Shad, Twaite	*Alosa fallax*
Shark, Basking	*Cetorhinus maximus*
Shrimp, Fairy	*Chirocephalus diaphanus*
Shrimp, Lagoon Sand	*Gammarus insensibilis*
Slow-worm	*Anguis fragilis*
Snail, Glutinous	*Myxas glutinosa*
Snail, Sandbowl	*Catinella arenaria*
Snake, Grass	*Natrix helvetica (otherwise known as Natrix natrix)*
Snake, Smooth	*Coronella austriaca*
Spider, Fen Raft	*Dolomedes plantarius*
Spider, Ladybird	*Eresus niger*
Squirrel, Red	*Sciurus vulgaris*
Sturgeon	*Acipenser sturio*
Toad, Common	*Bufo bufo*
Toad, Natterjack	*Bufo calamita*
Turtles, Marine (all species)	*Dermochelyidae and Cheloniidae*
Vendace	*Coregonus albula*
Vole, Water	*Arvicola terrestris*
Walrus	*Odobenus rosmarus*
Whale (all species)	*Cetacea*
Whitefish	*Coregonus lavaretus*

PLANTS

Common name	Scientific name
Adder's-tongue, Least	*Ophioglossum lusitanicum*
Alison, Small	*Alyssum alyssoides*
Anomodon, Long-leaved	*Anomodon longifolius*
Beech-lichen, New Forest	*Enterographa elaborata*
Blackwort	*Southbya nigrella*
Bluebell	*Hyacinthoides non-scripta*
Bolete, Royal	*Boletus regius*
Broomrape, Bedstraw	*Orobanche caryophyllacea*
Broomrape, Oxtongue	*Orobanche loricata*
Broomrape, Thistle	*Orobanche reticulata*
Cabbage, Lundy	*Rhynchosinapis wrightii*
Calamint, Wood	*Calamintha sylvatica*
Caloplaca, Snow	*Caloplaca nivalis*
Catapyrenium, Tree	*Catapyrenium psoromoides*
Catchfly, Alpine	*Lychnis alpina*
Catillaria, Laurer's	*Catellaria laureri*
Centaury, Slender	*Centaurium tenuiflorum*
Cinquefoil, Rock	*Potentilla rupestris*
Cladonia, Convoluted	*Cladonia convoluta*
Cladonia, Upright Mountain	*Cladonia stricta*
Clary, Meadow	*Salvia pratensis*
Club-rush, Triangular	*Scirpus triquetrus*
Colt's-foot, Purple	*Homogyne alpina*
Cotoneaster, Wild	*Cotoneaster integerrimus*
Cottongrass, Slender	*Eriophorum gracile*
Cow-wheat, Field	*Melampyrum arvense*
Crocus, Sand	*Romulea columnae*
Crystalwort, Lizard	*Riccia bifurca*
Cudweed, Broad-leaved	*Filago pyramidata*
Cudweed, Jersey	*Gnaphalium luteoalbum*
Cudweed, Red-tipped	*Filago lutescens*
Cut-grass	*Leersia oryzoides*
Deptford Pink (England and Wales only)	*Dianthus armeria*
Diapensia	*Diapensia lapponica*
Dock, Shore	*Rumex rupestris*
Earwort, Marsh	*Jamesoniella undulifolia*
Eryngo, Field	*Eryngium campestre*
Feather-moss, Polar	*Hygrohypnum polare*
Fern, Dickie's Bladder	*Cystopteris dickieana*
Fern, Killarney	*Trichomanes speciosum*
Flapwort, Norfolk	*Lieocolea rutheana*
Fleabane, Alpine	*Erigeron borealis*
Fleabane, Small	*Pulicaria vulgaris*

Pigmyweed	*Crassula aquatica*
Pine, Ground	*Ajuga chamaepitys*
Pink, Cheddar	*gratianopolitanus*
Pink, Childling	*Petroraghia nanteuilii*
Plantain, Floating Water	*Luronium natans*
Polypore, Oak	*Buglossoporus pulvinus*
Pseudocyphellaria, Ragged	*Pseudocyphellaria lacerata*
Psora, Rusty Alpine	*Psora rubiformis*
Puffball, Sandy Stilt	*Battarraea phalloides*
Ragwort, Fen	*Senecio paludosus*
Ramping-fumitory, Martin's	*Fumaria martinii*
Rampion, Spiked	*Phyteuma spicatum*
Restharrow, Small	*Ononis reclinata*
Rock-cress, Alpine	*Arabis alpina*
Rock-cress, Bristol	*Arabis stricta*
Rustworth, Western	*Marsupella profunda*
Sandwort, Norwegian	*Arenaria norvegica*
Sandwort, Teesdale	*Minuartia stricta*
Saxifrage, Drooping	*Saxifraga cernua*
Saxifrage, Marsh	*Saxifraga hirculus*
Saxifrage, Tufted	*Saxifraga cespitosa*
Solenopsora, Serpentine	*Solenopsora liparina*
Solomon's-seal, Whorled	*Polygonatum verticillatum*
Sow-thistle, Alpine	*Cicerbita alpina*
Spearwort, Adder's-tongue	*Ranunculus ophioglossifolius*
Speedwell, Fingered	*Veronica triphyllos*
Speedwell, Spiked	*Veronica spicata*
Spike-rush, Dwarf	*Eleocharis parvula*
Stack Fleawort, South: see above under Fleawort South Stack	
Star-of-Bethlehem, Early	*Gagea bohemica*
Starfruit	*Damasonium alisma*
Stonewort, Bearded	*Chara canescens*
Stonewort, Foxtail	*Lamprothamnium papulosum*
Strapwort	*Corrigiola litoralis*
Sulphur-tresses, Alpine	*Alectoria ochroleuca*
Threadmoss, Long-leaved	*Bryum neodamense*
Turpswort	*Geocalyx graveolens*
Violet, Fen	*Viola persicifolia*
Viper's-grass	*Scorzonera humilis*
Water-plantain, Ribbon leaved	*Alisma gramineum*
Wood-sedge, Starved	*Carex depauperata*
Woodsia, Alpine	*Woodsia alpina*
Woodsia, Oblong	*Woodsia ilvensis*
Wormwood, Field	*Artemisia campestris*
Woundwort, Downy	*Stachys germanica*
Woundwort, Limestone	*Stachys alpina*
Yellow-rattle, Greater	*Rhinanthus serotinus*

CLOSE SEASONS AND RESTRICTIONS ON GAME

Shooting game or hares at night is prohibited, with certain exceptions. Although there are no legal restrictions, it is not customary to kill game on a Sunday or Christmas Day. If shooting is to take place on a Sunday, it should begin after noon.

All dates are inclusive.

GAME BIRDS

Black game (heathfowl)	11 December to 19 August
Grouse (muirfowl)	11 December to 11 August
Partridge	2 February to 31 August
Pheasant	2 February to 30 September
Ptarmigan	11 December to 11 August

HUNTING AND GROUND GAME

There is no statutory close time for fox-hunting or rabbit-shooting. However, under the Hares Preservation Act 1892 the sale of hares (except imported ones) or leverets in Great Britain is prohibited from 1 March to 31 July inclusive. The recognised date for the opening of the fox-hunting season is 1 November, and it continues until the following April.

DEER

The statutory close seasons for deer are:

Fallow deer

Male	1 May to 31 July
Female	16 February to 20 October

Red deer

Male	21 October to 30 June
Female	16 February to 20 October

Roe deer

Male	21 October to 31 March
Female	1 April to 20 October

Sika Deer

Male	21 October to 30 June
Female	16 February to 20 October

Red/Sika Hybrids

Male	21 October to 30 June
Female	16 February to 20 October

ANGLING

BROWN TROUT

The statutory close time for fishing for brown trout is from 7 October to 14 March inclusive.

SALMON

The Scottish Parliament is responsible for the regulation of salmon fishing, through the Scottish Executive Rural Affairs Department. Local management is devolved to district salmon and fishery boards. The annual close time for salmon fishing in each salmon fishery is set by law. For further information contact the Association of Salmon Fishery Boards on 0131-343 2433 or at www.asfb.org.uk

SEA TROUT

The regulations on fishing for sea trout are the same as those on fishing for salmon.

COARSE FISHING

The Scottish Parliament is responsible for the regulation of coarse fishing, through the Scottish Executive Rural Affairs Department.

LICENCES

No licence is required to fish in Scotland. In the case of salmon fishing, a person must have a legal right to fish or written permission from a person having such right. To fish for freshwater fish, including trout, permission should be obtained from the riparian owner. Where a protection order is in force, it is an offence to fish for freshwater fish in inland waters without a permit.

THE PEOPLE

POPULATION

The first official census of population in Great Britain was taken in 1801 and a census has been taken every ten years since, except in 1941 when there was no census because of war. The last official census in the UK took place in April 2001. The average density of population at the 2001 census was 0.64 persons per hectare.

CENSUS RESULTS (SCOTLAND) 1801–2001

	Total	Male	Female
1801	1,608,000	739,000	869,000
1811	1,806,000	826,000	980,000
1821	2,092,000	983,000	1,109,000
1831	2,364,000	1,114,000	1,250,000
1841	2,620,000	1,242,000	1,378,000
1851	2,889,000	1,376,000	1,513,000
1861	3,062,000	1,450,000	1,612,000
1871	3,360,000	1,603,000	1,757,000
1881	3,736,000	1,799,000	1,936,000
1891	4,026,000	1,943,000	2,083,000
1901	4,472,000	2,174,000	2,298,000
1911	4,761,000	2,309,000	2,452,000
1921	4,882,000	2,348,000	2,535,000
1931	4,843,000	2,326,000	2,517,000
1951	5,096,000	2,434,000	2,662,000
1961	5,179,000	2,483,000	2,697,000
1971	5,229,000	2,515,000	2,714,000
1981	5,131,000	2,466,000	2,664,000
1991	4,998,567	2,391,961	2,606,606
2001	5,062,011	2,432,296	2,629,714

POPULATION BY SEX AND AGE, SCOTLAND, 2001

	Persons	Males	Females
All aged under 16	970,374	497,283	473,091
All aged under 18	1,097,605	562,065	535,540
All aged 16 and over	4,093,826	1,936,450	2,157,376
All aged 18 and over	3,966,595	1,871,668	2,094,927
All aged 16-29	882,508	438,546	443,962
All aged 30-44	1,163,357	563,430	599,927
All aged 45-64/59 (M/F)	1,103,851	607,764	496,087
All aged 65/60 (M/F) and over	944,110	326,710	617,400
All aged 75 and over	360,539	126,215	234,324
Dependants per 100 working age pop.	61		
Children per 100 working age pop.	31		
Pensionable[1] age per 100 working age pop.	30		

[1] Pensionable age is 65 for men, 60 for women

Source: *General Register Office for Scotland, 2001 Census (Crown Copyright 2003)*

INTERNATIONAL POPULATIONS AND VITAL STATISTICS RATES, SELECTED COUNTRIES,

	Estimated population (thousands)		Live births per 1,000 population		Stillbirths[3] per 1,000 total births (live & still)
	Year	Population	Year	Rate	Year
Scotland	2001	5,064	2001	10.4	2001
European Union					
Austria	2001	8,121	2000	9.6	1998
Belgium	2001[1]	10,262	2000[1]	11.3	1995
Denmark	2001	5,349	2000[1]	12.6	1996
Finland	2001	5,181	2000	11.0	1998
France	2001	59,521	2000[1]	13.1	1997
Germany	2001[1]	82,193	2000[1]	9.2	1997
Greece	2001	10,565	2000	9.6	1998
Irish Republic	2001*	3,820	2000*	14.3	1995
Italy	2001	57,844	2000	9.4	1997
Luxembourg	2001	441	2000	13.1	1998
Netherlands	2001[1]	15,983	2000[1]	13.0	1998
Portugal	2001*	10,023	2000*	12.0	1997
Spain	2001	39,490	2000*	9.8	1996
Sweden	2001	8,883	2000	10.2	1998
United Kingdom[4]	2000	59,756	2000	11.4	2000

Sources: *Eurostat and the Office for National Statistics.*

* Eurostat estimate
[1] Provisional.
[2] Excludes Isle of Man and Channel Islands.
[3] The definition of a stillbirth varies from country to country and over time. The position in the UK is described in the Notes and Definitions.
[4] The population for 2000 and corresponding rates for the UK do not take into account revised 2000 population estimates.

PROJECTED POPULATION FOR SCOTLAND 2006–21 (MID-YEAR)

Age	2006	2011	2021
Under 16	917,000	845,000	796,000
16-29	907,000	923,000	823,000
30-44	1,127,000	1,011,000	932,000
45-64/59	1,175,000	1,1274,000	1,428,000
65/60[1]-74	583,000	606,000	553,000
75+	583,000	387,000	441,000
All Ages	5,078,000	5,047,000	4,973,000

[1] Pensionable age is 65 for men, 60 for women until 2010, between 2010 and 2020 pensionable age for women increases to 65.
Source: *General Register Office for Scotland, 2001 Census (Crown copyright 2003).*

POPULATION OF ETHNIC MINORITIES IN SCOTLAND 2001

Known ethnic group	Males	Females	Total
White	2,380,586	2,579,748	4,960,334
Indian	7,965	7,072	15,037
Pakistani and other South Asian	20,762	19,208	39,970
Chinese	8,148	8,162	16,310
Other ethnic minority	15,033	15,327	30,360
All	2,432,494	2,629,517	5,062,011

Source: *General Register Office for Scotland, 2001 Census. (Crown Copyright 2003)*

BIRTHS

During the 20th-century, there has been an overall reduction in the size of families, with fewer large families with many children. In 2001, there were just over 52.5 thousand births in Scotland, the lowest level since civil registration began in 1855. This represents a fall of 22% from ten years ago and nearly half the level of 50 years ago. In 2001, 47.9 per cent of live births were to mothers aged over 30 and 17 per cent to mothers aged over 35, compared to 28 and 7 percent in 1989.

LIVE BIRTHS, SCOTLAND 1989–2001

Year	All Live Births
1989	63,480
1990	65,973
1991	67,024
1992	65,789
1993	63,337
1994	61,656
1995	60,051
1996	59,296
1997	59,440
1998	57,319
1999	55,147
2000	53,076
2001	52,527

Source: *General Register Office for Scotland, Crown Copyright 2003*

ABORTIONS

A total of 12,052 legal pregnancy terminations were performed in Scotland in 2001 (an increase of about 9 per cent since 1990), of which women aged between 20 and 34 accounted for over half. The number of girls under 16 undergoing abortions in 2001 was 276, 2.3 per cent of the total.

LEGAL ABORTIONS 2001 *by age of mother*

Under 16	276
16–19	2,706
20–34	7,553
35–44	1,494
45 and over	23
Total	12,052

Source: *Information and Statistics Division (ISD), Common Services Agency for NHS Scotland.*

DEATHS
Death Rates (Extract of Population and Migration)
Deaths per thousand population

	1991–95	1996–2000	2001
Deaths	11.9	11.6	11.3

Sources: *General Register Office for Scotland, Crown Copyright 2003.*

MARRIAGE AND DIVORCE

Year	Marriages		Divorces	
	No.	Rate*	No.	Rate*
1987	35,813	14.0	12,133	10.2
1988	35,599	14.0	11,472	9.8
1989	35,326	13.9	11,659	10.0
1990	34,672	13.6	12,272	10.5
1991	33,762	13.2	12,399	10.6
1992	35,057	13.7	12,479	10.8
1993	33,366	13.0	12,787	11.1
1994	31,480	12.3	13,133	11.5
1995	30,663	11.9	12,249	10.8
1996	30,242	11.8	12,308	10.9
1997	29,811	11.6	12,222	11.0
1998	29,668	11.6	12,384	11.2
1999	29,940	11.7	11,864	10.8
2000	30,367	11.7	11,143	
2001	29,621	11.7	10,631	

* Per 1,000 members of population.

Source: *General Register Office for Scotland, Crown Copyright 2003*

RELIGIOUS SCOTLAND

RELIGION

About a quarter of the population of Scotland professes active membership of a religious faith. Of this number, the overwhelming majority is Christian (in the Trinitarian sense); nearly two-thirds of Christians adhere to the Church of Scotland and other Presbyterian churches, over a fifth adhere to the Roman Catholic Church, just under 5 per cent to the Scottish Episcopal Church, 2 per cent to Orthodox churches, and 6 per cent to other Christian churches, including Methodists, Baptists, Pentecostal churches, Congregational churches, assemblies of Brethren, the Religious Society of Friends (Quakers) and the Salvation Army. About 14 per cent of the adult population regularly attends a Christian church.

Less than 1 per cent of the population is affiliated to non-Trinitarian churches, e.g. Jehovah's Witnesses, the Church of Jesus Christ of Latter-Day Saints (Mormons), the Church of Christ, Scientist and the Unitarian churches.

Just under 1 per cent of the population are adherents of other faiths, including Buddhism, Hinduism, Islam, Judaism, Sikhism and a number of new religious movements. There are sizeable Islamic communities in Glasgow and Edinburgh, and a significant Jewish community, particularly in Glasgow. The Samye Ling Tibetan Buddhist Centre, based in Eskdalemuir, Dumfriesshire, is building a Buddhist retreat centre on Holy Island, a small island off the Isle of Arran.

Over the past decade adherence to religion has been falling overall, but a steady decline in membership of the Trinitarian Christian churches and Judaism has been offset by a growth in non-Trinitarian churches, Islam and other faiths.

The 1999 Scottish Social Attitudes Survey found that 40 per cent of people in Scotland did not have a formal religion.

At the last census, which was carried out in April 2001, some 67 per cent of people in Scotland stated that they 'identified with a religion', however, 27.5 per cent said they had no current religion, and 17.5 per cent said they had no religion at birth. It was not compulsory to answer the census religion question, however, over 92 per cent of people in the UK chose to answer it.

SCOTLAND'S RELIGIOUS COMMUNITY 1990–2005

Religious Group	1990[1]	2000[2]	2005[1]
Church of Scotland	2,858,100	2,146,251	1,882,400
Roman Catholic	1,072,200	803,732	694,100
Other Christian	158,600	196,577	209,000
Non-Trinitarian	128,700	147,985	155,400
Muslim	26,500	42,557	48,400
Hindu	4,200	5,564	6,100
Sikh	4,900	6,572	7,200
Buddhist	2,800	6,830	8,300

Source: Religious Trends No 4 2003/4, Christian Research
[1] Estimate
[2] 2001 Population census figures

CHURCH ATTENDANCE IN SCOTLAND

	1995	2000	2005 (projected estimate)
Episcopal	20,600	20,100	19,400
Baptist	24,400	22,200	20,200
Catholic	308,800	278,200	247,200
Church of Scotland	290,500	262,100	235,600
Independent	48,600	49,000	50,300
Other Presbyterian	22,800	19,500	16,200
Other churches	32,200	32,700	33,400
Total	747,900	683,800	622,300

Source: UK Christian Handbook Religious Trends No. 3 2002–3

INTER-CHURCH AND INTER-FAITH CO-OPERATION

The main umbrella body for the Christian churches in the UK is the Council of Churches for Britain and Ireland (formerly the British Council of Churches). Ecumenical bodies in Scotland are Action of Churches Together in Scotland (ACTS) and the Churches Agency for Inter-Faith Relations in Scotland. The Church of Scotland, the Methodist Church, the Religious Society of Friends (Quakers), the Roman Catholic Church, the Salvation Army, the Scottish Episcopal Church and the United Reformed Church belong to both. ACTS also includes the Congregational Federation, the Scottish Congregational Church and the United Free Church; the Eastern Orthodox Church has associate membership. The Evangelical Alliance, representing evangelical Christians, has an office in Scotland.

The Scottish Inter-Faith Council is composed of Christians, Buddhists, Hindus, Jews, Muslims, Sikhs and representatives from other inter-faith groups. Churches Together in Britain and Ireland also has a Commission on Inter-Faith Relations.

Several of the UK-wide inter-church and inter-faith bodies do not have offices in Scotland; in these cases the contact details for the UK office are given.

ACTION OF CHURCHES TOGETHER IN SCOTLAND
Scottish Churches House, Kirk Street, Dunblane, Perthshire FK15 0AJ
Tel: 01786-823588 Fax: 01786-825844
Email: ecumenical@acts-scotland.org
Web: www.acts-scotland.org
General Secretary: Dr Kevin Franz

COUNCIL OF CHRISTIANS AND JEWS
5th Floor, Camelford House, 87–89 Albert Embankment London, SE1
Tel: 020-7820 0090 Fax: 020-7820 0504
Email: cjrelations@ccj.org.uk
Web: www.ccj.org.uk
Director: Sr M. Shepherd

CHURCHES TOGETHER IN BRITAIN AND IRELAND
Inter-Church House, 35–41 Lower Marsh, London SE1 7SA Tel: 020-7523 2121 Fax: 020-7928 0010
Email: info@ctbi.org.uk Web: www.ctbi.org.uk
General Secretary: Dr D. Goodbourn

EVANGELICAL ALLIANCE SCOTLAND
Challenge House, 29 Canal Street, Glasgow G4 0AD
Tel: 0141-332 8700 Fax: 0141-332 8704
Email: scotland@eauk.org Web: www.eauk.org
General Secretary: Revd D. Anderson

FREE CHURCHES FEDERAL COUNCIL
27 Tavistock Square, London WC1H 9HH
Tel: 020-7387 8413 Fax: 020-7383 0150

INTER FAITH NETWORK FOR THE UNITED KINGDOM
5–7 Tavistock Place, London WC1H 9SN
Tel: 020-7388 0008 Fax: 020-7388 7124
Email: ifnet@interfaith.org.uk
Web: www.interfaith.org.uk
Director: B. Pearce

SCOTTISH INTER-FAITH COUNCIL
St Mungo's Museum of Religious Life and Art, 2 Castle Street, Glasgow, G4 0RH
Tel: 0141-553 2557 Fax: 0141-552 4744
Web: www.scottishinterfaith.org

NON-CHRISTIAN FAITHS

Several non-Christian religions with significant membership in Scotland do not have representative bodies specific to Scotland. In the following list, contact details for the UK body, or bodies, are given where no Scottish representative body has been identified.

BAHÁ'Í FAITH

The Bahá'í faith was founded by Mirza Husayn-`Ali, known as Bahá'u'lláh (Glory of God), who was born in Iran in 1817.

The Bahá'í faith recognises the unity and relativity of religious truth and teaches that there is only one God, whose will has been revealed to mankind by a series of messengers, such as Zoroaster, Abraham, Moses, Buddha, Krishna, Christ, Muhammad, the Báb and Bahá'u'lláh, whose common purpose was to bring God's message to mankind. It teaches that all races and both sexes are equal and deserving of equal opportunities and treatment, that education is a fundamental right and encourages a fair distribution of wealth.

THE BAHÁ'Í OFFICE OF PUBLIC INFORMATION
27 Rutland Gate, London SW7 1PD
Tel: 020-7584 2566 Fax: 020-7584 9402
Email: nsa.bahai.org.uk Web: www.bahai.org.uk
Secretary: The Hon. Barnabas Leith

BUDDHISM

Buddhism originated in northern India in the teachings of Siddhartha Gautama, known to his followers as the Buddha ('the one who knows'). It is most generally accepted that he lived in the sixth/fifth centuries BC. Although Buddhism died out in its country of origin, it spread widely through Asia developing into a number of forms which are superficially very different. This diversity makes it difficult to summarise Buddhist doctrines in a form which would be accepted by all Buddhists, but the following points would likely be accepted by the majority: Buddhists do not believe in one kind of supreme deity central to religions more familiar in the West. Instead, the course of the universe is determined by the law of karma, a form of moral causation. According to this, the good and bad volitions of beings tend to produce pleasant or painful consequences in present and future lives. Karma generally operates to maintain beings in the familiar cycle of rebirth and death (samsara) which is inevitably a state of suffering (dukkha) in the long run notwithstanding the possibility of interludes of happiness and fulfilment. Buddhism teaches that escape from this cycle requires the threefold development of morality (including the practice of qualities such as generosity and patience), concentration (development of the powers of the mind, including loving-kindness and compassion for all beings) and wisdom (insight into the real nature of things, including out own mind and body). The methods of achieving this development vary from one school of Buddhism to another. The Buddhist Society seeks to raise awareness of Buddhist teachings and practice without favouring one school above another. It runs courses, gives lectures and publishes books about Buddhism.

THE BUDDHIST SOCIETY
58 Eccleston Square, London SW1V 1PH
Tel: 020-7834 5858 Fax: 020-7976 5238
Email: info@thebuddhistsociety.org.uk
Web: www.thebuddhistsociety.org.uk

KAGYU SAMYE LING MONASTERY AND TIBETAN CENTRE
Eskdalemuir, Langholm, Dumfriesshire DG13 0QL
Tel: 01387-373232 Fax: 01387-373223
Email: scotland@samyeling.org
Web: www.samyeling.org

NETWORK OF BUDDHIST ORGANISATIONS
6 Tyne Road, Bishopston, Bristol BS7 8EE
Tel: 0117-924 8819 Email: sally@bristol-chan.co.uk
Secretary: Sally Masheder

HINDUISM

Hinduism has no historical founder but had become highly developed in India by about 1200 BC. Most Hindus hold that satya (truthfulness), ahimsa (non-violence), honesty, physical labour and tolerance of other faiths are essential for good living. They believe in one supreme spirit (Brahman), and in the transmigration of atman (the soul). Most Hindus accept the doctrine of karma (consequences of actions), the concept of samsara (successive lives) and the possibility of all atmans achieving moksha (liberation from samsara) through jnana (knowledge), yoga (meditation), karma (work or action) and bhakti (devotion).

Most Hindus recognise the authority of the Vedas, the oldest holy books, and accept the philosophical teachings of the Upanishads, the Vedanta Sutras and the Bhagavad-Gita.

Brahman is formless, limitless and all-pervading,

and is represented in worship by murtis (images or statues). Brahma, Vishnu and Shiva are the most important gods worshipped by Hindus; their respective consorts are Saraswati, Lakshmi and Durga or Parvati, also known as Shakti. There are believed to have been ten avatars (incarnations) of Vishnu, of whom the most important are Rama and Krishna. Other popular gods are Ganesha, Hanuman and Subrahmanyam. All gods are seen as aspects of the supreme God, not as competing deities.

The commonest form of worship is a puja, in which offerings of red and yellow powders, rice grains, water, flowers, food, fruit, incense and light are made to the murti (image) of a deity.

ARYA PRATINIDHI SABHA (UK) AND ARYA SAMAJ LONDON
69A Argyle Road, London W13 0LY
Tel: 020-8991 1732

INTERNATIONAL SOCIETY FOR KRISHNA CONSCIOUSNESS (ISKCON)
Karuna Bhavan, Bankhouse Road, Lesmahagow, Lanarkshire ML11 0ES Tel: 01555-894790
Fax 01555-894526 Email: scotland@iskon.org.uk

NATIONAL COUNCIL OF HINDU TEMPLES (UK)
Bhaktivedanta Manor, Hilfield Lane, Aldenham, Watford WD2 8EZ
Tel: 01923-856269 Fax: 01923-856269
Email: bimal.krnsa.bcs@pamtio.net
Secretary: Bimal Krishna Das

SWAMINARAYAN HINDU MISSION
105–119 Brentfield Road, London NW10 8JB
Tel: 020-8965 2651 Fax: 020-8965 6313
Email: shm@swaminarayan-baps.org.uk

VISHWA HINDU PARISHAD (UK)
48 Wharfedale Gardens, Thornton Heath, Surrey
CR7 6LB Tel: 020-8684 9716
Web: www.vhp-uk.com
General Secretary: K. Ruparelia

ISLAM

Islam (which means 'peace arising from submission to the will of Allah' in Arabic) is a monotheistic religion which was taught by the Prophet Muhammad, who was born in Mecca (Makkah) in AD 570.

For Muslims (adherents of Islam), there is one God (Allah), who holds absolute power. His commands were revealed to mankind through the prophets, who include Abraham, Moses and Jesus, but his message was gradually corrupted until revealed finally and in perfect form to Muhammad through the angel Jibril (Gabriel) over a period of 23 years. This last, incorruptible message has been recorded in the Qur'an (Koran), and is held to be the essence of all previous scriptures. The Ahadith are the records of the Prophet Muhammad's deeds and sayings (the Sunnah) as recounted by his immediate followers. The Shari'ah is the sacred law of Islam based upon prescriptions derived from the Qur'an and the Sunnah of the Prophet.

There is no central organisation, but the Islamic Cultural Centre, which is the London Central Mosque, and the Imams and Mosques Council are influential bodies; there are many other Muslim organisations in Britain.

ISLAMIC COUNCIL OF SCOTLAND
275 Tantallon Road, Langside, Glasgow G41 3JT
Tel: 0141-632 8028
Chairman: Mr. Naqshbandi

IMAMS AND MOSQUES COUNCIL
20–22 Creffield Road, London W5 3RP
Tel: 020-8992 6636 Fax: 020-8993 3946
Chairman of the Council and Principal of the Muslim College: Dr M. A. Z. Badawi
Director: M.S. Raza

MUSLIM WORLD LEAGUE
46 Goodge Street, London W1P 1FJ
Tel: 020-7636 7568 Fax: 020-7637 5034
Acting Director: Abdelbasit E. Abdelbasit

UNION OF MUSLIM ORGANISATIONS OF THE UK AND ÉIRE
109 Campden Hill Road, London W8 7TL
Tel: 020-7221 6608 Fax: 020-7792 2130

JAINISM

Jainism was founded in the sixth century BC by Vardhamana Jnatiputra, known as Mahavira (The Great Hero), but it traces its roots to a succession of 24 Jinas (those who overcome), of which Mahavira is considered the last.

Jains believe that the universe is eternal and exists as a series of layers, including heaven, the earth and hell. Karma, the fruit of past actions, determines the place of every person and creature within the universe. Moksha (liberation from an endless succession of reincarnations) is achieved by enlightenment, which can be attained only through asceticism.

INSTITUTE OF JAINOLOGY
27 Lindsay Drive, Kenton, Middlesex HA3 0TD
Tel: 020-8206 1003

JUDAISM

The primary authority of Judaism is the Hebrew Bible or Tanakh. The first section (Torah) records how the descendants of Abraham were led by Moses out of their slavery in Egypt to Mount Sinai where God's law was revealed to them as the chosen people. The often two sections are Nevi'im (Prophets) and Ketuvim (Sacred Writings). The Talmud, which consists of commentaries on the Mishnah (the first text of rabbinical Judaism), is also held to be authoritative. Orthodox Jews regard Jewish law as derived from God and therefore unalterable; Reform and Liberal Jews seek to interpret it in the light of contemporary considerations; and Conservative Jews aim to maintain most of the traditional rituals but to allow changes in accordance with tradition.

The Chief Rabbi of the United Hebrew Congregations of the Commonwealth is the rabbinical authority of the Orthodox sector of the Ashkenazi Jewish community. His authority is not recognised by the Reform Synagogues of Great Britain (the largest progressive group), the Union of Liberal and Progressive Synagogues, the Union of Orthodox Hebrew Congregations, the Federation of Synagogues, the Sephardi community, or the Assembly of Masorti Synagogues. He is, however, generally recognised outside the Jewish community as the public religious representative of the totality of British Jewry. The Chief Rabbi is President of the Beth Din (Court of Judgement) of the United Synagogue. The Board of Deputies of British Jews is the representative body of British Jewry.

CHIEF RABBINATE
Adler House, 735 High Road, London N12 0US
Tel: 020-8343 6301 Fax: 020-8343 6301
Email: info@chiefrabbi.org
Web: www.chiefrabbi.org
Chief Rabbi: Prof. Jonathan Sacks
Executive Director: Mrs S. Weinberg
Director of Communications: Jeremy Newmark

BETH DIN (COURT OF THE CHIEF RABBI)
735 High Road, London N12 0US
Tel: 020-8343 6270 Fax: 020-8343 6257
Email: info@londonbethdin.fsnet.co.uk
Registrar: Mr D. Frei
Dayanim: Rabbi C. Ehrentreu; Rabbi I. Binstock; Rabbi C. D. Kaplin; Rabbi M. Gelley; Rabbi Y. Abraham

BOARD OF DEPUTIES OF BRITISH JEWS
6 Bloomsbury Square, London WC1A 2LP
Tel: 020-7543 5400 Fax: 020-7543 0010
Email: info@bod.org.uk Web: www.bod.org.uk
Director-General: Neville Nagler

ASSEMBLY OF MASORTI SYNAGOGUES
1097 Finchley Road, London NW11 0PU
Tel: 020-8201 8772 Fax: 020-8201 8917
Email: office@masorti.org.uk
Director: M. Gluckman

FEDERATION OF SYNAGOGUES
65 Watford Way, London NW4 3AQ
Tel: 020-8202 2263 Fax: 020-8203 0610
Email: office@masorti.org.uk
Web: www.masorti.org.uk
Director: G. D. Coleman

REFORM SYNAGOGUE OF GREAT BRITAIN
The Sternberg Centre for Judaism, 80 East End Road,
London N3 2SY
Tel: 020-8349 5640 Fax: 020-8349 5699
Email: admin@reformjudaism.org.uk
Web: www.reformjudiasm.org.uk
President: Sir Sigmund Sternberg

SPANISH AND PORTUGUESE JEWS' CONGREGATION
2 Ashworth Road, London W9 1JY
Tel: 020-7289 2573 Fax: 020-7289 2709
Email: howardmiller@sandpsyn.org.uk
Chief Executive: Howard Miller

UNION OF LIBERAL AND PROGRESSIVE SYNAGOGUES
The Montagu Centre, 21 Maple Street, London
W1T 4BE Tel: 020-7580 1663 Fax: 020-7436 4184
Email: montagu@ulps.org Web: www.ulps.org

UNION OF ORTHODOX HEBREW CONGREGATIONS
140 Stamford Hill, London N16 6QT
Tel: 020-8802 6226 Fax: 020-8809 7092
Principal Rabbinical Authority: Rabbi Ephraim Padwa

UNITED SYNAGOGUE
Adler House, 735 High Road, London N12 0US
Tel: 020-8343 8989 Fax: 020-8343 6262
Email: infogeneral@unitedsynagogue.org.uk
Web: www.unitedsynagogue.org.uk
Chief Executive: Rabbi Saul Zneimer

SIKHISM

The Sikh religion dates from the birth of Guru Nanak in the Punjab in 1469, who taught that there is one God and that different religions are like different roads leading to the same destination. He condemned religious conflict, ritualism and caste prejudices. 'Guru' means teacher but in Sikh tradition has come to represent the divine presence of God giving inner spiritual guidance. Nanak's role as the human vessel of the divine guru was passed on to nine successors, the last of whom (Guru Gobind Singh) died in 1708. The immortal guru is now held to reside in the sacred scripture, Guru Granth Sahib, and so to be present in all Sikh gatherings.

Every gurdwara (temple) manages its own affairs and there is no central body in the UK. The Sikh Missionary Society provides an information service.

SIKH MISSIONARY SOCIETY UK
10 Featherstone Road, Southall, Middx UB2 5AA
Tel: 020-8574 1902 Fax: 020-85741912
Hon. General Secretary: Mr Kirpal Singh Rai

WORLD SIKH FOUNDATION
33 Wargrave Road, South Harrow, Middx HA2 8LL
Tel: 020-8864 9228 Fax: 020-8931 2623
Managing Editor: Mrs H. B. Bharara

ZOROASTRIANISM

Zoroastrianism was founded by Zarathushtra in Persia around 1500 BC. Zarathushtra's words are recorded in five poems called the Gathas, which, together with other scriptures, forms the Avesta.

Zoroastrianism teaches that there is one God, Ahura Mazda (the Wise Lord), and that all creation stems ultimately from God; the Gathas teach that human beings have free will, are responsible for their own actions and can choose between good and evil: Zoroastrians believe that after death, the immortal soul is judged by God, and is then sent to paradise or hell.

In Zoroastrian places of worship, an urn containing fire is the central feature; the fire symbolises the presence of Ahura Mazda in every human being.

WORLD ZOROASTRIAN ORGANISATION
135 Tennison Road, London SE25 5NF
Web: www.w-z-o.org
Chairman: Rumi Sethna

THE CHRISTIAN CHURCHES

Christianity is believed to have reached the Roman province of Britain from Gaul in the third century or slightly earlier, but spread no further northwards than the limits of Roman rule, leaving the northern part of Britain to be evangelised by Celtic missionaries. The first Christian church in Scotland, at Whithorn, was established by St Ninian in AD 397. But it was with the arrival c. AD 563 of St Columba from Ireland on the island of Iona, and his creation there of an abbey and missionary centre, that Christianity in Scotland took firm root. It was slow to spread, however, despite the work of missionaries such as St Kentigern (also known as St Mungo), the patron saint of Glasgow. Iona remained the religious centre until the time of the Viking raids, in the early ninth century.

After the Synod of Whitby (AD 663) asserted the practices of the Roman Church over those of the Celtic, the Roman Church gradually became dominant throughout Scotland. In c. AD 850 the Pictish king Kenneth mac Alpin established a new religious centre at Dunkeld, but this too was destroyed by the Vikings and the religious centre shifted to St Andrews, where the cult of that saint was growing.

Malcolm III (1058–93) introduced a number of reforms in the Church, including the banning of Gaelic from use in church services. His wife Margaret encouraged monastic foundations and revived the monastery at Iona. In the reign of David I (1124-53), a full episcopal structure with nine bishoprics was established, with St Andrews as the leading see.

THE REFORMATION

By the late 15th-century the church was the largest and richest institution in the country, with revenues far exceeding those of the state. However, the widening gap between the higher clergy, who often combined religious and secular functions, and the underpaid parish priests provided fertile ground for dissent among the lower clergy when the new Reform doctrines of Luther and Calvin were introduced in the mid-16th-century from the continent by John Knox, a disaffected priest.

The Reformers' ideas quickly became popular, particularly in the east and among the lesser nobility. In 1555 nobles who favoured the Protestant cause were organised, with the help of Knox, into the Lords of the Congregation; in 1557, these reforming nobles signed the 'First Bond', in which they declared their intention to overthrow the Roman church. The regent, Mary of Guise, outlawed Knox and his followers, provoking riots by Protestants and a brief war in 1559.

A Parliament (the 'Reformation Parliament') called on 1 August 1560 in the name of Queen Mary but without a royal presence, abolished the Latin Mass and rejected the jurisdiction of the Pope; the first assembly of the Church of Scotland ratified the Confession of Faith, drawn up by a committee including John Knox.

In 1578, the Second Book of Discipline provided for the establishment of the Kirk session as the governing body for each church and set out the overall organisation of the Kirk into presbyteries, provinces and a general assembly.

THE BISHOPS' WARS

In 1592 Parliament passed an Act guaranteeing the liberties of the Kirk and its Presbyterian government, although James VI and I and later Stewart monarchs made several attempts to restore episcopacy. Scottish fears that Charles I would reinstate Roman Catholicism led to the signing in 1638 of the National Covenant, which reasserted the right of the people to keep the reformed church. At the end of 1638 the General Assembly abolished the episcopacy and proscribed the use of the Book of Common Prayer. In the ensuing Bishops' Wars of 1639–40, an army of Covenanters took Durham and Newcastle before peace was restored in 1641. When the civil war broke out in 1644, the Scottish Covenanters sided with Cromwell's army, concluding the Solemn League and Covenant with the English Parliament on condition that England would adopt a Presbyterian church.

The restoration of Charles II in 1660 brought a reinstatement of episcopacy and intolerance of Presbyterianism. Covenanters were persecuted and the Covenant declared illegal. Several waves of protest and repression followed. James VII and II issued decrees in 1687–8 allowing Catholics and Quakers, and later Presbyterians, to hold meetings in private houses; the various Presbyterian factions reunited, fearing a return to Catholicism. A Presbyterian church was restored in 1690 and secured by the Act of Settlement 1690 and the Act of Union 1707.

The 18th-, 19th- and early 20th-centuries saw a series of divergent and convergent movements in the Kirk and the formation of successive splinter groups, which subsequently regrouped. Five smaller Presbyterian churches exist today.

THE CHURCH OF SCOTLAND

The Church of Scotland is the established (e.g. national) church of Scotland. It was established in 1567, and its contractual relation with the state is expressed in a series of statutes from that year onward, concluding with an Act of 1921 setting out the constitution of the new Church and one of 1925 handing over the state endowments to the Church.

The Church is Reformed and Evangelical in doctrine, and Presbyterian in constitution, e.g. based on a hierarchy of councils of ministers and elders and, since 1990, of members of a diaconate. At local level the Kirk session consists of the parish minister and ruling elders. At district level the presbyteries, of which there are 47, consist of all the ministers in the district, one ruling elder from each congregation, and those members of the diaconate who qualify for membership. The General Assembly is the supreme authority, and is presided over by a Moderator chosen annually by the Assembly. The Sovereign, if not present in person, is represented by a Lord High Commissioner who is appointed each year by the Crown.

The Church of Scotland has about 570,000 members, 1,100 ministers and 1,500 churches. There are about 100 ministers and other personnel working overseas.

Lord High Commissioner (2003): The Rt. Hon Lord Steel of Aikwood
Moderator of the General Assembly (2003): The Rt. Revd Iain R. Torrance
Principal Clerk: Very Revd Dr F. A. Macdonald
Depute Principal Clerk: Revd Marjory MacLean
Procurator: P. S. Hodge, QC
Law Agent and Solicitor of the Church: Mrs J. S. Wilson
Parliamentary Agent: I. McCulloch
General Treasurer: D. F. Ross

CHURCH OFFICE

121 George Street, Edinburgh EH2 4YN.
Tel: 0131-225 5722

PRESBYTERIES AND CLERKS

Edinburgh: Revd W. P. Graham
West Lothian: Revd D. Shaw
Lothian: J. D. McCulloch
Melrose and Peebles: Revd A. J. Morton
Duns: Revd James Cutler
Jedburgh: Revd N. R. Combe
Annandale and Eskdale: Revd C. B. Haston
Dumfries and Kirkcudbright: Revd G. M. A. Savage
Wigtown and Stranraer: Revd D. Dutton
Ayr: Revd J. Crichton
Irvine and Kilmarnock: Revd C. G. F. Brockie
Ardrossan: Revd D. Broster
Lanark: Revd I. D. Cunningham
Greenock and Paisley: vacant
Glasgow: Revd A. Cunningham
Hamilton: Revd J. H. Wilson
Dumbarton: Revd D. P. Munro

South Argyll: Revd M. A. J. Gossip
Dunoon: Revd R. Samuel
Lorn and Mull: Revd J. A. McCormick
Falkirk: Revd Ian W. Black
Stirling: Revd M. MacCormick
Dunfermline: Revd W. E. Farquhar
Kirkcaldy: A. Moore
St Andrews: Revd P. Meager
Dunkeld and Meigle: Revd B. Dempsey
Perth: Revd D. G. Lawson
Dundee: Revd J. A. Roy
Angus: Revd M. I. G. Rooney
Aberdeen: Revd A. Douglas
Kincardine and Deeside: Revd J. W. S. Brown
Gordon: Revd E. Glen
Buchan: Revd M. M. McKay
Moray: Revd G. Melvyn Wood
Abernethy: Revd J. A. I. MacEwan
Inverness: Revd A. S. Younger
Lochaber: Revd A. Ramsay
Ross: Revd T. M. McWilliam
Sutherland: Revd J. L. Goskirk
Caithness: Mrs M. Gillies
Lochcarron-Skye: Revd A. J. Macarthur
Uist: Revd M. Smith
Lewis: Revd T. S. Sinclair
Orkney (Finstown): Revd T. Hunt
Shetland (Lerwick): Revd C. Greig
England (London): Revd W. A. Cairns
Europe: Revd J. A. Cowie

The minimum stipend of a minister in the Church of Scotland in 2003 was £19,486.

THE SCOTTISH EPISCOPAL CHURCH

The Scottish Episcopal Church was founded after the Act of Settlement (1690) established the presbyterian nature of the Church of Scotland. The Scottish Episcopal Church is in full communion with the Church of England but is autonomous. The governing authority is the General Synod, an elected body of approximately 170 members which meets once a year. The diocesan bishop who convenes and presides at meetings of the General Synod is called the Primus and is elected by his fellow bishops.

THE GENERAL SYNOD OF THE SCOTTISH EPISCOPAL CHURCH

21 Grosvenor Crescent, Edinburgh EH12 5EE
Tel: 0131-225 6357 Fax: 0131-346 7247
Email: office@scotland.anglican.org
Web: www.scotland.anglican.org
Secretary General: J. F. Stuart

PRIMUS OF THE SCOTTISH EPISCOPAL CHURCH

Most Revd A. Bruce Cameron (Bishop of Aberdeen and Orkney), elected 2000

DIOCESAN OFFICES

ABERDEEN AND ORKNEY
Monkmyre, Myreriggs Road, Coupar Angus, Blairgowrie PH13 9HS Tel: 01224-636653 Fax: 01224-636186
Bishop: Most Revd Bruce Cameron

ARGYLL AND THE ISLES
39 King's Crescent, Aberdeen AB24 3HP
Tel: 01631-570870 Fax: 01631-570411
Bishop: Rt. Revd Douglas Cameron

BRECHIN
Pine Grove, 334 Perth Road, Dundee DD2 1EQ
Tel: 01382-640007 Fax: 01382-630083
Bishop: Rt. Revd Neville Chamberlain

EDINBURGH
21a Grosvenor Crescent, Edinburgh EH12 5EL
Tel: 0131-538 7033 Fax: 0131-538 7088
Bishop: Rt. Revd Brian Smith

GLASGOW AND GALLOWAY
5 St Vincent Place, Glasgow G1 2DH
Tel: 0141-221 6911 Fax: 0141-221 6490
Bishop: Rt. Revd Idris Jones

MORAY, ROSS AND CAITHNESS
11 Kenneth Street, Inverness IV3 5NR
Tel/Fax: 01463-226255
Bishop: Rt. Revd John Crook

ST ANDREWS, DUNKELD AND DUNBLANE
28a Balhousie Street, Perth PH1 5HJ
Tel: 01738-643000 Fax: 01738-443174

THE ROMAN CATHOLIC CHURCH

The Roman Catholic Church is one worldwide Christian church, with an estimated 890.9 million adherents, acknowledging as its head the Bishop of Rome, known as the Pope (Father). The Pope is held to be the successor of St Peter and a direct line of succession is therefore claimed from the earliest Christian communities. The Pope exercises spiritual authority over the Church with the advice and assistance of the Sacred College of Cardinals, the supreme council of the Church. He is also advised about the concerns of the Church locally by his ambassadors, who liaise with the Bishops' Conference in each country.

The Roman Catholic Church universally and the Vatican City State are run by the Curia, which is made up of the Secretariat of State, the Sacred Council for the Public Affairs of the Church, and various congregations, secretariats and tribunals assisted by commissions and offices. The Vatican State has its own diplomatic service, with representatives known as nuncios and apostolic delegates.

THE BISHOPS' CONFERENCE

The Bishops' Conference of Scotland is the permanently constituted assembly of the Bishops of Scotland. To promote its work, the Conference establishes various agencies which have an advisory function in relation to the Conference. The more important of these agencies are called Commissions and each one has a Bishop President who, with the other members of the Commissions, is appointed by the Conference.

SECRETARIAT OF THE BISHOPS' CONFERENCE OF SCOTLAND

64 Aitken Street, Airdrie, ML6 6LT
Tel: 01236-764061 Fax: 01236-762489
President: HE Cardinal Thomas J. Winning
General Secretary: Very Revd Mgr Henry Docherty

ARCHDIOCESES

ST ANDREWS AND EDINBURGH
Archbishop: Most Revd Keith Patrick O'Brien, Con. 1985

Diocesan Curia: 113 Whitehouse Loan, Edinburgh EH9 1BB. Tel: 0131-623 8900
Web: www.edinburghdiocese.free.online.co.uk

GLASGOW
Archbishop: Mario Joseph Conti, cons. 1977, apptd 2002

Diocesan Curia: 196 Clyde Street, Glasgow G1 4JY.
Tel: 0141-226 5898 Web: www.rcag.org.uk

DIOCESES

ABERDEEN
Bishop: vacant

Bishop's House: 3 Queen's Cross, Aberdeen AB2 6BR.
Tel: 01224-319154
Web: www.dioceseofaberdeen.com

ARGYLL AND THE ISLES
Bishop: Rt. Revd Ian Murray, con. 1999

Diocesan Curia: Bishop's House, Esplanade, Oban PA34 5AB. Tel: 01631-567436
Web: www.dioceseofargyllandtheisles.org

DUNKELD
Bishop: Rt. Revd Vincent Logan, cons. 1981

Diocesan Curia: 24–28 Lawside Road, Dundee DD3 6KY Tel: 01382–225453
Web: www.dunkelddiocese.org.uk

GALLOWAY
Bishop: vacant

Diocesan Curia: 8 Corsehill Road, Ayr KA7 2ST.
Tel: 01292-266750
Web: www.gallowaydiocese.org.uk

MOTHERWELL
Bishop: Rt. Revd Joseph Devine, cons. 1977, apptd.1983

Diocesan Curia: Coursington Road, Motherwell ML1 1PW. Tel: 01698-269114
Web: www.rcdom.org.uk

PAISLEY
Bishop: Rt. Revd John A. Mone, cons. 1984, apptd. 1988

Diocesan Curia: Cathedral Precincts, Incle Street, Paisley PA1 1HR Tel: 0141-847 6130
Web: www.paisleydiocese.org.uk

PRESBYTERIAN CHURCHES

THE FREE CHURCH OF SCOTLAND

The Free Church of Scotland was formed in 1843, when over 400 ministers withdrew from the Church of Scotland as a result of interference in the internal affairs of the church by the civil authorities. In 1900, all but 26 ministers joined with others to form the United Free Church (most of which rejoined the Church of Scotland in 1929). In 1904 the remaining 26 ministers were recognised by the House of Lords as continuing the Free Church of Scotland. This Church is also known as the 'Wee Frees'.

The Church maintains strict adherence to the Westminster Confession of Faith of 1648 and accepts the Bible as the sole rule of faith and conduct. Its General Assembly meets annually. It

also has links with Reformed Churches overseas. The Free Church of Scotland has 6,000 members, 90 ministers and 140 churches.

For further information visit:
www.freechurchcontinuing.co.uk

UNITED FREE CHURCH OF SCOTLAND

The United Free Church of Scotland has existed in its present form since 1929, but has its origins in divisions in the Church of Scotland in the 18th-century. The Secession Church broke away from the Church of Scotland in 1733, and the Relief Church in 1761. In 1847 the Secession and Relief Churches united, becoming the United Presbyterian Church of Scotland. In 1900 this church united with a majority of the Free Church of Scotland to become the United Free Church of Scotland. The majority of members rejoined the Church of Scotland in 1929, with the minority continuing as the United Free Church.

The Church accepts the Bible as the supreme standard of faith and conduct and adheres to the Westminster Confession of Faith. It is opposed to the state establishment of religion. The system of government is presbyterian. It has approximately 6,000 members, 41 ministers and 70 churches.

General Secretary: Revd J. O. Fulton,
11 Newton Place, Glasgow G3 7PR.
Tel: 0141-332 3435
Email: gensec@ufcos.org.uk
Web: www.ufcos.org.uk

THE FREE PRESBYTERIAN CHURCH OF SCOTLAND

The Free Presbyterian Church of Scotland was formed in 1893 by two ministers of the Free Church of Scotland who refused to accept a Declaratory Act passed by the Free Church General Assembly in 1892. The Free Presbyterian Church of Scotland is Calvinistic in doctrine and emphasises observance of the Sabbath. It adheres strictly to the Westminster Confession of Faith.

The Church has about 3,000 members in Scotland and about 4,000 in overseas congregations. It has 23 ministers and 50 churches.

Napier House, 8 Colinton Road, Edinburgh EH10 5DS
Moderator: Revd H. M. Cartwright
Clerk of the Synod: Revd J. MacLeod

ASSOCIATED PRESBYTERIAN CHURCHES OF SCOTLAND

The Associated Presbyterian Churches came into being in 1989 as a result of a division within the Free Presbyterian Church of Scotland. Following two controversial disciplinary cases, the culmination of deepening differences within the Church, a presbytery was formed calling itself the Associated Presbyterian Churches (APC). The Associated Presbyterian Churches has about 1,000 members, 15 ministers and 20 churches.
For further information visit: ww.apchurches.org.uk

REFORMED PRESBYTERIAN CHURCH OF SCOTLAND

The Reformed Presbyterian Church of Scotland has its origins in the Covenanter movement. After the 'Glorious Revolution' of 1688, a minority of Presbyterians in southern Scotland did not accept the religious settlement and remained outside the Church of Scotland. Known as 'Cameronians', they met in 'Societies' and formed the Reformed Presbyterian Church of Scotland in 1743. In 1872 the majority of the church joined the Free Church of Scotland.

The Church regards the Bible as its sole standard and adheres strictly to the Westminster Confession of Faith. The Church is Presbyterian in structure, with the Synod the supreme court. At present there are four congregations and approximately 150 members and adherents.

OTHER CHURCHES

ASSEMBLIES OF GOD
PO Box 7643, Nottingham NG11 6ZY
Tel: 0115-921 7272
Web: www.aog.org.uk
Regional Superintendent: Peter Cochrane

BAPTIST UNION OF SCOTLAND
14 Aytoun Road, Glasgow G41 5RT
Tel: 0141-423 6169 Fax: 0141-424 1422
Email: admin@scottishbaptist.org.uk
Web: www.scottishbaptist.org.uk
General Secretary: Revd William G. Slack
In the Baptist Union for Scotland there are 13,991 members, 160 pastors and 176 churches.

CHURCH OF JESUS CHRIST OF LATTER-DAY SAINTS
Church Offices, 751 Warwick Road, Solihull B91 3DQ
Tel: 0121-712 1200 Fax: 0121-709 0180

GENERAL ASSEMBLY OF UNITARIAN AND FREE CHRISTIAN CHURCHES
Essex Hall, 1–6 Essex Street, Strand,
London WC2R 3HY
Tel: 020-7240 2384 Fax: 020-7240 3089
Email: ga@unitarian.org
Web: www.unitarian .org.uk

INDEPENDENT METHODIST ASSOCIATION
Fleet Street, Pemberton, Wigan WN5 0DS
Tel: 01942-223526 Fax: 01942-227768
Email: resourcecentre@imcgb.org.uk

INTER FAITH NETWORK FOR THE UNITED KINGDOM
5–7 Tavistock Place, London WC1H 9SN
Tel: 020-7388 0008 Fax: 0207-388 7124
Email: ifnet@interfaith.org.uk
Web: www.interfaith.org.uk

JEHOVAH'S WITNESSES
Watch Tower House, The Ridgeway, London NW7 1RN
Tel: 020-8906 2211 Fax: 020-8371 0051
Email: pr@wtbts.org.uk Web: www.watchtower.org

LUTHERAN COUNCIL OF GREAT BRITAIN
30 Thanet Street, London WC1H 9QH
Tel: 020-7554 2900 Fax: 020-7383 3081
Email: enquiries@lutheran.org.uk
Web: www.lutheran.org.uk

METHODIST CONFERENCE
Methodist Church, 25 Marylebone Road,
London NW1 5JR
Tel: 020-7486 5502 Fax: 020-7467 5226
Web: www.methodist.org.uk

THE RELIGIOUS SOCIETY OF FRIENDS (QUAKERS)
Friends House, 173–177 Euston Road,
London NW1 2BJ Tel: 020-7663 1000
Fax: 020-7663 1001 Web: www.quaker.org.uk

THE SALVATION ARMY
1 Houldsworth Street, Glasgow G3 8DU
Tel: 0141-226 2459

SEVENTH-DAY ADVENTISTS HEADQUARTERS
Stanborough Park, Watford WD25 9JZ
Tel: 01923-672251 Fax: 01923-893212

UNITED REFORMED CHURCH
PO Box 189, Glasgow G1 2BX Tel: 0141-332 7667

SCOTLAND AND THE WORLD

TIME ZONES

INTERNATIONAL DIRECT DIALLING CODES

CONSULATES IN SCOTLAND

SCOTLAND AND THE WORLD

TIME ZONES

Standard time differences from the Greenwich meridian
+ hours ahead of GMT
- hours behind GMT
* may vary from standard time at some part of the year
(Summer Time or Daylight Saving Time)
‡ some areas may keep another time zone
h hours
m minutes

	h	*m*
Afghanistan	+ 4	30
*Albania	+ 1	
Algeria	+ 1	
*Andorra	+ 1	
Angola	+ 1	
Anguilla	− 4	
Antigua and Barbuda	− 4	
Argentina	− 3	
*Armenia	+ 4	
Aruba	− 4	
Ascension Island	0	
*Australia		
ACT, NSW (except Broken Hill area)		
Qld, Tas., Vic, Whitsunday Islands	+10	
*Broken Hill area (NSW)	+ 9	30
*Lord Howe Island	+ 10	30
Northern Territory	+ 9	30
*South Australia	+ 9	30
Western Australia	+ 8	
*Austria	+ 1	
*Azerbaijan	+ 4	
*Bahamas	− 5	
Bahrain	+ 3	
Bangladesh	+ 6	
Barbados	− 4	
*Belarus	+ 2	
*Belgium	+ 1	
Belize	− 6	
Benin	+ 1	
*Bermuda	− 4	
Bhutan	+ 6	
Bolivia	− 4	
*Bosnia–Hercegovina	+ 1	
Botswana	+ 2	
Brazil		
western states	− 5	
central states	− 4	
N. and NE coastal states	− 3	
*S. and E. coastal states, including Brasilia	− 3	

	h	*m*
Fernando de Noronha Island	− 2	
British Antarctic Territory	− 3	
British Indian Ocean Territory	+ 5	
Diego Garcia	+ 6	
British Virgin Islands	− 4	
Brunei	+ 8	
*Bulgaria	+ 2	
Burkina Faso	0	
Burundi	+ 2	
Cambodia	+ 7	
Cameroon	+ 1	
Canada		
*Alberta	− 7	
*‡British Columbia	− 8	
*‡Labrador	− 4	
*Manitoba	− 6	
*New Brunswick	− 4	
*Newfoundland	− 3	30
*Northwest Territories		
east of 85° W.	− 5	
85° W.–102° W.	− 6	
*Nunavut	− 7	
*Nova Scotia	− 4	
Ontario		
*east of 90° W.	− 5	
west of 90° W.	− 5	
*Prince Edward Island	− 4	
Québec		
east of 63° W.	− 4	
*west of 63° W.	− 5	
‡Saskatchewan	− 6	
*Yukon	− 8	
Cape Verde	− 1	
Cayman Islands	− 5	
Central African Republic	+ 1	
Chad	+ 1	
*Chatham Islands	+ 12	45
*Chile	− 4	
China (inc. Hong Kong and Macao)	+ 8	
Christmas Island (Indian Ocean)	+ 7	
Cocos (Keeling) Islands	+ 6	30
Colombia	− 5	
Comoros	+ 3	
Congo (Dem. Rep.)		
Haut–Zaïre, Kasai, Kivu, Shaba	+ 2	
Kinshasa, Mbandaka	+ 1	
Congo–Brazzaville	+ 1	
Costa Rica	− 6	
Côte d'Ivoire	0	
*Croatia	+ 1	

	h m		h m
*Cuba	− 5	*Iran	+ 3 30
*Cyprus	+ 2	*Iraq	+ 3
*Czech Republic	+ 1	*Ireland, Republic of	0
*Denmark	+ 1	*Israel	+ 2
*Færøe Islands	0	*Italy	+ 1
*Greenland	− 3	Jamaica	− 5
Danmarkshavn, Mesters Vig	0	Japan	+ 9
*Scoresby Sound	− 1	*Jordan	+ 2
*Thule area	− 4	*Kazakhstan	
Djibouti	+ 3	western	+ 4
Dominica	− 4	central	+ 5
Dominican Republic	− 5	eastern	+ 6
East Timor	+ 9	Kenya	+ 3
Ecuador	− 5	Kiribati	+ 12
Galápagos Islands	− 6	Line Islands	+ 14
*Egypt	+ 2	Phoenix Islands	+ 13
El Salvador	− 6	Korea, North	+ 9
Equatorial Guinea	+ 1	Korea, South	+ 9
Eritrea	+ 3	Kuwait	+ 3
Estonia	+ 2	*Kyrgyzstan	+ 5
Ethiopia	+ 3	Laos	+ 7
*Falkland Islands	− 4	Latvia	+ 2
Fiji	+ 12	*Lebanon	+ 2
*Finland	+ 2	Lesotho	+ 2
*France	+ 1	Liberia	0
French Guiana	− 3	Libya	+ 2
French Polynesia	− 10	*Liechtenstein	+ 1
Guadeloupe	− 4	Line Islands not part of Kiribati	− 10
Martinique	− 4	Lithuania	+ 1
Réunion	+ 4	*Luxembourg	+ 1
Marquesas Islands	− 9 30	*Macedonia	+ 1
Gabon	+ 1	Madagascar	+ 3
The Gambia	0	Malawi	+ 2
*Georgia	+ 3	Malaysia	+ 8
*Germany	+ 1	Maldives	+ 5
Ghana	0	Mali	0
*Gibraltar	+ 1	*Malta	+ 1
*Greece	+ 2	Marshall Islands	+ 12
Grenada	− 4	Ebon Atoll	− 12
Guam	+ 10	Mauritania	0
Guatemala	− 6	Mauritius	+ 4
Guinea	0	*Mexico	− 6
Guinea–Bissau	0	*Nayarit, Sinaloa, S. Baja California	− 7
Guyana	− 4	Sonora	− 7
Haiti	− 5	N. Baja California	− 8
Honduras	− 6	Micronesia	
*Hungary	+ 1	Caroline Islands	+ 10
Iceland	0	Kosrae, Pingelap, Pohnpei	+ 11
India	+ 5 30	*Moldova	+ 2
Indonesia		*Monaco	+ 1
Java, Kalimantan (west and central), Madura, Sumatra	+ 7	Mongolia	+ 8
		Montserrat	− 4
Bali, Flores, Kalimantan (south and east), Lombok, Sulawesi, Sumbawa, West Timor	+ 8	Morocco	0
		Mozambique	+ 2
Irian Jaya, Maluku	+ 9	Myanmar	+ 6 30
		*Namibia	+ 1

	h	m		h	m
Nauru	+ 12		Sierra Leone	0	
Nepal	+ 5	45	Singapore	+ 8	
*Netherlands	+ 1		*Slovakia	+ 1	
Netherlands Antilles	− 4		*Slovenia	+ 1	
New Caledonia	+ 11		Solomon Islands	+ 11	
*New Zealand	+ 12		Somalia	+ 3	
*Cook Islands	− 10		South Africa	+ 2	
Nicaragua	− 6		South Georgia	− 2	
Niger	+ 1		*Spain	+ 1	
Nigeria	+ 1		*Canary Islands	0	
Niue	−11		Sri Lanka	+ 6	
Norfolk Island	+ 11	30	Sudan	+ 3	
Northern Mariana Islands	+ 10		Suriname	− 3	
*Norway	+ 1		Swaziland	+ 2	
Oman	+ 4		*Sweden	+ 1	
Pakistan	+ 5		*Switzerland	+ 1	
Palau	+ 9		*Syria	+ 2	
Panama	− 5		Taiwan	+ 8	
Papua New Guinea	+ 10		Tajikistan	+ 5	
*Paraguay	− 4		Tanzania	+ 3	
Peru	− 5		Thailand	+ 7	
Philippines	+ 8		Togo	0	
*Poland	+ 1		*Tonga	+ 13	
*Portugal	0		Trinidad and Tobago	− 4	
*Azores	− 1		Tristan da Cunha	0	
*Madeira	0		Tunisia	+ 1	
Puerto Rico	− 4		*Turkey	+ 2	
Qatar	+ 3		Turkmenistan	+ 5	
Réunion	+ 4		*Turks and Caicos Islands	− 5	
*Romania	+ 2		Tuvalu	+ 12	
*Russia			Uganda	+ 3	
Zone 1	+ 2		*Ukraine	+ 2	
Zone 2	+ 3		United Arab Emirates	+ 4	
Zone 3	+ 4		*United Kingdom	0	
Zone 4	+ 5		*United States of America;		
Zone 5	+ 6		Alaska	− 9	
Zone 6	+ 7		Aleutian Islands, east of 169° 30' W.	− 9	
Zone 7	+ 8		Aleutian Islands, west of 169° 30' W.	− 10	
Zone 8	+ 9		eastern time	− 5	
Zone 9	+ 10		central time	− 6	
Zone 10	+ 11		Hawaii	−10	
Zone 11	+ 12		mountain time	− 7	
Rwanda	+ 2		Pacific time	− 8	
St Helena	0		Uruguay	− 3	
St Christopher and Nevis	− 4		Uzbekistan	+ 5	
St Lucia	− 4		Vanuatu	+ 11	
*St Pierre and Miquelon	− 3		*Vatican City State	+ 1	
St Vincent and the Grenadines	− 4		Venezuela	− 4	
Samoa	− 11		Vietnam	+ 7	
Samoa, American	− 11		Virgin Islands (US)	− 4	
*San Marino	+ 1		Yemen	+ 3	
São Tomé and Princípe	0		Zambia	+ 2	
Saudi Arabia	+ 3		Zimbabwe	+ 2	
Senegal	0				
*Serbia and Montenegro	+ 1				
Seychelles	+ 4				

INTERNATIONAL DIRECT DIALLING (IDD)

International dialling codes are composed of four elements which are dialled in sequence:

(i) the international code
(ii) the country code (see below)
(iii) the area code
(iv) the customer's telephone number

Calls to some countries must be made via the international operator.

* Varies in some areas
** Varies depending on carrier

Country	IDD from UK	IDD to UK
Afghanistan	00 93	00 44
Albania	00 355	00 44
Algeria	00 213	00 44
Andorra	00 376	00 44
Angola	00 244	00 44
Anguilla	00 1 264	011 44
Antigua and Barbuda	00 1 268	011 44
Argentina	00 54	00 44
Armenia	00 374	810 44
Aruba	00 297	00 44
Ascension Island	00 247	00 44
Australia	00 61	00 11 44
Austria	00 43	00 44
Azerbaijan	00 994	810 44
Azores	00 351	00 44
Bahamas	00 1 242	011 44
Bahrain	00 973	0 44
Bangladesh	00 880	00 44
Barbados	00 1 246	011 44
Belarus	00 375	810 44
Belgium	00 32	00 44
Belize	00 501	00 44
Benin	00 229	00 44
Bermuda	00 1 441	011 44
Bhutan	00 975	00 44
Bolivia	00 591	00 44
Bosnia-Hercegovina	00 387 / 00 381	00 44
Botswana	00 267	00 44
Brazil	00 55	00 44
British Virgin Islands	00 1 284	011 44
Brunei	00 673	00 44
Bulgaria	00 359	00 44
Burkina Faso	00 226	00 44
Burundi	00 257	90 44
Cambodia	00 855	00 44
Cameroon	00 237	00 44

Country	IDD from UK	IDD to UK
Canada	00 1	011 44
Canary Islands	00 34	00 44
Cape Verde	00 238	0 44
Cayman Islands	00 1 345	011 44
Central African Republic	00 236	19 44
Chad	00 235	15 44
Chile	00 56	00 44
China	00 86	00 44
Hong Kong	00 852	001 44
Colombia	00 57	009 44
Comoros	00 269	00 44
Congo, Dem. Rep. Of	00 243	00 44
Congo, Republic of	00 242	00 44
Cook Islands	00 682	00 44
Costa Rica	00 506	00 44
Côte d'Ivoire	00 225	00 44
Croatia	00 385	00 44
Cuba	00 53	119 44
Cyprus	00 357	00 44
Czech Republic	00 420	00 44
Denmark	00 45	00 44
Djibouti	00 253	00 44
Dominica	00 1 767	011 44
Dominican Republic	00 1 809	011 44
East Timor	00 670	00 44
Ecuador	00 593	00 44
Egypt	00 20	00 44
El Salvador	00 503	0 44
Equatorial Guinea	00 240	00 44
Eritrea	00 291	00 44
Estonia	00 372	800 44
Ethiopia	00 251	00 44
Falkland Islands	00 500	0 44
Faroe Islands	00 298	009 44
Fiji	00 679	05 44
Finland	00 358	00 44**
France	00 33	00 44
French Guiana	00 594	00 44
French Polynesia	00 689	00 44
Gabon	00 241	00 44
The Gambia	00 220	00 44
Georgia	00 995	810 44
Germany	00 49	00 44
Ghana	00 233	00 44
Gibraltar	00 350	00 44
Greece	00 30	00 44
Greenland	00 299	009 44
Grenada	00 1 473	011 44
Guadeloupe	00 590	00 44
Guam	00 1 671	001 44
Guatemala	00 502	00 44
Guinea	00 224	00 44
Guinea-Bissau	00 245	099 44

Country	IDD from UK	IDD to UK	Country	IDD from UK	IDD to UK
Guyana	00 592	001 44	Moldova	00 373	810 44
Haiti	00 509	00 44	Monaco	00 377	00 44
Honduras	00 504	00 44	Mongolia	00 976	00 44
Hungary	00 36	00 44	Montenegro	00 381	99 44
Iceland	00 354	00 44	Montserrat	00 1 664	011 44
India	00 91	00 44	Morocco	00 212	00 44
Indonesia	00 62	001 44**	Mozambique	00 258	00 44
		00844**	Myanmar	00 95	00 44
Iran	00 98	00 44	Namibia	00 264	00 44
Iraq	00 964	00 44	Nauru	00 674	00 44
Ireland, Republic of	00 353	00 44	Nepal	00 977	00 44
Israel	00 972	00 44**	Netherlands	00 31	00 44
Italy	00 39	00 44	Netherlands Antilles	00 599	00 44
Jamaica	00 1 876	011 44	New Caledonia	00 687	00 44
Japan	00 81	001 44**	New Zealand	00 64	00 44
		004144**	Nicaragua	00 505	00 44
		006144**	Niger	00 227	00 44
Jordan	00 962	00 44*	Nigeria	00 234	009 44
Kazakhstan	00 7	810 44	Niue	00 683	00 44
Kenya	00 254	00 44	Norfolk Island	00 672	011 44
Kiribati	00 686	00 44	Norway	00 47	00 44
Korea, North	00 850	00 44	Oman	00 968	00 44
Korea, South	00 82	001 44**	Pakistan	00 92	00 44
		00244**	Palau	00 680	011 44
Kuwait	00 965	00 44	Panama	00 507	00 44
Kyrgystan	00 996	00 44	Papua New Guinea	00 675	05 44
Laos	00 856	00 44	Paraguay	00 595	00 44**
Latvia	00 371	00 44			003 44**
Lebanon	00 961	00 44	Peru	00 51	00 44
Lesotho	00 266	00 44	Philippines	00 63	00 44
Liberia	00 231	00 44	Poland	00 48	00 44
Libya	00 218	00 44	Portugal	00 351	00 44
Liechtenstein	00 423	00 44	Puerto Rico	00 1 787	011 44
Lithuania	00 370	810 44	Qatar	00 974	00 44
Luxembourg	00 352	00 44	Réunion	00 262	00 44
Macao	00 853	00 44	Romania	00 40	00 44
Macedonia	00 389	99 44			
Madagascar	00 261	00 44	Russia	00 7	810 44
Madeira	00 351 91	00 44*	Rwanda	00 250	00 44
Malawi	00 265	101 44	St Christopher		
Malaysia	00 60	00 44	and Nevis	00 1 869	011 44
Maldives	00 960	00 44	St Helena	00 290	0 44
Mali	00 223	00 44	St Lucia	00 1 758	011 44
Malta	00 356	00 44	St Pierre and		
Mariana Islands,			Miquelon	00 508	00 44
Northern	00 1 670	011 44	St Vincent and the		
Marshall Islands	00 692	011 44	Grenadines	00 1 784	01 44
Martinique	00 596	00 44	Samoa	00 685	0 44
Mauritania	00 222	00 44	Samoa, American	00 684	00 44
Mauritius	00 230	00 44	San Marino	00 378	00 44
Mayotte	00 269	10 44	Sao Tomé and		
Mexico	00 52	98 44	Principe	00 239	00 44
Micronesia, Federated			Saudi Arabia	00 966	00 44
States of	00 691	011 44	Senegal	00 221	00 44

Country	IDD from UK	IDD to UK
Serbia and Montenegro	00 381	99 44
Seychelles	00 248	00 44
Sierra Leone	00 232	00 44
Singapore	00 65	001 44
Slovak Republic	00 421	00 44
Slovenia	00 386	00 44
Solomon Islands	00 677	00 44
Somalia	00 252	16 44
South Africa	00 27	09 44
Spain	00 34	00 44
Sri Lanka	00 94	00 44
Sudan	00 249	00 44
Suriname	00 597	00 44
Swaziland	00 268	00 44
Sweden	00 46	00944**
Switzerland	00 41	00 44
Syria	00 963	00 44
Taiwan	00 886	002 44
Tajikistan	00 7	810 44
Tanzania	00 255	00 44
Thailand	00 66	001 44
Tibet	00 86	00 44
Togo	00 228	00 44
Tonga	00 676	00 44
Trinidad and Tobago	00 1 868	011 44
Tristan da Cunha	00 2 897	
Tunisia	00 216	00 44
Turkey	00 90	00 44
Turkmenistan	00 993	810 44
Turks and Caicos Islands	00 1 649	0 44
Tuvalu	00 688	00 44
Uganda	00 256	00 44
Ukraine	00 380	810 44
United Arab Emirates	00 971	00 44
Uruguay	00 598	00 44
USA	00 1	011 44
Uzbekistan	00 998	810 44
Vanuatu	00 678	00 44
Vatican City State	00 390 66982	00 44
Venezuela	00 58	00 44
Vietnam	00 84	00 44
Virgin Islands (US)	00 1 340	011 44
Yemen	00 967	00 44
Zambia	00 260	00 44
Zimbabwe	00 263	00 44

CONSULATES

The list below is of Consulates based in Scotland.

AUSTRALIAN HIGH COMMISSION
69 George Street, Edinburgh, EH2 2JG.
Tel: 0131-624 3333 Fax: 0131-624 3701

AUSTRIAN CONSULATE
Alderwood, 49 Craigcrook Road, Edinburgh, EH4 3PH.
Tel: 0131-332 3344 Fax: 0131-332 1777

CANADIAN CONSULATE
Standard Life House, 30 Lothian Road,
Edinburgh, EH1 2DH. Tel: 0131-220 4333

CHINESE CONSULATE-GENERAL IN EDINBURGH
55 Corstorphine Road, Edinburgh, EH12 5QG.
Tel: 0131-337 3220
Web: www.chinese-embassy.org.uk

DANISH CONSULATE
215 Balgreen Road, Edinburgh, EH11 2RZ.
Tel: 0131-337 6352 Fax: 0131-346 8737
Eadie House, 74 Kirkintilloch Road, Bishopbriggs,
Glasgow, G64 2AH.
Tel: 0141-762 2288 Fax: 0141-772 3854

FAROESE COMMERCIAL ATTACHE
150 Market Street, Aberdeen, AB1 2PP.
Tel: 01224-592777 Fax: 01224-592779

FINNISH CONSULATE & TRADE OFFICE
22 Hanover Street, Edinburgh, EH2 2EP.
Tel: 0131-225 1295
Broomage Avenue, Larbert, Stirlingshire, FK5 4NQ.
Tel: 01324-562241 Fax: 01324-556642

FRENCH CONSULATE GENERAL
11 Randolph Crescent, Edinburgh, EH3 7TT.
Tel: 0131-225 7954 Fax: 0131-225 8975
Web: www.consulfrance-edinbourg.org

GERMANY, HONORARY CONSUL OF THE FEDERAL REPUBLIC OF
16 Eglinton Crescent, Edinburgh, EH12 5DG.
Tel: 0131-337 2323 Fax: 0131-346 1578 Email:
germanttoncon@aol.com
Web: www.german-embassy.org.uk
Pentagon Centre, 36 Washington Street,
Glasgow, G3 8AZ.
Tel: 0141-226 8443 Fax: 0141-357 6605
12 Albert Street, Aberdeen, Aberdeenshire, AB25 1XQ.
Tel: 01330-844414 Fax: 01330-844486

ICELANDIC CONSULATE
24 Jane Street, Edinburgh, EH6 5HD.
Tel: 0131-555 3532

INDIA, CONSULATE GENERAL OF
17 Rutland Square, Edinburgh, EH1 2BB.
Tel: 0131-229 2144 Fax: 0131-229 2155
Email: indianconsulate@btconnect.com

IRISH CONSULATE GENERAL
16 Randolph Crescent, Edinburgh, EH3 7TT.
Tel: 0131-226 7711 Fax: 0131-226 7704
Web: www.irlgov.ir/ivragh

ITALIAN CONSULATE
32 Melville Street, Edinburgh, EH3 7PG.
Tel: 0131-226 3631
Italian Vice-Consulate, Brebner Court, Castle Street,
Aberdeen, AB11 5BQ.
Tel: 01224-647135 Fax: 01224-627406

JAPANESE CONSULATE GENERAL
2 Melville Crescent, Edinburgh, EH3 7HW.
Tel: 0131-225 4777 Fax: 0131-225 4828

THE NETHERLANDS CONSULATE
18 Garden Place, Aberdeen, AB10 1UQ.
Tel: 01224-561616 Fax: 01224-561616
Email: nlconsulab@aol.com
Web: www.netherlands-emabassy.org.uk
53 George Street, Edinburgh, EH2 2HT.
Tel: 0131-220 3226
Thistle Court, 1/2 Thistle Street, Edinburgh, EH2 1DD.
Tel: 0131-220 3226 Fax: 0131-220 6446

NORWEGIAN CONSULATE GENERAL
86 George Street, Edinburgh, EH2 3BU.
Tel: 0131-226 5701 Fax: 0131-220 4976
Email: cons.gen.edinburgh@mfa.no
Web: www.norway.org.uk
18 Woodside Crescent, Glasgow, G3 7UL.
Tel: 0141-333 0618 Fax: 0141-353 2190

PAKISTAN CONSULATE
137 Norfolk Street, Glasgow, G5 9EA.
Tel: 0141-429 5335 Fax: 0141-429 0808

POLISH CONSULATE
2 Kinnear Road, Edinburgh, EH3 5PE.
Tel: 0131-552 0301

PORTUGAL, CONSULATE OF
25 Bernard Street, Edinburgh, EH6 6SH.
Tel: 0131-555 2080

RUSSIAN CONSULATE GENERAL
58 Melville Street, Edinburgh, EH3 7HF.
Tel: 0131-225 7098

SPANISH CONSULATE GENERAL
63 North Castle Street, Edinburgh, EH2 3LJ.
Tel: 0131-220 1843 Fax: 0131-226 4568
Email: cgspedumburgo@mail.mae.es

SWEDISH CONSULATE GENERAL
22 Hanover Street, Edinburgh, EH2 2EP.
Tel: 0131-220 6050 Fax: 0131-220 6006

SWITZERLAND, CONSULATE GENERAL OF
66 Hanover Street, Edinburgh, EH2 1HH.
Tel: 0131-226 5660 Fax: 0131-226 5332

US CONSULATE GENERAL IN SCOTLAND
3 Regent Terrace, Edinburgh, EH7 5BW.
Tel: 0131-556 8315 Fax: 0131-557 6023
Web: www.usembassy.org.uk/scotland

SOCIETIES AND INSTITUTIONS

SOCIETIES AND INSTITUTIONS

ABERDEEN AND NORTH EAST SCOTLAND FAMILY HISTORY SOCIETY
164 King Street, Aberdeen, AB24 5BD.
Tel: 01224-646323 Fax: 01224-639096
Email: enquiries@anesfhs.org.uk
Web: www.anesfhs.org.uk
Chairperson: Mrs G. Murton

ADVOCATES FOR ANIMALS
10 Queensferry Street, Edinburgh, EH2 4PG.
Tel: 0131-225 6039 Fax: 0131-220 6377
Email: info@advocatesforanimals.org.uk
Web: www.advocatesforanimals.org.uk

AGE CONCERN SCOTLAND
Leonard Small House, 113 Rose Street, Edinburgh,
EH2 3DT. Tel: 0131-220 3345 Fax: 0131-220 2779
Email: enquiries@acscotland.org.uk
Web: www.ageconcernscotland.org.uk
Director: Ms M. O'Neill

ALCOHOL FOCUS SCOTLAND
2nd Floor, 166 Buchanan Street, Glasgow, G1 2LW.
Tel: 0141-572 6700 Fax: 0141-333 1606
Email: enquiries@alcohol-focus-scotland.org.uk
Web: www.alcohol-focus-scotland.org.uk

ALCOHOLICS ANONYMOUS
Baltic Chambers, 50 Wellington Street, Glasgow, G2.
Tel: 0141-226 2214 Helpline: 0845-769 7555
Fax: 0141-221 9450
Web: www.alcoholics-anonymous.org.uk

ALZHEIMER SCOTLAND – ACTION ON DEMENTIA
22 Drumsheugh Gardens, Edinburgh, EH3 7RN.
Tel: 0131-243 1453 Fax: 0131-243 1450
Email: alzscot@alzscot.org Web: www.alzscot.org
Chief Executive: Jim Jackson

AMNESTY INTERNATIONAL SCOTLAND
6 Castle Street, Edinburgh, EH2 3AT.
Tel: 0131-466 6200 Fax: 0131-466 6201
Email: members@amnesty.org.uk
Web: www.amnesty.org.uk

AN COMUNN GÀIDHEALACH
109 Church Street, Inverness, IV1 1EY.
Tel: 01463-231226 Fax: 01463-715557
Email: info@ancomunn.co.uk
Web: www.ancomunn.co.uk
Chief Executive: D. J. MacSween

APEX TRUST SCOTLAND
9 Great Stuart Street, Edinburgh, EH3 7TP.
Tel: 0131-220 0130 Fax: 0131-220 6796
Email: admin@apexscotland.org.uk
Web: www.apexscotland.org.uk
Director: Bernadette Monaghan

ARRAN NATURAL HISTORY SOCIETY
Woodside, Pirnmill, Isle of Arran, KA27 8HP.
Tel: 01770-850216
Secretary: Fiona Laing

ARTHRITIS CARE IN SCOTLAND
Unit 25A Anniesland Business Park, 242 Netherton
Road, Glasgow, G13 1EU.
Tel. 0141-954 7776 Fax: 0141-954 6171
Email: scotlandoffice@arthritiscare.org.uk
Web: www.athritiscare.org.uk/scotland
Director - Scotland: Ms P. Wallace
Administrator - Scotland: Ms K. Green

ARTS AND BUSINESS SCOTLAND
6 Randolph Crescent, Edinburgh, EH3 7TH.
Tel: 0131-220 2499 Fax: 0131-220 2296
Email: scotland@aandb.org.uk
Web: www.aandb.org.uk
Director: Barclay Price

ASSOCIATION FOR MENTAL HEALTH
Cumbrae House, 15 Carlton Court, Glasgow, G5 9JP.
Tel: 0141-568 7000 Fax: 0141-568 7001
Email: enquire@samh.org.uk Web: www.samh.org.uk

ASSOCIATION OF DEER MANAGEMENT GROUPS
Dalhousie Estate Office, Brechin, Angus, DD9 6SG.
Tel: 01356-624566 Fax: 01356-623725
Email: dalhousieestates@btinternet.com
Web: www.deer-management.co.uk
Chairman: S. C. Gibbs
Secretary: R. M. J. Cooke

ASSOCIATION OF HEAD TEACHERS IN SCOTLAND
Gardyne Road, Dundee, DD5 1NY.
Tel: 01382-458802 Fax: 01382-455622
General Secretary: J. C. Smith

ASSOCIATION OF REGISTRARS OF SCOTLAND
77 Bank Street, Alexandria, G83 0LE.
Tel: 01389-608980 Fax: 01389-608982
Hon. Secretary: Anothony Gallagher, MBE

ASSOCIATION OF SCOTTISH COMMUNITY COUNCILS
21 Grosvenor Street, Edinburgh, EH12 5ED.
Tel: 0131-225 4033 Fax: 0131-225 4033
Email: info@ascc.org.uk Web: www.ascc.org.uk

ASSOCIATION OF SPEAKERS CLUBS
Beanlands Chase, 20 Rivermead Drive, Garstang,
Preston, Lancashire, PR3 1JJ. Tel: 01995-602560
Email: natsecasc@lineone.net
Web: www.the-asc.org.uk
National Secretary: Ms D. M. Dickinson

ASSYNT FIELD CLUB
Calltuinn, Nedd, by Drumbeg, Sutherland, IV27 4NN.
Tel: 01571-833241
Secretary: Ian M. Evans

THE AUTOMOBILE ASSOCIATION
Fanum House, Erskine Harbour, Erskine, Renfrewshire,
PA8 6AT. Tel: 0141-848 8622 Fax: 0141-848 8623
Email: neil.greig@theaa.com Web: www.theaa.com
Head of Motoring Policy: N. Greig

AYRSHIRE ARCHAEOLOGICAL AND NATURAL HISTORY SOCIETY
17 Bellrock Avenue, Prestwick, Ayrshire, KA9 1SG.
Tel: 01292-479077
Hon. Secretary: Sheena Andrew

BAFTA SCOTLAND
249 West George Street, Glasgow, G2 4QE.
Tel: 0141-302 1770 Fax: 0141-302 1771
Email: info@baftascotland.co.uk
Web: www.baftascotland.co.uk

BANFFSHIRE FIELD CLUB
1 Alvah Terrace, Banff, AB45 1BG.
Tel: 01261-812563
Secretary: Caroline R. Leggat

BARNARDO'S SCOTLAND
235 Corstorphine Road, Edinburgh, EH12 7AR.
Tel: 0131-334 9893 Fax: 0131-316 4008
Web: www.barnardos.org.uk

BERWICKSHIRE NATURALISTS' CLUB
Borough Museum, The Barracks, Berwick-upon-Tweed,
TD15 1TQ. Tel: 01289-330933
Secretary: Dr G. A. C. Binnie

THE BIG ISSUE FOUNDATION SCOTLAND
14 Albany Street, Edinburgh, EH1 3QB.
Tel: 0131-467 4701

BIRTH RESOURCE CENTRE
40 Leamington Terrace, Edinburgh, EH10 4JL.
Tel: 0131-229 3667 Email: nadineedw@aol.com
Web: www.birthresourcecentre.freeserve.co.uk
Co-ordinators: Ms N. Edwards; Ms J. Crewe;
C. Milner

BOTANICAL SOCIETY OF SCOTLAND
c/o Royal Botanical Garden, Inverleith Row, Edinburgh,
EH3 5LR. Tel: 0131-552 7171 Fax: 0131-248 2901
Hon. General Secretary: Dr P. Cochrane

BOYS' BRIGADE – SCOTTISH HEADQUARTERS
Carronvale House, Carronvale Road, Larbert, FK5 3LH.
Tel: 01324-562008 Fax: 01324-552323
Email: carronvale@boys-brigade.org.uk
Web: www.boys-brigade.org.uk
Director for Scotland: Tom Boyle

BRITISH AGENCIES FOR ADOPTION AND FOSTERING
40 Shandwick Place, Edinburgh, EH2 4RT.
Tel: 0131-225 9285 Fax: 0131-226 3778
Email: scotland@baaf.org.uk Web: www.baaf.org.uk

BRITISH ASSOCIATION OF SOCIAL WORKERS
17 Waterloo Place, Edinburgh, EH1 3BG.
Tel: 0131-556 9525 Fax: 0131-556 5376
Email: r.stark@.basw.co.uk Web: www.basw.co.uk
Professional Officer: Mrs R. Stark

BRITISH DEAF ASSOCIATION SCOTLAND
3rd Floor, Princes House, 5 Shandwick Place,
Edinburgh, EH2 4RG. Tel: 0131-221 1137
Fax: 0131-221 7960 Web: www.bda.org.uk

BRITISH RED CROSS
Alexandra House, 204 Bath Street, Glasgow, G2 4HL.
Tel: 0141-332 9591 Fax: 0141-332 8493
Web: www.redcross.org.uk
UK Director: G. McLaughlin

BUCHAN FIELD CLUB
4 Ythan Place, Ellon, Aberdeenshire, AB41 9DQ.
Tel: 01358-720328
Secretary: May Forres

BUTESHIRE NATURAL HISTORY SOCIETY
5 Kerrycroy, by Rothesay, Isle of Bute, PA20 9LW.
Tel: 01700-502409
Secretary: Elizabeth Johnson

CAITHNESS FIELD CLUB
9 Tormsdale Place, Thurso, Caithness, KW14 8PZ.
Tel: 01847-892999
Secretary: Mrs M. Owen

CANCERBACUP
3rd Floor Cranston House, 104/114 Argyle Street,
Glasgow, G2 8BH.
Tel: 0141-223 7676 Fax: 0141-248 8422
Email: jwhelan@cancerbacup.org
Web: www.cancerbacup.org.uk
Chief Executive: Ms J. Rule

CAPABILITY SCOTLAND
11 Ellersly Road, Edinburgh, EH12 6HY.
Tel: 0131-313 5510 Fax: 0131-346 1681
Email: ascs@capability-scotland.org.uk
Web: www.capability-scotland.org.uk
Chief Executive: A. Dickson

CARERS SCOTLAND
3rd Floor, 91 Mitchell Street, Glasgow, G1 3LN.
Tel: 0141-221 9141 Fax: 0141-221 9140
Email: info@carerscotland.co.uk
Web: www.carersonline.org
Chief Executive: Ms D. Whitworth
Director - Scotland: Angela O'Hagan

CARNEGIE DUNFERMLINE TRUST
Abbey Park House, Dunfermline, Fife, KY12 7PB.
Tel: 01383-723638 Fax: 01383-721862
Email: admin@carnegietrust.com
Web: www.carnegietrust.org.uk
Executive Officer: Elizabeth East

CARNEGIE HERO FUND TRUST
Abbey Park House, Dunfermline, Fife, KY12 7PB.
Tel: 01383-723638 Fax: 01383-721862
Chief Executive: Bruce W. Anderson

CARNEGIE UNITED KINGDOM TRUST
Comely Park House, Dunfermline, Fife, KY12 7EJ.
Tel: 01383-721445 Fax: 01383-620682
Web: www.carnegieuktrust.org.uk
Secretary: Charles S. McConnell

CHARTERED INSTITUTE OF BANKERS IN SCOTLAND
Drumsheugh House, 38B Drumsheugh Gardens,
Edinburgh, EH3 7SW. Tel: 0131-473 7777
Fax: 0131-473 7788 Email: info@ciobs.org.uk
Web: www.ciobs.org.uk

CHEST, HEART AND STROKE SCOTLAND
65 North Castle Street, Edinburgh, EH2 3LT.
Tel: 0131-225 6963 Fax: 0131-220 6313
Email: admin@chss.org.uk Web: www.chss.org.uk

CHILDLINE SCOTLAND
18 Albion Street, Glasgow, G1 1LH.
Tel: 0141-552 1123 Helpline: 0800-1111
Fax: 0141-552 3089
Email: scotland@childline.org.uk
Web: www.childline.org.uk

CHILDREN 1ST
83 Whitehouse Loan, Edinburgh, EH9 1AT.
Tel: 0131-446 2300 Fax: 0131-446 2339
Email: info@children1st.org.uk
Web: www.children1st.org.uk
Chief Executive: Mrs M. McKay

CHILDREN IN SCOTLAND
Princes House, 5 Shandwick Place, Edinburgh, EH2
4RG. Tel: 0131-228 8484 Fax: 0131-228 8585
Email: info@childreninscotland.org.uk
Web: www.childreninscotland.org.uk

CHRISTIAN AID SCOTLAND
41 George IV Bridge, Edinburgh, EH1 1EL.
Tel: 0131-220 1254 Fax: 0131-225 8861
Email: edinburgh@christian-aid.org
Web: www.christian-aid.org.uk
National Secretary: John Wylie

THE CHURCH OF SCOTLAND GUILD
121 George Street, Edinburgh, EH2 4YN.
Tel: 0131-225 5722 Fax: 0131-220 3113
Email: guild@cofscotland.org.uk
Web: www.cos-guild.org.uk
General Secretary: Mrs A. M. Twaddle
Information Officer: Mrs F. J. Lange

CITIZENS ADVICE SCOTLAND
1st Floor Spectrum House, 2 Powderhall Road,
Edinburgh, EH7 4GB. Tel: 0131-550 1000
Fax: 0131-550 1001 Email: info@cas.org.uk
Web: www.cas.org.uk
Chief Executive Officer: Mrs K. Lyle

CLACKMANNANSHIRE FIELD STUDIES SOCIETY
Tower Square, Alloa, FK10 1PL. Tel: 01259-213954
Secretary: Mrs E. K. Roy

CLYDE AREA BIOLOGICAL RECORDS CENTRE
Foremount House, Kilbarchan, Renfrewshire, PA10 2EZ.
Tel: 01505-702419
Recorder: Dr J. A. Gibson

COMUNN NA GÀIDHLIG
5 Mitchell's Lane, Inverness, IV2 3HQ.
Tel: 01463-234138 Fax: 01463-237470
Email: oifis@cnag.org.uk Web: www.cnag.org.uk

COMMUNITY SERVICE VOLUNTEERS SCOTLAND
Wellgate House, 200 Cowgate, Edinburgh, EH1 1NQ.
Tel: 0131-622 7766 Fax: 0131-622 7755
Email: info@csvscotland.u-net.com
Web: www.csv.org.uk

SCOTTISH COUNCIL FOR SINGLE HOMELESS
5th Floor, Wellgate House, 200 Cowgate,
Edinburgh, EH1 1NQ.
Tel: 0131-226 4382 Fax: 0131-225 4382
Email: enquries@scsh.demon.uk.uk
Web: www.scsh.co.uk
Director: R. Aldridge

COUPLE COUNSELLING SCOTLAND
18 York Place, Edinburgh, EH1 3EP.
Tel: 0131-558 9669 Fax: 0131-556 6596
Email: enquiries@couplecounselling.org
Web: www.couplecounselling.org
Chief Executive: Hilary Campbell

COWAL NATURAL HISTORY SOCIETY
Allt na Blathaich, Loch Eck, Dunoon, PA23 8SG.
Tel: 01369-840606
Secretary: Nigel Scriven

CRUSE BEREAVEMENT CARE SCOTLAND
Suite A Riverview House, Friarton Road, Perth, PH2 8DF.
Tel: 01738-444178 Fax: 01738-444807
Email: info@crusescotland.org.uk
Chief Executive: Stewart Wilson

DEESIDE FIELD CLUB
Department of Geography, University of Aberdeen,
Regent Walk, Aberdeen, AB24 3FX.
Tel: 01224-272342
Secretary: Dr J. S. Smith

DIABETES UK
Savoy House, 140 Sauchiehall Street, Glasgow,
G2 3DH. Tel: 0141-332 2700 Fax: 0141-332 4880
Email: scotland@diabetes.org.uk
Web: www.diabetes.org.uk/scotland

DOWNS SYNDROME SCOTLAND
158–160 Balgreen Road, Edinburgh, EH11 3AU.
Tel: 0131-313 4225 Fax: 0131-313 4285
Email: info@dsscotland.org.uk
Web: www.dsscotland.orq.uk
Director: Ms K. Watchman
Office Manager: Ms P. Hernandez

THE DUKE OF EDINBURGH'S AWARD
69 Dublin Street, Edinburgh, EH3 6NS.
Tel: 0131-556 9097 Fax: 0131-557 8044
Email: scotland@theaward.org
Web: www.theaward.org

DUMFRIESSHIRE AND GALLOWAY NATURAL HISTORY AND ANTIQUARIAN SOCIETY
Acorn Bank, 6 Cracken Wood, Gatehouse of Fleet,
Dumfriesshire, DG7 2FA. Tel: 01557-814966
Secretary: Mrs M. Rochester

DUNDEE NATURALISTS' SOCIETY
34 Foggyley Gardens, Dundee, DD2 3LS.
Tel: 01382-611096
Secretary: Gordon Maxwell

DYSLEXIA IN SCOTLAND
Stirling Business Centre, Wellgreen, Stirling, FK8 2DZ.
Tel: 01786-446650 Fax: 01786-471235
Email: info@dyslexia-in-scotland.org
Web: www.dyslexia-in-scotland.org
Chairman: Mrs E. Reilly

DYSLEXIA INSTITUTE SCOTLAND
74 Victoria Crescent Road, Dowanhill, Glasgow,
G12 9JN. Tel: 0141-334 4549 Fax: 0141-339 8879
Web: www.dyslexia-inst.org.uk

EARL HAIG FUND SCOTLAND
New Haig House, Logie Green Road, Edinburgh,
EH7 4HR. Tel: 0131-557 2782 Fax: 0131-557 5819
Chief Executive: Cdr A. C. Herdman

EAST LOTHIAN ANTIQUARIAN AND
FIELD NATURALISTS' SOCIETY
Inchgarth, East Links, Dunbar, EH42 1LT.
Tel: 01368-863335
Secretary: Stephen A. Bunyan

EDINBURGH BIBLIOGRAPHICAL SOCIETY
c/o National Library of Scotland, George IV Bridge,
Edinburgh, EH1 1EW. Tel: 0131-226 4531
Fax: 0131-220 6662
President: Dr M. C. T. Simpson

EDINBURGH CHAMBER OF COMMERCE
AND ENTERPRISE
27 Melville Street, Edinburgh, EH3 7JF.
Tel: 0131-477 7000 Fax: 0131-477 7002
Email: information@ecce.org Web: www.ecce.org
Chief Executive: W. Furness

EDINBURGH NATURAL HISTORY SOCIETY
180 Granton Road, Edinburgh, EH5 1AH.
Tel: 0131-552 5026
Secretary: Dr Heather McHaffe

ENABLE
6th Floor, 7 Buchanan Street, Glasgow, G1 3HL.
Tel: 0141-226 4541 Fax: 0141-204 4398
Email: enable@enable.org.uk
Web: www.enable.org.uk
Director: N. Dunning

ENGENDER
18 York Place, Edinburgh, EH1 3EP. Tel: 0131-558 9596
Email: engender@engender.org.uk
Web: www.engender.org.uk

EPILEPSY SCOTLAND
48 Govan Road, Glasgow, G51 1JL. Tel: 0141-427 4911
Helpline 0141-427 5225 Fax: 0141-419 1709
Email: enquiries@epilepsyscotland.org.uk
Web: www.epilepsyscotland.org.uk
Chief Executive: Ms H. Mounfield

ERSKINE HOSPITAL
Bishopton, Renfrewshire, PA7 5PU.
Tel: 0141-812 1100 Fax: 0141-812 3733
Web: www.erskine.org/welcome.htm
Chief Executive: Col. M. F. Gibson, OBE, DL

THE EUROPEAN MOVEMENT (BRITISH
COUNCIL)
13A Melville Street, Edinburgh, EH3 7PE.
Tel: 0131-220 0377 Fax: 0131-220 0377
Email: scotland@euromove.org.uk
Web: www.euromove.org.uk
National Organiser: Ms B. MacLeod

EX-SERVICES MENTAL WELFARE SOCIETY
Hollybush House, Hollybush, by Ayr, KA6 7EA.
Tel: 01292-560214 Fax: 01292-560871
Email: contactus@combatstress.org.uk
Web: www.combatstress.com
Clinical Manager: Frances Robertson

FABB SCOTLAND
Norton Park, 57 Albion Road, Edinburgh, EH7 5QY.
Tel: 0131-475 2313 Fax: 0131-475 2685
Chief Executive: Fiona Hird

FAIR ISLE BIRD OBSERVATORY TRUST
Fair Isle Bird Observatory, Fair Isle, Shetland, ZE2 9JU.
Tel: 01595-760258 Fax: 01595-760258
Email: fairisle.birdobs@zetnet.co.uk
Web: www.fairislebirdobs.co.uk
Administrator: Mrs H. Shaw

FAMILY PLANNING ASSOCIATION
SCOTLAND
Unit 10, Firhill Business Centre, 76 Firhill Road,
Glasgow, G20 7BA.
Tel: 0141-576 5015 Fax: 0141-576 5006
Email: fpascotland@dial.pipex.com
Web: www.fpa.org.uk

FÈISEAN NAN GÀIDHEAL
Meall House, Portree, Isle of Skye.
Tel: 01478-613355 Fax: 01478-613399
Email: fios@feisean.org Web: www.feisean.org
Director: A. Cormack
Development Officer: D. Boag

FINDHORN FOUNDATION
The Park, Findhorn, Forres, Moray, IV36 3TZ.
Tel: 01309-690311 Fax: 01309-691301
Email: enquiries@findhorn.org
Web: www.findhorn.org
Co-Chairpersons: Ms M. Hollander

FRASER OF ALLANDER INSTITUTE FOR
RESEARCH ON THE SCOTTISH
ECONOMY
University of Strathclyde, Curran Building,
100 Cathedral Street, Glasgow, G4 0LN.
Tel: 0141-548 3958 Fax: 0141-552 8340
Email: fraser@strath.ac.uk
Web: www.fraser.strath.ac.uk
Policy Director: Prof. Brian Ashcroft
Research Director: Prof. Kim Swales

FRIENDS OF THE EARTH SCOTLAND
72 Newhaven Road, Edinburgh, EH6 5QG.
Tel: 0131-554 9977 Fax: 0131-554 8656
Email: info@foe-scotland.org.uk
Web: www.foe-scotland.org.uk

THE GIRLS' BRIGADE IN SCOTLAND
11a Woodside Crescent, Charing Cross, Glasgow,
G3 7UL. Tel: 0141-332 1765 Fax: 0141-331 2681
Email: hq@girls-brigade-scotland.org.uk
Web: www.girls-brigade-scotland.org.uk

GLASGOW NATURAL HISTORY SOCIETY
c/o Art Gallery and Museum, Kelvingrove, Glasgow,
G3 8AG. Tel: 0141-586 3164
Secretary: Kirsty Kennedy-Wylie

GRAND LODGE OF ANTIENT FREE AND ACCEPTED MASONS OF SCOTLAND
Freemasons' Hall, 96 George Street, Edinburgh,
EH2 3DH. Tel: 0131-225 5304 Fax: 0131-225 3953
Email: mail@grandlodgescotland.com
Web: www.grandlodgescotland.com
Grand Secretary: C. M. McGibbon
Grand Master Mason: Sir Archibald Orr Ewing

HAMILTON NATURAL HISTORY SOCIETY
1 Stonehouse Road, Sandford, Strathven, Lanarkshire,
ML10 6PD. Tel: 01357-520159
Secretary: Michael Pink

HEBRIDEAN WHALE AND DOLPHIN TRUST
28 Main Street, Tobermory, Isle of Mull, Argyll,
PA75 6NU. Tel: 01688-302620 Fax: 01688-302728
Email: hwdt@sol.co.uk Web: www.hwdt.org
Executive Director: Ms Cally Fleming

HELENSBURGH AND DISTRICT NATURAL HISTORY SOCIETY
109 West King Street, Helensburgh,
Dunbartonshire, G84 8DG.
Tel: 01436-676022
Secretary: Geoffrey Flann

HELP THE AGED
11 Granton Square, Edinburgh, EH5 1HX.
Tel: 0131-556 6331 Fax: 0131-557 5415
Email: infoscot@helptheaged.com
Web: www.helptheaged.co.uk
Scottish Executive: Ms E. Duncan

HIGHLAND CATTLE SOCIETY
59 Drumlanrig Street, Thornhill, Dumfries, DG3 5LY.
Tel: 01848-331866 Fax: 01848-331183
Email: info@highlandcattlesociety.com
Web: www.highlandcattlesociety.com

IMMIGRATION ADVISORY SERVICE
115 Bath Street, Glasgow, G2 2SZ.
Tel: 0141-248 2956 Fax: 0141-221 5388
Email: glasgow@iasuk.org Web: www.iasuk.org

INVERNESS FIELD CLUB
Swallowhill, Lentran, Inverness, IV3 8RJ.
Tel: 01463-831057
Email: invernessfieldclub@btinternet.com
Web: www.invernessfieldclub.btinternet.co.uk
Hon. Secretary: Mrs G. Cameron

ISLAY NATURAL HISTORY TRUST
Islay Field Centre, Port Charlotte,
Isle of Islay, PA48 7TX.
Tel: 01496-850288
Secretary: Dr Malcolm Ogilvie

JUBILEE SCOTLAND
41 George IV Bridge, Edinburgh, EH1 1EL.
Tel: 0131-225 4321 Fax: 0131-225 8861
Email: mail@jubileescotland.org.uk
Web: www.jubileescotland.org.uk
Co-ordinator: Vicki Clayton

KEEP SCOTLAND BEAUTIFUL
7 Melville Terrace, Stirling, FK8 2ND.
Tel: 01786-471333 Fax: 01786-464611
Email: ksb@tidybritain.org.uk
Director: John Summers

KILMARNOCK GLENFIELD RAMBLERS SOCIETY
88 Bridgehouse Hill Road, Kilmarnock,
Ayrshire, KA1 4QD.
Secretary: Mrs C. Rowan

KINTYRE ANTIQUARIAN AND NATURAL HISTORY SOCIETY
Craiglussa, Peninver, Campbeltown, Argyll, PA28 6QP.
Tel: 01586-553804
Secretary: Mrs Frances Hood

KIRKCALDY NATURALISTS' SOCIETY
50 Templars Crescent, Kinghorn, Fife, KY3 9XS.
Tel: 01592-890042
Secretary: Rosalind Ramage

LOCHBROOM FIELD CLUB
Strathan Moorfield, Ullapool, IV26 2TL.
Tel: 01854-612842
Secretary: Barry Dumughn

MACMILLAN CANCER RELIEF
Osborne House, 15 Osborne Terrace,
Edinburgh, EH12 5HG.
Tel: 0131-346 5346 Fax: 0131-346 5347
Web: www.macmillan.org.uk
Director for Scotland and Northern Ireland:
I. R. L. Gibson

**MENTAL HEALTH FOUNDATION
SCOTLAND**
5th Floor, Merchants House, 30 George Square,
Glasgow, G2 1EG.
Tel: 0141-572 0125 Fax: 0141-572 0246
Email: scotland@mhf.org.uk
Web: www.mentalhealth.org.uk

MOFFAT AND DISTRICT WILDLIFE CLUB
4 Park Circle, Moffat, Dumfriesshire, DG10 9AY.
Tel: 01683-221374
Secretary: Ian Anderson

**MONTROSE NATURAL HISTORY AND
ANTIQUARIAN SOCIETY**
97 High Street, Montrose, DD10 8QR.
Tel: 01674-676534
Secretary: Graham King

MORAY FIELD CLUB
59 Bruceland Road, Elgin, IV30 1SP.
Tel: 01343-543675
Secretary: Lorna Paterson

THE MORAY SOCIETY
Elgin Museum, 1 High Street, Elgin, IV30 1EQ.
Tel: 01343-543675

**NATIONAL ASTHMA CAMPAIGN
SCOTLAND**
2A North Charlotte Street, Edinburgh, EH2 4HR.
Tel: 0131-226 2544 Fax: 0131-226 2401
Email: enquiries@asthma.org.uk
Web: www.asthma.org.uk
Chief Executive: Donna Covey
Director: Marjory O'Donnell

**NATIONAL BLOOD TRANSFUSION
ASSOCIATION**
Scottish National Blood Transfusion Service, Protein
Fractionation Centre, 21 Ellen's Glen Road, Edinburgh,
EH17 7QT.
Tel: 0131-536 5700 Fax: 0131-536 5781
Director: Dr Bob Perry

NATIONAL CHILDBIRTH TRUST
Stockbridge Health Centre, 1 India Place, Edinburgh,
EH3 6EH. Tel: 0131-260 9201
Web: www.nct-online.org
Administrator: Ms K. McGlew

**NATIONAL HOUSE-BUILDING COUNCIL
(NHBC)**
42 Colinton Road, Edinburgh, EH10 5BT.
Tel: 0131-313 1001 Fax: 0131-313 1211
Web: www.nhbc.co.uk
Director: M. MacLeod

THE NATIONAL TRUST FOR SCOTLAND
28 Charlotte Square, Edinburgh, EH2 4ET.
Tel: 0131-243 9300 Fax: 0131-243 9301
Email: information@nts.org.uk
Web: www.nts.org.uk
Chief Executive: R. Pellew

**NATIONAL UNION OF STUDENTS
SCOTLAND**
29 Forth Street, Edinburgh, EH1 3LE.
Tel: 0131-556 6598 Fax: 0131-557 5679
Email: nus.scot@dircon.co.uk
Web: www.nusonline.co.uk

**NATURAL HISTORY AND ANTIQUARIAN
SOCIETY OF MID-ARGYLL**
Kirnan Farm, Lochgilphead, Argyll, PA31 8QL.
Tel: 01546-605316
Secretary: Dave Batty

**THE SCOTTISH NATIONAL WAR
MEMORIAL**
The Castle, Edinburgh, EH1 2YT.
Tel: 0131-226 7393 Fax: 0131-225 8920
Web: www.snwm.org

NCH ACTION FOR CHILDREN SCOTLAND
17 Newton Place, Glasgow, G3 7PY.
Tel: 0141-332 4041 Fax: 0141-332 7002
Web: www.ncha.org.uk
Director of Children's Services: Christopher Holmes

ONE PARENT FAMILIES SCOTLAND
13 Gayfield Square, Edinburgh, EH1 3NX.
Tel: 0131-556 3899 Fax: 0131-557 7899
Email: opfs@gn.apc.org Web: www.opfs.org.uk
Director: Ms S. Robertson

ORKNEY FIELD CLUB
Ardleigh, Dounby, Orkney, KW17 2JA.
Tel: 01856-771535
Secretary: Dennis Paice

ORKNEY NATURAL HISTORY SOCIETY
6 Franklin Road, Stromness, Orkney, KW16 3AN.
Tel: 01856-850190
Secretary: Steven Hogley

ORNITHOLOGISTS' CLUB
Harbour Point, Newhailes Road,
Musselburgh, EH21 6SJ.
Tel: 0131-653 0653 Fax: 0131-653 0654
Email: mail@the.soc.org.uk
Web: www.the.soc.org.uk
Administrative Officer: Caroline Scott

OXFAM IN SCOTLAND
Tel: 0141-331 1455 Web: www.oxfam.org.uk
Head of Oxfam Scotland: Mrs M. Hearle

PARKINSON'S DISEASE SOCIETY –
SCOTTISH RESOURCE
10 Claremont Terrace, Glasgow, G3 7XR.
Tel: 0141-332 3343 Fax: 0141-353 2701
Email: enquiries.pdsscotland@virgin.net
Web: www.parkinsons.org.uk
Regional Manager: Richard O'Grady

PDSA (PEOPLE'S DISPENSARY FOR SICK
ANIMALS)
Fundraising Office, Pet Aid Hospital, Muiryfauld Drive,
Tollcross, Glasgow, G31 5RT.
Tel: 0141-778 9229 Fax: 0141-778 9229
Email: crawford.lynn@pdsa.org.uk
Regional Fundraising Manager: Ms L. Crawford

PERTHSHIRE SOCIETY OF NATURAL
SCIENCE
Rosamount, 16 Pitheavlis Terrace, Perth, PH2 0JZ.
Tel: 01738-632488
Secretary: Rhoda Fothergill

POSTWATCH SCOTLAND
Queen Margaret University College, Clerwood Terrace,
Edinburgh, EH12 8TS.
Tel: 0845-601 3265 Fax: 0131-334 3972
Email: info@postwatch.co.uk
Web: www.postwatch.co.uk
Chairman: Dr Tom Begg
Director: Tricia Dow

THE POVERTY ALLIANCE
162 Buchanan Street, Glasgow, G1 2LL.
Tel: 0141-353 0440 Fax: 0141-353 0686
Email: admin@povertyalliance.org
Web: www.povertyalliance.org
Director: D. Killeen

PRINCE'S SCOTTISH YOUTH BUSINESS
TRUST
6th Floor, Mercantile Chambers, 53 Bothwell Street,
Glasgow, G2 6TS.
Tel: 0141-248 4999 Email: firststep@psybt.org.uk
Web: www.psybt.org.uk

QUEEN VICTORIA SCHOOL
Dunblane, Perthshire, FK15 0JY.
Tel: 01786-822288 Fax: 0131-310 2926
Email: enquiries@qvs.org.uk Web: www.qvs.org.uk
Headmaster: B. Raine

QUEEN'S NURSING INSTITUTE
31 Castle Terrace, Edinburgh, EH1 2EL.
Tel: 0131-229 2333 Fax: 0131-228 9066
Email: office@qnis.org.uk Web: www.qnis.org.uk
Treasurer: Fiona Watson

RENFREWSHIRE NATURAL HISTORY
SOCIETY
30 Wheatlands Drive, Kilbarchan,
Renfrewshire, PA10 2LJ.
Tel: 01505-702419
Secretary: Mr R. Anderson

ROYAL ACADEMY OF ENGINEERING
Department of Petroleum Engineering, Heriot-Watt
University, Riccarton, Edinburgh, EH14 4AS.
Tel: 0131-451 3128 Fax: 0131-451 3127
Email: brian.smart@pet.hw.ac.uk
Web: www.pet.hw.ac.uk
Head of Department: Prof. B. G. D. Smart

ROYAL BRITISH LEGION SCOTLAND
New Haig House, Logie Green Road,
Edinburgh, EH7 4HR.
Tel: 0131-557 2782 Fax: 0131-557 5819
Email: admin@rblscotland.org
Web: www.rblscotland.org
Administrative Officer: George Ross

ROYAL CALEDONIAN HORTICULTURAL
SOCIETY
6 Kirkliston Road, South Queensferry, EH30 9LT.
Tel: 0131-331 1011
Web: www.royalcaledonianhorticulturalsociety.org
Secretary: T. Mabbott

ROYAL CELTIC SOCIETY
23 Rutland Street, Edinburgh, EH1 2RN.
Tel: 0131-228 6449 Fax: 0131-229 6987
Email: gcameron@stuartandstuart.co.uk
Secretary: J. G. Cameron

ROYAL FACULTY OF PROCURATORS IN
GLASGOW
12 Nelson Mandela Place, Glasgow, G2 1BT.
Tel: 0141-331 0533 Fax: 0141-332 4714
Email: i.c.pearson@btinternet.com
Web: www.rfpg.org
General Manager: I. C. Pearson

ROYAL HIGHLAND AND AGRICULTURAL
SOCIETY OF SCOTLAND
Royal Highland Centre, Ingliston, Edinburgh,
EH28 8NF.
Tel: 0131-335 6200 Fax: 0131-333 5236
Email: info@rhass.org.uk Web: www.rhass.org.uk

ROYAL NATIONAL INSTITUTE FOR DEAF
PEOPLE
Crowngate Business Centre, Brook Street,
Glasgow, G40 3AP.
Tel: 0141-554 0053 Textphone: 0141-550 5750
Fax: 0141-554 5837
Email: rnidscotland@rnid.org.uk
Web: www.rnid.org.uk

ROYAL NATIONAL INSTITUTE FOR THE
BLIND SCOTLAND
Dunedin House, 25 Ravelston Terrace,
Edinburgh, EH4 3TP.
Tel: 0131-311 8500 Fax: 0131-311 8529
Web: www.rnib.org.uk

ROYAL NATIONAL LIFEBOAT
INSTITUTION SCOTLAND
Unit 3 Ruthvenfield Grove, Inveralmond Industrial
Estate, Perth, PH1 5RR.
Tel: 01738-642999 Fax: 01738-642998
Email: scotland@rnli.org.uk Web: www.rnli.org.uk
National Organiser, Scotland: Mrs M. Caldwell

ROYAL NATIONAL MISSION TO DEEP SEA
FISHERMEN
Scottish Regional Office, Haypark Business Centre,
Marchmont Avenue, Polmont, Stirlingshire, FK2 0NZ.
Tel: 01324-716857 Fax: 01324-716423
Email: ianbaillie@rnmdsf.org.uk
Director - Scotland: I. Baillie

ROYAL SCOTTISH ACADEMY
The Mound, Edinburgh, EH2 2EL.
Tel: 0131-558 7097 Fax: 0131-557 6417
Email: info@royalscottishacademy.org.uk
Web: www.royalscottishacademy.org.uk
Administrative Secretary: B. Laidlaw
Assistant Administrative Secretary:
Pauline Costigane

ROYAL SCOTTISH AGRICULTURAL
BENEVOLENT INSTITUTION
Ingliston, Edinburgh, EH28 8NB.
Tel: 0131-333 1023/1027 Fax: 0131-333 1027 Email:
rsabi@rsabi.org.uk Web: www.rsabi.org.uk
Director: John N. Macdonald

ROYAL SCOTTISH GEOGRAPHICAL
SOCIETY
Graham Hills Building, University of Strathclyde,
40 George Street, Glasgow, G1 1QE.
Tel: 0141-552 3330 Fax: 0141-522 3331
Email: rsgs@strath.ac.uk
Web: www.geo.ed.ac.uk/~rsgs/
Director: Dr D. M. Munro

ROYAL SOCIETY FOR THE PREVENTION
OF ACCIDENTS (ROSPA)
Slateford House, 53 Lanark Road,
Edinburgh, EH14 1TL.
Tel: 0131-455 7457 Fax: 0131-443 9442
Email: mmcdonnell@rospa.com
Web: www.rospa.co.uk
Road Safety Manager (Scotland): M. A. McDonnell

THE ROYAL SOCIETY FOR THE PROTECTION OF BIRDS
Dunedin House, 25 Ravelston Terrace,
Edinburgh, EH4 3TP.
Tel: 0131-311 6500 Fax: 0131-311 6569
Web: www.rspb.org.uk

ROYAL SOCIETY OF EDINBURGH
22–26 George Street, Edinburgh, EH2 2PQ.
Tel: 0131-240 5000 Fax: 0131-240 5024
Email: rse@rse.org.uk Web: www.royalsoced.org.uk

ROYAL ZOOLOGICAL SOCIETY OF SCOTLAND
National Zoological Park, Edinburgh Zoo,
134 Corstorphine Road, Edinburgh, EH12 6TS.
Tel: 0131-334 9171 Fax: 0131-314 0382
Email: marketing@rzss.org.uk
Web: www.edinburghzoo.org.uk
Chief Executive: David Windmill

RURAL SCOTLAND
3rd Floor, Gladstone's Land, 483 Lawnmarket,
Edinburgh, EH1 2NT.
Tel: 0131-225 7012/3 Fax: 0131-225 6592
Email: info@ruralscotland.org
Web: www.ruralscotland.org
Director: Mrs J. Geddes

SALTIRE SOCIETY
9 Fountain Close, 22 High Street, Edinburgh, EH1 1TF.
Tel: 0131-556 1836 Fax: 0131-557 1675
Email: saltire@saltiresociety.org.uk
Web: www.saltiresociety.org.uk
Administrator: Mrs K. Munro

SAMARITANS CORRESPONDENCE BRANCH
PO Box 90 90, Stirling, FK8 2SA.
Tel: 08457-90 90 90 Web: www.samaritans.org
Chairman: Richard Balkwill

SAVE THE CHILDREN IN SCOTLAND
2nd Floor, Haymarket House, 8 Clifton Terrace,
Edinburgh, EH12 5DR.
Tel: 0131-527 8200 Fax: 0131-527 8201
Email: scotland@scfuk.org.uk
Web: www.savethechildrenscot.org.uk
Programme Director: Alison Davies

SCOTTISH HUMAN RIGHTS CENTRE
146 Holland Street, Glasgow, G2 4NG.
Tel: 0141-332 5960 Fax: 0141-332 5309
Email: info@scottishhumanrightscentre.org.uk
Web: www.scottishhumanrightscentre.org.uk
Director: Rosemarie McIlwhan

SCOTS LANGUAGE RESOURCE CENTRE ASSOCIATION
A. K. Bell Library, 2–8 York Place, Perth, PH2 8EP.
Tel: 01738-440199 Fax: 01738-477010
Email: slrc@sol.co.uk
Web: www.pkc.gov.uk/slrc
Manager: Michael Hance
Convener: John Law

SCOTS LEID ASSOCIE
The A.K. Bell Library, York Place, Perth, PH2 8EP.
Tel: 01738-440199 Fax: 01738-477010
Web: www.lallans.co.uk

SCOTTISH ASSOCIATION FOR MARINE SCIENCE
Dunbeg, Oban, Argyll, PA37 1QA.
Tel: 01631-559000 Fax: 01631-559001
Email: mail@sams.ac.uk Web: www.sams.ac.uk
Director: Prof G. B. Shimmield, FRSE

SCOTTISH ASSOCIATION OF LAW CENTRES
c/o Paisley Law Centre, 65 George Street,
Paisley, PA1 2JY.
Tel: 0141-561 7266 Fax: 0141-561 7164
Email: lw@paisleylawcentre.co.uk
Secretary: Ms L. Welsh

SCOTTISH BUSINESS IN THE COMMUNITY
PO Box 408, Bankhead Avenue, Edinburgh, EH11 4HE.
Tel: 0131-442 2020 Fax: 0131-442 3555
Email: info@sbscot.com Web: www.sbcscot.com
Chief Executive: Ms S. Barber

SCOTTISH CAMPAIGN FOR NUCLEAR DISARMAMENT
15 Barrland Street, Glasgow, G41 1QH.
Tel: 0141-423 1222 Fax: 0141-243 1231
Email: scnd@banthebomb.org
Web: www.banthebomb.org
Co-ordinator: J. Ainslie

SCOTTISH CHAMBERS OF COMMERCE
30 George Square, Glasgow, G2 1EQ.
Tel: 0141-204 8316 Fax: 0141-221 2336
Director: Robert Leitch

SCOTTISH CHILD LAW CENTRE
54 East Cross Causeway, Edinburgh, EH8 9HD.
Tel: 0131-667 6333 Fax: 0131-662 1713
Web: www.sclc.org.uk

SCOTTISH CHURCH HISTORY SOCIETY
Crown Manse, 39 Southside Road, Inverness, IV2 4XA.
Tel: 01463-231140 Fax: 01463-230537
Hon. Secretary: Revd Dr P. H. Donald

SCOTTISH CIVIC TRUST
The Tobacco Merchants House, 42 Miller Streeet,
Glasgow, G1 1DT.
Tel: 0141-221 1466 Fax: 0141-248 6952
Email: sct@scottishcivictrust.org.uk
Web: www.scottishcivictrust.org.uk

SCOTTISH COUNCIL FOR NATIONAL PARKS
15 Park Terrace, Stirling, FK8 2JT.
Tel: 01786-465714 Web: www.scnp.org.uk
Hon. Secretary: B. K. Parnell

SCOTTISH COLLEGE OF COMPLEMENTARY MEDICINE
c/o The Complementary Medicine Centre, 11 Park
Circus, Glasgow, G3 6AX.
Tel: 0141-332 4924 Fax: 0141-353 3783 Email:
complementarymedecinecentre@compuserve.com
Web: www.complementarymedicinecentre.co.uk

SCOTTISH CONSERVATION BUREAU
Technical Conservation, Research and Education,
Historic Scotland, Longmore House, Salisbury Place,
Edinburgh, EH9 1SH.
Tel: 0131-668 8668 Fax: 0131-668 8669
Email: hs.conservation.bureau@scotland.gsi.gov.uk
Web: www.historic-scotland.gov.uk
*Director, Technical Conservation Research and
Education:* I. Maxwell

SCOTTISH COUNCIL FOR VOLUNTARY ORGANISATIONS (SCVO)
Mansfield Traquair Centre, 15 Mansfield Place,
Edinburgh, EH3 6BB.
Tel: 0131-556 3882 Fax: 0131-556 0279
Email: enquiries@scvo.org.uk
Web: www.scvo.org.uk
Chief Executive: M. Sime

SCOTTISH COUNCIL FOR INTERNATIONAL ARBITRATION
Albany House, 58 Albany Street, Edinburgh, EH1 3QS.
Tel: 0131-557 1545 Fax: 0131-525 8653
Web: www.simpmar.com

SCOTTISH COUNCIL ON DEAFNESS
Clerwood House, 96 Clermiston Road,
Edinburgh, EH12 6UT.
Tel: 0131-314 6075 Fax: 0131-314 6077
Email: admin@scod.org.uk Web: www.scod.org.uk

SCOTTISH COUNCIL OF LAW REPORTING
Darfaulds Cottage, Blairgowrie, Perthshire, PH10 6PY.
Tel: 0131-226 7411 Fax: 0131-226 2934
Secretary: Anthony Kinahan

SCOTTISH CROFTERS UNION
Old Mill, Broadford, Isle of Skye, IV49 9AQ.
Tel: 01471-822529 Fax: 01471-822799
Email: crofters.union@talk21.com
Web: www.scu.co.uk

SCOTTISH DRUGS FORUM
Shaftesbury House, 5 Waterloo Street,
Glasgow, G2 6AY.
Tel: 0141-221 1175 Fax: 0141-248 6414
Email: info@sdf.org.uk Web: www.sdf.org.uk
Information Officer: Ms I. Hendry

SCOTTISH KENNEL CLUB
Eskmills Park, Station Road, Musselburgh, EH21 7PQ.
Tel: 0131-665 3920 Fax: 0131-653 6937
Email: info@scottishkennelclub.org
Web: www.scottishkennelclub.org

SCOTTISH LANDOWNERS' FEDERATION
Stuart House, Eskmills Business Park,
Musselburgh, EH21 7PB.
Tel: 0131-653 5400 Fax: 0131-653 5401
Email: slfinfo@slf.org.uk Web: www.slf.org.uk
Director: Dr M. S. Hankey

SCOTTISH LANGUAGE DICTIONARIES
27 George Square, Edinburgh, EH8 9LD.
Tel: 0131-650 4149 Fax: 0131-650 4149
Email: mail@sldl.org.uk Web: www.sldl.org.uk
Editorial Director: Ms Marace Dareau

SCOTTISH LAW AGENTS' SOCIETY
11 Parliament Square, Edinburgh, EH1 1RF.
Tel: 0131-225 5051 Fax: 0131-225 5051
Email: secretary@slas.co.uk
Web: www.slas.co.uk
Secretary: Mrs J. H. Webster, LLB, WS

SCOTTISH MOTOR NEURONE DISEASE ASSOCIATION
76 Firhill Road, Glasgow, G20 7BA.
Tel: 0141-945 1077 Fax: 0141-945 2578
Email: info@scotmnd.sol.co.uk
Web: www.scotmnd.org.uk

SCOTTISH NATURAL HISTORY LIBRARY
Foremount House, Kilbarchan, Renfrewshire,
PA10 2EZ. Tel: 01505-702 419
Director: Dr J. A. Gibson

SCOTTISH NATIONAL FEDERATION FOR THE WELFARE OF THE BLIND
5 Balmashanner Rise, Forfar, Angus, DD8 1PD.
Tel: 01307-463099 Email: snfwb@care4free.net
Hon. Secretary and Treasurer: J. Duncan

SCOTTISH PARENT TEACHER COUNCIL
53 George Street, Edinburgh, EH2 2HT.
Tel: 0131-226 4378/1917 Fax: 0131-226 4378
Email: sptc@sol.co.uk Web: www.sol.co.uk/s/sptc
Administrator: Mrs L. Grant
Development Manager: Mrs J. Gillespie

SCOTTISH PROPERTY NETWORK
University of Paisley, Paisley, PA1 2BE.
Tel: 0141-561 7300 Fax: 0141-561 7319
Email: info@scottishproperty.co.uk
Web: www.scottishproperty.co.uk
Chief Executive: D. Martin
Systems Manager: P. McKay

SCOTTISH REFUGEE COUNCIL
5 Cadogan Square, 170 Blythswood Court,
Glasgow, G2 7PH.
Tel: 0141-248 9799 Fax: 0141-243 2499
Email: info@scottishrefugeecouncil.org.uk
Web: www.scottishrefugeecouncil.org.uk
Chief Executive: Sally Daghlian

SCOTTISH RIGHTS OF WAY AND ACCESS SOCIETY
24 Annandale Street, Edinburgh, EH7 4AN.
Tel: 0131-558 1222 Fax: 0131-558 1222
Email: info@scotways.com
Web: www.scotways.com

SCOTTISH SOCIETY FOR AUTISM
Hilton House, Alloa Business Park, Whins Road,
Alloa, FK10 3SA.
Tel: 01259-720044 Fax: 01259-720051
Chief Executive: D. Liddell
Director of Fundraising: B. Tait

SCOTTISH SOCIETY FOR THE PREVENTION OF CRUELTY TO ANIMALS
Braehead Mains, 603 Queensferry Road,
Edinburgh, EH4 6EA.
Tel: 0131-339 0222 Fax: 0131-339 4777
Email: enquiries@scottishspca.org
Web: www.scottishspca.org
Chief Executive: I. R. Gardiner
Support Services Director: Ms K. Bunyan

SCOTTISH SPINA BIFIDA ASSOCIATION (SSBA)
190 Queensferry Road, Edinburgh, EH4 2BW.
Tel: 0131-332 0743 Fax: 0131-343 3561
Email: mail@ssba.org.uk Web: www.ssba.org.uk

SCOTTISH WILDLIFE TRUST
Cramond House, Cramond Glebe Road, Edinburgh,
EH4 6NS. Tel: 0131-312 7765 Fax: 0131-312 8705
Email: enquiries@swt.org.uk Web: www.swt.org.uk

SCOTTISH WOMEN'S AID
Norton Park, 57 Albion Road, Edinburgh, EH7 5QY.
Tel: 0131-475 2372 Fax: 0131-475 2384
Email: swa@swa-l.demon.co.uk
Web: www.scottishwomensaid.co.uk

SCOTTISH YOUTH HOSTELS ASSOCIATION
7 Glebe Crescent, Stirling, FK8 2JA.
Tel: 01786-891400 Fax: 01786-891333
Email: enquiries@syha.org.uk
Web: www.syha.org.uk
Chief Executive: Lorna MacDonald

SCOTTISH YOUTH THEATRE
3rd Floor, Forsyth House, 111 Union Street, Glasgow,
G1 3TA. Tel: 0141-221 5127 Fax: 0141-221 9123
Email: admin@scottishyouththeatre.org
Web: www.scottishyouththeatre.org
Chief Executive: Ms M. McCluskey

SCOUT ASSOCIATION SCOTTISH COUNCIL
Fordell Firs, Hillend, Dunfermline, KY11 7HQ.
Tel: 01383-419073 Fax: 01383-414892
Email: shq@scouts-scotland.org.uk
Web: www.scouts-scotland.org.uk

THE SEA CADETS
Northern Area HQ, HMS Caledonia, Rosyth,
Fife, KY11 2XH.
Tel: 01383-416300 Fax: 01383-419772
Email: ao@seacadetsnorthern.org.uk
Web: www.seacadetsnorthern.org.uk
Area Office Manager: A. E. Parr

SHELTER SCOTLAND
4th Floor, Scotiabank House, 6 South Charlotte Street,
Edinburgh, EH2 4AW.
Tel: 0131-473 7170 Fax: 0131-473 7199
Email: shelterscot@shelter.org.uk
Web: www.shelterscotland.org.uk

SHETLAND FIELD STUDIES GROUP
Breckon, 4 West Baila, Lerwick, Shetland, ZE1 0SG.
Tel: 01595-696311
Secretary: Averill Dorrat

SOCIETY OF ANTIQUARIES OF
SCOTLAND
Royal Museum, Chambers Street, Edinburgh, EH1 1JF.
Tel: 0131-247 4115/4133 Fax: 0131-247 4163
Email: m.hardie@nms.ac.uk Web: www.socanscot.org
Director: Mrs F. Ashmore, FSA

SOCIETY OF SOLICITORS IN THE
SUPREME COURT OF SCOTLAND
SSC Library, Parliament House, 11 Parliament Square,
Edinburgh, EH1 1RF.
Tel: 0131-225 6268 Fax: 0131-225 2270
Email: enquiries@ssclibrary.co.uk
Web: www.ssclibrary.co.uk
Secretary: I. L. S. Balfour
Librarian: C. A. Wilcox

SOCIETY OF WRITERS TO HM SIGNET
Signet Library, Parliament Square, Edinburgh, EH1 1RF.
Tel: 0131-220 3426 Fax: 0131-220 4016
Email: manager@wssociety.co.uk
Web: www.signetlibrary.co.uk
General Manager: M. R. McVittie
Librarian: Miss A. Walker

SOUTH WEST ROSS FIELD CLUB
Culag, Carr Brae, Dornie, Kyle, Ross-shire, IV40 8HA.
Tel: 01599-555341
Secretary: Brian Neath

THE STANDING COUNCIL OF SCOTTISH
CHIEFS
Hope Chambers, 52 Leith Walk, Edinburgh, EH6 5HW.
Tel: 0131-554 6321 Fax: 0131-553 5319
Email: r.squire@virgin.net
Acting General Secretary: Romilly Squire, OSTJ

STEWART SOCIETY
53 George Street, Edinburgh, EH2 2HT.
Tel: 0131-220 4512 Fax: 0131-220 4512
Email: info@stewartsociety.org
Web: www.stewartsociety.org
Secretary: Mrs C. Larkins, MVO

STIRLING FIELD AND ARCHAEOLOGICAL
SOCIETY
East Murdieston, Thornhill, Stirling, FK8 3QE.
Tel: 01785-850271
Secretary: Rita Barth

SUSTRANS SCOTLAND
162 Fountainbridge, Edinburgh, EH3 9RX.
Tel: 0131-624 7660 Fax: 0131-624 7664
Email: scotland@sustrans.org.uk
Web: www.sustrans.org.uk
Manager in Scotland: Tony Grant
Chief Executive: J. Grimshaw

TAIN AND DISTRICT FIELD CLUB
2 Achandunie Cottages, Ardross, Alness, Tain,
Ross-shire, IV17 0YB.
Tel: 01349-884806
Secretary: Sean Meikle

THE THISTLE FOUNDATION
Niddrie Mains Road, Edinburgh, EH16 4EA.
Tel: 0131-661 3366 Fax: 0131-661 4879
Email: jfisher@thistle.org.uk
Web: www.thistle.org.uk
Chief Executive: Ms J. Fisher

TURNING POINT SCOTLAND
54 Govan Road, Glasgow, G51 1JL.
Tel: 0141-427 8200 Fax: 0141-427 8201
Email: info@turningpointscotland.com
Web: www.turningpointscotland.com
Chief Executive: Ms N. Maciver
Fundraising Co-ordinator: K. Blackie

UNIT FOR THE STUDY OF GOVERNMENT
IN SCOTLAND
Governance of Scotland Forum, Chisholm House, High
School Yards, Edinburgh, EH1 1LZ.
Tel: 0131-650 2456 Fax: 0131-650 6345
Email: l.adams@ed.ac.uk
Web: www.ed.ac.uk/usgs/unit

UNITED NATIONS ASSOCIATION
SCOTLAND
40 Grosvenor Lane, Glasgow, G12 9AA.
Tel: 0141-339 5408 Fax: 0141-339 5408
Email: frances.mildmay@btinternet.com
National Officer: Ms F. Mildmay

VARIETY CLUB OF SCOTLAND
437 Crow Road, Glasgow, G11 7DZ.
Tel: 0141-357 4411 Fax: 0141-334 4796
Email: hazelnorral@varietyclub.org.uk
Web: www.varietyclub.org.uk
Executive Secretary: Mrs Anne Wyper
Fundraiser: Hazel Norral

VICTIM SUPPORT SCOTLAND
15–23 Hardwell Close, Edinburgh, EH8 9RX.
Tel: 0131-668 4486 Fax: 0131-662 5400
Web: www.victimsupportsco.demon.co.uk
Chief Executive: Mr D. McKenna

WESTERN ISLES NATURAL HISTORY
SOCIETY
Scottish Natural Heritage, 135 Stilligarry,
South Uist, HS8 5RS.
Tel: 01876-510725
Secretary: Brian Lowe

WOODLAND TRUST SCOTLAND
Glenruthven Mill, Abbey Road, Auchterarder,
Perthshire, PH3 1DP.
Tel: 01764-662554 Fax: 01764-662553
Email: angeladouglas@woodland-trust.org.uk
Web: www.woodland-trust.org.uk
Chief Executive: M. J. Townsend
Operations Director - Scotland: Ms A. Douglas

YMCA SCOTLAND
11 Rutland Street, Edinburgh, EH1 2AE.
Tel: 0131-228 1464 Fax: 0131-228 5462
Email: info@ymcascotland.org.uk
Web: www.ymcascotland.org

YOUTH SCOTLAND
Balfour House, 19 Bonnington Grove,
Edinburgh, EH6 4BL.
Tel: 0131-554 2561 Fax: 0131-454 3438
Email: office@youthscotland.org.uk
Web: www.youthscotland.org.uk
Chief Executive: Ms C. Downie

YOUTHLINK SCOTLAND
Rosebery House, 9 Haymarket Terrace,
Edinburgh, EH12 5EL.
Tel: 0131-313 2488 Fax: 0131-313 6800
Email: info@youthlink.co.uk
Web: www.youthlink.co.uk

YWCA SCOTLAND
7B Randolph Crescent, Edinburgh, EH3 7TH.
Tel: 0131-225 7592 Fax: 0131-225 1052
Email: info@ywcascotland.org
Chief Executive: E. Samson
Operations Director: Candice Tait

INDEX

NOTES

NOTES

NOTES